D0374785

CRITICAL SURVEY
OF
DRAMA

CRITICAL SURVEY
OF
DRAMA

English Language Series

Authors
Cow-Gua

2

Edited by
FRANK N. MAGILL

SALEM PRESS
Englewood Cliffs, N. J.

LIBRARY OF CONGRESS CATALOG CARD NUMBER: 85-50962
Complete Set: ISBN 0-89356-375-7
Volume 2:   ISBN 0-89356-377-3

PRINTED IN THE UNITED STATES OF AMERICA

LIST OF AUTHORS IN VOLUME 2

NOËL COWARD

Born: Teddington, England; December 16, 1899
Died: Port Royal, Jamaica; March 26, 1973

Principal drama

I'll Leave It to You, pr. 1919, pb. 1920; *Sirocco*, wr. 1921, pr., pb. 1927; *The Better Half*, pr. 1922 (one act); *The Young Idea*, pr. 1922, pb. 1924; *London Calling*, pr. 1923 (music and lyrics by Noël Coward and Ronald Jeans); *Weatherwise*, wr. 1923, pb. 1931, pr. 1932; *Fallen Angels*, pb. 1924, pr. 1925; *The Rat Trap*, pb. 1924, pr. 1926 (wr. 1918); *The Vortex*, pr. 1924, pb. 1925; *Easy Virtue*, pr. 1925, pb. 1926; *Hay Fever*, pr., pb. 1925; *On with the Dance*, pr. 1925; *The Queen Was in the Parlour*, pr., pb. 1926; *This Was a Man*, pr., pb. 1926; *Home Chat*, pr., pb. 1927; *The Marquise*, pr., pb. 1927; *This Year of Grace!*, pr. 1928, pb. 1929 (musical); *Bitter Sweet*, pr., pb. 1929 (operetta); *Private Lives*, pr., pb. 1930; *Some Other Private Lives*, pr. 1930, pb. 1931 (one act); *Cavalcade*, pr. 1931, pb. 1932; *Words and Music*, pr. 1932, pb. 1939 (musical); *Design for Living*, pr., pb. 1933; *Conversation Piece*, pr., pb. 1934; *Point Valaine*, pr., pb. 1935; *Tonight at 8:30*, pb. 1935 (3 volumes; a collective title for the following nine plays, which were designed to be presented in various combinations of three bills of three plays: *We Were Dancing*, pr. 1935; *The Astonished Heart*, pr. 1935; *Red Peppers*, pr. 1935; *Hands Across the Sea*, pr. 1935; *Fumed Oak*, pr. 1935; *Shadow Play*, pr. 1935; *Family Album*, pr. 1935; *Ways and Means*, pr. 1936; *Still Life*, pr. 1936); *Operette*, pr., pb. 1938; *Set to Music*, pr. 1939, pb. 1940 (musical); *Blithe Spirit*, pr., pb. 1941; *Present Laughter*, pr. 1942, pb. 1943; *This Happy Breed*, pr. 1942, pb. 1943; *Sigh No More*, pr. 1945 (musical); *Pacific 1860*, pr. 1946, pb. 1958 (musical); *Peace in Our Time*, pr., pb. 1947; *Ace of Clubs*, pr. 1950, pb. 1962; *Island Fling*, pr. 1951, pb. 1956; *Relative Values*, pr. 1951, pb. 1952; *Quadrille*, pr., pb. 1952; *After the Ball*, pr. 1954 (musical; based on Oscar Wilde's play *Lady Windermere's Fan*); *Nude with Violin*, pr. 1956, pb. 1957; *South Sea Bubble*, pr., pb. 1956; *Look After Lulu*, pr., pb. 1959; *Waiting in the Wings*, pr., pb. 1960; *High Spirits*, pr. 1961 (musical; based on his play *Blithe Spirit*); *Sail Away*, pr. 1961 (musical); *The Girl Who Came to Supper*, pr. 1963 (musical; based on Terence Rattigan's play *The Sleeping Prince*); *Suite in Three Keys: Come Into the Garden Maude; Shadows of the Evening; A Song at Twilight*, pr., pb. 1966; *Cowardy Custard*, pr. 1972, pb. 1973 (also as *Cowardy Custard: The World of Noel Coward*); *Oh! Coward*, pr. 1972, pb. 1974 (also as *Oh Coward! A Musical Comedy Revue*).

Other literary forms

Noël Coward was an extraordinarily prolific playwright, lyricist, and composer, writing more than fifty plays and musicals during his lifetime. He did not limit his literary endeavors solely to the drama, but ventured into other genres as well. These diversions into the realm of fiction, nonfiction, and poetry proved equally successful for him. In addition to his plays, Coward wrote three novels (two unpublished), several collections of short stories, satires, a book of verse, and three autobiographical works, *Present Indicative* (1937), *Middle East Diary* (1944), and *Future Indefinite* (1954).

Coward's versatility is further apparent in his original scripts for five films, his screenplays and adaptations of his hit plays, and his several essays on the modern theater which appeared in popular journals and in *The Times* of London and *The New York Times*. Like his plays, Coward's other works reveal his distinctive satiric style, sharp wit, and clever wordplay.

Achievements

In 1970, Coward was knighted by Queen Elizabeth II for "services rendered to the arts." The succinct phrasing of this commendation is as understated as some of Coward's best dialogue, considering his long and brilliant career in the theater. Coward wrote plays specifically designed to entertain the popular audience and to provide an amusing evening in the theater. Few of his plays champion a cause or promote a social issue. His most noteworthy achievement came in the writing of scores of fashionable comedies, revues, and "operettes" which were resounding successes on the English, American, and Continental stages and which continue to enjoy success today. For this insistence on writing light comedy, he received substantial criticism, and several of his works were brusquely dismissed as "fluff" by critics. These same plays, however, never wanted for an audience, even during the most turbulent, politically restless years.

Coward came to be associated with the 1920's in England in much the same way that F. Scott Fitzgerald was identified with the Jazz Age in America. Whereas Fitzgerald seriously examined the moral failings of his prosperous characters, however, Coward treated them lightly. His plays chronicle the foibles, fashions, and affairs of the English upper class and provide satirical vignettes of the social elite. Coward's life and work reflect the same urbane persona; indeed, he wrote his best parts for himself. Coward's world was that of the idle rich, of cocktails, repartee, and a tinge of modern decadence; this image was one he enjoyed and actively promoted until his death.

For all their popularity, most of Coward's plays are not memorable, save for *Private Lives*, *Blithe Spirit*, *Design for Living*, and possibly one or two others, yet his song lyrics have become part of the English cultural heritage. "Mad Dogs and Englishmen," from *Words and Music*, achieved immortality when its famous line "Mad dogs and Englishmen go out in the mid-day sun" was included in *The Oxford Dictionary of Quotations*.

Coward's reputation rests less on the literary merits of his works and more on the man, who as an accomplished actor, entertainer, and raconteur displayed enormous resilience during his five decades in the public eye. One of the obvious difficulties in producing a Coward play is finding actors who are able to handle the dialogue with the aplomb of "the master." What made Coward's plays successful was not so much a strong text, but virtuoso performances by Gertrude Lawrence, Jane Cowl, Alfred Lunt and Lynn Fontanne, and Coward himself. The public continues to be amused by his works in revivals, but the brilliance of the plays fades perceptibly without these performers. Though there is still interest in the vintage Coward plays, on the whole, his star seems to be waning as the twentieth century moves to a close.

Biography

Noël Pierce Coward was born December 16, 1899. He was the child of Arthur Sabin Coward and Violet Agnes Veitch, who married late in life after meeting in a church choir. Coward's family on his father's side was very talented musically. They helped nurture the natural virtuosity of the child, instilling in him a lifelong love of music.

Since his birthday was so close to Christmas, Coward always received one present to satisfy both occasions, but on December 16, his mother would take him to the theater as a special treat. He first attended a matinee at the age of four, never realizing he would spend the next seventy years of his life in service to the dramatic muse. As he grew older, he found these junkets to the theater more and more fascinating, and upon returning home would rush to the piano and play by ear the songs from the production he had just seen.

Coward made his first public appearance, singing and accompanying himself on the piano, at a concert held at Miss Willington's School. Though obviously a very talented child, Coward's precocity did not carry over to his formal education. At best, his schooling was sporadic. For a time, he attended the Chapel Royal School at Clapham in hopes of becoming a member of the prestigious Chapel Royal Choir. Failing his audition as a choir member, he was taken from school and did not attend any educational institution for six months, at which time he was sent to school in London. He was ten years old.

Coward was an incorrigible, strong-willed child, given to tantrums when he did not get his way. These traits, inherited from both sides of his argumentative family, are evident in his characters, and each of his plays contains a rousing altercation scene. He was indulged by his mother, who became the stereotypical stage mother during his early years, and it was at his mother's insistence that he began attending Miss Janet Thomas' Dancing Academy in addition to his regular school in London. Soon, Miss Thomas' school usurped the position of importance held by traditional academic fare, and Coward became a child performer.

Coward's first professional engagement, and that which launched his long career, was on January 28, 1911, in a children's play, *The Goldfish*. After this appearance, he was sought after for children's roles by other professional theaters. He was featured in several productions with Sir Charles Hawtrey, a light comedian, whom Coward idolized and to whom he virtually apprenticed himself until he was twenty. It was from Hawtrey that Coward learned comic acting techniques and playwriting. He worked in everything from ballets to music halls and made it a point to study the more experienced performers to learn to "catch" the audience quickly. This skill was one he actively drew upon in the writing of his plays.

At the tender age of twelve, Coward met one of the actresses who would help contribute to his overwhelming success, Gertrude Lawrence; she was then fifteen and a child performer as well. The occasional acting team of Coward and Lawrence would become synonymous with polished, sophisticated comedy during the 1920's, 1930's, and 1940's.

When he was fifteen, Coward was invited to stay at the country estate of Mrs. Astley Cooper. This stay, and subsequent visits, influenced his life markedly in two ways: He grew to know intimately the manners and mores of the upper class, and, through Mrs. Cooper, he came to meet Gladys Calthrop, who was to become his lifelong friend and the designer for his productions.

Coward began his writing career when he was sixteen by writing songs and selling them for distribution. He turned his hand to playwriting when he was seventeen and found that he was very good at writing dialogue. Success came quite early to Coward. He was already accepted as an accomplished actor on the London stage when he began writing. By 1919, his play *I'll Leave It to You* was produced in the West End with Coward in the leading role. One of the idiosyncracies of Coward's writing is that often he wrote "whacking good parts" for himself or for people he knew. Some of his best plays are essentially vehicles for his own talents or those of Gertrude Lawrence and later of the Lunts.

I'll Leave It to You met with moderate success, and Coward received great praise from critics for his playwriting abilities, although Sir Neville Cardus, writing in the *Manchester Guardian*, faulted the play for its narrow focus on the world of the idle rich. This criticism dogged Coward throughout his career.

. Coward went to New York for the first time in 1921 and arrived virtually penniless. He sold three satires to *Vanity Fair* in order to support himself. Though he may have begun the 1920's in penury, Coward's position as the most popular playwright in the English theater became secure during this decade. In 1924, *The Vortex* was produced in London. Coward's most important serious play, *The Vortex* broke with English theatrical tradition in its choice of subject matter: drug addiction. This Ibsenesque approach to a problem created quite a sensation. It was hailed by many as an important play but also found dissenters who labeled it "filth" and "dustbin drama."

In late 1927, Coward purchased 139 acres in Kent called Goldenhurst Farm. This was the first residence he used as a retreat to escape the glitter of the stage. Eventually, he would own others in Jamaica, Paris, Geneva, and London. The years from 1928 to 1934 are regarded by many as Coward's "golden years." His string of successes during this period include some of his best and most famous plays and revues: *This Year of Grace!*, *Bitter Sweet*, *Private Lives*, *Cavalcade*, *Words and Music*, *Design for Living*, and *Conversation Piece*. According to Coward, in a letter written to his mother, *Bitter Sweet* was the only show that played to capacity houses in New York during the stock market crash of 1929. By the 1930's, the opening of a Coward play in London was regularly attended by royalty and other prominent socialites.

Coward took his success and the responsibility of fame seriously. When asked to aid the Actors' Orphanage, he did so willingly and subsequently became president of the organization, a position he retained from 1934 to 1956.

After World War II, Coward fell from grace with many critics, who regarded him as being past his literary prime. The year 1949-1950 proved the lowest point in his career as he received poor reviews for his plays and scathing reviews for his film, *The Astonished Heart*. The drama was changing during these restless years that would produce playwrights such as John Osborne, and Coward was momentarily out of step with the times. He turned to the writing of fiction and produced several short stories and his autobiographical work *Future Indefinite*.

By the late 1950's, audiences were once again in love with Coward. His plays, revues, and nightclub appearances were extremely successful. The critics, however, remained vitriolic, but their rancor failed to dim the enthusiasm of the general theatergoing public, who clamored for more Coward plays. In 1969, there was a seventieth birthday tribute to Coward in London which lasted a full week. On January 1, 1970, Coward's name appeared on the Queen's New Year's list as a Knight Bachelor, for services rendered to the arts. For the remaining years of his life, he was Sir Noël Coward. In the same year, he was awarded a special Tony Award by the American theater for Distinguished Achievement in the Theatre. In 1972, he received an honorary Doctor of Letters from the University of Sussex.

Coward died of a heart attack in Jamaica on March 26, 1973, bringing to an end a career of more than sixty years in the theater. The most lasting tribute awarded to Coward is the continued success which meets revivals of his plays and musicals. Coward created a mystique about himself during his lifetime, and this intangible quality of wit and sophistication has become part of the Coward legend, which has become a part of the colorful heritage of the theater.

Analysis

Betty Comden and Adolph Green observe of Noël Coward in Roddy McDowall's book *Double Exposure* (1966), "To us he represented class . . . and we don't mean that in a superficial sense. We mean the highest of wit, of style, of discipline, and craftsmanship." As a playwright, composer, lyricist, producer, director, author, and actor, Coward spent his life entertaining the public. This he did with a flair, sophistication, and polish that are not readily found in twentieth century drama. He wrote farce, high comedy, domestic and patriotic melodramas, musical comedies, and revues. His plays were popular fare in England and America for years because Coward recognized that the "great public" for which he wrote his plays wanted, above all, to be entertained.

All of Coward's plays fall into easily recognizable stylized patterns. Essentially, Coward wrote modern comedies of manners which are as reflective of twentieth century mores and sentiments as their Restoration forebears were of those in the seventeenth century. For the most part, his plays are set in drawing rooms and usually have a couple involved in a love relationship as the central characters. He draws heavily on his theatrical background and populates his plays with theatrical and artistic characters. These temperamental personages allow Coward to involve them easily in the constant bickering and verbal fencing that came to be the trademarks of a Coward play. Each of his characters vies to get the upper hand over the others. Arguments are central to his work, and much of his humor relies on sophisticated insults. Coward's dialogue bitingly exposes hypocrites and the petty games played by the upper class; his plays parody Mayfair society mercilessly. Unfortunately, his plays involve little else. There is little motivation of character, less development of theme, and what thin remnant of plot remains, is swept along in the incessant bantering of the characters. Robert Greacen, referring to *Fumed Oak*, remarked that "an observant foreigner might sit through the entire play . . . and simply hear people talking and believe that no action was taking place at all." Such statements apply to most of Coward's plays.

This criticism reveals both the strongest and the weakest aspects of Coward's theater. He was capable of writing brilliant, naturalistic dialogue with an astonishing economy. In spite of this enormous talent for writing dialogue, however, little happens in his plays to advance the plot. Most of his plays remain structurally flawed, relying heavily on the use of *deus ex machina* and coincidence for plot resolutions.

Thematically, Coward's comedies examine true love, adulterous affairs, and domestic upheavals. His more serious plays focus on a variety of topics, including drug addiction, infidelity, and patriotism. The few patriotic plays he attempted strongly support solid middle-class values and promote a stereotyped image of the stoical Englishman.

Though his works appear to have identifiable themes, they lack a thesis. Coward's plays realistically depict modern characters in absorbing situations, but the characters are not as fully developed as the situations in which they find themselves. Their motivations remain obscured. Even in the serious plays, his position on his subject is never clearly revealed. Most of his serious dramas fail because he never brings the moment to a crisis, and so his plays end anticlimactically. According to Milton Levin, Coward's plays "raise no questions, they provide few critical footholds, they simply ask to be praised for what they are, sparkling caprices."

Generally, the success of Coward's plays depended on the ability of the actors to carry his rapier-sharp dialogue. He freely admitted tailoring choice roles to his talents and those of his friends. Coward and Gertrude Lawrence in *Private Lives*, Coward and the Lunts in *Design for Living*, Coward with Beatrice Lillie in *Blithe Spirit* mark legendary moments in theatrical history that cannot be replicated. When criticizing drama, one must consider the text in production. It is this consideration that elevates the relatively weak scripts of Coward's plays to modern classics.

One finds embodied in Coward a theatrical trinity of actor, playwright, and producer. The inability to separate completely one from the other in studying his works contributes to the mystique which surrounds the man. Rarely are his works found in academic anthologies of the genre, but the imprint of his productions is still discernible in the theater today.

Design for Living was the end result of a plan by Coward, Alfred Lunt, and Lynn Fontanne to act in a play together, written specifically for them. They originally conceived of this idea in the early 1920's, and the gestation period required for Coward actually to write and produce the play lasted eleven years. *Design for Living* scrutinizes a free-spirited and occasionally painful *ménage à trois* comprising Gilda, an interior decorator, Otto, a painter, and Leo, a playwright. The most striking quality of the play is its completely amoral stance on marriage, fidelity, friendship, and sexual relations. Pangs of conscience are fleeting in these characters as their relationships as friends and lovers become apparent to one another and to the audience.

It is the amorality of the characters, rather than a perceived immorality, that has provoked criticism of this play. Coward forms no conclusions and passes no judgment: The play ends with the three characters embracing and laughing wildly on a sofa, and the audience is provided no clue as to how they should judge these amorous individuals. They are asked to watch and accept without being given a resolution to the plot. Most of the criticism directed at the production resulted from a misunderstanding of the title on the part of the critics. Coward intended his title to be ironic. It was taken to be an admonition that the Bohemian life-style depicted onstage was not merely acceptable but was actually preferable to conventional ways as a "design for living."

Design for Living was a vehicle for the formidable talents of Coward and the Lunts. The dialogue is quick and sharp as the three characters alternately pair off, argue, and reunite. The theme stressed most strongly in this play, and the one which offers its most redemptive qualities, is that of friendship. Gilda, Otto, and Leo value their mutual companionship, but their active libidos complicate their relationships. *Design for Living* was judged to be "unpleasant" by the critics, but it enjoyed a phenomenal success with audiences in England and America.

Private Lives, considered one of Coward's best plays, "leaves a lot to be desired," by the author's own admission. The protagonists, Amanda and Elyot, are divorced and meet again while both are honeymooning with their new spouses. Their former affection for each other is rekindled, and they abandon their unsuspecting spouses and escape to Paris. Here, they are reminded of what it was in their personalities that prompted them to seek a divorce. The scene is complicated by the arrival of the jilted spouses, who come seeking reconciliation, but who eventually are spurned as Amanda and Elyot, after arguing violently, leave together, presumably to lead a life of adversarial bliss.

Amanda and Elyot are interesting, fairly well-drawn characters; these roles were written with Gertrude Lawrence and Coward in mind. The secondary characters, the spouses, Victor and Sibyl, are two-dimensional and only provide a surface off which to bounce the stinging repartee of the reunited couple. Coward himself has described *Private Lives* as a "reasonably well-constructed duologue for two performers with a couple of extra puppets thrown in to assist the plot and to provide contrast."

Coward was a highly developed product of the 1920's and the 1930's and of the social milieu he frequented, and, to a not inconsiderable extent, the current popularity of his work originates in the nostalgic hunger of contemporary audiences for an age more verbally sophisticated and carefree than their own. Nevertheless, at their best, Coward's plays continue to sparkle with their author's lively sense of wit, talent for dramatic dialogue and construction, and genius for the neat twist in dramatic action. These significant talents make Coward's theater instructive as well as delightful.

Other major works

NOVEL: *Pomp and Circumstance*, 1960.

SHORT FICTION: *Terribly Intimate Portraits*, 1922; *Chelsea Buns*, 1925; *Spangled Unicorn*, 1932; *To Step Aside*, 1939; *Star Quality: Six Stories*, 1951; *The Collected Short Stories*, 1962; *Pretty Polly Barlow and Other Sto-*

ries, 1964; *Bon Voyage and Other Stories*, 1967.

POETRY: *Not Yet the Dodo*, 1967.

NONFICTION: *Present Indicative*, 1937; *Australia Visited*, 1941; *Middle East Diary*, 1944; *Future Indefinite*, 1954.

SCREENPLAYS: *Bitter Sweet*, 1933; *In Which We Serve*, 1942; *This Happy Breed*, 1944; *Blithe Spirit*, 1946; *Brief Encounter*, 1946; *The Astonished Heart*, 1949.

TELEPLAY: *Post Mortem*, 1931.

MISCELLANEOUS: *The Lyrics of Noel Coward*, 1965.

Bibliography

Greacen, Robert. *The Art of Noel Coward*, 1953.

Lesley, Cole. *The Life of Noël Coward*, 1976.

Levin, Milton. *Noel Coward*, 1968.

Mander, Raymond, and Joe Mitcheson. *The Theatrical Companion to Coward*, 1957.

Marchant, William. *The Privilege of His Company: Noël Coward Remembered*, 1975.

Morley, Sheridan. *A Talent to Amuse*, 1969.

Susan Duffy

JOHN CROWNE

Born: Shropshire, England; c. 1640
Died: London, England; April, 1712

Principal drama

Juliana: Or, The Princess of Poland, pr., pb. 1671; *The History of Charles the Eighth of France: Or, The Invasion of Naples by the French*, pr. 1671, pb. 1672; *Calisto: Or, The Chaste Nymph*, pr., pb. 1675 (music by Nicholas Staggins); *The Country Wit*, pb. 1675, pr. 1676; *The Destruction of Jerusalem by Titus Vespasian, Parts I and II*, pr., pb. 1677; *The Ambitious Statesman: Or, The Loyal Favorite*, pr., pb. 1679; *Thyestes*, pr., pb. 1681; *City Politiques*, pr., pb. 1683; *Sir Courtly Nice: Or, It Cannot Be*, pr., pb. 1685 (adaptation of Agustín Moreto y Cabaña's comedy *No puede ser: O, No puede ser guardar una mujer*); *Darius, King of Persia*, pr., pb. 1688; *The English Friar: Or, The Town Sparks*, pr., pb. 1690; *Regulus*, pr. 1692, pb. 1694; *The Married Beau: Or, The Curious Impertinent*, pr., pb. 1694; *Caligula*, pr., pb. 1698; *The Dramatic Works of John Crowne*, pb. 1872-1874 (4 volumes; James Maidment and W. H. Logan, editors); *The Comedies of John Crowne*, pb. 1984 (B. J. McMullin, editor).

Other literary forms

John Crowne is remembered primarily for his plays, although he also wrote some verse and a novel, *Pandion and Amphigenia: Or, The History of the Coy Lady of Thessalis* (1665).

Achievements

Crowne was one of many playwrights who flourished in the small but intense theatrical world of Restoration London. In some ways, he is the archetypal dramatist of the time. He wrote to gain royal favor and to advance socially; he wrote in several genres to satisfy the taste of his aristocratic audience: court masques, historical tragedy, heroic tragedy, comedy of wit, and tragicomedy. Crowne's plays commented, directly and indirectly, on contemporary political and social issues. Despite the attention to relevance, Crowne patterned his plays on the best models: Seneca, William Shakespeare, and Jean Racine in tragedy; Lope de Vega and Molière in comedy. That Crowne's career spanned a quarter of a century suggests that he was popular and skillful, and an important playwright.

From the dramatic variety of the time, two genres emerge as characteristically Restoration. The first is heroic tragedy. John Dryden was the preeminent practitioner of the form in plays such as *All for Love* and *The Conquest of Granada by the Spaniards*. Crowne is somewhat beneath Dryden's level of achievement. Lacking Dryden's skill in poetry and subtlety in psychological conflict, Crowne successfully created larger-than-life heroes and placed them amid spectacular action.

The second genre is the comedy of wit. Here again, Crowne ranks immediately below the best writers, such as Sir George Etherege and William Wycherley. Though somewhat weak in plotting, Crowne excelled in creating ingenious situations, introducing farcical stage business, and portraying eccentric *dramatis personae*—the sort good character actors very much like to play.

Though his tragedies are badly outdated by their idealism about monarchy and their relevance to Restoration politics, his comedies are less so. Several were revived occassionally in the 1700's. The gem among them is *Sir Courtly Nice*, which remained a staple of the eighteenth century theater and is refreshingly amusing still.

Biography

John Crowne was the son of William Crowne, who fought on the Parliamentary side in the English Civil War. In 1657, he accompanied his father to America, and while the elder Crowne established a proprietorship in Nova Scotia province, young Crowne enrolled in Harvard College. William Crowne's claim to Nova Scotia was made doubtful by a partner's perfidy and by the Restoration of Charles II; thus, in 1660 John Crowne accompanied his father to London, where they sought royal protection for the proprietorship. In the meantime, Crowne earned a living by becoming a gentleman-usher to an elderly lady and by writing a prose romance in the style of Sir Philip Sidney's *Arcadia* (1590). The family's hopes for reclaiming the proprietorship ended in 1667 when Charles II ceded Nova Scotia to the French.

Most scholars agree that Crowne wrote plays in order to provide an income and to secure Charles II's royal favor that might compensate the family for its lost lands. Crowne succeeded in the first goal but not in the second. For fourteen years (1671-1685), Crowne strove mightily to please Charles and his court. He wrote plays virtually on command, often following the king's advice for themes, characters, or Continental models to imitate. Crowne's dramas in these years are clearly Royalist in sentiment: They articulate aristocratic values, and they defend Charles against his enemies. Unfortunately for Crowne, Charles had more people who sought favors than he had resources with which to favor them.

After Charles's death in 1685, Crowne continued to support himself by his pen. He wrote, saw produced, and had published six plays in the next thirteen years. By the late 1690's, however, his health was failing; he was plagued by what he described as "a distemper, which seated itself in my head, and threatened me with an epilepsy." Crowne secured an annual pension from Queen Anne which lasted until 1706. After that, it is unclear how he was able to live; presumably, he resided in poverty and went unremarked by a new generation. In 1712, he died.

Analysis

John Crowne wrote seven tragedies and five comedies, frequently repeating character-types, plot devices, and thematic concerns from play to play. His method and his achievement can be best understood by a close analysis of three plays. *The Destruction of Jerusalem by Titus Vespasian* was his most popular tragedy and remains a good example of the peculiar type of Restoration tragedy called "heroic drama." In *Sir Courtly Nice*, Crowne's most successful comedy of wit, clever men and women of fashion compete with one another in wordplay and intriguing. *City Politiques* is unlike Crowne's other comedies; it relies on farce and on the ridicule of specific contemporary personalities for its impact, but even the modern reader who does not understand the political allusions can appreciate Crowne's ability to keep the stage filled with interesting characters and action.

Like Restoration tragedies in general, *The Destruction of Jerusalem by Titus Vespasian* interweaves complex love plots and complicated political plots. The complexities of love Crowne borrowed from the same source that all of his fellow dramatists used: French romances and tragedies of the early and middle 1600's. The political complications Crowne took from the world around him. The restoration of the monarchy in 1660 had neither ended the competition for power between the king and Parliament nor stilled the loud debate over whether the English throne should be occupied by a Protestant or a Catholic monarch.

Crowne's *The Destruction of Jerusalem by Titus Vespasian* was patterned after John Dryden's *The Conquest of Granada by the Spaniards*, which had been a great success in the early 1670's. Like Dryden, Crowne wrote his play in rhyming couplets (imitating the French tragedies that Charles II loved) and doubled the normal length to ten acts. In both plays, the action centers on several monarchs who are caught in a maze of political and romantic obligations. Finally, Crowne followed Dryden in using special stage effects to heighten the tension. If Crowne had lived three centuries later, he could have easily written scripts for cinema epics.

The action of *The Destruction of Jerusalem by Titus Vespasian, Part I* commences on the eve of Passover, A.D. 72. The city of Jerusalem awaits the arrival of a Roman army under Titus Vespasian. The city's high priest and governor, Matthias, works to prepare the defenses, but he faces insubordination from John, leader of the Pharisee party, who believes that Matthias is secretly in the Romans' pay. Matthias governs in the place of the Jewish king, recently killed under mysterious circumstances. The dead monarch's sister Berenice, appointed by the Romans to rule, has returned to the city in the hope of preventing resistance to the imperial army.

Berenice's heart, however, is not in her mission, because she is in love with Titus, the son of the Emperor Vespasian.

Also present in the city are two exiled monarchs, Phraartes and Monobazus, who have fallen in love with Jewish noblewomen. Phraartes, who believes that religion is a myth supporting the divine right of kings, loves Matthias' daughter Clarona, a vestal virgin of the temple. Clarona is attracted to Phraartes but refuses to violate her vow of eternal virginity. Monobazus loves Berenice, but his ability to woo is inhibited by his secret knowledge that he is her brother's murderer. Berenice, smitten by Titus, hardly notices Monobazus.

Though neither king makes progress in courting his beloved, both use their swords effectively. First they fight off the Edomites, a neighboring tribe invited by John to invade the city on the pretext of forestalling the Romans. Next they rescue Matthias when John leads the Pharisees in open rebellion and captures the Temple. Phraartes demands from Matthias Clarona's hand in marriage as his reward. The high priest is willing if a loophole can be found in the law which would release Clarona from her vows. As they deliberate his daughter's fate, a messenger announces that the Roman army has made camp on nearby hills. On this ominous note, *Part I* ends.

Part II opens with Titus pacing in his tent, torn between his love for Berenice and his duty to the empire. Titus' second-in-command convinces him that duty is superior to love, and two allied kings convince Titus to conquer before the Jews can rally under a new leader. Berenice arrives at the Roman camp soon afterward, but after a long and passionate interview, Titus pushes her away.

Inside Jerusalem conditions worsen as food supplies dwindle. John continues his efforts to kill or capture Matthias. Phraartes is wounded in a second skirmish against the Pharisees; as Clarona binds his wound, she admits her love and hints that if the two of them can save the city, she might renounce her vow. In the meantime, the Jews lose an ally: Monobazus follows Berenice to the Roman camp.

Phraartes departs in search of food supplies. Returning with some provisions, he finds Matthias again in the hands of the Pharisees and once more rescues him. Phraartes now promises Clarona that he will bring in his own Parthian troops to save the city. Titus acts to counter Phraartes' plans even though Berenice attempts to distract the Roman general by threatening to kill herself if her love is not requited. With a heavy heart, Titus chooses duty over love. Berenice fails to carry out her threat.

Monobazus, now ashamed of his beloved and his love, returns to join Phraartes in the city's defense. The two kings find the Temple desecrated by John's forces and discover Matthias and Clarona mortally wounded. After his beloved dies in his arms, Phraartes decides to give up his life fighting the invaders. Monobazus decides to do the same after passing up the chance to flee the doomed city. They die like brothers, side by side in combat.

Titus enters the city in triumph and spares the survivors. Berenice visits him one last time, and when he again refuses to return her love, she goes into permanent and secret exile. As the play ends, Titus stands alone onstage, still agonizing whether duty can be worth such a sacrifice.

It is easy to discern political themes in the play in which the Restoration audience could see their own concerns reflected. The Jews face aggression from the greatest power in the world, Rome, just as England feared domination by neighboring France, which, under Louis XIV, was Europe's most potent nation. The Jewish resistance against the invader is hampered by internal dissension, just as Charles's policies were hampered by opposition from anti-Royalist groups.

The most important political theme centers on the rulers in the play: Phraartes, Monobazus, Matthias, and Titus. The hero is not any of these but rather the institution of kingship itself. The four represent facets of Charles II, his life, his obligations, and his privileges. Phraartes and Monobazus are kings in exile, echoes of the Charles who was in exile in the 1650's. Although they have no kingdoms that obey them, Phraartes and Monobazus speak and act with a natural and convincing authority; clearly, they believe that the authority of kingship flows from divine approbation rather than from popular will. Matthias represents the besieged ruler who struggles bravely against the odds when domestic rebels join foreign enemies in threatening the State. Titus shows the personal sacrifice that kingship demands: For the good of the State, he must deny the longings of his own soul and reject the woman he loves. There is not a consistent political allegory in the play; rather, Crowne presents several vantage points from which to survey the character of a king.

All of the rulers speak eloquently about political obligation: Their diction is elegant and their imagery rich in metaphor. Phraartes and Titus speak with the same poetic force about love. Phraartes with Clarona and Titus with Berenice engage in lengthy debates that reveal the depth of their commitment. What makes the lovers' anguish such good stage business is that each pair is caught in an inescapable dilemma: Clarona has made eternal vows to a religion Phraartes despises; Berenice and Titus must be traitors in order to be lovers. As Crowne devises the situations, lifelong doubt, exile, or death are the only solutions.

Spectacular staging heightens the emotional impact of the play's political themes and romantic dilemmas. An angel appears against the ceiling of the temple to prophesy the doom of the city, and the ghost of Herod walks abroad to do the same. The laments of enslaved citizens and dying warriors are heard offstage, and there is an abundance of swordplay, chases, and stabbings onstage. In the tenth act, the temple catches fire, and Phraartes and Monobazus (seen in silhouette) fall from a prominent battlement as they are fighting Romans. The stage itself is an ambitious multilevel setting whence Matthias can look down at rebel Pharisees, the exiled kings can glare down at invaders, and the nightdress-clad Clarona can gaze down at her lover. No wonder *The Destruction of Jerusalem by Titus Vespasian* was Crowne's greatest success in the 1670's.

Among his comedies, *Sir Courtly Nice* was Crowne's most popular play, and it has retained its reputation as his best. Like other Restoration comedies of wit, it combines a love plot with social commentary. Its themes are love, marriage, and independence: *Sir Courtly Nice*'s dual heroines struggle to achieve the third without sacrificing the first two.

Violante, in love with Lord Bellguard, hesitates to marry him because of his treatment of his unmarried sister Leonora. Bellguard has set a maiden aunt and two eccentric kinsmen (the religious fanatic Testimony and the antireligious zealot Hothead) to watch over the girl. These three sentinels hinder Leonora's romance with Farewel, the son of a rival noble family. Bellguard is cautious because he thinks that all women are promiscuous by nature. Violante and Leonora decide to teach Bellguard a lesson.

Violante asks Farewel to help, and he suggests that they employ Crack, a poor but ingenious scholar expelled from the university for studying magic. Their first victim is Surly, a cynical and unpleasant man in love with Violante. She promises to respond to Surly's awkward advances if he chases away Bellguard's choice of suitor for Leonora, Sir Courtly Nice. Meanwhile, Crack, disguised as a traitor, gains access to Leonora and gives her a locket containing Farewel's picture.

Surly visits Sir Courtly, a man of elegant, even fastidious, manners. Arriving drunk, Surly annoys Sir Courtly by announcing his intention to woo Leonora. Surly annoys him to an even greater extent when he exhales his foul-smelling breath.

Bellguard meanwhile finds Farewel's picture in Leonora's possession and accuses her of being a wanton. With the sentinels in an uproar over the accusation, Crack enters in a new guise and manages to right the situation. Pretending to be Bellguard's crazy but rich cousin, Sir Thomas Calico, he provides Leonora with an absurd alibi. Bellguard, deferring to the wisdom of the wealthy, accepts the lame excuse. Crack tells Leonora that Farewel will visit her that night.

Sir Courtly comes courting. Leonora's aunt wishes to remain behind to supervise the lovers, but Bellguard escorts her out of the room. Leonora listens to Courtly's smug and silly avowals of love and responds mockingly. Surly interrupts to woo Leonora himself and to taunt Courtly. Against his will, Courtly timorously challenges Surly to a duel in order to save face.

Meanwhile, Crack sneaks Farewel into Leonora's room. Her aunt discovers his presence, and an alarmed Bellguard hunts for the intruder throughout the house. Crack comes to the rescue again by declaring that it was he who let Farewel, whom he identifies as his future brother-in-law, into the house. Bellguard is willing to forgo suspicion if Leonora promises to listen once more to Courtly's proposal. She tries, but she indignantly leaves the room as Courtly professes love and offers marriage as he stands gazing fondly on himself in a mirror. The aunt, entering the room and seeing no other woman, takes Courtly's words as applying to herself. When she loudly accepts, Courtly is too preoccupied to notice her misinterpretation.

Leonora takes her fate into her own hands, leaving Bellguard's house to marry Farewel. Violante praises her friend's love and brave spirit, contrasting it with the aunt's betrayal of trust at the first opportunity. Bellguard is finally convinced that not all women need close supervision. As a final test, Violante teases Bellguard by flirting with Surly. When Bellguard responds with passionate declarations rather than jealous accusations, Violante knows she has a man on her terms. No longer afraid that Bellguard will try to control her as he did Leonora, Violante agrees to become his wife.

Crowne wrote *Sir Courtly Nice* as an adaptation of a Spanish comedy, *No puede ser: O, No puede ser guardar una mujer* (1661), by Agustín Moreto y Cabaña. Charles II himself suggested the adaptation to Crowne, who revised the original to suit an English audience and his own dramatic skills. The Spanish play had used the framing device of a debate about the nature of women which leads to a wager. Crowne abandoned that device and began his comedy *in medias res*. One of Crowne's favorite techniques was to multiply character-types; thus, in *Sir Courtly Nice*, he uses not one eccentric kinsman but two and has Crack appear in a variety of disguises. The effect is a more lively play; more characters enter and leave the stage than in most comedies.

Crowne's strength was not in the creation of memorable leading characters but in forming a cast with several strong roles. Indeed, the enduring popularity of *Sir Courtly Nice* can in part be attributed to its appeal to acting companies. There are numerous good parts, and even the smaller roles add distinctively to the whole. It is a play that depends for success not on one or two stars but on the successful interaction of the company. Crowne worked closely with actors and actresses, often tutoring them about the way he imagined his characters being played. *Sir Courtly Nice* is an actor's play as much as it is the author's play.

All of Crowne's characters are strong. Violante and Leonora are atypical Restoration heroines who possess more initiative and spirit than women—real or fictitious—were allowed in the seventeenth century. Testimony and Hothead are bold caricatures of mentalities that were powerful and respected in the age. Sir Courtly is a magnificent fop whose folly is not exposed by others so much as it is revealed by his own actions; his every mannerism betrays the narcissism that leads to his comeuppance in the mirror scene. Surly is a delightful foil to Courtly—one of the crudest of numerous ill-mannered Restoration rakes. These characters interact in a comedy that is always funny, though not always kind. Their story is one that does not pale, the perennially interesting tale of young lovers who must use ingenuity to circumvent the objections of the older generation— or of their peers who prematurely think like the older generation.

Crowne's other important play, *City Politiques*, does not fit into any established genre of comedy. It is too politically oriented to be a romantic comedy; it has too many scenes of farce to be a comedy of wit or a comedy of manners. It is a play of its time, when a playwright employed his dramatic skills on behalf of his patron or of his party. The years from 1678 to 1682 were a time of serious political crisis in England, and when King Charles emerged victorious from that crisis, Crowne celebrated the triumph with a satiric production that ridiculed the Whigs, the enemies of royal rule. *City Politiques* laughs at the issues and personalities of the Popish Plot from the safe vantage of hindsight.

The Popish Plot crisis began in 1678 when an ex-clergyman, Titus Oates, claimed that he had uncovered a plan by which English Catholics, the pope, and the French king intended to assassinate the Protestant Charles II and replace him with his Catholic brother, James. On the sworn testimony of Oates and several others, thousands of Catholics were implicated and arrested; two dozen were put to death. Charles's opponents united to campaign for the Exclusion Bill, which would remove the incentive for a plot by barring James from the succession. Charles opposed the measure, but for the next two years, both Parliament and the city of London were dominated by the bill's supporters. With many of his nobility and the country's major city hostilely disposed, Charles's reign became difficult. In 1681, after much of Oates's testimony had been discredited, the king dissolved the Whig-dominated Parliament. By 1682, the Whig control of London had collapsed, and many leaders of the party fled the country. Except for the emotional scars, the crisis was over.

City Politiques, a series of connected sketches more than a coherent play, ridicules the assumptions and practices of the Whigs during the Popish Plot. It shows ambitious statesmen relying on false oaths to gain selfish ends, citizens defying authority under the cover of respectability but actually motivated by mere whimsy, and lawyers using the laws against the source of all law, the king. Contemporaries delighted in drawing connections between the characters Crowne put on the stage and the actual persons who had important roles in the plot. Modern readers do not enjoy such identifications long after the fact, but they can enjoy Crowne's clever dramatization of mankind's less respectable motives for action.

The action of *City Politiques* occurs in Naples, where the rakish nobleman Florio plans to seduce Rosaura, the young second wife of the newly elected Podesta (mayor of the city). To attain his goal Florio pretends to be a supporter of the Podesta; he also pretends to be incapacitated by venereal disease. In the course of his scheme, Florio befriends the Podesta's son, Craffy, who confides one day that he is in love with his stepmother. When Florio threatens to tell the Podesta, Craffy replies that he will get a dozen paid informants to swear that Florio is the woman's lover.

The Podesta and his followers, openly called Whigs, celebrate his election by acting rudely to the royal governor. When the governor refuses their request to have the Podesta knighted, the mayor vows to gain revenge by fomenting rebellion. One of his supporters is the lawyer Bartoline, who has recently married a much younger woman, Lucinda. Her beauty immediately attracts the eye of another rake, Artall, who disguises himself as Florio. Thinking "Florio" a dying man, Bartoline leaves Lucinda with him while he goes about the Podesta's business. Artall uses the opportunity to teach her the difference between a virile nobleman and an impotent lawyer.

The Podesta continues to harass the governor. He calls the citizens to arms by spreading rumors that a foreign army is poised to invade, and he hires Bartoline to prepare a false indictment against the governor. Bartoline, however, is playing a double game: at the same time he helps the Podesta indict the governor, he is helping the governor press charges against the Podesta and his followers. Florio meanwhile harasses the Whigs by publishing a mock proclamation against them.

Florio goes to Rosaura's apartment. A drunken Craffy interrupts their assignation, attempting to seduce Rosaura while Florio pretends to be the Podesta asleep on the couch. When the real Podesta enters the house, Rosaura tricks Craffy into attacking his father while Florio escapes. Father and son wrestle each other to the ground before realizing their mistake.

Later, Artall again tricks Bartoline. Hoping that the dying Florio (Artall in disguise) will include Lucinda in his will, Bartoline allows his wife to visit Florio's bedroom. At the same time, Craffy discovers the real Florio making love to Rosaura in a nearby room. Craffy calls the Podesta, but the mayor is assured by Bartoline that Florio is with Lucinda and must not be disturbed. Thus, the two rakes complete the double cuckolding while Craffy is deemed mad. Afterward, "Florio" brazenly carries Lucinda from her husband's house while Bartoline watches helplessly.

Florio plays one more trick on the Podesta. His servant Pietro pretends to be a Spanish nobleman with influence upon the governor. Pietro promises to help the Podesta become lord treasurer if he will betray his followers, and the Podesta enthusiastically agrees. When the governor arrives at the mayor's house, however, it is with a warrant, not a knighthood, in hand. The Podesta is under arrest for causing false alarms among the citizens. Bartoline, too, is under arrest: To gain revenge upon "Florio," he paid several informants to accuse him of treason. When he identifies Artall as Florio, Bartoline is arrested for harassing an innocent bystander. The governor concludes the play by warning everyone to leave politics to those properly in authority.

City Politiques shows that once a citizen has broken faith with his legitimate ruler, he can expect no one to keep faith with him. After the Podesta begins to plot against the governor, his son attempts to steal his wife, his best friend succeeds in seducing her, and his lawyer tries to frame him. Likewise, if a man has betrayed his ruler, he will betray anyone, as the Podesta plans to betray his followers. Political rebellion leads to the loss of fidelity at all levels of society.

Phrased this way, the theme of *City Politiques* is indeed serious, but its onstage execution is humorous. Florio and Artall are witty seducers, as anxious to puncture the husband's pomposity as to enjoy the wife. Craffy is a zany and incompetent would-be rake, so infatuated with Rosaura that he talks to himself about his passion even in his father's presence. Bartoline lisps peculiarly and gratingly, making numerous inadvertent puns. The stage business is as inventive as the characters' speaking habits. Craffy's wrestling match with his father wrecks the entire room; the dual cuckolding unfolds daringly and rapidly.

Proof that Crowne's satire struck home was his fate after the play opened: Outraged Whigs assaulted him on the street. Whatever pains Crowne suffered on that occasion must have been eased by his knowledge that the play was a success. London audiences relished his satiric depiction of those who, only months before, had been powerful and feared enemies.

Other major works
NOVEL: *Pandion and Amphigenia: Or, The History of the Coy Lady of Thessalis*, 1665.
POETRY: "A Poem on the Death of King Charles," 1685; "The History of a Love Between a Parisian Lady and a Young Singing Man," 1692.

Bibliography
Backscheider, Paula. "Sir John Crowne," in *Restoration and Eighteenth Century Drama*, 1980. Edited by Arthur H. Scouten.
Hughes, Charlotte Bradford. "Introduction," in *Sir John Crowne's 'Sir Courtly Nice': A Critical Edition*, 1966.
Staves, Susan. *Players' Sceptres: Fictions of Authority in the Restoration*, 1979.
White, Arthur F. *John Crowne: His Life and Dramatic Works*, 1922.
Wilson, John Harold. "Introduction," in Crowne's *City Politiques*, 1967.

Robert M. Otten

RICHARD CUMBERLAND

Born: Cambridge, England; February 19, 1732
Died: Tunbridge Wells, England; May 7, 1811

Principal drama
The Banishment of Cicero, pb. 1761; *The Summer's Tale*, pr., pb. 1765; *The Clandestine Marriage*, pr. 1766; *The Brothers*, pr. 1769, pb. 1770; *The West Indian*, pr., pb. 1771; *The Fashionable Lover*, pr., pb. 1772; *The Choleric Man*, pr. 1774, pb. 1775; *The Walloons*, pr. 1782, pb. 1813; *The Mysterious Husband*, pr., pb. 1783; *The Carmelite*, pr., pb. 1784; *The Natural Son*, pr. 1784, pb. 1785; *The Box-Lobby Challenge*, pr., pb. 1794; *The Jew*, pr., pb. 1794; *The Wheel of Fortune*, pr., pb. 1795; *First Love*, pr., pb. 1795; *Don Pedro*, pr. 1797, pb. 1831; *False Impressions*, pr., pb. 1797.

Other literary forms
Richard Cumberland is remarkable for the volume and variety of his literary output, if for nothing else. Experimenting in several different genres, he earned a reputation in his day as a distinguished man of letters. Most of his works, however, have not survived.

Cumberland had early ambitions as a poet, his first publication being an imitation of Thomas Gray, *An Elegy Written on St. Mark's Eve* (1754). He was to publish *Odes* in 1776, and a volume entitled *Miscellaneous Poems* two years later. A religious epic, *Calvary: Or, The Death of Christ* (1792) sold well, which encouraged him to collaborate with Sir James Bland Burgess in *The Exodiad* (1807). Cumberland rendered some fifty psalms into English meter in *A Poetical Version of Certain Psalms of David* (1801) and reflected on his life in verse in *Retrospection* (1811).

Cumberland also won renown as an essayist for his multivolume work *The Observer*, which first appeared in 1785, with editions following in 1788 and in 1798. It featured a discussion of the early Greek drama with some original translations (notably of Aristophanes' *The Clouds*, 1798). Cumberland wrote pamphlets—defending his grandfather's reputation, among other causes—and a religious tract. He entered the realm of art history with his *Anecdotes of Eminent Painters in Spain During the Sixteenth and Seventeenth Centuries* (1782) and published the first catalog of the paintings housed in the royal palace at Madrid.

The pathetic scenes which mark Cumberland's drama are also found in his fiction: *Arundel* (1789), an epistolary novel of the form popularized by Samuel Richardson, and *Henry* (1795), a conscious imitation of Henry Fielding. Cumberland's active involvement in the theater resulted in numerous prologues and epilogues as well as an edition of *The British Drama* with biographical and critical comments, published posthumously in 1817.

In 1809, Cumberland also founded *The London Review*, which invited signed articles from contributors; it appeared only twice. His *Memoirs of Richard Cumberland, Written by Himself* (1806-1807), perhaps the most lasting of his nondramatic productions, preserved for posterity the record of his long and productive career.

Achievements

Cumberland is remarkable for his long and varied contribution to the theater. During his career, which spanned forty years, he wrote some fifty dramatic pieces, including musical comedies and operas, a masque, classical historical and domestic tragedies, translations and adaptations, farces, and occasional pieces. The genre in which he excelled was sentimental comedy, and for years he was the most successful writer in the field. His held the stage against the masterpieces of Oliver Goldsmith and Richard Brinsley Sheridan. His very preeminence, however, made him vulnerable to attack, and unfortunately he has been handed down to posterity, through the eyes of his opponents, as "the Terence of England, the mender of hearts," according to Goldsmith in *Retaliation* (1774).

Indeed, Cumberland is remembered primarily for his place in the debate between sentimental and laughing comedy. The issues were hotly contested: What is the primary purpose of the stage? Should comedy be realistic or idealistic; should it ridicule vices and follies or present models worthy of imitation? Should the playwright appeal to the intellect or to the emotions? Should he aim to provoke superior laughter or sympathetic tears? Stated in these terms, the answers seem obvious, with the common verdict in favor of "true," or laughing, comedy. One should not forget, however, the response of Cumberland's contemporaries. In his day, he was enormously popular as well as influential. Many imitators followed Cumberland's lead, ensuring the dominance of the sentimental school to the end of the century.

Cumberland was convinced of the moral utility of the drama and took his role seriously as reformer of the age. He created characters specifically to combat national prejudices, and he attacked fashionable vices. This was done both by means of admonitory examples (the ruined gambler in *The Wheel of Fortune*) and by direct statement. Aphorisms are to be found throughout Cumberland's plays, and a useful lesson is often expounded at the end.

Cumberland was unusual as a "gentleman" playwright and was considered a credit to the profession. He was well educated in classical as well as English stage tradition and drew on his knowledge for his works. His writing was admired for its elegance and accurate portrayal of high life. The refined sensibility of his heroines and the tearful pathos they inspired were highly commended.

Cumberland was superior to other writers in this genre in that he was able to blend humor with sentiment. In almost all of his plays, one finds "low" characters, included for comic relief, as well as sprightly ladies, amorous spinsters, and henpecked husbands. Strongly patriotic, he liked homegrown English characters and created some memorable types, such as the Irishman, Major O'Flaherty. He could also employ local color to advantage, as he did in the seaside scenes in *The Brothers*.

Through his long acquaintance with the theater, Cumberland developed a good sense of what would work onstage; it was often remarked that his plays performed better than they read. He was able to utilize all the resources at his disposal (scenery, costumes, and so on) to enhance his plays. He also knew the abilities of the performers and could write parts which would exploit their talents. Some of these roles—Penruddock or Belcour, for example—were favorite acting parts.

Famous in his own time, Cumberland was the last and the best of the sentimental dramatists. Of his many plays, *The West Indian* survives as a classic.

Biography

Richard Cumberland was born on February 19, 1732, in the Master's Lodge at Trinity College, Cambridge, into a family of clergymen and scholars of whom he was justly proud. His father, Denison Cumberland, later Bishop of Clonfert and Kilmore, was descended from the Bishop of Peterborough, who wrote an influential treatise in refutation of Thomas Hobbes, *De Legibus Naturae, Disquisito Philosophica* (1672). Cumberland's mother, Joanna, was the daughter of the famous classics scholar Richard Bentley. Cumberland cherished fond memories of this learned man and upheld Bentley's reputation all of his life.

At the age of six, Cumberland was sent to school at Bury St. Edmunds, where, encouraged by headmaster Arthur Kinsman, he stood first in his class. In 1744, he entered Westminster School contemporaneously with Warren Hastings, George Colman, and William Cowper. In Cumberland's school days, an interest in the drama was awakened by his mother's reading of William Shakespeare; on an early trip to the theater, he was much impressed by the innovative acting of the young David Garrick.

In 1747, Cumberland was admitted to Trinity College, Cambridge, where he enjoyed the quiet life of study and intellectual exertion. He took his bachelor of arts degree in 1751 with high honors and was elected to a fellowship two years later. He felt drawn to an academic or clerical career and relinquished his calling with some regret when more worldly prospects presented themselves.

The great Whig Sir George Montagu Dunk, second Earl of Halifax, out of gratitude to Cumberland's father, offered to take Cumberland as his private secretary. Cumberland moved to London to take up the post, which gave him the opportunity to move in political circles. In 1759, he married Elizabeth Ridge, by whom he was to have four sons and three daughters. Fortunately for his growing family, he was appointed the Crown Agent for Nova Scotia and Provost Marshal of South Carolina, which added to his income.

Cumberland accompanied Lord Halifax to Ireland in 1761 as Ulster Secretary. This experience was later to bear fruit in Cumberland's drama, when he brought original Irish characters to the stage. The relationship with his patron cooled upon Cumberland's refusal of a baronetcy, and when Halifax became Secretary of State in 1762, he appointed a rival as Under Secretary. Cumberland was forced to accept a minor position as Clerk of Reports on the Board of Trade.

With little to do and in need of money, Cumberland began in earnest his career as a dramatist. His first play, *The Banishment of Cicero*, was refused, but in 1765, *The Summer's Tale* was produced, a musical comedy imitative of Isaac Bickerstaffe. This provoked a charge from which Cumberland was often to suffer, that of plagiarism, and he turned his efforts to a genre more conducive to his talents, that of sentimental comedy. In 1769, *The Brothers* played at Covent Garden to great applause. An unexpected compliment to Garrick in the epilogue won Garrick's friendship and led to a very productive association between the two. As actor-manager of Drury Lane Theatre until 1776, Garrick produced several of Cumberland's plays, which benefited from Garrick's expert knowledge of stagecraft. Their first effort was also the most successful: *The West Indian*, which appeared in 1771, enjoyed an extraordinary first run of twenty-eight nights, was frequently revived and held the stage to the end of the century. When his third comedy, *The Fashionable Lover*, also won favor, in 1772, Cumberland was established as the leading dramatist of the sentimental school.

Cumberland's preeminence in the theater won for him his entrée into the leading social and literary circles of the time. At the British Coffee House, he met Samuel Johnson, Sir Joshua Reynolds, Edmund Burke, and Samuel Foote. He patronized the painter George Romney. He dined at Elizabeth Montagu's ("Queen of the Blues"); he knew Hester Thrale and irritated Horace Walpole. As to the latter, although Cumberland moved in society with ease, proud of his dignified position as "gentleman playwright," he had a temperament that provoked as much enmity as friendship.

Most unsatisfactory were his relationships with fellow dramatists, for Cumberland was reputed to be envious of all merit but his own. His discomfiture at the success of Sheridan's *The School for Scandal* (pr. 1777) was widely reported. As the most popular exponent of sentimental comedy, Cumberland was vulnerable to attack by those who preferred laughing comedy, and when Goldsmith's famous essay on the subject, "An Essay on the Theatre," appeared in 1773, Cumberland took it as a personal affront. He replied in a vitriolic preface to his (appropriately entitled) play *The Choleric Man*. Proud of his accomplishments though professing humility, and sensitive to criticism though pretending to lofty indifference, he exasperated even Garrick, who called him a "man without a skin." Cumberland was identified by contemporaries as the original of Sheridan's caricature in *The Critic* (pr. 1779) and was known as Sir Fretful Plagiary.

Cumberland's literary career was interrupted in 1780 by involvement in political affairs. He had been appointed Secretary to the Board of Trade in 1775 through the interest of his patron and friend Lord George Germain. For this nobleman, then Colonial Secretary, Cumberland undertook a secret mission to Spain to arrange a separate peace treaty. When negotiations failed in 1781, Cumberland was recalled and was treated ungratefully by the government, which refused to reimburse him for his expenses. Moreover, he lost his post when the Board of Trade was abolished in 1782. Disappointed and in need of money, Cumberland retired to Tunbridge Wells, where he tried through unceasing literary activity to recoup his fortunes.

The first work produced after Cumberland's return, *The Walloons*, a play with a strong Spanish flavor, failed to please, but he had more success with a domestic tragedy, *The Mysterious Husband*, in 1783. *The Carmelite*, staged in 1784 with an impressive Gothic setting, displayed the extraordinary talents of actress Sarah Siddons as the heroine. Cumberland won little approval for his next few ventures, and it was not until 1794 that he again found his audience.

The Box-Lobby Challenge, produced early that year, was amusing fare, and a few months later *The Jew* was widely acclaimed. For the title role of the latter, Cumberland created a sympathetic character whose apparent avarice cloaked benevolent actions. Another powerful figure animated *The Wheel of Fortune* in 1795, giving actor John Philip Kemble one of his favorite roles. *First Love*, in the old vein of sentimental comedy, also won favor. These plays briefly restored Cumberland to his former popularity, but in the years to come, he was unable to match their success. He continued to write prolifically up to his death but for the most part failed to suit the taste of the audience and complained of the degeneracy of the stage.

Perhaps for this reason, Cumberland turned to other channels, and the years of his retirement saw a tremendous outpouring of fiction, poetry, and prose. This unremitting literary activity was at least partly a result of financial pressure. Toward the end of his life, his unfortunate situation attracted notice, as one unworthy of a venerable man of letters.

By 1800, Cumberland had outlived his own generation and was viewed by his younger contemporaries as a figure from another era. He enjoyed his position as elder statesman and was accorded respect for his age and accomplishments. He liked to encourage young writers of talent, entertaining them with anecdotes of his own younger days. Always staunchly patriotic, he raised a corps of volunteers to meet the threat of a Napoleonic invasion; two of his sons died serving their country. At his death, at the age of seventy-nine, Cumberland left a modest estate to his youngest daughter. He lies buried in the Poets' Corner of Westminster Abbey.

Analysis

Richard Cumberland took seriously his role as moralist and reformer and set himself a novel didactic task:

> I thereupon looked into society for the purpose of discovering such as were the victims of its national, professional or religious prejudices; . . . and out of these I meditated to select and form heroes for my future dramas, . . .

In his popular play *The West Indian*, he defends the character of a Creole. The basic plot is a familiar testing device, set up in the opening scene. Stockwell awaits the arrival from Jamaica of his unacknowledged son; he decides to defer acknowledgment of their relationship until he has had an opportunity to evaluate the young man's behavior. Should his son, Belcour, satisfy this scrutiny, Stockwell will reward him with legitimacy, a fortune, and a place in English society.

Interest in Belcour is awakened before his entrance and increased by the parade of black porters. Nor is he likely to disappoint expectations; he enters breezily, complaining of the rapacious mob at the waterside. As a stranger to English society, he is able to view it objectively and provide satiric commentary. Moreover, as a "child of nature," his viewpoint should be a healthy corrective. Generous and honorable himself, he does not suspect duplicity in others; while this makes him an easy dupe of the scheming Fulmers, it redounds to his credit as a proof of his innocence.

Belcour's lack of guile is an endearing trait: The candor with which he acknowledges his faults to Stockwell disarms reproof, and his ingenuous confession to Charlotte of the loss of her jewels wins an easy forgiveness. This West Indian shows the human heart in its natural state—impulsive, mercurial, and uncontrolled. He himself bemoans the violence of his passions, blaming them on his tropical constitution. He is driven by his powerful urges; inflamed by the beauty of Louisa Dudley, he sacrifices every other tie to possess her. Plunging headlong into error, he is chastened by the mischief that ensues. Like so many other libertines, Belcour is reclaimed by a virtuous woman. Kneeling at her feet, he pledges his love, grounded now on principle. In their union, the ideal of a feeling heart tempered with reason will be achieved.

Belcour is valued above all for his benevolence. A creature of instinct, his first impulse on hearing of distress is to relieve it. His follies and virtues proceed from the same source—a warm heart. He reflects the fundamental belief of sentimental drama in the natural goodness of man and contradicts the orthodox Christian view of man's sinfulness. Sympathy with one's fellow creatures is the moral touchstone for all the characters in the play—a quality conspicuously lacking in Lady Rusport, who represents the Puritan position: She was taught never to laugh; she abhors the playhouses; and she upholds the letter of the law over the spirit of charity. She is rightfully excluded from the happy ending.

Cumberland's fallible but generous hero, who would not be out of place in a laughing comedy, resembles Fielding's Tom Jones and Sheridan's Charles Surface. The play abounds with high spirits; besides the amusing peccadilloes of Belcour, there is a subplot involving the lively Charlotte Rusport. She is unexpectedly forthright, avowing her love for Charles although uncertain of its return. This reversal of roles, where a lady takes the active part in the wooing, is frequently seen in Cumberland's plays. Charlotte's witty repartee, directed even at the sentimental heroine, prevents Louisa's distresses from appearing too pathetic.

A similar defusing of sentiment is accomplished by Major O'Flaherty. He is a stage Irishman with a difference; while retaining some national traits, he has many admirable qualities, showing courage, loyalty, and generosity. It is he, after all, who discovers and delivers the will which brings about the happy reversal of fortune. His joyful exuberance animates this otherwise tearful scene. He punctures the Dudleys' formal rhetoric with irreverent comments, undercuts Lady Rusport's tirade, and interrupts the highly emotional father-son reunion.

In *The West Indian*, Cumberland skilfully blends comic and sentimental elements. It is unique in this regard; more often, his plays are thoroughly imbued with sentiment. *The Fashionable Lover*, for example, shows more clearly what is meant by the "tearful Muse."

The opening of *The Fashionable Lover* is reminiscent of a comedy of humors, in which each character appears onstage to exhibit his particular foible. A Scotsman complains of extravagance to a foppish French valet; a railing misanthrope irritates a dissolute aristocrat; and a musty Welsh antiquary squares off with a vulgar merchant. The tone is one of satire until the introduction of the sentimental plot. This involves a poor orphan, surprised by the rakish lord into a compromising situation. Wherever Miss Augusta Aubrey turns in her hapless state, tears are sure to follow.

Cumberland aims to inspire pity through the picture of virtue in distress. He presents characters in a middle walk of life, with whose problems the audience can identify. The appeal to the heart is beneficial and instructive; it enlarges one's sympathies and strengthens one's affections. To evoke this response, Augusta is cast upon the world bemoaning her hard lot. Nor is she likely to minimize her sorrows: "I have no house, no home, no father, friend, or refuge, in this world." The smallest problems are magnified in her eyes; the awesome prospect of independence overwhelms her. Preoccupied as she is with her troubles, it is difficult to rouse her from self-pity. Even when informed of her good fortune, Augusta weeps, reflecting how unaccustomed she is to happiness.

As Augusta is unlikely to show stoic fortitude, so she is incapable of acting spiritedly on her own behalf. Her most likely resource at this critical pass would be her fiancé, but rather than appeal for his aid, she advises him to forget her. When he demands an explanation, she replies ambiguously that she accepts her fate. It is not surprising that Mr. Tyrrel concludes that she is guilty, for she makes no effort to deny it.

The heroine's extraordinary passivity is the result of her extreme sensibility; she is tremblingly alive to every sensation and fearful of aggression. Ushered into the presence of a man who eyes her keenly, Augusta complains, "his eyes oppress me." She is delicate of body as well as of spirit, and the least exertion exhausts her. Reunited with her long-lost father, she weeps, faints, and has to be carried away. Her feminine frailty endears her to the hero, since she so evidently depends on his protection.

Such a pathetic heroine requires a rescuer. A conventional figure is an elderly gentleman somewhat removed from the action who wanders through the play doing good. He appears at propitious moments to solve difficulties, remove obstacles, and shower benefits on the needy. In *The Fashionable Lover*, there are at least three rescuers. Colin MacLeod is the most colorful of these and the linchpin of the plot. He is on hand at every critical juncture: He meets Augusta in the street and later saves her from rape; he intercepts her father on his return and masterminds the final discovery. An attractive character with his homely, forceful dialect and blunt humor, he was intended by Cumberland to combat prejudice against the Scots. It is clear that Colin is economical on principle and not parsimonious; he disapproves of wasteful expenditure and lives frugally that he may be the more generous to others. He is the mouthpiece for several moral maxims which serve the playwright's didactic purpose.

Colin's confederate is a stock type, not quite so original. Like Tobias Smollett's Matthew Bramble, Mortimer cloaks his charitable deeds under an affected cynicism. Extremely susceptible to human suffering, he hides his soft heart within a crusty shell. He succors the afflicted, expecting no reward but his own gratification. He proves that one acts benevolently for purely selfish reasons and calls himself a voluptuary in virtue. Besides protecting Augusta, he is determined to extricate Lord Abberville from the snares of evil. The return of the prodigal is a familiar motif in Cumberland. He frequently attacks fashionable vice in his plays: Dueling is discussed in *The West Indian* and condemned as ignoble murder. Gambling is another favorite topic and is treated as a serious crime; typically, it leads to other follies. Lord Abberville, for example, comes to realize that "gaming has made a monster of me"; grateful for his reprieve on the brink of ruin, he promises to reform.

The ending is conventional: The dishonest are chastised, the wicked repent, and the chaste lovers, blissfully united, are lavishly endowed with fortune. This is the "tin money" of which Goldsmith complained; the conclusion demonstrates the sentimentalist's rather simplistic view of poetic justice. Virtue need not wait for the hereafter; Cumberland himself takes on the role of Providence, distributing appropriate rewards and punishments before the curtain falls.

Romantic love is often at the center of Cumberland's plots, which typically revolve around a young couple who encounter difficulties in bringing their attachment to fruition. The obstacles they face recur: parental opposition, difference of class or fortune, misleading appearances, or the waywardness of one of the parties. A conventional pair of star-crossed lovers appears in *The Wheel of Fortune*. What is surprising is that their affair is secondary, significant only for its effect on the protagonist.

Roderick Penruddock is an unusual hero for a Cumberland play in that he is well past the age of courtship. In his youth, he was cruelly betrayed by his friend and robbed of his beloved. Bitter and disillusioned, he has withdrawn into gloomy seclusion. The play opens on his inheritance of a vast estate, to which the property of his enemy has been mortgaged. His accession to wealth gives him the power to destroy his foe and rouses in him long-suppressed emotion. The conflict of the play is internal, as he is tempted by, contends with, and eventually vanquishes the spirit of revenge.

In this brooding figure, the play shows signs of the taste for melodrama that was to dominate the English stage in the nineteenth century. There are also certain Romantic tendencies that link it to a later era. Immediately striking is the setting; the first scene takes place in a wild and remote landscape, extremely picturesque. The character of the misanthrope is well adapted to his environment: Penruddock is not only an isolated but also an alienated man. Deeply passionate, he has never forgiven his injuries. Inexorable in anger, he is equally tenacious in love. Though rejected and forgotten by his betrothed, he retains her image fresh in his mind and is haunted by her voice. The anguish of his loss has driven him close to madness.

The turbulence of Penruddock's mind is shown by the intemperance of his language. He rails at the beguiling world which entices only to destroy: "Away with all such snares! There's whore upon the face of them." At home in a stormy wasteland, he is out of place in London. In a gaily festooned ballroom, he looks "like a gloomy nightpiece in a gilded frame." In the streets, the beggars shrink away from his grim visage, which bears the "mark of Cain." He is almost Byronic in his role as a man set apart by a fateful destiny.

Penruddock also shows the Romantic need to escape the corrupting influence of society. He is more content in a simple cottage than in the splendid mansions of the city. He is loath to leave his humble abode and anxious to return. When he has won his battle of conscience, he looks forward to the solace of a self-approving conscience in his rural retreat.

This is a familiar notion in a sentimental play, that good deeds are also pleasurable. One finds an increasingly greater emphasis as the century progresses on sensual gratification, on luxuriating in emotions for their own sake. Penruddock shows signs of this preoccupation; he is completely engrossed by his own subjective experience. Wandering the streets of London, he considers the tumult outside as a reflection of his own state of mind. At every stage of the action, he feels his own mental pulse. Moreover, he deliberately seeks out potentially stimulating situations. He rereads Mrs. Woodville's letter for the tender melancholy it produces, which he indulges to the full. His self-consciousness is characteristically Romantic.

Despite these innovative features, Penruddock is contained within the structure of a sentimental play, and in the end he is reclaimed. The change begins in the third act, when he abandons his aloof and ironic pose to defend his actions. He sympathizes strongly with Henry and is finally able to forgive his debtor. Consonant with Cumberland's philosophy, the spirit of vengeance has been a brief aberration in an otherwise benevolent soul. Apparently, Penruddock's former state of alienation has also been a distortion of his true nature, to which he is now restored. By the end of the play, he has grown remarkably sociable. He compares his heart, overflowing with sympathy, to a river flooding its banks. The bonds have been reestablished, and Penruddock has been accepted back into society.

In *The Wheel of Fortune*, enormously popular in its day, Cumberland demonstrated his ability to adapt to the latest literary trends, yet he was later to fall back on his old recipes for success, despite the fact that these outmoded forms failed to please. In his last years, he complained of the deterioration of standards, to which he would not accommodate himself, and pleaded for tolerance. Cumberland's influence on the theater effectively ended in 1795.

Other major works

NOVEL: *Arundel*, 1789; *Henry*, 1795.

POETRY: *An Elegy Written on St. Mark's Eve*, 1754; *Odes*, 1776; *Miscellaneous Poems*, 1778; *Calvary: Or, The Death of Christ*, 1792; *A Poetical Version of Certain Psalms of David*, 1801; *The Exodiad*, 1807 (with Sir James Bland Burgess); *Retrospection*, 1811.

NONFICTION: *Anecdotes of Eminent Painters in Spain During the Sixteenth and Seventeenth Centuries*, 1782; *The Observer*, 1785; *Memoirs of Richard Cumberland, Written by Himself*, 1806-1807.

TRANSLATIONS: *The Clouds*, 1798 (of Aristophanes' play).

MISCELLANEOUS: *The London Review*, 1809 (editor); *The British Drama*, 1817.

Bibliography

Detisch, Robert J. "The Synthesis of Laughing and Sentimental in *The West Indian*," in *Educational Theatre Journal*. XX (1970), pp. 291-300.

Dircks, Richard J. *Richard Cumberland*, 1976.

Waith, Eugene M. "Richard Cumberland, Comic Force and Misanthropy," in *Comparative Drama*. XII (1978-1979), pp. 283-299.

Williams, Stanley T. "The English Sentimental Drama from Steele to Cumberland," in *Sewanee Review*. XXXIII (1925), pp. 405-426.

_____. *Richard Cumberland: His Life and Dramatic Works*, 1917.

Lorna Clarke

SIR WILLIAM DAVENANT

Born: Oxford, England; February, 1606
Died: London, England; April 7, 1668

Principal drama
The Cruell Brother, pr. 1627, pb. 1630; *The Tragedy of Albovine, King of the Lombards*, pb. 1629; *The Just Italian*, pr. 1629, pb. 1630; *The Siege: Or, The Collonell*, pr. 1629, pb. 1673; *Love and Honour*, pr. 1634, pb. 1649; *The Witts*, pr. 1634, pb. 1636; *News from Plimouth*, pr. 1635, pb. 1673; *The Temple of Love*, pr., pb. 1635 (masque); *The Platonick Lovers*, pr. 1635, pb. 1636; *The Triumphs of the Prince d'Amour*, pr., pb. 1636 (masque); *Britannia Triumphans*, pr., pb. 1638 (masque); *The Fair Favorite*, pr. 1638, pb. 1673; *Luminalia: Or, The Festival of Light*, pr., pb. 1638; *The Unfortunate Lovers*, pr. 1638, pb. 1643; *The Distresses*, pr. 1639, pb. 1673 (also as *The Spanish Lovers*); *Salmacida Spolia*, pr., pb. 1640 (masque); *The First Days Entertainment at Rutland House*, pr. 1656, pb. 1657 (music by Henry Lawes); *The Siege of Rhodes, Part I*, pr., pb. 1656, *Part II*, pr. 1659, pb. 1663; *The Cruelty of the Spaniards in Peru*, pr., pb. 1658; *The History of Sir Francis Drake*, pr., pb. 1659; *Hamlet*, pr. 1661, pb. 1676 (adaptation of William Shakespeare's play); *Twelfth Night*, pr. 1661 (adaptation of Shakespeare's play); *The Law Against Lovers*, pr. 1662, pb. 1673; *Romeo and Juliet*, pr. 1662 (adaptation of Shakespeare's play); *Henry VIII*, pr. 1663 (adaptation of Shakespeare's play); *Macbeth*, pr. 1663, pb. 1674 (adaptation of Shakespeare's play); *The Playhouse to Be Lett*, pr. 1663, pb. 1673; *The Rivals*, pr. 1664, pb. 1668; *The Tempest: Or, The Enchanted Island*, pr. 1667, pb. 1670 (with John Dryden; adaptation of Shakespeare's play); *The Man's the Master*, pr. 1668, pb. 1669.

Other literary forms
Apart from his plays, Sir William Davenant is best known for his unfinished heroic poem, *Gondibert* (1651).

Achievements
Sir William Davenant began his career as a playwright in the age of Ben Jonson and ended it in the age of John Dryden. Already a well-established playwright and poet laureate before the closing of the playhouses at the beginning of the English Civil War in 1642, Davenant managed a limited revival of theatrical entertainments toward the end of the interregnum. Despite the Puritan prohibition against staging plays, Davenant succeeded in obtaining government consent to present "entertainments" at Rutland House in London in 1656. These "entertainments" were musical rather than strictly dramatic, with set declamations instead of plots and entries in-

stead of acts and scenes, but their popularity kept the theater from vanishing entirely during the protectorate of Oliver Cromwell and kept it poised for a revival after the restoration of Charles II in 1660.

Davenant may be credited with having introduced the first actress on the English stage, when Mrs. Edward Coleman sang the role of the heroine Ianthe during the production of his "opera" *The Siege of Rhodes* at Rutland House in the fall of 1656. This production also made use of the changeable scenery hithertofore restricted to private theaters and court masques. After the Restoration, Davenant retained and expanded his use of changeable scenery, designing his new theater in Lincoln's Inn Fields to take advantage of its possibilities and spurring imitation by his competitors. Thus, the staging of almost every kind of drama was radically altered.

Davenant operated his theater under a patent that was granted to him by Charles II. In need of plays to produce, he revived some of Ben Jonson's and adapted several of William Shakespeare's. Indeed, Davenant's adaptation of *Macbeth* held the stage well into the eighteenth century, and his adaptation of *The Tempest* well into the nineteenth. As an innovator and an impresario, Davenant changed the course of English theatrical history and extended his influence well beyond his own age.

Biography

Sir William Davenant (or D'Avenant), son of John Davenant, a vintner, was born at Oxford, England, near the end of February, in 1606. As a young man, he wrote his first plays while living in the household of Sir Fulke Greville, and by 1638, he was sufficiently established as a poet and playwright to succeed Ben Jonson as poet laureate. When civil war broke out in 1642, Davenant, a staunch Royalist, risked his life for the Stuart cause. He fled to the Continent for a time, and in 1650 he was on his way to America to become lieutenant governor of Maryland when his ship was intercepted and he was captured and imprisoned in the Tower of London. It was there that he wrote most of his unfinished heroic poem *Gondibert*. Influential friends finally secured his release from the Tower, after which Davenant managed to live on good terms with the Puritan government. He eventually secured official permission to stage operatic entertainments at Rutland House in London, beginning in May of 1656.

Four years later, when the monarchy was restored, Davenant expected court preferment on the basis of his past service to the Stuarts. Although Charles II did grant him a patent to operate a theater, Davenant never regained the favor he had enjoyed under Charles I. Therefore, instead of relying on the patronage of the court, he busied himself with writing and staging plays for the Duke's Company, which he managed at Lincoln's Inn Fields in the public playhouse that he himself built to accommodate the changeable scenery that had been the prerogative of the earlier private theaters. His post-Restoration career lasted only seven years, but during that time, he managed to establish actresses on the English stage, to change play production radically, and to create a new appreciation of Shakespeare's plays, even if in a greatly altered version.

Davenant was married three times. In 1632, he wed a still unidentified woman to whom he was reputed to have been unfaithful. After her death (the date of which is unknown), Davenant married Dame Anne Cademan in 1652. She died in 1655; in that same year, he married Henrietta-Maria du Tremblay, who had four sons by previous marriages. She subsequently bore Davenant nine sons. He had only one daughter, by one of his first wives. After Davenant's death in 1668, Henrietta-Maria helped prepare an edition of his works. Davenant was buried in Westminster Abbey. His epitaph epitomizes his achievements: "O rare Sir Will. Davenant."

Analysis

Thematically and technically, Sir William Davenant's plays link the theater of Charles I with that of Charles II. For example, the seeds of Restoration comedy are embedded in *The Witts*, in which Davenant explores the subject of wit, using heroes and heroines who prefigure those of Sir George Etherege, William Wycherley, and William Congreve. His early tragedies and tragicomedies, such as *Love and Honour*, explore the love and honor conflicts that later dominate Restoration heroic drama, beginning with Davenant's own *The Siege of Rhodes*. His court masques for Charles I and his queen, Henrietta Maria, used the movable scenery that he would popularize in the public theater after the Restoration. His revivals of the plays of Ben Jonson and his adaptations of Shakespeare's plays preserved and advanced the reputations of those writers during the reign of Charles II.

The Witts is perhaps the best of Davenant's early comedies. During the seventeenth century, the term "wit" came to have multiple meanings. It could mean simply verbal cleverness expressed in appropriate and sustained repartee; it could mean the synthetic faculty of the mind that could see similarities in apparently dissimilar things; it could mean the ornamentation of discourse; it could mean gamesmanship, implying a superior understanding of "the way of the world."

Gamesmanship comes closest to the meaning that concerns Davenant in *The Witts*. Most of the characters in this work are concerned with outmaneuvering their opponents in games of love and legacy. The contest is between the Truewits—those who truly have wit—and the Witwouds—those who think they have wit but do not. Davenant represents the first in the characters of Young Pallatine and Lady Ample; the second, in the characters of the Elder Pallatine and his companion, Sir Morglay Thwack, a country squire.

These last two characters come to London to live by their wits, which to them means seducing rich women who will afterward support them lavishly. Young Pallatine, already in London, has been successful at this game, having gone so far as to persuade his mistress Lucy to sell her belongings to pay for his indulgences. When the brothers Pallatine meet in London, the elder rejects his younger brother's plea for money, and Young Pallatine plots how he may reap both revenge and reward at his brother's expense.

Young Pallatine enlists Lucy in his plot. When Lucy's aunt finally turns her out of her house, she seeks aid from a friend, the wealthy Lady Ample, who, of all the play's characters, turns out to be the wittiest because she can best understand and control her own and others' actions. Lady Ample eventually uses that wit to foil her guardian, Sir Tirant Thrifty, who has picked out an inappropriate husband for her.

In one of the play's key scenes, Lady Ample discusses her wit with Lucy, whom she first takes to task for being so dull-witted and traitorous to her sex as to support a man. Lady Ample, who says she draws her wit from nature, argues instead for tempting "the Fowl" until it can be "caught" and "plume[d]." She then proceeds to demonstrate the application of this principle by acquiring complete mastery over the Elder Pallatine.

After a series of twists, turns, and deceits, engineered by Young Pallatine, Lucy, and Lady Ample herself, the Witwouds are totally humiliated. Sir Morglay Thwack resolves to return to the country while the Elder Pallatine is forced to recant his pretensions to wit. Surprisingly, however, Lady Ample, eager to escape the match arranged by her miserly guardian, agrees to marry the Elder Pallatine because she likes being able to dominate one who has so much money and so little wit.

Lady Ample further demonstrates her mastery over him by forcing him to sign certain bonds without him knowing what it is he is signing. It turns out to be a deed to part of his estate that he has unwittingly signed over to his younger brother. This generous settlement allows Young Pallatine and Lucy to marry. That done, Lady Ample confirms her intention to marry the Elder Pallatine, whom she "has the wit to govern." This scene, in which an independent woman sets the terms upon which she will be married, is a forerunner of the famous "proviso" scenes of Restoration comedy in which like-minded heroines set forth the terms upon which they will consent to marry. Thus, Lady Ample clearly proves to be the best gamester, and therefore the greatest wit, among all the characters. With the addition of more polished repartee and a worthier adversary, Congreve at the end of the seventeenth century would refine a charming Lady Ample into the brilliant Millamant of his *The Way of the World* (pr. 1700).

The English Civil War temporarily halted Davenant's playwriting career, but toward the end of the interregnum, Davenant succeeded in convincing the Puritan government that theatrical entertainments could be useful in teaching morality. Davenant was granted permission to set up a semiprivate stage at Rutland House, his London residence, and to present *The First Days Entertainment at Rutland House* on May 23, 1656. Carefully avoiding even the semblance of drama, Davenant's entertainment was little more than two debates, interspersed with musical interludes. The first debate concerned the usefulness and morality of public entertainments. Indeed, *The First Days Entertainment at Rutland House* was itself designed to demonstrate that public entertainments need not threaten either public morals or the Puritan government. The second debate concerned the relative merits of Paris and London, with, of course, English nationalism triumphant.

Encouraged by the success of this initial enterprise, Davenant again used Rutland House to present his "opera" *The Siege of Rhodes* in the fall of 1656. This time Davenant was more daring, moving his entertainment a step closer to drama by giving it a thin plot and characters developed beyond those of the debaters in *The First Days Entertainment at Rutland House*. In fact, Edward J. Dent in his *Foundations of English Opera* (1928) argues persuasively that *The Siege of Rhodes* was originally written as a play but altered to include instrumental and vocal music to circumvent the Puritan prohibition against the staging of plays. Nevertheless, Davenant was careful to call his work neither drama nor opera, but *The Siege of Rhodes: Made a Representation by the Art of Prospective in Scenes, and the Story Sung in Recitative Musick*. He even avoided the designation "act" by borrowing the term "entry" from the court masques, which he had composed during the reign of Charles I. Thus, *The Siege of Rhodes* has five "entries" instead of five "acts."

From the court masque, Davenant also borrowed the idea of using changeable scenery in his entertainments at Rutland House. Scenes were changed in full view of the audience and indeed were themselves sometimes the most important part of the entertainment. In his preface to *The Siege of Rhodes*, Davenant complains that the narrowness and shallowness of the stage at Rutland House greatly limited his use of spectacle. To create his effects, Davenant used a proscenium arch to frame movable backflats and wings. No attempt at realism was made; instead, the various scenes merely suggested an appropriate atmosphere (though not without inevitable incongruities). Generally, the actors played on the stage apron in front of the proscenium rather than close to the scenery behind it.

Women had long taken part in the court masques. Usually the queen and some of her ladies-in-waiting would appear as goddesses, often accompanied by spectacular scenic effects. On the English public stage, however, men customarily acted women's roles. The closing of the theaters in 1642 meant that by 1656 Davenant had no readily available young actors specifically trained to interpret female roles. Furthermore, Davenant's exile in France had accustomed him to seeing actresses rather than actors in women's roles. Thus, his first production of *The Siege of Rhodes* also marked the first appearance of an actress on the English public stage, when Mrs. Edward Coleman sang the role of the heroine, Ianthe.

After the Restoration, Davenant converted this work into a heroic play. The essence of this genre was the conflict between love and honor. Its heroes and heroines either were exemplary in virtue or were Herculean figures not subject to customary moral niceties. Its verse form was the heroic couplet—the rhymed iambic pentameter closed couplet—deemed most suitable for the expression of heroic ideals. Finally, it emphasized spectacle, sometimes at the expense of sense, as George Villiers, Duke of Buckingham, was to point out in *The Rehearsal* (pr. 1671), which burlesqued the conventions of the genre.

The Siege of Rhodes is a quasi-historical drama. In 1522, the Ottoman Turks besieged Rhodes, garrisoned by the Knights of St. John, under the command of Villiers de L'Isle-Adam. The knights fought valiantly and, though defeated, won the respect of the Turks and safe conduct from the island. Into this story Davenant inserts his hero, Alphonso, and his heroine, Ianthe. Alphonso is one of the defenders of Rhodes; Ianthe, his bride, having sold her jewels in Sicily to procure arms for the garrison, sets sail for Rhodes but is intercepted by the Turkish Fleet and taken prisoner by its commander, the sultan Solyman. Ianthe conquers the sultan by her virtue, and he grants her safe passage to Rhodes. Alphonso is less than happy to see her, since he assumes her safe conduct has been granted because Solyman has enjoyed her favors. Overcareful of his honor, Alphonso fails to recognize honor in others. His resultant jealousy momentarily overwhelms his love, but when the siege resumes and both he and Ianthe are wounded, he at last realizes his folly, and the pair are reconciled, though the outcome of the siege is left in doubt.

To balance Alphonso's jealousy, Davenant introduces Roxolana, Solyman's wife, who is jealous of her husband's appreciation of and attention to Ianthe. Their marital discord is less definitely and happily reconciled, since their marital peace is achieved not by love or trust but by the watchfulness of Roxolana's waiting-women, who have been charged to report any infidelity of Solyman.

Indeed, the notion of reconciliation is crucial to an understanding of *The Siege of Rhodes*, since much of the play's structure seeks a creative rather than a destructive tension between opposites, especially between love and honor. Thus, antitheses abound. For example, West and East are represented by the Rhodians and the Turks respectively, Christian and Muslim by Alphonso and Ianthe and by Solyman and Roxolana; the play's diction is liberally sprinkled with references to order and chaos, public and private worlds, harmony and discord, passion and reason, and light and darkness.

Viewed from this perspective, the marital discords of Alphonso and

Ianthe and of Solyman and Roxolana take on new meaning. The former resolve their discord through the creative power of love and thereby reach a new harmony; the latter achieve only the appearance of a resolution, since the destructive power of jealousy still mars their relationship. These private reconciliations, however, are played out against the backdrop of a larger and much more public discord—the siege itself, which is left unresolved.

This larger conflict was not resolved until Davenant wrote part 2 of *The Siege of Rhodes*. Always the impresario, he staged parts 1 and 2 on alternate days at Lincoln's Inn Fields Theatre. Part 2 continues Davenant's theme of love and honor. This time, the defenders of Rhodes, threatened by famine and by the inevitability of a direct Turkish assault, must choose either an honorable death or an ignoble surrender. Ianthe is sent to negotiate with Solyman, who once again treats her honorably. Alphonso's jealousy is reawakened but eventually subordinated to his fear for Ianthe's safety. Roxolana's jealousy, also rekindled, is somewhat assuaged by her awe of Ianthe's virtue, which lies not so much in Ianthe's reputation as in a sense of personal integrity that allows her to risk her reputation by returning to Solyman's camp. Similarly impressed, Solyman allows Ianthe to set honorable conditions for the surrender of Rhodes. Thus, Ianthe's virtue reconciles both private and public tensions—a happy ending indeed for an England still struggling with the destructiveness of its civil war and the uncertainties of its restored monarchy.

A different sort of reconciliation must be effected in Davenant's *The Playhouse to Be Lett*. The prologue likens this work to a new-fashioned "monster" whose disproportionate limbs "are disjoyn'd and yet united too." Davenant, the successful theater manager, takes his audience behind the scenes to observe the workings of a Restoration playhouse, empty for the summer but about to be rented for various entertainments. The housekeeper and a player must choose among such prospective tenants as a dancing master, a musician, a gentleman, and a poet.

Four entertainments are selected, three of which are by Davenant himself. The French farce presented in act 2 is Davenant's own translation of Molière's *Sganarelle: Ou, Le Cocu imaginaire*. Acts 3 and 4 revive two of Davenant's Rutland House entertainments: *The History of Sir Francis Drake* and *The Cruelty of the Spaniards in Peru*. Act 5 is a travesty of Katherine Philips' tragedy *Pompey* (1663).

Interesting as each of these entertainments may be, it is the action of the frame story that is of most importance, for *The Playhouse to Be Lett* is really a play about the problems of managing a playhouse. Together with plays about the problems of producing a play, it belongs to the sizable group of Restoration plays concerned with theatrical self-consciousness. Many of these plays use a frame story in which a playwright and one or more critics attend the rehearsal of a play, whose action is often interrupted by their comments or by those of the actors themselves, who step out of character momentarily. The epitome of this genre was *The Rehearsal*, which satirized John Dryden and poked fun at the absurdities of heroic drama.

Davenant, whose work preceded *The Rehearsal*, uses a rehearsal framework only in the loosest sense of that word. There is a rehearsal of what will be presented for the summer season, but there is no attempt to interrupt or to correct the individual presentations. In fact, the player and the housekeeper are not even the final judges of what is to be presented. Near the end of the first act, a crowd is gathering outside the theater in order to "see strange things for nothing." The player sends a dozen laundry maids with "tough hands" to keep them out. Nevertheless, at the end of *The Playhouse to Be Lett*, this imaginary audience is revealed to be, in reality, the actual theater audience that has been watching Davenant's entertainment. The player observes that somehow their neighbors have been let in; if they elect to stay, they are likely to hear "An Epilogue, since they have seen a Play." Thus, Davenant's audience is suddenly brought into the action of *The Playhouse to Be Lett*, and the frame characters' awareness of the audience is responsible for the abrupt ending of Davenant's entertainment with no judgments among the prospective renters having been made by the player and the housekeeper. Instead, those judgments will be made by the spectators themselves—a process Dryden was later to term the law of "pit, box, and gallery." The audience alone will determine the profitability of an entertainment. Indeed, throughout act 1, the housekeeper and the player discuss possible audience responses to the kinds of entertainments proposed by the prospective renters and even discuss packing the audience with favorable critics, including a one-handed man who claps by striking his hand against his cheek. Therefore, in giving the audience a look behind the curtain of the playhouse, Davenant also gives the audience a look at itself. His parading before them of the popular entertainments of the town, generated by his audience's insatiable appetite for novelty, would later be enlarged upon by Henry Fielding in the third act of *The Author's Farce* (pr., pb. 1730), in which emblematic representations of the "pleasures of the town" vie for a chaplet to be awarded by the Goddess of Nonsense to her favorite devotee—an honor which eventually goes to Signior Opera.

Davenant's jest at the expense of his playhouse audience illustrates his capacity to play with the paradoxes of the imagination. One of the primary meanings of "imagination" in Davenant's day was the capacity to form images. As the player and the housekeeper in the first act of *The Playhouse to Be Lett* discuss the anticipated responses of their projected audience, they create the image of an early Restoration audience eager for novel entertainments. At the end of act 5, this image fuses with its underlying reality when this imaginary audience is identified with the audience present at Davenant's play. In turn, *The Playhouse to Be Lett*, termed a dramatic "monster" in its prologue, becomes an image of the audience, since it reflects their tastes.

In this sense, Davenant's plays as a whole reveal the "imagination" of two ages—that of Charles I and that of Charles II. The heroes and heroines of Restoration tragedy and comedy are nascent in Davenant's early plays and reach their maturity in his later plays, reflecting the heroic ideals and pragmatic cynicism of the age of Charles II. Indeed, the unpleasantness of the English Civil War and the uncertainties of the restored monarchy seem both to have enhanced expectations for a new heroic age and to have tempered those expectations with the wisdom of the recent past.

However well Davenant may have reflected his world, he also dared to try to shape it, both politically and theatrically. He was no mere spectator during the English Civil War but risked his life in the service of the Crown. In the theater, he risked Puritan opposition to present his entertainments at Rutland House, and he risked introducing actresses and innovative staging in the public playhouse. Like Young Pallatine in *The Witts*, Davenant had wit; like Alphonso in *The Siege of Rhodes*, he had heroic ideals; but above all, like the player and the housekeeper, he had a "playhouse to be lett." To his credit, he filled its stage with exceptional entertainments.

Other major works

POETRY: *Madagascar: With Other Poems*, 1638; *Gondibert*, 1651 (unfinished); *The Seventh and Last Canto of the Third Book of Gondibert*, 1685; *The Shorter Poems and Songs from the Plays and Masques*, 1972 (A. M. Gibbs, editor).

NONFICTION: *The Preface to Gondibert with an Answer by Mr. Hobbes*, 1650 (with Thomas Hobbes).

MISCELLANEOUS: *Works*, 1673, 1968.

Bibliography
Bordinat, Philip, and Sophia B. Blaydes. *Sir William Davenant*, 1981.

Deane, Cecil V. *Dramatic Theory and the Rhymed Heroic Play*, 1968.

Hotson, Leslie. *The Commonwealth and Restoration Stage*, 1928.

Nethercot, Arthur H. *Sir William D'Avenant: Poet Laureate and Playwright Manager*, 1938.

Southern, Richard. *Changeable Scenery: Its Origin and Development in the British Theatre*, 1952.

Valerie C. Rudolph

ROBERTSON DAVIES

Born: Thamesville, Canada; August 28, 1913

Principal drama

Overlaid, pr. 1947, pb. 1949 (one act); *Eros at Breakfast*, pr. 1948, pb. 1949; *Hope Deferred*, pr. 1948, pb. 1949; *The Voice of the People*, pr. 1948, pb. 1949; *At the Gates of the Righteous*, pr. 1948, pb. 1949; *Eros at Breakfast and Other Plays*, pb. 1949 (includes *Hope Deferred*, *Overlaid*, *At the Gates of the Righteous*, *The Voice of the People*); *At My Heart's Core*, pr., pb. 1950; *King Phoenix*, pr. 1950, pb. 1972; *A Jig for the Gypsy*, pr. 1954 (broadcast and staged), pb. 1954; *Hunting Stuart*, pr. 1955, pb. 1972; *Love and Libel: Or, The Ogre of the Provincial World*, pr. 1960 (adaptation of his novel *Leaven of Malice*); *Hunting Stuart and Other Plays*, pb. 1972 (includes *King Phoenix* and *General Confession*); *Question Time*, pb. 1975.

Other literary forms

Robertson Davies is known primarily as a novelist. His most highly acclaimed novels form the Deptford Trilogy: *Fifth Business* (1970), *The Manticore* (1972), and *World of Wonders* (1975). These three novels were preceded by another trilogy, set in the fictional community of Salterton: *Tempest Tost* (1951), *Leaven of Malice* (1954), and *A Mixture of Frailties* (1958). His earliest success was the publication of three books based on a newspaper column, "The Diary of Samuel Marchbanks," in which he offered witty observations on the social pretensions of a small Ontario town: *The Diary of Samuel Marchbanks* (1947), *The Table Talk of Samuel Marchbanks* (1949), and *Samuel Marchbanks' Almanack* (1957).

Davies also has written a teleplay, *Fortune, My Foe* (1948), and he enjoys a considerable reputation as a critic. His articles, essays, and observations have been collected in several books, including *A Voice from the Attic* (1960), *One Half of Robertson Davies* (1977), *The Enthusiasms of Robertson Davies* (1979), and *The Well-Tempered Critic* (1981). Subjects to which he has turned his sharp pen include contemporary Canadian theater, the manners and mores of small-town residents, the humor of Stephen Leacock, the history of the Stratford Shakespearean Festival, and the Canadian national identity. His scholarly writing has centered on theater history and dramatic literature, particularly of the nineteenth century.

In all of his nondramatic writing, Davies demonstrates a keen sense of the absurdity of social pretension, an awareness of the dark world of the unconscious, and a love of magic. In many of his fictional works, the theater plays an important part, whether it be the amateur production of William Shakespeare's *The Tempest*, which sets the stage for *Tempest Tost*, or the flamboyant actor-manager of the melodramatic school who holds center stage in *World of Wonders*. Regardless of genre, Davies' perspective is that of the ironic, detached, urbane, yet sensitive observer, a reporter of the quirks of fortune which act upon human existence and which serve to reveal the inner workings of the heart.

Achievements

Davies is recognized as one of Canada's leading writers, and, although his influence is predominately in fiction, his impact on the emergence of drama and theater uniquely Canadian is widely appreciated. The source of this influence is divided between his position as a respected critic and scholar and his original and striking dramatic writing. As Master of Massey College, a position he held from 1962 to 1981, and as founder and senior scholar of the Graduate Centre for the Study of Drama, Davies influenced two generations of students at the University of Toronto.

The period immediately following World War II was of great significance to the development of indigenous Canadian drama. A spirit of nationalism, arising in large part from the important contribution of Canadian regiments to the victory in Europe, fueled a renewed interest in plays about the Canadian experience. At the same time, there was a sharp increase in the number of plays being performed in theatrical centers such as Toronto. The new professional theater companies were looking for new plays which would appeal to local audiences and with which they could make their reputations. One such company was the Crest Theatre, and several of Davies' plays were written for this group. Other influential plays by Davies were written for amateur companies and became staples of the amateur repertoire in Canada. As a result, between 1945 and 1965 Davies was the dominant English-Canadian playwright.

Davies was awarded the Leacock medal for humor in 1955, the Lorne Pierce medal for contribution to Canadian literature in 1961, and, in 1973, the Governor-General's Award for Fiction. He is a fellow of the Royal Society of Canada, the recipient of honorary degrees from more than ten universities, an honorary member of the American Academy (the first Canadian to be so honored), and a Companion of the Order of Canada.

Biography

William Robertson Davies was born on August 28, 1913, in Thamesville, Ontario, to William Rupert Davies, editor of the *Thamesville Herald*, and Florence Sheppard McKay Davies. In 1926, the Davies family moved to Kingston, where William Rupert Davies became owner and editor of the Kingston *Whig* and later, when the two local papers merged, of the Kingston *Whig Standard*. The fictional town of Salterton, which provides the environment for three of Davies' novels, bears a remarkable resemblance to the town of Kingston.

Davies was greatly influenced by the literary and dramatic activities of his parents, both of whom had a lively interest in music and theater. At that time, there was little professional theater in the small towns of Ontario, but the family traveled regularly to Toronto, Ottawa, and Detroit to see productions touring out of New York or London. The influence of the great masters of the art of acting is felt in much of Davies' work, but most notably in *World of Wonders*, which is a fictional treatment of the Canadian tour of John Martin-Harvey, one of the last proponents of the nineteenth century school of Romantic acting.

Davies' love of theater was evident throughout his academic career. As a schoolboy, he dramatized classic novels for his fellow students to perform. He acted in local amateur theater productions in the community and at school. At Balliol College, Oxford, he was active in the Oxford University Dramatic Society as an actor, stage manager, and director. He also did his bachelor of literature thesis on Shakespeare's boy actors, publishing it in 1939.

The young Davies determined to make his career in theater, and, as there was virtually no professional theater in Canada at the time, he remained in England and found employment at the Old Vic Repertory Company. He performed only minor roles and proved more valuable in teaching theater history in the company school and doing literary work for the director, Tyrone Guthrie, an old school friend from Oxford. It was there that he met Brenda Mathews, a young Australian actress and stage manager, whom he married in 1940.

The theaters in London closed with the outbreak of World War II, and the Davies returned to Canada, where Davies became literary editor of *Saturday Night*, a monthly cultural magazine. In 1942, they moved to Peterborough, and Davies became the editor and publisher of the *Peterborough Examiner*, a position he held until 1962. In 1943, he began the syndicated column "The Diary of Samuel Marchbanks," featuring satiric observations and anecdotes about fictional characters, situations, and attitudes in a small Ontario town, as seen through the eyes of a thinly disguised Robertson Davies. Selections from this column were collected in three books: *The Diary of Samuel Marchbanks*, *The Table Talk of Samuel Marchbanks*, and *Samuel Marchbanks' Almanack*.

It was also at this time that Davies and his wife became active in local amateur theatricals. He began to write full-length and short plays, submitting one of them, *Overlaid*, to a play competition in Ottawa in 1947. As the winning play, it was produced by the Ottawa Drama League. The same group produced his next short comedy, *Eros at Breakfast*, the following year, and entered their production in the national amateur dramatic competition, the Dominion Drama Festival. The production won a trophy for best production of a Canadian play and Davies won the prize for author of the best Canadian play. Moreover, the production was selected to represent Canada at the Edinburgh Festival in Glasgow in 1949.

With this encouraging beginning, Davies went on to write, in quick succession, *Fortune, My Foe* (which carried off the same prizes as *Eros at Breakfast*), *At My Hearts' Core*, and *King Phoenix*. By 1948, Davies had become the most produced English-Canadian playwright, with amateur groups across Canada performing his plays.

Nevertheless, at this time, Davies' energies were being directed more and more toward the writing of full-length fiction. *Tempest Tost, Leaven of Malice*, and *A Mixture of Frailties* were published in the 1950's, and in 1953, Davies discontinued the Marchbanks column. He did not, however, entirely turn his back on the theater; on the contrary, his writing benefited from two exciting new developments in Canadian drama. In 1953, the Stratford Shakespearean Festival was founded, and Davies became a member of the board of directors, a position he held until 1971. From 1953 to 1955, he published an annual record of the history of the festival, which was then under the leadership of his friend Tyrone Guthrie. These volumes were published as *Renown at Stratford* (1953), *Twice Have the Trumpets Sounded* (1954), and *Thrice the Brinded Cat Hath Mew'd* (1955). The second development was the emergence of a fully professional theater company in Toronto, the Crest Theatre, for which Davies wrote several plays. The company produced his *A Jig for the Gypsy* in 1954 and *Hunting Stuart* in 1955. *General Confession* was written in 1956 for the same group but was never performed.

Davies' considerable energies were further diverted when, in 1962, he was appointed by Vincent Massey to be the first Master of Massey College, a college for graduate students at the University of Toronto. In 1960, Davies had been appointed a professor of English and began his teaching career. He remained a member of the academic community for twenty years but was always skeptical about his adopted world, as is evident in the pointed satire in his novel *The Rebel Angels* (1981).

In 1960, Davies attempted a dramatization of his novel *Leaven of Malice*, entitled *Love and Libel*, which Tyrone Guthrie directed for the New York Theatre Guild. Reviews were mixed; the production closed after four days, and Davies himself was dissatisfied with his adaptation. He consented to rework the script for an amateur production at Hart House Theatre at the University of Toronto in 1973 under the same title as the novel, and it was this version which was produced at the Shaw Festival in 1975. In 1975, Davies wrote *Question Time* for Toronto Arts Productions, a leading Toronto professional company. Again, the results were not entirely positive. The reviews were mixed, and audiences were puzzled by the play's nonrealistic style. Davies was more comfortable writing for amateur groups, including the theater group at his old school Upper Canada College, which produced *A Masque of Aesop* in 1952 and *A Masque of Mr. Punch* in 1962. In 1967, the year of the centennial celebrations in Canada, he contributed one segment to *The Centennial Play*, which was written expressly for amateur audiences. It was given its first full-scale production by a group with which Davies had been associated at the beginning of his writing career, the Ottawa Little Theatre.

In 1981, Davies retired from his duties as Master of Massey College to dedicate himself full-time to his writing. Thereafter, he continued to contribute to scholarly and popular periodicals on a regular basis but concentrated on his novel writing.

Analysis

The dramatic writing of Robertson Davies stands far removed from the mainstream of mid-twentieth century drama. The majority of modern drama is realistic in language and characterization, if not in form. Davies rejects this trend for older and blatantly theatrical models such as medieval masques and morality plays and nineteenth century Romantic comedies and melodramas. In his commentary on his own plays, Davies confirms his commitment to alternatives to realism. He rejects the naturalistic school of drama, which seeks to reproduce daily life on the stage, for, as Davies notes, it is the paradox of the theater that plays are sometimes most like life when they are least like a photograph of reality.

Davies' love for some of the older forms of drama springs from his conviction that these forms were closer in spirit to the original, primal function of all art. He seeks theater that will fill audiences with a sense of wonder. The theater, in Davies view, should be a place of spiritual refreshment, and this is particularly the case, he suggests, in melodrama and in the earliest forms of drama. Theater began, he reminds his audience, as a temple, a place where people expected to experience the full range of human emotion—the glorification of the godlike in man as well as his invigorating wickedness.

Davies readily admits to being an old-fashioned playwright longing for a theater which has perhaps entirely disappeared. He writes plays which call for acting in the classic Romantic style he remembers so fondly from visits to the theater during his youth. His plays necessitate this larger-than-life manner because they deal with fundamental conflicts between archetypal forces.

Davies is equally unfashionable in the strongly didactic tone of his plays. He defines himself as a moralist, one who perceives several insidious diseases of the spirit and seeks to cure them with the powerful antidote of laughter. So strong are Davies' opinions that he eschews subtlety in favor of direct statement, as well as a decidedly oracular tone thinly disguised with a sugary coating of wit.

Davies recognizes that his attitudes run against the *Zeitgeist*, but he remains true to his original commitment to the magical rather than the ordinary. As a result, his dramatic writing is remarkably unified in style.

The predominant identifying feature of Davies' plays is their language. Modern fashion leans toward dramatic dialogue that is colloquial, filled with slang and expletives, and minimal. Davies has chosen the opposite extreme, and his plays are linguistic feasts of wit, flights of fancy, and lucidity. Davies defends his style by pointing out that, for those with intelligence, style, sensitivity, and the wit to give form to random human discourse, conversation is an art. Davies' attitude toward conversation is expressed in *Fortune, My Foe* by Professor Rowlands, who describes himself as having a gift for something which is undervalued: good talk. Rowlands claims to be an artist, a master of poetry that is verbal and extempore but that is still poetry. Indeed, in general, the characters in the plays of Robertson Davies speak in a manner remarkably reminiscent of that of the playwright himself.

Davies' carefully constructed sentences are the perfect vehicle for another dominant attribute of his writing, his satire and parody of Canadian institutions and attitudes. There is nothing oblique about this element of Davies' dramas: the incorporation of the satiric element is very much a part of the moral thrust of the plays. Virtually every character in every play is given at least one well-constructed aphorism, and characters have a decided tendency to address one another in short moral lectures. At times these digressions threaten to slow the dramatic movement of the plot to a standstill, but the sheer pleasure of Davies' language retains the goodwill of the audience.

The witty repartee characteristic of a Davies play is generally given plausible motivation, given the setting and the intellectual attributes of the speakers. Chilly Jim and Idris Rowlands, who exchange quips and aphorisms in *Fortune, My Foe*, are two such plausible moral wits. Rowlands, as noted above, is a university professor who describes himself as a professional talker, a poet of conversation, while Chilly confesses that language is his hobby. Their conversations, which are filled with the most carefully crafted language, are entirely believable. Modern audiences are used to fast-paced and tightly edited forms of entertainment, but Davies crafts his plays for a premodern, slow-moving dramatic form and for audiences who prefer to savor *bons mots*.

In dramatic structure, Davies' plays are also strongly influenced by archaic forms. Several of his plays, most notably *Question Time*, take the form of a morality play, with a central character representing mankind interacting with personifications of the human psyche on a journey toward self-discovery. In *Question Time*, Peter MacAdam is a representative of humanity (his name means "son of Adam") and of all Canadians (as Prime Minister of Canada) who is launched upon a journey into his unconscious mind after a plane crash in the Arctic. While he lies in a coma, his mind is freed to explore his inner landscape in search of his true identity. He encounters personifications of his own attributes—totem animals—and finally convenes the Parliament of the Irrational, wherein two versions of himself lead the debate as to whether he should live or die.

Debate is another traditional element of the morality play, and Davies' characters frequently engage in such contests. Many of his plays focus on two essential forces in conflict, with the balance clearly weighted toward one of the two parties. This is the case in *Overlaid*, where Pop represents life-affirming forces (Eros), and Ethel, life-denying forces (Thanatos).

In drawing on an archaic form such as the morality play, Davies does not stifle audiences with dusty scholarship. Rather, he adapts the model to realize the potential of the modern stage to become a forum for an exploration of those deep concerns humanity shares. Davies replaces the absolute Christian moral doctrines espoused by the medieval morality plays with a standard of judgment that is not external but internal. Davies is concerned with each individual's judgment of himself, his perception of his soul in its entirety, and his recognition of the unlived lives that, if unattended, are sure to have their revenge.

In characterization, Davies also rejects the expected naturalistic layering of details or the question-filled outlines of the contemporary theater. Instead, he relies on character-types as symbolic vehicles for his morality lessons. He generally structures a play around a single protagonist whom he presents in the most exciting and positive manner. He surrounds this character with a variety of less fully developed creations, all of whom exist to fulfill a thematic function, to embody a force against which the hero reacts. Minor characters are given single and striking identifying characteristics and then allowed to interact within situations that are crafted to bring essential conflicts to the surface.

Davies' heroes share the attributes of the artist, and those characters who stand in opposition embody those forces which seek to destroy or limit the artistic function. Davies' sharp juxtapositions of these forces indicate his condemnation of certain attitudes. Ranged against the positive force of art, which is linked with spiritual enrichment, intuition, sensitivity, perception, and wonder, are narrow materialism, ignorant respectability, cultural philistinism, dogmatic religion, science, modern impatience, insufficient education, and the absence of laughter. Those characters who lack a sense of humor are perhaps the most barren, pretentious, and emotionally undernourished (as well as the least appealing to the audience). Their grim devotion to principle—whether it be religious, social, or scientific—is the most effective force against the joyful spirit of the healthy soul.

In his most successful novels and plays, Davies explores the relationship between human consciousness, trapped as it is in the perceptions of daily reality and blinded by the limitations of sensibility, and the unconscious, that vast, uncharted, terrifying world whence springs all art, all vitality, and all meaning. From Davies' perspective, the conflicts of the unconscious mind are more real than the trivial, day-to-day concerns of observable reality.

Davies' fascination with the internal workings of an individual dates, he reports, from the health dialogues in which he acted as a child. These little skits were set in such locales as the stomach and featured naughty foods as well as the angelic Miss Milk and Mr. Apple. In one of his earliest plays, *Eros at Breakfast*, Davies returns to this idea and shows us a young man's soul when he first experiences love. With this fantasy, Davies is able to teach a few lessons about the inner workings of the mind: Love comes, we learn, not from the mind, but is initiated by sentiment, enhanced by the liver, and finally affects the soul. In his later plays, Davies takes on increasingly complex aspects of human experience, until he comes to grips with the nature of identity and strives to define more clearly the soul itself. En route, Davies' expert knowledge of and defiant admiration for melodrama is transferred to the interior landscape, so that striking character-types merge with psychological allegory. In this method, he is greatly influenced by the theories of Carl Jung, in particular the definition of the three attributes of the personality: the persona, the anima, and the shadow. In his scholarly writing, Davies has explored the relationship between Jungian archetypes and melodramatic character-types, and scholars have traced a similar correspondence in Davies' fiction. In melodrama, they appear as the hero, the heroine, and the villain; in Davies' plays, they emerge in a variety of forms as he experiments with the dramatic presentation of this theory.

An early, unproduced experiment is *General Confession*, which Davies has singled out as his favorite play. An elderly Casanova entertains two young lovers with three conjured figures: the philosopher Voltaire, the evil magician Cagliostro, and an unnamed beautiful woman. The figures act out scenes from Casanova's past, and in the last act, Casanova is put on trial for his sins, with the philosopher as adviser, the woman as defender, and the magician as accuser. Finally, Davies gives these last three figures allegorical titles: they are, respectively, Casanova's Wisdom, his Ideal of Womanhood, and his Contrary Destiny. Casanova and his two young friends learn an important lesson in identity: Everyone has within him a wise adviser; an ideal, to provide direction; and an enemy, against which to test himself.

This dramatization of Jung's theory of the personality has injected Davies' writing with an atmosphere of the mystical, which underlies the surface narrative he presents. In *Question Time*, he jettisons the external reality within which he tried to work in *General Confession*, using the patterns of dreams for his dramatic form and the images of Jungian theory for characters and setting. The *terra incognita* into which Peter MacAdam journeys in *Question Time* is the world of the unconscious, here made remarkably theatrical by Davies' image of the Arctic as the last unchartered realm of our world and so the perfect metaphor for the unchartered territory of the mind. His description of the stage presentation indicates the mystical atmosphere he wished to evoke; he asks for music that is not the conventional movie sound track, but something truly mysterious, embracing, alive. The set, he suggests, should create the effect of a landscape that, although unfriendly, is of transporting beauty.

Along with his old-fashioned dramatic form, Davies often alienates audiences by expressing attitudes which it is unfashionable to state publicly, though they may be widely held. In two areas, in particular, he has incurred the wrath of sectors of the public. Davies has strong feelings about class divisions, as is evident in the characterization in his plays. In *Question Time*, the representatives of the working classes are Madge and Tim, and the portrait is not at all flattering. Crude language, cruder vision, and the most narrow-minded selfishness characterize these figures. Tim is much given to simplistic, clichéd pronouncements against the rich, and he makes several references to his union. He is particularly irritating in the second half of the play, where he disrupts the formal rituals with obnoxious and ignorant objections. Davies seems to be implying that the common people are easily led, uneducated, brutish, and totally lacking in any sensitivity to the world of the spirit. Regardless of the veracity of this portrait, it is in sharp contrast to the egalitarian ideals mouthed by most contemporary playwrights.

Davies is openly elitist about the world of art and espouses an aristocracy of the soul: Some people are open to its magic, and some are closed. This capacity is not always tied to class and education, for some of Davies' most obtuse and closed characters suffer from an excess of money and schooling. More often than not, however, the most appealing, witty, sensitive, and attractive of Davies' characters are members of the social elite. Davies describes repeatedly the natural grace and acquired good taste of the ladies in *At My Heart's Core*, qualities which are very much part of their breeding as gentlewomen. Contrast is provided by Sally and Honour, the first an Indian servant whom Davies describes as giggling at the most inopportune moments or brandishing a skillet, and the second an uneducated Irish settler who has just borne a child to her foster father. In a telling scene, Mrs. Frances Stewart, whom Davies portrays as the most beautiful and gracious of the ladies, suggests that, if Honour does not wish to stay in bed to recover from the birth of her child, she might just as well go out into the kitchen and help Sally. Frances means no insult here, nor does Davies. Honour is more comfortable serving Frances, and both women accept the responsibilities and privileges of their different positions. There is no hint of these two having been born equal.

Another issue on which Davies has expressed decided and unpopular ideas is gender. In direct statement as well as by implication, Davies communicates his belief that women and men are different and that the world runs most smoothly when both sexes know their strengths and limitations and do not attempt to shatter the natural order. For Davies, women are the more sensitive, the givers, the supporters. This does not mean that they are incapable of intelligence, of spirit, or of strength, but theirs is a distinctly feminine intelligence, spirit, and strength. Frances Stewart is a woman witty enough to match swords with the devilish tempter Edmund Cantwell, intelligent enough to admit his success and attempt to deal with the dissatisfaction with which he attempts to poison her life, and strong enough to deliver a baby, outface a drunken settler, and remain alone in the forest eight miles from her closest neighbor. When her husband returns, however, she bows to his masculine wit, intelligence, and strength and allows him to solve the social entanglement in which she finds herself. It is Thomas Stewart who hands out justice to the erring settler, who gets to the bottom of the plotting of Edmund Cantwell and who embodies the most vital and theatrical love of life, exemplified by his mimicry of the music-hall clown Grimaldi.

The explanation for Davies' attitude toward his female characters rests partially in his personal Victorian sensibilities but also in his use of the female gender to embody the values of the spirit. The most striking example of this occurs in *Question Time*, in the figure of La Sorcière des Montagnes de Glace. In the final moments of the play, Davies explicates her symbolic function: She is the ultimate authority in the world of the soul, the final reality, the life force, a power so old that she "makes all monarchies seem like passing shadows on her face, and all forms of power like games children tire of." Women cannot complain that Davies dislikes their sex, but they are perhaps correct when they say that he does not portray them realistically on the stage.

Given Davies' concern with the interior of the human mind, it is no surprise to discover two perennial themes in his dramatic writing: the quest for personal identity and the magic of art. These are not new themes, and Davies' treatment of the importance of self-knowledge and the unique properties of art and artists is not new. What is striking is the way in which he unites these two themes with a third concern which figures largely in his dramatic writing: the relationship between art, personal identity, and the national identity of Canadians. When asked to describe the theme of *Question Time*, Davies' reply was brief and to the point; he stated that the play was about the relationship of the Canadian people to their soil and about the relationship of a man to his soul, both of which we neglect at our peril.

These relationships, and the parallels between the two, form the thematic content of many of Davies' plays. Canada, he suggests, suffers from a lack of emotional stimulation, from a denigration of the arts which might have been appropriate in a pioneer society but which is sadly out of place in the twentieth century. By evoking the magic and power of art, Davies hopes to awaken his audiences to the need for the life-giving spirit of art in their lives.

Nowhere is the pure magic of the performing arts more powerfully evoked than in *Fortune, My Foe*. Here the art form is puppetry, and the artist is Franz Szabo, a refugee who has brought to Canada a European artistic discipline and awareness. Franz gives voice to Davies' view of artistic creation when he describes his profession. It takes sixteen years to acquire the skill of a marionette master, but once acquired, it allows the puppet master to infuse his creation with a part of his own soul, so that the figure is more real, more truly alive, than the puppet master himself. Although his new Canadian friends warn him that Canada is a cold country, inhospitable to artists, Franz is determined to remain and find an audience for his puppets. In the course of the play, he is partially successful in this quest.

The individual most deeply affected by his encounter with the artist Szabo is Nicholas, a young university professor on the brink of leaving Canada for a more lucrative career in the United States. Nicholas has despaired of ever achieving a decent income in Canada, a country where the questions he asks meet only with blank incomprehension and where the yearnings he feels find no understanding. He realizes the importance of art to the health of the soul: Art fills a need in the heart; it provides brilliant color, the warmth and gaiety that people crave. Others who come in contact with Franz Szabo respond less favorably. Vanessa Medway is enchanted and eager to become involved, but her impatience bars her from partaking of an artistic experience which requires a minimum of two years' training. Vanessa exemplifies a worldview that Davies labels as distinctively modern: detached, unemotional, fast-moving, quickly tiring of things and people, yet capable of perception and honesty. Ursula Simonds wants to alter Szabo's art to pure didacticism; she claims that art without a message is worthless, while Szabo argues that art is not to be trusted unless it is in the hands of artists, not educators or revolutionaries.

The least appealing response comes from Mrs. E.C. Philpott and Ovrille Tapscott, representatives from the local recreation board, whom Davies uses to satirize certain educational theories that emphasize the scientific approach. Tapscott and Mrs. Philpott regard puppets as ideal for instruction in oral hygiene and for developing manual dexterity in young girls.

Their belief in their power to do good is so powerful that it blinds them to the simple, pure message of Szabo's little theater. They are, Davies suggests, the half-educated, who are the least likely to appreciate art. They find Szabo's dramatization of the story of Don Quixote immoral, offensive, and antisocial. Terrified of any art which ventures into the area of deep personal concerns, they are blind to their own need for art to save them from emotional starvation.

Szabo has the strength to survive the condemnation of the emotionally barren and the impatience of the modern. He reminds his friends that a real artist is tough; as long as he keeps the image of his work clear in his heart, he will not fail. Canada is his country now, and though he foresees struggle, he will continue his search for an audience. His optimism tips the balance for Nicholas, and the play ends with the young man's announcement that he, too, will stay in Canada.

It is the cynical Chilly Jim, however, who voices Davies' most powerful evocation of the potential of the theater. Chilly has seen three murders, but nothing has moved him like Szabo's puppets. The theater makes him feel something he has not experienced since he was a boy, a kind of religious wonder:

> You've always suspected that something existed, and you've wished and prayed that it did exist, and in your dreams you've seen little bits of it, but to save your life you couldn't describe it or put a name to it. Then, all of a sudden, there it is, and you feel grateful, and humble, and wonder how you ever doubted it. That little stage makes me feel like that—quiet and excited at the same time.

This is the power of the theater that Robertson Davies celebrates in his writing.

Other major works

NOVELS: *Tempest Tost*, 1951; *Leaven of Malice*, 1954; *A Mixture of Frailties*, 1958; *Fifth Business*, 1970; *The Manticore*, 1972; *World of Wonders*, 1975; *The Rebel Angels*, 1981.

NONFICTION: *Shakespeare's Boy Actors*, 1939; *The Diary of Samuel Marchbanks*, 1947; *The Table Talk of Samuel Marchbanks*, 1949; *Renown at Stratford*, 1953 (with Tyrone Guthrie); *Twice Have the Trumpets Sounded*, 1954; *Thrice the Brinded Cat Hath Mew'd*, 1955 (with Guthrie); *A Voice from the Attic*, 1960; *Samuel Marchbanks' Almanack*, 1967; *Stephen Leacock*, 1970; *The Well-Tempered Critic*, 1981.

TELEPLAY: *Fortune, My Foe*, 1948.

MISCELLANEOUS: *One Half of Robertson Davies*, 1977; *The Enthusiasms of Robertson Davies*, 1979.

Bibliography
Canadian Drama. VII, no. 2 (Summer, 1981).

Grant, Judith S. *Robertson Davies*, 1978.
Monk, Patricia. *The Smaller Infinity*, 1982.
Morley, Patricia. *Robertson Davies*, 1977.

Leslie O'Dell

OWEN DAVIS

Born: Portland, Maine; January 29, 1874
Died: New York, New York; October 14, 1956

Principal drama

For the White Rose, pr. 1898; *Through the Breakers*, pr. 1899; *The Confessions of a Wife*, pr. 1905; *The Family Cupboard*, pr. 1913, pb. 1914; *The Detour*, pr. 1921, pb. 1922; *Icebound*, pr., pb. 1923; *The Nervous Wreck*, pr. 1923; *The Haunted House*, pr. 1924, pb. 1926; *The Good Earth*, pr. 1932 (with Donald Davis; adaptation of Pearl Buck's novel); *Jezebel*, pr. 1933; *Ethan Frome*, pr. 1936 (with Donald Davis; adaptation of Edith Wharton's novel); *Mr. and Mrs. North*, pr. 1941 (adaptation of Frances and Richard Lockridge's novel).

Other literary forms

In addition to more than three hundred plays, Owen Davis wrote a radio series entitled *The Gibson Family* (1934), which lasted for thirty-nine weeks. He was also a screenwriter in Hollywood, where his work included *Icebound* (1924), *How Baxter Butted In* (1925), *Frozen Justice* (1929), and *Hearts in Exile* (1929).

In 1930, dissatisfied with Hollywood and its exploitation of the writer, Davis returned to writing for the stage. In 1931, he published a volume of autobiography, *I'd Like to Do It Again*; he updated his life story in 1950 with *My First Fifty Years in the Theatre*.

Achievements

Owen Davis' career spanned almost sixty years, and during that period he wrote more than three hundred plays, most of which were performed professionally. Inasmuch as his work was produced in New York for thirty-seven consecutive seasons, and twenty of his plays were produced in Hollywood as movies, he was, from 1900 to 1950, America's most prolific playwright. Indeed, drama critic George Jean Nathan called Davis "the Lope de Vega of the American Theatre."

Davis began his career as a writer of "ten-twenty-thirt" melodramas, and by 1910 he achieved recognition as the dominant writer in this dramatic form. Motivated to be a serious writer, Davis wrote *The Family Cupboard*, which enabled him to move from the visually dominated melodramas to comedy. Always seeking to grow as an artist, Davis shifted from situation comedy to psychological melodrama; perhaps his finest work in this form was the 1923 play *Icebound*, for which he received the Pulitzer Prize and for which he was inducted into the National Institute of Arts and Letters. Later, he would serve on the Pulitzer Prize selection committee.

In addition to his work as a dramatist, Davis sought to free the writer from managerial abuse and plagiarism. Thus, he became actively involved in founding the Dramatists' Guild, serving as its president in 1922. As president, he addressed himself to such issues as film rights, actors' homes, loans, and other issues germane to the theater profession. Davis had a gift for organization and administration and was drafted continually into leadership positions.

Biography

Writing plays like "a freshman writes home for money—as frequently and with as little effort," Owen Davis became America's most prolific dramatist. Born in 1874, Davis was one of eight children of Abbie Gould Davis and Owen Warren Davis. His father, a graduate of Bowdoin College and a Civil War veteran, was primarily in the iron business, owning the Kathodin Iron Works and serving one term as president of the Society of American Iron Manufacturers. Later, he operated a photography studio on New York's Forty-second Street. He died in 1920 of a heart attack.

Davis went to school in Bangor, Maine, and at the age of nine wrote his first play, "Diamond Cut Diamond: Or, The Rival Detectives." At the age of fourteen, he enrolled as a subfreshman at the University of Tennessee. To satisfy his father, Davis left after one year and attended Harvard. Because Harvard did not have a theater and drama department, Davis first majored in business and then transferred, in 1893, to the sciences to become a mining engineer. While at Harvard, Davis participated in football and track and organized the Society of Arts, under the auspices of which he produced his verse dramas. In 1893, he left Harvard without a degree and followed his family to Southern Kentucky, where he was hired by the Cumberland Valley Kentucky Railroad as a mining engineer. Dissatisfied, Davis decided that he wanted to become a playwright or an actor. In 1895, with twelve dollars in his pocket, he quit his job and went to New York City. Meeting with continual discouragement, Davis was finally aided by theater manger A. M. Palmer, whose influence helped Davis get work as a utility actor, stage manager, press agent, advance man, company manager, and in some instances assistant director for the Fanny Janauschek Troupe. Davis left the company in 1896, committed to becoming a writer.

Giving full attention to writing, Davis tried to sell his first play, *For the White Rose*. Meeting with rejection after rejection, he became determined to figure out a formula for the then-running successful plays. After studying the melodramas and the audiences, Davis discovered that he needed to write for the "eye rather than the ear"—that is, he needed to emphasize scenic elements. Davis also concluded that the successful melodramas depended on such common features as a strong love interest, the triumph of good over evil, and stock comic characters. Although *For the White*

Rose was finally produced in 1898, *Through the Breakers* was to be Davis' first successful play.

In January, 1901, Davis met Elizabeth Drury "Iza" Breyer, whom he married on April 23, 1902. They remained married for fifty-five years and had two sons. In 1902, Davis and Al "Sweetheart" Woods signed an agreement that led in 1905 to the well-known "Owen Davis-Al Woods Melodrama Factory," from which fifty-nine plays were produced, the first being *The Confessions of a Wife* in 1905. While pouring out "Davidrama" after "Davidrama," as his particular brand of melodrama was labeled, at a rate of eight or more per year, Davis began using such pseudonyms as Arthur Lamb, Martin Hurly, Walter Lawrence, George Walker, and John Oliver.

Not satisfied with his success as a popular playwright, Davis struggled to write serious drama. In 1918, he moved from the melodrama of the "ten-twenty-thirt" theaters to try his luck on Broadway. Success on Broadway was not easy to achieve, and Davis again studied the work of other successful writers (such as Clyde Fitch) to ascertain the necessary formula. Besides writing plays, he also published articles on the theater in *The New York Times* and other periodicals.

Disturbed and sobered by World War I, Davis read works by Henrik Ibsen, Maxim Gorky, Gerhart Hauptmann, and other serious dramatists whose naturalistic emphasis on the influence of heredity and environment is apparent in such Davis plays of the early 1920's as *The Detour* and *Icebound*. Another departure in Davis' work occurred with his farce *The Nervous Wreck*, which Davis called "the terrible play which made us all rich." Whereas his Pulitzer Prize drama, *Icebound*, made one thousand dollars weekly, *The Nervous Wreck* brought in twenty-one thousand dollars a week. Made into the musical *Whoopee* (1928), remade as *Up in Arms* (1944), and later adapted for the screen (Davis was not involved in these projects), *The Nervous Wreck* was Davis' most popular and most lucrative work. During the years from 1924 to 1941, Davis worked on movies, on radio, and on drama at the Lakewood Theatre in Skowhegan, Maine (known as "Broadway in Maine"), as well as on Broadway. His play *Jezebel* failed in New York, but as a 1938 movie it earned for Bette Davis an Academy Award. Davis' last major achievement was his adaptation of Edith Wharton's *Ethan Frome* (1911). Failing eyesight and bad health slowed his output, and his last substantial work was *Mr. and Mrs. North*. Davis died in New York City on October 14, 1956.

Analysis

Under the influence of naturalistic drama, Owen Davis wrote one of his finest plays, *The Detour*. Still using the melodramatic form, Davis varied his approach with a realistic style. The characters are thus depicted as products of heredity and environment, placed in circumstances in which they struggle physically and psychologically against these forces. Despite their efforts to circumvent their fate, the destiny that shapes their ends prevails. The central character, Helen Hardy, exemplifies this determination in the face of hardship.

For ten years, Helen has scrimped and sacrificed for the sake of her daughter, Kate, who aspires to be a painter. Helen's dream for Kate is in reality her own unfulfilled dream "to get away and go to New York, or somewheres where bein' born and bein' dead wasn't the only things that ever happened." Her efforts to escape her environment, however, fail when fate intercedes in the guise of Stephen Hardy. Helen admits that, in her loneliness, "somehow I got to loving him before I knew it." Married and feeling trapped, Helen doggedly tells Kate, "Your life isn't going to be like this:" Helen's struggle against destiny becomes the central conflict of the play.

The struggle focuses on Kate's suitor, Tom Lane, and takes on larger proportions when Tom, echoing a widely held viewpoint, affirms that "women ought to just cook, and clean, and sew, and maybe chop a little wood, and have the babies. . . . And if a woman sometimes gets to thinkin it ain't quite fair" and decides to alter the situation, "she's flyin' in the face of Providence." In order to expedite Kate's departure to New York, Helen sells her bedroom wardrobe and with the additional money plans for Kate to leave immediately. Again, Stephen Hardy intercedes. Obsessed with owning land, and needing money to buy what he considers a prime section, Stephen takes the money intended for Kate. This makes the men happy: Stephen will get his land, and Tom will get Kate. Stephen's act is a villainous one, and inasmuch as Tom supports Stephen, he must share that guilt. Thus, the men in *The Detour* symbolize society and its failure to guarantee equal rights for women. The play ends with the forces of tradition victorious: An art critic seriously questions Kate's talent, and Kate decides to remain with her family and Tom. Despite this defeat, Helen is undaunted; "she stands, her face glorified, looking out into the future, her heart swelling with eternal hope."

The influence of naturalism is also apparent in Davis' prizewinning play *Icebound*. In this work, despite his intention to move away from melodrama, Davis retained many of the basic elements of that form. Unlike tragedy, which contains highly serious action that probes the nature of good and evil, melodrama generally lacks moral complexity; in melodrama, good and evil are clearly defined. While the plot of *Icebound* is essentially melodramatic, the play also features an element of psychological complexity that distinguishes it from straight melodrama.

Jane Crosby is an adopted second cousin to the Jordan family. Taken in by the family's matriarch, Jane is considered an outcast by the rest of the family, especially as the mother is dying and the Jordan wealth is to be inherited. Responding to her enemies, Jane asserts her "hate" for the Jordans and her plans "to get away from them." As for the dying mother, "she was the only one of you worth loving, and she didn't want it." When the mother dies, fate intervenes in the guise of the dead woman's will: Jane is left the Jordan home and money. When the will's contents are revealed, the Jordan family's sentiments are summed up: "We'll go to the law, that's what we'll do." Thus, Jane is pitted against the greedy and vengeful Jordan clan. The conflict is clearly defined, and the audience is sympathetic to Jane.

Had Davis kept the focus solely on the conflict between Jane and the Jordans, the play would be a simple melodrama; instead, he chose to emphasize the role of Mrs. Jordan's son Ben, the black sheep of the family. Ben is a "wild, selfish, arrogant fellow, handsome but sulky and defiant"; indicted by the grand jury for his "drunken devilment," he has run away to avoid state prison. While he is still a fugitive, Ben, risking capture, returns to see his dying mother, and after her death, he is arrested. Alone and without money, Ben is befriended by Jane, in whose custody the court places him. Four months later, Ben comes to grips with his past. Ashamed and feeling remorse about his past behavior, Ben struggles to express his repressed emotions. Admitting love for his mother and for Jane, Ben beseeches Jane to "help me to be fit." With Ben's reformation, society's positive values emerge triumphant over the baneful influence of the Jordan family. No longer emotionally icebound, Ben marries Jane, who gives him his rightful inheritance.

Davis was active as a playwright for many years after the appearance of *Icebound*, but the only significant work of this later period was his adaptation of *Ethan Frome*, Edith Wharton's short novel set in a harsh New England landscape. Ethan "lives in a depth of moral isolation too remote for casual access." He is married to Zenobia, whom Davis characterizes as cruel, harsh, impersonal, and drab, like the play's New England winter setting. In that she represents those forces which seek to enslave Ethan's body and soul, and in that she drives the action to catastrophe, Zenobia (or Zeena) is the villain.

Despite her sickly appearance, Zeena is a forceful personality, and on issues of importance to her, her strength surfaces. For example, she demands that her cousin Mattie Silver be allowed to come and live with them as a hired girl. Citing a complete lack of money, Ethan protests against this demand, but Zeena settles the issue by curtly asserting, "Well—she's comin' just the same, Ethan!" The consequences, however, are not what Zeena intended: Mattie's presence "thaws" Ethan, and eventually, the two fall in love. Jealousy rages within Zeena, who conspires to get rid of Mattie. For years, Ethan has felt trapped by the farm that he inherited, and with Mattie leaving, Ethan's "desire for change and freedom" are resurrected. Ethan tells Zeena that he plans to go West for a fresh start and that Zeena may have the farm. Zeena, however, wishes to keep Ethan enslaved, and, playing on his strong sense of duty, she makes Ethan realize that he is a "poor man, the husband of a sickly woman, whom his desertion would leave alone and destitute." Ethan and Mattie decide to kill themselves by sledding at high speed "into that big elm . . . so't we'd never have to leave each other any more." Their decision gives the play an element of high seriousness; it is a tragic action rather than a melodramatic one. The act of crashing into the elm is also symbolic in that it dramatizes the perennial conflict between man and nature. Typical of characters in tragedy whose decisions cause their undoing, Ethan and Mattie survive. Not only does their survival create a reversal in the action, but also it suggests nature's superior force. Although crippled, Ethan can walk, but Mattie is partially paralyzed and is confined to a wheelchair. Ethan and Zeena are tied down to a daily existence of caring for the farm and for Mattie. Nature has demonstrated its mastery over man's destiny.

Other major works

NONFICTION: *I'd Like to Do It Again*, 1931; *My First Fifty Years in the Theatre*, 1950.

SCREENPLAYS: *Icebound*, 1924; *How Baxter Butted In*, 1925; *Frozen Justice*, 1929; *Hearts in Exile*, 1929.

RADIO PLAY: *The Gibson Family*, 1934 (series).

Bibliography

Davis, Robert. "Owen Davis: A Study in Mass Production," in *Theatre Magazine*. XLV (September, 1929), p. 17.

Goff, Lewis. "The Owen Davis-Al Woods Melodrama Factory," in *Educational Theatre Journal*. XI (October, 1959), pp. 200-207.

Loud, R. O. "America's Most Prolific Playwright," in *Green Book Album*. April, 1911, pp. 844-847.

Moses, Montrose J. *The American Dramatist*, 1925.

_____ . "The Metamorphosis of Owen Davis," in *Theatre*. May, 1922, pp. 300-332.

Witham, Barry B. *The Dramaturgy of Owen Davis*, 1968 (dissertation).

Loren Ruff

THOMAS DEKKER

Born: London, England; c. 1572
Died: London, England; August, 1632

Principal drama

The Whole History of Fortunatus, pr. 1599, pb. 1600 (commonly known as *Old Fortunatus*); *The Shoemaker's Holiday: Or, The Gentle Craft*, pr., pb. 1600 (based on Thomas Deloney's narrative *The Gentle Craft*); *Patient Grissell*, pr. 1600, pb. 1603 (with Henry Chettle and William Haughton); *Satiromastix: Or, The Untrussing of the Humourous Poet*, pr. 1601, pb. 1602; *Sir Thomas Wyatt*, pr. 1602 (as *Lady Jane*), pb. 1607; *The Honest Whore, Part I*, pr., pb. 1604 (with Thomas Middleton); *Westward Ho!*, pr. 1604, pb. 1607 (with John Webster); *Northward Ho!*, pr. 1605, pb. 1607 (with Webster); *The Honest Whore, Part II*, pr. c. 1605, pb. 1630; *The Whore of Babylon*, pr. 1606-1607, pb. 1607; *The Roaring Girl: Or, Moll Cutpurse*, pr. c. 1610, pb. 1611 (with Middleton); *If This Be Not a Good Play, the Devil Is in It*, pr. 1610-1612, pb. 1612 (as *If It Be Not Good, the Devil Is in It*); *Match Me in London*, pr. c. 1611-1612, pb. 1631; *The Virgin Martyr*, pr. c. 1620, pb. 1622 (with Philip Massinger); *The Witch of Edmonton*, pr. 1621, pb. 1658 (with William Rowley and John Ford); *The Noble Soldier: Or, A Contract Broken, Justly Revenged*, pr. c. 1622-1631, pb. 1634 (with John Day; thought to be same as *The Spanish Fig*, 1602); *The Wonder of a Kingdom*, pr. c. 1623, pb. 1636; *The Sun's Darling*, pr. 1624, pb. 1656 (with Ford); *The Welsh Embassador: Or, A Comedy in Disguises*, pr. c. 1624 (revision of *The Noble Soldier*); *The Dramatic Works of Thomas Dekker*, 1953-1961 (4 volumes; Fredson Bowers, editor).

Other literary forms

Thomas Dekker was also known in his time as a prolific pamphleteer. His pamphlets are characterized not by a failure of moral judgment, as some critics have charged, but by a deliberate strategy of refraining from gratuitous finger-pointing. *The Wonderful Year* (1603), for example, presents two long poems that are supposed to be the prologue to a play and a summary of its action and, in a prose section, that action—stories of English reaction to the death of Elizabeth I; Dekker leaves the reader to decide whether there is a thematic relationship in the tripartite structure of the work which links the death of Elizabeth and the devastating plague of 1603, whether these disasters are to be regarded as retribution for England's sins, and whether the accession of James represents God's gift of unmerited grace. Such implications are there, but the author draws no final conclusions. In this and other pamphlets, Dekker typically adopts the role of observer-reporter, who, like the Bellman of London, carries his lantern into the darkest corners of his dystopian world to reveal the deepest degradations of the human spirit. In this regard, like modern social critics, he is content to "tell it like it is"; the selection of specific detail furnishes the didactic underpinning of his vision. In works such as *The Bellman of London* (1608) and the different versions of *Lanthorn and Candlelight* (1608, 1609; revised as *O per se O,* 1612; *Villanies Discovered,* 1616, 1620, and *English Villanies,* 1632, 1638, 1648), the reader discovers an alarming truth: The social and political organization of the underworld is a grotesque parody of polite society and the Jacobean Establishment. Thus, rogues and thieves have their own laws, codes of ethics, and standards of "scholarship" which hold a wide currency in both town and country. As demonstrated in *The Gull's Hornbook* (1609), they have even developed their own professional language. In this world, God is not an immediate presence, although He may work out His providential purposes in the hearts and minds of men; Dekker, however, is chiefly interested in sociological rather than theological sins, as seen in *The Seven Deadly Sins of London* (1606), in which he carefully adapts the traditional medieval framework to fit his own experience of life in the city of London. Even in his numerous descriptions of Hell, Dekker presents an essentially secular view of the afterlife, designed to show that the community of rogues is an integral part of the Jacobean commonwealth.

Another significant feature of the pamphlets—significant for an understanding of the plays—is the evidence they give of Dekker's familiarity with and manipulation of a wide range of literary forms and conventions. *The Wonderful Year* combines elements of narrative journalism, the frame-tale, the morality play, and the jestbook. *The Seven Deadly Sins of London* involves not only some knowledge of the medieval tradition of the sins but also of morality drama, estates satire, and pageants. *The Bellman of London* parodies the Utopian travelogue, while *The Gull's Hornbook* should be read in the tradition of education books such as Baldassare Castiglione's *The Courtier* (1528). Such a review only scratches the surface of Dekker's diverse reading and interests; it is only in works such as *Four Birds of Noah's Ark* (1609), modeled upon contemporary prayer books, that the author maintains a relatively simple structure. An awareness of Dekker's breadth is of the first importance for a reading of his plays, which also draw on a multiplicity of forms. To some extent, the plays also represent a necessary thematic balance to the moral vision of the pamphlets, for in his drama, Dekker provides the role models usually missing in his prose works—protagonists such as Moll in *The Roaring Girl,* the saintly Dorothea in *The Virgin Martyr,* and the Subprior in *If This Be Not a Good Play, the Devil Is in It,* who rise above worldly temptations. Such characters suggest that, while it is often impossible to make clear moral distinctions in a world where knaves and politicians are easily confused, one can successfully rely upon one's own moral intelligence. The key to this steadfast vision might well be summarized by a brief passage from *The Seven Deadly Sins of London*: "Wee are moste like to God that made us, when wee shew love to another, and doe most looke like the Divell that would destroy us, when wee are one anothers tormentors."

Achievements

Although he had a hand in some aspect of the creation of at least seventy plays, it is unfair to dismiss Dekker as a mere refurbisher of old plays, for there is no question that his frequent collaboration with lesser dramatists was a necessity forced upon him in his constant struggle against bankruptcy. His equally frequent collaborations with such outstanding dramatists as Thomas Middleton, John Webster, and John Ford indicate that he was held in high esteem as a playwright. In fact, a fair estimate of his achievement may never be possible, since at least forty-five of his plays have not survived, and much of the work attributed to him remains a matter of critical conjecture. On the other hand, extant plays, such as *Old Fortunatus* and *Satiromastix*, that are attributed solely to Dekker reveal little sense of moral, thematic, or structural unity. The playwright's handful of genuine masterpieces, including *The Shoemaker's Holiday*, the two parts of *The Honest Whore*, and *If This Be Not a Good Play, the Devil Is in It*, conclusively prove, however, that he was capable of transcending the difficulties which mar his lesser works.

At his best, Dekker was an excellent lyric poet, as illustrated in the pastoral scenes of *The Sun's Darling* and the poignant love songs and laments which appear throughout his works. He was also the master of lively and racy dialogue, particularly in the characterization of clowns, rogues, citizens' wives, and old men. Owing to his creation of such memorable characters as the voluble Eyre and his uppity wife Margery (*The Shoemaker's Holiday*), Orlando Friscobaldo and the scoundrel Matheo (*The Honest Whore*), Scumbroth and the devils (*If This Be Not a Good Play, the Devil Is in It*), and Elizabeth Sawyer (*The Witch of Edmonton*), Dekker has gained a reputation as a "realist"; while it is true that he is at his best among the shops and stalls of London, it is more accurate to recognize Dekker as a dramatist who breathed new life into essentially old forms and conventions, for the roots of his invention lie in the chronicle play, folklore, the mystery plays, and moral interludes of the previous age. His dramatic preferences are clearly revealed in his typical choice of subject, such as legendary biography (in *The Shoemaker's Holiday*), Prudentian psychomachia (in *Old Fortunatus*), medieval hagiography (in *Patient Grissell* and *The Virgin Martyr*), anti-Catholic polemic (in *The Whore of Babylon*), and the use of diabolical temptation similar to that found in such old plays as Christopher Marlowe's *Doctor Faustus* (in *If This Be Not a Good Play, the Devil*

Is in It). Dekker's drama, more fully than that of any of his contemporaries, demonstrates the continuing vitality of medieval themes and conventions in Renaissance theater. His greatest achievement was to re-create these traditions upon the Jacobean stage with moral force and perspicuity.

Biography

The phrase "my three-score years" in the dedicatory epistle to the 1632 edition of *English Villanies* suggests that Thomas Dekker was born in 1572, probably in the City of London. His broad knowledge of Latin literature suggests that he received a grammar school education, although all such speculation about his early years is mere conjecture. Since he was ranked by Francis Meres, in 1598, among the best English writers of tragedy, he must have begun writing plays as early as 1595; his name first appears in Philip Henslowe's diary in 1598 as the author of the lost play *Phaeton*, and he may also have collaborated with Anthony Munday, Henry Chettle, Thomas Heywood, and William Shakespeare in *The Booke of Sir Thomas More* (c. 1595-1596). Numerous other references in Henslowe's papers and on the title pages of published plays show that Dekker remained extremely busy from 1598 to 1613, writing for the Lord Admiral's Men and occasionally for the Children of Paul's. He was also constantly in debt during this period and was forced to supplement his income by the publication of pamphlets. In 1613, he was imprisoned for debt for the third time and remained in the King's Bench prison until his eventual release in 1619. During his last years, Dekker wrote several plays for the Palsgrave's Men and published several more pamphlets. He apparently refused to attend church from 1626 to 1629 in order to avoid being arrested for debt and was consequently indicted for recusancy. It is believed that he was buried in the parish of St. James, Clerkenwell, on August 25, 1632. The fact that his widow, Elizabeth, refused administration of his will suggests that Dekker had no estate to administer and that death came as his final release from the specter of debtors' prison.

Analysis

Critical condemnation of Thomas Dekker as "a moral sloven" or as a hack with a marginal understanding of dramatic structure is chiefly based upon unsympathetic readings of such early plays as *Old Fortunatus*, *Patient Grissell*, and *Satiromastix*. To some extent, the adverse assessments are justified, for these plays are quite severely lacking in structural coherence. Part of the problem, however, may lie in the sheer intransigence of Dekker's sources. The fact that Dekker did possess a keen sense of dramatic structure and moral integrity can easily be demonstrated by an analysis of two of his finest works, *The Shoemaker's Holiday* and *The Honest Whore, Part II*.

Based upon Thomas Deloney's prose narrative *The Gentle Craft* (1597–c. 1598), *The Shoemaker's Holiday* reveals its structural strategy in the opening scene, in which a discussion between Sir Roger Otley, Lord Mayor of London, and Sir Hugh Lacy, the powerful Earl of Lincoln, is animated by the latent hostility which divides the landed nobility and the wealthy, self-made citizenry of London. Both men fear an elopement between the earl's nephew, Rowland Lacy, and Rose, the Mayor's daughter. Rather than expose his treasury to the frivolous exploitation of a courtly son-in-law, Sir Roger has ordered his daughter into rustic banishment. The earl, to avoid besmirching the family dignity and turn his nephew's attention elsewhere, has arranged to have his nephew lead one of the regiments about to invade France. Lacy, however, leaves his command in charge of his cousin Askew, but before he can escape, he is temporarily interrupted by a shoemaker, Simon Eyre, and his men, who try, unsuccessfully, to intercede for the newly married journeyman Rafe, who has been pressed for service in France. Realizing the futility of his plea, Eyre then encourages Rafe to fight for the honor of the gentle craft of shoemakers. The poignant departure scene is highlighted by the generous monetary gifts showered upon Rafe and by Rafe's gift of a pair of monogrammed shoes he has made for Jane, his bride. Rafe's obedience provides a stark contrast to the irresponsibility of Lacy, who, though he insists upon Rafe's loyalty, has no intention of fulfilling his own patriotic duty. Meanwhile, Jane's distress is reflected in a parallel scene in which Rose learns of Lacy's orders to leave for France. Lacy, however, has decided to use his knowledge of the shoemaker's trade learned on an earlier trip to Germany, to find work with Eyre, who will be shorthanded without Rafe's services. In the following scene, the audience is entertained by the lively bustle of Eyre's shop as he drives his men into honest industry and heaps torrents of loving abuse upon his wife, Margery, when she tries to exert a little domestic authority over his employees. Lacy, now posing as Hans Meulter, a Dutchman who speaks only broken English, appears to apply for a job but only is hired because of the strong support of Hodge and Firke, Simon's other workmen. This scene reinforces the central theme of class conflict, because it demonstrates both that true love knows no social barriers and that a resourceful courtier can humble himself to the level of mere apprentice.

By stark contrast, in act 2, Dekker introduces the character of Hammon, an upstart citizen who, in the hope of impressing the exiled Rose, dresses in the height of fashion and ludicrously affects the language of courtly love. Even though his suit is favored by Sir Roger, Hammon is sternly rebuffed when he proposes marriage to Rose. Ironically, Sir Roger is far more impressed by the citizen who apes courtly manners and speech than by the true nobility of Lacy, who is willing to sacrifice all, including social status, for the sake of love. In the third scene, Lacy repays his employer's kindness by introducing him to a Dutch captain who sells Eyre a cargo of valuable merchandise at a great bargain. In order to impress the captain and effect the deal, Simon disguises himself as an alderman, a post he later achieves.

The first scene of act 3 renews Sir Roger's entertainment of Hammon as a suitable husband for Rose, but once again Rose firmly rejects the proposal, much to her father's disgust, and when he learns of Lacy's desertion, Sir Roger's suspicions are highly aroused. In the second scene, Simon's men play upon Margery's vanity by suggesting how she should respond to the news that Simon has been elected High Sheriff of London. The festivities are dampened by the unexpected return of Rafe, who has suffered the amputation of a leg. His grief is doubled when he discovers that Jane has secretly left the Eyre household. His distress, however, is swept aside by the triumphal entrance of Eyre, wearing the sheriff's chain of office. The third scene, in which Sir Roger honors Eyre at a banquet, is pivotal to the main plot, for it provides an opportunity, when Simon's men perform a morris dance, for Lacy to reveal his identity to Rose. This scene also reinforces the striking contrast between the pretentious gravity of Sir Roger and the bluff good nature of Simon Eyre. Margery's amusing efforts at courtly decorum also provide an ironic commentary upon citizen snobbery. Having been unsuccessful in his pursuit of Rose, Hammon subsequently proposes to Jane, now working as a seamstress, and when she rejects him on the grounds that she is still married, Hammon concocts a false report of Rafe's death in battle. In spite of her evident grief, Hammon relentlessly presses his case until Jane agrees to marry him.

Act 4 begins with excited speculation that Simon will become the next Lord Mayor, but the shoptalk is interrupted by Rose's maid, Sybil, who has been sent to arrange a secret meeting between Rose and Lacy. In the following scene, Rafe learns that Jane is going to marry Hammon when Hammon's servant is dispatched to Eyre's shop to have a pair of shoes made after the exact model of those which Rafe had given Jane. The wily Firke promises to devise a scheme to prevent the marriage. In scene 3, Lacy is surprised during his secret assignation with Rose by Sir Roger, yet he eludes detection by pretending, in the character of Hans, to measure Rose for shoes. When, shortly after, Sir Hugh is announced, Hans and Rose manage to slip away undetected. When Sybil eventually reveals their elopement, Sir Hugh, fully aware of his nephew's experience as a shoemaker in Wittenberg, realizes how he has been duped. At this point, Firke enters with the shoes which Rose had actually ordered and, seeing the danger to Hans, manufactures a story that misdirects the two enraged elders to St. Faith's, where a marriage, but that of Hammon and Jane, is scheduled. It is important to note that Dekker uses pairs of shoes throughout act 4, in both the main plot and the subplot, to effect the union or reunion of souls.

In the opening scene of act 5, Simon Eyre, who has been elevated to the office of Lord Mayor, agrees to intercede on behalf of Rose and Lacy to the king himself, who has accepted an invitation to dine with him that same day. Simon undertakes this potentially dangerous mission because he will not "forget his fine Dutch journeyman." In the scene following, Rafe, Firke, and Hodge intercept Hammon and his men who are escorting Jane to St. Faith's. Realizing that her husband still lives, Jane immediately rejects Hammon, while the shoemakers give his men a sound thrashing. Sir Hugh and Sir Roger appear at this moment, only to discover that Firke has deceived them, for Rose and Lacy have already been married at the Savoy. Finally, Eyre and his men entertain the king at a great banquet, dedicating the day to their gentle craft and their patron Saint Hugh. This saint's association with the city of Lincoln not only suggests good fortune for shoemakers but also for Lacy, who as the Earl of Lincoln's heir and as a shoemaker himself, embodies the best of both worlds. In spite of the earl's vigorous objections, the king, responding graciously to Eyre's humble petition, pardons Lacy's desertion. The shoemaker-mayor, "one of the merriest madcaps" in the land, carries the day, and the king reconciles Sir Roger and Sir Hugh to the marriage of Lacy and Rose.

In adapting Deloney's novel for the stage, Dekker drastically revised the character of Simon Eyre, who in Deloney's work seems much more like Dekker's Sir Roger Otley, a ceremoniously grave and ambitious man who plots his rise to power. Thus, Dekker suppresses the darker side of the bargaining for the Dutch merchandise and creates in Simon an irrepressible force for good. Furthermore, although Deloney's Eyre believes in thrift and hard work, Dekker's Eyre is less motivated by purely economic considerations than he is by an exhilarating sense of the value of work *as* work. It is also important to note that *The Shoemaker's Holiday* is not a dynamic play, for Dekker's treatment of his main characters permits no internal conflict, no self-discovery, and no essential growth. Simon, Lacy, Rose, and the shoemakers remain, throughout, perfectly secure in the holiness of their hearts' affections, and their knowledge is instinctive rather than based upon systems of moral philosophy or codes of social behavior. In the very integrity of their words and actions, their lives exemplify the theme of the comedy: that love and nobility transcend such considerations as wealth, class consciousness, or political status. Although Simon Eyre achieves all the social distinctions which mean most to men such as Sir Roger and Sir Hugh, he remains completely oblivious to them. His love of life, his concern for his men, and his innate patriotism are never corrupted. From beginning to end, he remains "the merriest madcap" in the land, whose triumphs are based upon goodwill and honest industry. It is also significant that his victory over class prejudice is realized through the royal intervention of the legendary King Henry V, who recognizes in Eyre's raucous good humor a strain of genuine nobility which escapes the pettier understanding of such men as Sir Hugh and Sir Roger. In fact, it is tempting to see in Eyre and his men a group of individuals who represent the exact social obverse of Shakespeare's Falstaff and his predatory followers.

Throughout the play, Dekker skillfully interweaves the various strands of plot to achieve both a structural and thematic unity, not only in the resolution of the romantic intrigues but also in the establishment of a new social order that sweeps aside the trivial differences which divide courtiers and citizens. Beginning with the class conflict developed in the initial debate between Sir Roger and Sir Hugh, each consecutive scene either opposes or reinforces the class harmony which must eventually prevail in the final scene. Lacy's decision to work as a tradesman and the friendship and loyalty he finds in the assistance of Hodge and Firke counterpoise the noble pride of the Earl of Lincoln. The truth of Lacy's love for Rose, for which he risks all, is neatly balanced against the unscrupulous conduct of Hammon, whose romantic affectations and courtly love language are offset by Lacy's true nobility and Rafe's simple devotion to Jane. Rose and Jane suffer the anguish of forced separation from their lovers, and both are reunited in scenes which involve the manufacture and delivery of shoes from Eyre's premises. Sir Roger's preference for Hammon provides a ludicrous commentary upon the blindness of class snobbery, as do Margery's feeble attempts at gentility and decorum. The one flaw in Lacy's behavior, his desertion from patriotic duty, is structurally necessary to justify his employment in Eyre's shop and thematically essential to provide the reason for the king's intervention against the feuding parents. The act of royal clemency, in turn, affirms the primacy of love and resolves the theme of class conflicts, and the royal pardon itself is based upon the king's affirmation of Simon Eyre as the exemplar of social and political harmony.

Dekker's greatest work, however, is *The Honest Whore, Part II*, a tragicomedy utilizing most of the characters from the first part (written in collaboration with Thomas Middleton), in which is dramatized the moral conversion of the whore Bellafronte by Hippolito, the son-in-law of the Duke of Milan. In the resolution of *The Honest Whore, Part I*, the scoundrel Matheo has been forced to marry Bellafronte because he had been initially responsible for leading her into a life of sin. The subplot of the first part features the tempting of Candido, a patient man who triumphs over the constant humiliations heaped upon him by his shrewish wife Viola.

The second part of *The Honest Whore* begins with Bellafronte and an unnamed scholar waiting to make petitions to Hippolito. His summary dismissal of the scholar is ominous, for the clear implication is that the scholar is willing to sell his genius for money. The suggestion that the scholar is an intellectual prostitute, however, may be more a reflection upon the prince's mind than upon the scholar's integrity. On the other hand, Hippolito does listen to Bellafronte's request that he intercede on behalf of the profligate Matheo, who has been condemned for killing a man in a duel. At the same time, finding himself strangely attracted to the fallen woman whom he had once redeemed, he also promises to reconcile her, if he can, to her estranged father Orlando Friscobaldo, who had abandoned his support when she resorted to prostitution. Hippolito makes good his promise in the following scene when he intercepts Orlando and urges him to forgive his daughter, who has turned away from sin. The old man appears totally intransigent in his repugnance for Bellafronte and rebukes Hippolito for disturbing his peace, although secretly he resolves to keep an alert watch over Bellafronte and her disreputable husband. In the third scene, a number of gallants visit the linen-draper Candido, who has remarried after Viola's unexpected death. Urging him to subdue the pettish whims of his new bride, lest she too turn into an untamable shrew, they together devise a scheme in which Ludovico Sforza, in the role of an apprentice, will test her mettle.

Act 2 begins with Matheo's return from prison, although it is immediately apparent that he has not changed his ways, a fact which sorely distresses Bellafronte, who has now been reduced to virtual destitution. Their quarreling is interrupted by Orlando, who has disguised himself as his own servingman, Pacheco. When he and Matheo exchange disparaging remarks about her father's honesty, Bellafronte will not tolerate their insults, even though the old man has abandoned her to humiliation and direst poverty. Reassured by this successful testing of his daughter's virtue, Orlando offers his services to Matheo and gives him money for safekeeping. When Hippolito visits Bellafronte, Orlando quickly discerns the drift of the prince's interest in his daughter and watches anxiously to see how she will react to even greater temptations. Later, however, she dispatches Pacheco with a letter and a diamond she wishes to return to Hippolito. She also gives the old man a cryptic message which rejects the prince's lecherous designs. In the following scene, Candido reduces his new wife to submission after challenging her to a duel with yardsticks. This scene highlights the virtue of a wife's loyalty and obedience to her husband in a test which clearly parallels Bellafronte's support for a far less worthy husband.

Act 3 opens with Orlando's delivery of Bellafronte's letter not to Hippolito but to Infelice, who subsequently confronts her husband with positive proof of his treachery. Hippolito feigns contrition but nevertheless resolves to give full rein to his lust. With "armed Devils staring in [his] face," like Angelo in William Shakespeare's *Measure for Measure*, the young prince is less captivated by Bellafronte's beauty than by her persevering virtue. In the meantime, Orlando returns to find that Matheo has squandered all the money he had entrusted to him and has even robbed his wife of her gown, which he intends to sell to satisfy his desire for a cloak and rapier. Matheo even urges her to return to her profession in order to keep him supplied with ready cash. After the husband's angry departure, Orlando consoles his daughter and plots an appropriate revenge. Bella-fronte's trial is further reflected in the following scene, in which Candido's wife is tested by the gallants who lure the husband into a protracted discussion of his wares while Lieutenant Bots, a denizen of the local stews, tries unsuccessfully to lure her into prostitution.

Orlando appears in his own person, in the first scene of act 4, to accuse Matheo and Bellafronte of maintaining a bawdy house, but his daughter disclaims her past and pleads with the old man not to leave her destitute, since poverty may drive her back into a life of sin. After engaging in a shouting match with Matheo, Orlando storms out of the house, only to return moments later in the guise of Pacheco, who commiserates with Matheo and promises to help him burglarize his father-in-law's house. After the husband's departure, Hippolito appears and argues with Bellafronte in the hope of making her turn "whore/ By force of strong perswasion." His argument, however, is unconvincing, because he merely reverses the claims he had presented in his earlier conversion speech in *Part I*; Bella-fronte triumphs because her arguments are firmly based upon the real shame and degradation she has actually experienced as a whore. Though soundly defeated in this exchange, the prince swears to press his case "even to Hell's brazen doores." In scene 2, Orlando enlists the duke's aid in having Matheo arrested for theft committed against two peddlers who are actually Orlando's own men in disguise. Aware of Hippolito's infidelity to Infelice, the duke also orders the arrest of all harlots and bawds, including Bellafronte. In the third scene, the gallants, including Matheo, entertain Bots and Mistress Horseleach and lure the unsuspecting Candido into drinking their health while Orlando delivers the stolen goods for their appraisal. When the trap is set, the constables arrive, first to arrest the bawdy-house keepers and Candido, and second to apprehend Matheo for theft and possession of stolen goods.

The final act begins with Ludovico informing Hippolito of Bellafronte's arrest, the news of which drives the prince into a frenzy of rage. He races off to storm the Bridewell, where the duke and Infelice lie in wait for him. All the interwoven threads of intrigue are carefully drawn together in the long final scene as Orlando and the duke confront Matheo and Hippolito with the enormity of their behavior. Still disguised as Pacheco, Orlando orchestrates the arraignment of Matheo, who first tries to pin the blame upon Bellafronte and then upon Pacheco himself. He even accuses Hippolito and Bellafronte of whoring, claiming to have caught them together in bed. When Infelice demands justice against the bewildered Bellafronte, Hippo-lito confesses his miserable failure in trying to tempt Bellafronte; at this moment, Orlando casts off his disguise to exonerate his daughter of Matheo's malicious accusation, while at the same time certifying the veracity of the prince's confession. Matheo is saved from the charge of theft, since the men he had robbed are Orlando's own servants. Matheo is not pardoned for his merits, or even in the hope that he will reform, but as a reward for Bellafronte's patient loyalty to him. Similarly, Candido, who remains the soul of patience, is elevated to the rank of "king's counselor." Hippolito is ignored but is doubtless restored to Infelice's good graces.

It was a stroke of realistic genius on Dekker's part to leave Matheo only grudgingly repentant at the end of the play, for his insolent prodigality and his cruelty toward Bellafronte make it impossible for his crimes merely to be whitewashed. The main point of the resolution is to demonstrate how completely the "whore" has overcome the obstacles which have constantly threatened her progress. In *Part I*, Bellafronte's conversion becomes the continuing butt of scurrilous jests and innuendos, which partly suggest that she will be unable to sustain her penitence and purity of moral purpose. Her final victory in *Part II* is earned against almost insuperable odds, in spite of the seemingly mitigating fact that her father has been watching over her, for there is no question that Orlando undertakes his role with a view to testing fully her reformed character. The implication is clearly that he will once again abandon Bellafronte if she suffers a relapse. In fact, her conversion to chastity in *Part I* would ultimately have proven unconvincing had not Dekker submitted her to the protracted trials and grief of *Part II*, for which Matheo's thorough, unrelenting evil is thematically essential.

It seems likely that Dekker was attracted to a reexamination of the temptation theme after his less than successful effort at reworking the legend of patient Griselda. Unlike the saintly Grissell, who has never experienced the pleasures of forbidden life and who is never seriously threatened by Gwalter's cruelty, Bellafronte undergoes a series of much more realistic temptations. Her chastity is severely tested not because her resolution is weak but because she faces the constant fear of degrading poverty and starvation. In this light, Hippolito's importunate lust represents no serious threat, since her resistance is firmly based upon the clear recollection of the disgust and shame she has actually experienced as a prostitute. On the other hand, Matheo's repulsive suggestion that she return to her "profession" poses a genuine threat because it represents a terrifying dilemma; she must choose between a return to prostitution or continued resistance to her husband's will. The stripping away of her self-respect reaches its nadir with Matheo's theft of her gown, which is sold to feed his uncontrollable greed. It is at this point that Orlando knows he must intervene to uncloak Matheo's villainy, but he only makes this decision when he is thoroughly convinced that her steadfast resistance to temptation is genuine.

Structurally, the subplot provides consistently strong reinforcement of the trial theme in the main plot, particularly since it involves not only the enduring patience of Candido, whose unassailable virtue reminds one of Grissell's, but also the successful resistance of Candido's new wife to the schemes of Bots, Horseleach, and Ludovico. The duke's Milan, plagued as it seems by all the seven deadly sins, is Dekker's re-creation of the Jacobean London so vividly depicted in the rogue pamphlets. In such a world, Hippolito, Matheo, the bawds, prostitutes, and gallants "doe most looke like the Divell that would destroy us, when wee are one anothers tormentors," and they are frequently described in terms of diabolic imagery. Furthermore, true to Dekker's basically Arian moral thought, Bellafronte demonstrates that love, obedience, and perseverance are the constant virtues of a distinctly possible reformation. In this play and in *The Shoemaker's Holiday*, Dekker left at least two works which demonstrate architectonic unity and a keen sense of moral values. For this achievement, he deserves to be ranked among the excellent second-rank dramatists of the Elizabethan-Jacobean stage.

Other major works

MISCELLANEOUS: *The Magnificent Entertainment Given to King James*, 1603 (with Ben Jonson and Thomas Middleton); *The Wonderful Year*, 1603 (prose and poetry); *The Seven Deadly Sins of London*, 1606; *News from Hell*, 1606; *The Bellman of London*, 1608; *Lanthorn and Candlelight*, 1608, 1609 (revised as *O per se O*, 1612; *Villanies Discovered*, 1616, 1620; *English Villanies*, 1632, 1638, 1648); *The Gull's Hornbook*, 1609; *Four Birds of Noah's Ark*, 1609; *A Work for Armourers*, 1609; *Dekker, His Dream*, 1620 (prose and poetry); *Penny-Wise and Proud-Foolish*, 1630.

Bibliography

Berlin, Normand. "Thomas Dekker: A Partial Reappraisal," in *Studies in English Literature*. VI (1966), pp. 263-277.
Conover, James H. *Thomas Dekker: An Analysis of Dramatic Structure*, 1969.
Hunt, Mary Leland. *Thomas Dekker: A Study*, 1964.
Kaplan, Joel H. "Virtue's Holiday: Thomas Dekker and Simon Eyre," in *Renaissance Drama*. New Series, II (1969), pp. 103-122.
Manheim, Michael. "The Construction of *The Shoemaker's Holiday*," in *Studies in English Literature*. X (1970), pp. 315-323.
_____. "The Thematic Structure of Dekker's *2 Honest Whore*," in *Studies in English Literature*. V (1965), pp. 363-381.
Price, George R. *Thomas Dekker*, 1969.
Waage, Frederick O. *Thomas Dekker's Pamphlets, 1603-1609*, 1977 (2 volumes).

E. F. J. Tucker

MERRILL DENISON

Born: Detroit, Michigan; June 23, 1893
Died: Bon Echo, Ontario; June 13, 1975

Principal drama

Brothers in Arms, pr. 1921, pb. 1923 (one act); *From Their Own Place*, pr. 1922, pb. 1923 (one act); *Balm*, pr. 1923, pb. 1926; *Marsh Hay*, pb. 1923, pr. 1974; *The Weather Breeder*, pb. 1923, pr. 1924 (one act); *The Unheroic North*, pb. 1923 (includes *Brothers in Arms*, *From Their Own Place*, *Marsh Hay*, *The Weather Breeder*); *The Prizewinner*, pr., pb. 1928; *Contract*, pr. 1929; *Haven of the Spirit*, pb. 1929 (one act); *The U.S. vs Susan B. Anthony*, pb. 1941 (one act).

Other literary forms

Merrill Denison not only contributed to the emergence of indigenous Canadian drama for the stage but also was involved in the establishment of radio as a medium for drama. On the invitation of the radio department of the Canadian National Railways, Denison wrote a series of radio dramas based on incidents from Canadian history, which were broadcast as the *Romance of Canada* series in the winter of 1930-1931. He produced a similar series for American radio, entitled *Great Moments in History*, broadcast during 1932 and 1933. He continued to write original radio dramas and adaptations until 1944. Denison's historical writing also took the form of company biographies, histories of large corporations which were more than mere self-serving eulogies or lists of directors. The first of these was *Harvest Triumphant* (1948), about Massey-Harris Company, the farm equipment manufacturers. He also wrote about Canada's largest brewery in *The Barley and the Stream: The Molson Story* (1955) and about the Royal Bank, in *Canada's First Bank: A History of the Bank of Montreal* (1966-1967). Denison's major prose works are *Boobs in the Woods* (1927), a series of comic anecdotes about tourists and residents of the backwoods of Ontario, and *Klondike Mike* (1943), a biography of the Yukon Gold Rush prospector Michael Ambrose Mahoney. Both books have been praised as essentially accurate accounts freed from the restrictions of factual documentation. Denison also regularly contributed both fiction and nonfiction to newspapers and magazines. His collected papers are housed at Queen's University in Kingston, Ontario.

Achievements

Denison was the first and most successful of a group of writers in the 1920's who sought a truly indigenous Canadian dramatic literature. He has been called Canada's first nationalist dramatist and the founder of modern

Canadian drama. This reputation is based on but four short comedies and one full-length drama. When these plays were first presented to the public, critics agreed that Denison showed great promise. Edith Isaacs, editor of *Theatre Arts Monthly*, in reviewing the publication of *The Unheroic North*, a collection of Denison's plays, called him a Canadian Eugene O'Neill. Ironically, this praise appeared at the same time Denison was turning his back on the theater and beginning his exploration of radio as a forum for his writing. It was not until 1971, on the fiftieth anniversary of the production of *Brothers in Arms*, that the Canadian literary community attested unequivocally Denison's contribution to the evolutionary growth of Canadian literature, and it was not until 1974, one year before his death, that his best play, *Marsh Hay*, received a public performance. Given the small quantity of his contributions to theater and the admittedly flawed nature of his dramatic writing, how can it be that Denison holds such a significant position in the history of Canadian drama?

The answer to that question lies only partly in the barren nature of Canadian dramatic literature before the 1960's. W. S. Milne, in reviewing *The Unheroic North* for *Canadian Forum* in 1932, commented with bitter sarcasm, "Some half dozen plays, mostly of one act; four of them dealing with the same restricted milieu; not a bit of imagination in one of them, unless by accident. A small thing almost perfectly done. That is the dramatic achievement of Merrill Denison, and he is Canada's greatest dramatist." At that time, Denison was one of the very few playwrights exploring issues of interest to Canadians and presenting a realistic picture of life in Canada. As a leading member of the first wave, his position in history books is assured, but the achievement of his dramatic writing is not limited to its historical significance. A close examination of the plays allows for a rebuttal to Milne's condemnation of "not a bit of imagination in one of them" and supports the praise given by those dramatists who followed Denison's leadership and innovation. In his attitude toward contemporary social issues, Denison provided a model for the social realism that became the mainstay of several of Canada's leading playwrights and theater companies. The same is true of Denison's commitment to historical subjects. His influence was apparent in the lively theater scene in Toronto in the 1960's, which was dominated by plays that bore a remarkable resemblance, in form, content, and impact, to Denison's work. In particular, the docudramas of this period, based on incidents from history or observation of real-life situations and people, followed Denison's commitment to dramatizing only those situations which he himself had observed.

In retrospect, Denison is worthy of the title Father of Canadian Drama not only because he was the first, but also because his plays demonstrate all the potential of a great dramatist as well as all of the flaws of a young writer. The tragedy is that Denison, for whatever reasons, turned his back on playwriting before the promise of his first works could be fulfilled. He needed an ongoing relationship with professional actors and directors and a sympathetic public in order to grow as a writer, and in Canada at that time he was cut off from these. One can only speculate that he might indeed have become the Canadian O'Neill—if only he had had a Canadian Provincetown Players.

Biography

Merrill Denison was born in Detroit, Michigan, on June 23, 1893. That he was born an American rather than a Canadian resulted from the fact that his mother wanted her child not to be a subject of the British Crown. Shortly prior to the birth, she had traveled from her home in Toronto to Detroit in order to accomplish this. A well-known feminist, Flora MacDonald Denison was a descendant of Nathaniel Merrill, who had left Connecticut in 1774 to settle in Kingston as part of the second exodus of United Empire Loyalists. Flora continued the family tradition of outspoken individualism. In 1905, after five years as a manager of the women's wear department of a large department store, Flora refused to punch in on the newly installed time clock, on the grounds that the newfangled system fostered class distinctions.

Merrill Denison was an only child, and the influence of his mother on his private and public life was strong. He supported her stand on women's issues; he was president of the University Men's League for Women's Suffrage in Canada. By contrast, Denison's father, Howard, had little influence. A commercial traveler, he was at home only irregularly, although his son remembers him as a friend. Flora was responsible for Merrill's literary bent as well as his social awareness. She contributed a regular column on women's suffrage to the *Sunday World* of Toronto and took every opportunity to speak and write about religious, social, and political controversies. Another enduring love that passed from mother to son was of the Bon Echo resort on Lake Mazinaw in northern Ontario. This backwoods area not only became Denison's holiday and retirement home, but also provided the setting and characters for his most significant dramatic writing. Flora first took the eight-year-old Denison to Bon Echo in 1901; in 1910, she bought the twelve-hundred-acre resort; Denison managed a summer hotel there from 1921 to 1929; and in 1959 he turned the property over to the Ontario government for use as a provincial park.

As a young man, Denison studied at the University of Toronto for one semester and then departed "by mutual consent." After a series of odd jobs, including work as a journalist, drama critic, advertising agent, and timekeeper in a steelworks plant, he returned to the University of Toronto to study architecture. In 1916, he departed to serve two years with the American Ambulance Field Service in France. In 1919 and 1920, he worked as an architectural draftsman in Boston and New York, but architecture was not to be his career. In fact, he wrote a critique of his architectural education, which appeared in 1922 in *The American Architect*. The magazine's publishers reportedly offered him the editorship, which he refused. After he returned to the family home in Toronto, he was approached by Roy Mitchell, the dynamic and forward-looking director of Hart House Theatre at the University of Toronto, to become the theater's art director. His first stage designs were for a production of Euripides' *Alcestis* in February of 1921. He also tried his hand at acting and became a playwright by the end of the season.

Denison tells an amusing story of how this came about. Mitchell had planned an evening of three Canadian plays for April, but only two, both tragedies, had been found. Five weeks before the opening, Denison and Mitchell were joking about where to find a true Canadian. Denison claimed that the only untainted Canadians he had known were the backwoodsmen near Bon Echo, the subject of so many of the amusing stories with which he had regaled his friends. The result: He was locked in the director's room and told to turn out a play based on his famous story of the Upper Canada College principal trying to acquire the use of a boat from a backwoodsman. As Denison reports, "Well, with no inhibitions and a deadline, I was able to accomplish the feat in about four and a quarter hours."

Brothers in Arms, as this play was called, enjoyed remarkable popularity, appearing in ten editions from 1923 to 1975, and was performed an estimated fifteen hundred times from 1921 to 1971. The initial response, however, was not undivided. Hart House was governed by a theater committee which had to give approval to all scripts. This group, shocked by the ungrammatical language of backwoodsmen and by the satire of patriotism that fuels the comedy, rejected Denison's script. After Mitchell threatened to resign, however, the play was added to the program, and theater history was made.

Denison continued with Mitchell at Hart House Theatre and saw productions of *The Weather Breeder* on April 21, 1924, and *The Prizewinner* on February 27, 1928. The one-act format was necessitated by Mitchell's commitment to an evening of short plays by three different writers, but in 1929, Denison was given a chance to provide an entire evening's entertainment. He wrote *Contract*, described by the Toronto *Star* as "good-natured satire . . . charged with local allusions . . . convincing and clever." Other reviews were equally positive, but this was to be Denison's last major stage production. The first twentieth century English-Canadian playwright to attempt to make a living from his writing in Canada was forced to abandon the stage in order to earn enough money to survive.

In 1929, Denison was approached by Austin Weir, who was then in charge of radio programs for the Canadian National Railways, with the idea of presenting episodes from Canadian history over the air. At first, Denison was dubious about the potential of such a venture, having an ambivalent regard for the medium and questioning, as he later admitted, anyone's ability to discover in Canadian history the material out of which half a dozen, let alone twenty-five, romantic dramas could be written. He soon warmed to the task, however, and became fascinated with the potential of radio for dramatic presentation. The result was the radio series known as *Romance of Canada* directed by Tyrone Guthrie and broadcast in the winter of 1930-1931 over a transcontinental chain by Canadian National Railways' Radio Department. Six of the scripts were published in 1931 under the title *Henry Hudson and Other Plays*. So successful was this series with both audiences and critics that Denison was commissioned by the J. Walter Thompson Company to write a similar series dealing with American history. Denison produced a forty-week series of half-hour programs, broadcast during 1932 and 1933, entitled *Great Moments in History*, and he continued to earn his living writing for American radio networks through World War II. He was best known for his ability to dramatize historical events in a manner both educational and entertaining. During the war, he wrote for American, British, and Canadian radio, including the British Broadcasting Corporation's *Home Hour*, for which he produced dramatized commentaries explaining the American war effort to United Kingdom listeners.

Denison's storytelling skills led him to several prose treatments in both short and full-length form. *Klondike Mike*, a biography of Michael Ambrose Mahoney, a survivor of the Klondike Gold Rush, was a best-seller within weeks of its publication and was a Book-of-the-Month Club selection. It was reprinted in 1965 and received the accolades of another generation of Canadians. Nevertheless, playwriting and storytelling were insufficient sources of income, and Denison's attempt at resort management was also not a financial success. His alternative career was in journalism; as a regular contributor to leading daily newspapers and monthly magazines, Denison spoke out on cultural and social issues that concerned him deeply. These included the state of drama in Canada, the potential of radio as a social and cultural force, the hardships endured by those trying to survive in the less developed regions of Canada, and the need for a strong conservationist policy to protect the natural beauty of the unspoiled north.

In 1922 and 1923, Denison was a contributing editor of *The Bookman*, from which position he analyzed the causes of the slow emergence of indigenous Canadian literature. His theory, that Canadians suffer from an inferiority complex—or "an intellectual timidity born of a false feeling of inadequacy or inability"—has profoundly influenced subsequent theories and later practitioners. Being an American by birth and citizenship and a

Canadian by choice of residence, Denison was also able to comment insightfully on relations between these neighbors. Though against nationalism as a divisive international force, Denison remained throughout his life an ardent advocate of Canadian nationalism because of his sense of the feelings of inferiority suffered by Canadians, despite prodigious accomplishments in many areas. "You will have to find out about yourselves and know and appreciate yourselves before you can expect other people to know and understand you," he advised in 1949. In 1967, the year of the Canadian Centennial, his message had altered as little as the problem he addressed: the ignorance of Canadians about their own past achievements.

An interest in history, biography, and journalism made Denison a logical choice for the Massey-Harris Company when they celebrated their one hundredth birthday in 1947 with a booklet outlining their history. Denison admitted that "farm implements had never been numbered my irrepressible enthusiasms," but he soon became fascinated with the technological advancements pioneered by the firm, as well as the position of the company in the social, economic, and international history of Canada. He received permission to prepare a full-length biography which was published in 1948 as *Harvest Triumphant*. Company biographies usually are of little interest save to those members of past and present management who receive the praise which seems to be the sole motive for their production, but in this case, Denison's book not only was an overwhelming commercial success but also set a creative precedent for the company biographies that followed.

Denison was much in demand, following the success of *Harvest Triumphant*, to record the achievements of other companies. The most respected of these biographies were *The Barley and the Stream*, a history of the powerful Molson brewery empire; *The People's Power: The History of Ontario Hydro* (1960); and *Canada's First Bank*. In each of these company biographies, which involved several years of historical research and for which Denison demanded freedom from interference by company management, Denison remained true to his commitment to the importance of the country's history for an understanding of what it meant to be a Canadian. He did not limit his definition of history to political events. History, he said,

is to be found in the nature of the land itself, dominated by the Laurentian Shield. It is to be found in the struggles of a tiny population to subdue that and other regions, in the long wait for the tools with which to master the Prairies and the Far North, the Shield and its inaccessible forests and once-useless water power. It is linked to canals, railroads, hydro-electric power, diamond drills, airplanes and caterpillar tractors, far more than it is to fluctuating fortunes of political parties or the decisions of the Privy Council. The story is to be found in the mineshafts and the lumber camps and the holds of the Great Lakes Freighters; in the tellers' cages of banks from Canso to the Yukon; in the custom brokers' records of a hundred ports around the world.

Merrill Denison, master storyteller, dedicated his life to transmitting, in a variety of forms, incidents from real life, contemporary and historical, that would hold a mirror up to the Canadian people, in which they might more clearly see themselves. He tried to battle the inferiority complex that he saw around him in order to give the citizens of his adopted country the same love for the land and its people that he so fervently felt.

Analysis

Merrill Denison was one of the group of Canadian writers who, in the 1920's, first attempted to dramatize the uniquely Canadian aspects of their national experience. If this were his only achievement, he would be a provincial writer of interest only to his immediate contemporaries and to theater historians. It is his unique attitude to the Canadian experience that marks his contribution to dramatic literature and gives it enduring value.

Three aspects of Denison's dramatic writings distinguish his work. His plays are first and foremost realistic, based entirely on personal experience and observation and written with careful attention to believable dialogue, setting, action, and characterization. Second, he is both antiheroic and antiromantic, dedicated to debunking the false image of Canada as the home of Mounties and noble, simple hunters—natural heroes of the virgin wilderness. Finally, he brings to his writing a sense of comedy tempered with commitment to justice—a commitment that leads him to explore social problems objectively and in defiance of contemporary morality. The result is a group of plays that have not become dated with the passage of time.

In his short comedies, Denison uses character-types, two-dimensional creations that function within a limited plot line. The plays turn on a single narrative device, usually a reversal. In *From Their Own Place*, city dweller Larry Stedman turns the tables on the backwoodsmen who have attempted to sell him the furs from illegally trapped animals for an inflated price (while arguing over who is the rightful owner of the furs) by calling in the game warden to witness all three men deny ownership. The tricksters are tricked into parting with the furs, and the naïve city dweller pays only for the cost of the trapping license.

Even within the limitations of the one-act structure, Denison creates evocative and well-crafted explorations of life in the northern areas of Ontario. His attention to language demonstrates the fine ear of a raconteur adept at mimicry. The ungrammatical utterances of the locals might offend university committees, but this language provides authenticity and a rich comic texture. Denison does not use foul language, but he still manages to capture the flavor of backwoods speech. When Alec, one of the tricksters, swears that half of the furs are his, he vows, "If they aint will the Lord strike me down right here where I'm stanin and send me to burnin hell for ten thousand years wiv a cup of cold water just beyond my lips and me not able to reach it."

Denison does not incorporate these vivid colloquialisms for mere comic effect; language is always tied to the characters and to their social environment. Sandy, caretaker for the Stedmans, and Cline, who habitually sells them worthless objects, debate the relative morality of their positions: Sandy attacks first, saying, "You've sold him enough trash now to satisfy anybody but a MacUnch." Cline indignantly defends his family name with "That's a fine thing for you to say, and you married to a MacUnch yourself and had three children by her. And the hull of you half starved till you got a job from the old lad. It aint everyone can get a job caretakin and not have nothin to do." Sandy retorts, "No, there aint but one can get it and that's me and it wouldn't matter if Emmy had twelve children and all of them twins, I wouldn't be like yous MacUnches trying to sponge off'n the only friend the backwoods has." Buried in this amusing exchange is the presentation of a serious socioeconomic situation. The duplicity of Sandy and Cline evolves into a hilarious farce of entrance and exit, lie and counterlie, as they conspire to cheat Stedman and then betray each other, but their convoluted relationship also points to a condition of inbreeding that Denison had observed and on which he had commented in his letters and articles, and their actions are motivated by a poverty that is tragic. "It's a hopeless country to try and make a living in. Even if it is the most beautiful spot in the world," comments Harriet Stedman, in an effort to excuse the stealing and lying of Sandy, Cline, and Alec.

Brothers in Arms, like *From Their Own Place*, features two-dimensional characters, simple plot devices, comic exchanges, and serious social commentary. J. Altrus Browne, a businessman, and his wife, Dorothea, have ventured to a hunting camp in the backwoods. Dorothea exhibits all of the romanticism of an outsiders' view of Canada; she wants to meet a *coureur de bois* (a French or half-breed trapper), one of the romantic figures of whom she had read in books or seen in movies about Canada. Her husband is presented even less sympathetically, as an impatient, insensitive, and pompous fool. Having received word of a business deal worth twenty-five thousand dollars, he is determined to catch the next train to Toronto but must wait for Charlie to drive them out in the only car. Dorothea views her environment through a glaze of romanticism: "I think your camp is adorable. It's so simple, and direct. So natural." Browne judges by a different standard: "I should never have come up into this God-forsaken hole at all." Syd, an authentic *coureur de bois*, unrecognized by Dorothea, and a fellow veteran (a brother-in-arms), unrecognized by Browne, sees his surroundings with the clear vision of a man who is resigned to the reality of survival in a "wild, virgin country," where there are a few deer left, although most have been scared off by the neighbor's hounds. Although

Syd lives far from civilization, that "keeps folks outa here in the summer. City folks is a kinda bother. . . . They's always tryin to get a feller to work. One way and another they figger they's doin a feller a favour to let him work for em." Dorothea tries to fit Syd into her preconceived notions, suggesting to him that he wants to be left alone to lead his own simple life, but Syd defies romanticism. His relaxed manner and unconventional attitudes might entice audience sympathy, but Denison undercuts this by also presenting his laziness and destructive shortsightedness. The hunters tear up the floorboards rather than split firewood, so the abandoned farmhouse they use for their camp is slowly being destroyed.

Denison has some pointed comments to make about the army. Syd and Browne were both soldiers, but their experiences in the war were quite different. Syd's view of "their war" is "they wasn't no sense to it to my way of thinkin." Syd's version of sentry duty—"They wasn't a German this side of the ocean and they wasn't no sense hangin around in the cold. So I went in and went to bed"—horrifies Browne but arouses in Dorothea continued romanticism: "Don't you love his sturdy independence? It's so Canadian." Denison tempers this satire with a bitter image when Syd voices his most pointed criticism of officers and businessmen: "Perhaps you ain't used to listenin much in your business. We got a feller up here that got his eyes blew out in France can hear most a mile away." Finally, Denison, having created a vehicle for his satiric portrait of romanticism and the army, ends the piece with the comic reversal. Charlie arrives at last, only to inform the Brownes that Syd, with whom they have been talking all along, could just as well have driven them to the train, being half owner of the car. Browne explodes with the question, "Why didn't you say you could drive us?" to which Syd replies, "You never ast me."

In *The Weather Breeder*, Denison explores a theme which plays a part in all of his dramatic writing: the relationship between character and natural environment. Old John, a backwoods farmer, is gloomy when the weather is glorious because he is certain that a storm is blowing. When the storm arrives, he is overjoyed because his sour predictions have come true; when the storm passes by and causes minimal damage to the vulnerable crops, he becomes gloomy again. Old John's attitude toward the weather becomes a metaphor for his pessimistic outlook: "It aint natural to have three weeks without a storm and the longer she waits the worse she'll be. We'll have to pay for it." As Jim, John's young helper, notes, John makes life miserable for everybody with his sour prophesying of inevitable doom. Even the most perfect of days becomes merely an excuse to prophesy that an entire summer's worth of bad weather is building up, waiting to descend on them all at once.

Denison based *The Weather Breeder*, like all of his plays, on attitudes that he had observed in the communities around Bon Echo. For the bare subsistence farming such an environment provides, weather can destroy the hopes of a lifetime. Old John expects a certain amount of hardship every year, and, when it holds off for a time, he expects his share of disaster to occur in one huge cataclysm. This bleak outlook, ingrained in Old John's personality, is largely played for comic effect, and the serious implications of his pessimism are further undermined by a rather mundane motivation for his sour spirits: Old John has been laid up with a serious injury; his foot was caught in a thresher.

Thus, in his short plays, Denison did not give full expression to his harsh vision of Canadian life. In his full-length drama *Marsh Hay*, however, he directly addressed the devastated state of the northern backwoods, where, as a result of unrestricted lumbering from 1850 to 1890 and ravaging forest fires, the land had been transformed. As Barnood, a struggling farmer in *Marsh Hay*, recalls, "I can remember when a man could drive a team through a stand of white pine for days ... but the lumber companies and the fire gouged her clean. Turned it into so much bare rock and scrub popple." The farms of the area were abandoned by those with the resources and vision to escape. Those who remained were forced into a cruel, grasping search for survival. Outsiders such as Thompson, the city lawyer (a less satiric portrait than Browne), might call them lazy and shift-less, but Barnood defends his fellow survivors: "I don't know as you call a man that works fourteen or sixteen hours a day, lazy. They don't make much of a livin, Mr. Thompson. Pick up a few dollars from the city people that summers on the lakes back here ... do a little trappin ... kill a deer or two ... raise a few potatoes between the rocks and cut marsh hay."

Marsh Hay tells the story of the Serang family. John, the father, like the John in *The Weather Breeder*, is a sour, bitter man, so broken by the desperation of his effort to scratch a living in this desolate region that he is incapable of any positive feeling. He summarizes his life thus: "Twenty years of a man's life gone into workin fifty acres of grey stone ... cuttin marsh hay to keep a couple of sows and a half dead horse alive. Cuttin marsh hay because the land won't raise enough fodder to winter a rat. A dozen scrawny chickens ... twelve children. Five dead, thank God. Twenty years of a man's life." There is an alternative, to travel west to the fertile land of the prairies, but for John Serang, this is the bitterest twist of fate he must endure: When he was young enough to go, he could not break free, and now he is too worn out to summon the energy and too poor to finance the trip. As he ironically notes, "If we'd lived in England they'd a paid our fare."

John sees no hope for change in his situation and expects no help from a change in government. As he says to his neighbor Barnood, "Andy, the only thing a change in government ever changes, Andy, is the government." A government cannot make the weather good or make the hay stand shoulder high in the marshes, nor is the government even likely to build railroads all through the back country, a more realistic hope at which John also sneers.

John's wife, Lena, shares this desolation, so reflective of the barren environment. Their marriage is one of continued accusation and bitterness. John calls her a damned sow, and she replies, "It's a wonder I aint killed you before this John. Callin me... look at me! Look at me! Worn out before my time... bearin your children. And you call me that. It's a wonder I aint killed you." Denison's stage direction notes, "Lena comes slowly to John, vehemence and heat forgotten and nothing but cold, bitter rage left her." John replies, indifferently, "I wish you had."

In this sort of home, it is not surprising to find that the children are dispirited, cruel, and desperate for any means of escape. John's bitterness has been passed on like a disease to his surviving offspring. Sarilin, fifteen years old, says, "Paw don't like us to do nothin. It don't make no difference to him but he won't let nobody have no fun. He never has done hisself and he don't know what it is." Her solution is to follow in the path of her sister Tessie, who runs off with a boy at the beginning of the play. The result is that Sarilin finds herself pregnant. Walt, who is the father of the child, tries to escape an enforced marriage which, as even old John admits, would be a cruel trap. This has been John's own experience, but Denison does not wholly doom the next generation to this horrible cycle. Pete, John's youngest, is determined to continue to attend school despite the eight-mile walk each way. "I want to get some learnin so's I can get out a this back country and go out front. I aint goin to spend my life workin this farm."

The most profound hope for the family comes from an unlikely source. Sarilin's pregnancy, which is viewed by the community as a shameful and tragic event and by the minister as a heinous sin, is for Lena an inspiration for dignity and renewed caring. This comes about through a chance meeting with a city woman (based on Denison's mother), who shares with Lena the unconventional philosophy that no child is illegitimate. As Lena reports it, "She said it was natural . . . she told me people is ruled by laws . . . just like a tree is . . . and she says no one was to blame." Lena resolves to follow unflinchingly the woman's recommendation never to let Sarilin feel ashamed, and to give the baby the best chance they can. The strength of her conviction has a profound effect on the family. The two boys, Jo and Pete, share in her caring for Sarilin, and even John finds himself half believing her. The house itself reflects the transformation. In his stage direction, Denison says, "Where before was a feeling of extreme squalor, poverty, tragic futility, there is a feeling of regeneration. The place lacked self-respect before... all echo the evident attempt to make the place decent to live in."

The regeneration, however, is short-lived. Tessie infects her younger sister with a cynical realism that arises naturally out of being reared in hatred. Children are only another mouth to feed, another link on the chain of entrapment. She suggests a self-induced abortion, and Sarilin complies. The final act of the play brings us full circle, to a scene of abject misery. The despair is palpable, made all the more bitter by John's begrudging respect for Sarilin's decision: "I don't know but what she showed pretty good sense, too." The same recriminations are voiced by John and Lena, and even Lena's last residue of gentle feeling, "We must've been kinda fond of each other to stick together all these years, John?" is shattered by John's brutal and uncompromising reply, "Fond? Fond be damned. We stuck together because we couldn't get away from each other. That's why we stuck. We're chained here. That's what we are. Just like them stones outside the door, there. Fond? Bah!"

The dramatic writings of Merrill Denison exhibit many of the weaknesses of any young dramatist. He has been criticized for simplistic characterization, particularly of the women in his short plays, who have a tendency to utter the most inane superficialities. Even *Marsh Hay*, his most ambitious work, suffers from a lack of complexity in the delineation of the relationships and emotions of the central characters. In dramatic structure, his plays rely on twists of plot that are at times difficult to believe, and his language, though vigorous and amusing, is also repetitious, particularly in the longer drama, which is weighted with so many references to "fifty acres of grey stone" that it begins to read as though it were "fifty acres of grey prose."

These flaws, however, do not outweigh Denison's real achievement. It is his unflinching commitment to the recording of events, attitudes, and problems he observed in the area around his beloved Bon Echo that merits most praise. Unfortunately, his most exciting attribute as a dramatist may well have been a factor in Denison's unwillingness to write another play after *Marsh Hay*. The documentation of observed social phenomenon was fine when it was sugarcoated with comedy, but in a serious form it was unpalatable to audiences.

Denison was passionately committed to the social message he wished to convey, but the public was not ready to hear it. It is to be regretted that this gifted playwright did not find the environment within which to fulfill his early promise.

Other major works

SHORT FICTION: *Boobs in the Woods*, 1927.

NONFICTION: *Klondike Mike*, 1943, 1965; *Harvest Triumphant*, 1948; *The Barley and the Stream: The Molson Story*, 1955; *The People's Power: The History of Ontario Hydro*, 1960; *Canada's First Bank: A History of the*

Bank of Montreal, 1966-1967 (2 volumes).
RADIO PLAYS: *Henry Hudson and Other Plays*, 1931 (6 plays from the *Romance of Canada* series).

Bibliography

Goldie, Terence. "A National Drama and a National Dramatist: The First Attempt," in *Canadian Drama*. III, no. 2 (Spring, 1977), pp. 9-11.
MacDonald, Dick. *Mugwump Canadian: The Merrill Denison Story*, 1973.
Milne, W. S. "Merrill Denison," in *Canadian Forum*. XIII (November, 1932), p. 64.
Wagner, Anton. "Introduction," in *Canada's Lost Plays, Volume IV*, 1982.

Leslie O'Dell

JOHN DRINKWATER

Born: Leytonstone, England; June 1, 1882
Died: London, England; March 25, 1937

Principal drama

Ser Taldo's Bride, pr. 1911 (one act; adaptation of Barry Jackson's play); *Cophetua*, pr., pb. 1911; *An English Medley*, pr., pb. 1911 (masque; music by Ruthland Boughton); *Puss in Boots*, pr., pb. 1911; *The Pied Piper: A Tale of Hamelin City*, pr., pb. 1912 (masque; music by S. W. Sylvester); *The Only Legend: A Masque of the Scarlet Pierrot*, pr., pb. 1913 (masque; music by J. Brier); *Rebellion*, pr., pb. 1914; *Robin Hood and the Pedlar*, pr., pb. 1914 (masque; music by Brier); *The Storm*, pr. 1914, pb. 1915 (one act); *The God of Quiet*, pr., pb. 1916 (one act); *The Wounded*, pr. 1917; *X=O: A Night of the Trojan War*, pr., pb. 1917 (one act); *Abraham Lincoln*, pr., pb. 1918; *Oliver Cromwell*, pb. 1921, pr. 1923; *Mary Stuart*, pr., pb. 1921; *Robert E. Lee*, pr., pb. 1923; *Robert Burns*, pb. 1924; *Collected Plays*, 1925 (2 volumes); *The Mayor of Casterbridge*, pr., pb. 1926 (adaptation of Thomas Hardy's novel); *Bird in Hand*, pr., pb. 1927; *John Bull Calling: A Political Parable in One Act*, pr., pb. 1928; *A Man's House*, pr. 1931, pb. 1934; *Napoleon: The Hundred Days*, pr., pb. 1932 (adaptation of Giovacchino Forzano and Benito Mussolini's play *Campo di Maggio*); *Laying the Devil*, pr., pb. 1933; *Garibaldi: A Chronicle Play of Italian Freedom in Ten Scenes*, pb. 1936.

Other literary forms

Starting in 1903 with *Poems*, John Drinkwater published a number of volumes of poetry, the most significant of which are *Poems 1908-1914* (1917), *Poems 1908-1919* (1919), *Selected Poems* (1922), *New Poems* (1925), and *The Collected Poems of John Drinkwater* (in three volumes, two published in 1923 and one in 1937). His most important critical and biographical studies are *William Morris: A Critical Study* (1912), *Swinburne: An Estimate* (1913), *Lincoln, The World Emancipator* (1920), *The Pilgrim of Eternity: Byron—A Conflict* (1925), *Mr. Charles, King of England* (1926), *Cromwell: A Character Study* (1927), *Charles James Fox* (1928), *Pepys: His Life and Character* (1930), and *Shakespeare* (1933). His autobiographical volumes are *Inheritance* (1931) and *Discovery* (1932); they cover only the period to 1913.

Achievements

For three decades, from early in the twentieth century until he died in 1937, Drinkwater was a consummate man of the theater—a playwright, actor, producer, director, and critic. Foremost among his achievements was his role in the organization and development of the Birmingham Repertory Theatre, one of Great Britain's most innovative and influential companies. In addition, the popular success of his verse dramas encouraged other playwrights to work in the same genre, and his prose play *Abraham Lincoln* was the most notable historical-biographical play of its time. Both it and the earlier verse drama $X = O$ were important expressions of antiwar sentiment, to which audiences responded enthusiastically, and *Abraham Lincoln* enjoyed long runs in London and New York. Active as he was in the theater, Drinkwater was also a prolific man of letters. He wrote critical studies of Algernon Charles Swinburne, William Morris, and William Shakespeare; biographies of such famous men as Abraham Lincoln, King Charles I, Oliver Cromwell, Samuel Pepys, and Lord Byron; a novel; essays; and film scripts. He also was a major poet in the Georgian movement; according to John Middleton Murry (in 1922), only John Masefield rivaled Drinkwater in popularity. (His popularity notwithstanding, critics did not regard his poetry favorably, labeling it derivative, unimaginative, and sentimental.)

Though public and critical interest in him had faded by the time of his death, and he and his work have been largely ignored in the half century since, Drinkwater merits at least a footnote in studies of modern English drama for his attempts to revitalize poetic drama in the twentieth century and to develop the chronicle play into a viable modern dramatic form. More than most playwrights, he brought to his craft (as Arnold Bennett put it) "a deep, practical knowledge of the stage."

Biography

John Drinkwater was born on June 1, 1882, in Leytonstone, Essex, England, to Albert Edwin and Annie Beck Brown Drinkwater. His father, headmaster of the Coburn Foundation School at Bow, in East London, had been active in amateur theatricals and, in 1886, embarked on a career in the theater as an actor, playwright, and manager (setting a pattern for his son to follow years later). Because his mother was terminally ill, young Drinkwater was sent to live with his maternal grandfather in Oxford when he was nine. An indifferent student, he left Oxford High School in 1897 for Nottingham, where he worked for the Northern Assurance Company and did some acting in amateur productions. His transfer in 1901 to the Birmingham branch of the firm was a fortuitous move, for there he met Barry Jackson, a well-to-do theater enthusiast (two years older than Drinkwater) who presented plays at his father's palatial home. When Jackson's group went public as the Pilgrim Players, Drinkwater joined them, and, in 1909, he gave up his career in insurance to work for the Players, becoming general manager in 1913 (by which time the Pilgrim Players had become the Birmingham Repertory Theatre and had a theater). By the time he left

Jackson's employ in 1918, Drinkwater had directed more than sixty productions, had appeared (under the name of John Darnley) in about forty roles, and had written a number of plays, including $X = O$ and *Abraham Lincoln*. His wife, Kathleen Walpole, whom he had married in 1906, also acted in the company (as Cathleen Orford).

The presentation of *Abraham Lincoln* at Sir Nigel Playfair's theater, the Lyric, in a London suburb, starting on February 19, 1919 (it had a run of four hundred performances), and its subsequent New York production made Drinkwater a celebrity on two continents. Birmingham gave him an M.A. in 1919, and he was in demand for lecture tours of the United States. On his return home, in 1921, from his second trip to the United States, Drinkwater met and fell in love with the violinist Daisy Kennedy. This shipboard romance led to an affair which culminated in the breakup of Drinkwater's marriage to Kathleen Walpole and of Kennedy's to Russian pianist Benno Moiseiwitsch. Drinkwater and Kennedy married in 1924 and during the next decade traveled widely on concert, lecture, and stage tours in the United States, on the Continent, and in Britain. They also became major figures on the London social circuit. Through this entire period, Drinkwater wrote for the stage; wrote articles, poems, and biographical and critical studies; did screenplays as well as lyrics for films; wrote two volumes of autobiography; and edited anthologies. He also continued to act, and shortly before he died—at his London home on March 25, 1937—appeared in the role of Prospero in a Regent's Park, London, production of Shakespeare's *The Tempest*.

Analysis

In the preface to his collected plays, John Drinkwater says that his "affections have never been divided between poetry and drama, " and he recalls that he hoped "to help as far as one could towards the restoration of the two upon the stage in union." Despite John Galsworthy's admonition to him that "the shadow of the man Shakespeare is across the path of all who should attempt verse drama in these days," Drinkwater was not deterred, and his first solo venture as a playwright (he previously had put a Barry Jackson sentimental comedy, *Ser Taldo's Bride*, into rhymed verse) was *Cophetua*, a one-act play in verse about a stubborn king who resists the demands of his mother and counselors that he wed but then decides to marry a beggar-maid, whose beauty and purity win over the aghast mother and counselors. Though the play has neither literary nor dramatic merit, it is of some interest, for the independent-minded Cophetua is a character-type that reemerges in later Drinkwater plays. Drinkwater wrote the play as a conscious experiment: "I used a variety of measures for the purpose of seeing whether a rapid and changing movement of rhyme might not to some extent produce the same effect on the stage as physical action." The effort failed, but Drinkwater concluded: "The experiment, I think, showed that there were exciting possibilities in the method, and if I had been born into a theatre that took kindly to verse as a medium I believe that interesting things might have been done in its development."

Drinkwater's only full-length poetic drama, *Rebellion*, also was a failure, in large part because of its overly rhetorical blank verse (which Drinkwater "stripped . . . of a little of its rhetoric" in the printed version). Nevertheless, it remains interesting because it recalls William Butler Yeats's *The King's Threshold* (pr. 1904), also about a struggle between a king and a poet, and foreshadows later Drinkwater plays that focus on war and the conflict between liberty and tyranny.

Little more than a curtain raiser, *The Storm* also has an Irish connection, for it is a contemporary rural tragedy that echoes John Millington Synge's *Riders to the Sea* (pb. 1903). The only one of Drinkwater's poetic dramas with a contemporary setting, *The Storm* is about women vainly awaiting the return of the man of the house, who is lost in a storm. The conflict centers on the boundless optimism of the young wife and the insistent pessimism of an old neighbor. Though blank verse is too stately a measure for the occasion, the play does possess tragic intensity, primarily because of the fully developed character of the wife, Alice, who is Drinkwater's most memorable creation.

The death in 1915 of poet Rupert Brooke, who was serving in the Royal Naval Division, heightened Drinkwater's antipathy toward war. He had met Brooke through Sir Edward Marsh, editor of *Georgian Poetry* (1912-1922), in which both were represented, and the two had become close friends. Drinkwater's last verse plays, *The God of Quiet* and *X = O*, are complementary works that reflect both sorrow over Brooke's death and disdain for war. The earlier of these one-act plays is the lesser of the two.

In *The God of Quiet*, war-weary people (young and old beggars, a citizen, and a soldier) meet at a life-size statue of their god, a Buddha-like figure, where they are joined by their king, who also has tired of the lengthy conflict and now preaches humility and love. The enemy king comes in prepared to resume the battle, denounces the God of Quiet for having "slacked the heat" and turned the people against war, and drives his dagger into the god's heart. The effigy comes to life, cries out "Not one of you in all the world to know me," and collapses. The first king is angered ("Why did you do it? He was a friendly god,/ Smiling upon our faults, a great forgiver . . . / He gave us quietness—"), curses his enemy, draws his sword, and vows "to requite the honour of this god." The din of war is heard as the curtain falls. Although the message is clear, the play lacks impact because the generalized characters are merely two-dimensional (not at all universal types), the dialogue is stilted, and the setting lacks precision.

On the other hand, *X = O*, the theme of which is the same, is a play of enduring sensitivity and impact. Briefer even than *The God of Quiet*, $X = O$ was a critical and popular success when first presented, and the passage of time has not dimmed its luster. Its structure is simple: Set during the ninth year of the Trojan War, the parallel scenes of the play show a pair of Greek soldiers and then two Trojan warriors lamenting what they consider a futile war, regretting the need to kill their adversaries, and yearning to return home. Each man is named and distinctively individualized, and all share an appreciation of the beauty and promise of life; as the mathematical equation in the title suggests, the erstwhile enemies are portrayed as sharing character traits and aspirations.

One of the youths in each camp must leave for his daily chore of killing an enemy soldier. The Greek who remains, a poet, is killed by the Trojan who is a would-be statesman with a dream of "Troy regenerate"; the Trojan who stays behind, a sculptor, is killed by the Greek who wants to become a politician. On each side, then, an artist is slain by an aspiring politician, a representative of the state, a detail that surely has its genesis in the deaths of Brooke and other young poets of Drinkwater's generation in World War I, which was at its height when Drinkwater wrote the play.

In writing his five verse plays, Drinkwater attempted "to find some other constructional idiom whereby verse might be accepted as a natural thing by a modern audience." By 1917, however, despite the popular success of $X = O$, Drinkwater had (as he reports in his autobiography) "a growing conviction that if I was to take any effective part in the practical theatre of my time, I should have to abandon verse for prose. Full of reforming ideas as we all were, I soon began to realise that in this fundamental matter of expression it would be futile, and indeed pointless, to try to alter the habit of an age." Somewhat defensive about his decision, he says in the preface to the collected plays:

> The transition from verse to prose, from $X = O$, that is, to *Abraham Lincoln*, was not a surrender, but a recognition that any chance of development in one's dramatic technique depends upon an acceptance of the fact that if one insists on staying in the theatre at all one may be anything one likes so long as one is not doctrinaire. The problem to be solved was how to keep in the sparest prose idiom something of the enthusiasm and poignancy of verse. In the days when verse was the natural speech of the theatre, its beauty, like the beauty of all fine style, reached the audience without any insistence upon itself. The guiding principle of the speech of these plays later than $X = O$ has been, so far as I could manage it, to make it beautiful without letting anybody know about it.

Abraham Lincoln was a transitional work for Drinkwater; although it was his first prose play, the dramatic tableaux that dominate this chronicle are linked by choral odes in verse. The play was closely tied to its immediate predecessors by its theme as well, for it is as obviously an antiwar drama as is $X = O$. It also set the pattern for Drinkwater's plays *Oliver*

Cromwell and *Robert E. Lee*; all three of these historical plays dramatize the problem of leadership, and each is developed in a series of episodes that chronologically traces the development of the hero and cumulatively delineates his personality. Indeed, Drinkwater said that he conceived of the three plays as a unit and according to "a more or less definite plan."

In a note included in the first edition of *Abraham Lincoln*, Drinkwater says that his "purpose is not that of the historian but of the dramatist . . . of the dramatist, not that of the political philosopher," and that his "concern is with the profoundly dramatic interest of [Lincoln's] character, and with the inspiring example of a man who handled war nobly and with imagination." Given his primary aim, he has "freely telescoped [historical] events, and imposed invention upon [their] movement, in such ways as I needed to shape the dramatic significance of my subject."

Abraham Lincoln begins in Springfield, Illinois, with townsmen talking of their neighbor's nomination for the presidency; it concludes with the assassination of the President at Ford's Theatre. Lincoln is portrayed as a peace-loving man who endures the agonies of war for the sake of lasting freedom. His last speech, given to the theater audience immediately before his assassination, epitomizes his character; he concludes: "With malice toward none, with charity for all, it is for us to resolve that this nation, under God, shall have a new birth of freedom; and that government of the people, by the people, for the people, shall not perish from the earth." Drinkwater's use of Lincoln's words in this context typifies the dramatic license that he exercises throughout the play.

When originally produced at the Birmingham Repertory Theatre on October 12, 1918, the play was a great hit. This provincial success did not assure a West End opening, however; in fact, managers either ignored or rejected it, and the London production was at Hammersmith, a suburb. Enlightened by its popularity there, West End managers tried unsuccessfully to convince Sir Nigel Playfair to bring it to the city. Finally, the city came to the play. The public loved it, for *Abraham Lincoln* was timely and obviously touched a responsive chord, a pervasive concern among the people with war and a desire for peace, and also admiration for a strong, principled leader who could guide his country through a dangerous period. Another determining factor in the popular success of the play was that the United States and Great Britain had jointly fought in a common cause, and the British, who had become increasingly interested in American history, saw in the play a reflection of their own sufferings and triumphs. In like manner, when *Abraham Lincoln* was produced in New York (for which production Drinkwater made his first trip to the United States, appearing in the play as a chronicler), Americans responded favorably to the patriotic theme and noted the intended parallels between Lincoln and Woodrow Wilson. In sum, it matters not that today, *Abraham Lincoln* seems closer to melodrama than it is to tragedy; it was the right play for its time.

Among Drinkwater's other plays (and masques, a form of which he was fond), *Bird in Hand* merits attention, in part because it is an atypical light comedy in the tradition of Oliver Goldsmith's *She Stoops to Conquer* (pr. 1773), but also because it shows Drinkwater's skill at orchestrating a varied group of well-developed characters in a realistic Midlands setting. His familiarity with the Cotswolds, where he rented a cottage for a time and about which he wrote in *Cotswold Characters* (1921), is apparent. The plot revolves about the reluctance of an innkeeper to permit his daughter to marry the son of a local baronet, since he believes that people should keep to their station in life. The efforts of his daughter, wife, and assorted guests fail to persuade him to renounce his prejudices, and he is moved to consent only through trickery. Although the plot is not very original, the play succeeds because Drinkwater gave his characters—stereotypical though they are—a measure of individuality, and he had them speak realistic dialogue. Further, the frivolity of the complications and the lightness of style and tone do not obscure the serious dimension of the play: an examination of the perennial problem of the generation gap. Coming almost ten years after the success of *Abraham Lincoln*, which prompted him to move to London, *Bird in Hand* marked Drinkwater's triumphant return to the Birmingham Repertory Theatre. The play was first produced there, with Drinkwater directing and including Peggy Ashcroft and Laurence Olivier as the young lovers. Its subsequent popularity in London and New York rivaled that of *Abraham Lincoln*, and reviewers on both sides of the Atlantic were generally more enthusiastic than they had been about any of Drinkwater's other plays.

In an early essay, "The Nature of Drama," Drinkwater says that a man chooses to write drama "quite definitely with the response of a theatre audience in his mind, and it is for this, and not because of any inherent virtue which he finds in this form and in no other, that his choice is made." The public reaction to at least three of his plays—*X = O*, *Abraham Lincoln*, and *Bird in Hand*—suggests that he chose well.

Other major works

POETRY: *Poems*, 1903; *Poems 1908-1914*, 1917; *Poems 1908-1919*, 1919; *Selected Poems*, 1922; *New Poems*, 1925; *The Collected Poems of John Drinkwater*, 1923, 1937 (3 volumes).

NONFICTION: *William Morris: A Critical Study*, 1912; *Swinburne: An Estimate*, 1913; *Lincoln, The World Emancipator*, 1920; *Cotswold Characters*, 1921; *The Pilgrim of Eternity: Byron—A Conflict*, 1925; *Mr. Charles, King of England*, 1926; *Cromwell: A Character Study*, 1927; *Charles James Fox*, 1928; *Pepys: His Life and Character*, 1930; *Inheritance*, 1931; *Discovery*, 1932; *Shakespeare*, 1933.

Bibliography

Abercrombie, Lascelles. "The Drama of John Drinkwater," in *Four Decades of Poetry 1890-1930, I,* 1977.

Cunliffe, John W. *Modern English Playwrights: A Short History of the English Drama from 1825,* 1927.

Gowda, H. H. Anniah. *The Revival of English Poetic Drama,* 1972.

Pearce, Michael. *John Drinkwater: A Comprehensive Bibliography of His Works,* 1977.

Sutton, Graham. *Some Contemporary Dramatists,* 1924.

Thouless, Priscilla. *Modern Poetic Drama,* 1934.

Gerald H. Strauss

514

JOHN DRYDEN

Born: Aldwinckle, England; August 9, 1631
Died: London, England; May 1, 1700

Principal drama

The Wild Gallant, pr. 1663, pb. 1669; *The Indian Queen*, pr. 1664, pb. 1665 (with Sir Robert Howard); *The Rival Ladies*, pr., pb. 1664; *The Indian Emperor: Or, The Conquest of Mexico by the Spaniards*, pr. 1665, pb. 1667; *Secret Love: Or, The Maiden Queen*, pr. 1667, pb. 1668; *Sir Martin Mar-All: Or, The Feign'd Innocence*, pr. 1667, pb. 1668 (adaptation of Molière's *L'Étourdi*; with William Cavendish, Duke of Newcastle); *The Tempest: Or, The Enchanted Island*, pr. 1667, pb. 1670 (adaptation of William Shakespeare's play; with Sir William Davenant); *An Evening's Love: Or, The Mock Astrologer*, pr. 1668, pb. 1671 (adaptation of Thomas Corneille's *Le Feint Astrologue*); *Tyrannic Love: Or, The Royal Martyr*, pr. 1669, pb. 1670; *The Conquest of Granada by the Spaniards, Part I*, pr. 1670, pb. 1672; *The Conquest of Granada by the Spaniards, Part II*, pr. 1671, pb. 1672; *Marriage à la Mode*, pr. 1672, pb. 1673; *The Assignation: Or, Love in a Nunnery*, pr. 1672, pb. 1673; *Amboyna: Or, The Cruelties of the Dutch to the English Merchants*, pr., pb. 1673; *Aureng-Zebe*, pr. 1675, pb. 1676; *The State of Innocence, and Fall of Man*, pb. 1677 (libretto; dramatic version of John Milton's *Paradise Lost*); *All for Love: Or, The World Well Lost*, pr. 1677, pb. 1678; *The Kind Keeper: Or, Mr. Limberham*, pr. 1678, pb. 1680; *Oedipus*, pr. 1678, pb. 1679 (with Nathaniel Lee); *Troilus and Cressida: Or, Truth Found Too Late*, pr., pb. 1679; *The Spanish Friar: Or, The Double Discovery*, pr. 1680, pb. 1681; *The Duke of Guise*, pr. 1682, pb. 1683 (with Lee); *Albion and Albanius*, pr., pb. 1685 (libretto; music by Louis Grabu); *Don Sebastion, King of Portugal*, pr. 1689, pb. 1690; *Amphitryon: Or, The Two Socia's*, pr., pb. 1690; *King Arthur: Or, The British Worthy*, pr., pb. 1691 (libretto; music by Henry Purcell); *Cleomenes, the Spartan Hero*, pr., pb. 1682; *Love Triumphant: Or, Nature Will Prevail*, pr., pb. 1694; *The Secular Masque*, pr., pb. 1700 (masque); *Dramatick Works*, 1717; *The Works of John Dryden*, 1808 (18 volumes).

Other literary forms

If one follows the practice of literary historians and assigns John Milton to an earlier age, then John Dryden stands as the greatest literary artist in England between 1660 and 1700, a period sometimes designated "the Age of Dryden." In addition to his achievements in drama, he excelled in poetry, translation, and literary criticism. He wrote some two hundred original English poems over a period of more than forty years, including the best poetic satires of his age, memorable odes, and a variety of verse epistles, elegies, religious poems, panegyrics, and lyrics. His prologues and epilogues, attached to his dramas and those of his contemporaries, stand as the highest achievements in English in that minor poetic genre.

For every verse of original poetry Dryden wrote, he translated two from another poet. Moreover, he translated two long volumes of prose from French originals—in 1684, Louis Maimbourg's *Histoire de la Ligue* (1684) and, in 1688, Dominique Bouhours' *La Vie de Saint François Xavier* (1683)—and he had a hand in the five-volume translation of Plutarch's *Parallel Lives* published by Jacob Tonson in 1683. The translations were usually well received, especially the editions of Juvenal and Persius (1693) and Vergil (1697).

Dryden's literary criticism consists largely of prefaces and dedications published throughout his career and attached to other works, his only critical work published alone being *An Essay of Dramatic Poesy* (1668). As a critic, Dryden appears at his best when he evaluates an earlier poet or dramatist (Homer, Vergil, Ovid, Geoffrey Chaucer, William Shakespeare, Ben Jonson, John Fletcher), when he seeks to define a genre, or when he breaks new critical ground, as, for example, in providing definitions of "wit" or a theory of translation.

Achievements

In a period of just over thirty years (1663-1694), John Dryden wrote or coauthored twenty-eight plays, an output which made him the most prolific dramatist of his day. His amplitude remains even more remarkable when one considers the amount of poetry, criticism, and translation he produced during the same period. This prolific production is equaled by the variety of the plays: heroic plays, political plays, operas, heroic tragedies, comedies, and tragicomedies. In his prefaces and other prose works, Dryden commented at some length upon the various types of plays, seeking to define and to clarify the dramatic forms in which he wrote.

Yet Dryden himself recognized that his dramas were not likely to wear well, and his literary reputation today rests largely upon his poetry and criticism. The operas *King Arthur* and *The State of Innocence* (which was not produced during his lifetime) survive primarily in their lyrics; like other operas of the time, they were somewhat primitive, judged by modern standards, with relatively little music—something more akin to the masque or to modern musical comedy than to grand opera. The heroic plays are too artificial to appeal to any but the most devoted scholars of the period, and Dryden's comedies and tragicomedies suffer in comparison with those of his contemporaries, Sir George Etherege, William Wycherley, and William Congreve, not to mention his predecessors in English drama. As an index to the taste of the Restoration, however, the plays remain valuable and instructive, reflecting the levels of achievement and prevalent values of dramatic art of the time. Further, a study of Dryden reveals much about both aesthetic and intellectual influences on the drama of his period and the development of the dramatic genres of his age.

Biography

John Dryden was the eldest of fourteen children in a landed family of modest means whose sympathies were Puritan on both sides. Little is known of his youth in Northamptonshire, for Dryden, seldom hesitant about expressing his opinions, was reticent about details of his personal life. At about age fifteen, he was enrolled in Westminster School, then under the headmastership of Dr. Richard Busby, a school notable for its production of poets and bishops. Having attained at Westminster a thorough grounding in Latin, he proceeded to Cambridge, taking the B.A. in 1654. After the death of his father brought him a modest inheritance in the form of rents from family land, Dryden left the university and settled in London. Though little is known of his early years there, he served briefly in Oliver Cromwell's government in a minor position and may have worked for the publisher Henry Herringman. He produced an elegy on the death of Cromwell, yet when Charles II ascended the throne, Dryden greeted the new ruler with a congratulatory poem, *Astraea Redux* (1660). After the Restoration, he turned his main interest to the drama, producing an insignificant comedy, *The Wild Gallant*, and collaborating with Sir Robert Howard on a heroic play, *The Indian Queen*. He married Lady Elizabeth Howard, Sir Robert's sister, a marriage which brought him a generous dowry and, eventually, three sons in whom he took pride.

Throughout his career, Dryden was no stranger to controversy, whether literary, political, or religious; in fact, he seemed all too eager to seize an occasion for polemics. In literature, he challenged Sir Robert Howard's views on the drama, Thomas Rymer's on criticism, the Earl of Rochester's and Thomas Shadwell's on questions of literary merit and taste. After receiving encouragement from Charles II, Dryden entered the political controversy over succession to the throne with *Absalom and Achitophel* (part 1, 1681; part 2, with Nahum Tate, 1682). Later, he explained his religious views by attacking Deists, Catholics, and Dissenters in *Religio Laici* (1682); then, he shifted his ground and defended Catholicism in *The Hind and the Panther* (1687).

For a variety of reasons, Dryden was the most often assailed among major poets in his time, a fact attributable in some measure to envy. In an age when almost everyone prized his own wit, Dryden attained eminence without obviously possessing more of that quality than many others. Yet his willingness to plunge into controversy won him a host of enemies, and his changes of opinions and beliefs—literary, religious, political—made him vulnerable to criticism. Examining Dryden's changes of allegiance and point of view one by one, a biographer or critic can provide a logical explanation for each. This task is perhaps most difficult in literary criticism, where Dryden defended a position with enthusiasm only to abandon it later for another, which he advocated with an equal enthusiasm. To his contemporaries, some of his changes were to be explained by self-interest, and, rightly or wrongly, the charge of timeserving became a potent weapon in the hands of his critics.

In 1668, Dryden was appointed poet laureate, a position he held for twenty years, and he also signed a lucrative contract with the Theatre Royal to produce three new plays each year. Though he was unable to produce this stipulated number over the decade of the contract, he nevertheless received his share of theater revenues. During his term as laureate, he received a two-hundred-pound annual stipend, an amount that was later increased to three hundred pounds when he became historiographer royal, but irregularly paid. He was active as a dramatist throughout the 1670's, though he gradually turned his interest to poetic satire, beginning with *MacFlecknoe* (1682).

With events surrounding the Popist Plot (1678) posing a threat to the government of Charles II, Dryden all but abandoned the theater, writing instead satires, translations, and then his religious poems. Initially, he carried the field for the king, but after the fall of James II and the loss of his political cause, he also lost the laureateship and its accompanying pension.

During the final period of his life, 1688-1700, Dryden made a brief return to the theater, producing an additional five dramas, but he devoted most of his considerable energy and talent to translations of poetry, achieving success with his patrons and public.

Analysis

Marriage à la Mode is usually considered John Dryden's best comedy. His others rely heavily upon farcical situations and double entendre and, at times, inept licentiousness that makes comedies such as *The Assignation* and *The Kind Keeper* seem unnecessarily coarse even by the standards of his time. *Marriage à la Mode* combines in its two distinct plot lines the conventions of the romantic tragicomedy and the Restoration comedy of manners, a genre not fully established when Dryden produced his play.

The tragicomic plot involves the theme of succession, perhaps Dryden's most frequent dramatic theme after love and honor. Polydamas, having usurped the throne of Sicily, discovers two young persons of gentle birth but unknown parentage who have been living among fisher folk under the care of Hermogenes, a former courtier. When Hermogenes tells the usurper that Leonidas is his son, born after his wife had fled from him, the king accepts this as correct, even though Leonidas is actually the son of the king he had deposed. When Polydamas insists that Leonidas marry the daughter of his friend, Leonidas refuses because of his love for Palmyra, the girl with whom he had been discovered. To frustrate this passion, Polydamas seeks to banish her, whereupon Hermogenes declares that Palmyra is the king's daughter and claims Leonidas as his own son, for he cannot risk revealing the truth about Leonidas, in reality the rightful successor. Polydamas than seeks to have Palmyra marry his favorite, Argaleon, and banishes Leonidas, later changing the sentence to death. Facing execution, Leonidas manages to proclaim his right to the throne, to bring his captors over to his side, and to oust Polydamas, whom he generously forgives as the father of his beloved Palmyra.

The tragicomic characteristics are all present—the unusual setting; the usurper; the long-lost noble youth; the faithful servant; the idealization of romantic love, struggling successfully against the odds and triumphing. To heighten the tone, Dryden uses blank verse rather than prose and, in the most serious passages, employs rhymed heroic couplets. The tragicomic plot, in the manner of John Fletcher, reveals a significant debt to Elizabethan and Jacobean tragicomedies.

Whereas in the main plot the attitude toward love is idealistic, the subplot represents a sharp contrast in the value placed upon both love and marriage. Dryden creates two witty couples—Rhodophil and Doralice, Palamede and Melantha—the first pair married and the second engaged by arrangement of their parents. Their attitudes toward marriage and love are as cynical and sophisticated as is standard in the comedy of manners. Palamede hopes before marriage to carry off an affair with his friend Rhodophil's wife, while Rhodophil hopes to make Melantha his mistress. They freely satirize Puritans and country folk, and the prevailing attitude of society toward marriage is indicated by Rhodophil when he speaks of his wife, "Yet I loved her a whole half year, double the natural term of any mistress; and I think, in my conscience, I could have held out another quarter, but then the world began to laugh at me, and a certain shame, of being out of fashion, seized me." Disguises, masked balls, and assignations keep the plot lively and suspenseful, though the couples' goals are never realized because all plans either are intercepted or go awry, and at the end, they part still friends. Throughout, the dialogue sparkles with repartee unequaled in any of Dryden's other plays. It includes Melantha's affected French expressions along with much double entendre and innuendo, yet it is never brutally licentious in tone, as is true of dialogue in comedies such as *The Kind Keeper*.

Though the two plots are loosely connected, Rhodophil does bring the newly found gentlefolk to the court, and both he and Palamede unite to support Leonidas in the final act. Further, the attitudes of parents who arrange marriages are condemned in both plot lines. For the most part, however, the plots occur in two separate worlds—the witty and sophisticated world of the comedy of manners and the idealistic and sentimental world of tragicomedy.

During the period from 1663 to 1680, Dryden wrote, entirely or in part, twenty-one plays. His initial success came with his heroic plays from *The Indian Queen* to *Aureng-Zebe*, by which time the genre had almost run its course. The heroic play was influenced by a variety of sources, including the English dramas of John Fletcher, the French tragedies of Pierre Corneille, and the French poetic romances of Madeleine de Scudéry and Gautier de Costes de La Calprenède. The most prominent feature which set the genre apart from the usual tragedy was the dialogue in heroic couplets, attributed to the playwrights' efforts to please Charles II, who, it was said, had come to enjoy the rhymed French drama he saw during his years in exile. Dryden defended the artificiality of rhymed dialogue on the grounds that the plays dealt with conflicts and characters above the commonplace; thus, the stylistic elevation provided by rhyme was appropriate. The characters, however, engage in lengthy rhymed speeches, usually with two characters confronting each other, and the result has seemed in a later time excessively artificial.

The plays frequently employ spectacle, enhanced by songs, dances, and elaborate costumes. The settings are usually exotic rather than English, thus heightening their romantic appeal. *The Indian Queen* and *The Indian Emperor*, for example, are set in Mexico, whereas both parts of Dryden's *The Conquest of Granada by the Spaniards* are set in Spain. Warfare, conquest, and striving dominate the plays.

The characters belong to a set of types that include as the protagonist the love-honor hero, who finds himself involved in intrigues and power-struggles which put those virtues to the test. Like the other characters, he does not change; the tests the characters encounter are intended to show the strength of their virtue or the depth of their depravity. The hero is surrounded by such Fletcherian types as the sentimental maiden, whom he loves; the evil woman, who shamelessly attempts to gain him for herself; the weak king, whom others are attempting to topple from the throne; the faithful friend; and an antagonist who is almost but not quite a Machiavellian villain motivated solely by ambition. The hero is sometimes fortunate and prevails over all of the obstacles he encounters; at other times, he dies without any success other than preserving his love and honor.

The romantic excesses of heroic plays were satirized by George Villiers, Duke of Buckingham, in his burlesque *The Rehearsal* (pr., pb. 1672), which has as its major character John Bayes, a brilliant satiric depiction of Dryden. Villiers parodies many of the absurd and inflated lines of Dryden and others who wrote in the form, yet *The Rehearsal* failed to drive the heroic drama from the stage. The genre remained viable for nearly two decades, until the late 1670's, when the playwrights began shifting their efforts to a less flamboyant form of tragedy.

Aureng-Zebe, the last of Dryden's heroic plays, was judged by him to be his best, though in the prologue he announced that he had grown weary of rhyme, an indication of his imminent shift to blank verse as the appropriate meter for serious drama. By comparison to Dryden's earlier heroic dramas, *Aureng-Zebe* makes less use of song and dance and includes less rant and bombast, yet it clearly preserves the major elements of the genre.

Set in India at the time of the Mogul Empire, it derives events and characters from history, though Dryden freely alters the sources. The aging emperor, a stereotypical weak king, finds his throne challenged by several of his sons, the loyal Aureng-Zebe being an exception. Aureng-Zebe is depicted by his friend Arimant, Governor of Agra, as "by no strong person swayed/ Except his love," a hero of unshakable loyalty who hopes that he will attain the hand of the captive queen Indamora for his support of the emperor.

While *Aureng-Zebe* is tame by earlier standards of the heroic play, echoes of the swashbuckling, superhuman hero remain. In armed conflict, the hero defeats two rebellious brothers, Darah being the first, "Darah from loyal Aureng-Zebe is fled,/ And forty thousand of his men lie dead." The threat represented by Morat, the ambitious villain of the play, is not so easily parried, for he has raised an immense force thus described by Abbas: "The neighb'ring plain with arms is coverd o'er;/ The vale an iron harvest seems to yield/ Of thick-sprung lances in a waving field." The hyperboles, typical of the genre, suggest the physical threat posed by Morat; his character also serves as a foil to that of Aureng-Zebe, for he does not properly control his passions. Primarily motivated by a desire for power, he also wishes to abandon his faithful wife, Melesinda, for Aureng-Zebe's beloved Indamora, who finds him repulsive. Further complications arise when the emperor falls passionately in love with Indamora, and the Empress Nourmahal, Aureng-Zebe's stepmother and the "evil woman" of the play, conceives a strong passion for her stepson. Confronted with news of his father's love for Indamora and his placing her under arrest, the hero accepts the challenge involving both his love and honor.

Aureng-Zebe finds himself threatened from many directions when he intercedes with the emperor and attempts to prevent the emperor's petulant imprisonment of Nourmahal. No sooner has the emperor seen Nourmahal taken away than he summons the rebellious Morat with the intent of making him his heir, all because of Aureng-Zebe's love for Indamora. Boldly entering unannounced, Aureng-Zebe attempts to end the alliance between the emperor and Morat by offering to disband his army if Morat will withdraw his forces from the city, leaving the emperor in control. Despite these peace-making efforts, the emperor orders Aureng-Zebe's arrest when he will not renounce his love for Indamora. When

Indamora pleads for Morat to spare the life of Aureng-Zebe, he demands her love in exchange, which she curtly refuses. The alliance between the emperor and Morat is broken when the emperor learns of Morat's passion for Indamora. After Aureng-Zebe has been released through the efforts of Indamora and Arimant, Indamora finds great difficulty in convincing the jealous hero that she has remained faithful and has not betrayed him with Morat. Meanwhile, having lost the favor of the emperor, Morat rebels against him.

The outcome is obscured when Arimant, in a disguise that results in his being mistaken for Aureng-Zebe, is killed and Morat has to break off a long seductive speech to Indamora to quell an uprising. In the final battle, Aureng-Zebe leads the emperor's forces to victory, and Morat, mortally wounded, manages to prevent his mother from murdering Indamora. Her violent passion frustrated, Nourmahal poisons herself, and the Emperor grants Aureng-Zebe both the state and Indamora.

In *Aureng-Zebe*, the characters who retain their honor reap the rewards of both love and honor, whereas those who do not control their passions and ambition encounter misfortune. The abruptness and violence of passions are appropriately accompanied by abrupt and violent actions in the plays. A major difference between good and evil characters becomes the measure of control over passions, not the violence of the passion itself. As D. W. Jefferson has pointed out, Dryden's characters, both the good and the bad, express themselves blatantly where sexual passions are concerned, a phenomenon not limited to the characters of the heroic plays.

Of *All for Love*, his tragedy based upon Shakespeare's earlier great work *Antony and Cleopatra*, Dryden himself commented that he had never written anything "for myself but *Antony and Cleopatra.*" The drama reflects Dryden's vision of tragedy, sometimes designated by critics as "heroic tragedy" to indicate certain similarities to the heroic play. The chief among Dryden's works in the type include *Oedipus, Troilus and Cressida, Don Sebastian, King of Portugal* and *Cleomenes, the Spartan Hero.* Unlike the heroic plays, these are written in blank verse and their sources are Shakespearean or classical. They demonstrate fewer of the epic dimensions of the heroic play, and the heroes are more nearly realistic characters. Although Dryden succeeds more fully in presenting human emotions in these dramas, in part because the medium of blank verse is more suited to emotional expression, he achieves the effects of pathos and sentiment rather than pity and fear.

In *All for Love*, Dryden follows the dramatic unities of time, place, and action, which he regarded as ornaments of tragedy, though not indispensable. The hero, Antony, is presented on the final day of his life, which happens to be his birthday. Facing imminent defeat at the hands of Octavius, he encounters temptations to abandon the great passion of his life, Cleopatra, in order to prolong the contest or to minimize the consequences of the loss. Restrictions inherent in the dramatic unities result in characters which are not nearly so complex as those of the source, Shakespeare's *Antony and Cleopatra*. Cleopatra neither wavers in her devotion to Antony nor reflects at length upon her role as queen, as she does in Shakespeare's tragedy. Dryden's Ventidius shares qualities drawn from Shakespeare's character of the same name but also from Shakespeare's Enobarbus, the devoted adviser who abandons Antony. Ventidius strives to deliver Antony from his passion for Cleopatra, while, at the same time, her servant Alexas is scheming with Cleopatra to keep Antony's devotion. Caught in the struggle between love and duty, Antony appears a weak hero. Ventidius first offers Antony, then under attack by Octavius, the support of twelve legions if he will abandon Cleopatra, pointing to this as a necessary condition since the legionnaires refuse to come to Egypt and insist that Antony join them to assume command. Seizing upon this chance for victory, Antony agrees, only to change his mind when he receives a parting gift, a bracelet, from Cleopatra, who unexpectedly arrives to put her gift on his arm.

Ventidius next arranges for Antony to make an honorable peace with Caesar, leaving him with limited power, if he will return to his wife Octavia. When Octavia appears with their two daughters, Antony is unable to withstand their pleas and agrees to return to her, dispatching Dolabella to deliver a farewell to Cleopatra. This episode reveals the flaws in Alexas' and Ventidius' calculations. Alexas reasons that Cleopatra may win Antony back by arousing his jealousy through Dolabella, whereas Ventidius assumes that jealousy will convince Antony that Cleopatra was worthless. Thus, both adversaries steer Antony in the same direction for different ends. The result is that Octavia becomes so distressed at Antony's obvious jealousy over their reports that she leaves him. In return for Antony's hostility and anger and after the loss of a battle at sea, Cleopatra sends word of her death, which Antony cannot bear. Following his self-inflicted mortal wound, he is taken to Cleopatra, whose death following his brings a sense of triumph.

While scenes such as that between Antony and Octavia involve a generous amount of sentimentality, Dryden achieves in *All for Love* an intensity that is lacking in most of his plays, one whose emotional effects are not dissipated through digressions or loosely related subplots. The play reveals a tightly unified plot line in which characters' motives and actions are influenced primarily by strong romantic love.

Dryden's tragedy *Don Sebastian, King of Portugal*, written after the Glorious Revolution, is his longest drama and, in the view of critics from Sir Walter Scott to Bruce King, his finest dramatic achievement. In the play's preface, Dryden acknowledges that the players cut more than twelve hundred lines from the acted version. Though the play's themes are universally appropriate for tragedy, it includes a closely related comic subplot, and it ends not with the death of the hero or heroine but with their retirement from the world of affairs. The play incorporates numerous qualities and dramatic techniques that Dryden employs elsewhere in his work and may be the most fruitful play to examine for clarifying his dramatic art.

The play is set in North Africa, where Don Sebastian, King of Portugal, and his allies have been defeated and captured after warring against the Moors. Sebastian's chief desire is to marry the woman he loves, Almeyda, Christian Queen of Barbary, also held captive. This he manages to do after the Emperor Muley-Moluch has given him a measure of freedom so that Sebastian can attempt to win Almeyda's hand for the emperor. Sebastian and Almeyda escape the emperor's retribution for their marriage, because he is slain in a rebellion, but they do not escape fate. In the final act, they learn from the old counselor Alvarez, who has just been freed from captivity, that they are half brother and sister, having had the same father. The incestuousness of their relationship, unknowing though it was, forces them to part, with each retiring to a separate religious house.

The Moors are portrayed throughout the play as riven by factions, the chief threat being the effort of the emperor's favorite, Benducar, to topple him from the throne, ostensibly in favor of the emperor's brother, Muley-Zeydan, but in reality for himself. In this attempt, he involves the populace, the religious leader Mufti Abdalla, and Dorax, a Christian who has turned against Sebastian and has joined the Moors. Dorax later joins Sebastian, after the fall of the emperor, to defeat the uprising and restore worthy leaders to their places. A comic subplot involves the efforts of the Christian captive Don Antonio to flee the household of the Mufti with his daughter Morayma and his treasure, in much the same way that Lorenzo and Jessica flee Shylock in Shakespeare's *The Merchant of Venice*.

The exotic setting, the theme of heroic love, the stock characters, and the broils and warfare represent familiar themes and situations of Dryden's dramas. Occasionally, one also finds in the dramas some exceptional improbabilities. In this play, for example, Dorax, having lost the confidence of the Moors, is poisoned by two of them, Benducar and the Mufti, but survives because each poison neutralizes the effect of the other. Yet *Don Sebastian, King of Portugal* illustrates other characteristics of Dryden's dramatic art that are less obvious but more influential and significant: the theme of incest, actual or suppressed; anticlericalism; political satire and allusions; and scenes of reconciliation. In *Don Sebastian, King of Portugal*, unwitting incest occurs between Sebastian and Almeyda after they are married, and such is their consternation when they discover they have violated the taboo that Sebastian believes suicide the only escape until Dorax dissuades him. The situation resembles somewhat that of Oedipus in the version of the old Greek drama that Dryden and Nathaniel Lee produced for the Restoration stage. It is as though love in Dryden is so exalted, wrought up to such a pitch, that introduction of the taboo acts to heighten it and make the plight of the lovers more poignant. In *Don Sebastian, King of Portugal*, the theme is counterbalanced by the story of Violante, who denied affection to the husband Sebastian had chosen for her and awaited for many years her beloved Dorax.

It is unclear why anticlericalism becomes such a prominent theme in the works of Dryden, though it seems plausible that his profound distrust and dislike of Puritan influence on political affairs may in part explain it. The Mufti represents the typical clergyman in Dryden, usually the object of satire in both the poems and the plays. He is ambitious, avaricious, sensual, officious, and usually hypocritical. The Mufti appears ridiculous in both political and personal affairs, becoming the object of humor and scorn. Dryden does not, of course, ridicule clergymen of the Church of England, but wherever he introduces a pagan, a Moslem, or a Catholic religious figure, the character becomes the object of satire.

In its political theme, the play concerns betrayal and misappropriation of power. The emperor, having usurped the throne, discovers that he can trust no one, least of all Benducar, his closest adviser. Benducar incites the mob to rebellion, and they manage to defeat and kill the emperor, barbarously showing his head on a pike as that of a tyrant. Like a true Machiavellian, Benducar muses on the thesis that might makes right: "And I can sin but once to seize the throne; all after-acts are sanctified by power." Such passages as this in Dryden's plays, poems, and translations following the Glorious Revolution usually serve as oblique satire of the new monarchs, and his distrust of the judgment of the common people where political affairs are concerned is a recurring theme throughout his work.

A final characteristic of Dryden's theater is evident in act 4, scene 3, often considered the most successful scene of the play. It depicts the intense quarrel of the two friends, Dorax and Sebastian, and their reconciliation. Dryden may have based this scene on the quarrel of Brutus and Cassius in Shakespeare's *Julius Caesar*; similar scenes occur in other works of Dryden, notably in *Troilus and Cressida* and *Cleomenes, the Spartan Hero*. Although Dorax has fought on the side of the Moors, he defends and spares the life of Sebastian—so that he can kill him to exact his own revenge. He holds a powerful grudge because Sebastian did not adequately reward him for his prior service and awarded the hand of Violante to another courtier, Henriquez. Facing an imminent fight to the death with Dorax, Sebastian explains that Henriquez had sought the hand of Violante first, that Henriquez had died defending Sebastian, and that Violante now waits for Dorax. Accepting Sebastian's explanation, Dorax submits, is restored to favor, and promises that he will serve Sebastian as faithfully as Henriquez had done. In the final act, Dorax helps Sebastian bear manfully his sense of guilt and loss. Scenes of intense confrontation permit the dramatist to display a range of emotions in a brief space, as well as a heightening and diminution of passions. Dryden's ability to capture such a range of tones compensates to a degree for his lack of a greater gift as a dramatist—the ability to show growth and development of his characters.

Other major works

POETRY: *Heroic Stanzas*, 1659; *Astraea Redux*, 1660; "To My Lord Chancellor," 1662; *Prologues and Epilogues*, 1664-1700; *Annus Mirabilis*, 1667; *Absalom and Achitophel*, 1681; *Absalom and Achitophel, Part II*, 1682 (with Nahum Tate); *MacFlecknoe*, 1682; *Religio Laici*, 1682; *Threnodia Augustalis*, 1685; *The Hind and the Panther*, 1687; "A Song for St. Cecilia's Day," 1687; *Britannia Rediviva*, 1688; *Eleonora*, 1692; "To My Dear Friend Mr. Congreve," 1693; *Alexander's Feast: Or, The Power of Music*, 1697; "To My Honour'd Kinsman, John Driden," 1700.

NONFICTION: *An Essay of Dramatic Poesy*, 1668; "A Defense of *An Essay of Dramatic Poesy*," 1668; "Preface to *An Evening's Love*," 1671; "Of Heroic Plays: An Essay," 1672; "Preface to *All for Love*," 1678; "The Grounds of Criticism in Tragedy," 1679; "Preface to *Sylvae*," 1685; "Dedication of *Examen Poeticum*," 1693; "A Discourse Concerning the Original and Progress of Satire," 1693; "Dedication of the *Aeneis*," 1697; "Preface to *The Fables*," 1700.

TRANSLATIONS: *Ovid's Epistles*, 1680; *The History of the League*, 1684 (of Louis Mainbourg's *Histoire de la Ligue*); *The Life of St. Francis Xavier*, 1688 (of Dominique Bouhours' *La Vie de Saint François Xavier*); *The Satires of Juvenal and Persius*, 1693; *The Works of Virgil*, 1697.

Bibliography
Barbeau, Anne T. *The Intellectual Design of John Dryden's Heroic Plays*, 1970.
Brown, John Russell, and Bernard Harris, eds. *Restoration Theatre*, 1965.
King, Bruce. *Dryden's Major Plays*, 1966.
Kirsch, Arthur. *Dryden's Heroic Drama*, 1965.
Larson, Richard Leslie. *Studies in Dryden's Dramatic Techniques*, 1975.
Moore, Frank Harper. *The Nobler Pleasure: Dryden's Comedy in Theory and Practice*, 1963.
Ward, Charles E. *The Life of John Dryden*, 1961.
Wilson, John Harold. *A Preface to Restoration Drama*, 1965.
Zebouni, Selma A. *Dryden: A Study of Heroic Characterization*, 1965.

Stanley Archer

WILLIAM DUNLAP

Born: Perth Amboy, New Jersey; February 19, 1766
Died: New York, New York; September 28, 1839

Principal drama

The Father: Or, American Shandyism, pr., pb. 1789 (revised as *The Father of an Only Child*, pb. 1806); *Fountainville Abbey*, pr. 1795, pb. 1806; *The Archers: Or, Mountaineers of Switzerland*, pr., pb. 1796 (opera; music by Benjamin Carr); *The Man of Fortitude: Or, The Knight's Adventure*, pr. 1797, pb. 1807; *Tell Truth and Shame the Devil*, pr., pb. 1797 (adaptation of A. L. B. Robineau's play *Jérome Pointu*); *André*, pr., pb. 1798; *False Shame: Or, The American Orphan in Germany*, pr. 1798, pb. 1940 (adaptation of August von Kotzebue's play *Falsche Schaam*); *The Stranger*, pr., pb. 1798 (adaptation of Kotzebue's play *Menschenhass und Reue*); *Don Carlos*, pr. 1799 (adaptation of Friedrich Schiller's play *Don Carlos, Infant von Spanien*); *Lovers' Vows*, pr. 1799, pb. 1814 (adaptation of Kotzebue's play *Das Kind der Liebe*); *The Italian Father*, pr. 1799, pb. 1800; *The Virgin of the Sun*, pr., pb. 1800 (adaptation of Kotzebue's play *Die Sonnen Jungfrau*); *Pizzaro in Peru: Or, The Death of Rolla*, pr., pb. 1800 (adaptation of Kotzebue's play *Die Spanier in Peru: Oder, Rollas Tod*); *Fraternal Discord*, pr. 1800, pb. 1809 (adaptation of Kotzebue's play *Versöhnung: Oder, Bruders Twist*); *Abaellino, the Great Bandit*, pr. 1801, pb. 1802 (adaptation of J. H. D. Zschokke's play *Abällino der Grosse Bandit*); *The Glory of Columbia—Her Yeomanry!*, pr. 1803, pb. 1817 (adaptation of *André*); *Ribbemont: Or, The Feudal Baron*, pb. 1803 (originally as *The Mysterious Monk*, pr. 1796); *The Wife of Two Husbands*, pr., pb. 1804 (adaptation of Guilbert de Pixérécourt's play *La Femme à deux maris*); *Leicester*, pb. 1806 (originally as *The Fatal Deception: Or, The Progress of Guilt*, pr. 1794); *The Dramatic Works of William Dunlap*, pb. 1806, 1816 (3 volumes); *Thirty Years: Or, The Life of a Gamester*, pr. 1828, pb. 1940 (adaptation of Prosper Goubaux and Victor Ducange's play *Trente Ans*); *A Trip to Niagara: Or, Travellers in America*, pr. 1828, pb. 1830.

Other literary forms

Many of William Dunlap's nondramatic works have earned for him solid status among students of literature and visual art. His biography of his contemporary Charles Brockden Brown, America's first major Gothic novelist, remains a standard reference tool. Dunlap's other biographical works—a shorter piece on Brown, sketches of Gilbert Stuart and Thomas Abthorpe Cooper, and a book on George Frederick Cooke—are valuable portraits by one who was on the scene for many of the events presented. Because of his career as a painter, Dunlap's *A History of the Rise and Progress of the*

Arts of Design in the United States (1834) also remains a work worth consulting for this aspect of America's early cultural history.

Still more important is *A History of American Theatre* (1832). Dunlap's account of the American theater from the 1790's through the first third of the nineteenth century is at times blurred by faulty memory. Nevertheless, before the work of George O. Seilhamer, George C. D. Odell, Arthur Hornblow, and Arthur Hobson Quinn, Dunlap offered a rich history of American drama. His firsthand account also furnishes an autobiography of its author, and altogether, it remains a classic in the annals of the American stage.

Dunlap also wrote verse, and several of his short stories, published in periodicals during the final decade of his life, merit critical attention. Many of his periodical pieces were unsigned, making definite attribution difficult. Dunlap intended to bring out a collected edition of his plays, in ten volumes. Only three volumes of *The Dramatic Works of William Dunlap* appeared, however, the first in 1806, the following two in 1816.

Achievements

Customarily designated the "Father of American Drama," Dunlap lived a long life through a period of extraordinary historical change in American culture. He was the first American playwright who turned to writing plays and managing theaters for a livelihood. His output of original plays and adaptations or translations from foreign dramas adds up to more than fifty titles. He gained considerable fame, as well as the love of many who were connected with early American theater, during his management of playhouses in Philadelphia and New York. Dunlap also deserves praise for his interest in and knowledge of German language and literature, as a result of which he was able to bring plays by August von Kotzebue, Friedrich Schiller, and J. H. D. Zschokke to the American stage at the turn of the nineteenth century. Such fare continued to be popular for many years. Dunlap also adapted from French theater, particularly from the then fairly new melodrama. His own pleasure in melodramatic and sensational scenes informs many of his original productions; he adapted many sentimental-sensational plays for his theaters because he well comprehended the desires of his audiences. His striving in his writing and in his theaters for high standards of morality, however, countered common tendencies to cater mainly to less admirable impulses of audiences eager for thrills and sexually suggestive titillation. At times, too, Dunlap's intense patriotism, centered on his admiration for George Washington, saved his own plays from running overmuch into sleazy melodramatics. On the other hand, that overt patriotism emphatically dates these plays and limits their appeal today, except as valuable literary history.

Dunlap as dramatist furnishes a curiosity in the accounts of anthologists and scholars of our national literature, in that most collections of eighteenth and early nineteenth century American plays have featured only *André*. Richard Moody, however, in his anthology *Dramas from the American Theatre, 1762-1909* (1966), provides other specimens from Dunlap's canon, *The Glory of Columbia—Her Yeomanry!* and *A Trip to Niagara*. The first is a reworking of *André*; the second demonstrates Dunlap's experimental combination of dramatic and visual-arts techniques. Dunlap's interests as playwright and painter make such a blending understandable. Possibly more than any other playwright of his age, Dunlap has come down through chronicles of American drama, such as those of Arthur Hobson Quinn, Montrose J. Moses, and Oral Sumner Coad, as the author of a single play, although Quinn's account in his history of early American drama does reveal other facets of Dunlap's work.

Dunlap's decided inclination toward the Gothic, obvious in *Leicester*, *Fountainville Abbey*, and other plays and clearly coursing through works in which other concerns are primary, has been sadly neglected, although this interest led to some of Dunlap's outstanding achievements. The early historians of American literature tended to follow too closely in the footsteps of Ralph Waldo Emerson, championing a distinctly national literary art. As a result, they generally regarded Gothicism as a product of European decadence, a genre not conducive to the production of a genuinely indigenous American literature. Dunlap himself recognized the excesses to which literary Gothicism was prone, as is evident in his short stories: There, as often as not, such exaggerations were subjected to hoax treatment. In the manner of Washington Irving and Edgar Allan Poe, Dunlap deftly mingled horror and humor.

Dunlap's partiality toward the Gothic has not been the only aspect of his work to be noted unfavorably by critics and historians. Dunlap's twin interests, the theater and painting, have often been used against him by those who believe that he achieved slightly less than greatness in either, simply because he was engaged in two careers. Partly as a result of such prejudices, Dunlap's work as a playwright has been undervalued. At a time when bombast clouded much of American literature, Dunlap experimented with vernacular speech on the stage. He managed to effect compelling characters by such means. His practical experience of theater management gave him a command of his medium that many of his contemporaries did not enjoy, as, for example, the career of James Nelson Barker reveals. All of his limitations notwithstanding, William Dunlap merits greater attention than he has received from students of American drama.

Biography

William Dunlap, the only child of Samuel and Margaret Sargeant Dunlap, spent his early years in Perth Amboy, New Jersey, where he was born. The wealth of his father, a merchant specializing in the china and looking-glass trade, enabled the boy to receive a fine education. He was particularly fortunate in studying classical literature with the elderly Thomas Bartow, whose store of learning in the classics enriched the mind of his young friend. In the spring of 1777, Samuel Dunlap, whose sympathies were Loyalist, moved his family to New York City, where William was first introduced to stage drama. This interest was to continue throughout his life, and although reverses in fortune later dogged Dunlap, he never lost his enthusiasm for any aspect of the stage. In 1783, after the close of the Revolutionary War, the Dunlaps returned to Perth Amboy. Shortly thereafter, during the convening of Congress at Princeton, Dunlap first saw George Washington, and during the winter of 1783-1784, the young man painted a portrait of his hero.

From 1784 to August, 1787, Dunlap spent time in London, studying painting with Benjamin West and increasing his acquaintance with playgoing and with theater personages. Richard Brinsley Sheridan's plays were among his favorites. Returning to the United States, Dunlap tried to establish himself as a portrait painter, but the theater soon came to be uppermost in his mind and work. The success of Royall Tyler's *The Contrast* (pr. 1787) inspired Dunlap to create his own first play, a comedy entitled "The Modest Soldier: Or, Love in New York," which was accepted by the American Company but never performed; the young playwright had failed to fashion parts suitable for the manager and his wife. Correcting that circumstance in his next work, *The Father*, written in 1788 and performed in 1789, Dunlap launched himself on a career as a dramatist that lasted for the next thirty years and made him famous. His experiments with numerous dramatic forms, his introduction of Kotzebue and other European playwrights to the American stage, and his career as a manager in Philadelphia and New York, as well as his ventures into painting (most notably portraits) and into other forms of writing, filled his life.

Dogged by financial misfortunes after he lost his fortune as a theater manager, Dunlap maintained a good temper, as well as the respect and love of a wide circle of friends. His marriage, in 1789, to Nabby Woolsey, of an old New York family, brought him into contact with many well-known figures of his day, including Timothy Dwight, his wife's brother-in-law, who was to become President of Yale University. Always a social being, Dunlap also maintained connections with several literary clubs. The Friendly Club numbered among its members, in addition to Dunlap, many who shaped the cultural history of the United States during its early national period. Dunlap died in New York on September 28, 1839, after suffering a stroke.

Analysis

The Father: Or, American Shandyism was William Dunlap's first play to be performed; it was also the second comedy by an American playwright to enjoy public notice. As such, it deserves examination as a follow-up to Tyler's *The Contrast*. *The Father* still can entertain readers; its comic misunderstandings and mishaps, its portraiture of the typical Yankee character, and its lively dialogue retain their power to amuse.

The marriage of the Rackets has entered the doldrums; Mr. Racket believes that solace will come in the arms of country-bred Susannah, a pert household maid, while Mrs. Racket hopes to intensify her husband's love by inciting him to jealousy of their friend, Ranter. Ranter, however, has designs on her sister, Caroline. At an inopportune moment, Colonel Duncan, guardian to the sisters, enters and discovers Mrs. Racket fainting into Ranter's arms—and suspects the worst. The colonel and his servant, Cartridge, function, as Cartridge observes, like Laurence Sterne's Mr. Toby Shandy and Corporal Trim from the novel *The Life and Opinions of Tristram Shandy, Gent.*, (1759-1767), a tale abounding in comic high jinks such as Dunlap tries to approximate with American characters. Ultimately, a solid reunion of the Rackets is effected by means of the exposure of Ranter's rascalities, the revelation that Caroline's lover, the long-lost son of Colonel Duncan, is alive, and the proper disposition of Susannah to Dr. Quiescent, a comic figure who has provided relief to tempestuous or grave incidents.

Dunlap deftly revised this play into *The Father of an Only Child*, which was possibly never performed, although it certainly reads well and could be a lively performance piece. A more distinctly American tinge is emphasized by means of comic reference to the *American Monthly Magazine*, in the vernacular speech of some of the characters, principally the maid Susannah, and in diminishing the Latinate names (Dr. Quiescent becomes Dr. Tattle). The Rackets are still the bibulous Irishman who has an eye for the ladies, and the long-suffering, determined wife who wrongheadedly tries to use jealousy to regain her husband's affections. The Colonel, renamed Campbell (his aide is renamed Platoon), with his concern for the only son he left to others long ago, gives the new title to the play. The background (the recent adoption of the United States Constitution) provides plausibility for the drunken revelry at the opening of the play. The menial, Jacob, adds to the cast a comic "Dutch" character, soon to become a stereotype in American plays. The outcome of this play is similar to that of *The Father*, except that Susannah is destined for Platoon.

Susannah's speeches in particular are noteworthy for their colloquial flavor, as when she repulses Racket's advances: "I'm a poor Yankee girl, and you are a rich town gentleman, and I'm sartin sich are no more fit to go together than a *pumpkin* and a pine-apple. Now mister Platoon don't go for higher than a good ripe ear of Indian corn, and a pumpkin needn't be ashamed of coming upon the same table any day." She remarks at this same juncture that "a body ought to keep company with a body's likes. Some folk's place is the keeping-room, and some folk's place is the stirring-room." Along with Platoon's praise for Colonel Campbell freeing his slaves (Dunlap's own action upon his father's death), such speeches serve to add homey, American touches to *The Father of an Only Child*. The exposure of the villainous servant's machinations against his master—the long-lost lover of Mrs. Racket's sister—in both versions suggests that European villainy is more vicious than the rather tame misdoings of Americans (the Rackets are new Americans). Ranter-Marsh-Rushport has his disguise stripped from him, and the revelation that he is the ne'er-do-well son whose misdeeds killed his clergyman father and whose ring is that of Caroline's betrothed recalls the confusions of identity, duplicitous and otherwise, characteristic of the Gothic romance so much in vogue at that time.

Similar comedies wherein misapprehension of motives furnishes the dramatic conflict are *False Shame*, adapted from Kotzebue, *Thirty Years*, adapted from Goubaux and Ducange, and Dunlap's original *A Trip to Niagara*. In this last play, Dunlap put together suitable dramatic action to enhance a diorama or revolving set of scenery that moves the audience from New York Harbor to Catskill Landing, during which action the merits of the United States, as Dunlap's audience knew it, were debated—to the final yielding to its excellences by the British antagonist. Too easily dismissed by critics, *A Trip to Niagara* is not poor dramatic art. The dialogue is spirited, the situation—of Amelia Wentworth's lover having to win her brother to things American in order to marry her—is good comic material, and the portraiture of comic stage types (French, Irish, Yankee) is compelling. The dialects, especially the American colloquial (although John Bull, Amelia's lover, merely impersonates a familiar Yankee figure), are well handled. Dunlap also presented the first serious portraiture of a black character of the American stage in Job Jerryson, who is a far cry from the amusing black minstrel who became a popular stage type during the nineteenth century. Despite Dunlap's apparent writing of this play upon commission, he managed to create a comedy of no mean order.

Dunlap's tragic muse also inspired him to write several plays of high quality; these tragedies often derive from Gothic tradition. *Leicester*, *Fountainville Abbey*, *Ribbemont* (originally staged as *The Mysterious Monk* in 1796), and *The Man of Fortitude* abound in eerie scenery; foreboding characters and settings in equally mysterious situations; intense, emotion-filled scenes; and death—with accompanying moral loftiness triumphing. Derivative as it is from William Shakespeare's *Macbeth*—itself an inspiration for Gothic fiction—*Leicester* conveys splendidly the tensions of characters motivated by ambition, thwarted or illicit passion, and murderous impulses. The shifts in scenes, physical and psychological, through numerous shadows and glooms or fears and hysteria artistically support the strained verbal interchanges among the *dramatis personae*.

Fountainville Abbey, even more literary than historical in inspiration, was founded on Ann Radcliffe's famous Gothic novel, *The Romance of the Forest* (1791), and a play that was based on it, by the British dramatist James Boaden, *Fountainville Forest* (pr. 1794). Dunlap's play, first performed in 1795, is another of his works that has been neglected in favor of historical-patriotic creation, although Elihu Hubbard Smith, thoroughly knowledgeable in cultural currents at the time, pronounced it the best tragedy he had seen in twenty years, adding that if Dunlap fulfilled his promise, he might well become the most respected dramatist of his time.

In Dunlap's hands, the British sources are transmuted into exceptional verse drama. Fleeing creditors, La Motte, his wife, and his servant, old Peter, along with Adeline, a girl mysteriously brought along by La Motte, find shelter in abandoned Fountainville Abbey. The darkness and obscurity of that locale blend well with a seeming ghost—who in the end turns out to be old Peter harmlessly going to and fro—to produce a rational supernaturalism, after the manner of Radcliffe and akin to what Dunlap's contemporary, the novelist Charles Brockden Brown, would soon purvey in his fiction. (Dunlap, however, should be credited with being the first American Gothicist.) The wicked Marquis de Montalt, whom La Motte had attempted to rob, soon appears on the scene, lusts after Adeline, and then tries to browbeat La Motte into murdering the girl when he discovers that she is his niece, daughter of the brother and rightful marquis, whom he had murdered. In the end, justice and virtue triumph, but that happy conclusion occurs only after moments of great trauma. Adeline is restored to her rightful status, and with her wealth she will bring good fortune to La Motte as well. The Marquis unsuccessfully tries to commit suicide—and thus departs from his origins in Radcliffe and Boaden, wherein he does kill himself. La Motte, a man dogged by guilt, finally, and symbolically, is brought from darkness, in setting and spirit, to light and salvation. The backdrops are functional in enhancing the psychic upsets (more significant than physical action) in *Fountainville Abbey*. Dunlap's poetic heights in this play are not matched in *Ribbemont*. Reminiscent of the *Romeo and Juliet* situation of poisoning, this play of apparently illicit love and murder is marred by too many overstrained speeches and too little action.

The Man of Fortitude, *The Stranger*, *The Italian Father*, *Don Carlos*, and *Abaellino, the Great Bandit*—adaptations from older English or from German plays—contain fine scenes. They are interesting in that they exemplify types of stage fare, such as the Gothic, the robber play, or the sentimental, much sought in the period of Dunlap's career. Overall, however, these works do not measure up to the high standards achieved in dramas such as *Leicester* or *Fountainville Abbey*.

André, Dunlap's best-known drama, though unsuccessful in its 1798 performance, reaches heights of psychological tension that are matched only in the Gothic plays written shortly before, in the 1790's. It has also appealed to those whose tastes in early American drama turn decidedly toward the patriotic. The plot is simple: Major John André, en route to Benedict Arnold, is captured and sentenced to hang as a spy against the American cause during the Revolution. He ultimately goes off to die after successive emotionally charged attempts to save him fail. The dramatic interest centers on delineating the psychological workings of those who argue for André's life. Even George Washington finds admirable traits in André's personality, although he realizes that to pardon him would be to encourage treason. The action of young Bland, André's great friend, in throwing down his cockade before Washington, was hissed by the American audience on the opening-night performance, but his subsequent repentance of his rashness toned down the suggestion of treason in his anger. Dunlap did not observe strict historical accuracy in creating his play—only one, but the best, of several on the popular André theme. Documents reveal that the love affair between André and Honora, who in Dunlap's play appears to plead for him, was romanticized by the playwright. He also invented the Blands, a mother and son who, in their pleadings, doubtless appealed to an American audience's love of sentimentality.

The André theme is reworked in *The Glory of Columbia—Her Yeomanry!*, nine of the fifteen scenes of which were taken from *André*, but to no great advantage. As the title change suggests, the center of interest shifts from André, who in both plays recalls the villain-hero of many tragedies, to the common people of America. Dunlap's handling of colloquial idiom is the single positive feature in this otherwise too fervently patriotic play, so blatantly calculated to wring the nationalistic hearts of American playgoers. Nevertheless, *The Glory of Columbia—Her Yeomanry!* was for some time revived each year to celebrate the Fourth of July.

Other major works

NONFICTION: *Memoirs of the Life of George Frederick Cooke*, 1813 (2 volumes), 1815 (revised as *The Life of Cooke*); *The Life of Charles Brockden Brown*, 1815 (2 volumes); *A History of American Theatre*, 1832; *A History of the Rise and Progress of the Arts of Design in the United States*, 1834 (2 volumes); *Thirty Years Ago: Or, The Memoirs of a Water Drinker*, 1836 (as *Memoirs of a Water Drinker*, 1837); *A History of New York for Schools*, 1837 (2 volumes); *Diary of William Dunlap*, 1931, 1969 (Dorothy C. Barck, editor).

Bibliography
Canary, Robert H. *William Dunlap*, 1970.
Coad, Oral Sumner. *William Dunlap: A Study of His Life and Works and*

of His Place in Contemporary Culture, 1917, 1962.

Halline, Allan Gates, ed. *American Plays*, 1935, 1976.

Hodge, Francis. *Yankee Theatre: The Image of America on the Stage, 1825-1850*, 1964.

——————, ed. *American Drama to 1900*, 1980.

Meserve, Walter J. *An Emerging Entertainment: The Drama of the American People to 1828*, 1977.

Moody, Richard. *America Takes the Stage: Romanticism in American Drama and Theatre, 1750-1900*, 1955, 1977.

——————, ed. *Dramas from the American Theatre, 1762-1909*, 1966.

Moramarco, Fred. "The Early Drama Criticism of William Dunlap," in *American Literature*. XL (March, 1968), pp. 9-14.

Moses, Montrose J., ed. *Representative Plays by American Dramatists, Volume I: 1765 to 1819*, 1918, 1964.

Odell, George C. D. *Annals of the New York Stage*, 1927-1949.

Quinn, Arthur Hobson. *A History of the American Drama from the Beginning to the Civil War*, 1923, 1943.

——————, ed. *Representative American Plays from 1767 to the Present Day*, 1953, 1966 (7th edition).

Seilhamer, George O. *A History of the American Theatre During the Revolution and After*, 1889, 1968.

Vaughn, Jack. *Early American Dramatists: From the Beginnings to 1900*, 1981.

Wilkens, Frederick H. *Early Influences of German Literature in America*, 1899.

"William Dunlap," in *The New York Mirror*. February 23, 1833, pp. 265-266.

Benjamin Fisher

LORD DUNSANY
Edward John Moreton Drax Plunkett

Born: London, England; July 24, 1878
Died: Dublin, Ireland; October 25, 1957

Principal drama

The Glittering Gate, pr. 1909, pb. 1914; *King Argimenes and the Unknown Warrior*, pr. 1911, pb. 1914; *The Gods of the Mountain*, pr. 1911, pb. 1914; *The Golden Doom*, pr. 1912, pb. 1914; *The Lost Silk Hat*, pr. 1913, pb. 1914; *Five Plays*, pb. 1914; *The Tents of the Arabs*, pr. 1914, pb. 1917; *A Night at an Inn*, pr., pb. 1916 (one act); *The Queen's Enemies*, pr. 1916, pb. 1917; *The Laughter of the Gods*, pb. 1917, pr. 1919; *Plays of Gods and Men*, pb. 1917; *If*, pr., pb. 1921; *Cheezo*, pr. 1921, pb. 1922; *Plays of Near and Far*, pb. 1922; *Lord Adrian*, pr. 1923, pb. 1933; *Alexander*, pb. 1925, pr. 1938; *Mr. Faithful*, pr. 1927, pb. 1935; *The Old Folk of the Centuries*, pb. 1930; *Plays for Earth and Air*, pb. 1937.

Other literary forms

Lord Dunsany did not limit himself to a particular literary format; his prolific output comprised novels, short stories, poems, translations, extensive periodical publication, and a wide range of literary and social criticism presented as lectures. Although his drama is historically significant, he is best remembered for his short tales and stories, which are still available in various reprints and anthologies. In these works, his fertile imagination best combined with a natural style to produce an appropriate single effect. Dunsany made little attempt to develop character or to probe the nuances of an individual mind. Instead, he created self-contained mythological worlds which depend upon plot and highly stylized language to move the action to its inevitable conclusion. Dunsany's novels suffer from an excess of invention without a firm grounding in reality or psychological depth; as a remarkable curiosity of verbal ingenuity and fantasy, however, *The King of Elfland's Daughter* (1924) remains a classic. The critical reception of his poetry has been kind, but his work in this genre has never been considered anything but minor. Distinguished by an enviable range of interest in all aspects of art, Dunsany believed that the task of the artist is to create or reveal beauty; for him, the beauty evoked by the written word could be expressed in any form.

Achievements

Dunsany's first play, *The Glittering Gate*, was commissioned by William Butler Yeats for production at the Abbey Theatre, Dublin, in 1909. Having read Dunsany's earlier tales, Yeats thought him a genius and wished to include his work as part of the Irish Renaissance. Although public response to the play did not equal the furor provoked by John Millington Synge's *The Playboy of the Western World* (pr. 1907), Dunsany's delineation of the capriciousness of the gods and the emptiness of Heaven on the other side of the gate nevertheless raised a minor disturbance which seemed to ensure Dunsany a place in the group.

Yeats, however, was interested in developing a literature that was purely Irish in tone and subject matter, and his desire to include Dunsany as part of this movement seems to have been based upon a misperception of Dunsany's point of view. While Dunsany may have been technically Irish, his was not the mystical outlook of Yeats or James Stephens but rather the sensibility of a certain type of Englishman, in the same strain as Rudyard Kipling, John Buchan, or J. R. R. Tolkein, a direct inheritor of the Romantic tradition of Lord Byron and Samuel Taylor Coleridge. In his youth, Dunsany's imagination was fueled more by the Brothers Grimm, Hans Christian Andersen, Edgar Allan Poe, and the Greek writers of the Golden Age than by Irish legends. His closest affinity to Ireland came through his appreciation of the lush beauty of its landscape, evoked with power and mystery in the best of his works.

His early plays were well received, the English casts often featuring respected actors such as Claude Rains (in *The Gods of the Mountain* and *The Golden Doom*), Cathleen Nesbit (in *The Queen's Enemies*), and Gladys Cooper (in *If*). *The Laughter of Gods* was translated into Czech (as *Smich Boha*) and was also performed at the Moscow Art Theatre. Another of his early plays, *The Lost Silk Hat*, was produced in Russia, in 1915, and, even more unexpectedly, in China, at the end of World War I. Americans were his most admiring audiences, however, responding to the initial production of *A Night at an Inn*, according to *The New York Times*, "half-hysterical with excitement for the play is stirring beyond belief." His American biographer Edward Hale Bierstadt declared, "The three great contemporary dramatic poets of Ireland are Synge, Dunsany and Yeats."

Although Dunsany's literary influence has not been widespread, it has been important to the minor fictional area of fantasy. His successful Billiards Club series, for example—stories related by a retired adventurer to his cronies at the club—is echoed in Arthur C. Clarke's *Tales of the White Hart* (1957) and also in the Gavigan's Bar stories of Fletcher Pratt and L. Sprague de Camp. Both C. S. Lewis and H. P. Lovecraft were directly indebted to him, and today many of their followers, although not familiar with Dunsany's work at first hand, pursue the same tradition.

Dunsany was a fellow of the Royal Literary Society and of the Royal Geographical Society as well as president of the Authors' Society. He won the Harmsworth Award and was accorded an honorary doctor of letters degree, in 1939, from Dublin University.

Biography

Lord Dunsany was born Edward John Morton Drax Plunkett, becoming eighteenth Baron Dunsany upon the death of his father in 1899. He spent his early boyhood at Dunstall Priory in Kent, but in later years his principal residence was Dunsany Castle in Meath, Ireland. The influence of the Irish side of his heritage was muted greatly by political connections to England, his grandfather being seated in the House of Lords and his father and two uncles holding seats in the House of Commons. Dunsany himself stood as Conservative candidate for the Commons but lost in a local election.

Educated in England at Eton, Cambridge, and Sandhurst Military Academy, Dunsany accepted his role in the conventional upper-class life and adopted most of the attitudes and habits current among his peers. While writing was important to him, he gave every evidence of pursuing his literary career in a gentlemanly fashion, claiming that it engaged no more than three percent of his time.

In the spirit of the country gentleman, Dunsany led an active life as a sportsman, enjoying fishing, horseback riding, cricket, and hunting. He was a crack shot and became pistol-shooting champion of Ireland. A yearning for adventure led him to more serious pursuits in the military, and he first saw action at age twenty in the Coldstream Guards, fighting for the British in the Boer War. While in South Africa, he met Rudyard Kipling, a man similar in temperament and outlook, who was to remain his friend for life. Like Kipling, Dunsany was preoccupied with the conflict between the instinctive, primitive nature of man and the rational, respectable façade of civilization.

After leaving the army and experiencing the disappointments of political life, Dunsany married Lady Beatrice Villiers, the daughter of the Earl and Countess of Jersey, in 1904. Two years later, the Dunsanys' only child, Randall, was born. During this period, Dunsany wrote three volumes of stories, beginning with *The Gods of Pegana* (1905). In these early tales, Dunsany set the tone for much of his later writing, evoking magical worlds of his own creation with great originality and humor. The language in which they are presented is poetic, biblical; they stress the beauty of the land, the power of fate, and the impotence of human intellect.

Dunsany's first play, commissioned by Yeats, was received with some acclaim by Abbey Theatre audiences, but when his second opened there, it was given little notice. He offered at least two other plays, *The Golden Doom* and *The Tents of the Arabs*, to Yeats and the Abbey Theatre and was rather hurt when they were rejected as "unsuitable." Because of this rejection, their differing views of the purpose of "Irish drama," and an awkward social situation created when Dunsany learned of some rather malicious remarks made about him, Dunsany's friendship with Yeats and

Lady Augusta Gregory cooled and he severed his relationship with their group.

Many of the great and near-great of his time did like Dunsany, however, including writers Padraic Colum, George Russell (Æ), George Moore, Oliver St. John Gogarty, and H. G. Wells, as well as members of the nobility. His position on political affairs, particularly the Irish question, was hard to categorize. As a landlord in Ireland, Dunsany thought the Sinn Fein rebels and traitors. On the other hand, the reviews of his novel *Up in the Hills* (1935), a good-natured satire on the Troubles, were as enthusiastic in Ireland as in England.

Dunsany's brief flirtation with the Irish National Theatre at least induced him to continue writing plays, and from 1909 to 1922 he produced drama of interest, including *King Argimenes and the Unknown Warrior, The Gods of the Mountain, A Night at an Inn, The Tents of the Arabs*, and *If*. These plays often reached the stage in Britain and the United States, but with the return of realism in the 1920's, they were judged to be dated and facile.

Dunsany was thirty-six when World War I began in 1914. He enlisted in the National Volunteers and, shortly after, joined the Royal Inniskilling Fusiliers. After seeing action in France, Dunsany was wounded in Dublin during the Easter Rebellion in 1916; while out on a weekend pass, he was shot in the face and spent a week in a rebel hospital before his release. Subsequently, Dunsany joined the War Office to write propaganda.

Between the two world wars, Dunsany wrote with extraordinary energy and, although unsuccessful as a playwright, enjoyed popular acclaim for such novels as *The King of Elfland's Daughter* and *The Blessing of Pan* (1927), for his collections of poetry, and for the tales of his most ambitiously rendered character, Mr. Joseph Jorkens. The demand for Jorkens, the boastful, Dickensian drunk of the fictional Billiards Club, became so extraordinary that Dunsany was forced to write four more volumes to satisfy his growing public. Ever restless in his creativity, Dunsany also took up painting as a hobby and perfected his chess game enough to reign as Irish champion. His victories led to friendship with the famed world chess master José Raul Capablanca, who became a regular visitor at Dunsany Castle. Dunsany's taste for a fight did not diminish, either; at the age of sixty-two, he joined the Local Defence Volunteers in preparation for a possible Nazi invasion. When this service proved uneventful, he accepted an invitation from the British Council to take the Byron Chair of English Literature at the university in Athens and set off for that city in 1940, an experience that culminated in *Guerilla* (1944), a novel about the war of resistance in Greece. One of his few semirealistic books, this novel demonstrated that he could control conventional fiction and also receive favorable response from tough-minded modern critics.

From 1945 to the end of his life, Dunsany's inventiveness never failed, but old age moderated his productivity. Eccentric, but no longer embittered by the brave new world's lack of appreciation for his work, Dunsany lived contentedly until his death after an appendix operation in 1957.

Analysis

Lord Dunsany's writing consists of many elements found in his early reading of the tales of the Brothers Grimm, of Anderson, and of Greek mythology. His religious temperament was formed intuitively by the beauty and terror of mysterious fictional worlds rather than by formal theology. Dreamlands of mystery and mythology, filled with marvels and the exotic, confrontations between gods and heroes—or mere mortals—these were the center of most of his works. He found such subjects attractive in part because without them, life was less fun, less exciting, less colorful. While he managed to retain a childlike wonder at the vastness of the universe and the power of external forces which people disregard at their own peril, Dunsany was also a well-educated, sophisticated man of the world, and this dichotomy shows through. Just when his work seems ready to lapse into sentimentality, irony, satire, or an unexpected twist is encountered. Instead of bemoaning the dimness of the Celtic Twilight, Dunsany celebrated the adventuresome spirit of mankind. He continually pointed out that the dawning of the Age of Reason may have been announced, that worship of industrialization and technology may have swept the earth, but whenever humans become too confident in themselves and think they have safely pigeonholed the universe, the universe will surprise them by upsetting their pet ideas.

In his essay on playwriting, "Carving the Ivory" (1928), Dunsany claims that, as a playwright, he follows no formal rules of dramatic composition. He merely carves the play, "the ivory block," as a sculptor carves his material. The result is a finished shape which assumes a natural form, refined to its fruition as if no authorial hand was implicated in its making. Dunsany wrote quickly, with little revision—*A Night at the Inn*, for example, was completed between his noon meal and teatime—but his preoccupation with the mysteries of aesthetic romanticism is quite deceptive. The poetic language of his plays, often delivered in perfect hexameters, and their effective rhetorical devices reveal a thoughtful and cunning artist at work, adept at rendering a limpid style.

The Glittering Gate, which Dunsany said he had written chiefly to please Yeats, is not characteristic of Dunsany's work. It opens in a lonely place of rock suspended in an abyss hung with stars. Close to the landscape littered with thousands of beer bottles is a golden gate hinged in a wall of granite. Jim, a thief hanged for crimes on earth, wearily and cynically uncorks the bottles, but none of them contains beer. He is joined by Bill, formerly his student of burglary, who has died from a gunshot wound while attempting to break into a house. At various points, there is faint and unpleasant laughter in the background. Bill is convinced that his jemmy, his "old nutcracker" burglary tool, can open the heavenly gate; beyond it, he hopes to find angels, gold, apples, and his mother. Jim has a moment of astonishment as Bill succeeds in prying the door ajar. As they look out at the emptiness, cruel, violent laughter rises.

Dunsany's cynicism is apparent in this play, and although many critics downplay this quality in him, it is not uncharacteristic of his work. The case against the gods is one-sided in that the reader or viewer is not allowed to see what eventually happens to "good people"—unless, in ultimate cynicism, Dunsany wishes to indicate that even the best of mankind is, to the gods, no better than Jim or Bill. Each of the characters pays for his actions in the world and is abandoned to a form of punishment particularly suited to him: Jim will be perpetually thirsty, possibly more for hope than for beer, and Bill will never see his mother again. Even in the afterlife, each continues to be true to his criminal nature. Instead of feeling remorse, they seek a way out; they do not give in to the gods any more than the gods give in to them.

The play has parallels to the myth of Sisyphus. Like Sisyphus, forever rolling his stone up the mountainside only to have it roll back down again, Jim opens his beer bottles to find them empty. He knows he will not find beer, but he hopes that, if only once, the gods' trick might not work. His placid statement at the end, as he looks into nothingness, is that it is characteristic of the gods to have arranged such an anticlimax. In a similar way, Sisyphus understands his predicament but must nevertheless repeat the cycle of his condemnation. Jim's monologue on the meaninglessness of the years and the futility of confinement with Bill is also reminiscent of Jean-Paul Sartre's *No Exit* (pr. 1944).

Two closely related plays, *The Gods of the Mountain* and *A Night at an Inn*, clearly illustrate Dunsany's major theme of the arrogance of men provoking retribution at the hands of intransigent gods. In *The Gods of the Mountain*, set somewhere in the East, a group of beggars, led by Agmar, wish to enter the city to seek riches at a time when the gods seem to be asleep and the divine in men seems to be dead. The beggars suggest posing as lords or kings, but Agmar insists that they impersonate gods. Disguised as the seven green jade idols of Marma, they fool a skeptical populace through the will and intellect of Agmar. Dunsany's admiration of Friedrich Nietzsche's *Thus Spake Zarathustra* (1883-1885) is reflected in the characterization of Agmar. Agmar dismisses the idea of subservience to anyone, but when the real gods enter to seek vengeance on the usurpers, Agmar's genius fails, and all the beggars are turned to stone.

A Night at an Inn, a slighter play, demonstrates that human pride is as dangerous close to home as it is in the mysterious East. Three merchant sailors and their leader, A. E. Scott (the Toff), steal the ruby eye from a green idol, Klesh. The Toff remains aloof and calm upon hearing that the priests of Klesh are following them. He says that they will not come until he is ready to receive them. After all, he says, he is able to see into the future. When the three priests appear, the Toff formulates and carries out a clever plan to murder them. The blind idol, however, claims his ruby eye and leaves the inn; offstage, a seductive voice calls the names of the sailors, and, against their will, they exit into the darkness. On his way out, the Toff comments in despair that he did not foresee this conclusion.

These two works read better than they play. Unlike *The Glittering Gate*, both melodramas call for the physical presence of the gods, which lessens the mystery considerably in a staged version: The problem for Dunsany was to make the audience believe that an abstraction could operate on the material level; the attention commanded by the idols leaves the message out of focus and depersonalized. In reading, at least, each individual can create his own image of the idols.

It may always be difficult to evaluate Dunsany's work fairly, since it is an admixture of so many strains. Audiences conditioned by the work of filmmakers George Lucas and Steven Spielberg may not object to the speaking statues or the ominous laughter of the gods, and audiences accustomed to Samuel Beckett, Eugène Ionesco, and T. S. Eliot may enjoy the stylized soft-edge mysticism—unfortunately, the two types rarely overlap.

In his search for eternal values in imaginative expression, Dunsany produced a body of work of considerable diversity and quality. His private mythological universe may seem too arcane for today's taste, but it is one of surprising richness and beauty. Dunsany's provocative plays are models of sophistication and verbal precision and certainly deserve more recognition than they have been afforded.

Other major works

NOVELS: *The Chronicles of Rodrigues*, 1922; *The King of Elfland's Daughter*, 1924; *The Charwoman's Shadow*, 1926; *The Blessing of Pan*, 1927; *Up in the Hills*, 1935; *Rory and Bran*, 1936; *Guerilla*, 1944; *His Fellow Man*, 1952.

SHORT FICTION: *The Gods of Pegana*, 1905; *Time and the Gods*, 1906; *The Sword of Welleran and Other Stories*, 1908; *A Dreamer's Tales*, 1910; *Tales of Wonder*, 1916 (also as *The Last Book of Wonder*); *Tales of War*, 1918; *Tales of Three Hemispheres*, 1919; *Unhappy Far-off Things*, 1919; *The Travel Tales of Mr. Joseph Jorkens*, 1931; *Jorkens Remembers Africa*, 1934; *Jorkens Has a Large Whiskey*, 1940; *The Man Who Ate the Phoenix*, 1947; *The Fourth Book of Jorkens*, 1948; *The Little Tales of Smethers*, 1952; *Jorkens Borrows Another Whiskey*, 1954.

POETRY: *Fifty Poems*, 1929; *War Poems*, 1940; *To Awaken Pegasus and*

Other Poems, 1949.
NONFICTION: *My Ireland*, 1937; *Patches of Sunlight*, 1938; *While the Sirens Slept*, 1944; *The Sirens Wake*, 1945; *A Glimpse from a Watchtower*, 1946.
TRANSLATION: *The Odes of Horace*, 1947.

Bibliography
Amory, Mark. *A Biography of Lord Dunsany*, 1972.
Bierstadt, Edward Hale. *Dunsany the Dramatist*, 1917.
Lovecraft, H. P. *Marginalia*, 1944.
Smith, H. *Lord Dunsany, King of Dreams: A Personal Portrait*, 1959.

James C. MacDonald

T. S. ELIOT

Born: St. Louis, Missouri; September 26, 1888
Died: London, England; January 4, 1965

Principal drama

Sweeney Agonistes, pb. 1932, pr. 1933 (fragment); *The Rock*, pb., pr. 1934; *Murder in the Cathedral*, pb., pr. 1935; *The Family Reunion*, pb., pr. 1939; *The Cocktail Party*, pr. 1949, pb. 1950; *The Confidential Clerk*, pr. 1953, pb. 1954; *The Elder Statesman*, pr. 1958, pb. 1959; *Collected Plays*, pb. 1962.

Other literary forms

In addition to being a successful liturgical dramatist, T. S. Eliot was an editor, an essayist, and a poet of great distinction. He became assistant editor of *The Egoist* in 1917 and founded *The Criterion* in 1922, serving as editor of the latter from then until its demise in 1939. As an essayist, Eliot explored the place of modern literature with regard to tradition, discussed the relationship between literature and ethics, and emphasized the need for a modern idiom. Among his extremely influential collections of essays are *The Sacred Wood* (1920) and *After Strange Gods* (1934), both dealing with the individual's debt to tradition, the latter propounding a moral standpoint; *The Use of Poetry and the Use of Criticism* (1933); and *On Poetry and Poets* (1957). In *For Lancelot Andrewes* (1928) and *The Idea of a Christian Society* (1939), the impact of his 1927 confirmation in the Church of England on his life and letters is particularly evident.

Eliot's poetry has had a greater influence, not only in England and America but also in world literature, than that of any of his contemporaries. *Prufrock and Other Observations* (1917), *Poems* (1919; printed by Leonard and Virginia Woolf), and *The Waste Land* (1922) illustrate his growing despair over personal problems as well as modern social trends; *Ash Wednesday* (1930) and *Four Quartets* (1943), produced following his confirmation, are meditations concerning spiritual illumination. In *Old Possum's Book of Practical Cats* (1939), Eliot demonstrated his talent for writing comic verse with equal success. That work has been reprinted widely in many formats and even, in 1983, provided the basis for a Tony Award winning musical, *Cats*.

Achievements

Any assessment of T. S. Eliot's achievements as a dramatist must be made in the light of his own comments about the relationship between past and present, between "tradition and the individual talent." For Eliot, a new work of art causes a rearrangement of the ideal, preexisting order. As

Carol Smith points out, his comments about "historical perspective" are not innovative; what is new is his idea that the "given" order defines the artist, whose chief responsibility is to subsume his individual talent as part of the progress of literary history. Eliot's dramatic works are therefore "classical" in the altered sense of his attempting to employ a modern idiom in the service of the imperatives of history, both literary and religious.

One of Eliot's achievements was the presentation of liturgical drama on the modern stage to a commercial audience. His endeavor in this regard began with his writing both a pageant, *The Rock*, and a ritual drama, *Murder in the Cathedral*, for the limited audiences provided respectively by a benefit to promote church building in London and the Canterbury Festival, audiences preconditioned to dramas of redemption. (*Sweeney Agonistes*, an experimental fragment, was not produced until 1933.) With his later plays, however, Eliot undertook the task of convincing secular audiences that traditional ideas about redemption were viable within a modern framework. *The Family Reunion*, his first full-length experiment in turning drawing-room comedy into religious fable, was not immediately successful; as his close friend and adviser Elliott Martin Browne reports, critics found the work mixed—the most negative reviews said that the play was characterized by "lifeless smoothness" and "difficulty" and was guaranteed to leave the audience "vexed and exhausted." Some modern critics, however, such as Eliot's biographer T. S. Matthews, find the play "extraordinary, . . . far superior to his later, 'better made' plays." *The Cocktail Party*, on the other hand, was better received; even those who wrote negative reviews acknowledged that the production bordered on greatness. Browne notes that similar comments were made about *The Confidential Clerk*, although critical reception was influenced by the general belief that Eliot's attempt "to combine the esoteric with the entertaining" was no longer innovative. *The Elder Statesman*, Browne believes, was overinterpreted by gossipmongers intent on reading the play in the light of Eliot's marriage to his secretary, Valerie Fletcher, the previous year.

Quite aside from their mixed commercial appeal, Eliot's plays illustrate his critical theories not only about the connection between drama and poetry but also about the failure of realistic theater. As C. L. Barber notes, Eliot's Aristotelian viewpoint prompted him to criticize modern drama for its lack of rhythm. For Eliot, poetry was more than a distraction, more than an attempt to prettify dramatic diction; never extrinsic to the action, poetry provides an underlying musical pattern that strengthens the audience's response. The presence of such an abstract pattern suggests, as Eliot says in "Four Elizabethan Dramatists" (written in 1924), that the great vice in English drama is realism, for it detracts from the unity of the play. As his large essay *Poetry and Drama* (1951) makes clear, such unity is more than a technical matter of form and content, for the literary is handmaiden to the religious. Eliot's ideal vision of verse drama is one in which "a design of human action and of words" is perpetuated in such a way that the connection between the everyday world and the universal design is illustrated; such a drama, Eliot believed, would provide the proper feeling of "reconciliation" to lead the audience to a spiritual awakening.

Biography

Thomas Stearns Eliot was born on September 26, 1888, in St. Louis, Missouri. His celebrated statement of his allegiances in *For Lancelot Andrewes*—"classicist in literature, royalist in politics, and Anglo-Catholic in religion"—ran counter to the family tradition of Unitarianism; his grandfather, William Greenleaf Eliot, descendant of a pastor of Boston's Old North Church, established the Unitarian Church of the Messiah in St. Louis. Eliot's father himself was a renegade, refusing the ministry for what was eventually the presidency of the Hydraulic-Press Brick Company. His mother, Charlotte Stearns, was a descendant of one of the judges in the Salem witch trials; an intellectual woman, Stearns began a career as a schoolteacher and eventually became active in children's causes.

As Matthews notes, the family saying *"Tace et fac* ('Shut up and get on with it')" suggests a household in which indulgence gave way to duty. As a child, Eliot was considered delicate but precocious; at Smith Academy, he took the Latin prize and excelled in English. Deemed too young at seventeen to enter Harvard, he was sent first to Milton Academy. At Harvard, he was conservative and studious. He became an editor of the *Advocate*, a literary magazine, but his decision to accelerate his undergraduate work in order to pursue a master's degree left him small leisure for such friends as Conrad Aiken. Important influences during his college years included his discovery of Arthur Symons' *The Symbolist Movement in Literature* (1899), a book that led him to imitate the verse of Jules Laforgue; his love for Elizabethan drama; and, finally, his acquaintance with Irving Babbitt, the leader of the New Humanism, an anti-Romantic movement that stressed the ethical nature of experience. Certainly, Babbitt's influence led Eliot to spend one of his graduate years in France, where, resisting the attractive Bohemianism open to a writer of his talents, he decided to pursue a degree in philosophy at Harvard, where he came under the influence of Bertrand Russell.

The fellowship that Harvard awarded Eliot in 1914 proved to alter the course of his life. Enrolled in Merton College, at Oxford, he began his long friendship with Ezra Pound, under whose aegis Eliot published "The Love Song of J. Alfred Prufrock" in *Poetry* magazine in 1915. In England, Eliot met and married his first wife, Vivienne Haigh-Wood. Described as a beautiful and entrancing individual, she nevertheless suffered from a nervous disability that had devastating emotional effects. In increasing financial difficulty, Eliot worked as an usher at a boys' school, an employee at Lloyd's Bank, or free-lance journalist, and an assistant editor of *The Egoist.*

Eliot enjoyed many fruitful friendships, among them those with Bertrand Russell, Virginia Woolf, and I. A. Richards. From 1921 to 1925, when he was publishing reviews in the *Times Literary Supplement,* Eliot's health deteriorated; the unforeseen result of an enforced vacation was *The Waste Land.* In 1922, he founded *The Criterion,* a literary quarterly that was sponsored financially by Lady Rothermere. After a long period of ill health and self-doubt, he joined the Anglican Church. His biographer suggests a number of reasons for the decision, including certain social and "aesthetic" attractions of this particular denomination, the authoritarian cast of the Church, and the long Church "pedigree" that satisfied Eliot's belief in the importance of tradition. His decision to become a British citizen followed soon thereafter, partly, Matthews believes, because Eliot felt that in America "the aristocratic tradition of culture was dead."

Eliot's 1932 return to his native land was, like his first journey away, a new start, for it began his separation from Vivienne, for whom he had become more nurse than husband. To be sure, the attempt to escape from her neurotic persecution made his middle years unhappy ones, years complicated further by the exigencies of World War II. Despite such distractions, however, these were the years in which Eliot began his career as a playwright.

Quite clearly, Eliot's religious conversion provided the themes not only for his poetry but also for his plays. Events in Eliot's personal life, including the death of his estranged wife in 1947, are also reflected in his plays. Conceivably, his sense of alienation and guilt found its way into the portrait of Harry, the putative wife-killer in *The Family Reunion,* as well as into the depiction of the dreary marriage faced by the Chamberlaynes in *The Cocktail Party.* Other elements are identifiable, such as the figure of Agatha in *The Family Reunion*; the only one to understand Harry's spiritual search thoroughly, Agatha is said to be based on Emily Hale, Eliot's longtime friend, who had been a schoolmistress at Scripps College, Smith College, and Abbot Academy. Emily was as shocked by Eliot's second clandestine marriage as she was by his first; at the age of sixty-nine, Eliot married Valerie Fletcher, his secretary.

Before the arrival of that emotional security, however, Eliot had achieved other triumphs. He was awarded the Nobel Prize in 1948, and, in the same year, received the British Empire's Order of Merit. While he was drafting *The Cocktail Party,* he traveled to Princeton, New Jersey, to accept a fellowship at the Institute for Advanced Study. His last two plays—*The Confidential Clerk* and *The Elder Statesman*—were not as popular as *The Cocktail Party*; they do, however, show an increasing understanding of the way in which human relationships may be ameliorated. Indeed, in *The Elder Statesman*, the love experienced by Monica and Charles seems a reflection of the happiness that Eliot himself found with his second wife. For the first time in his dramatic writing, the possibility of redemption through human love is adequately broached; indeed, for the first time, human love seems a model of divine love rather than, as Celia observes in *The Cocktail Party*, a distraction or a second-best choice.

On January 4, 1965, Eliot died in London. At his request, his ashes repose at East Coker, the birthplace of his ancestors and the titular locale of one of the *Four Quartets*; the memorial plaque in the Poets' Corner at Westminster Abbey was placed on January 4, 1967.

Analysis

T. S. Eliot's conservative dramaturgy is clearly expressed in his 1928 essay "Dialogue on Dramatic Poetry" in which, as C. L. Barber notes, he suggests that "genuine drama" displays "a tension between liturgy and realism." To be sure, Eliot differed sharply from the advocates of Ibsenite realism, maintaining throughout his career that untrammeled realism operating outside the limitations of art did not produce classic harmony. In consequence, Eliot relied on a number of traditional forms, including the Mass and Greek drama. On the other hand, he created new verse forms, convinced that traditional forms such as Shakespearean blank verse would be inadequate to express modern experience. In *Sweeney Agonistes*, he made use of the rhythms of vaudeville, believing that such robust entertainment contained the seeds of a popular drama of high artistic quality, comparable to the achievements of the great Elizabethan and Jacobean playwrights.

Modern religious drama, Eliot believed, "should be able to hold the interest, to arouse the excitement, of people who are not religious." Redemption is the theme of all of his plays, a theme explored on different levels. For example, Becket's understanding, in *Murder in the Cathedral*, that salvation is a willing submission to a larger pattern is developed and tempered in the later social comedies.

In almost all of his plays, Eliot presents characters on a continuum of spiritual understanding, including the martyr or saint figure, the "guardians" (the spiritual advisers), the common folk (capable of limited perception or at least of accommodation), and the uncomprehending. In *The Family Reunion* and *The Cocktail Party*, respectively, Harry and Celia experience a sense of having sinned and the desire to atone. Celia's illumination is also characterized by a sense of having failed another person. Her martyrdom is correspondingly more moving, not because it is graphically described, but because it seems inexorable. In *The Confidential Clerk*, Colby, whose search for a human father parallels his desire for a divine one, experiences his *éclaircissement* as a private moment in a garden and works out his salvation as an organist. In the aforementioned plays, guardian figures abound. Agatha councils Harry to follow attendant Eumenides if he wishes to expiate the family curse; Julia, Alex, and Reilly not only show Celia the way to enlightenment but reinstate the Chamberlaynes' marriage; the retired valet Eggerson offers Colby a job as an organist and predicts his eventual entry into holy orders. Eliot's last play, *The Elder Statesman*, is the only one in which human love is an adequate guide to divine love; in that sense, Monica, in her affection for her fiancé and in her unwavering love for her father despite his faults, is a guardian figure.

A development in the characterization of the common people may be seen as well. Because of their foolishness or their attempt to dominate, all of Harry's relatives seem lost to perceptiveness, except, perhaps, for his Uncle Charles, who begins to feel "That there is something I *could* understand, if I were told it." A wider hope is held out in *The Cocktail Party*, for while not all may follow Celia's path, the Chamberlaynes learn to accept the "good life" that is available to them, and even Peter, in love with Celia, may learn to "see" through the same qualities that make him a film producer. Again, while Colby withdraws from the family circle, those who remain—no matter how superficially mismatched—engage in a communion characterized most of all by a desire to understand and to love. Finally, in *The Elder Statesman*, Eliot achieves a balance in his continuum of characters, for he presents the salvation of the Calvertons by love as well as the possibility that, through Monica, Michael might return to find his self-identity, while both Gomez and Mrs. Carghill become lost souls as they pursue their revenge.

Although originally produced for the Canterbury Festival, *Murder in the Cathedral* has achieved the most lasting interest of all Eliot's plays. It is a psychological and historical exploration of martyrdom that, as David R. Clark points out, speaks directly not only to current disputes about the interconnection between Church and State but also to the ever-present contemporary threat of assassination. It is Eliot's most successful attempt to adapt verse forms to drama, particularly in the speeches of the Chorus, whose function, Eliot believed, was to interpret the action to the viewers and to strengthen the impact of the action by reflecting its effects. In the speeches of the Knights and Tempters (characters doubled when the play is staged) as well, attitudes are mirrored by poetic cadence—a fine example of form following content. As Grover Smith notes, the title itself, while commercially attractive, is somewhat misleading, as were other possibilities Eliot considered, among them "The Archbishop Murder Case" and "Fear in the Way," for *Murder in the Cathedral* is less a whodunit than an attempt to startle the unimpassioned believer into percipience and the nonbeliever into understanding.

Like Eliot's first venture into ritualistic drama, *The Rock*, *Murder in the*

Cathedral is based on an actual event, the martyrdom of Thomas à Becket in the year 1170 in the chapel of Saint Benedict in Canterbury Cathedral. Unlike *The Rock*, however, which is a spectacle play delineating the history of the Church, *Murder in the Cathedral* is focused on a dramatic event of great intensity. The play traces the spiritual education of Thomas, whose greatest temptation is self-aggrandizement; the education of the Chorus, who seek to escape both suffering and salvation; and the education of the Knights and the audience, whose worldliness implicates them jointly in the assassination.

Eliot's addition of a Fourth Tempter to Becket's "trial" in part 1 is crucial. The first three tempters are expected and easily rejected. The first, who offers sensual pleasures, resigns Becket to "the pleasures of [his] higher vices." One such vice is offered by the Second Tempter: "Temporal power, to build a good world," power that requires submission to secular law. Becket, who rejects this exercise in intelligent self-interest, also rejects the Third Tempter's offer of a coalition with the barons to overthrow the King; such an action would bestialize Becket, make him "a wolf among wolves." The Fourth Tempter is, however, not so easily answered, for he brings the temptation of spiritual power through martyrdom. Counseling the Archbishop to seek death, he offers as its rewards the joy of wielding power over eternal life and death, the adulation of the masses, the richness of heavenly grandeur, and, finally, the sweetness of revenge, for Becket will then be able to look down and see his "persecutors, in timeless torment."

For Becket, the only way to escape the damning effects of his own spiritual pride is to give up self-will so that he may become part of a larger pattern. As Grover Smith notes, the counsel that Becket gives to the Chorus (ironically quoted to him by the Fourth Tempter) has its roots in Aristotle's image of the still point—on a wheel, for example—as the source of action:

> You know and do not know, that acting is suffering,
> And suffering action. Neither does the actor suffer
> Nor the patient act. But both are fixed
> In an eternal action, an eternal patience
> To which all must consent that it may be willed
> And which all must suffer that they may will it,
> That the pattern may subsist, that the wheel may turn and still
> Be forever still.

In theological terms, Eliot is suggesting that the nature of the relationship between action and suffering depends on the conception of God as the first mover, just as the still point is centered in the wheel. Becket, in willing martyrdom, has substituted his will for God's will. When he understands that he was doing the right deed for the wrong reason, he enters the ideal relationship between man and God—one of submission, of man's consent to be an instrument. In that condition of bringing one's will into conformity with that of God, one paradoxically does not suffer, for he acts as an instrument; neither does he act, for he gives up will. Both Grover Smith and David E. Jones explore the extension of this idea from Aristotle to Dante to clarify the sources of Eliot's vision.

For the women whose barren lives are spent among small deeds, Becket becomes a new center; with their wills in conformity to his, they too become the instruments of God's will, even as the Knights are in the murder of Becket. For Grover Smith, whereas Becket's language is abstract and passionless, his decision hidden in difficult, paradoxical words, that of the women is overtly sensual; for Carol Smith, such language shows that the women have accepted their "Christian responsibility." The women's unwilling participation in the event is a violent disturbance of their willed attitude of noninterference; through Becket, they are touched not only by life but also by death. The key is in the homily delivered by Becket as an interlude in the play, a sermon in which he speaks of an attitude of mourning and rejoicing in martyrdom. Before his death, he warns the women that their joy will come only "when the figure of God's purpose is made complete"—when, in other words, they understand that his martyrdom is the answer to their despair.

The prose in which the Knights speak after the murder has taken place is to some critics jarring, but it is deliberately so on Eliot's part; a far graver criticism is that it is either amusing, or, as Grover Smith suggests, misleading, insofar as the emphasis on the "contest . . . between brute power and resigned holiness" is shifted to an argument about Church and State. Jones disagrees; for him, the prose shakes the audience's sanctimonious complacency. The arguments offered by the Knights are familiar rationalizations. The Second Knight pleads disinterested duty as his reason for the murder, the Third that "violence is the only way in which social justice can be secured," and the Fourth that, since Becket's overweening egotism prompted the murder, the correct "verdict" is "Suicide while of Unsound Mind." The final words of the Chorus, spoken to a Te Deum in the background, serve as a corrective to any distorted view, for they, the "type of common man," not only accept responsibility for "the sin of the world" but also acknowledge that human consciousness is an affirmation of the ultimate design, of which they have willingly become a part.

Produced in March, 1939, *The Family Reunion* was considerably less successful than Eliot's first full-length play, partly because he was attempting to appeal to a secular audience; moreover, his evocation of the Aeschylean Eumenides—the Furies—as a group of well-dressed aunts and uncles and his deliberate blurring of the hero's motives and fate contribute to the weakness of the play. Various critics have traced the antecedents of *The Family Reunion*, including Henry James's "The Jolly Corner," William Shakespeare's *Hamlet*, and Aeschylus' *Oresteia*, sources discussed thoroughly by Grover Smith and David Jones. Eliot attempted to wed the classical and the modern, believing that poetry brought into the audience's world would help to heal social disintegration.

The two levels of the play—the realistic and the spiritual—are not always mutually illuminating. On the surface, the play depicts the homecoming of Harry, Lord Monchensey, to Wishwood, the family mansion that his mother, Amy, has maintained, unchanged, for his benefit. Harry, convinced that he murdered his wife a year ago, is unable to agree with the conventional wishes of his mother or of his featherheaded aunts, Ivy and Violet, or of his blundering uncles, Gerald and Charles. On another level, he arrives convinced that he is pursued by the Furies, only to learn from his Aunt Agatha that to *follow* the "bright angels" is the way to redemption through suffering.

The Family Reunion reflects Eliot's recurring preoccupation with original sin. While Harry's own uncertainty about his responsibility for his wife's death may be unsettling to the audience, the point is surely that for Eliot the *fact* is irrelevant; what is important is that Harry (and Eliot, because of his own marital situation) feels guilty about the wish itself. Indeed, Harry seems to be burdened with a family curse that he must expiate. As Agatha tells him, his father wanted to murder Harry's mother but was prevented from doing so by Agatha, who loved him; Harry has lived to reenact his father's will. Harry's guilt thus is shifted to the larger framework of the *felix culpa*, or fortunate fall.

Again, Harry's character is so unappealing that to call him, as Agatha does, "the consciousness of your unhappy family,/ Its bird sent flying through the purgatorial fire," is not acceptable on the metaphoric level. His rudeness and abrupt repudiation of his mother (which leads to her death) conspire against the suggestion that he is to become a Christian mystic or saint—that, as Agatha says, he is destined for "broken stones/ That lie, fang up" or that, as he says, he is headed for "A stony sanctuary and a primitive altar" or "A care over lives of humble people."

The transformation of the Eumenides from "hounds of hell" to "bright angels" is justified not only by the *Oresteia* of Aeschylus but also by the idea, developed in *Murder in the Cathedral*, that suffering precedes atonement; on a psychological level, however, the idea poses problems. As the evocation of the watchful eyes possessed by both mother and wife, the Eumenides suggest a developing Oedipus complex; interpreted by Agatha as helpful guardians, they suggest a childish transference of affection to Agatha, an affection that is at once incestuous and spiritual. As both Barber and Grover Smith point out, Mary, Harry's childhood sweetheart, simply presents the desired but now impossible fulfillment of human love. For Agatha, however, and eventually for Harry, the Eumenides posit a frontier beyond which all experience is private, save that it is a confrontation between the human spirit and the divine, a purgatorial confrontation under "the judicial sun/ Of the final eye."

In the final analysis, the play is not a triumph of comedy—or of tragedy. With Amy dead, Harry's father has ironically gotten his wish; Wishwood is to be ceded to Harry's brother John, about whom Harry says brutally, "A minor trouble like a concussion/ Cannot make very much difference to John." In the ritualistic chorus performed by Agatha and Mary at the end of the play, Eliot emphasizes the inexorability of the curse around which he has built his plot as well as the possibility of salvation. What is lacking is an explanation of the nature of expiation.

First produced for the 1949 Edinburgh Festival, *The Cocktail Party* is, like *The Family Reunion*, an attempt to express modern concerns in the guise of ritualistic drama. In this case, however, Eliot depends on Euripides' *Alcestis* as his classical antecedent, wisely eliminating the embodiment of the Furies that proved to be so dramatically disruptive. In one view, he effectively reproduced the sophisticated patois of cocktail-party chatter to distract his secular audience from what Grover Smith calls the play's theological "underpattern." Other critics, among them Barber and Carol Smith, suggest that the comic approach was a deliberate attempt at a reversal in which "surfaces" become "depths" and the comic resolution an indication of divine order.

A number of this play's themes are taken from Eliot's earlier plays. There is a reunion, although not in the sense of Harry Monchensey's mythopoeic experience, for the Chamberlaynes literally as well as figuratively re-create their marriage; again, there is the figure of the mystic, this time, however, a more convincing one, in Celia; moreover, there is a guardian, Reilly, who achieves expressed validity in his role as a psychologist. Finally, and perhaps most important, there is a sense that spiritual illumination is not restricted, except in its intensity, to martyr figures.

Superficially, the plot is familiar drawing-room comedy, entailing a series of love affairs. Edward's wife, Lavinia, has inexplicably left him; Peter Quilpe, a filmmaker, is in love with Celia Coplestone, Edward's mistress, while Lavinia is in love with Peter. Comic relief is provided by the scatter-brained Julia Shuttlethwaite, the peripatetic Alexander MacColgie Gibbs, and Sir Henry Harcourt-Reilly, an enigmatic, gin-swilling psychologist. As in the well-made play, the plot revolves around a secret: Julia and Alex have conspired with Reilly to reinvigorate the Chamberlaynes' marriage, in an association called variously "the Christian conspiracy" or, as Jones puts it, "the Community of Christians."

The marital difficulties would be familiar to the audience, but not Eliot's interpretation of them. Having confused desire with affection in his attachment to Celia, Edward must face the fact that he is essentially unloving, whereas Lavinia is by nature unlovable: Thus, Eliot suggests, they are perfectly matched. In addition, Edward, who is indecisive, must learn to face the consequences of making a decision—in this case, the decision that Lavinia should return to him. What he realizes is that her return is tantamount to inviting the angel of destruction into his life.

Possessed by the belief that he is suffering "the death of the spirit," that he can live neither with the role Lavinia imposes on him nor without it, Edward goes to Reilly for help. The language that this counselor uses indicates his role of spiritual guardianship. He speaks of Edward's "long journey" but refuses to send him to his "sanatorium," for to do so would be to abandon him to the "devils" that feast on the "shadow of desires of desires." Instead, he brings him face to face with Lavinia to convince him that the unloving and the unlovable should make the best of a bad job—or, in terms of the blessing he administers, must "work out [their] salvation with diligence." Carol Smith's review of Christian mysticism as a background to the play makes clear that Reilly encourages the Chamberlaynes to follow the "Affirmative Way," in which "all created things are to be accepted in love as images of the Divine," rather than the "Negative Way," which is characterized by detachment from "the love of all things."

Reilly's interview with Celia is substantially different, for while she, like Edward, complains of an awareness of solitude, she focuses less on herself than on a perception that loneliness is the human condition and that communication is therefore illusory. She also complains, unlike Edward, of a sense of sin, of a feeling that she must atone for having failed "someone, or something, outside." She attributes her failure to a self-willed fantasy: In Edward, she loved only a figment of her imagination. Unlike Edward, she has had a vision of the Godhead, an ecstatic exhaltation "of loving in the spirit." It is this vision that she chooses to follow, although Reilly emphasizes that it is an unknown way, a blind journey, a way to being "transhumanized," the "way of illumination." Her way, the "Negative Way" of mysticism, culminates in her crucifixion "very near an ant-hill" in the jungles of Kinkanja.

What Eliot offers in *The Cocktail Party* is a series of gradations of spiritual understanding, gradations that were not presented adequately in *The Family Reunion*. Celia's way of illumination is undoubtedly more believable because her developing perceptions are not expressed in sibylline pronouncements; likewise, the guardians are given authenticity by the comic role their very eccentricity engenders. The common way, represented by the Chamberlaynes, is not appealing but understandable, and, as Reilly says, "In a world of lunacy,/ Violence, stupidity, greed . . . it is a good life." Finally, Peter Quilpe, shocked by the news of Celia's death, comes to understand that he had been loving only the image he had created of her. As Grover Smith comments, "the kind of comedy Eliot devised has been compared generically by some critics to Dante's *Commedia*, for in it the characters either fulfill their greatest potentialities or else are set firmly on the way toward doing so."

In Eliot's fourth play, *The Confidential Clerk*, the theme of redemption is again explored, this time through a dependence on Euripides' *Ion*, a play that deals with hidden paternity. Eliot examines the sense of aloneness expressed so effectively by Celia and the human penchant for re-creating other individuals to conform with one's own desires. In addition, Eliot shows the path that a mystical vocation may take.

Denis Donoghue pertinently remarks that Eliot solved the "false tone" occasioned by Celia's death by shifting his terms: Illumination becomes Art, and the worldly way, Commerce, both terms that avoid doctrinal problems. Metaphorically, an escape into Art (illumination) becomes an escape into a garden, one in which real communication is possible. So it is for the musical Colby Simpkins, about whom Lucasta Angel, Sir Claude Mulhammer's illegitimate daughter, notes that he has his "own world." Taken in by Sir Claude as his presumptive son, Colby is immediately claimed by Lady Elizabeth Mulhammer, a fashionable reincarnation of Julia Shuttlethwaite, as the lost son of her former lover, a poet. Each imagines Colby in terms of personal wish-fulfillment. To Colby, the failed musician, Sir Claude reveals his early yearnings to be a sculptor and his decision to follow in the family business. For Sir Claude, the act of creation is "a world where the form is the reality" and an "escape into living" from an illusory world. Indeed, for Sir Claude, life is a constant compromise, just as it is for the Chamberlaynes, a constant coping with two worlds, neither of which offers perfect fulfillment. It is, as he says, a substitute for religion.

Despite this analogy, Colby is unwilling to accept Sir Claude as a father. Colby expresses his yearning for an ideal father in words that may be read for their religious connotation. He wishes, as he says, to have a father "Whom I had never known and wouldn't know now/ . . . whom I could get to know/ Only by report, by documents," a father, he continues, "whose life I could in some way perpetuate/ By being the person he would have liked to be." The analogues to Christ are unmistakable. The revelation that Colby is actually the son of Herbert Guzzard, a "disappointed musician," suggesting a harmony between the mystical and the commonplace that is seldom achieved in *The Family Reunion*, adds to the success of *The Confidential Clerk*.

Like Celia, Colby chooses a life of service, if one more prosaic than joining a nursing order and perishing in Kinkanja. He acknowledges his inheritance by becoming the organist at a small church (rather than continuing to live on Sir Claude's generosity, for Sir Claude is eager to think of Colby as one with whom he shared disillusionment); Eggerson, the retired confidential clerk—who, as Jones notes, was for Eliot "'the only *developed* Christian in the play'"—suggests that Colby will enter the ministry.

As Barber points out, the play presents a succession of individuals who are reaching out after Colby, essentially as a way of gratifying their own expectations. It is only, however, when the audience knows the secret of Colby's birth that many of the early conversations make sense; consequently, Barber suggests, the play is weak in its early acts. Despite this criticism, *The Confidential Clerk* offered Eliot's most convincing and optimistic treatment to that time of the possibility of human communion, pointing the way to his hopeful treatment of human love in his last play, *The Elder Statesman*. It seems less important that Lady Elizabeth's up-to-date spiritualism, her substitute for religion, fails her in her perception that Colby is her son than that she is willing to accept as her real offspring B. Kaghan, a brash, successful businessman, a diamond in the rough. Again, it seems less important that Sir Claude has lost his desired son than that, in the end, he emotionally accepts Lucasta as a daughter. Indeed, the note that Eliot strikes—that, as the Mulhammers say, they are "to try to understand our children" and that both Lucasta and B. Kaghan desire to "mean something" to their newfound parents—is exceptionally conciliatory and suggestive of greater amelioration in the "good life" than is posited in the earlier plays.

Eliot's final play, *The Elder Statesman*, is an extension not only of the idea that one must come to terms with his past, just as Harry Monchensey and the Mulhammers attempt to do, but also that this is, indeed, the only way to redemption. Such atonement on the part of Lord Claverton is presented in words that are less mystical than prosaic; indeed, his past is populated by the blackmailers Federico Gomez, who seeks to capitalize on his knowledge that Lord Calverton had run over a dead man after a drinking party, and Mrs. Carghill, who, as the actress Maisie Montjoy, possesses incriminating love letters. Certainly Calverton's immediate problem—that of being a terminally ill, newly retired man of consequence, suffering from the loneliness of "sitting in an empty waiting room"—is one with which the audience can quickly identify. As Jones points out, T*he Elder Statesman* has a "naturalistic surface": The more plays Eliot wrote, the more muted the spiritual enlightenment became, so that eventually the social relationships became primary. Carol Smith, on the other hand, sees the play as a culmination of Eliot's development of the "dramatic fable" that serves as a "transparent mask" for permanent, religious meanings.

The corollary to Calverton's loneliness takes on sinister (and existential) connotations when it is present in Gomez, who has adopted a new name and new country after a prison sentence. As he says, he has returned to face Lord Calverton in order to find the self he left behind. Gomez charges Calverton with "creating him," with engineering his tastes and altering his career. In revenge, he threatens to make others see Calverton for what he really is—a murderer and a hypocrite. Calverton, in fact, has created his own ghosts by dominating the lives of others. The lesson that he must take responsibility for meddling in others' lives is reinforced by his realization that he is no better than those he created. Both Jones and Carol Smith point out that Calverton's and Gomez's careers parallel each other in that their ethical standards merely mirror the society of which they are a part and in that both have changed identities, the "statesman" Dick Ferry having adopted his wife's name for its impressiveness and the Oxford student having changed his name to blend into his new country. Gomez's desire to amalgamate his two personalities and his desire for revenge are satisfied when he meets Calverton's ne'er-do-well son Michael, to whom he offers the lure of easy money and a new identity. Gomez is, in short, reenacting Calverton's earlier role of tempter.

The other ghost that Calverton must face—Maisie Montjoy, known as Mrs. Carghill—has also been "created" by him. As his mistress, who sued him for breach of promise, she was irrevocably affected by his offer of and withdrawal of love. Indeed, their relationship is a parody of the fruitful, redeeming love that comes to Monica Calverton and Charles Hemington. Like Gomez, Mrs. Carghill has gone through a series of name changes reflecting a progressive confusion in identity. Like him, she resorts to blackmail to gain companionship, insisting on what Jones calls the "uncomfortable Christian conception of a man and a woman becoming the inseparable unity of 'one flesh,'" and like him, she seeks revenge by encouraging the weak-willed Michael to emigrate to South America.

The cure that Eliot proposes for Calverton's loneliness, for his series of façades, and for his discomfort with the past also exorcises his ghosts by allowing him to face them: love. Accompanying that love is the relinquishment of power; understanding that Michael is a free agent, Calverton recognizes that he has been trying to dominate his son's choice of friends, lifestyle, and career. If Michael is a free agent, then Gomez and Carghill's revenge has lost its sting, because Calverton is no longer responsible for his son's actions. The model for the cure is the love shared by Monica and Charles, a love that creates a new, viable personage out of the you and the I. Unlike the kind of false images projected by Calverton's desire to dominate, the new individual is created by a submission of wills, a voluntary merging of the selves. It is, in short, a model of divine love. Eliot thus points to an achievable salvation unspoiled by artificial dramatic techniques such as the evocation of the Eumenides or the awkward ritualistic libation in *The Cocktail Party.*

While Jones notes that for one reviewer, at least, the language of the lovers is abstract and lacking in evocative details, Calverton's illumination is clearly expressed: As Calverton says, if an individual is willing to confess everything to even one person—willing, that is, to appear without his mask—"Then he loves that person, and his love will save him." Calverton further realizes that his wish to dominate his children arises not from love but from the desire to foist upon them an image so that he "could believe in [his] own pretences." At peace with himself and with Monica, who has promised to remember Michael as he really is so that he may one day shed his mask and return to his real self, Calverton approaches death with serenity: "It is worth dying," he says, "to find out what life is."

Other major works

POETRY: *Prufrock and Other Observations*, 1917; *Poems*, 1919; *Ara Vos Prec*, 1920; *The Waste Land*, 1922; *Poems, 1909-1925*, 1925; *The Journey of the Magi*, 1927; *A Song for Simeon*, 1928; *Animula*, 1929; *Ash Wednesday*, 1930; *Marina*, 1930; *Triumphal March*, 1931; *Words for Music*, 1934; *Collected Poems, 1909-1935*, 1936; *Old Possum's Book of Practical Cats*, 1939; *Four Quartets*, 1943; *The Cultivation of Christmas Trees*, 1954; *Collected Poems, 1909-1962*, 1963; *Poems Written in Early Youth*, 1967; *The Complete Poems and Plays*, 1969.

NONFICTION: *Ezra Pound: His Metric and Poetry*, 1917; *The Sacred Wood*, 1920; *Homage to John Dryden*, 1924; *Shakespeare and the Stoicism of Seneca*, 1927; *For Lancelot Andrewes*, 1928; *Dante*, 1929; *Charles Whibley: A Memoir*, 1931; *Thoughts After Lambeth*, 1931; *John Dryden: The Poet, the Dramatist, the Critic*, 1932; *Selected Essays*, 1932, 1950; *The Use of Poetry and the Use of Criticism*, 1933; *After Strange Gods*, 1934; *Elizabethan Essays*, 1934; *Essays Ancient and Modern*, 1936; *The Idea of a Christian Society*, 1939; *The Classics and the Man of Letters*, 1942; *The Music of Poetry*, 1942; *Notes Toward the Definition of Culture*, 1948; *Poetry and Drama*, 1951; *Religious Drama: Medieval and Modern*, 1954; *The Three Voices of Poetry*, 1954; *The Literature of Politics*, 1955; *The Frontiers of Criticism*, 1956; *On Poetry and Poets*, 1957; *To Criticize the Critic*, 1965.

Bibliography

Barber, C. L. "The Power of Development . . . in a Different World," in *The Achievement of T. S. Eliot*, 1935.

Behr, Caroline. *T. S. Eliot: A Chronology of His Life and Works*, 1983.

Browne, Elliott Martin. *The Making of T. S. Eliot's Plays*, 1969.

Clark, David R., ed. *Twentieth Century Interpretation of "Murder in the Cathedral,"* 1971.

Donoghue, Denis. *The Third Voice: Modern British and American Verse Drama*, 1959.

Jones, David E. *The Plays of T. S. Eliot*, 1960.

Matthews, T. S. *Great Tom: Notes Towards the Definition of T. S. Eliot*, 1973.

Matthiessen, F. D., ed. *The Achievement of T. S. Eliot*, 1935.

Smith, Carol. *T. S. Eliot's Dramatic Theory and Practice: From "Sweeney*

Agonistes" to *"The Elder Statesman,"* 1963.
Smith, Grover. *T. S. Eliot's Poetry and Plays: A Study in Sources and Meaning,* 1956.

Patricia Marks

ST. JOHN ERVINE

Born: Belfast, Northern Ireland; December 28, 1883
Died: London, England; January 24, 1971

Principal drama

The Magnanimous Lover, wr. 1907, pr., pb. 1912 (one act); *Mixed Marriage*, pr., pb. 1911; *Jane Clegg*, pr. 1913, pb. 1914; *John Ferguson*, pr., pb. 1915; *The Ship*, pr., pb. 1922; *The Lady of Belmont*, pb. 1923, pr. 1924; *Anthony and Anna*, pb. 1925, pr. 1926; *The First Mrs. Fraser*, pr., pb. 1929; *Boyd's Shop*, pr., pb. 1936; *Robert's Wife*, pr. 1937, pb. 1938; *Private Enterprise*, pb. 1938, pr. 1947; *William John Mawhinney*, pr. 1940 (also as *Ballyfarland's Festival*, pr. 1953); *Friends and Relations*, pr. 1941, pb. 1947; *My Brother Tom*, pr., pb. 1952; *Esperanza*, pr. 1957.

Other literary forms

St. John Ervine was the author of several novels which were highly regarded in their day. His novels, such as *Mrs. Martin's Man* (1914) and *The Foolish Lovers* (1920), display the same strengths as the best of his plays—realism and clarity of design and structure. Ervine also wrote abrasive and controversial drama criticism for several newspapers. Finally, he was the author of several opinionated biographies of literary and public figures, including Oscar Wilde and George Bernard Shaw.

Achievements

Ervine holds an honorable place in the Irish Renaissance; as such, he is aligned with William Butler Yeats, Lady Augusta Gregory, and the Abbey Theatre. His greatest achievements are his early Irish plays, two of which, *Jane Clegg* and *John Ferguson*, have long been recognized as minor classics. After a brief time as manager of the Abbey Theatre followed by wartime military service, Ervine settled in England and was chosen as a member of the Irish Academy. He served as professor of dramatic literature for the Royal Society of Literature from 1933 through 1936. His critical theory supports his practice in his early plays: Dramatic value resides in the author's attempt to present real people dealing with believable human situations. Though he turned from playwriting to novels, criticism, and political and biographical essays, Ervine is best remembered as a spokesman for and practitioner of dramatic realism. His influence on a later generation of Irish playwrights, while indirect, may be seen in the continuation of the realistic tradition. Ervine serves as an exemplar of honest, realistic, economically plotted, straightforward playwriting.

Biography

St. John Greer Ervine was born in Belfast in Northern Ireland on December 28, 1883. He did not take a university degree but was writing plays by his twenty-fourth year. In 1911, he married Leonora Mary Davis and became associated with the Abbey Theatre in Dublin. He served for a brief time as manager of the Abbey Theatre, and, while in that capacity, produced his best play, *John Ferguson*. His British sympathies caused an estrangement between him and the theater players, and on May 29, 1916, the actors declared their unwillingness to work under Ervine's direction. The resultant break with the Abbey Theatre, combined with the escalation of World War I, led Ervine to turn away from Ireland and exclusively Irish subject matter. His service in a regiment of the British Household Battalion and, later, with the Royal Dublin Fusiliers ended in 1918, when he was severely wounded and suffered the loss of a leg.

After the war, Ervine settled in London. His first London success was in 1929, when his play, *The First Mrs. Fraser*, enjoyed an extended run; that success was repeated the next year in New York. His career expanded to include novels, essays on political and ethical subjects, drama criticism, and biographies. He was drama critic for *The Sunday Observer* of London, and in 1929, he was guest drama critic for *The World* in New York. His criticism was controversial, which is usually attributed to Ervine's plainspoken, even harsh criticism of American plays. His reputation for acerbity rests additionally upon his style: Abandoning his polished, sophisticated prose, he wrote in an approximation of a "Broadway" dialect; this caused at least as much outrage as his astringent critical judgments. Indeed, this choice of dialect seems to have been a mistake. As dialect, it is not accurate, and its use seems patronizing, even if that was not Ervine's intent.

After his return to London, Ervine served for three years as professor of dramatic literature for the Royal Society of Literature. His later plays, written after he left Ireland, are less serious than his early work. These later plays, written for a British audience, are sophisticated comedies of manners that rely on wit and topicality for their very considerable effect. Ervine's biographical subjects included men of letters such as Shaw and Wilde; William Booth, founder and General of the Salvation Army; and Lord Craigavon, the first prime minister of Ulster. His biographies reflect his literary, ethical, and political interests; they are partisan rather than objective, polemical rather than scholarly.

With the production of *William John Mawhinney* in 1940, Ervine renewed his association with the Abbey Theatre; one of his next plays, *Friends and Relations*, was produced at the Abbey Theatre in 1941. These were the last of Ervine's works to premiere at the Abbey Theatre, however, and in 1957, Ervine completed his theatrical career with the production of *Esperanza*.

Ervine died in 1971, at the age of eighty-seven, in a nursing home in Sussex.

Analysis

St. John Ervine's early Irish plays are his finest, displaying the strengths characteristic of his best work in all genres. *Mixed Marriage, Jane Clegg, John Ferguson,* and *The Ship* are uniformly serious in plot and theme, realistic in subject matter, and economical in structure. Ervine's virtues as a playwright are traditional ones; each play has a single, unified plot and an unambiguous, uncomplicated theme. Each play displays great economy of construction and a modest level of aspiration, and within this deliberately simple, unassuming framework, it succeeds because of certain very real strengths of structure and characterization.

In his drama criticism, Ervine's touchstone is economy. In every important way, the early plays illustrate that Ervine believed in and followed his own theory: Economy is not a negative value of limiting, cutting, and leaving out; it is, rather, a positive principle. Good theater, to Ervine, is that which exhibits restraint and simplicity in cast size, subject matter, plot line, dialogue, and characterization.

The casts, for example, are uniformly small. *John Ferguson* has the largest cast; there are eleven characters. *Jane Clegg* has seven; *The Ship*, eight; and *Mixed Marriage*, six. There are simply no minor characters whose dramatic function may be described as merely decorative. Every character is important and necessary to the development of the action of the play.

The action of each play is also dictated in part by Ervine's rule of economy. On a superficial level, his plays are devoid of luxuries such as tableau scenes, offstage voices, and unnecessary dramatic business. There is a minimum of exposition; for the most part, each play consists only of those events which are seen by the audience. The exposition in *John Ferguson*, for example, is limited to the information that the Fergusons are going to lose their farm unless they manage to pay the mortgage; the audience learns of the successive trials of John Ferguson's faith in a just God as Ferguson himself experiences them. The exposition in *Jane Clegg* is limited to the information that Henry Clegg has been unfaithful to his wife in the past. This immediacy of action is present in all the early plays. Nothing *has* happened; everything happens onstage during the course of the play.

The plays are all limited to a single plot, which is usually a familiar one and which is uniformly serious. Each of the long plays consists of a single story whose content is that of everyday life. *Jane Clegg* deals with the failure of a marriage, *John Ferguson* with the loss of a farm and the destruction of a family through violence. *The Ship* is a study of the lack of communication between a strong-willed father and his son. *Mixed Marriage* deals with the public forces which destroy the private romance of a Protestant boy and a Catholic girl. The stories are familiar ones, and Ervine does not alter his material so that it appears to be anything other than what it essentially is—newspaper realism, known territory to everyone. At the same time, there is always a single sustained idea which informs and illuminates the play.

The dialogue of Ervine's plays also exhibits his characteristic economy. The language of all the early plays is simple and easily understood and has as its function the furthering of the plot and the revelation of character. Dialogue, Ervine believed, should sound artlessly natural but should actually be an artful construct. None of Ervine's characters chatters aimlessly; no one repeats himself or leaves a sentence or thought unfinished. Ervine eliminates those parts of ordinary talk which would produce conversation rather than dialogue. Even when his characters are supposed to be merely making conversation, there is no excess. Each seemingly meaningless sentence is working to establish character. Again, the principle of economy is used as a positive force to shape an element of Ervine's plays.

The characters in Ervine's plays are, like his plots, familiar and instantly recognizable types, yet they are also extremely believable and vital. The character of Jane Clegg is strong and able to bear suffering; Rainey of *Mixed Marriage* and John Thurlow of *The Ship* are egotists. In each character, there is a single, prevailing element of personality, and each character becomes real and believable within his own "humor." The characters are drawn with little internal complexity; they are not cowardly *and* brave, but rather cowardly *or* brave. Like his dialogue, Ervine's characters appear to be natural but are in fact artful constructs.

One can appreciate Ervine's art most fully by examining the elements of plot and character in his early plays. In general, the plot is the weakest element of each play. All the plays have plots associated with melodrama. *John Ferguson* is the story of a family whose farm is lost to the evil landlord who forecloses, rapes the daughter, and is murdered by the son. *Jane Clegg* is the story of the strong, long-suffering wife who holds her family together while her husband loses her money, embezzles company funds, and finally runs away with a younger woman. *Mixed Marriage* deals with young lovers surrounded by the chaos of a strike which rapidly becomes a religious war; ultimately, the lovers are destroyed by the religious bigotry of the Protestant father. *The Ship* is the story of a strong-willed father who builds a ship that "God couldn't sink" and forces his son to sail on her maiden voyage. The son, who has refused to enter the family business, dies when the ship is sunk after colliding with an iceberg. The plots are both melodramatic and highly conventional; there are no surprising turns, no innovative twists in the action.

An important technique that Ervine used to control the response of the audience is one that is closely related to satire. Within the structure of the plot, there is always an explicit norm with which the audience can identify. The plots of the early plays make, in some way, an attack on stupidity, and there is usually a character who explicitly represents the sane, moral position of playwright and audience. Jane Clegg, John Ferguson, Old Mrs. Thurlow, and Mrs. Rainey are articulate spokespersons for the standards of good sense and morality. One recognizes the standard they offer and judges the other characters and the plot development by this explicit norm.

The plots of the four plays hinge upon dramatic irony of the simplest, most basic sort. John Ferguson's family is destroyed because his brother forgot to mail the money that would have saved the farm; Jack Thurlow dies because his father asks him to sail with the ship just this once. John Rainey loses his children because his religious prejudice is stronger than his desire to unite the Protestant and Catholic strikers.

Although the plots of these plays are simple and melodramatic, this is not a serious weakness in Ervine's art. Perhaps a playwright cannot create great drama from this material, but he can create great theater. Ervine asks his audience to respond in a rather uncomplicated, unsophisticated manner; he manages to get an audience, conditioned to dismiss plots of this nature as slight and hackneyed, to believe implicitly in his stories. The audience understands the familiar, unambiguous plots and themes, applauds the hero and hisses the villain, but not with the self-conscious condescension that one would bring to minstrel-show melodrama. The audience reacts in an unsophisticated way to the plays, but it reacts sincerely.

In large part, this response can be attributed to the vitality of Ervine's characters. His best characters are universal types: The audience recognizes the villainous landlord or the foolish, irritating mother-in-law with a shock of pleasure. Each character is also, within his type, absolutely individual.

Ervine is particularly good with certain types of characters. His villains are all lifelike and effective. They are of two types: the unpleasant little vermin such as Jimmy Caesar in *John Ferguson*, Henry Clegg and the racing tout, Munce, in *Jane Clegg*, and Captain Cornelius in *The Ship*; and the monster of evil, such as Witherow in *John Ferguson*. The villain Witherow has no redeeming qualities; he is unalterably evil. He is a brilliantly drawn one-dimensional character; the audience hates him and is appeased by his death.

Jimmy Caesar and the other little villains are villainous because they are weak and mean-spirited. They are more satisfactory characters than is Witherow because they are more complex, and the audience is able to despise them as well as hate them. They are all incapable of anything as large and important as a foreclosure or a rape. Their villainies are secret and unsavory; they are all cowards. Captain Cornelius is willing to accept money from John Thurlow in return for ruining Jack's farm; Munce is quite willing to ruin lives to get his money from Henry Clegg; Henry himself leaves his wife, children, and mother penniless for another woman and cannot understand why no one is terribly sorry to see him go. Jimmy Caesar, the most vividly drawn of the weak villains, is the unsavory suitor of Hannah Ferguson; he grovels at Witherow's feet, nauseates Hannah when he tries to kiss her, goes home to bed when he is supposedly avenging her honor, eats a hearty breakfast while he confesses his cowardice, and offers to marry Hannah even though her rape has made her "unworthy" of him.

In Mrs. Rainey, Old Mrs. Thurlow, and John Ferguson, Ervine creates strong, sympathetic moral characters. John Ferguson, for example, is uniformly good without being unrealistic. He is devout, gentle, and forgiving, yet, unlike many virtuous characters, absolutely convincing. His moments of doubt are canceled by his monumental Christian goodness and faith. He is a truly decent man who keeps his faith in a just God even as he mourns his ruined son and daughter. Like John Ferguson, Mrs. Rainey in *Mixed Marriage* is consistently good, tender and protective toward her sons, sensible and tolerant toward Michael O'Hara, their Catholic friend, and gentle with Nora, Hugh's girlfriend; most important, she manages to love her husband even though she has no respect for him and disapproves of his tenaciously held prejudices. Mrs. Rainey, Old Mrs. Thurlow, and John Ferguson are all voices of sanity in situations which have suddenly gone insane. Mrs. Rainey pleads for religious tolerance in the middle of a religious war; John Ferguson tries to love and protect the man who has taken his farm and raped his daughter; Old Mrs. Thurlow of *The Ship* tries to reconcile her son and grandson, and when Jack dies in his father's place, she comforts and encourages John Thurlow to continue to live with unchanged goals even though she believes him to be wrong.

St. John Ervine's early plays are good plays, strong and believable in their economy and in characters who force the viewer to accept plots that have become clichés. The deliberate simplicity of construction, the unity of tone and theme, the absolutely vital characters, make Ervine an important playwright. He is not great, but he is very good. His plays are not complex or difficult to understand; their value lies precisely in their accessibility and believability.

Other major works

NOVELS: *Francis Place, the Tailor of Charing Cross*, 1912; *Mrs. Martin's Man*, 1914; *Alice and a Family*, 1915; *The Foolish Lovers*, 1920; *The First Mrs. Fraser*, 1931 (novelization of his play); *Private Enterprise*, 1948.

NONFICTION: *The Organized Theatre: A Plea in Civics*, 1924; *Parnell*, 1925; *How to Write a Play*, 1928; *God's Soldier: General William Booth*, 1934; *The Christian and the New Morality*, 1940; *Oscar Wilde*, 1951; *Bernard Shaw: His Life, Work and Friends*, 1956.

Bibliography
Blythe, Ernest. *The Abbey Theatre*, 1963.
Ellis-Fermor, Una. *The Irish Dramatic Movement*, 1939.
Fay, Gerard. *The Abbey Theatre, Cradle of Genius*, 1958.
Hogan, Robert. *After the Irish Renaissance*, 1967.
_____. *"Since O'Casey" and Other Essays on Irish Drama*, 1983.
Howard, Paula. "St. John Ervine: A Bibliography of His Published Work," in *Irish Booklore*. I (August, 1971), pp. 203-207.
Kavanagh, Peter. *The Story of the Abbey Theatre*, 1950.
Robinson, Lennox. *Ireland's Abbey Theatre*, 1951.

Elizabeth Buckmaster

SIR GEORGE ETHEREGE

Born: Maidenhead(?), England; c. 1635
Died: Paris(?), France; c. May 10, 1692

Principal drama
The Comical Revenge: Or, Love in a Tub, pr., pb. 1664; *She Would if She Could*, pr., pb. 1668; *The Man of Mode: Or, Sir Fopling Flutter*, pr., pb. 1676.

Other literary forms
In addition to his drama, Sir George Etherege wrote poetry, collected and published posthumously in *The Poems* (1963). His correspondence is collected in *The Letterbook* (1928) and *Letters* (1973).

Achievements
In the amazingly vital and varied drama that developed, flourished, and faded in London within a few decades after the restoration of Charles II to the throne in 1660, the most important type was the so-called comedy of manners. The comedy of manners was characterized by strong contemporary realism, by resolution of the main plot in marriage, and by pairs of characters arranged in a hierarchy of wit, from the most witty down to the most foolish. In the Restoration drama, wit is determined in part by a person's ability to get his own way and in part by his social grace, best exemplified in the witty (meaning comic, ingenious, and psychologically astute) verbal duels with which the plays abound. It was Sir George Etherege's achievement to develop and define this distinctive Restoration form in *The Comical Revenge* and *She Would if She Could* and to bring it to full maturity in *The Man of Mode*.

Biography
Sir George Etherege's life resembled those of the wits, courtiers, and rakes who populated his plays. When he was born, his father had a small place at Court. In 1644, during the Civil War, when the queen escaped to France, Etherege's father followed her into exile, where he died in 1650. Etherege himself was probably reared by his grandfather in England, obtaining along the way a good education and an excellent knowledge of French. In 1654, he was appointed a clerk to George Goswold, an attorney at Beaconsfield. In 1668, *The Comical Revenge*, Etherege's first play, was performed at Lincoln's Inn Fields. It was well received, and Etherege's reputation was at once established. His next play, *She Would if She Could*, was performed at Lincoln's Inn Fields in 1668; although a better play than the first, it was poorly rehearsed and badly performed, and it fared very

poorly. By this time, Etherege was a member of the circle of courtiers and wits that included Sir Charles Sedley and the Earl of Rochester. He was made a Gentleman of the Privy Chamber and went, as secretary to the ambassador, to Constantinople. Etherege returned to London in 1671, and for the next few years he, along with the Earl of Rochester, was mixed up in several wild and rather unsavory scrapes, resulting in at least one death.

In 1676, *The Man of Mode* was performed at the Duke's Theatre in Dorset Garden. Remembering his earlier failure, Etherege was careful to have a first-class performance, with the top actors of the period playing the principal parts, particularly with Thomas Betterton, the most famous actor of his time, taking the role of Dorimant. This major play was, as it deserved to be, an enormous success. During this period, Etherege was knighted and then married a rich old widow, daughter of a London merchant. By 1683, he was rapidly squandering his wife's wealth on cards and dice at Locket's, a popular coffeehouse. He was offered a minor diplomatic post, under King James II, at the Diet of the Holy Roman Empire in Regensburg, Bavaria. He gladly accepted the appointment, possibly escaping heavy gambling debts in London and certainly leaving his unloved wife behind. He outraged and antagonized the staid and pompous German ministers there with his informal behavior. During this period, he carried on a large correspondence. Almost four hundred letters have been preserved, which give the best existing portrait of the life and thoughts of a Restoration playwright and wit. When James II was deposed in 1689, Etherege left his post to try to join him in France. Etherege died, possibly first converting to Roman Catholicism, in 1692.

Analysis

Sir George Etherege's first play, *The Comical Revenge*, has no discernible main plot. Rather, it has four more or less unconnected subplots. Three of the plots are derivative of earlier drama; the fourth constitutes Etherege's real contribution to dramatic form. The first of the derivative plots is the "heroic" plot, based no doubt on the romantic plays of Francis Beaumont and John Fletcher (still very popular during this period) and of Sir William Davenant. When the characters of this plot, with their characteristically romantic names, come onstage, the play's usual prose dialogue shifts to rhyming verse. The action in this subplot revolves around highly stylized conflicts between love and honor. Graciana and Lord Beaufort are madly in love; by mischance, however, Graciana's brother has told his best friend, Colonel Bruce, that Graciana will marry him. Colonel Bruce does not care particularly about Graciana, whom he has not met, but would like to be connected to the family of his best friend. Secretly, Graciana's sister Aurelia is madly in love with Bruce, but out of honor cannot tell him. When Colonel Bruce discovers that Beaufort might be his rival for

Graciana, he fights a duel with him, is disarmed, but is magnanimously given his life by Beaufort. Not to be outdone in honor, Bruce falls on his sword. As he lies grievously wounded, Graciana feels honor-bound to pretend to Beaufort that she never loved him but only led him on to test Bruce's love for her. She pledges to Bruce that if he survives she will marry him; if he dies, she will remain forever a virgin. At the last minute, everybody accidentally overhears everybody else confessing his and her true thoughts, all are overcome by how honorable all the rest are, and the right couples get together and live happily ever after.

The second plot is low farcical comedy of a kind to delight those who guffaw at dialect jokes and pratfalls. The humor is meant to come in part from the nearly unintelligible French accent of the servant, Dufoy ("Begar me vil havé de revengé"), and in part from his situation. He looks pale and unhealthy, and when people ask the cause, he claims he is languishing from unrequited love for Betty, a waiting woman. Actually, it soon comes out, he is languishing from a venereal disease. Betty, highly indignant when she discovers that he has been pretending to love her, locks him up in a wash-tub (the "comical revenge," or "love in a tub" of the title), providing opportunities for various farcical jokes. In the "happy ending," it appears that Dufoy and Betty actually *are* to get married. It is difficult to guess how boisterously audiences may have responded to this kind of comedy.

The third plot seems to derive from the comedy of Ben Jonson, or perhaps of Thomas Middleton. It involves Sir Nicholas Cully, who, as his name suggests, is a gull waiting to be swindled. He falls into the clutches of Wheadle and Palmer, two con artists; thinking all the time that he is the one who is doing the swindling, Cully gets the treatment he deserves. What separates this plot from the first two is its astonishing, almost documentary realism: The language of the street plays against the absurdly elevated "torments" and "despair" of the heroic scenes and the theatrically conventional burlesque French accent of Dufoy. For example, Wheadle and Palmer, having maneuvered Cully into a tavern to play cards, want to shift from the public table where they are seated to a back-room table, where they can cheat their victim in private. Finding a pretext for this move, one of them says, "this table is so wet, there's no playing upon it." That may be the first time in the history of the drama that a character mentions something so homely and realistic as the wetness of a table that has had several glasses and bottles sitting on it.

The fourth plot, which in the play gets no more emphasis than the other three, constitutes Etherege's major contribution to Restoration drama and was to become the central plot of his two comedies to follow. It involves Sir Frederick Frollick, a young rake and gallant and wit about town. Audiences were no doubt accustomed to the nonspecific, timeless settings of William Shakespeare, to the remote and imaginary settings of the romantic plays of Beaumont and Fletcher. Suddenly, Sir Frederick walks in off the very London streets the playgoers themselves have just quitted to see this play. The language he speaks is their language; the class to which he belongs is theirs. His conversation is topical. He is indeed a sad young rake, keeping his wench, intriguing with dozens of women, drinking, carousing, fighting, breaking windows, and otherwise tearing about. He is also, at least to a degree, witty, fashionable, and genteel. As the wealthy widow he is chasing throughout the play admits, he is "the prettiest, wittiest, wildest gentleman about the town." Having gone through his fortune, he must court and wed the widow to mend his estate, as Etherege himself was to do a few years later.

The play as a whole is not memorable. Except for the moments of fine realism in the swindling scenes, the motivation for actions and the conflicts to be overcome are all weakly contrived. The four plots are but faintly connected. At the end, all the players—servants, whores, swindlers, rakes, and romantic lovers—are improbably brought onstage together in a mass marriage ceremony. With the exception of this unlikely event, they could as easily have been in separate plays.

Still, the play contained important innovations, and Etherege, shrewdly observing his audience, must have seen their delight and response to his contemporary rake speaking their language, frequenting the same places of pleasure as they did. He must also have recognized his facility in rendering such a character (so like himself) and his witty language. He made such characters the center of his subsequent plays, wisely phasing out the other subplots or, rather, disguising, shifting, and transforming them until they were no longer recognizable, serving instead as underpinnings to his main plot.

Etherege's second play, *She Would if She Could*, is a considerable refinement upon *The Comical Revenge*. The structure is clearer, simpler, the actions more logically motivated. Three plotlines are discernible, but one of these is clearly the major plot, and the two minor plots are closely integrated with it, supporting its actions and commenting on it thematically. Most important, in the play as a whole, the contrast between the Truewit and the Witwoud, or would-be wit, has become central, setting the pattern for the great comedies of manners of the period.

The Witwouds are at the center of the two minor plots. In one subplot, Sir Oliver Cockwood is a "country knight." In the social geography of the Restoration stage, the courtiers, rakes, and the stylish and witty women all live in the "town," the fashionable West End of London. The "city" is the commercial part of London, where the "cits," the much despised middle class, live. Worst of all, however, is the country. For the wits, the chief pleasures in life were found in association with town and court: the coffeehouses, the playhouses, the pleasure resorts, the fashionable clothing. The severest penance, therefore, would be to live in the country, where every-thing is several years out of date, where the only diversion is going for long walks. Witty young people forced to live in the country by cruel parents who do not trust them among the seductions of London are justified in using any means to escape to the town. Older people from the country are automatically assumed to be foolish and out of fashion.

Sir Oliver Cockwood is typical of the country knights. His name, to begin with, is appropriate (the "wood" having the sense of "would-be"), since his annoyed wife charges that he is impotent. If he stayed in the country, got drunk every night, and hunted foxes during the day, no one would object to him. His fault is that he has come to town to spark it like a young rake and to boast of all of his amorous adventures. He spends most of his time running away from his wife to make ineffectual dates with prostitutes. He becomes a comic butt because of his pretensions to being a man of honor (that is, a duelist and a lover) when he is actually timid and impotent.

In the other subplot, his wife, Lady Cockwood, is equally well named, though with an opposite signification. She tries to make assignations with any young man who will look at her. The problem is that she also wants to maintain her reputation for honor and virtue. She becomes a comic butt because of her pretensions to being modest and chaste, when it is obvious to everyone that she would readily be unchaste if she could. Interestingly, Lady Cockwood's language is a burlesqued echo of the heroic or romantic scenes of *The Comical Revenge*. Her dialogue is filled with such words as "honor," "ruined," "undone," "betrayed," and "false," but with the mean-ings comically reversed. If a young rake fails to keep his assignation with her, he is "wicked." If he finally does show up to commit adultery with her, "truly he is a person of much worth and honor."

The subplots in which these foolish persons partake, by giving examples of Witwouds—failed Truewits—provide a backdrop against which the Truewits of the main plot can be measured. These Truewits are the young men Courtall and Freeman and the young women Gatty and Ariana. The young men are considerable refinements upon Sir Frederick Frollick of *The Comical Revenge*. For example, Frollick's idea of courtship is to get drunk and go to his lady's window in the wee hours of the morning to shout out ribald suggestions to her. He marries at the end a wealthy widow, behavior that Etherege himself was not above. Courtall is above it. He is much more self-assured than Frollick and has his drives, emotions, and true feelings absolutely under control—an important sign of the Truewit. Losing con-trol, however, and thus putting himself at the mercy of others, is the un-mistakable sign of the Witwoud. Courtall needs to marry a rich heiress but will not consider a widow. His wife, in addition to being rich, must also be young, beautiful, as witty as he, and untouched by other men.

Of particular interest in this play are the roles of the female characters. Lady Cockwood is an archetypal character—the lustful woman—who has appeared in both comedy and tragedy from the classical drama onward. Etherege, however, makes specific Restoration uses of her. She is made comic by her pretension to heroic virtue and by the fact that she has so little control of her emotions that she gives herself away at every word. By the lights of the Restoration society, she is not wrong in wishing to have a reputation for chastity, for without such a reputation a woman was lost (with the exception of mistresses of high royalty). At the same time, she was not wrong to possess sexual desire, for women, in this realistic society, were allowed to have at least moderate appetites. She was wrong, and therefore comic, in her extreme pretension of virtue, in her extreme libidinousness, and in her consequent inability to control herself. Control of self was highly valued in Restoration theater because only through self-control, so it was believed, could one's external world be controlled. The world of Restoration theater is one in which a person must control himself or be controlled. Courtall, for example, by pretending to be interested in her, used Lady Cockwood in order to gain access to Gatty and Ariana, who are staying in her house, and then uses her desire to save her reputation to fend her off. He fends her off, interestingly, because her overeagerness has rendered her undesirable.

Gatty and Ariana represent the feminine witty ideal. Envious of the men for their freedom (which the women cannot have, for reputation is important), they decide, while resolving "to be mighty honest" to have as much fun as circumstances will allow. They put on masks (very popular at the time) to disguise their identities, and go strolling in the fashionable Mulberry Garden in hopes of flirting innocently with some handsome and witty men. Though the men whom they encounter (Courtall and Freeman) are tremendously attractive to them, the women easily fend them off with witty conversation and a dissembling of their emotions. This response does not mean that they lack emotions, for in private they admit to each other how much the men tempt them. As Gatty says to Ariana: "I hate to dissemble when I need not. 'Twould look as affected in us to be reserved now we're alone as for a player to maintain the character she acts in the tiring [dressing] room." The scene is in direct contrast with the scene in which Lady Cockwood sends out her maid to pimp for her, and then scolds her (even though they are in private) for doing so.

She Would if She Could, in short, is a didactic play, suggesting which emotions, which pretenses, which modes of behavior are proper—that is, witty—and which are not. The modern theatergoer, losing sight of this and responding to the play as simply a realistic social document, can misinterpret it in certain ways, seeing cruelty, for example, where a Restoration theatergoer would see a didactic point being made.

The finest thing of all in *She Would if She Could* is the witty love dialogue between Courtall and Freeman and the two women. Their first encounter is quite delightful. The girls, in their masks, are strolling through the Mulberry Garden. When Courtall and Freeman see them, they immediately set out after them, planning to engage them in witty repartee, but the women, who have been brought up in the country, are such swift walkers that the men are soon panting and puffing, quite unable to overtake them. Freeman says, "Whatever faults they have, they cannot be broken-winded."

When the men finally do catch up, the women are equally nimble verbally. When the men insist on kissing their hands, Ariana says, "Well, I am not the first unfortunate woman that has been forced to give her hand where she never intends to bestow her heart." They part, agreeing to meet again the next day, each side immensely pleased with the other (though of course the women have not admitted their feelings). The jealous Lady Cockwood, hoping to win the two men for herself, starts a rumor that the men have spoken slightingly of Gatty's and Ariana's honor. The next time Gatty and Ariana meet with the innocent and unsuspecting men, their witty banter suddenly has real bite and sting to it. The men, puzzled by the shift in tone, scarcely know how to reply. The dialogue is wonderfully witty; at the same time, it is subtly and dramatically revelatory of the inner states of the characters.

Etherege's last play, *The Man of Mode*, is in every respect a major work and remains the central document of Restoration comedy. The brilliant opening act is so relaxed and casual as to seem like a slice of life rather than the first act of a tightly constructed play. A minor poet of the time even alluded to Etherege as "one that does presume to say,/ A plot's too gross for any play." Such an impression is deceptive, however, for every word in the first act carefully defines characters and sets up the complex chain of events to follow. On the surface, the first act is a very naturalistic presentation of Dorimant (whose name suggests "the gift of love") in the morning. He is composing a letter to his current mistress, whose suggestive name is Loveit. When his friend Medley drops in on him, it emerges in conversation between them that he is tired of Loveit and wants to break off with her so he can begin with a new girl, Bellinda. He plans to use Bellinda in his plot to break with Loveit, who is passionately jealous; Bellinda will call on her just before Dorimant is expected to arrive, and will insinuate that Dorimant has been seeing someone else. Dorimant will walk in, and Loveit, who has no control of her emotions, will fall on him in a passion; he will then instantly break with her and stalk out. While Dorimant is recounting his plot to Medley, an old woman selling fruit arrives at his door. She is, in addition, a bawd who keeps a watchful eye out for young women in whom young men might be interested. She brings information to Dorimant that an extremely beautiful and wealthy heiress has come to town and has seen Dorimant and is attracted to him. The woman's name is Harriet, and she has been brought to town from the country by her mother, Lady Woodvill. Dorimant immediately begins plotting to get to know her. Young Bellair, another friend, drops in, and Medley and Dorimant begin teasing him about his coming marriage to Emilia. Marriage, to the young rakes, is nearly equivalent to suicide, as it means the end of their bachelor freedom and a limitation on their openly chasing after new mistresses. Young Bellair is in love and takes their teasing lightly. Then they discuss Sir Fopling Flutter, newly arrived in town from a long stay in Paris. Fopling wants desperately to be a true-wit, but he is in every way the opposite of Dorimant. Where Dorimant dresses well, Fopling dresses extravagantly. Where Dorimant has several affairs, Fopling strives only for the reputation of having several affairs. Where Dorimant is casually witty and literate, Fopling works hard to achieve these graces, even affecting a French accent (the last lingering echo of Dufoy in *The Comical Revenge*) to let everyone know he has been abroad. Dorimant decides to use him in his plot to break with Loveit: He will pretend to be jealous himself, and charge her with chasing after Fopling.

At this point, a messenger calls Young Bellair outside the room, and while he is out, Dorimant confesses to Medley that he has encouraged Young Bellair to marry Emilia. Dorimant has tried in the past to seduce her, with no luck. He thinks that once she is married and no longer needs to worry about her maidenhood, she will be more accessible to him. Young Bellair comes back in with the news that his father, Old Bellair, is in town. The father, not knowing anything about Emilia, has conspired with Lady Woodvill to arrange a marriage between Young Bellair and Harriet. If Young Bellair does not agree to the marriage, he will lose his inheritance. Young Bellair leaves in distress. As a last bit of business in the act, before Dorimant and Medley go off to dine, Dorimant receives a note from a former girlfriend fallen on hard times and sends her some money.

No brief summary can hope to render the quality of this act, one of the finest things in Restoration drama. The witty repartee, the different levels of language, the naturalness, all make it a virtuoso performance, but one should not lose sight of the function of the act in terms of the unfolding action of the play. First, it has introduced Dorimant, the main character. He is witty, relaxed, capable of dealing with all social classes on their own terms, shamefully indulgent of his servants, most of whom have not yet got out of bed by the end of the act. At the same time, he is the supreme gallant, with, as Medley says of him, "more mistresses now depending" than the most eminent lawyer in England has cases. The audience sees abundant proof of this. In the course of one morning, he is forming plans to cast off one mistress, Loveit, as he begins to close with a new one, Bellinda, and tries to get Emilia married off in hopes that matrimony will make her more vulnerable to him. At the same time, he is already beginning to think ahead to Harriet, whom he has not even met, and, at last, sends money to a girlfriend from sometime in the past. The audience also gets an insight into Dorimant's *modus operandi*. He thinks in terms of power plays and manipulation. People, to him, are to be used: He employs the fruiterer to bring him information of new beauties come to town; he uses his mistress-to-be to help him break off with Loveit; he uses Young Bellair to make Emilia more accessible; he plans to use Fopling also in his plot to rid himself of Loveit. He states his attitude more baldly in a later scene: "You mistake the use of fools, they are designed for properties and not for friends." In this respect, almost all are fools to Dorimant.

In addition to Dorimant, the first act introduces the audience to two other major characters, Medley and Young Bellair, and gives capsule profiles to prepare the audience in advance for seeing the other important characters: Loveit, Fopling, Old Bellair, Lady Woodvill, and Harriet. Finally, the groundwork is laid for the main action of the play, Dorimant's pursuit of Harriet, and for the four subplots: Dorimant's breaking off with Loveit; his coming to terms with his new mistress, Bellinda; Young Bellair's attempt to marry the woman he loves without being disinherited; and the fun they will all have with the foolish Sir Fopling Flutter, especially when Dorimant tries to foist him off on Loveit.

The play now unrolls quickly. Old Bellair meets Emilia and, not knowing she is his son's fiancée, begins chasing her himself. She humors him in his infatuation, hoping it will help later when she confesses her love for his son. In the meantime, Young Bellair has met Harriet. Harriet has no intention of marrying him but has only pretended to go along with the match as an excuse to get out of the country and come to London. She and Young Bellair act out a courtship for the sake of their parents, in order to buy time. At the proper moment, Young Bellair and Emilia sneak off and get married. They fall on their knees before Old Bellair, and he is prevailed upon to give them his blessing. He cannot say his son has made a bad choice, since it was the choice he was thinking of making himself. In the meantime, Dorimant's plans go off almost but not quite perfectly. Loveit rages at him jealously, and he storms off, charging her with chasing after Fopling. Bellinda is timid but at last submits to a meeting with him in his room, but Loveit is suspicious and almost catches Bellinda in the act, so that Bellinda would have lost her reputation on her very first fall from grace. She cleverly talks her way out of being discovered but vows never to take such a chance again. Dorimant, though charging Loveit with receiving Fopling's advances (as an excuse for dropping her), still wants her to spurn Fopling publicly, thus showing that he holds complete power even over a cast-off mistress. He even brings Medley along to be a witness of Fopling's discomfiture. Loveit, however, realizing that Dorimant is using her, greets Fopling with open arms and walks off with him. Medley jibes: "Would you had brought some more of your friends, Dorimant, to have been witnesses of Sir Fopling's disgrace and your triumph." Dorimant begs Medley not to tell everyone for a few days, to give him a chance to make amends. He wants his reputation as a perfect manipulator of women to remain intact. In the meantime, Dorimant has met Harriet, and they have a duel of brilliant repartee, almost like the love song of two wary but amorous birds of prey. The final scene shows Dorimant in high gear, running from woman to woman, keeping all bridges unburned. First, he convinces Loveit that he is courting Harriet only for her fortune, as he has gone through his own inheritance, and that he will come back to her as soon as he can. She is sufficiently satisfied to snub Fopling publicly the next time he enters—and Medley declares Dorimant's reputation clear. Dorimant convinces Bellinda that she should take another chance with him, keeps his lines of communication open with Emilia, and gains permission from Lady Woodvill to pay his court to Harriet. A marriage seems in the offing, but it has not happened by the end of the play, and Dorimant is still free to go in any direction he chooses.

It is a play, then, in which a vain, arrogant man, renowned for his deceptions, seductions, cruel manipulations, and constant infidelities, has by the end achieved the admiration of all the men, has all the women at his beck, and has the prospect of a rich, witty, beautiful young girl's hand in marriage. It may seem a considerable leap to maintain that *The Man of Mode* is a didactic play (even liberated modern audiences have difficulty with the morality of the play), but such it is. Although courtship is at the center of Restoration drama, *The Man of Mode* and similar masterpieces of the period are not romantic works; on the contrary, they are cynically realistic. The plays abound with cautionary examples of bad marriages—marriages inappropriately arranged by parents, resulting in spouses who detest each other, are rude to each other in public, and betray each other at every chance—or, at the other extreme, "love" matches in which neither partner has any money, condemned to sink into sordidness. The appropriate marriage is one in which at least one of the partners has enough money to make them both comfortable for life (since a gentleman, by definition, does not work for a living) and the partners are so perfectly matched in wit and attractiveness that they can continue to be interesting and exciting to each other even after the novelty of the chase is over. It is a serious and realistic business, and a misstep has the lifetime repercussion of an unhappy marriage. That is why this drama can be so ruthless and competitive. The stakes are high. The good-natured, trusting person is the one who will be exploited; the shrewd, perceptive person has the best chance of winning.

Since accurate judgment of one's partner is of the utmost importance in this dangerous game, part of the didactic purpose of the play is to serve as a sort of field guide to help the audience tell true-wit from would-be wit—and, of course, through poking fun at the fools and fops, to laugh members of the audience out of any foolishness or foppery they may have acquired. With these practical purposes in mind, the Restoration comedy of manners, by its end, will have arranged the characters into a hierarchy from the most witty—in other words, most desirable (if most dangerous)—down to the least witty (or most to be reviled and mocked).

An examination of the hierarchy of wit in *The Man of Mode* will demonstrate how complex and subtle this ranking can be. The characters are divided, first, into young characters and old characters, and the audience is asked to judge each character according to the behavior appropriate to his station in life. Dorimant is obviously at the top of the pecking order among the young men. He is the cleverest and wittiest in speech, he dresses in perfect taste, he is the most perceptive in judging the motives and the weaknesses of others yet the most astute in concealing his own. Another essential quality is his "malice." His pleasure in manipulating others and triumphing over them—which can seem so ugly to modern audiences—is the very quality that gives him the competitive edge over others.

Young Bellair is next in the pecking order. He is attractive and clever, and some modern audiences prefer him to Dorimant. That is to miss the point. In Dorimant's accurate summation: "He's handsome, well-bred, and by much the most tolerable of all the young men that do not abound in wit." Young Bellair's crippling defect is that he has not as much malice as Dorimant, so he does not disguise his emotions, being genuinely in love with Emilia. Because of his lack of malice, he is unsuspicious of malice in others, and Dorimant, pretending friendship, is using him. In the play's most cruel—if most realistic and psychologically astute—line, Dorimant says that, since he has been unable to seduce Emilia, he is encouraging the marriage between her and Young Bellair because "I have known many women make a difficulty of losing a maidenhead, who have afterwards made none of making a cuckold."

Sir Fopling Flutter obviously finishes last. With his Frenchified language and excessively fashionable clothing, he is the laughingstock of the town. He attempts to maintain a reputation as a lover, but all the characters easily see through him, and correctly so, for underneath, he appears to be all but sexless. Dorimant has an easy time making Fopling a tool in his plot to cast off Loveit.

Harriet is at the top of the pecking order of the young women. She is the wittiest in dialogue, the most handsomely yet naturally dressed, and, as the characters admiringly point out, she is as full of malice—of pleasure in using and abusing others—as Dorimant. Although she has been described and discussed throughout the play, Etherege, for dramatic effect, does not allow her to appear onstage until the third act. That act is a replay of the first act, as Harriet rises in the morning, the scene almost point for point paralleling the first, to underline what an even and perfect match Dorimant and Harriet are. She is constantly on guard against him, and so she is the only female who can resist him, meaning, at the end, the only one who might possibly get him in marriage.

Emilia, Young Bellair's fiancée, is next in line. Like Young Bellair, her single failing is that she has not enough malice, and for that reason, she is not suspicious enough of it in others. Like Young Bellair, she is sufficiently clever to make use of Old Bellair and Lady Woodvill to get them into a position to agree to the marriage between her and Young Bellair, but again like Young Bellair, she is no match for Dorimant. She is second in the pecking order because, by play's end, she still has not been seduced by Dorimant, but she is clearly in danger. When Bellinda tries to warn her that Dorimant is not to be trusted, she innocently disputes this, saying he is a completely good, trustworthy man—thus indicating that she has her guard down.

Bellinda is third, because she has let Dorimant seduce her. Still, she is shrewd, clever, and witty enough to keep herself from being found out by the others, so she has, for the time being, preserved her reputation. Loveit is last because, unable to control her jealous passions, she has let everyone in town know that she is having an affair with Dorimant. It is her lack of self-control that has allowed Dorimant to work his will on her to begin with, and to continue triumphing over her even after he has cast her off. An outward sign of her lack of wit is in her language. Instead of the repartee of the others, she speaks in the exaggerated tones of the heroic lovers of *The Comical Revenge*: "Traitor! . . . Ingrateful perjured man!"

What is the proper role for the older characters, who are beyond the courtship stage of their lives? Medley and Lady Townley are good examples. They do not come forward and obtrude their advice where it is not wanted, but help out the young lovers when they are asked and generally provide the gracious and civilized background against which the young people play out their courtship. They also—somewhat like a Greek chorus—keep track of the young people's reputations and make judgments (which young ladies' reputations are unblemished, which are in danger, which young men are the most perfect gallants with women). The negative examples of the older characters are Old Bellair and Lady Woodvill, who both feel that they can choose marriage partners for their children and yet whose language immediately marks them as so far behind the times, so out of touch socially, that they would make disastrous choices. Luckily, however, they are also so socially inept that the young people manipulate them easily.

The Man of Mode suggests that self-interest—Dorimant's "malice"—is necessary to the successful functioning of society. In a reaction against this Restoration worldview in the eighteenth century, later playwrights left out the cruelty and malice in their dramas of courtship. The result was sentimental theater, frankly unrealistic. Remove Dorimant and Harriet from the play, and Young Bellair and Emilia come to the top of the pecking order. Like them, the sentimental dramas of the eighteenth century are "tolerable" but do not "abound with wit."

Other major works

POETRY: *The Poems*, 1963.

NONFICTION: *The Works of Sir George Etherege Containing His Plays and Poems*, 1704; *The Works of Sir George Etherege*, 1888 (A. W. Verity, editor); *The Letterbook*, 1928; *Letters*, 1973.

Bibliography

Brett-Smith, H. F. B. "Introduction," in *The Dramatic Works of Sir George Etherege*, 1927.

Hume, Robert D. *The Development of English Drama in the Late Seventeenth Century*, 1976.

Mann, David O. *Sir George Etherege: A Reference Guide*, 1981.

Underwood, Dale. *Etherege and the Seventeenth Century Comedy of Manners*, 1957.

Norman Lavers

GEORGE FARQUHAR

Born: Londonderry, Ireland; 1678(?)
Died: London, England; late May, 1707

Principal drama

Love and a Bottle, pr. 1698, pb. 1699; *The Constant Couple: Or, A Trip to the Jubilee*, pr. 1699, pb. 1700; *Sir Harry Wildair, Being the Sequel of a Trip to the Jubilee*, pr., pb. 1701; *The Inconstant: Or, The Way to Win Him*, pr., pb. 1702 (adaptation of John Fletcher's play *The Wild Goose Chase*); *The Twin Rivals*, pr. 1702, pb. 1703; *The Stage Coach*, pr., pb. 1704 (with Peter Anthony Motteux; adaptation of Jean de La Chapelle's play *Les Carosses d'Orléans*); *The Recruiting Officer*, pr., pb. 1706; *The Beaux' Stratagem*, pr., pb. 1707.

Other literary forms

George Farquhar wrote a few short poems, one long occasional poem entitled *Barcellona* (1710), numerous prologues and epilogues for plays, a short novel called *The Adventures of Covent Garden* (1698), and one miscellany entitled *Love and Business* (1702), besides contributing letters to two other miscellanies.

Achievements

Farquhar was one of the most popular dramatists at the end of the Restoration period. His success is illustrated by the number of prologues and epilogues he was asked to write for other plays, and by his contributions to popular miscellanies such as *Familiar and Courtly Letters* (1700) and *Letters of Wit, Politicks, and Morality* (1701). The popularity of his plays with actors, particularly *The Beaux' Stratagem* and *The Recruiting Officer*, accounted in no small measure for their survival during the eighteenth century and has played a large part in their continued visibility in the twentieth century.

Farquhar's skill in modifying typical Restoration themes and characters accounted for much of the success of his work. He reintroduced a significant degree of realism into drama and used topical issues for comic effect. Although classed among the Restoration playwrights, he stands somewhat apart from them in his craftsmanship and his philosophy of drama, showing greater variety of plot and depth of feeling. In his later work, he sought to reconcile the liberal sexual attitudes of early comedy of manners with the more severe, increasingly moralistic tone of the early eighteenth century. He thus produced a type of comedy that stands between the traditional Restoration comedy of wit and the later sentimental comedy.

The influence of Farquhar's approach to comedy is most apparent not in the work of succeeding dramatists (although Oliver Goldsmith reveals an indebtedness to Farquhar, particularly in *She Stoops to Conquer*, pr., pb. 1773), but in the novels of Henry Fielding, both in terms of sense of humor and breadth of social milieu. Oddly enough, Farquhar was to exert a considerable influence on the development of eighteenth century German drama, mainly as a result of Gotthold Ephraim Lessing's great enthusiasm for him. His continued influence on the history of German theater is displayed in the work of a major twentieth century dramatist, Bertolt Brecht.

Biography

Many traditions and legends have developed around the sparse facts known about the life of George Farquhar. The earliest documented evidence is contained in the records of Trinity College, which list him as entering in July, 1694, at the age of seventeen, establishing his year of birth as either 1677 or 1678. These records also note Londonderry, Ireland, as his place of birth, and Walker as the name of his previous teacher. Farquhar entered Trinity College, presumably to study for the Church, with a sizarship which entitled him to an allowance of bread and ale in return for serving duties. He won a scholarship less than a year after entering. This four pounds a year was suspended for a time, however, because of his riotous behavior at the Donnybrook Fair. Sometime after February, 1696, he left Trinity without taking a degree.

Not long after, Farquhar became an actor at the Smock Alley Theatre, the only theater in Dublin. His not particularly successful career as an actor ended after he wounded a fellow player in a duel scene, having forgotten to use a blunted foil. It was supposedly on the advice of his friend Robert Wilks, who was later to become one of the most popular actors on the London stage, that Farquhar went to London, probably in 1697, to write plays. *Love and a Bottle*, his first play, was produced at the Theatre Royal in Drury Lane in December, 1698. It reportedly ran for nine nights, a successful debut for the young playwright. That same month, a pamphlet entitled *The Adventures of Covent Garden* appeared anonymously. It has been attributed with some certainty to Farquhar on the basis of hints in the preface, the technique of the writer, and the fact that one of the poems appears in a later text, this time signed by Farquhar.

About a year later, again at Drury Lane, *The Constant Couple* was performed, which Farquhar later described as drawing some fifty audiences in a five-month period. Robert Wilks, who had probably joined the company at Farquhar's request, was immensely popular as Sir Harry, and another actor gained the lifelong nickname of "Jubilee Dicky" as a result of the play. Suddenly, Farquhar had become the most popular dramatist in London.

Between 1700 and 1703, three more plays appeared, all relatively unsuccessful: *Sir Harry Wildair*, a sequel to *The Constant Couple*; *The Incon-stant*, an adaptation of John Fletcher's *The Wild Goose Chase* (pr. 1621, pb. 1652); and *The Twin Rivals*. Sometime between the fall of 1700 and the spring of 1702, a date earlier than the once-proposed 1704, Farquhar—in collaboration with Peter Anthony Motteux—adapted Jean de La Cha-pelle's *Les Carosses d'Orléans* into a farce entitled *The Stage Coach*. The authors probably did not make much money from it, since one-act plays could not stand alone on a program. Adding to his increasing financial dif-ficulties, Farquhar was married, probably in 1703, to Margaret Pemell, a widow by whom he was to have two daughters. Knowing that Farquhar needed money, Pemell tricked him into marriage by having rumors spread that she was an heiress.

During the period from 1704 to 1706, Farquhar did not stage any plays. In 1704, he received a lieutenancy from the Earl of Orrery's Regiment of Foot, which was sent for service in Ireland. This commission assured him of a small yearly income of about fifty pounds. He was soon sent into west-ern England on a recruiting campaign. In 1705, he wrote his poem *Bar-cellona* on the occasion of the taking of that city by the Earl of Peterbor-ough; the poem was not published until after his death. It was also in 1705, supposedly during a stay at the Raven Inn while recruiting at Shrewsbury, that *The Recruiting Officer* was written. In the spring of 1706, this play was an overwhelming success, first at Drury Lane, then at the Queen's Theatre when some of the Drury Lane players moved to the new rival company.

Despite this success, Farquhar still seems to have had financial difficul-ties. In the fall or winter of 1706, he sold his commission to pay his debts, reportedly after a promise by the Duke of Ormonde that he would obtain for him another commission. This promise apparently came to nothing. In the meantime, Farquhar became ill. Wilks, seeking him out after an absence from the theater, advised him to write a new play and loaned him twenty guineas. The result was *The Beaux' Stratagem*, written in six weeks during his continued illness. The new play, produced in March, 1707, proved to be another success.

The register of St. Martin's in the Fields lists Farquhar's funeral, paid for by Wilks, on May 23, 1707, although his death must have occurred a few days earlier, rather than on the traditionally accepted date, that of the third performance of *The Beaux' Stratagem* in April. He may have died of tuberculosis.

Analysis

In general, past criticism of George Farquhar's plays has centered on two basic areas: finding possible autobiographical references in both characters and settings, and comparing Farquhar's moral attitudes to those of previous Restoration dramatists. In fact, many critics view Farquhar as the harbinger of the eighteenth century sentimental comedy. Both these views fail to deal adequately with Farquhar's artistic development of comedy. Unlike the writers of previous Restoration drama and subsequent sentimental comedy, Farquhar presents a balanced view of man and an equal appeal to the intellect and the emotions. His notion of the proper function of comedy, as expressed in a letter entitled "A Discourse upon Comedy" from *Love and Business*, includes the responsibility to portray the times accurately; the playwright's diversions must be realistic if he is also to carry out his task of instruction. Following these ideas, Farquhar produced drama which rests at some point of balance between the earlier cynical, witty comedy of manners and the later melodramatic sentimental comedy. Thematic development, dramatic conflict, and sources of comedy in Farquhar's three most popular plays—*The Constant Couple, The Recruiting Officer*, and *The Beaux' Stratagem*—illustrate his philosophy of comedy.

The Constant Couple is characterized by a light, often farcical atmosphere centered on situational comedy which instructs both by positive and by negative example. The efforts of several of the characters to attend the Jubilee in Rome gave the play a topical flavor.

Farquhar's habit of sustaining dramatic tension by action rather than by dialogue is a primary characteristic of *The Constant Couple*. The main actions center on Lady Lurewell, Colonel Standard, Sir Harry Wildair, and Angelica Darling, whose names alone suggest positive and negative examples. Angelica virtuously rejects a hypocritical suitor in the beginning, quickly establishing her character. In revenge, this suitor, appropriately named Vizard, tells Sir Harry that Angelica is a prostitute. Sir Harry, who has followed Lady Lurewell from Europe in hopes of a conquest, makes several humorous attempts to solicit Angelica's services; the best he can do is to look foolish and to hum when he discovers his mistake. Meanwhile, Lady Lurewell is involved in making all of her would-be lovers pay for the trickery of a man who seduced her at a young age. Her revenge takes the form of getting her suitors into foolish, farcical situations. Sir Harry finally abandons his wooing of Lady Lurewell to marry Angelica, and Standard is revealed as Lady Lurewell's seducer, who has been faithful to his previous engagement with her. All potentially sentimental situations, such as the reconciliation of Lady Lurewell and Standard, are short and factual rather than long and emotional.

Another aspect of *The Constant Couple* that is typical of Farquhar's plays is his modification of the usual Restoration characters. Sir Harry is not the stereotyped rake, cool and polished, living by his wit alone. Above all, he is good-natured and full of contradictions. He has been a good soldier, but he avoids a duel. He loves fashion as well as French phrases.

In *The Recruiting Officer*, typical Restoration characters and themes are similarly modified. The action centers on recruiting antics and the difficulties of the relationships of two couples: Plume and Sylvia, and Worthy and Melinda. At the play's end, both couples plan to be married. This theme of marriage, a typical Restoration theme, is a common motif in the play, but marriage is no longer a loveless relationship with both parties finding pleasure in affairs. Much of the play is devoted to the growing companionship between Plume and Silvia. This marriage, unlike the marriages in earlier Restoration drama, is not for money alone.

Farquhar's characters are also modified from the previous extremes of the Restoration. Farquhar's fop figure, Brazen, who has hopes of marrying Melinda, represents a fragmentation of the usual Restoration fop. Brazen has none of the typical clothes and affectations of the Restoration fop, and much less of the foolish gullibility. Farquhar instead takes the social qualities of a fop, exaggerates them, and fits them into a military atmosphere. Brazen's bragging, traditional for the fop, encompasses the world of battle and the world of the beau. The social memory and name-dropping tendency of a fop are exaggerated; it is precisely these characteristics of Brazen which leave him open to ridicule by other characters within the play.

The rake figure also undergoes modification in *The Recruiting Officer*. Plume asks the country girl, Rose, to his lodging not to debauch her, but to get her to aid in his recruiting, his main area of manipulation. Plume has a definite share of kindness and good nature. He provides for the subsistence of his bastard and provides a husband for the mother. He releases the disguised Silvia from her enlistment because he values an obligation to her father above money. Plume's dialogue has its share of wit, but it also reveals his fundamentally kind nature.

Although wit is used to produce comedy in *The Recruiting Officer*, the dialogue also features puns, farce, and comical treatment of social issues. The greater use of the latter as one of the major sources of comedy distinguishes Farquhar from other Restoration dramatists. The recruiting issue underlies a large part of the comedy in *The Recruiting Officer* and often provides for major dramatic conflict. The light atmosphere is set in the prologue, when the action is foretold and ironically compared to heroic times. The recruiting tricks of Kite play upon possibilities, however improbable, of military advancement and even upon the superstitions of the people when he dons his fortune-telling disguise. Less gentle is the comedy of Plume's entering his bastard as a recruit and wanting no one in his company who can write or who is a gentleman.

In Farquhar's *The Beaux' Stratagem*, social issues and modification of traditional Restoration themes and characters again play a prominent role. *The Beaux' Stratagem* is regarded by most critics as Farquhar's finest achievement; its great sense of naturalness, of fidelity to life, continue to make it a great favorite with actors and audiences alike. The action centers on Aimwell's courtship of Dorinda, first of all for her money, but later for love. Archer, Aimwell's friend disguised as a servant, also courts Cherry, the innkeeper's daughter, and Mrs. Sullen, an unhappily married woman. In the meantime, a series of scenes alternates between the inn, whose owner is a highwayman, and the manor, in which a robbery and a midnight love scene occur.

Farquhar's use of the social issue of the recent war against France and the resulting anti-French sentiment pervades all levels of the play. In the inn, Frenchmen pay double the regular fee. Scrub, Mr. Sullen's servant, parodies the French, while Aimwell quips that he would not like a woman who was fond of a Frenchman. Count Bellair, Mrs. Sullen's suitor, and Foigard, Bellair's chaplain, both come in for a large portion of the anti-French comedy.

The concept of social equality also becomes a major source for comedy, including the financial inequality created by primogeniture. Gibbet, the highwayman, excuses himself because he is a younger brother. Aimwell initiates dramatic conflict because of his status as a younger brother. In *The Beaux' Stratagem*, Farquhar stresses the fact that class differences do not correspond to levels of virtue. He achieves this emphasis by showing the same goodness in Cherry and Lady Bountiful, and the same corruption in Boniface and Sullen. In the robbery scene, Archer himself is cleverly associated with the thieves by Mrs. Sullen's cry of "Thieves, Murder." The same fundamental human qualities are thus shown to exist both in the inn and in the country mansion.

As in *The Recruiting Officer*, the plot of *The Beaux' Stratagem* deals with a modified marriage theme. The subject of marriage is not discussed using the common gaming imagery of the earlier Restoration drama, and the only slave imagery is used to describe Mrs. Sullen's marriage. In this instance, the marriage conflict is a conflict between law and nature. Sullen lies with his wife because of the law, and the natural differences between them do not come within the bounds of divorce law. In the conclusion, however, the maxim of nature as the first lawgiver is upheld.

The roster of traditional figures, as in *The Recruiting Officer*, is again modified. Count Bellair in *The Beaux' Stratagem* is a different variety of fop. He is obviously less foolish than the traditional fop since Mrs. Sullen chooses the Count to be part of her manipulations. Bellair shows extraordinary intelligence, for a fop, in initiating his own manipulation to get into Mrs. Sullen's closet. In creating Count Bellair, Farquhar took one aspect of the traditional fop, the beau, and exaggerated it. Bellair functions exceedingly well in this role, but he is also ridiculed because of his French qualities and becomes emblematic of the deeper conflict of social ideas in Farquhar.

In these three plays, the treatment of theme, dramatic conflict, and sources of comedy contributes to an increased realism. The stiff, artificial characters of early Restoration drama have no place in Farquhar's theater. A Dorinda who admits to Aimwell that she does not know herself would not have been understood by earlier audiences; a Mrs. Sullen who verbalizes her unhappiness would have astonished them. The audience at the turn of the century, however, was different: It was mainly a middle-class audience with an awakening sense of social consciousness.

Farquhar opened the window to a blast of fresh air for English comedy. By placing his characters in the world of innkeepers, military recruits, and highwaymen, Farquhar directed attention to humor rather than wit, and, in so doing, broadened the scope for comedy. His plays may well be less sharp-tongued than those of the dramatists who preceded him, but his work displays a greater naturalness and a deeper sense of life. His is the more human view of the world.

Other major works

SHORT FICTION: *The Adventures of Covent Garden*, 1698.

POETRY: *Barcellona*, 1710.

MISCELLANEOUS: *Love and Business*, 1702; *The Complete Works of George Farquhar*, 1930 (Charles Stonehill, editor).

Bibliography

Archer, William, ed. *George Farquhar*, 1906.

Farmer, A. J. *George Farquhar*, 1966.

James, Eugene Nelson. *The Development of George Farquhar as a Comic Dramatist*, 1972.

Perry, Henry Ten Eyck. *The Comic Spirit in Restoration Drama*, 1925.

Rothstein, Eric. *George Farquhar*, 1967.

Eril Barnett Hughes

EDNA FERBER

Born: Kalamazoo, Michigan; August 15, 1885
Died: New York, New York; April 16, 1968

Principal drama

Our Mrs. McChesney, pr., pb. 1915 (with George V. Hobart); *$1200 a Year*, pr., pb. 1920 (with Newman A. Levy); *Minick*, pr., pb. 1924 (with George S. Kaufman); *The Royal Family*, pr. 1927, pb. 1928 (with Kaufman); *Dinner at Eight*, pr., pb. 1932 (with Kaufman); *Stage Door*, pr., pb. 1936 (with Kaufman); *The Land Is Bright*, pr., pb. 1941 (with Kaufman); *Bravo!*, pr. 1948, pb. 1949 (with Kaufman).

Other literary forms

Edna Ferber hoped she would be remembered as a playwright, but even during her lifetime, she was considered primarily a novelist and writer of short stories; nevertheless, the ease with which several of her major novels, among them *Show Boat* (1926), *Saratoga Trunk* (1941), and *Giant* (1952), have been adapted to musical theater and film proves that memorable characterization is the greatest strength her works possess. Strong characterization appears even in her first novel, *Dawn O'Hara* (1911), and Ferber achieved national success with the Emma McChesney stories, which were published originally in *American* and *Cosmopolitan* magazines, quickly reprinted as collections from 1913 to 1915, and finally distilled as Ferber's first dramatic collaboration, *Our Mrs. McChesney*.

Ferber's works were perfectly attuned to American popular taste. This was especially true of the novels and short stories written in the years between the two world wars, when her career was at its height. Her first venture in autobiography, *A Peculiar Treasure* (1939), written just prior to the outbreak of World War II, appropriately finishes this period. This work especially shows Ferber's identification with European Jewry suffering under Nazi persecution and ominously foreshadows the horrors of the Holocaust.

Giant was Ferber's last successful major novel, and it appears that even as she wrote her somewhat anticlimactic second autobiographical volume, *A Kind of Magic* (1963), she was aware that her popularity had waned. She continued to write until her death, however, managing to sell film rights to her unsuccessful last novel, *Ice Palace* (1958), even before its publication.

Achievements

Ferber's reputation as a novelist and writer of short stories made possible her ventures into drama and autobiography. Paradoxically, the adaptation of several of her major novels to musical theater (*Show Boat*), film (*Saratoga Trunk*, *So Big*, *Giant*, *Ice Palace*), and even television (*Cimarron*, 1929), has served to reduce public recognition of the novels from which the adaptations were derived. Correspondingly, two substantial autobiographies, coupled with a biography by Ferber's great-niece Julie Goldsmith Gilbert, have discouraged scholarly research less than twenty years after Ferber's death.

Ferber's novels are large in scope yet regional in character, and Ferber considered it an accomplishment that she was able to write with apparent ease about so many locations in which she had never lived, describing not only the Midwest, where she was reared, but the South, the West, and even the Arctic. She rightly believed that her strength lay in the ability to isolate the distinctive character of each region and describe it in terms appropriate to the popular imagination.

The Midwest of Emma McChesney, the South of *Show Boat*, even the Texas of *Giant* no longer exist, however, and this has served to make some of Ferber's finest works period pieces. Stronger, more contemporary statements have been made about the plight of minorities; anonymous corporate greed has exceeded that of individual families; and novels of manners are generally out of favor. The works of Willa Cather and William Faulkner, although also regional, can survive on the universal applicability of the situations they describe, but Ferber's work cannot.

Ferber's greatest popularity came in the nostalgic period between the two world wars and during the Depression, when Americans sought escape from overwhelming reality. *So Big* won the Pulitzer Prize in 1925, and this led to a flurry of publication which slowed only after 1941. Today, most of her works are out of print, even some of her best-known books—books which sold thousands of copies before the advent of the paperback and which won the unsolicited plaudits of Rudyard Kipling and both Theodore and Franklin D. Roosevelt.

The situation is even more dismal in the case of Ferber's plays, this despite her often brilliant collaborations with George S. Kaufman. When *The Royal Family*, *Dinner at Eight*, or *Stage Door* are mentioned, a glimmer of recognition comes to the eye of a well-read person, but even these works are not generally associated with Ferber's name. Sometimes they are remembered as Kaufman's work, perhaps because his name always preceded Ferber's on the title page and in billing, but they are as likely to be recalled only as films.

Ferber was adept at female characterization, and strong women, who were also usually amiable, fill the pages of her works. This was considered by many an innovation which made Ferber in her own time a popular counterweight to Ernest Hemingway, but it has not continued to save her literary reputation.

Biography

Edna Ferber considered her earliest years turbulent and unhappy, particularly the time before her family's move to Appleton, Wisconsin. This unhappiness had essentially two causes: awareness that as the child of middle-class Jewish merchants, she was often not accepted by rough-edged Midwestern farmers, and her recognition of the isolated and difficult nature of plains life in the last quarter of the nineteenth century. Her parents, Jacob and Julia, made several moves, evidently seeking a more comfortable life for the family, and Edna was born in Kalamazoo, Michigan, on August 15, 1885. (Ferber, perhaps from the vanity to which she confesses in her autobiography, gave the date as 1887, and this was the year published in *The New York Times"* obituary.) By 1888, Jacob, though he seems to have prospered moderately in Kalamazoo, moved his family to Chicago, where his wife, Julia Neumann Ferber, had been reared, and the Ferbers lived for a year in the large Neumann house on Calumet Avenue. Jacob's desire for independence, as well as his idea that his dry goods business would be more successful in an isolated town, prompted him to move the family again, this time to Ottumwa, Iowa, and the Ferbers lived in this farming and coal-mining town from 1890 to 1897. Edna Ferber always considered the place brutal and crude; it was a struggle to maintain even a modicum of comfort in this primitive town, which quite often was openly anti-Semitic. Jacob's progressive blindness was first diagnosed in the Ottumwa years, and this served to place more business and family responsibilities on Julia. A successful lawsuit for slander brought by a fired employee cost the Ferbers several thousand dollars and hastened their move to Wisconsin.

Appleton provided more congenial surroundings. There was a small Jewish community there, good schools, and the pleasant atmosphere of a Midwestern college town. Ferber excelled in declamation and debate for Ryan High School's Forum Debating Society, and her first prize at a statewide declamation contest paved the way at age seventeen for her position as reporter on the Appleton *Daily Crescent*, the town's newspaper. Ferber, like Willa Cather, planned a career in journalism, and in 1905, she accepted an offer to work on the Milwaukee *Journal*.

Milwaukee proved a big change for the nineteen-year-old Ferber. She was suddenly on her own, living in a boarding house whose principal tenants were German-speaking engineers employed in the steelworks and engineering plants in and around the city. She drew on this experience for her first novel, *Dawn O'Hara*, a few years later. Milwaukee also provided more chances than ever to attend the theater, and some of Ferber's earliest writings were drama and music reviews published in both the *Journal* and the *Daily Crescent*. Her health suffered, however, and forced her return to Appleton after three years.

Though Ferber had planned to return to Milwaukee after recovering her strength in Appleton, she never did. On a secondhand typewriter, she wrote an essay entitled "Why I Lost My Job," entered it in a contest sponsored by the Chicago *Tribune*, and won first prize; encouraged by this success, she began to write *Dawn O'Hara*. Upon Jacob's death in 1909, Julia returned to Chicago with Edna and her older sister Fannie (the Fannie Fox who wrote the famous cookbook); this was the beginning of Ferber's Chicago period, and for the next thirteen years, she lived in hotels and furnished apartments. She continued to write free-lance articles for the *Tribune*, but she directed her energies primarily toward fiction.

Short stories in the style of O. Henry poured from her typewriter, and her 1911 success with *Dawn O'Hara* enabled her to publish much of this material. Good reviews for *Buttered Side Down* (1912) continued the momentum, but it was the McChesney stories, which were published in nationally circulated magazines, that brought her popular success. They introduced an admirable and determined traveling saleswoman named Emma McChesney, a character derived from Ferber's mercantile and Midwestern background. These successes led Ferber to divide her time, somewhat awkwardly, between Chicago and New York. She was able to use her training in journalism to cover the 1912 Republican and Democratic National Conventions for the Franklin P. Adams syndicate; it was at this time that she met William Allen White, who would remain a friend and confidant for the rest of her life. The dramatic rights to the McChesney stories were sold to Joseph Brooks at the end of 1913, and in 1915 they appeared as the play *Our Mrs. McChesney*, a difficult collaboration with George V. Hobart. Ethel Barrymore, as Emma McChesney, saved this mediocre play, although Ferber always maintained that Barrymore had been miscast.

Although Ferber could have allowed her reputation to rest on the McChesney character alone, she wisely sought new literary horizons. Returning by ship from a European holiday, she met a young Chicago lawyer, Newman A. Levy, who was a playwright and artist by avocation, and this meeting resulted in the play *$1200 a Year*. Although a dismal failure, the play anticipated the direction her future works in drama would take and led to more successful collaborations with George S. Kaufman. *The Royal Family*, *Dinner at Eight*, and *Stage Door* remain minor classics, although they stand more effectively as literature than as revivals. Her novel *Fanny Herself* (1917), which enjoyed only moderate success, enabled Ferber to see that her greatest abilities lay in the novel, the direction her career would ultimately take.

So Big, *Show Boat*, and *Cimarron* appeared in quick succession during the post-World War I years, and Ferber was firmly established as a New York-based writer and a popular success. She frequented the Algonquin Round Table and met Marc Connelly, Robert E. Sherwood, Deems Taylor,

Alexander Woollcott, George Oppenheimer, and other literary notables in that circle. These were her most productive years.

Ferber's move to Connecticut and Treasure Hill, the country home she built there in the late 1930's, continued to feed her muse. Her autobiography *A Peculiar Treasure* was written while her house was being built, and *Nobody's in Town* (1938), a collection of short stories, also appeared at this time. The onset of World War II, however, reduced her literary output considerably, and it was only at the war's end that her novel *Great Son* (1945) appeared. It was not until 1952 that *Giant*, her novel on life among the oil-rich families of Texas, brought her new acclaim.

In the early 1960's, Doubleday, the publisher with which Ferber had enjoyed such a successful association, encouraged her to write a novel that she had been planning on the American Indian, tentatively entitled "The Squaw." Ferber was doing research for this projected work even as she was suffering from a painful facial nerve disease and finally from the stomach cancer that eventually took her life. She carried on gallantly to the last, dining regally at her favorite restaurants and enjoying the company of her sister's family. She had never married.

Analysis

"Stagestruck" Edna Ferber, as she described herself, could not help writing plays, though she never attempted to do this alone. It appears, from a reading of those she wrote with George S. Kaufman, that she relied on Kaufman's skill for timing and dialogue but that the characterizations are essentially her own. A consistent development in Ferber's dramatic skills can be traced, beginning with her collaboration with Newman A. Levy, *$1200 a Year*.

Ferber wrote *$1200 a Year* with Levy during 1920, which was a transitional year in her life. Still living in Chicago but contemplating a permanent move to New York, she was at once attracted and repelled by city life and the large sums of money that could be earned there. She wrote to William Allen White that she hated the play even as she and Levy were writing it, that everyone but she seemed to be earning $100,000 a year, and that she was eager to work on her novel *The Girls* (1921). She describes the multiple coats of "paint" and "varnish" that she and Levy were applying to the play in an effort to make it stageworthy. This less than enthusiastic approach to the task may well have been one of the reasons for the play's dismal failure. Sam Harris, who had agreed to produce the play, closed it after a week of Baltimore tryouts. Nevertheless, *$1200 a Year* reveals a good deal about Ferber as a developing playwright.

Broadly drawn characterizations and stereotypes developed through hyperbole appear throughout the work. The once-moneyed Massachusetts aristocracy, represented by the appropriately named Winthrop family, contrasts with the prosperous immigrant Cyrus McClure, the Scot who built the Wickley, Pennsylvania, steel mill, which supports most of the town's affluent working class. These personalities, in turn, contrast with those of the mill workers, recent immigrants who have supplied the brawn that the system demands and so have prospered. Paul Stoddard, the protagonist, is a professor of economics at Dinsmore, the university maintained by McClure's money. Stoddard teaches his students, among them McClure's son Steven, the mysteries of political economy, and although he understands theoretically how to make great sums of money, he struggles to survive on his meager professor's salary of $1200 a year.

Stoddard's lectures and research have dealt with the growth of fifteenth century English trade guilds. This has angered Cyrus McClure, who is a member of the Dinsmore Board of Trustees and who fears that the mill workers' children attending the university will convince their parents to agitate for the establishment of unions at the mill.

When Stoddard first appears, McClure and the other trustees have already issued an ultimatum that the young professor delete this potentially inflammatory material from his lectures. Stoddard has met these demands by submitting his resignation. He decides to leave the threadbare aristocracy of college life and apply for a worker's job at McClure's mill. He completes the transformation to worker by living among the workers of the mill district.

Six months later, he has acquired all the material things he and his wife, Jean, have always wanted and has acquired as well a new group of friends, among whom is mill hand Chris Zsupnik. In his free time, Stoddard lectures to receptive audiences, outlining his theories on the potential power of workers, and his words soon have an effect. Significantly, the effect is most pronounced among American academics and other underpaid professionals who flock to join the ranks of unskilled laborers. These new workers create such an imbalance in the labor supply that colleges and universities all over America begin to close. What is more, factory and mill owners such as McClure threaten to cut wages to absorb the new supply of workers and maintain a market for the goods they produce. Another group of casualties includes academics who cannot make the transition to the working class. Jean's older brother, Henry Adams Winthrop, who knows little of any historical event that has occurred since the Peloponnesian War, is now utterly unemployable.

Of necessity, a reversal now occurs. Stoddard's fellow workers become convinced that the academic is merely doing a form of practical research and attempting to see if his theories really work. Jean is never comfortable with her working-class neighbors, even though she does like what Stoddard's higher salary can buy. Jean is a characteristic Ferber heroine: She takes decisive action and bargains with McClure on her own. McClure shrewdly uses his interview with Jean to convince his mill workers that he, and not Stoddard, is their true friend.

The play is now at an impasse, which can be solved only by *deus ex machina*, which arrives in the form of Cleveland Welch, talent scout for the Mastodon Art-Film Company. He offers Stoddard five thousand dollars a week to play the lead in a great new heartthrob film to be entitled *Brains and Brawn*. The film will be the life story of Paul Stoddard, who has put theory to practice in order to conquer the illiterate tyrant Cyrus McClure. When McClure hears Welch's offer, he asks what Stoddard would consider a fair salary for a university professor. The audience never hears Stoddard's reply, for the curtain descends just as he is about to name a figure.

Ferber's first autobiographical memoir, *A Peculiar Treasure*, describes the special affection she had for immigrants to the United States, an affection apparent in the sympathetic portrait of the Zsupnik family in *$1200 a Year*. Her father's background and her life at Appleton and Milwaukee provided inspiration for many of these characters in her comedy.

Although a failure, *$1200 a Year* foreshadows themes that would be developed in subsequent Ferber plays. Topics such as socialism in America following the Russian Revolution, immigration, unfair distribution of wealth, the advancing labor movement, and how America chooses its heroes provide the play's background. Still, *$1200 a Year* never becomes a diatribe on American life. Hyperbole allows the audience to see absurdity where it exists and to draw the obvious conclusion that the common interest is served only by fair dealing; anything else is merely a short-term advantage.

Dinner at Eight was successful in its first production and shows a more mature development of similar themes. In this play, Ferber and Kaufman explore American classes and manners against the background of New York during the Depression. The changed circumstances in which many Americans found themselves in 1932 are obviously at the root of the play's action, but once again, the audience is allowed to discover this on its own. The Jordan family, described in terms Ferber had earlier used for the Winthrops, represents the Yankee aristocracy. Oliver Jordan has come to realize that the family shipping line, which had always seemed a sure source of continuing income, is threatened with bankruptcy. His wife, Millicent, seems blissfully unaware of this; her greatest concern is planning a pretheater dinner for Lord and Lady Ferncliffe, who have just arrived in town.

The guest list is planned to combine business and social requirements. Don Packard, whose manners still betray his Western mining days, and his Passaic-born wife, Kitty, receive Millicent's invitation only through Oliver's urgent petition. Oliver hopes to enlist Dan's aid to rescue the Jordan line. One of Oliver's old flames, Carlotta Vance, an apparently wealthy but faded actress, also receives an invitation; Larry Renault, an equally faded actor, is to be her dinner companion. Oliver's physician, J. Wayne Talbot, and his wife, Lucy, will complete the guest list. (Kaufman worried that the social complications that the play relates would invite comparisons with *The Grand Hotel*, which had been produced the same year; this was indeed the case, for *Dinner at Eight* rivaled *The Grand Hotel* in complexity.)

As the dinner preparations continue, the audience learns that Oliver, struggling to keep the Jordan Line afloat, has an incurable heart disease; that Carlotta has sold her Jordan stock, thereby making Oliver's business problems more acute; that Dan has been maneuvering behind the scenes to acquire control of the Jordan company; that Kitty has been having an affair with Wayne Talbot; and that the Jordans' daughter Paula, though engaged, has been enjoying her own liaison with the alcoholic actor Larry Renault. Ironically, the Ferncliffes, who leave New York for Florida at the last moment, never appear at the party in their honor, and their place is filled, somewhat unwillingly, by Millicent's sister Hattie and her husband, Ed. Larry Renault never appears either, for he commits suicide after learning that he cannot get even a supporting part in an upcoming play.

As usual in Ferber's plays, external events influence the action but are never incorporated into the play. The audience recognizes that the Depression is the fundamental cause of much of what happens, but beyond an occasional reference to difficult times, no one mentions it. Each of the characters has brought on personal disaster by some individual failing: Oliver through lack of diligent management; Dan because of his preoccupation with money-making; Larry by his alcoholism; Talbot through his womanizing. This allows Ferber to maintain her fundamentally optimistic view of American life. The seeds of decadence are present, and a few succumb to them, but others, such as Hattie and Ed, retain the common sense and attachment to simple pleasures that allow them to avoid the disasters that afflict the major characters.

In *Stage Door*, her next play after *Dinner at Eight*, Ferber introduces a large cast of characters to portray manners and emphasize conflict. This 1936 collaboration with Kaufman features thirty-two actors, each of whom plays a character with a remarkably different personality. Even the minor characters become essential to advance the play's action.

The plot is relatively simple. There is only one scene, at the Footlights Club, a boardinghouse for aspiring actresses. Life at the club is one of genteel and somewhat Bohemian poverty. The young women are without jobs more often than with them. They discreetly jockey for position and sometimes grant their favors to assorted "stage-door-Johnnys," writers, producers, and movie moguls.

Terry Randall is the single exception. She refuses a film offer made through David Kingsley, a Broadway producer who has sought greener pastures in Hollywood. She encourages an idealistic writer named Keith Burgess but does not criticize his decision to write screenplays for Hollywood. She resents, though silently, Jean Maitland's exploitation of the Footlights Club to publicize an already successful film career. Rather than rely on the financial support of her father, she works at Macy's department store and seeks auditions during her lunch hour. In short, Terry remains in control of her life throughout the play and never sacrifices her idealism. Inspired by her example, Kingsley decides to return to Broadway as the producer of a play that he rescues from the clutches of movie executive Adolph Gretzl, who had planned to use the play only to publicize Maitland's latest film. *Stage Door* concludes with idealism triumphant. Terry will star in the rescued play and will marry Kingsley, the man whom she has rescued from the dangers of materialism.

It is interesting that Julie Cavendish, in the Ferber-Kaufman collaboration *The Royal Family*, best sums up the way Ferber saw her relationship to the theater. (Indeed, Ferber's single experience as an actress was her portrayal of Julie in a 1940 revival of the play staged in Maplewood, New Jersey.) Julie, a character based on Ethel Barrymore, Ferber's girlhood stage heroine, sees her life as a grand drama. Like Ferber, she is a woman who wants all that life can offer. Ferber, however, had infinitely more common sense and considerably more business acumen than Julie possessed. Her popular appeal made possible the unquestioned success that she enjoyed during her lifetime, even if it has not assured her immortality as a writer.

Other major works

NOVELS: *Dawn O'Hara*, 1911; *Fanny Herself*, 1917; *The Girls*, 1921; *So Big*, 1924; *Show Boat*, 1926; *Cimarron*, 1929; *American Beauty*, 1931; *Come and Get It*, 1935; *Saratoga Trunk*, 1941; *Great Son*, 1945; *Giant*, 1952; *Ice Palace*, 1958.

SHORT FICTION: *Buttered Side Down*, 1912; *Roast Beef Medium*, 1913; *Personality Plus*, 1914; *Emma McChesney & Co.*, 1915; *Cheerful—By Request*, 1918; *Half Portions*, 1919; *Mother Knows Best*, 1927; *They Brought Their Women*, 1933; *Nobody's in Town*, 1938; *One Basket*, 1947.

NONFICTION: *A Peculiar Treasure*, 1939, 1960 (revised with new introduction); *A Kind of Magic*, 1963.

Bibliography

Davidson, Colleen Tishe. "Behind the Sentimental Heroine: The Feminist Character in American Novels, 1899-1937," in *Dissertation Abstracts International*. XXXVII (1976), p. 306A.

Francis, Michelle. "The James Adams Floating Theatre: Edna Ferber's *Show Boat*," in *Carolina Comments*. XXVIII, no. 5 (1980), pp. 135-142.

Gilbert, Julie Goldsmith. *Ferber: A Biography*, 1978.

Goldstein, Malcolm. *George S. Kaufman: His Life, His Theatre*, 1979.

Horowitz, Stephen P., and Miriam J. Landsman. "The Americanization of Edna: A Study of Ms. Ferber's Jewish-American Identity," in *Studies in American Jewish Literature*, 1982.

Shaughnessy, Mary Rose. *Women and Success in American Society in the Works of Edna Ferber*, 1975.

Teichmann, Howard. *George S. Kaufman: An Intimate Portrait*, 1972.

Uffen, Ellen Serlen. "Edna Ferber and the 'Theatricalization' of American Mythology," in *Midwestern Miscellany*. VIII (1980), pp. 82-93.

Robert J. Forman

HENRY FIELDING

Born: Sharpham Park, England; April 22, 1707
Died: Lisbon, Portugal; October 8, 1754

Principal drama

Love in Several Masques, pr., pb. 1728; *The Temple Beau*, pr., pb. 1730; *The Author's Farce, and The Pleasures of the Town*, pr., pb. 1730; *Tom Thumb: A Tragedy*, pr., pb. 1730 (revised as *The Tragedy of Tragedies*, pr., pb. 1731); *Rape upon Rape: Or, Justice Caught in His Own Trap*, pr., pb. 1730 (also known as *The Coffee-House Politician*); *The Letter-Writers: Or, A New Way to Keep a Wife at Home*, pr., pb. 1731; *The Welsh Opera: Or, The Grey Mare the Better Horse*, pr., pb. 1731 (revised as *The Grub-Street Opera*, pb. 1731); *The Lottery*, pr., pb. 1732; *The Modern Husband*, pr., pb. 1732 (five acts); *The Old Debauchees*, pr., pb. 1732; *The Covent Garden Tragedy*, pr., pb. 1732; *The Mock Doctor: Or, The Dumb Lady Cur'd*, pr., pb. 1732 (adaptation of Molière's *Le Medecin malgré lui*); *The Miser*, pr., pb. 1733 (adaptation of Molière's *L'Avare*); *Don Quixote in England*, pr., pb. 1734; *The Intriguing Chambermaid*, pr., pb. 1734 (adaptation of Jean-François Regnard's *Le Retour imprévu*); *An Old Man Taught Wisdom: Or, The Virgin Unmask'd*, pr., pb. 1735; *The Universal Gallant: Or, The Different Husbands*, pr., pb. 1735 (five acts); *Pasquin: Or, A Dramatic Satire on the Times*, pr., pb. 1736; *Tumble-Down Dick: Or, Phaeton in the Suds*, pr., pb. 1736; *Eurydice: Or, The Devil's Henpeck'd*, pr. 1737, pb. 1743 (one act); *Eurydice Hiss'd: Or, A Word to the Wise*, pr., pb. 1737; *The Historical Register for the Year 1736*, pr., pb. 1737 (three acts); *Miss Lucy in Town*, pr., pb. 1742 (one act); *The Wedding Day*, pr. 1743 (five acts; also known as *The Virgin Unmask'd*); *The Fathers: Or, The Good-Natured Man*, pr., pb. 1778 (revised for posthumous production by David Garrick).

Other literary forms

The focus of Henry Fielding's work progressed from drama to satire to the novel to legal inquiries and proposals, with some overlap and with a nearly constant overlay of critical and political journalism. Among his novels, his masterpiece *Tom Jones* (1749) is a monument of English literature, though *Joseph Andrews* (1742) is highly regarded and *Amelia* (1751) was his own favorite. *Shamela* (1741) burlesques Samuel Richardson's novel *Pamela* (1740-1741), and the strongly satiric *Jonathan Wild* (1743) attacks the contemporary prime minister of England, Sir Robert Walpole. Political satire formed the staple of *The Champion*, a thrice-weekly journal in which Fielding was a leading partner in 1739 and 1740, but social commentary and drama criticism played a large role in *The Covent-Garden Journal*, which came out during 1752. In the early 1750's, Fielding authored several influential tracts aimed at reforming his country's criminal and poor laws, and in 1754 he wrote a moving and contemplative travel book, *The Journal of a Voyage to Lisbon* (1755).

Achievements

Fielding was a central figure in the theatrical world of the 1730's, and he continued to be influential as a literary and social critic almost up to his death in 1754. He wrote in popular and established forms, but his cleverness and vigor raised his work well above the level set by his contemporaries. Fielding exploited the ballad opera, a form originated by John Gay, with particular success. By adding broad farce and often surreal fantasy to Gay's inspiration of setting satiric lyrics to popular tunes sung in operatic style, Fielding produced one of his best plays, *The Author's Farce*. He combined farce, burlesque, and fantasy to create *The Tragedy of Tragedies*, another masterpiece. Both plays, often classified as dramatic satires, were hugely popular by the standards of the time.

Beyond his contribution as a playwright, Fielding's management of the Little Theatre in the Haymarket set a dangerously bold pace in terms of showmanship and satire. He attacked the shortcomings of society in general and of the theater in particular but found his chief target in the Whig government of Robert Walpole. Fielding's popularity, his influence in the theater, and the potency of his satire are usually credited with bringing on the Licensing Act of 1737, an instrument of political censorship which limited the staging of plays to a select list of theaters and required the Lord Chamberlain's approval before a new play could be staged or an old one altered. The Licensing Act ended Fielding's theatrical career on an ironic note; he had made the stage at once so lively and so central to England's political life that its control and suppression had become a political necessity.

Shorn of topical relevance and their original sense of daring, only two or three of his plays are still performed. They have wit and pace, and they certainly repay the discriminating reader, but they no longer exert the tremendous popular appeal that was Fielding's first goal. As a contributor to dramatic tradition, Fielding presents another irony; he was restless within the forms he chose, but his experimentation forced and complicated those forms rather than breaking through and extending them. Had his career as a playwright not ended so early—in part through his own doing—he might well have made a more substantial contribution to the genre. As it was, his interest turned to the novel, and he joined Daniel Defoe and Richardson in establishing a great new English literary tradition.

Biography

Born on April 22, 1707, Henry Fielding grew up quietly in Somerset and

Dorset. When he was eleven, however, his mother died, and after a year of turmoil, during which his father remarried and quarreled violently with his mother's relatives, young Henry was sent to Eton. After making as much as possible of the excellent if strict and structured education offered by this famous school, Fielding chose, about 1724, to enjoy life in London rather than enter a university.

In 1728, his comedy *Love in Several Masques* was staged at the Theatre Royal. Instead of pursuing a stage career at once, however, Fielding enrolled at the University of Leyden, where he remained for a year, probably studying classical literature. In 1729, Fielding returned to England, where his second play, *The Temple Beau*, was accepted by the theater in Goodman's Fields. This coup inaugurated ten years of immersion in the London theater world, a brilliant career in the course of which Fielding became both widely known and respected and widely disparaged and attacked. His third play, a ballad opera called *The Author's Farce*, opened at a more prestigious theater, the Little Theatre in the Haymarket, where it met with great success; it was followed immediately by *Tom Thumb*, a minor masterpiece which Fielding reworked the following year as *The Tragedy of Tragedies*. This satire on Robert Walpole, a parody of heroic tragedy, is today Fielding's most widely known dramatic production.

After his spectacular initial success, Fielding's ability to please the public became less certain. *Rape upon Rape* was found only acceptable, and its afterpiece, *The Letter-Writers*, had to be withdrawn. A new and highly political afterpiece, however, *The Welsh Opera*, played to enthusiastic houses. Already the government was aware of Fielding; the play's even more outspoken revision, *The Grub-Street Opera*, was suppressed before it could open.

In 1732, Fielding continued to increase the pressure he had caused by his inflammatory satire with *The Lottery*, an attack on the combination of financial corruption and public foolishness represented by lottery-ticket jobbers. This play did well, but *The Modern Husband*, a strong satire on public—rather than political or financial—morals, had a mixed reception, as did *The Old Debauchees*, which is a much darker work than Fielding's lighthearted style usually produced. *The Old Debauchees*' afterpiece, *The Covent Garden Tragedy*, was a flat failure and had to be replaced by *The Mock Doctor*. This ballad opera was the first of Fielding's two successful adaptations of Molière. The second, a highly successful farce entitled *The Miser*, was produced the following year, followed by another ballad opera, *The Intriguing Chambermaid*.

Fielding was now well established as a popular London playwright, a figure to be reckoned with among his literary peers, and a man well able to earn a decent, if uneven, income through his art. At the same time, he had already made enemies among both politicians and literary critics and had himself been the butt of sharp satiric comment.

At this juncture, late in 1734, Fielding married. For information about how he lived, passed his days, dealt with his necessities, and satisfied his tastes—whatever these were—one must rely on generalizations about the period. No Fielding diaries have been found and very little of his correspondence exists. He and his new wife, the former Charlotte Cradock, lived in the heart of London while he opened *An Old Man Taught Wisdom*, a successful ballad opera/farce, and *The Universal Gallant*, a comedy which failed emphatically.

The death of Fielding's mother-in-law, which came soon after this failure, left his wife with a small estate. After dealing with financial matters related to the estate, the couple managed to spend a good deal of the year 1735 at Fielding's family home in East Stour, but Fielding apparently did not take well to rural life. By the time he was back in London for the fall season, he had succeeded in gaining control of the Little Theatre, where he organized a group of young actors referred to as the "Great Mogul's Company of Comedians." *Pasquin*, a dramatic satire, which was more specific in its personal reference than any of Fielding's other works, made the new company's name. This was followed with a farce, *Tumble-Down Dick*, which was aimed at his theatrical compatriots.

Fielding continued to provide competition and stimulation to the new theatrical season with a provoking and innovative schedule at the Little Theatre, also offering a short farce of his own, *Eurydice*, to Drury Lane, a rival house. *Eurydice* failed, giving Fielding the opportunity to rework it (twice), ending up with *Eurydice Hiss'd*, a short farce which played for more than a month as a popular afterpiece to *The Historical Register for the Year 1736*. The latter, while it provides the broad social satire suggested by its title and takes aim at the theatrical world as well, is largely a political allegory to which Walpole's government, hard-pressed and near its end, was sensitive. Fielding's next offering, a play called *The Fall of Bob, Alias Gin* (now lost), apparently did much to end his career in the theater, although after his works had lost some of their notoriety, he did produce a few minor pieces.

The Licensing Act of 1737 closed the Little Theatre as well as those in Lincoln's Inn Fields and Goodman's Fields. Moreover, it closed all stages to Fielding, whose development as a dramatist had increasingly led him to the kind of material that would never pass a government censor. Fielding's engagement in anything with which he was involved had been intensely energetic and provocative; he was always searching, pushing, and trying something new. Faced with chains and muzzles, he simply shifted his energies to two, or perhaps three, new careers.

Ostensibly, Fielding became a lawyer instead of a playwright. He resumed his formal education, studying at the Middle Temple, and was admitted to the bar in 1740. He practiced as a barrister, riding the Western Circuit and generally working hard for small financial reward. In 1748, however, he was made a Justice of the Peace for the city of Westminister, and for the next six years he served as a stern but sympathetic judge, concerned with discerning and remedying the causes of crime as well as reforming and improving the city's means of protecting itself, its rudimentary police force. During this period, Fielding continued to interest himself in politics and the drama through three journals, *The Champion* (1739-1741), *The Jacobite Journal* (1747-1748), and *The Covent-Garden Journal* (1752).

Not satisfied by law and journalism, Fielding channeled into prose fiction the creative powers cut off from the stage. In 1741, very soon after he abandoned *The Champion* and less than a year after he began to practice law, Fielding published *Shamela*, a parody of Richardson's *Pamela*. This led the next year to *Joseph Andrews*, the first of his three great novels. *Joseph Andrews*, published anonymously, begins as another attack on Richardson's ethical and moral vision but soon goes off in its own direction, a picaresque work—in the tradition of *Don Quixote de la Mancha*—which is centered on the inscrutable character of Parson Adams. Fielding next published his *Miscellanies* (1743), a collection of both old and new works that was especially notable for the inclusion of *Jonathan Wild*. This intense and bitter satire equates political greatness with criminal notoriety, insisting that greed, ruthlessness, cunning, and singleness of vision propel men to success in crime and government alike. Six years later, *Tom Jones*, Fielding's masterpiece and one of the world's great novels, made original literary contributions, which the plays had not managed to produce. *Amelia*, which Fielding published at the end of 1751, lacks the robust spirit and characters of *Tom Jones* but sold well when it first appeared. Fielding himself favored the book and was disappointed with its critical reception.

By the time *Amelia* was published, Fielding was nearing the end of his life. Making do with the inadequate resources of the legal system, constantly exposed to the diseases of those brought before him in court, and fundamentally weakened, perhaps, by the pace of his own somewhat intemperate life, Fielding required constant medical attention. He did not, however, slow down until the summer of 1754, when he decided to travel to Portugal for his health. During the slow, uncomfortable journey, he wrote *The Journal of a Voyage to Lisbon*, a work of shrewd, humorous observation. It was his last effort. On October 8, 1754, Fielding died, widely mourned by friends who, however much they had valued him, were unlikely to appreciate the scope and variety of his achievements or grasp the extent of the contributions he had made in the forty-seven years of his life.

Analysis

In a period of only nine years, Henry Fielding wrote and staged more than twenty plays. Such a sustained outburst recalls the careers of Elizabethan dramatists Thomas Dekker and John Fletcher, who in the early 1600's turned out three or four scripts a year to feed London's voracious appetite for new plays. The decade of the 1730's was another theatrically hungry period. Five theaters competed for reputation, audience, and income; their managers vied for the best authors, plays, and actors. The pressure of competition added farces, burlesques, operas, pantomime, and even puppet shows to the repertory of drama by standard playwrights. In the struggle to keep up and get ahead, authors and companies freely borrowed material from the French and Italian theaters and readily used singers, dancers, jugglers, and anything else that attracted customers. Innovative theater often brought quick profits, but it challenged many dramatic conventions (especially notions of genre) and often sacrificed dramatic quality to gain immediate impact.

A review of Fielding's plays shows that he attempted to work in one traditional dramatic style, the comedy of manners, but, more important, to cater to the popular taste for new dramatic entertainments. Fielding first tried his hand at five-act comedies in the style of William Congreve and Sir John Vanbrugh. When he met limited success with this form, Fielding turned to farce, one- and two-act plays designed as afterpieces to the main performance. These short plays, at which Fielding proved adept, emphasized broad characterization, limited plots, and busy stage action. If Fielding had worked only in these two styles, however, his modern reputation as a dramatist would be negligible. The theatrical rivalry of his era led Fielding to experiment with dramatic form and stage technique; he experimented both to find innovations that would please audiences and to poke fun at rival playwrights. His experimental dramas (which he once called the "unshaped monsters of a wanton brain") defy categorization because they mix freely and imaginatively elements of manners comedy, farce, burlesque, and ballad opera. Fielding's plays represent different levels of achievement. Skillful as he could be at following convention or manipulating it, Fielding often pursued thematic concerns at the expense of form. His themes are as numerous as the plays themselves: the moral state of London society, the political health of the nation under the administration of Prime Minister Robert Walpole, the condition of modern marriage, and the quality of contemporary theater.

The emphasis on theme made Fielding only a mediocre practitioner of the five-act comedy. His Congrevian comedies were progressively ill-received by audiences, and modern scholarship has devoted attention to them primarily because of Fielding's reputation in other genres. The thematic emphasis was more congenial in farce, where conventions were less firm, but at the same time, the form worked against any substantial thematic exploration or revelation. Fielding's "unshaped monsters," plays in which form is shaped almost organically as a means of expressing theme, are his major achievement. They are amusing, imaginative, and energetic; even though two centuries have dulled some of the pointed satire, they are a delight to read. In the 1730's these experimental plays, mingling dramatic elements in unexpected ways for irreverent purposes, sometimes pleased and sometimes puzzled. Modern readers—accustomed to Gilbert and Sullivan operettas, Marx Brothers films, and Monty Python skits—can easily visualize these works in performance. A term Fielding used for one of this group, "dramatic satire," might serve for all of them.

Tracing the sequence of Fielding's five-act comedies, one sees clearly how the conventions of the genre and Fielding's interests grew steadily. The Congrevian comedy of manners followed patterns that had codified during four decades of Restoration theater. The staple plot presents a witty hero in pursuit of love and fortune through fashionable London society. Love begins as a hunt for pleasure—like a fox hunt, a chase of elaborate ceremony—with the hunter well equipped by a solid inheritance. The hero, a skeptic about the virtues of marriage, enjoys the hunt until he meets a woman whose wit and intelligence match his own. Now the hero's pursuit changes: Love's quality matters more to him than variety, and his wealth enables him to avoid mindless conformity to society's customs. The lovers display their attractive characters and mutual affection in brilliant dialogue, and they overcome whatever obstacles arise: rival lovers, disagreeable guardians, legal complexities. By manipulating other characters, the lovers bring their courtship to a successful conclusion which sees deserving heads, hearts, and fortunes united. Although the dramatist might make, in the course of things, satiric points about contemporary values and attitudes, Congrevian comedy emphasizes the mutual attraction of the young lovers. John Loftis has called this celebration of attraction, as it matures from a physical desire to incorporate intellectual parity, the "gaiety of sex." Congrevian comedy entertains and improves by championing the pursuit of love.

Fielding's first two comedies, *Love in Several Masques* and *The Temple Beau*, remain faithful to the conventions and emphases of the type. In the first play, Merital seeks to win Helena, whose guardians, an aunt and uncle, wish to marry her to the foolish man-about-town, Apish. The aunt, Lady Trap, is an obstacle in another sense: She is trying to seduce Merital. The lovers elope after Merital pretends friendship with Apish to gain access to Helena. In the second play, Veromil, though defrauded of his inheritance by a rascally brother, pursues Bellaria because he loves her. His rival is a high-living rake and supposed law student, Henry Wilding, who courts Bellaria as a means of recouping his wasted fortune. The timely intervention of an old family servant exposes the fraud and secures social recognition for Veromil's marriage to Bellaria. Although the plays attack the contemporary feeling that money and concern for the family name are more important than love, their satire does not obscure the zesty pursuit of love.

This is not the case, however, in Fielding's other five-act comedies. Perhaps because comedy is a traditional vehicle for lashing vice and exposing folly, Fielding increasingly gave precedence to theme over conventions of character and plot. A moralist, like many eighteenth century authors, he could not help paying more attention to political, professional, and social corruption than he did to literary traditions. Though this emphasis weakened the public appeal of his five-act plays, it shows his thinking and underlies his growing sense of dramatic freedom.

Rape upon Rape, which claims to present contemporary life as any observer could remark it, is more a thesis play than a comedy. The title (which offended Fielding's contemporaries and had to be changed) both describes the literal action and also becomes a symbolic indictment of the English judicial system. Hilaret's plans to elope with Captain Constant are upset when she is accosted by the rakish Ramble. Her cry of "rape" causes Ramble to be apprehended, but he then charges her with swearing a false accusation. Both are hauled before Justice Squeezum, who solicits bribes from men and women alike: money from the former and sex from the latter. Managing to escape Squeezum's solicitations, Hilaret learns that Constant has been carried to the same court on a false rape charge. Although Hilaret and Constant are true lovers, who proceed to expose Squeezum's corruption and manage to marry, little attention is paid to celebrating their mutual attraction. The play offers some amusing moments, but there is, not surprisingly, little gaiety in the themes of pandering, attempted rape, and injustice.

Fielding's subsequent five-act comedies move even further from the model. There are courting lovers in *The Modern Husband*, but they are not the central couple; there are no unmarried lovers in *The Universal Gallant*, nor are the married people especially attractive people in either play. The main action of *The Modern Husband* is a strong indictment of aristocratic power and middle-class groveling: Lord Richly awards power and prestige to men who prostitute their wives to him and then uses those couples to seduce others. The play shows Richly attempting to use Mr. and Mrs. Modern to bring Mr. and Mrs. Bellamant within his circle. Fortunately, the Bellamants are faithful to each other and clever enough to thwart Richly's design. *The Universal Gallant* contrasts the overly suspicious Sir Simon Raffler, whose wife is faithful, with the trusting Colonel Raffler, whose wife is regularly unfaithful. Entangled with these couples are Captain Spark, who boasts (without justification) of numerous conquests, and the beau Mondish, who goes quietly about several amours. Sex abounds in both plays, but, again, little of it is lighthearted. The Bellamants and the

Simon Rafflers find only distress in love; the couples endure, but with little sense of celebration.

Fielding found farce a better medium than comedy for exaggerated characterization and pointed satire. Eighteenth century farce did not have as many conventions as manners comedy, but its assumptions were well understood. In the prologue to *The Lottery*, Fielding comments on two important differences between the types. First, while "Comedy delights to punish the fool,/ Farce challenges the vulgar as her prize"; that is, the characters satirized in farce are more mean-spirited than self-deluded (and probably of a low social class). Second, farce identifies and attacks its targets by a "magnifying right/ To raise the object still larger to the sight"; that is, it allows exaggeration, hyperbole, and caricature. Formally, farce differs from comedy by dispensing with subplot, speeding up the pace, and emphasizing humor rather than wit in dialogue.

The Lottery is a good example of the latitude that farce gave Fielding's interests. The play exposes the foolishness of those who literally mortgage their futures to a one-in-ten-thousand chance and deplores the corruption of those who capitalize on foolish hopes. Mr. Stocks, who sells lottery tickets, knows "what an abundance of rich men will one month reduce to their former poverty." The brief plot follows the rocky love affair of Mr. Stock's younger brother Jack, who has no inheritance and whose beloved puts all their hopes for a happy married life on winning a ten-thousand-pound first prize. Fortunately, the lovers' natural affection survives the inevitable disappointment when their ticket does not win.

Eurydice shows a more imaginative use of farce's freewheeling style. The play depicts the visit of Orpheus to the Underworld in pursuit of his wife, Eurydice. Orpheus, singing ballad opera instead of strumming the lyre, charms Pluto, god of the Underworld, into granting permission for Eurydice to return to earth. Eurydice, however, is reluctant to return to modern London, where married love is accorded little respect; if Orpheus is like other modern husbands, he will soon lose interest in her. She wonders if she is not better off in a kingdom where she is free to govern herself. After much singing about the advantages and disadvantages of either choice, Eurydice finally decides to stay, and Orpheus departs alone, warning other husbands to appreciate their wives while they have them. *Eurydice* was not well received by its first audience, which took an unexpected dislike to one character, the ghost of an army beau. This reception led Fielding to write a sequel, *Eurydice Hiss'd*, about an author whose play, though imperfect, is unjustly scorned by theatergoers.

The Lottery and *Eurydice* are typical English farces, with a certain zaniness that results from making the plot fit the satiric theme. There was another tradition of farce, however, that Fielding explored in the 1730's. This other tradition was French; its major practitioner was Molière. Its sat-

ire is general (the incompetence of doctors, the social vanity of the nouveau riche), its structure built on the traditional devices of fast-paced
action, intrigue, and disguise rather than on ludicrous situations. One
might call it the "well-made farce": The plot leaves no loose ends. Such
plays demand especially skillful actors; Fielding, who was always aware of
how much a play's success depended upon its cast, twice adapted material
from the French to match the talent of a specific actress—in *The Intriguing
Chambermaid* and *The Mock Doctor*. Taking stock situations such as the
clever servant who outwits a master and the couple for whom marital life
and marital strife are synonymous, these farces move briskly to unfold,
develop, and tie together the action. *The Intriguing Chambermaid* and *The
Mock Doctor*, both successful pieces, show that Fielding could adapt as
well as be original in the art of farce.

Fielding, like many of his contemporaries, spoke slightingly of farce
because it was without classical precedent and therefore less literary: "The
stage . . . was not for low farce designed/ But to divert, instruct, and mend
mankind" through comedy. Fielding moved progressively away from comedy, however, as his own interests and theatrical developments in the 1730's
did more to shape his drama than did the desire to succeed as a regular
dramatist. Fielding found two vehicles, ballad opera and burlesque, ideal
for presenting satire in drama. Ballad opera combined farce, music, and
ingenious paralleling; it originated with John Gay's *The Beggar's Opera* (pr.
1728), a tale of London's underworld in which thieves and prostitutes sing
arias (set to native English tunes) about their lives, which show embarrass-
ing similarities to those of the rich and powerful. Burlesque exaggerated
theatrical conventions in order to poke fun at them and to indict a public
taste for such inferior entertainment. (Sometimes, however, "inferior"
meant only "what was currently successful at a rival theater.")

Fielding never wrote pure burlesque or ballad opera, preferring to draw
on these forms for devices which, when mixed with elements of comedy
and farce, could produce ingenious and distinctive plays. As suggested earlier, Fielding's subtitle to *Pasquin—A Dramatic Satire on the Times*—may
be the most useful way of describing these plays. "Satire" comes from the
Latin *satura*, which means a medley; Fielding's dramatic satires are indeed
medleys for the stage, collections of parts and techniques and themes
which the critical purist may find offensive but which the responsive reader
often finds delightful. Fielding, never able to give up hope of becoming
famous for his five-act comedies, often apologized for the dramatic satires,
calling them products of "his unskilled muse," because they pleased the
fancy more than the judgment. Those who read the dramatic satires today
could hardly disagree more. Written to "combat the follies of the town,"
these plays do suffer somewhat because some contemporary allusions are
lost, but Fielding is one of the great detectors of human folly, and the truth

of his observations is not limited to any time, any place, or any social class. Four plays—*The Tragedy of Tragedies*, *The Author's Farce*, *Pasquin*, and *The Historical Register for the Year 1736*—are Fielding's masterpieces in dramatic satire. They demonstrate his inventiveness, his versatility, his wit, and his thematic concerns. *The Tragedy of Tragedies* (a three-act version of the two-act afterpiece *Tom Thumb*) is a fantastic burlesque of heroic tragedy. The court of King Arthur and Queen Dollalolla is attacked by a race of warriors led by the giantess Glumdalca. The invaders are defeated by Arthur's champion, Tom Thumb, a knight as big as the digit whose name he bears. In reward, Tom is allowed to marry the Princess Huncamunca, but the proposed union causes much jealousy. Lord Grizzle, who loves Huncamunca, refuses to see her wed to one "fitter for [her] pocket than [her] bed." The queen and Glumdalca despair because they both love Tom. The giantess must forsake Tom because of their physical difference, and the queen's marriage vows intrude, although Dollalolla finds that in Cupid's scale, "Tom Thumb is heavier than my Virtue."

While Tom celebrates his engagement by murdering two bailiffs who arrest his courtier friends for debt, Grizzle attempts to woo Huncamunca. He succeeds quickly, but only because the Princess is ready to marry either man—or any man. Grizzle vows to kill Tom by leading a rebellion. Meanwhile, King Arthur is visited by a ghost who prophesies Tom's death. When the loyal army confronts the rebels, Grizzle kills Glumdalca, but Tom slays Grizzle. The celebration at court is spoiled, however, when news comes that upon meeting the victors in their march home, "a Cow, of larger size than usual/ . . . in a Moment swallowed up Tom Thumb."

As farce, *The Tragedy of Tragedies* is humorous, but as burlesque it is brilliant. As he exaggerates tragic conventions, Fielding also mocks their language by mimicking it. Inflated rhetoric, overblown metaphor, inappropriate diction, and ironic simile provide an aural equivalent of the visual farce. The king inquires thus about Dollalolla's health: "What wrinkled Sorrow,/ Hangs, sits, lies, frowns upon thy knitted brow?" Huncamunca describes pining for Tom: "For him I've sighed, I've wept, I've gnawed my Sheets." The parson prays for the fruitfulness of Tom's marriage: "So when the Cheshire Cheese a Maggot breeds,/ . . . By thousands, and ten thousands they increase,/ Till one continued Maggot fills the rotten Cheese." Glumdalca laments the emotional storm raised in her by the sight of Tom: "I'm all within a Hurricane, as if/ The World's four winds were pent within my Carcass." A giantess filled with one wind to expel is awsome; the notion of four winds pent within her is catastrophic.

The printed text of the play adds another target to the burlesque: It is a mock scholarly edition with critical apparatus. Fielding names his editor H. Scriblerus *Secundus* in the tradition of Martinus Scriblerus, whom Alexander Pope and Jonathan Swift had created to satirize pedantic scholarship. In a preface filled with Latin tags and authoritative references, Scriblerus argues that *The Tragedy of Tragedies*, conforming perfectly to classical precedent, is renowned throughout Europe. The footnotes increase the fun. Fielding had borrowed lines from actual plays (sometimes crucially altered, sometimes not) for his burlesque; the footnotes invert the procedure by demonstrating that *The Tragedy of Tragedies* was actually written in Elizabethan times and has itself been borrowed from and pillaged by all subsequent dramatists.

The Author's Farce also ridicules, in a somewhat freer form than *The Tragedy of Tragedies*, theatrical tastes of the day. It tells of a struggling playwright named Luckless who is having great difficulty getting his piece performed or published. Luckless is sure the work is just the thing to please contemporary audiences: a puppet show, called *The Pleasures of the Town*, which uses live actors. The inversion is typically Fielding; he teases the current rage for puppet actors performing cut-down standard plays by positing live actors performing Punch-and-Joan (as Judy was universally known then) antics.

The play is not pure burlesque but a mixture of comic traditions. Act 1 is traditional manners comedy. It shows Luckless unable to pay his rent because he is unable to sell his play. Witty though impoverished, Luckless fends off the financial and amorous demands of his landlady, Mrs. Moneywood, because he is really in love with her daughter, Harriot. Luckless' friend Witmore aids him in his battles against dunning creditors and stingy booksellers. When Witmore pays off the back rent, the ingenious Luckless dupes Moneywood into turning the cash over to him. When the publisher Bookweight refuses Luckless an advance, Bookweight is abused and thrown out of the apartment. At least Luckless gains some emotional satisfaction, and he possesses the pluck, the hauteur, and the quick-wittedness of the Congrevian hero.

Act 2 is closer to farce. Ten rapid scenes show Luckless trying to get his puppet show staged immediately. Two theater managers (representing Colley Cibber and Robert Wilks of Drury Lane) turn the play down because the author has no "interest"—that is, no standing within the ruling theatrical clique. Taking his case directly to other managers and to the actors, Luckless arranges for a performance that very night. Bookweight, discovered at his shop overseeing instant dedications and rapid translations written by his stable of hacks, now willingly listens to Luckless because he has "interest." A crier advertises the performance, "in which will be shown the whole Court of Dullness with abundance of singing and dancing and several other entertainments . . . to be performed by living figures, some of them six foot high."

The third act, the actual performance of Luckless' play, combines farce and burlesque. *The Pleasures of the Town* opens with a scene of the archetypal feuding couple, Punch and Joan; the arguing, singing, and dancing please popular taste but in no way relate to what follows. The next scene introduces a deceased poet on his way to the Goddess of Nonsense's Underworld court; the poet meets several other travelers fresh from London who are on the same route. There is Don Tragedio, who died after one performance; Sir Farcical Comic, who was hissed to death; Mr. Pantomime, whose neck the audience wrung; and Madam Novel, who went unread. Preeminent among these victims of shifting audience taste is Don Opera, who was so overwhelmed with the audience's approbation and his own dying aria that he swooned to death. Don Opera has been chosen as the fittest spouse for the Goddess of Nonsense. After an irrelevant scene presenting a card game among four shrieking harridans, the stage is set for the wedding. At this moment, *The Pleasures of the Town* turns into a ballad opera and emotional outbursts are rendered in song. There is plenty of passionate carrying-on: Nonsense discovers that Opera is already wed to Novel, and Opera protests that death has freed him from his vows. Unconvinced, Nonsense invites wooing from Farcical, Pantomime, and the others. Spurned, Opera proclaims his undying affection for Novel.

This dramatic moment is interrupted by Parson Murdertext, who has brought Constable to arrest Luckless for staging a sacrilegious play. The characters in the puppet show argue with Murdertext and Constable, thus blurring the line between play and play-within-the-play. That line grows even fainter as Harriot and Witmore enter with the ambassador from the Javanese kingdom of Bantom. The newcomer proclaims Luckless as the long-lost heir to Bantom's throne. A messenger enters to announce that the old Javanese king has just died, and Luckless is immediately proclaimed Henry I of Bantom. He appoints all the characters (not the actors) in the puppet-show to important government posts. Punch returns to identify himself as Harriot's lost brother, and Moneywood proclaims herself the impoverished Queen of Brentford. The play concludes with a dance.

Without a well-annotated text, modern readers will miss many of the in-jokes, yet none will miss Fielding's general indictment of the foolishness that passes as entertainment. Sudden reversals of fortune, reliance upon spectacle in place of development, and heavy use of coincidence are all marks of amateurishness or incompetence that mar drama, whether their victim is an eighteenth century play, a Hollywood movie, or a television sitcom.

Pasquin, a dramatic satire that shows Fielding's seemingly limitless inventiveness, follows one of the few traditions for a satiric play: a rehearsal of another play. George Villiers' *The Rehearsal* (pr. 1671), which mocked the heroic plays of John Dryden and Robert Howard, originated the form, which became standard in the self-conscious theater of the late seventeenth and early eighteenth centuries. Fielding's twist on the formula is to include two rehearsals—one of a comedy and one of a tragedy—in the same play. For two and a half acts, *Pasquin* shows Trapwit leading the actors through a comedy about how to win an election; for another two and a half acts, *Pasquin* presents Fustian taking the cast through his tragedy on the death of Queen Commonsense.

There is much comment and satire in *Pasquin* on now-familiar theatrical topics: the plight of actors and actresses, the looming specter of debtor's prison for authors and performers, hasty production of plays, scenes written by formula, reliance in dialogue upon bombast and innuendo (Trapwit, for example, protests that "except about a dozen, or a score, or so, there is not an impure joke" in his comedy), and production opportunity allowed only to already-successful authors. Fielding's main target in *Pasquin*, however, is not the theater; his subjects are political and intellectual. *Pasquin* has more in common with Swift's *Gulliver's Travels* (1726) and Pope's *The Dunciad* (1728-1743) than it does with other plays of the period. Trapwit's comedy is a merciless exposure of election campaigning, and Fustian's tragedy is an indictment of three professions: law, medicine, and religion. The play's title suggests the wide-ranging assault: Pasquin was the name of a Roman statue that was annually festooned with satiric epigrams and verses.

Like Swift, Fielding shows that people get the politicians they deserve. Trapwit's comedy observes the conduct of a contemporary election. Lord Place and Colonel Promise, the court's candidates (representing the Whig party of Sir Robert Walpole), vie for seats in Parliament with Sir Henry Foxchase and Squire Tankard, the country candidates (representing the Tory party). As the Mayor and aldermen sit in a tavern discussing the election, Place and Promise arrive and begin campaigning; they simply bribe each voter. In contrast to this method, which Trapwit calls "direct bribing," Foxchase and Tankard engage in indirect bribing: They buy meat and drink freely for the tavern crowd, patronize the merchants with prodigious orders for silks and clothing, and lament the corruption of courtiers who openly buy votes. The Mayor and aldermen rally for a moment to the newcomers and their slogan of "Liberty, property, and no excise."

Meanwhile, Place and Promise have been active among the ladies of the town, filling their ears with stories about the masquerades and fashionable gowns which could be theirs if the Court candidates win. Mrs. Mayoress and Miss Mayoress conclude that the lord and the colonel are "the finest men ... the prettiest men ... the sweetest men" and that the Mayor must vote for them. Miss Mayoress also persuades Miss Stitch, by the gift of a fan, to seek her beau's vote for the Court. The ladies carry the day with the Mayor, and when Foxchase and Tankard win the election, the Mayor is much chagrined that he has supported the losing party. Unable to give up her dreams of Court preferment, Mrs. Mayoress convinces her husband to certify that the losers are really the victors. As she announces this startling development to the surprised courtiers, she encourages them, "when we have returned you so [that is, duly elected] it will be your fault if you don't prove yourself so." Mrs. Mayoress refers to the wonderful knack of eighteenth century incumbents, especially Walpole's supporters, for keeping their seats by parliamentary maneuvering—regardless of an election's outcome.

Fustian's play, more allegorical than Trapwit's, is set at the court of Queen Commonsense in the days when she ruled England. Three of her chief ministers—Law, Physic, and Firebrand (who stands for religion)—are unhappy because the reign of logic and reason in the land has diminished their power. For example, when two men suing each other over property lose it to their own lawyers, the queen is ready to reform the legal system, but Law sees only a decline in his authority and income. When news comes that Queen Ignorance, with an army of "singers, fiddlers, tumblers, and rope-dancers," has invaded the island, the disgruntled courtiers threaten to join the rebels unless Commonsense yields them more power. Nevertheless, the queen bravely contends:

> Religion, law, and physic were designed
> By Heaven, the greatest blessings of mankind;
> But priests and lawyers and physicians made
> These general goods to each a private trade;
> With each they rob, with each they fill their purses,
> And turn our benefits into our curses.

Commonsense's refusal to surrender brings on a battle. Gradually, her followers are slain until only a poet remains; his support of Commonsense has been so weak of late that he readily goes over to the enemy. Firebrand stabs Commonsense, and the reign of Ignorance is established. Only the ghost of Commonsense remains to harass Ignorance's minions on occasion. The play ends, like Pope's *The Dunciad*, with universal darkness covering just about all.

In neither *The Author's Farce* nor *Pasquin* is Fielding's satire subtle. No characters are fully realized, plots jump as need be, and the dialogue has more sarcasm than wit. Fielding's ingenuity is in the juxtaposition of diverse and eclectic elements; the plays please through surprise and bluntness.

The Historical Register for the Year 1736 is less imaginative in its theatrical technique but more daring in its political attack. It, too, is cast as a rehearsal, this time of the playwright Medley's work about the previous year's events on the island kingdom of Corsica (which is obviously a symbol of Walpolian England). Medley's play alternates comments on the theater and on the nation because "There is a ministry in the latter as well as the former, and I believe as weak a ministry as any poor kingdom could boast of."

In linking the two worlds of the prime minister and the theater manager, Medley observes that "though the public damn both, yet while they [the ministers] receive their pay, they laugh at the public behind the scenes." Through Medley's play, Fielding takes the audience behind the scenes.

Act 1 begins by assembling some observers of the rehearsal and showing what kind of reception Medley might expect. Medley and the actors, happy merely to have a script to perform and a stage to use, convene. The critic Sourwit joins them, immediately damning whatever he sees. Lord Dapper looks on, so weak-brained that the most obvious satire must be explained to him. As the rehearsal commences, Medley reads a prologue, an ode to the New Year (with immortal lines such as "This is a day in days of yore/ Our fathers never saw before") which burlesques the vapid verse of the poet laureate and theater manager Colley Cibber. The first scene displays a cabal of politicians who respond to financial crisis by voting another tax. Finding everything already taxed, one politico proposes a tax on learning, but another counters, "I think we had better lay it on Ignorance," which "will take in most of the great fortunes in the Kingdom." Lord Dapper is present proof that the speaker is right. Fielding manages to abuse both politicians and, through them, the masters they serve.

Act 2 continues the assault with an opening scene in which fashionable ladies (formula comedies always open the second act with fashionable ladies) adore the latest opera singer, whose performances currently pack the theaters. They display their enthusiasm by carrying his "babies" (little wax dolls in his image), certainly an ironic tribute to a castrato. Since these dolls are more valuable than lapdogs or spouses, one lady protests, "If my husband was to make any objection to my having 'em, I'd run away from him and take the dear babies with me." In the next scene, the women attend an auction (the current faddish pastime), where the satire turns political. Up for sale are items such as a cloth remnant of political honesty, a piece of patriotism big enough to show off but too small to hold attention, a few grains of modesty, and an unopened bottle of courage; the buyers disparage the goods. Fielding's comment is twofold: There is only enough virtue in political society to give the illusion of honesty, and even that little claims no great market. The act ends with the entrance of the madman Pistol, who claims the title of "Prime Minister Theatrical"; when a mob hisses, he takes the sound as a sign of approbation. Pistol is a caricature of Theophilus Cibber, who, like his father, Colley, aspired to this title by hearing applause in a round of catcalls.

The third act dramatizes Medley's thesis that in the contemporary world "a man of parts, learning, and virtue is fit for no employment whatever . . . that honesty is the only sort of folly for which a man ought to be utterly neglected and condemned." The theatrical and political implications of this view are worked out as a modern-day Apollo casts the players for a performance of Shakespeare's *King John* with little regard to their competency. Like the theater managers of *The Author's Farce*, the god makes his decisions on the basis of "interest," the auditioner's relationship to someone in power. The consequences of such thinking are dramatized as Pistol becomes Prime Minister Theatrical by usurping his father and as Quidam, the model of a modern politician, bilks five citizens of the little money with which he had bribed them at election time. Quidam's fraud is accomplished through a pantomime dance which demonstrates that politics is nothing but theater; Pistol's accession shows how political theater is. The dance concludes the play, yet it is not a proper dramatic ending, simply one that caters to the people's taste. If the actors laugh while they dance, the target of their laughter is clear. Though Fielding's plays are diverse in method and form, they are alike in motivation. Fielding used the stage as early eighteenth century writers used every literary genre: as a forum for the discussion of current events. With journalistic promptness and intensity, Fielding (like other dramatists of the 1730's) built plays around current events in London: examples of private morality and immorality, political issues and personalities, and trends in the theater. Like a journalist, Fielding wrote rapidly. If a play succeeded, it was imitated or redone in a bigger and better version; if a play failed, it was pulled from the stage and replaced. Fielding was adept at writing quickly as well as ingeniously, whether reviving old material or concocting new combinations of dramatic staples. These "unshaped monsters of a wanton brain" could never bring Fielding the literary fame that successful five-act comedies would have brought, but several of them are masterpieces of the 1730's, one of the liveliest and most experimental eras of English theater.

Other major works

NOVELS: *An Apology for the Life of Mrs. Shamela Andrews*, 1741 (commonly known as *Shamela*); *The History of the Adventures of Joseph Andrews, and His Friend Mr. Abraham Adams*, 1742 (commonly known as *Joseph Andrews*); *The History of the Life of the Late Mr. Jonathan Wild the Great*, 1743, 1745 (commonly known as *Jonathan Wild*); *The History of Tom Jones, a Foundling*, 1749 (commonly known as *Tom Jones*); *Amelia*, 1751.

NONFICTION: *The Journal of a Voyage to Lisbon*, 1755.

MISCELLANEOUS: *Miscellanies*, 1743 (3 volumes).

Bibliography

Bateson, F. W. *English Comic Drama, 1700-1750*, 1929.

Butt, John. *Fielding*, 1959.

Donaldson, Ian. *The World Upside Down: Comedy from Jonson to Fielding*, 1970.

Loftis, John. *Comedy and Society from Congreve to Fielding*, 1959.

───────── . *The Politics of Drama in Augustan England*, 1963.

Paulson, Ronald, ed. *Fielding: A Collection of Critical Essays*, 1962.

Rawson, C. J. *Henry Fielding and the Augustan Ideal Under Stress*, 1972.

───────── , ed. *Henry Fielding: A Critical Anthology*, 1973.

Rogers, Pat. *Henry Fielding: A Biography*, 1979.

Robert M. Otten
Richard N. Ramsey

CLYDE FITCH

Born: Elmira, New York; May 2, 1865
Died: Châlons-sur-Marne, France; September 4, 1909

Principal drama

Beau Brummell, pr. 1890, pb. 1908; *Frederick Lemaître*, pr. 1890, pb. 1933 (one act); *Betty's Finish*, pr. 1890; *Pamela's Prodigy*, pr. 1891, pb. 1893; *A Modern Match*, pr. 1892; *The Masked Ball*, pr. 1892 (adaptation of Alexandre Bisson and Albert Carré's play *Le Veglione*); *The Social Swim*, pr. 1893 (adaptation of Victorien Sardou's play *Maison neuve*); *The Harvest*, pr. 1893; *April Weather*, pr. 1893; *A Shattered Idol*, pr. 1893 (adaptation of Honoré de Balzac's novel *Le Père Goriot*); *An American Duchess*, pr. 1893 (adaptation of Henri Lavedan's play *Le Prince d'Aurec*); *Mrs. Grundy*, pb. 1893; *His Grace de Grammont*, pr. 1894; *Lovers' Lane*, wr. 1894, pr. 1901, pb. 1915; *Gossip*, pr. 1895 (with Leo Ditrichstein; adaptation of Jules Claretie's play); *Mistress Betty*, pr. 1895; *Bohemia*, pr. 1896 (adaptation of Henri Murger's novel *Scènes de la vie de Bohème*); *The Liar*, pr. 1896 (adaptation of Bisson's play); *The Superfluous Husband*, pr. 1897 (with Ditrichstein; adaptation of Ludwig Fulda's play); *Nathan Hale*, pr. 1898, pb. 1899; *The Moth and the Flame*, pr. 1898, pb. 1908 (revision of *The Harvest*); *The Head of the Family*, pr. 1898 (adaptation of Adolf L'Arronge's play *Hasemanns Töchter*); *The Cowboy and the Lady*, pr. 1899, pb. 1908; *Barbara Frietchie*, pr. 1899, pb. 1900; *Sapho*, pr. 1899 (adaptation of scenes by Alphonse Daudet and Adolphe Belot and adaptation of Daudet's novel); *Captain Jinks of the Horse Marines*, pr. 1901, pb. 1902; *The Climbers*, pr. 1901, pb. 1906; *The Last of the Dandies*, pr. 1901; *The Marriage Game*, pr. 1901 (adaptation of Émile Augier's play *Le Mariage d'Olympe*); *The Way of the World*, pr. 1901; *The Girl and the Judge*, pr. 1901; *The Stubbornness of Geraldine*, pr. 1902, pb. 1906; *The Girl with the Green Eyes*, pr. 1902, pb. 1905; *The Bird in the Cage*, pr. 1903 (adaptation of Ernst von Wildenbruch's play *Die Haubenlerche*); *The Frisky Mrs. Johnson*, pr. 1903, pb. 1908 (adaptation of Paul Gavault and Georges Berr's play *Madame Flirt*); *Her Own Way*, pr. 1903, pb. 1907; *Major André*, pr. 1903; *Glad of It*, pr. 1903; *The Coronet of the Duchess*, pr. 1904; *Granny*, pr. 1904 (adaptation of Michel Georges-Michel's novel *L'Aïeule*); *Cousin Billy*, pr. 1905 (adaptation of Eugène Labiche and Édouard Martin's play *Le Voyage de M. Perrichon*); *The Woman in the Case*, pr. 1905, pb. 1915; *Her Great Match*, pr. 1905, pb. 1916; *The Toast of the Town*, pr. 1905 (revision of *Mistress Betty*); *Wolfville*, pr. 1905 (with Willis Steell; adaptation of Alfred Henry Lewis' stories); *The Girl Who Has Everything*, pr. 1906; *Toddles*, pr. 1906 (adaptation of André Godfernaux and Tristan Bernard's play *Triplepatte*); *The House of Mirth*, pr. 1906 (with Edith Wharton; adaptation of Wharton's novel); *The Straight Road*, pr. 1906; *The Truth*, pr. 1906, pb. 1907; *Her Sister*, pr. 1907; *Girls*, pr. 1908 (adaptation of Alexander Engel and Julius Horst's play *Die Welt ohne Männer*); *The Blue Mouse*, pr. 1908; *A Happy Marriage*, pr. 1909; *The Bachelor*, pr. 1909; *The City*, pr. 1909, pb. 1915; *Plays*, pb. 1915 (4 volumes).

Other literary forms

Clyde Fitch's nondramatic works have never been collected. He wrote one novel, *A Wave of Life*, which appeared in *Lippincott's* magazine in February, 1891, and which was later published by Mitchell Kennerley, with a foreword by Montrose J. Moses. Before the novel was published, Fitch had served his literary apprenticeship by writing short stories for a variety of commercial and church-related magazines. In 1889 alone, *The Independent*, *The Christian Union*, *The Churchman*, *Puck*, *Life*, and the children's magazine *Young Hearts* had accepted his stories, and in 1891, Fitch gathered a number of his vignettes of childhood into a volume entitled *The Knighting of the Twins*, which was published by Roberts Brothers in Boston; one of the stories, "An Unchronicled Miracle," was dedicated to Walter Pater. Known for his association with the Pre-Raphaelite movement, the author of *Studies in the History of the Renaissance* (1873) answered Fitch's whimsical verse that suggested that "even a cat may look on a king" with a pleasant, congratulatory note. *Some Correspondence and Six Conversations* (1896) and *The Smart Set* (1897), both collections of letters and discussions, were published by Stone and Kimball in Chicago. Fitch's nondramatic works are out of print and difficult to obtain; some of the short stories in such magazines as *Puck* and *Life* have not been identified.

Achievements

While Fitch was awarded no prizes or honors, he deserves mention as one of the first American playwrights to achieve popular success on his home ground. Indeed, the theatrical climate was ripe for his combination of romance and realism with purely American settings; most Broadway plays were either comedies of manners imported from England or farces translated from the French or German. Fitch wrote, then, when many serious as well as satiric publications were concerned not only with "Anglomania" but also with the development of a national literature. Given such a receptive audience, Fitch frequently produced a number of plays within one season.

To be sure, he was criticized for his "artificial" plotting, for tailoring his plays to available actresses, and for both borrowing from successful foreign plays and taking poetic license with history. Nevertheless, his development from farce to drama was sure and steady, and his careful attention to scenic detail and acting method earmarked him as a major influence on the realistic stage. Fitch's later experimentation, notably in 'The City, would make him memorable.

Fitch's works generally met with wildly enthusiastic responses from audiences but were often less generously received by critics, many of whom felt that his mechanical, "well-made" plots were indicative of a superficial point of view. Others, however, believed that his carefully tailored dramatic structures were foils for a social consciousness that would not be accepted in an undisguised form. In one sense, at least, such negative criticism was justified. The lighthearted *Captain Jinks of the Horse Marines*, starring Ethel Barrymore as the enterprising and charming Bronxite who pretends to be an Italian soprano, was resoundingly successful; the more serious *The Truth*, treating the marital consequences of inveterate lying, was not—at least in the United States. Marie Tempest made the play one of the first American successes throughout Europe, but at home, reception was cool, perhaps because the title betokened a more serious treatment than the public wished. Certainly, *The Climbers* had similar trouble, refused by all the New York producers because of what they believed to be a twin disability: a death and a suicide. The producers were wrong: Fitch's audience, which was both nurtured on the new realism of Theodore Dreiser and Stephen Crane and rooted in the nostalgia of the nineteenth century, appeared in droves, not only to witness the January-May marriage of the widowed Mrs. Hunter and the wealthy, socially inept Johnny Trotter, but also to hear about the self-denying love between Blanche Sterling and Edward Warden.

Critics and audiences agreed that Fitch excelled in the details of his settings. Producers were content to give him free rein, knowing that the playwright who worked almost eighteen hours a day and who was concerned in *Barbara Frietchie*, for example, that a fan failed to blow the curtains realistically enough to simulate a Maryland breeze, would mount a production with the finest attention to detail. Such attention came from his own aesthetic predilections: Once he achieved financial success, he traveled to Europe every spring, collecting the Della Robbias, the Louis IV furniture, the rare books, and the Watteaus that spilled over in his New York salon.

For Fitch, the collection of such paraphernalia, which might be regarded as mere affectation, was much in concert with his immersion in the theater. Without family attachments, he saw his work as defining his life; in words reminiscent of Henry James, Fitch wrote that he spent his time "studying and observing life" and that he had one goal—"to develop always." Praised for his "psychology," ideas, and theatrical savvy abroad, he failed to win serious critical acclaim at home, yet a modern reassessment suggests that his enthusiastic audiences were wiser than the savants. Fitch is important, not simply as one of the first American playwrights to achieve solid popularity but also as a transitional figure between nineteenth century melodrama and twentieth century realism.

Biography

Born in Elmira, New York, on May 2, 1865, William Clyde Fitch was the first of five children and the only son of Alice Maud Clark of Hagerstown, Maryland, and William Goodwin Fitch, a staff member to General Heintzelman during the Civil War. When he was four, the family moved to Schenectady, where he later joined with friends to form the Amateur Club and the Hookey Club and edited *The Rising Sun*, the pages of which express Fitch's early verve and vitality. His childhood frailty and love of beauty, learned from his charming, vivacious mother and sisters, made him an anomaly as he grew older; preferring the company of girls, to whom he wrote precocious love notes, and affecting individualistic aesthetic costumes, he marked himself as an original as early as his attendance at the Hartford Public High School.

Fitch's reputation followed him through preparatory school in Holderness, New Hampshire, and to Amherst College, where his classmates and Chi Psi fraternity brothers found his picturesque appearance no deterrent to his good humor and inventiveness. In fact, his first dramatic effort was a second act to a *Harper's* operetta, *Il Jacobi*, written in haste to complete an evening program for his fraternity. During his college years, he acted, produced, and painted scenery, frequently transposing effects from, for example, Daly's theater in New York, where he was an avid visitor. His college acting career included performances in Oliver Goldsmith's *She Stoops to Conquer* (pr. 1773) and in Richard Brinsley Sheridan's *The Rivals* (pr. 1775).

After graduating from Amherst College in 1886, Fitch went to New York, attempting both journalism and tutoring—which he disliked—to support himself. His novel *A Wave of Life* and short stories for *The Churchman* were written at a boardinghouse on West Fifty-third Street. The beginnings of his successful career can be traced to two experiences: He presented a letter of introduction to E. A. Dithmars, the drama critic for *The Times*, who provided the entrée to opening nights; and he spent some time in Paris with his mother in 1888, where he composed and read the one-act original play *Frederick Lemaître*.

By 1889, Fitch had established himself in New York and increased his circle of acquaintances to include such artists and writers as Oliver Herford of *Life* and William Dean Howells. His old friend Dithmars spurred Fitch's dramatic career by introducing the young playwright to the actor Richard Mansfield, who wanted a tailor-made play about Beau Brummell. After several false starts, including an argument with Mansfield about the ending, the play opened on a shoestring budget on May 17, 1890, at the Madison Square Theatre, where it was a huge success. Five months later, Felix Morris produced *Frederick Lemaître* in Chicago with the Rosina Vokes Company.

Soon before Fitch went to London to work on the unsuccessful comedy *Pamela's Prodigy*, he countered the critic William Winter's charges that Mansfield's kindness had made him only the titular author of *Beau Brummell*. His apprenticeship years, from 1890 to 1892, were devoted to adapting and rewriting, commissions appearing at financially opportune times. Of his works in this period, his adaptation of *The Masked Ball* from Bisson and Carré's French play *Le Veglione* proved the most important, catapulting John Drew and Maude Adams to stardom and assuring the reputation of Charles Frohman.

Fitch's output of plays produced between 1891 and 1898 (the two biggest successes were *Nathan Hale*, which opened at Hooley's Theatre in Chicago, and *The Moth and the Flame*, first produced in Philadelphia) testifies to his unremitting industry, broken only by his lavish entertainment for his growing circle of theatrical acquaintances and his frequent trips abroad. He became, in fact, one of the first commercially successful American dramatists; Frohman, who had looked to the British playwrights Arthur Wing Pinero and Henry Arthur Jones for his productions, tapped the young playwright. *Barbara Frietchie*, which opened at the Philadelphia Broad Street Theater on October 10, 1899, surpassed even *Nathan Hale* in popularity, bringing in ten thousand dollars in a single week. Inspired by a photograph of Fitch's mother as a girl and written for Julia Marlowe, the play, a romanticized version of the events surrounding the American revolutionary war hero, evoked an ongoing discussion about poetic license. His next major success was *The Cowboy and the Lady*, which was well received on the circuit and in New York in 1899, but it was criticized because of the swearing which Fitch, who had never been West, employed as local color. Clearly, Fitch proved himself a master of versatility. As the year 1901 opened, no fewer than three Fitch plays, aside from *Barbara Frietchie*, were on the boards in New York: *The Climbers*, a comedy of manners; *Lovers' Lane*, a rural romance; and *Captain Jinks of the Horse Marines*, described as a "fantastic comedy."

Indeed, Fitch frequently had more than one play running at the same time. His Greenwich, Connecticut, homesite, purchased in March, 1902, and christened Quiet Corner, was to alleviate some of the intense pressure under which he worked in his studio in New York, a studio crammed with keepsakes and theatrical books, flowers and memoirs—and guests. In addition, Fitch traveled some six months of the year, sometimes taking a "cure" such as the one at Parma, Italy, where he met actress Lily Langtry. Throughout all, he continued to write; in 1902, suffering from illness and exhaustion, he produced both *The Stubbornness of Geraldine* in November and *The Girl with the Green Eyes* in December, both with the same attention to fine detail that fostered his reputation as a realist.

Although many of Fitch's plays were written while he was traveling—as, for example, was *Her Own Way*, written for Maxine Elliott partly in Florence and read aloud to friends in London—Fitch's plays are thoroughly American, a fact recognized by William Dean Howells, who favorably reviewed *Glad of It* in *Harper's Weekly* early in 1904. In a letter of thanks to Howells, Fitch acknowledged the novelist's influence, writing that, although he himself was lost in the midst of "shams," Howells' name was a signpost to the true path.

The composition and rehearsal of the less than successful *The Coronet of the Duchess* in 1904 were typical of Fitch's work habits at Quiet Corner, where he and his menagerie of pets entertained a constant flow of visitors and where he composed his plays under a favorite apple tree, his birdcages hanging above him and his company chattering around him. After the next year, in which *Her Great Match*, *Wolfville*, and *The Toast of the Town* were produced, Fitch gave a series of lectures in Philadelphia and New York and at Yale and Harvard, in an attempt to educate the public, as he put it, about their responsibility: "Hardened theater" was the result, he believed, of a constant and unhealthy cry for novelty and a refusal to take the drama seriously.

In one sense Fitch heeded his own words when, in 1906, in the midst of *Toddles*, *The House of Mirth* (produced with the cooperation of Edith Wharton), and *The Girl Who Has Everything*, he began to write *The Truth* for Clara Bloodgood. This play, which depicts the effect of inveterate lying, seems to be an oblique commentary on the falseness of the theatergoing public itself, which *prefers* to trivialize the truth into melodrama, just as the heroine *prefers* to jeopardize a happy marriage for the sake of fibbing and flirtation. Perhaps not surprisingly, the initial reception was not as enthusiastic as that of *The Straight Road*, opening the same night. Reviewers became more warm in their praise, however, even comparing Fitch to Henrik Ibsen; the French wildly applauded Marie Tempest in the foreign presentation of the play.

Fitch's years of overwork began to take their toll; suffering from perpetual indigestion and a weak heart, he virtually retired to Katonah, New York, in 1907. The last year of his life found him writing *The City*, a play that justifies his self-assessment as a major contributor to the American drama. Indeed, his last reading of the play, five days before he left for his last trip to Europe, left him exhausted. His continued illness on the trip ended in his death in Châlons-sur-Marne on September 4, 1909.

Analysis

Clyde Fitch's generally undeserved reputation as a playwright who wrote exclusively for star performers gained currency with his first success, *Beau Brummell*, written at the request of Richard Mansfield through the influence of the reviewer E. A. Dithmars. Mansfield, unhappy with Blanchard Jerrold's version, was initially pleased with Fitch's script. With the play in rehearsal at Palmer's Theatre in January, 1890, Mansfield suddenly withdrew the play, then decided to go ahead at the Madison Square Theatre in May. Even then, the production was fraught with problems; Mansfield, financially overdrawn, was forced to cut corners. Costumes were at a premium, borrowed or provided out of the actors' own trunks. In addition, actor and playwright argued over the last act, Mansfield insisting on a happy ending. Fitch's compromise—bringing back the king and Brummell's old friends at the very moment of the Beau's death—made the play a success.

Based on the life of the eighteenth century dandy George Bryan Brummell, the friend of the prince regent George IV, the play is a potpourri of romance, wit, and nostalgia that does, nevertheless, depict enough character development in Beau to gain the audience's sympathy when he finally dies impoverished in France. His first-act appearance is characterized by superficial wit, polished manners, and exquisite sensibility as contrasted with the bluff, natural mien of his nephew, Reginald Courtenay. The romantic interest involves Reginald's clandestine love for an unnamed woman whose father refuses consent, and Beau's financially motivated proposal to Mariana Vincent, Reginald's beloved.

While Beau's mistaken identification of Mr. Vincent as a merchant peddler and his difficulty in disentangling himself from his mistress, Mrs. St. Aubyn, provide comic relief, the second act presents Brummell in a more ennobling light as he confesses to Mariana that, although he proposed because of her wealth, he finds that he loves her in her own right. His quarrel with the prince regent is occasioned by his attempt to protect her father; flustered by having his flirtation with Mrs. St. Aubyn exposed to public scrutiny by the clumsiness of Mr. Vincent, the prince is offended by Brummell's familiarity.

Again, in act 3, Brummell becomes more humanized as Mariana, convinced that he has saved her father's honor by snubbing the prince regent, refuses to give up her engagement at the urging of Mrs. St. Aubyn, who, out of jealousy, offers to intercede with the prince if Mariana will not marry. Knowing that her wealth can save Beau from his creditors, Mariana agrees to marry him; then she meets Reginald, whose letters have been stopped by connivance between the servants. Beau, in a self-sacrificing gesture, releases her from her engagement and is led away by the bailiffs.

Beau, with his "glory gone," is depicted in the fourth act in abject poverty, his faithful servant Mortimer having pawned all of his possessions. Fitch's melodramatic genius created the act in which Brummell sees his old friends in a vision, Mortimer assisting as he goes through the empty formalities of greeting his nonexistent guests. That the guests actually return to play their parts at the end of the play satisfied both Mansfield's desire for a happy ending and Fitch's realization that no happy ending was possible.

The Truth began as a casual remark in 1906 to Fitch's business agent about a character who could not avoid telling lies. He elaborated the plot in less than two hours after being asked to write a play for the actress Clara Bloodgood and was convinced that the result was "psychologically and technically" his best work. Initially, the critics were less convinced; reviews after the first night, on which he also opened *The Straight Road*, were unenthusiastic. As the record shows, however, the second tour of the play, in October, 1907, was very successful; in addition, European audiences and reviewers were extraordinarily enthusiastic over the performance of Marie Tempest, whom Fitch met at Versailles. Indeed, her success abroad was the indirect cause of the suicide of Bloodgood, depressed over the lack of American response.

Becky Warder, the play's protagonist, seems to lie for the sheer inventiveness and challenge of juggling varieties of truth. Perhaps if Fitch had been a greater playwright, he would have explored, as the twentieth century playwright Luigi Pirandello did, the existential ramifications of such a condition. Fitch, however, concentrated on the effects of Becky's lying upon her marriage. Like his later play *The City*, *The Truth* ends with a reconciliation based on self-knowledge.

Act 1 is reminiscent of the eighteenth century comedy of manners. Becky carries on a flirtation with Lindon, under the pretext of reconciling him with his wife, Eve; she entertains his wife between his visits; she deceives her husband not only about Lindon but also about the price of a bonnet and about money sent to her sponging father. Through it all, she protests that she loves her husband. The audience can judge that she does indeed try to convince Lindon to return to Eve; nevertheless, she cannot stop lying.

The converse, that a sincere man can awaken a woman to good, is only suggested, not underscored, because it is the character of Becky that is emphasized, not that of Warder. Indeed, the sudden appearance of Becky's father and Mrs. Crespigny—the landlady with whom he has been living, from whom he has been borrowing, and whom he has been refusing to marry—interrupts the theme. Mrs. Crespigny, both comic and sincere in her awe at the Warders' residence, is a variation of the "prostitute with the heart of gold," yet she encourages Roland in his profligate habits rather than helping him. The act seems to fall into two halves: Tom Warder confronts his wife with the detectives' evidence that Eve has gathered against Lindon and Becky, and Roland and Mrs. Crespigny arrive to ask for money. Warder, who discovers that Becky has lied about sending money to her father and that she has indeed seen Lindon, no longer trusts her when she does tell the truth concerning her refusal to give in to Lindon's propositioning.

The function of the Crespigny subplot becomes clear when the third act opens; Becky decides to live with her father once Tom has left her, and the act takes place at the landlady's cheap boardinghouse. In this play as in *The City*, Fitch merely touches on the effect of upbringing and heredity in shaping character. Becky's father himself is a consummate liar—in fact, his scheme to reconcile Becky and her husband is based on a lie. Its double function—to save him from a second marriage and to resume his life-style without Becky's interference—is predicated on her agreeing to play a charade. His telegram to Tom that Becky is seriously ill brings Tom to the boardinghouse; Becky is to play the part of an invalid and so evoke her husband's pity.

At the final moment, Becky cannot play the game. "If I can't win his love back by the truth I'll never be able to keep it, so what's the use of getting it back at all?" she asks. In a scene reminiscent of the one with which Fitch ends *The City*, Tom forgives Becky—not because she is without fault, but because she has finally learned to be herself without shamming. "We don't love people because they are perfect," he says. "We love them because they are themselves."

In the final analysis, the play presents a problem that borders on the tragic; thus, the denouement seems too easy, although Fitch made an effort not to provide a *deus ex machina*, a solution achieved by external means, but rather one brought about by character change. The change in Becky wrought by her father's confession of his own propensity for lying and by the disagreeable surroundings of the boardinghouse seems, however, temporary at best.

Fitch's last play, *The City*, produced posthumously in New York in 1909, was conceived while he was at work on an English adaptation of a German farce, *The Blue Mouse*. *The City* is said to contain the best and the worst of Fitch: While it is a thesis play—arguing that the city is a crucible which reveals a person's essential strengths and weaknesses—it is also a melodrama, and while the dialogue is witty, it calls attention to itself at the expense of the plot. The play displays Fitch's gifts as a distinctively American playwright, dealing with a theme that is one of the staples of modern American literature: urbanization and its consequences.

Fitch was convinced that he had written his best play, and modern assessments agree. As usual, he read the script to a circle of friends in Katonah. The reading, which took place only five days before he sailed on his annual trip to Europe, lasted until two o'clock in the morning, during which time Fitch rewrote and removed scenes as he read. Although the play was not produced until December, 1909, some three months after his death, his production notes were clear, and his company, under the direction of stage manager John Emerson, attempted to reproduce Fitch's directions. Perhaps encouraged by the death of a favorite playwright, the audience's mood of expectation reportedly became hysterical at the end of the play. For once, the critics agreed with the audience, and *The City* finally earned for Fitch the critical acceptance that he had wanted.

In part, the play is an examination of the secret tensions that underlie an average American home and therefore may be seen within the context of Ibsen's realism; like Ibsen, Fitch was not reluctant to confront, onstage, matters such as incest, adultery, and suicide. Fitch was considerably more conventional than Ibsen, however, and so even *The City* presents the audience with a satisfying "happy" ending.

In the opening act, the tension in the Rand family, comfortably established in Middleburg, seems to lie between the security of the small town and the lure of the city. The father, a successful banker, opposes the social aspirations of his wife and daughters, Teresa and Cicely, and the professional ambitions of his son, George, Jr., all of whom want to move to New York. Underlying that tension, however, is the idea that to stay in Middleburg, or in any small town, for that matter, is not to be "safe." George Rand, the pillar of the community, has engineered illegal bank deals; moreover, he is being blackmailed by George Frederick Hannock, his illegitimate son. Before the close of the act, Rand falls dead, a victim of a heart attack apparently precipitated by another demand from Hannock and the necessity of confessing his hypocrisy to his son George.

For the family, the death means release to go to the city, where George establishes himself as a financier and political aspirant. Fitch does more, however, than simply show that Rand was wrong to force his family to stay in Middleburg or that the city offers unlimited opportunity. George, it is revealed, copies his father's suspect business practices by gambling with his partner's investment and selling at a favorable time; Hannock threatens to publicize the deal, which could send George to prison.

With every event, George is put to the test: Honesty will lose for him not only the nomination but also his fiancée, as plain dealing would have lost him money. His political success is threatened by Teresa's pending divorce and by Hannock's drug addiction and dubious associates. The realistic depiction of family problems becomes melodrama, however, when George tries to tell Cicely that in her secret marriage to Hannock, she has committed incest; Hannock shoots Cicely to prevent her knowing the truth. Fitch piles incident upon incident. George's final test in the second act is whether to allow Hannock to kill himself before the police arrive. Hiding his shady financial dealings protected his reputation; likewise, he has made a deal with Teresa: To save his nomination, she will live in apparent harmony with her husband. Hannock's death, which might be passed off as an accident, would hide the worst of the story of incest and crime and salvage George's own engagement to Eleanor, a woman who, as her father says, must "look up to" the man she marries.

The brief third act opens with George's confession to his fiancée's father and his old friend and political supporter. His determination is not to return to Middleburg, a decision that underlines Fitch's refusal to draw the conventional good/bad distinction between country and city. In perhaps the best speech in the play, George defends the city:

> *She* gives the man his opportunity; it is up to *him* what he makes of it! A man can live in a small town all his life, and deceive the whole place and *himself* into thinking he's got all the virtues, when at heart he's a hypocrite! . . . But *the City*! . . . there she strips him naked of all his disguises—and all his hypocrisies . . . and then she says to him, Make good if you can, or to Hell with you! And what is in him comes out to clothe his nakedness, and to the City he can't lie! *I know*, because *I tried!*

His truth-telling has an immediate effect on others: Teresa and her husband drop their twin divorce suits, convinced that unselfish consideration of their children is more rewarding than personal gratification.

George's more difficult confession is to Eleanor, to whom he says that he disguised lying and cheating as "business diplomacy" and as "the commercial code." His excuse—that he simply patterned himself on others around him—is, he says, finally no excuse at all, since, as a grown man, he was in possession of his own judgment. Eleanor's response, that someone who makes a fresh start because "it is the right thing to do" and because "he *had to be honest with himself*" is "twice the man" he was the day before, provides the kind of satisfying ending that Fitch's audiences enjoyed.

Fitch is noteworthy, then, in giving the theme of the city a new twist: As the small town is no guarantor of virtue—not only because it does not provide a test but also because it allows one to deceive oneself with the approval of one's neighbors—so the city is no guarantor of vice. Indeed, for George Rand, it is a place where, in the midst of millions of people, he has learned to live with himself.

Other major works

NOVEL: *A Wave of Life*, 1891.

NONFICTION: *Some Correspondence and Six Conversations*, 1896; *The Smart Set*, 1897; *Clyde Fitch and His Letters*, 1924 (Montrose J. Moses and Virginia Gerson, editors).

CHILDREN'S LITERATURE: *The Knighting of the Twins*, 1891.

Bibliography

Andrews, Peter. "More Sock and Less Buskin," in *American Heritage*.

‑ XXIII (April, 1972), pp. 48-57.

Bell, Archie. *The Clyde Fitch I Knew*, 1909.

Moses, Montrose J., and Virginia Gerson, eds. *Clyde Fitch and His Letters*, 1924.

Phelps, William Lyon. *Essays on Modern Dramatists*, 1921.

Quinn, Arthur Hobson. *A History of the American Drama from the Civil War to the Present Day*, 1927.

Patricia Marks

JOHN FLETCHER

Born: Rye, England; December 20, 1579 (baptized)
Died: London, England; August, 1625

Principal drama

The Woman's Prize: Or, The Tamer Tamed, pr. c. 1604, pb. 1647; *The Woman Hater*, pr. c. 1606, pb. 1607 (with Francis Beaumont); *The Faithful Shepherdess*, pr. c. 1608-1609, pb. 1629; *The Coxcomb*, pr. c. 1608-1610, pb. 1647 (with Beaumont); *Philaster: Or, Love Lies A-Bleeding*, pr. c. 1609, pb. 1620 (with Beaumont); *The Captain*, pr. c. 1609-1612, pb. 1647 (with Beaumont); *Bonduca*, pr. 1609-1614, pb. 1647; *Valentinian*, pr. 1610-1614, pb. 1647; *Monsieur Thomas*, pr. 1610-1616, pb. 1639; *The Maid's Tragedy*, pr. c. 1611, pb. 1619 (with Beaumont); *A King and No King*, pr. 1611, pb. 1619 (with Beaumont); *The Night Walker: Or, The Little Thief*, pr. c. 1611, pb. 1640; *Cupid's Revenge*, pr. 1612, pb. 1615 (with Beaumont); *Four Plays, or Moral Representations, in One*, pr. c. 1612, pb. 1647 (commonly known as *Four Plays in One*; with Beaumont); *The Two Noble Kinsmen*, pr. c. 1612-1613, pb. 1634 (with William Shakespeare); *The Masque of the Inner Temple and Grayes Inn*, pr., pb. 1613 (masque; with Beaumont); *Henry VIII*, pr. 1613, pb. 1623 (with Shakespeare); *Wit Without Money*, pr. c. 1614, pb. 1639; *The Scornful Lady*, pr. c. 1615-1616, pb. 1616 (with Beaumont); *The Nice Valour: Or, The Passionate Madman*, pr. 1616(?), pb. 1649; *The Mad Lover*, pr. 1616(?), pb. 1647; *Love's Pilgrimage*, pr. 1616(?), pb. 1647; *The Queen of Corinth*, pr. 1616-1617, pb. 1647; *The Knight of Malta*, pr. 1616-1618, pb. 1647; *The Tragedy of Thierry, King of France, and His Brother Theodoret*, pr. 1617(?), pb. 1621 (commonly known as *Thierry and Theodoret*; with Beaumont); *The Chances*, pr. c. 1617, pb. 1647; *The Loyal Subject*, pr. 1618, pb. 1647; *Sir John van Olden Barnavelt*, pr. 1619, pb. 1883 (with Philip Massinger); *The Humorous Lieutenant*, pr. 1619, pb. 1647; *The Custom of the Country*, pr. c. 1619-1620, pb. 1647 (with Massinger); *The Little French Lawyer*, pr. 1619-1623, pb. 1647 (with Massinger); *Women Pleased*, wr. 1619-1623, pb. 1647; *The Island Princess: Or, The Generous Portugal*, pr. 1619-1621, pb. 1647; *The False One*, pr. c. 1620, pb. 1647 (with Massinger); *The Double Marriage*, pr. c. 1621, pb. 1647 (with Massinger); *The Wild Goose Chase*, pr. 1621, pb. 1652; *The Pilgrim*, pr. 1621, pb. 1647; *The Beggar's Bush*, pr. before 1622, pb. 1647 (with Massinger); *The Prophetess*, pr. 1622, pb. 1647 (with Massinger); *The Sea Voyage*, pr. 1622, pb. 1647; *The Spanish Curate*, pr. 1622, pb. 1647; *The Maid in the Mill*, pr. 1623, pb. 1647 (with William Rowley); *The Lover's Progress*, pr. 1623, pb. 1647 (revised by Massinger, 1634); *A Wife for a Month*, pr. 1624, pb. 1647; *Rule a Wife and Have a Wife*, pr. 1624, pb. 1647; *The Elder Brother*, pr. 1625(?), pb. 1637 (with Massinger); *The Fair*

Maid of the Inn, pr. 1626, pb. 1647 (with Massinger?); *Wit at Several Weapons*, pb. 1647 (with Beaumont?).

Other literary forms

John Fletcher apparently wrote very little or no poetry. He may have collaborated with other playwrights in the composition of court masques, but no direct evidence has been introduced identifying his hand in entertainments of that kind.

Achievements

Although Fletcher wrote many plays alone, he is best known for those he composed in collaboration with Francis Beaumont. In fact, much of the criticism of these playwrights' work regards them as an inseparable team. This practice has tended to obscure the technical brilliance of Fletcher's own plays, many of which were revived successfully on the Restoration stage. In their collaboration, however, the two dramatists came to be recognized as the inventors and chief practitioners of a style of drama, tragicomedy, that won enthusiastic applause from audiences at the Jacobean public theaters. Fletcher published a definition of the new genre in the preface to one of his earliest plays, *The Faithful Shepherdess:*

> A tragi-comedy is not so called in respect of mirth and killing, but in respect it wants deaths, which is inough to make it no tragedie, yet brings some neere it, which is inough to make it no comedie: which must be a representation of familiar people, with such kinde of trouble as no life be questioned, so that a God is as lawfull in this as in a Tragedie, and meane people as a comedie.

While the play to which this preface was appended proved unpopular with its audience, Fletcher, with the older Beaumont, went on to instant success in *Philaster*, one of his first collaborative efforts in the new form. This event was also notable because it cemented the playwrights' connection with William Shakespeare's company, the King's Men. Beaumont and Fletcher continued to write for that company for the rest of their careers.

What attracted Jacobean playgoers to *Philaster* was its complicated but relatively fresh plot (no sources have been identified), romantic setting, and suspenseful denouement: The heroic prince discovers that the page who has served him faithfully throughout the play is in fact a woman—a woman who is deeply in love with him. The happy ending, however, leaves the audience with a sense of having been manipulated; Beaumont and Fletcher take little care to develop their characters or to motivate action. Even so, *Philaster* won the playwrights a reputation with the gentlemen and ladies who increasingly made up the audience at the Blackfriars playhouse.

Before Beaumont's retirement in 1613, he and Fletcher worked together on several other plays, only a few of which were in fact tragicomedies. Other than *Philaster*, *A King and No King* is probably the best example of the genre. *A King and No King*, like many Jacobean plays, depends on the frisson of an incestuous love: The hero believes that he has engaged in intercourse with his sister. As it turns out, the two are not in fact brother and sister, the hero's parentage having been misrepresented by a deceitful queen. Despite this happy evasion of tragedy, the purpose of titillating the viewers was deftly accomplished. The dramatic rhythm of relaxation and sudden surprise is reinforced by a style of verse that alternates between realistic conversation and high-flown rhetoric. This characteristic of the verse (informal talk that suddenly gives way to elevated poetry) was widely admired by the audiences of Beaumont and Fletcher's era and by Restoration audiences, for whom the plays became regular revival fare. Indeed, their tragicomedies were staged more frequently in the period from 1660 to 1700 than were the works of Shakespeare, who was judged too rough-edged, or Ben Jonson, who was regarded as too satiric.

Beaumont and Fletcher also composed tragedies—*Cupid's Revenge*, *The Maid's Tragedy*—and witty comedies—*The Coxcomb*, *The Scornful Lady*—in the Jonsonian vein. These plays demonstrate the versatility and range of these playwrights, but they helped propel the Jacobean stage into decadence. The dominant scene in *The Maid's Tragedy*, for example, contains a wedding-night confession by the heroine to her warrior-hero husband that she has been and intends to continue to be the king's mistress. This situation brings the style and tone of *The Maid's Tragedy* perilously close to the realm of soap opera.

After Beaumont's death, Fletcher continued to work in collaboration, primarily with Philip Massinger and William Shakespeare. The plays produced during this period were largely tragedies and tragicomedies that responded to the audience's desire for spectacular entertainment. The teaming of Fletcher and Shakespeare likewise suggests that the style of tragicomedy developed by Fletcher strongly influenced Shakespeare's own play production. Romances such as *Pericles, Prince of Tyre* (pr. c. 1607-1608), *The Winter's Tale* (pr. c. 1610-1611), and *The Tempest* (pr. 1611) display the same fascination for plot turns, type characters, exotic settings, and elevated verse found in Beaumont and Fletcher's tragicomedies. When left to his own devices, however, Fletcher also turned his hand to comedy that explored the manners of upper-class Englishmen. Most of these plays are distinguished by complicated plots, humorous characters, and witty dialogue. His ease in writing comedy has led many critics to conclude that Fletcher was the author of the comic scenes in the tragicomedies, while Beaumont was responsible for the tragic scenes and characters. Fletcher's comedies, with their themes of youthful love and sexual combat, caught the fancy of Stuart courtiers and helped to lay the groundwork for the Restoration comedies of manners.

Although he ended his career by composing sophisticated comedies, Fletcher has been recognized by commentators on the Jacobean stage as the innovator of tragicomedy and as the period's foremost dramatic collaborator. His name seems destined to be linked with that of Beaumont or Massinger in future critical analyses as well. The body of work turned out by Fletcher with his fellow playwrights is truly impressive: some fifty plays in the Second Folio (1679). Considerable time and print have been spent in attempts to determine the relative contributions of each playwright to the comedies, tragedies, and tragicomedies printed in the First and Second Folios—a task that is still going on and may never be satisfactorily completed. As a result, much valuable criticism of the style and content of the individual plays still remains to be done.

Biography

John Fletcher was born in Rye, Sussex, where he was baptized on December 20, 1579. His father, Richard, was a clergyman who attended Cambridge and was later made president of Corpus Christi College, Cambridge, Dean of Peterborough, and eventually Bishop of London. Elizabeth I reportedly admired his talent as a scholar and bestowed special favor on him. John Fletcher's uncles, Giles and Phineas Fletcher, were poets with respected reputations, and their successes added honors to the family name. These conditions of birth and social standing were somewhat unusual among playwrights of the age and doubtless helped to reinforce Fletcher's reputation as an entertainer of gentlemen.

Although John Fletcher no doubt attended lectures at his father's alma mater, he may have been forced to leave Cambridge in 1596 when, perhaps in part because of an ill-advised second marriage, Bishop Fletcher was suspended by the queen. Later in that same year, he died, and Fletcher was probably taken under the wing of his uncle Giles, who may have helped to pay off the family's large debts. Just when Fletcher began writing plays is not known, but it is certain that he was hard at work in collaboration with Beaumont early in the first decade of the seventeenth century. After Beaumont left the profession in 1613, Fletcher continued as the chief playwright for the King's Men, working alone or with Philip Massinger, William Shakespeare (on *The Two Noble Kinsmen* and *Henry VIII*), and several others. Fletcher's death in August, 1625, was caused by the plague; he was buried in St. Saviours Church, Southwark, the district in which he had resided throughout his career in London.

Analysis

Una Ellis-Fermor (*The Jacobean Drama: An Interpretation*, 1936) observes that the "names of Beaumont and Fletcher are often associated so closely with tragi-comedy that their work and that form of play are loosely spoken of as if they were coexistensive." Although she goes on to state that only five plays in the tragicomic genre are accepted as bearing the stamp of their mutual authorship, recent critical assessments have not been very successful in altering the prevailing opinion. Certainly, there are good reasons for the tenacity of the popular view, including the fact that Fletcher named and defined the genre in the preface to one of his earliest plays, *The Faithful Shepherdess*. The play may have been inspired by Giambattista Guarini's *Il pastor fido* (1585), but it bears little resemblance to the realistic "sad shepherd" plays, marked by dancing and festivity, with which the English audience of that day was familiar. In fact, with its shepherd and shepherdess lovers poeticizing about passion and lust, *The Faithful Shepherdess* more nearly approximates the prose romances of Edmund Spenser and Sir Philip Sidney.

Set in Thessaly, the play introduces the virgin shepherdess Clorin who, having vowed to purge all passion from her heart in memory of her dead lover, lives beside his grave and dispenses healing herbs to those wounded by love or lust. This devotion sets the standard against which one is to judge the behavior of all the other characters—especially the central couple, Perigot and Amoret, pastoral lovers who vow to exchange only chaste kisses. The comedy of errors that develops tests this resolve, and their love. Amarillis, Amoret's rival, wantonly pursues Perigot, who dutifully rejects her. She vows to gain revenge against Amoret by magically transforming herself into Amoret's double. Despite her altered appearance and her use of every conceivable weapon of seduction, Amarillis finds Perigot unable to love in any but a chaste fashion. As might be expected, when Perigot next encounters the true Amoret, he is so incensed by what he believes is her blatant cynicism that he strikes her with his sword. Later, Amarillis takes pity on the grieving Perigot, who believes he has killed his true love; she admits to disguising herself as Amoret and offers to do so again to prove her case. When the real Amoret reappears, seeking to reassure Perigot of her love, he believes she is intentionally deceiving him and once again wounds her with his sword. Through the good offices of Clorin, however, the two lovers are finally reconciled and Amarillis, along with two other unchaste lovers, is cured of her affliction. In the main plot and in subplots involving other pastoral characters (among them, a satyr, a river god, and the Caliban-like Sullen Shepherd), Fletcher sets up moral and ethical contrasts: He disguises vice as virtue and virtue as vice in an attempt to dramatize conflicts between essentially one-dimensional characters. Although the action is occasionally brought to the brink of tragedy only to be saved by some intervention of fortune, the plot depends on a kind of mechanical alteration of moods. Almost more an exercise in poetic composition—with impressive variations in sound effects and imagery, for example, used to indicate subtle differences between characters—the play's style has been nicely characterized by Eugene Waith as "the product of refined sensationalism." Whether because the contemporary audiences perceived this flaw or were simply unprepared to believe or care about the rather stylized figures delivering, in long poems of closely rhymed verse, explanations for their attitudes and desires, the play proved a failure on the stage.

As in *The Faithful Shepherdess, Cupid's Revenge* turns on the contrast between lust and love. Princess Hidaspes, a virtuous woman who recalls Clorin, is given one wish on her birthday, and she wishes for the destruction of Cupid's altars. When this occurs, a vengeful Cupid forces Hidaspes to fall in love with the court dwarf, who is later killed by the king. Hidaspes then expires from a broken heart. In a second story, Prince Leucippus, Hidaspes' brother, falls in love with Bacha, an unchaste woman who has wooed both the prince and the king (Leontius) by means of a mask of chastity. Thus, male and female members of the royal household are made to suffer because of love—degradation (in the case of Leucippus and Leontius) and death (Hidaspes). As in *The Faithful Shepherdess, Cupid's Revenge* is filled not with well-motivated dramatic characterizations but rather with representations of the moral dimensions of love.

An incident inserted in *Cupid's Revenge* primarily to play upon the sympathies of the viewers concerns Urania, daughter to Bacha, who loves Leucippus and disguises herself as a page in order to be near him after his banishment. She is murdered when she rushes between her lover and a messenger sent by Bacha to kill him. Leucippus' discovery of Urania's true identity provides the occasion for a melodramatic statement on the fortunes of true love. This situation was repeated by Fletcher and Beaumont in the popular and dramatically fresh *Philaster*. The hero, a disinterested prince who has been compared by many critics to Hamlet, finds himself living in the court of an evil king, usurper of his throne. Philaster falls in love with Arethusa, the king's daughter, but is informed by Megra, a scheming, lascivious lady of the court, that his beloved has deceived him with Bellario, a young page who has served as their messenger. Aroused to a sudden anger, Philaster attacks Bellario and Arethusa but is quickly arrested by the usurping king. After a revolt by the people helps Philaster win back his throne, his marriage to Arethusa is made public. Megra revives the old charge against Arethusa, and Philaster orders Bellario stripped and beaten. Only then is the page revealed to be Euphrasia, a noble's daughter who is hopelessly in love with Philaster; the revelation results in the banishment of Megra. Hero and heroine live happily ever after, although the continued presence of Philaster's "loyal" servant (often compared to Viola in *Twelfth Night*) seems to strike a melancholy note.

Philaster carries on the debates about love and lust, loyalty and deceit,

that were a part of Fletcher's earlier work. By setting the action in a distant time not associated with the pastoral, Beaumont and Fletcher manage
to avoid much of the confusion that resulted from a pastoral setting. The
characters here are types—the lover, the lustful lady, the usurper—whose
actions are not carefully motivated; they behave in a manner required by
the situation. There can be little doubt that the poetry spoken by these
characters, which is often refined and beautiful, helped considerably in
holding the contemporary playgoer's attention. More than any other element, however, the scenes depicting Philaster striking his loyal servant and
Bellario disclosing her true identity are typical of Beaumont and Fletcher's
successful plays. They are suspenseful and surprising; they wrench potentially tragic situations into the realm of romantic happiness, usually at the
last possible moment.

A somewhat different, more serious tone prevails in *A King and No
King*. As in *Philaster*, King Arbaces faces a romantic dilemma, but unlike
Philaster, he falls in love with his sister—when they meet after a long separation. Although promised to Arbaces' rival Tigranes, the captured King of
Armenia, Panthea returns her brother's love, thereby setting the stage for
what appears to be an incestuous affair. The shock of this situation is created through dubious maneuvering, but one can readily see that it is the
type of dilemma requiring the radical, even sensational resolution typical of
Beaumont and Fletcher's tragicomic style.

Just as Arbaces concludes that the only course for a sinner like him is
suicide, he learns that his real father is the Lord-Protector, who had helped
the queen "produce" an heir, allowing her to present his newborn infant as
her own son. Panthea emerges as the true heir to the throne, thereby
legitimating Arbaces' love for her. The two are married, Tigranes finds
Spaconia to be his true love, and the terrible atmosphere of evil that domi-
nates the play in its earlier stages seems banished like a bad dream. The
audience has followed the hero and heroine to the brink of tragedy, but
once again, through a miraculous discovery, a happy ending has been
imposed. What gives this play greater weight than even *Philaster* is the way
in which Arbaces' struggle with his emotions has been thoroughly explored.
He emerges as more than a type, although his flaws, which have seemed so
real throughout the body of the play, seem to disappear with the discovery
and resolution. Arbaces emerges in this regard as a "problem" character
similar to Shakespeare's Angelo (*Measure for Measure*) and Bertram (*All's
Well That Ends Well*).

Although the central dilemma of *The Maid's Tragedy*—what a worthy
man should do after learning that his bride is the king's mistress—could
have been resolved through the devices of tragicomedy, Beaumont and
Fletcher chose instead to make the play into a tragedy. The result is a
compelling, artful play. Amintor is persuaded to marry Evadne by the

predictably evil king; in order to do so, Amintor breaks off his engagement with Aspatia—and breaks her heart. When Evadne informs Amintor that their marriage is only a cover-up, he swears vengeance, but when he learns he has been cuckolded by the king, he decides against taking revenge because of his strong feeling of loyalty toward the throne. Amintor does divulge his awful secret to his fellow warrior Melantius, who also happens to be Evadne's brother. Melantius confronts his sister with the truth and says that she must repair the damage to her marriage—and to the country—by murdering the king: "All the gods require it." In another of those contrived but riveting scenes so typical of Beaumont and Fletcher plots, Evadne comes to Amintor, her hands covered with the king's blood, to ask his forgiveness, only to find him weeping over the body of Aspatia. Aspatia, despairing of happiness, had disguised herself as a man (a favorite convention in the tragicomedies) and provoked a duel with Amintor, falling on his sword and killing herself. When Amintor realizes what Evadne has done, he rejects her, in blank verse that rivals Shakespeare's in sheer dramatic strength. Evadne cannot withstand his rebuke and soon commits suicide. Finally, Amintor, struck by the horrible sight of these women who died for him, likewise gives up the struggle.

Despite the tragic impact of this final scene, it is difficult to describe either Amintor or Aspatia as characters with the capacity for suffering of a Hamlet or Ophelia. Both are sentimental figures. Whether, as one critic has observed, Aspatia represents the pure heroine of the Elizabethan period brought down by the sophisticated and corrupt Jacobean heroine is a matter for debate. She certainly traces her origins back to the disguised page characters of the earlier tragicomedies. The regular introduction of debates over honor and loyalty, the sudden twists of plot, the prominence of an intriguing and vengeful figure such as Melantius, and the almost operatic verse style are all elements that look ahead to the heroic drama of John Dryden and Sir William Davenant. Other than *A King and No King*, *The Maid's Tragedy* is probably the most carefully constructed and emotionally rich of the plays written by Beaumont and Fletcher.

In addition to tragicomedy and tragedy, the two playwrights also worked together on a number of comedies. Two of the best of these are *The Scornful Lady* and *The Coxcomb*. In *The Scornful Lady*, a play originally written for the Queen's Revels Children, two pairs of male lovers woo different ladies. The brothers Loveless, the older a sober fellow who engages in combats of wit with the Lady and the younger a prodigal who woos and wins a rich widow, are the comic heroes of this comedy of manners. The main action concerns Elder Loveless' attempt to purge the humor of the Lady, who longs for her lover when he is away but abuses and mocks him when he is present; he vies for her favor with the good-looking Walford, who, upon losing the contest, settles for the Lady's sister. In this situation one can clearly see the influence of Jonson on Fletcher; the humor scheme is worked in similar fashion in Jonson's *Epicoene: Or, The Silent Woman* (pr. 1609, pb. 1616). Young Loveless also woos a lady, a beautiful and wealthy widow, but in a style that is considerably more boisterous than that of his brother, and he, too, faces a rival—Morecraft, a moneylender who had previously fleeced him. Young Loveless might be called a "playboy" in modern usage, and he and his companions nearly drive the steward of his beloved's house mad with their drinking and carousing. Although his speech lacks the verbal pyrotechnics to be found in the dialogue of Restoration comedy, Young Loveless does stand for the power of revelry and good fun, and the stratagems and spicy wit which finally bring him and his brother their desired prizes were a model for subsequent playwrights.

Like *The Scornful Lady*, *The Coxcomb* follows a dual plot structure and depends somewhat heavily on the humor scheme for its effects. Antonio, the coxcomb or cuckold, proves to be so generous that the moment he learns of his friend Mercury's love for his wife (Maria), he literally forces her into Mercury's arms. Antonio even resorts to a disguise to bring the two together for what appears to be a lust-satisfying tryst. To the end, however, Antonio apologizes profusely for his wife's "excessive" virtue. The subplot (really a second story) concerns Viola, a fair maid who is scorned by her lover Ricardo. Forced to wander the countryside alone, Viola is robbed and nearly raped by an oversexed "gentleman." She is finally befriended by two milkmaids, a circumstance that allows her to praise the inherent virtues of country life. Her short verse encomium provides an effective contrast to the rough-and-tumble prose speech of the rustic characters. When Ricardo is finally reunited with Viola, he begs forgiveness for the wanton behavior that led him to scorn her. How this romantic tale relates to the more tragicomic one involving Antonio, Maria, and Mercury, however, remains unclear. Both heroes might be viewed as humor types who are, because of their blindness, susceptible to being cuckolded. Despite its disjointed plot, *The Coxcomb* is a comedy of lively contrast between city and country life, urban and rustic foolery.

A similar farce, *Wit at Several Weapons*, has been variously attributed to Fletcher alone, to Beaumont and Fletcher, and even to such revisers as Middleton. It is the story of Sir Perfidious Oldcraft, who strives to make his son, Wittypate, less of a dunce. After a complicated series of intrigues, the father discovers that Wittypate has been deceiving him from the beginning and, in fact, truly does possess wit. This recognition makes Oldcraft so happy that he immediately gives the boy a large allowance. In the subplot, a character named Sir Gregory Fop also finds himself the victim of trickery, but the result is a happy one: marriage to an attractive heiress. Even though the action, with its emphasis on intrigue and duping, smacks of Jonson, Beaumont and Fletcher do not intrude the element of keen satire here. Indeed, the mood is one of high spirits, involving stock characters speaking humorous but not ingenious verse.

When Beaumont retired from the stage in 1613, Fletcher continued to write plays on his own and in collaboration with others. He had become a valued member of the King's Men, recognized as a skilled and popular creator of tragicomedies, tragedies, and comedies. Indeed, there is convincing evidence that Fletcher was composing successful plays on his own even during the period of his collaboration with Beaumont. *Bonduca* and *Valentinian* are two tragedies written by Fletcher that appealed to the Globe and Blackfriars audiences. *Bonduca* dramatizes events related to the wars between Britons and Romans, and it may have been inspired by Shakespeare's *Cymbeline* (pr. c. 1609-1610). Although the play is named after the English queen Bonduca, she has very little part in it. The tragic hero is a brave lad named Hengo, who is deceitfully killed by the Roman Judas. Caratach, a courageous old soldier who is the other major figure in the play, avenges the murder by slaying Judas. The death scene, with its rhapsodizing about Britain and youthful death, smacks of the kind of pathos that Fletcher achieves in the verse of the tragicomedies. Whether Caratach was intended as a dramatic copy of Sir Walter Raleigh, at that time a prisoner in the Tower and widely regarded as a champion of the good old cause, is difficult to determine. There can be no doubt, however, that *Bonduca* was intended to be a play about English patriotism and loyalty.

Valentinian achieves a greater tragic impact than does *Bonduca*, primarily because its villain is the Roman emperor who rapes Lucina, the honest wife of a brave soldier named Maximus. Fletcher spins out the action by means of contrast between the brave and loyal army captains and the dissolute world of the court, with the emperor Valentinian announcing to the prostrate Lucina: "Justice shall never hear you; I am justice." Here is the mood and style of a work such as *The Maid's Tragedy*, with its helpless victims and seemingly omnipotent villains. When Lucina dies, Maximus, instead of seeking direct revenge against Valentinian, becomes a Machiavellian intriguer who employs servants to taunt and then poison the villain, betraying his own friend Aecius as one step toward this end. After Maximus marries the emperor's widow, he foolishly tells her of his deeds, and she proceeds to poison him in turn, by crowning him with a poisoned wreath. This serpentine plotting corrupts the tragic mood of *Valentinian*, which is also marred by special effects and what one critic has called "Fletcher's flamboyant declamation."

Fletcher's chief collaborator after Beaumont was Philip Massinger. The two men produced at least ten plays together, most of them tragedies and comedies. *The False One* and *Sir John van Olden Barnavelt* are two representative examples of this collaboration. The former tragedy depicts Caesar's affair with Cleopatra in Egypt, although the title does not refer to the queen but to a Roman named Septimius, who is responsible for the murder of his old general, Pompey. In a bold move, Septimius vows to murder Caesar, and much of the action concerns the intrigues against him. In the end, however, Caesar outwits and defeats his enemies, which makes it difficult to regard the ending as tragic. Massinger was probably responsible for the opening and closing scenes of the play, while Fletcher depicted the love scenes involving Caesar and Cleopatra and invented the breathtaking masque of Nilus. Honor and nobility are at stake throughout, but the action and characters do not achieve the heights or complexity found in Shakespeare's play dealing with similar materials.

Sir John van Olden Barnavelt deals with a contemporary rather than an ancient event in history—the downfall and death of the well-known Dutch statesman in May, 1619. There are also allusions in this tragedy to the execution of Sir Walter Raleigh, which had taken place the previous year, making it difficult to understand how the play was allowed on the stage (it was not published until 1883). Massinger's interest in political themes and foreign policy (see his *Believe as You List*, pr. 1631) is evident in this aspect of the play, while Fletcher no doubt wrote the scenes that deal with Barnavelt's emotional side. The play suffers from hasty composition: It was written and put into production within three months of Barnavelt's death. Of particular importance, however, is the fact that Fletcher lent his talent to a play dealing with the topic of absolutism. He is no doubt the author of a sensational scene in which three executioners throw dice to decide who will carry out the beheading.

Besides Massinger, Fletcher was also working with Shakespeare during this period (1613-1620), and *Henry VIII* and *The Two Noble Kinsmen* bear the mark of Fletcher's hand. In *Henry VIII*, the spectacular celebrations and the episodic plot are reminiscent of the style of *A King and No King* and *Thierry and Theodoret*. Little attention is given to Henry himself, the best speeches and scenes going to Wolsey (whose famous farewell may indeed have been written by Fletcher) and Cranmer. The same emphasis on spectacle, especially scenes of pageantry, can be seen in *The Two Noble Kinsmen*.

Although Fletcher collaborated with other playwrights after 1616, the main body of his work in this period was in his own hand and in his favorite genres: comedy and tragicomedy. Tragicomedy was apparently more attractive for him than tragedy because he was either incapable of or uninterested in exploring internal conflict by means of the soliloquy. As William Appleton has put it in *Beaumont and Fletcher: A Critical Study* (1956), "Rarely can Fletcher conceive of the tragedy of the individual caught in an infernal machine of his own making. He concentrates instead on the tragedy of circumstance."

A few tragicomedies from Fletcher's later works should suffice to illustrate his dramatic style at this stage in his career. In some ways, Fletcher's interests reveal a return to the themes and characters of his earliest plays. *The Mad Lover* features a hero named Memnon, who leaves his career as a vainglorious warrior to woo the beautiful Princess Calis. This rejection of war in favor of love was a subject treated in earlier tragicomedies, such as *Philaster* and *A King and No King*. Memnon, however, follows a rigid code of honor in his love that is mocked by other characters in the court of Paphos, where a cynical view of romance prevails. His chief rival for Calis' hand turns out to be his own brother, Polydor, who wins the princess' heart even as he tells her she must love his brother. In a spectacular denouement typical of Fletcher, Polydor has himself sent to Calis in a coffin, bearing a will that directs her to marry Memnon. When Memnon enters, however, he sees his apparently dead brother and declares his intention to follow him to the grave. At this point, Polydor arises, still pleading for his brother as suitor. Memnon, however, perceives the truth—that Calis loves Polydor deeply—and decides to return to war. This heroic gesture places Memnon in the first order of heroic lovers that will come to dominate the Restoration stage. He also qualifies as one of Fletcher's most memorable tragicomic figures, changing from an essentially foolish soldier to a romantic Platonist.

In *The Loyal Subject*, Fletcher likewise gives the action coherence by organizing it around the theme of duty to self and sovereign. Based on an earlier play by Thomas Heywood (*The Royal King and Loyal Subject*, pr. 1602?, pb. 1637), Fletcher's tragicomedy concerns the staunch loyalty of the general Archas to the weak and easily flattered Duke of Moscow. That devotion is contrasted to the Machiavellianism of Boroskie, who seeks to widen a rift that has resulted in Archas' resignation. Archas is then subjected to exile, imprisonment, and torture, but at every instance of national crisis, he acts to aid his country. Only after Archas' daughters are able to convince the duke of their father's loyalty is he allowed to live. Before this happens, Archas is brought to a point at which he threatens to kill his son Theodore for speaking out against the cruel duke and Boroskie. This disaster is deftly avoided by a general resolution in which Archas is forced to relent when his youngest son is threatened with death. The resolution allows Archas to remain true to his personal and political codes of honor. It also has suggested to certain critics that Fletcher meant his audience to be thinking about the fate—and principled character—of Sir Walter Raleigh as it listened to Archas' declamations (particularly when added to numerous contemporary references related to Raleigh). Certainly the extravagant rhetoric, overwrought scenes of conflict, and surprising convolutions of plot serve to place the play squarely in the Fletcher canon.

One final tragicomedy gives some sense of the range of Fletcher's last plays. *The Island Princess* has as its central character a woman, the Princess Quisara, who offers her hand to any suitor brave enough to rescue her brother, the King of Sidore, from captivity. When the Portuguese captain Armusia manages the release, it appears as if a joyous marriage will follow. The king, however, fears the Portuguese will attempt to take over his island and requires that Armusia change his religion before he marries Quisara. Armusia refuses and is thrown in prison, where Quisara, moved by her love's defiance, decides to join him. They are soon rescued by friends of Armusia, who also manage to unmask a priest responsible for poisoning the king's mind against Armusia. (He turns out to be the enemy king who held Quisara's brother captive at the opening of the action.) The king now welcomes his new brother-in-law, declaring that he is "half-persuaded" to become a Christian. As this happy resolution takes place, it becomes clear that the play has not really concerned religion or the conflict of East and West. The exotic setting proves to be only the backdrop for a tragicomic study of honor. It should also be added that *The Island Princess* looks forward to such Restoration plays as John Dryden's *The Indian Emperor* (pr. 1665), where the setting provides the occasion for spectacle and heroic flights of rhetoric. Fletcher's late comedies, in particular *The Chances*, *The Wild Goose Chase*, and *Rule a Wife and Have a Wife*, likewise foreshadowed the comedy of manners, which was to prove so popular during the Restoration.

The rich legacy of Fletcher's work, and that of his collaborators, was warmly received in the Restoration. It appears that the complex and suddenly turning plots, remote but familiar settings, effectively imitated manners, and high-flown rhetoric of the tragicomedies accurately reflected the taste of the age. Fletcher was also skilled at capturing the rhythm and diction of elevated conversation, which clearly contributed to his talents as a writer of comedy. "Sophistication" is a word that recurs in critical commentary on the comedies and tragicomedies, while assessments of the tragedies written alone and in collaboration often employ the words "facile" or "extravagant." That Fletcher was an innovator cannot be denied, but he (along with Beaumont and Massinger) was also an entertainer. He was to some extent lucky in sensing the taste of the age and in devising plays to indulge that taste. Even though one rarely finds a Fletcher play in theatrical repertories today, many of the comedies and some of the seriocomic pieces one sees on the modern stage feature scenes and characters that trace their lineage back to the theatrical genius of John Fletcher.

Bibliography
Appleton, William. *Beaumont and Fletcher: A Critical Study*, 1956.
Danby, John. *Poets on Fortune's Hill*, 1952.
Ellis-Fermor, Una. *The Jacobean Drama: An Interpretation*, 1936, 1947.
Hatcher, Orie L. *John Fletcher*, 1905.

Maxwell, Baldwin. *Studies in Beaumont, Fletcher and Massinger*, 1939.
Oliphant, E. H. C. *The Plays of Beaumont and Fletcher*. New Haven: Yale University Press, 1927.
Sprague, Arthur Colby. *Beaumont and Fletcher on the Restoration Stage*, 1926.
Thorndike, Ashby H. *The Influence of Beaumont and Fletcher on Shakespeare*, 1901.
Waith, Eugene M. *The Pattern of Tragicomedy in Beaumont and Fletcher*, 1952.
Wallis, Lawrence B. *Fletcher, Beaumont and Company: Entertainers to the Jacobean Gentry*, 1947.

Robert F. Willson, Jr.

SAMUEL FOOTE

Born: Truro, England; January 27, 1720 (baptized)
Died: Dover, England; October 21, 1777

Principal drama

The Diversions of the Morning, pr. 1747-1754 (series of vaudeville sketches); *The Auction of Pictures*, pr. 1748; *The Knights*, pr. 1749 (revised, pr., pb. 1754); *Taste*, pr., pb. 1752; *The Englishman in Paris*, pr., pb. 1753; *The Englishman Returned from Paris*, pr., pb. 1756; *The Author*, pr., pb. 1757; *The Minor*, pr., pb. 1760; *The Liar*, pr. 1762, pb. 1764; *The Orators*, pr., pb. 1762; *The Mayor of Garratt*, pr., pb. 1763; *The Patron*, pr., pb. 1764; *The Commissary*, pr., pb. 1765; *The Tailors*, pr. 1767, pb. 1778; *The Devil upon Two Sticks*, pr., pb. 1768; *The Lame Lover*, pr., pb. 1770; *The Maid of Bath*, pr., pb. 1771; *The Nabob*, pr. 1772, pb. 1778; *The Handsome Housemaid: Or, Piety in Pattens*, pr. 1773 (as *Piety in Pattens*); *Primitive Puppet Shew*, pr. 1773; *The Bankrupt*, pr. 1773, pb. 1776; *The Cozeners*, pr. 1774, pb. 1778; *The Trip to Calais*, pr. 1775, pb. 1778; *The Capuchin*, pr. 1776, pb. 1778 (revision of *The Trip to Calais* with new last half); *Dramatic Works*, pb. 1929 (M. M. Belden, editor).

Other literary forms

Although Samuel Foote is known chiefly for his dramatic works, he wrote several critical essays and letters and translated a French comedy. His *The Roman and English Comedy Consider'd and Compar'd* (1747) and *A Treatise on the Passions* (1747) are well written and sound, but they are short and reflect traditional, conservative Augustan literary and dramatic criticism. *A Letter from Mr. Foote, to the Reverend Author of the "Remarks, Critical and Christian," on "The Minor"* (1760) and *Apology for "The Minor"* (1771) are significant because in them Foote delineates his critical ideas concerning affectation, hypocrisy, comedy, farce, the humorist, and the man of humor. Foote's thinking as presented in these two essays is strikingly similar to Henry Fielding's ideas on these topics as stated in the famous preface to *Joseph Andrews* (1742). Several of Foote's prologues and prefaces, such as the preface to *Taste* and the preface to *The Minor*, are critically important for their discussions of the aims and purposes of his satires. (The prologue to *Taste* that was written and spoken by actor David Garrick seems also to present some of Foote's views.) Foote's *The Comic Theatre, Being a Free Translation of All the Best French Comedies, by Samuel Foote and Others* (1762) was an ambitious undertaking, and although he wrote the preface for it, he translated only one play, *The Young Hypocrite*, leaving "the others" to translate the remainder of the five volumes.

Achievements

In his time, Foote was known as the English Aristophanes, a sobriquet originally used by the opposition in a libel suit but one which stuck because of Foote's dramatic satires of living persons and of contemporary scandals. G. H. Nettleton has described Foote as Henry Fielding's direct descendant, because he fully developed the latter's personalities, localized mimicry, and contemporary satire. In formulating his comic theory, Foote emphasized the corrective purpose of comedy, whose ridicule he considered to be more effective than law or reason in combating folly and vice. There were indeed times when Foote's satire achieved this purpose. When Foote played Lady Pentweazel in his comedy *Taste*, for example, he wore a huge headdress made with large, loose feathers that fell off his head to litter the stage throughout the play. His ridicule of the absurd hats then in vogue was credited with reforming this extreme fashion.

Perhaps Foote's greatest achievement was breaking the monopoly of Drury Lane and Covent Garden, the only two theaters in London that had official permission to produce plays and that did so primarily during the winter, when the social season was at its height. Foote made significant strides in breaking this monopoly when he evaded the 1737 Stage Licensing Act by advertising his performances not as drama but as entertainments, scheduling them for early in the day, and describing them under various names such as *The Diversions of the Morning*, *The Auction of Pictures*, "a dish of chocolate," or "an invitation to a dish of tea." None of these had a set content but instead contained combinations of successful old material, reworked material, and new material based on the latest social and political gossip—much like television shows such as *Laugh In* and *Saturday Night Live* two hundred years later. The result of Foote's "diversions," according to Simon Trefman (in his 1971 book on Foote), was the first theatrical matinee.

Foote finally broke the monopoly when the king awarded him a summer patent to the Haymarket Theatre that allowed him to operate between May fifteenth and September fifteenth of each year. Foote's resourcefulness and energy were tremendous, and so was his success. He wrote, produced, and directed his plays and, for most of the season, played the leading roles in them. Most of his plays enjoyed long runs, commanding large audiences not only at his establishment but elsewhere. *The Englishman in Paris*, for example, became part of the repertoire at Drury Lane and Covent Garden and was regularly played for more than twenty years. In addition, Foote was able to give steady employment to almost fifty actors during each season and to run his performances for fifty to sixty nights. Trefman claims that no one else in the history of English theater had ever drawn such crowds by the sheer power of satiric invention.

Foote was interested in new and experimental theatrical devices. The framing techniques he used in *Taste* and *The Orators* provided both unity for the segments that made up the pieces and a plausible explanation for poor and inexperienced performers, with whom they might be staged. He also experimented with puppets in his *Primitive Puppet Shew*. Foote's performances were successful not only in England but also in Ireland and Scotland.

Biography

Samuel Foote, although he receives very little attention today, was one of the leading playwrights, actors, and theater managers in mid-eighteenth century England. Foote's father was an attorney and magistrate who served as mayor in Truro, Cornwall, as Member of Parliament for Tiverton, as commissioner of the Prize Office, and receiver of fines. His mother was Eleanor Dinely Goodere, the daughter of baronet Sir Edward Goodere of Hereford.

Samuel was the youngest of three sons. The oldest son, Edward, was trained as a clergyman but was unable to support himself financially and depended on Samuel. There is very little recorded about the second son, John.

Foote attended Truro Grammar School and, in 1737, entered Worcester College, Oxford, whose founder, Sir Thomas Cookes, was related to the Foote family. During his tenure at Oxford, Foote is said to have become a competent Greek and Latin scholar. He was an undisciplined student, however, and his frequent unauthorized absences led the College to disenroll him on January 28, 1740.

After leaving Oxford, Foote entered London's Inner Temple to study law, but he soon left to replenish his depleted fortune. On January 10, 1741, he married Mary Hicks, an old acquaintance from Truro. After spending her dowry, Foote neglected and deserted her. This marriage produced no children, but Foote's will mentions two sons, Francis and George, and Trefman suggests that these children were the result of a short-lived liaison between Foote and one of his servants.

Foote made his first appearance as a professional actor on February 6, 1744, at the Haymarket Theatre in the role of Othello. Foote's forte, however, was not tragedy but comedy and impersonation. Foote mimicked many of the luminaries of his day, including Charles Macklin, Thomas Sheridan (father of playwright Richard Brinsley Sheridan), David Garrick, Arthur Murphy, and Henry Fielding. This comedic flair marked his private life as well, and he was a noted conversationalist. Even Samuel Johnson found Foote's humor attractive, observing " . . . he has wit too, and is not deficient in ideas, or in fertility and variety of imagery . . . he never lets truth stand between him and a jest, and he is sometimes mighty coarse."

Foote had friends at court, including the Duke of York, although these relationships often seemed to be troublesome rather than advantageous. His lifelong connection with wealthy, handsome, socialite Francis Blake Delaval, for example, did lead to many high times at Delaval's family seat. On the other hand, when Delaval commissioned Foote to facilitate the marriage between a supposedly wealthy elderly widow, Lady Isabella Pawlett, and Delaval, the result was strikingly similar to a stage farce: legal battles, social scandal, and very little money for either Foote or Delaval— most of Lady Isabella's wealth proving to be part of an irrevocable trust for her daughter. Another scheme—in which Foote and some demimondaines were to accompany Delaval and Sir Richard Atkins on a yacht trip to Corsica and help Delaval secure the vacant throne of that country—ended in the death of Sir Richard.

The temptations of high-living friends with money to waste led to other problems for Foote. Although he worked hard, was a prolific playwright, and was much in demand as an actor, debts plagued him for most of his life. A low point was reached in 1742, when he was imprisoned for nonpayment of debts, having been charged by creditors ranging from his mother to Lady Viscountess Castlecoma. The passage of a bill for the relief of insolvent debtors led to Foote's release, but although his economic difficulties were never to become that acute again, they never entirely disappeared.

Foote traveled often for both work and recreation. It became habitual for him to travel to Dublin and Edinburgh to act, and he regularly spent his holidays in Paris. His trips to Paris inspired *The Englishman in Paris* and *The Englishman Returned from Paris.*

Foote's strongest competition as a theater manager came from the licensed winter theaters, Drury Lane and Covent Garden. In order to make a living, Foote rented and managed the Little Theatre in the Haymarket during the summer months—an insecure undertaking because he did not have legal permission to operate his theater. There he began what came to be a wildly popular form of entertainment consisting of imitations of various actors and celebrities and satiric sketches loosely grouped in programs that were commonly called *The Diversions of the Morning.*

This situation changed in 1765 as a result of a sad accident. While visiting the aristocratic Lord and Lady Mexborough, Foote's friends teased him into claiming that he was a good horseman. In backing up this false claim, Foote mounted the Duke of York's spirited horse and was thrown immediately. The hard fall shattered Foote's leg in several places and the duke's personal physician had to amputate it. Feeling guilty for his role in this affair, the duke used his influence to obtain for Foote the summer patent rights to the theater, a patent good for the remainder of Foote's life.

In 1767, Foote bought and refurbished the Haymarket Theatre. He successfully managed it and played most of the lead roles or acted in the afterpieces until 1776, when George Colman was finally able to rent the patent from him. Several times before this, Foote had contemplated retiring and leasing his theater rights, but his reluctance to give up his extremely favorable position in the theater world had always made him reconsider. He only gave the lease to Colman because of the mounting pressure of a battle Foote was waging against the Duchess of Kingston, the last and perhaps most disastrous lawsuit resulting from Foote's habit of satirizing persons involved in contemporary scandals. (An earlier lawsuit over Foote's lampoon in *The Orators* of the one-legged Dublin printer George Faulkner had been won by Faulkner.)

The Duchess of Kingston, the one-time Countess of Bristol, had begun life as Elizabeth Chudleigh. While Chudleigh was maid of honor to the Princess of Wales, she met and married the heir to the Earl of Bristol—in secret, so that her standing at Court was not jeopardized. A few years later, she found a man she preferred, the wealthy and elderly Duke of Kingston. Becoming the duchess involved a series of shady legal maneuvers, but the transfer was accomplished; after the duke's death, however, the duchess was indicted for bigamy and her trial became the focus for gossip in the best social circles.

Almost inevitably, Foote made the duchess' greed and hypocrisy the subject of a satire, *The Trip to Calais*, enraging the duchess. She retaliated by using her connections to prohibit the play's continued production. Foote did rewrite the play, with a new second act, as *The Capuchin*, but the duchess and her supporters were not appeased. A newspaper war ensued. One of Chudleigh's hangers-on, William Jackson, editor of *The Public Ledger*, bribed a servant whom Foote had discharged, John Sangster, to sue Foote for homosexual assault, and covered the matter extensively in his scandal sheet.

When the matter finally came to trial, the charge was found to be totally unsubstantiated, and Foote was acquitted. Although Foote appeared in forty-nine mainpieces and twenty-six afterpieces while awaiting trial, the most acting he had done since the loss of his leg, after the verdict was rendered, he began to suffer from recurring seizures.

In order to rebuild his health, Foote started for Paris, but he died en route at the Ship Inn at Dover. On October 27, 1777, his friends buried him in Westminster Abbey.

Analysis

Samuel Foote developed his theory of comedy over a fifteen-year period in several critical works. According to Foote, the main purpose of comedy is to correct vice and folly by ridiculing them while pleasing and delighting the imagination. By representing fashionable foibles and extravagant humors, comedy teaches people to avoid folly. Foote's comic design was to amend the heart, improve the understanding, and please the imagination.

In his *A Letter from Mr. Foote*, Foote outlined the requirements of comedy: Comedy should be true to nature; it must represent exactly the peculiar manners of a people; it must faithfully imitate singular absurdities and particular follies. Comic imitation and representation provide an example to the entire community.

Foote himself likened his comic-satiric method to that employed by Aristophanes, William Shakespeare, Molière, John Dryden, Alexander Pope, Jean de La Bruyère, and Nicolas Boileau. For Foote, character was the greatest comic requisite, and his definitions of two comic character-types— the "humorist" and the "man of humor"—constitute his major contribution to comic theory. According to Foote, the humorist possesses some internal disposition which makes him say or do absurd and ridiculous things while firmly convinced that his actions are correct and acceptable. Foote's man of humor is the pleasant person who enjoys the humorist's eccentricities or affectations and exposes them.

Foote's plays *Taste* and *The Orators* exemplify his comic method, although an analysis of any of Foote's plays must necessarily be incomplete since it depends on the printed version, while almost every performance was different. *Taste* was first produced at Drury Lane on January 11, 1752. Foote's target in this play was the booming art market of the time, the notoriously ignorant and gullible society poseurs who craved antiques and works of old masters only because of the current fad, and the dishonesty of dealers and auctioneers who preyed upon them. The play, staged only five times during the 1752 season, was a failure because, according to the critical judgment of the day, the audience lacked taste and did not understand the method or objectives of Foote's satire. Foote's satiric approach was high burlesque. In order to appreciate high burlesque, an audience must be aware of certain standards of true taste and judgment and therefore be able to recognize the discrepancy between these standards and the pretensions of the characters in the play. Audiences who were devoted to a similar mad pursuit of trends were unlikely to appreciate Foote's humor on the subject.

Foote's theory of taste is similar to the theories of the leading formulators of a standard of taste in the eighteenth century such as David Hume, Edmund Burke, Sir Joshua Reynolds, James Beattie, Oliver Goldsmith, and Joseph Addison. All held the same fundamental requisites to a standard of taste: sensibility, imagination, judgment, education, common sense, morality, and objectivity. In *Taste*, Foote develops these principles by exhibiting the follies of people who lack these requisites. Foote's "connoisseurs," Lord Dupe, Novice, Lady Pentweazel, Squander, and Sir Positive Bubble, are so overcome by the fashionable craze for mutilated objects that are promoted as antiques, for foreign artworks, and for foreign artists that what little intellect they may have suspends operation.

Foote, in the preface to *Taste*, presents his views on education and morality as necessary to a standard of taste. He says that he is determined to satirize the barbarians who have prostituted the study of antiquity to trifling superficiality, who have blasted the progress of the elegant arts by unpardonable frauds and absurd prejudices, and who have vitiated the minds and morals of youth by persuading them that what serves only to illustrate literature is true knowledge and that active idleness is real business.

In the context of the play itself, the virtuosi do not know art. Lady Pentweazel thinks that the *Mary de Medicis* and the *Venus de Medicis* were sisters in the Medici family instead of paintings. Novice and Dupe think that they can evaluate the age and worth of a coin or medal by tasting it. Puff, the auctioneer, is able to convince Dupe, Novice, and Sir Positive that broken statuary and china are more valuable than perfect pieces. Lord Dupe demonstrates a complete lack of common sense when he purchases a canvas that has all the paint scraped off it. Carmine, Puff, and their associates even convince the dupes that a head from Herculaneum dates from before the biblical account of the Creation.

Satire is invariably based on human foibles evident in the time in which it is written, but in good satire, such as that of Aristophanes, the point being made is more widely applicable. *Taste* reflects conditions that existed in Foote's day, but its humor is generalizable not merely to any era in which works of art are bought and sold by fashionable and ignorant collectors; it also has something to say about the way in which people come to be so easily misled, no matter what the issue or era.

The Orators, a three-act comedy which presented different aspects of another currently fashionable preoccupation, was first produced on Wednesday, April 28, 1762, in Foote's Haymarket Theatre. Unlike *Taste*, *The Orators* was highly successful, appearing thirty-nine times in the first year.

The Orators is a framed play. In the printed version (as was the case with many of Foote's plays, the staged version varied from one performance to the next), this play comprises three parts. The first is a long satire on oratory, the second is a mock trial of the Cock-Lane ghost (introduced so that students at Foote's onstage oratory class could practice judicial oratory in the trial of a currently notorious apparition), and the third features amateur debating clubs such as the Robin Hood Society. The parts are united by the four or five principal characters that appear in each, not by plot, because there is none—even within the individual parts.

Originally advertised as "A Course of Comic Lectures on English Oratory," the play is set in a theater. Harry Scamper and Will Tirehack, two Oxford dandies looking for amusement, enter, seat themselves in a side box, and after questioning the candle-snuffer about what the lectures will contain, call for the theater's manager, Mr. Foote, played by the author himself. They want him to assure them that they will be amused. From a box on the other side of the stage, Ephraim Suds, a soap-boiler, wants reassurance that the lectures will be educational—that he will learn to give speeches. Foote declares that both needs will be met; in the course of his explanation, it is revealed that Foote operates a school of oratory guaranteed to train even the most burr-tongued Scotsman to be a golden-throated speaker. This prepares the way for the introduction of the other major character, Donald, a young Scot with a broad accent.

After the opening lecture on the principles of oratory, Foote allows his "students" to practice what they have learned in various professions and situations. This framework provides not only unity but also an excuse for poor performers. In one scene, the actors are merely beginning students, in another they are rehearsing. This device enabled Foote to use a series of less skilled (and less expensive) actors and to vary lines on short notice without in any way diminishing the humor of the play.

Foote wrote *The Orators* primarily to satirize the British Elocutionary Movement and its leader, Thomas Sheridan, whose success as an actor gave weight to his pronouncements on delivery. From the days of the early Greeks, rhetoric had been regarded as possessing five aspects: *inventio*, *dispositio*, *elocutio*, *pronuntiatio*, and *memoria* (or discovery of a thesis, arrangement of argument, style, delivery, and memory). It was the belief of more conservative rhetoricians of Foote's day that Sheridan had devalued rhetoric by extending Cicero's definition of *pronuntiatio* and making it seem that it was the whole of the art of ancient rhetoric rather than merely one of five parts, and a lesser one at that.

Foote gives a good picture, though satirized and therefore exaggerated, of the tenets of Sheridan's elocutionary theory in act 1 of *The Orators*. At the beginning of his lecture he refers to Sheridan's *Lectures on Elocution* (1762), which delineates Sheridan's plan "to revive the long-lost art of oratory, and to correct, ascertain, and fix the English language." To achieve these goals, Sheridan wanted to establish an academy, but the institution had to be structured on his plan alone. Foote ridicules Sheridan's egocentrism by saying that he (Foote) wants to be made perpetual professor of his own academy.

Foote mimics Sheridan's intention to "correct, ascertain, and fix the English language" in the character of Ephraim Suds, who has just finished taking Sheridan's course of oratory. Suds has learned little from Sheridan's teaching, for he mispronounces words, such as "empharis" for "emphasis," and speaks ungrammatical English.

Sheridan not only believed his academy could perfect the English language; he also envisioned his school as an Irish center for the study of correct English speech, and he thought that students would flock to it from

Scotland, Wales, America, and the other British colonies abroad, in order to correct provincialisms in speech. Foote satirizes these ideas by demonstrating the effects of Sheridan's education on Donald, a Scottish orator who has studied for one year under Sheridan and six weeks under Foote. Donald continues to speak with a heavy Scottish accent and uses dialectal diction which Scamper and Tirehack cannot understand.

Foote also uses Donald to satirize Sheridan's emphasis on pronunciation—his belief that a good orator could, by following proper accents, read a work he did not understand. In an exaggerated paraphrase of Sheridan's discussion of pronunciation, Donald contradicts the ancient rhetoricians Demosthenes and Cicero, who called delivery the fourth rather than the first part of oratory. Scamper and Tirehack notice the contradiction and complain. Again, Foote attacks Sheridan and the Elocutionists for their emphasis on voice and gesture to the exclusion of the other four major procedures in rhetoric.

Donald becomes furious at Scamper and Tirehack's correction, and they tell him that he must tell the truth. Donald replies that he can tell the truth "logically," satirizing internal or artistic proofs which are based not upon empirical evidence but upon probability. The Elocutionists wanted to persuade and to win debates through a grandiloquent style, and they did not care about truth; they excluded from rhetoric considerations of subject matter and arrangement of argument and thereby reduced it to style, voice, and gesture alone.

Foote suggests a motto for a treatise that Sheridan planned to write. He adds, however, that Sheridan is probably already well provided with an apt Latin or a Greek one. Here, Foote's comment is most likely a strike at Sheridan's greatest shortcoming, his total inability to understand the Greek and Latin rhetoricians from whom he quoted so often, and the consequential diminishing of ancient oratory.

Although today his work is known only to specialists, Foote's colorful and successful theatrical career offers rich insights concerning the practical exigencies and the underlying values of the eighteenth century English style.

Other major works

NONFICTION: *The Roman and English Comedy Consider'd and Compar'd*, 1747; *A Treatise on the Passions*, 1747; *A Letter from Mr. Foote, to the Reverend Author of the "Remarks, Critical and Christian," on "The Minor,"* 1760; *Apology for "The Minor,"* 1771.

Bibliography
Belden, Mary M. *The Dramatic Works of Samuel Foote*, 1929, 1970.
Bogorad, Samuel N., and Robert G. Noyes. "Samuel Foote's *Primitive*

Puppet-Shew," in *Theatre Survey*. XIV (Fall, 1973).

Cooke, William. *Memoirs of Samuel Foote, Esq. With a Collection of His Genuine Bon-Mots, Anecdotes, Opinions, &c. Mostly Original, and Three of His Dramatic Pieces, Not Published in His Works*, 1805 (3 volumes).

Fitzgerald, Percy. *Samuel Foote: A Biography*, 1910.

Trefman, Simon. *Sam. Foote, Comedian, 1720-1777*, 1971.

Wilkinson, Tate. *The Wandering Patentee: Or, A History of the Yorkshire Theatres, from 1770 to the Present Time*, 1795.

Mary C. Murphy

JOHN FORD

Born: Near Ilsington, England; April 17, 1586 (baptized)
Died: Unknown; after 1639

Principal drama

The Witch of Edmonton, pr. 1621, pb. 1658 (with Thomas Dekker and William Rowley); *Perkin Warbeck*, pr. c. 1622-1632, pb. 1634; *The Sun's Darling*, pr. 1624, pb. 1656 (with Dekker); *The Broken Heart*, pr. c. 1627-1631, pb. 1633; *The Lover's Melancholy*, pr. 1628, pb. 1629; *'Tis Pity She's a Whore*, pr. 1629(?)-1633, pb. 1633; *The Fancies Chaste and Noble*, pr. 1631(?) or 1635-1636(?), pb. 1638; *Love's Sacrifice*, pr. 1632(?), pb. 1633; *The Lady's Trial*, pr. 1638, pb. 1639; *The Queen: Or, The Excellency of Her Sex*, pb. 1653.

Other literary forms

In addition to his plays, John Ford published two long poems and three prose pamphlets. *Fame's Memorial: Or, The Earl of Devonshire Deceased* (1606) is an elegy praising Charles Blount, who had married Penelope Devereux (on whom Sir Philip Sidney based his Stella) after her divorce from Lord Rich. *Christ's Bloody Sweat: Or, The Son of God in His Agony* (1613) is a religious poem on the efficacy of repentance. *Honor Triumphant: Or, The Peer's Challenge* (1606) argues four propositions in mock style; *The Golden Mean* (1613) praises Stoicism; and *A Line of Life* (1620) describes the Stoic conduct of a man, a public man and a good man.

Achievements

Many critics have acclaimed John Ford as the outstanding dramatist of the Caroline period (1625-1649), and his plays give ample evidence of the justice of this claim. Today, almost any full-year course on the drama surrounding William Shakespeare will include *The Broken Heart*, *'Tis Pity She's a Whore*, and *Perkin Warbeck*. These plays are being produced and evoke a positive response from modern audiences. Although he is not known for innovation, Ford creatively employed such common forms of the age as tragicomedy, revenge tragedy, and the visual elements of the masque. His plays are rich in resonances from other dramatists of the period (particularly Shakespeare, Ben Jonson, and John Webster), but what he borrows, he transforms for his own use. In no way is Ford a surface dramatist. He was deeply interested in Burtonian psychology, but he was never a slave to its formulas; in his drama, he was continually probing into the depths of personality, and he was particularly interested in exploring the human psyche in relationship to or confrontation with other human beings.

Biography

Very little is known about John Ford's life other than a few isolated facts. He was baptized on April 17, 1586, the second son of a Devonshire country gentleman. He was admitted to Middle Temple in 1602, expelled for not paying a board bill in 1606, readmitted in 1608, and involved in a dispute over the wearing of hats in 1617. His father died in 1610, leaving Ford a paltry ten pounds, and six years later, his income was increased by a bequest of twenty pounds a year from his elder brother's estate. Nothing is known of his style of life—whether he was ever married or engaged in a profession—and no record has yet been found of his death.

Analysis

John Ford's fascination with the psychology of love in its many-faceted applications to social life is evident in his earliest produced play, *The Witch of Edmonton*, which he wrote in collaboration with Thomas Dekker and William Rowley. Here also is evident Ford's propensity to the sensational as well as the association of love with death, which was to reappear in many of his subsequent plays. In the first scene, Frank Thorney has just been married to Sir Arthur Clarington's serving maid, Winnifride, who is with child. The marriage is to be kept in the dark until Frank can secure his inheritance. Sir Arthur abets this deception by writing a letter certifying that no marriage has taken place, even though he is frustrated in his hopes of maintaining a relationship with Winnifride, who takes her marriage and her new status most seriously. The reason for the secrecy becomes gradually yet shockingly apparent as the audience realizes that Frank, who seems to have a strong and genuine love for his bride, nevertheless intends to secure his inheritance through a bigamous marriage with his longtime neighbor Susan Carter. There is irony throughout the scene of his second courtship, but particularly in Susan's outburst of hymeneal joy at having her heart settled with her one true love and winning the right to dismiss her unwanted suitors. Frank, who seems to like Susan well enough, blames his situation on fate—an ever-present force in Ford's dramas.

The violent outcome of this wedding is predicted in the imagery as Susan's father remembers a proverb relating weddings with hangings. One of her former suitors remarks on the unity of the newly married couple, but with an undesirable cutting edge as he compares them to a "new pair of Sheffield knives, fitted both to one sheath." To Susan as to Ford, real love involves unity and the sharing of souls, and she is disturbed to discover that Frank is unable to share with her the source of his obvious discontent. In a pleading not unlike Portia's to Brutus in Shakespeare's *Julius Caesar*, she coaxes him to display his mind: "You shall not shut me from partaking/ The least dislike that grieves you; I'm all yours. . . . I must know/ The ground of your disturbance." Frank assures Susan that the cause has nothing to do with her, blaming his unrest on "the poison'd leeches twist about my heart." He comes close to revealing his bigamy, telling of a palmist who predicted that he should have two wives, but Susan naturally assumes that the second will appear only after her death and, with saintly humility, wishes that "fate" might give him a second wife to outmatch his first—that is, herself.

Frank's two wives are brought together for a brief scene in which Frank is leaving on a journey with his first wife, dressed as a page for the occasion, and stops to say a farewell to Susan. Winnifride, apprised of the situation, is horrified at Frank's lawlessness and callousness in committing bigamy for money, but she has little choice but to follow his lead, and her love for him seems to survive. Susan, in ignorance of the situation, ironically pleads with Frank's "page" to be servant, friend, and wife to him on their journey. Susan contrives to bid farewell to Frank privately; she delays their parting as long as possible, exacerbating Frank's impatience until a white dog enters the scene and Frank suddenly murders Susan, wounds himself, ties himself up (with the dog's help), and cries out "murder." In the supernatural scenes of the play, from which it gets its title and which are generally ascribed to Dekker, the dog is both the witch's familiar and the representative of the Devil himself. In the scenes by Ford, such as this, the dog almost seems to be a bodily representation of the force of fate, tainted as it is in this play with more than a touch of evil.

Later, in Frank's sickroom, where he is recovering from his wound, the dog enters just as Susan's sister discovers the incriminating knife. When she leaves, Frank is visited by the ghost of Susan and by a very live Winnifride before the authorities enter, and both Frank and his remaining wife are carted off to jail. In the final scene of the play, Winnifride is free but faints under the heaviness of her emotion and the weight of her continuing love for her condemned husband. A wave of pity for the bigamist-murderer seems to come over the crowd—a pity which Ford would evidently induce in his audience. This is strengthened by Frank's final speech on his way to execution. In deep penitence, he comments on the rightness of his own death, asks for forgiveness, and seeks to obtain financial security for Winnifride, whom he has never ceased to love, though his ways of demonstrating that love are aberrant in the extreme. Ford's obvious sympathy for the murderer, who planned the bigamy long before any "dog" urged him to go further, is an indication of a moral ambiguity which many critics have found in his plays, but it is also an empathetic examination of a kind of love, pure on the part of both Susan and Winnifride and tainted on Frank's, which can survive in spite of circumstances and a society which would threaten to smother it completely.

Dekker also collaborated with Ford on another early play (it is almost impossible to date Ford's plays precisely), a delightful marriage of morality play and masque entitled *The Sun's Darling*. Raybright, an Everyman figure who is the offspring of the sun, travels through the domains of the four seasons, each of which attempts to entice him to stay, while his companion, Humour, enlists counterforces to lure him on the the the next segment of the year. Each act, representing a season, is a masque in its own right, and each introduces separate masquelike episodes, with songs, dances, and poetic combats presenting various virtues and vices. The most insidious vice of the play is undoubtedly the Spanish confectioner in Spring's entourage, who brags that he "can teach sugar to slip down your throat a thousand ways." Perhaps the most outlandish is the personified Detraction, who claims that scholars are merely "petty penmen [who] covet/ Fame by Folly." The production ends with a final masque performed by the four elements and the four humours, after which the Sun itself descends to make its comments on health and harmony in the perfect interaction of these eight dancers.

There is much about love in the play, as each of the seasons courts Raybright, but he discerns that much of what is presented as love is merely an attempt to buy him with the various gifts the seasons offer. In Autumn and Winter, the season-acts most often ascribed to Ford on the basis of style, it is interesting to note that the ideas of love grow more complex. There is mutuality in the love offered by Autumn, who recognizes that Raybright, in representing the sun, has as much to offer the season as Autumn has to offer him. "Let us be twins in heart," she suggests, after which Humour and her companion Folly have a harder time convincing Raybright to leave. He does leave eventually, and as he approaches Winter, the love imagery of the play becomes theological if not downright messianic. Raybright, the son of the Sun, is the "excellently good" one for whom they have been waiting. He comes with justice and impartial law. The clowns who oppose his coming are waging "war against heaven" and thereby subject themselves to the "thunder-stroke" which is able to cast them "From heaven's sublime height to the depth of hell." In terms of the Book of Revelation, Raybright will appear like a star, and "Night shall be chang'd into perpetual day."

The Lover's Melancholy, which is probably the first play Ford wrote without a collaborator, examines love in what is almost a clinical study. The play opens with a veritable symphony of frustration. When Menaphon returns from a year's trip abroad, he is met by his soul-friend Amethus, who laments that his loved Cleophila (a kinswoman of Menaphon) has remained cold to him, because she cares only for her aging and infirm father. Menaphon, in return, discovers that his love, Thamasta, who also happens to be Amethus' sister, is still "intermured with ice"—absence having done nothing to make her heart grow fond. The illness of Cleophila's father, Meleander, is related to love, since its genesis was the disappearance of his loved daughter, Eroclea. The classic case of love melancholy, however, is that of Palador, the Prince of Cyprus, whose kingdom has been in a sharp decline since Eroclea's departure. She had been promised to him in marriage by his tyrant father, but only as a trick to lure her to court, where she was to be raped by lecherous courtiers—a fate from which she had been saved by her father, who was promptly dismissed from court as his reward. This was certainly a factor in producing his melancholy state.

The sickness suffered by the prince has descended through him to the state. Ford presents this on the stage via another returned traveler, Rhetias, who determines to play the role of court railer. His soliloquy against court foolery at the beginning of the second scene of the play is aided by the entrance of two court sycophants, Pelias and Cuculus, who provide excellent targets for his barrage of satire. At the end of the scene, Rhetias finds a partner in raillery in Corax, the physician who has been called into court to heal the prince's malady. The description of a sick court is enhanced by Meleander himself, as, in beautifully mad poetry, he pictures the decadence perpetrated by the former tyrant, moans over the futility of court life, and pleads for a funeral without pomp, ceremony, or expense. Even Thamasta shows a side of love melancholy as she conceives of herself in love with the youth, Parthenophill, whom Menaphon has brought back from his travels. "Love is a tyrant/ Resisted," she proclaims—a complaint which might have come from any one of the multifarious treatises on melancholy produced in the sixteenth and seventeenth centuries. This aberrant love, however, is easily treated when she discovers at the end of one particularly well-wrought scene that the object of her misguided affection is indeed a woman. "Cupid," Parthenophill points out, "Comes to make sport between us with no weapon."

The presence of a physician in the court, and hence in the play, gives Ford his chance to examine love melancholy as a form of diseased love. When Prince Palador enters like the melancholy Hamlet, reading a book, Corax caustically reminds him that he had prescribed exercise, not sonnets. Later, two court counselors open the door for a lecture by asking Corax to explain the nature of melancholy, which he does fairly directly out of Robert Burton's *The Anatomy of Melancholy* (1621). Being a master of stagecraft, Ford, through Corax, arranges for a "masque of melancholy" to be presented before the prince, in which Burtonian characters of Lycanthropia, Hydrophobia, Delirium, Phrenitis, Hypochondriacal Melancholy (including a delightful poem against tobacco), and Wanton Melancholy all make their appearance on the stage with appropriate speeches. Prince Palador perhaps assumes that he is getting off lightly, since love melancholy is not among the characters, but thus relaxed (as Claudius perhaps relaxed after the dumb show), he is an easy target for Corax, who, claiming that the condition is too serious and complex to be presented by art

(art versus nature being one of the concerns of the play), describes love melancholy to him and suggests that Parthenophill, pale and wan for a lad, is a *living* example of the disease. As visibly moved as Claudius, Palador abruptly dismissess the gathering, and Corax has his diagnosis confirmed: "Love . . . will be seen." Corax's cure is surely made easier by the fact that Parthenophill is in truth Eroclea, who had been in Athens under the care of Rhetias and opportunely found a way to return with Menaphon after the death of Palador's tyrannical father. Even so, the prince has to be prepared for her return with a closely paralleled parable, and he accepts her actual presence only very slowly, thinking it might be some trick—perhaps Parthenophill disguised as Eroclea. Ford fashions their meeting with another demonstration of the mutuality necessary for real love. When she enters the scene, she finishes his speech as if she were privy to the thoughts of his mind, and she also reveals that she has been carrying his picture next to her breast in exactly the same fashion that, it has been earlier revealed, he has been carrying hers.

In addition, the healing of Meleander is carefully wrought by the scholar-physician Corax. He first prepares Meleander (who enters raging, with a poleax) by staring him down, having donned a frightful mask. He then tries to establish empathy with him by claiming that he, Corax, has a daughter who has been snatched away, leaving him with a crazed head and an acute lack of sleep. It works; Meleander does thereafter claim a special affinity for Corax, admits "I hug my afflictions," and fetches Cleophila to praise her virtues and compare them with those of the lost Eroclea. In the final scene of the play, Meleander is reached with another court device, perhaps even more dramatic than the masque of melancholy. Meleander has been drugged, delivered to a barber to have his four-years' beard removed, and carted to a tailor to fit him with fresh clothes. When he wakes, to the sound of music, he is met with a procession of messengers. First Aretus, the court tutor, announces that all of Meleander's honors have been restored, and Amethus then presents him with a staff of office, indicating a healing to take place in the state as well as in the individual. Sophronos, Meleander's brother and the father of Menaphon, hands him the picture of Eroclea which Palador had worn next to his heart and which he no longer needs, further announcing that the prince is ready to address Meleander as father. When Cleophila enters with her sister, the meeting of father and daughter is natural and joyful as the story of her disappearance is related. When Prince Palador finally enters, he joyfully greets Meleander as father with the "prince's sweetness," which completes his cure. He makes all necessary explanations and arranges for the marriages, bringing the comedy to a healthy close.

In many ways, *The Broken Heart* is a study in courtship and marriage. The play opens with Orgilus discussing his relationship with his betrothed,

Penthea, which has been thwarted by, to use his words, a "poisonous stalk/ Of aconite" in the person of Penthea's brother, Ithocles, who, in spite of the betrothal, has compelled Penthea to marry Bassanes, an older and richer, though hardly wiser, nobleman. At first, Orgilus, who is later referred to as a married bachelor, seems to show some real concern for Penthea as he informs his father, Crotolon, that he is leaving Sparta for Athens not only to escape from the jealousies of Bassanes and to ease the pain he feels in Penthea's presence, but also to free her "from a hell on earth," caught between her present husband and her former lover. All of this, however, turns out to be little more than subterfuge, of which Orgilus is a master. He soon returns in disguise as a scholar, spies on her in an unconscionable way, continually describes his love for her in terms bordering on the lascivious, and even in one painful scene tries by psychological pressure to force her to violate her marriage vows, claiming that their prior betrothal was the more valid contract. His attempts on her honor fall little short of attempted rape, and her resistance serves but to whet his already sharp appetite for revenge.

Orgilus' lack of integrity is also manifest in his extraction of a promise from his own sister, Euphrania, that she will never marry without his consent. In doing this, Orgilus is taking control of his sister's marriage in the same way that Ithocles had manipulated Penthea's. Euphrania's love for Prophilus seems genuine, pure, and controlled throughout. It outlasts the delay imposed upon them by having to wait for permission from the supposedly absent Orgilus, and it survives his close examination of the relationship, disguised as student who by accident becomes the messenger by whom they exchange letters while their love is still secret. Because Prophilus is a close friend of the hated Ithocles, Orgilus' permission is wrenched from him only with the greatest difficulty, although once it is given, his rancor seems to be forgotten if not totally dissipated.

The marriage between Penthea and Bassanes is indeed a hellish affair. Orgilus deems it a "monster-love" because she had been previously betrothed to him, but surely it is monstrous in its own right. The cliché of an older man's fear of cuckoldry when married to a young, attractive woman comes to life on the stage. In the audience's first glimpse into their home, Bassanes is arranging for a mason to have the front window "dammed up" lest it afford passersby a glimpse of Penthea's beauty. She is continually spied upon by Brausis, a delightfully doughty old woman described in the *dramatis personae* as her overseer. Bassanes is even jealous of Penthea's brother, but perhaps this is not untoward in a Ford play. In spite of this oppressive picture of his personality, there is also a note of pathos in it. Although he was the benefactor of Ithocles' pandering, he did not devise it; the court he describes is indeed a dangerous place for an attractive woman; and his appreciation of her beauty has a numinous quality to it. At her first entrance, he exclaims: "She comes, she comes! So shoots the morning forth,/ Spangled with pearls of transparent dew." His own intoxication with her beauty justifies his belief that others might be equally affected.

The mad jealousy of Bassanes is dramatically revealed to all when he breaks in on a conference between his wife and her brother and imagines their incest. Ithocles, long since repentant of this marriage which he forced on his sister, now takes decisive steps to remove her from the oppression of this home and put her under his own protection. The shock of public horror at his behavior and the losing of his wife bring Bassanes to a sudden but believable repentance, and he genuinely laments the loss of a love he was not fit to enjoy. Ironically, his repentance comes too late to transform him into a fit husband at the same moment that Ithocles, through painful repentance, has belatedly become a fit brother.

In this state, Ithocles earnestly attempts to elicit his sister's forgiveness, but every opening gesture he makes is met with scornful barbs forged in the deep center of pain which Penthea feels from having been wrenched from her betrothed love and forced into a relationship which she therefore considers adulterous. She relents only when, sensitized to the psychological conditions of impossible love, she senses the nature of her brother's recent illness and evokes from him a confession of his love for Calantha, the daughter of his king, who is at the moment being newly courted by Nearchus, prince of neighboring Argos. Penthea recovers from her bitterness to visit Calantha, in the guise of asking her to be the executrix of her will. Using a familiar Renaissance form, she prettily bequeaths her youth to chaste wives who marry "for ties of love,/ Rather than ranging of their blood"; then her fame is left to memory and truth. Calantha is beginning to enjoy the game, when suddenly Penthea shatters the tradition and unexpectedly leaves Ithocles her brother to Calantha. The princess is irate at the presumption of this suggestion but withholds any comment on the suggestion itself. In the next scene, however, Calantha takes a ring that has been given to her by Nearchus and rejects it by tossing it to Ithocles, suggesting that he "give it at next meeting to a mistress." It is Ithocles' turn for presumption now, as he returns the ring to the princess herself, causing some resentment among the supporters of Nearchus. The love between Calantha and Ithocles is evidently genuine and reciprocal, and Nearchus, making a choruslike comment on the theme of marriage, shows genuine humility and understanding.

By the next scene, Calantha and Ithocles have courted and grown mature in their love, and she asks her dying father, the king, for permission to marry, which is readily granted. Ithocles has proved himself worthy on the battlefield and in the court and through repentance has cleansed himself of his earlier inclinations to control the lives of others. Calantha is a magnificent woman, a queen, knowing herself and her own love and managing to keep love, passion, and will in perfect balance. Unfortunately, however, their love is to be consummated only in death. Ithocles dies magnificently under the revenger's dagger as Orgilus first catches him fast in a trick chair and then coolly deprives him of life. Calantha is leading the festivities at the wedding celebration for Euphrania and Prophilus when, on successive changes of the dance, she hears of the deaths of her father, her best friend Penthea, and her betrothed. Giving no evidence of the shock she feels at the news brought by successive messengers, she continues the dance to its conclusion. Then, as the reigning queen, she comments on Penthea's death; provides for the continuing rule of her country in a wedding contract with Nearchus which, as Bassanes comments, is actually her will and testament; and then, placing her mother's wedding ring on Ithocles' lifeless finger as a symbol of the consummation of a timeless love, she dies, indeed of a "broken heart."

In *Love's Sacrifice*, Ford is concerned with human relationships between the sexes in which no fulfillment is possible. The play opens with the banishment of Roseilli, an honest courtier, from the court. The only explanation he can surmise for his banishment is that somewhere behind the action is Fiormonda, the woman he has been unsuccessfully wooing for some time and who wants only to be rid of him.

When the duke enters with his duchess, Bianca, it at first seems as if they are a well-mated pair. Their entrance is announced by courtiers praising the duke for choosing Bianca not because of family or connections but simply because of her beauty, to which Fernando adds virtue. Onstage, the duke affirms that he values only two things: his duchess and his trusted friend Fernando. Intimations of things to come present themselves shortly after their departure, however, when the trusted Fernando laments his all-consuming love for the duchess. He is hardly through with this speech when Fiormonda enters to court him. He deftly puts her off by praising not only her beauty but also her loyalty to her dead husband, but this serves only as a cue for Fiormonda to produce the ring that her husband instructed her to give to the one she could love as much as she had loved him. The scene is interrupted (a blessing to Fernando and a curse to Fiormonda) by the entrance of Bianca, asking Fernando's help in convincing the duke to recall Roseilli, the man Fiormonda had just succeeded in getting out of her way.

The intrigue does not stop here. The beginning of the second act discloses still another courtier enamored of Fiormonda, and the court gets a good laugh as, from the upper stage, it overhears and sees Mauruccio practicing ridiculous speeches, designing outlandish costumes, and devising foolish gifts as he outlines his assault upon his beloved—the only member of the court who is not in stitches at the entire proceeding. Thus, the audience is introduced to a court with its love triangles, quadrangles, and octangles, none of which promises to produce anything but pain.

The unhealthy quality of the love in this play is underscored by a quantity of disease imagery, with love referred to as a leprosy at least three times. The center of this disease in the court is the duke's new counselor, Ferentes, who initiates an intriguing scene in which two young ladies and one older one all discover they are pregnant, having been bribed into bed with a promise of marriage from the same man. This source of the disease is effectively purged, however, in a scene reminiscent of Thomas Kyd, in which Ferentes is stabbed by all three of the women in a court masque presented in honor of a visiting abbot (Bianca's uncle). To justify this action, each woman displays her newborn infant.

The primary love business of the play, between Fernando and Bianca, is strong, poignant, and confusing. At his first opportunity, Fernando speaks most eloquently of his love, evidently for the third time, and is put down with equal force and eloquence by a diatribe on chastity from Bianca, who takes her marriage vows seriously. In spite of being charged never to speak of love again, upon pain of exposure and certain death, Fernando cannot contain himself and once more pleads his plight. The situation is ominous. D'Avolos has noted Fernando's passion and, by means of displaying a pair of pictures, has trapped him into disclosing the object of his desire. With the duke away, Fiormonda has maneuvered the couple into a chess game (fraught with double entendre) and then, pleading sickness, has managed to leave them alone except for D'Avolos, who is sent back to spy upon them. The situation is too much for Fernando; even though warned, he is soon on his knees declaring his love. Again he is chastely humbled by Bianca, who deplores his "bestial dalliance" and warns that if he opens his "leprous mouth"again on the subject, it will mean "the forfeit of thy life." Fernando agrees to silence, but with Donne-like eloquence declares that if his heart is ripped open at his death, there the observer will read "Bianca's name carv'd out in bloody lines." From his observation post, D'Avolos completely misreads this scene and reports to Fiormonda that the couple are on their way to bed, to which she, playing the role of a good revenger, vows "to stir up tragedies as black as brave."

This misreading is the only preparation there is in the play for the next turn in the relationship, which surprises the reader in the very next scene. Bianca suddenly becomes the initiator in the game of love, appears in Fernando's bedroom while he is fast asleep, and wakes him with her declaration of mutual love. Even though she comes with "shame and passion," caught up by the "tyranny" of love, there is also an invitation in her words: "if thou tempt'st/ My bosom to thy pleasures, I will yield." Her invitation, however, has a barb in it; though she is torn by the passion of her love, she is also constant to her "vow to live a constant wife." Her impossible solution to this dilemma is to follow her passion in offering herself to Fernando but also to follow her conscience in declaring that, should he accept, "Ere yet the morning shall new-christen day,/ I'll kill myself." Fernando at first hopes this is some jest, but finally he takes her at her word, vowing to master his passion and sublimate their love into a spiritual relationship, though he is still uneasy enough to ask if she will later laugh at him for refusing the wondrous gift. At the end of the scene, she echoes Fernando's own avowal of constancy.

The reader is never quite sure of her mood after this. In one scene she contrives, in public, to wipe Fernando's lips and adds in an aside, "Speak, shall I steal a kiss? believe me, my lord, I long." There is something too coquettish in these lines coming from the woman vowed to death should her lover go beyond the kiss. Furthermore, in the final scenes of the play, she confesses to the duke, her husband, that she desired Fernando madly, tried her best to seduce him, but was unable to overcome his scruples. Perhaps she wanted both Fernando and death; this would not, certainly, be beyond the scope of Ford's imagination. Perhaps in this scene, she was merely trying to save his life in the face of the revenge-fury that Fiormonda had worked up in the duke. The latter seems most likely, in that she attributes Fernando's technical chastity not to the concern for her life but rather to his constant loyalty to the duke himself—an idea which, as far as the audience can tell, never entered Fernando's head, though perhaps it should have.

Typical of Ford's plays, the love which is impossible in life finds its consummation in death, as has been foreshadowed throughout the play. There is something noble about the way in which Bianca bravely bares her breast to receive death from her husband's dagger. She may be seeking death as the only way out of her dilemma, using her cruel and seemingly needless taunting of the duke (by proclaiming Fernando's superiority) as a device to be sure he is angry enough to complete the deed. She warns him that he will suffer when he comes to accept the validity of her physical chastity, but he cannot believe this, and his one moment of relenting is quickly overcome by the urging of Fiormonda, the real revenger, from the upper stage. The duke's anger is inflamed, the murder committed.

When the duke, again at Fiormonda's urging, approaches Fernando to complete his revenge, he finds him armed and unhesitatingly challenges him to a duel to the death. Fernando, however, upon hearing that Bianca is dead, drops his sword and bares his breast, willing to be sacrificed in the same manner that she had been, thus joining her in a death union symbolically apparent on the stage. He is denied this symmetry, however, for the duke, finally convinced of his wife's chastity if not her constancy, tries to stab himself, though he is stopped before completing his self-immolation. Instead, he arranges for a coffin and a funeral procession for his wife's body, and the abbot returns in time to add his dignity and pomp to the occasion. After an eloquent tribute to his dead wife, the duke opens the burial vault, only to find Fernando there ahead of him, still quite alive but dressed in his winding sheet. He answers the duke's attempt to drag him out by gulping poison to join his Bianca. The bliss of their union in death (assuming that such is possible) is, however, short-lived. The duke, after proclaiming that when the day comes that he should die he would like to be buried in one monument with his wife and friend, makes the waiting time short by stabbing himself to join them. The love triangle presumably moves from the human stage into an eternal tension.

Whether Ford is trying to say that all attempts at a solution by means of death are in vain or is quietly mocking himself, the situation suggests that there is neither glory nor promise nor fulfillment in love's sacrifice, which seeks to find on the other side of the grave what it is denied in life. On this side of the tomb, life goes on. The dukedom is perpetuated when Fiormonda, the sole surviving heir, offers the dukedom along with herself to Roseilli, who seems to be worthy of the post and establishes justice by consigning D'Avolos to the hangman. Fiormonda, however, who is the real source of evil in the play, lives to become the new duchess. Roseilli vows to live a celibate life within marriage. This, given his love for her, punishes him almost as much as it does Fiormonda, but it also reiterates the theme of the play, which is dominated by love, or at least by passion, without any fulfillment.

The play widely regarded as Ford's best, *'Tis Pity She's a Whore*, is a study of a single but hopelessly tainted love—that between Giovanni and his full sister Annabella. The other loves that emerge serve but to cast light upon the central pair of lovers.

In the opening speech of the play, the friar is in the process of urging young Giovanni to abandon love. For several lines, Ford artistically delays revealing the nature of the friar's objection until Giovanni reveals the state of his psyche by genuinely asking a question, the answer to which is totally obvious both to the friar and to the play's audience: "Shall then, for that I am her brother born,/ My joys be ever banish'd from her bed?" What Giovanni wants from the friar is some means of justifying his love and of consummating it, but what he gets is a formula for exorcising the "leprosy of lust/ That rots thy soul," as the friar describes his condition. Giovanni agrees to the regime, even though it seems obvious that it will not succeed, and the scene ends by introducing two powerful forces at work within the play: revenge and fate.

Undoubtedly the greatest critical problem in this play is the simple fact that although Giovanni's passion is by common definition a sick love, it is by far the healthiest love in the play. Giovanni and Annabella join strengths, not weaknesses; they augment each other's personalities through giving, never by preying upon each other. Giovanni is praised for his "government, behaviour, learning, speech,/ Sweetness, and all that could make up a man," and Annabella's virtues are lauded throughout the play as she is courted by at least three others and described by father, brother, and nurse. The quality most conducive to a genuine love in Ford's plays is mutuality, and this brother-sister love abounds with it. Giovanni justifies his love to the friar by describing their unity, and it is the primary mark of their first love scene when it is discovered that Annabella has long had the same feeling for her brother but has not dared to speak it. In this scene, both brother and sister seem to be free from a sense of guilt. Their mutual vows, "love me or kill me," speak of the strength of their love in the face of the opposition of the world, not a mutual guilt. By their next meeting, their love has been consummated, and the poetry of their union marks it as complete. When Giovanni tries to rationalize his love to the friar in terms of school principles, it turns out to be mere sophistry, but the real and convincing argument is her beauty, in which almost every cliché of Renaissance poetry is created anew.

It is also in the presence of the friar that some hint of division comes between Giovanni and Annabella. Although little noted by critics, it is surely her pregnancy that brings Annabella to her knees, weeping in contrition before the friar, who responds by offering her a fine condensation of Dante's *Inferno*. The means to salvation he suggests is for her to marry her suitor, Soranzo, not only to cover her pregnancy but also to live totally loyal to him all her days. The marriage is easily achieved, and that very day Annabella and Soranzo exchange vows. Loyalty and commitment, however, are harder to muster, and when Soranzo discovers the pregnancy and excoriates her as a common whore engaging in "belly sports," she taunts him with high praise of her former lover, a man whom Soranzo could never match. He ought to be proud, she insists, to "have the glory/ To father what so brave a father got." Though she is hardly an obedient wife (evidently continuing her relations with Giovanni), Annabella does grow in penitence, wishing in love, like John Milton's Eve, to take the penalty due Giovanni upon herself. When the friar enters in the middle of her soliloquy, he is delighted and agrees to deliver a letter to Giovanni, both suggesting that he join her in repentance and also warning him against the revenge-fury of Soranzo.

The change in Giovanni is more subtle, but there is a definite shift in his attitude from love of a woman to love of the pleasure itself. Ford has underlined this in the structure of his play, for just as the friar interrupted Annabella's soliloquy of repentance, he enters in the middle of Giovanni's soliloquy glorying that even after her marriage, he finds "no change/ Of pleasure in this formal law of sports." Annabella was once more than a sport, and though he can still speak of "united hearts" and a love to the death, the emphasis is on the pleasure. In their final meeting, "lying on a bed," Giovanni is upset at Annabella's sudden resolve to "be honest," and certainly his anger and resentment at being denied his pleasure contributes to the impetus to murder. Even after he is convinced that their end is near and the talk turns to eschatology and life after death, his mind is on pleasure: "May we kiss one another, prate or laugh,/ Or do as we do here?" Annabella, however, does not know the answer, but Giovanni, convinced that death is on the way and that only after death is there any possibility for their love, frustrates Soranzo's elaborate plans for revenge by sacrificing his love upon his own dagger. Like Shakespeare's Othello, he exacts three kisses from her, finally resolving to "kill thee in a kiss" as she begs Heaven to forgive him and cries for mercy. The final scene of the play, in which Giovanni, quietly and rationally demented, enters the banquet scene carrying her bleeding heart on the tip of his dagger, is one that few can forget.

It is not only the sensationalism of this final scene or the disturbingly sympathetic treatment of an incestuous love that makes this play memorable. The poetry is of a consistently high caliber, forming a mirror of the souls of the characters. Recurring motifs, particularly of music and the full and ebbing sea, bind the play together. The pervasive resounding of love associated with death, accentuated by images of piercing and ripping, artistically creates a unified tone and foreshadows the end. Further, Ford's masterful use of the irony inherent in the situation, in which only the audience and the friar know of the clandestine love, adds enjoyment and understanding to the experience of the play.

This work also receives Ford's most complete examination of the role fate plays in life, a topic which obsessed him. In the very first scene of the play, Giovanni is convinced that he is compelled into his love by a force beyond him, not by what the friar describes as his "wilful flames." When Giovanni resolves to tell his sister of his love, he proclaims (perhaps protesting too much), " 'tis not, I know,/ My lust, but 'tis my fate that leads me on." He uses the idea of fate in pleading his love, insisting, " 'tis my destiny/ That you must either love, or I must die," and fate justifies the incest: "Wise nature first in your creation meant/ To make you mine; else't had been sin and foul." Annabella also uses fate to justify her actions, as she unconvincingly tries to convince Soranzo that he should accept an impregnated bride: "Why, 'tis thy fate." Later, in soliloquy, she echoes an earlier pair of star-crossed lovers as, regarding Giovanni, she laments: "Would thou hadst been less subject to those stars/ That luckless reign'd at my nativity." The friar tries to make a distinction between fate as nature's dictates and the destiny which is the will of Heaven. Both of the minor, bungling revengers, Richardetto and Hippolita, indicate that they are trying to control fate, and against this background it is interesting that Giovanni also, as he begins to assume the role of avenger, changes from a victim of destiny to one who would manufacture his own fate. He does not, however, outlive his revenges, and a sword in the fist of Vasques deals him the final blow, which otherwise he had determined to inflict upon himself. He dies declaring the irrelevance of mercy in the fact of the justice he has met, and wishing to "enjoy this grace,/ Freely to view my Annabella's face."

Perkin Warbeck has been termed a tragedy by some critics and a history play by most. It is about a legitimate king and an infamous claimant to the throne, yet it has no villain, unless it be Margaret of Burgundy, who never appears in the play, although her murky influence is felt behind Warbeck's claim to the throne. Henry himself is presented as an efficient king who rules well, with both foresight and insight, keeping always the good of his kingdom as his first goal and using mercy and goodness whenever they coincide with his major purpose. James of Scotland joins forces with Perkin Warbeck, out of a genuine though misguided sense of right. He is a weak but not a sinister character. He quickly takes the expedient course when he perceives that no English forces are rising to back Warbeck and when the forces of Spain and the empire are discovered to be totally behind the current English king. Warbeck himself is not without dignity in the play. Totally convinced that he is the duke who should rightfully have inherited the throne of England, he behaves in all respects like a king. Ford heightens his sense of nobility in the closing act of the play by contrasting him with Lambert Simnel, a previous pretender to the throne who is presented on the stage as a tempter of Warbeck. Simnel has bought his life by accepting the abject position of the king's falconer, and it is made plain that a similar choice is open to Warbeck. Convinced that he is indeed of royal blood, however, he will have none of it, and in a conventional but moving speech on the nobility of death, he is taken off to his own in royal dignity, a genuine, almost heroic figure who has almost persuaded the audience.

Interested as Ford is in the proper rules of succession and in affirming the legitimacy of the Tudor and Stuart lines, the play is just as much concerned with the quality of love, the dominant theme in his plays. In *Perkin Warbeck*, there are two examples of deep spiritual love of man for man. One instance is King Henry's attachment to his counselor, Lord Stanley. When Clifford reveals Stanley's complicity in the Warbeck plot, the king is shaken; Stanley had saved Henry's life on the battlefield and placed the crown on his head. Since that time, there had been nothing the king would not have done for him. The king's feelings for Stanley are poignantly evident in the scene of Stanley's condemnation. The king confides to his couselors that his heart would pardon Stanley, that there is "a chancery of pity in our bosom," but his better sense (awakened by a few strong words from his advisers) knows that this is impossible. Even so, he absents himself from the trial, fearing his own strong emotions. Stanley himself seems to underline the strength of their relationship as he responds to his sentence: "O the king,/ Next to my soul, shall be the nearest subject/ Of my last prayers!" In the face of this love, the reasons for his complicity in the plot remain a mystery.

Even stronger than this relationship is that between the Scots' Lord Huntley and Daliell, the suitor for his daughter Katherine's hand. Since she is an attractive girl with royal blood flowing in her veins, her father feels that she might well be a fit choice for King James himself, yet he is so fond of Daliell that he finally agrees to give his blessing to the match if Katherine should answer Daliell's plea with proper passion, though he does not agree to recommend the match to her. When Kate shatters the dreams of both men by turning her passion toward Warbeck, whom her father sees as a mere impostor, the relationship between Huntley and Daliell deepens and the older man invites Daliell to "Come with me, for I feel thy griefs as full/ As mine; let's steal away and cry together." This friendship is deepened at the wedding feast, where the music sounds to Huntley "Like to so many choristers of Bedlam/ Trolling a catch." In spite of a good nature which has learned to make light of hardships and a determination to be merry in a court where flattery keeps him secure, there is a touch of bitterness in Huntley's resignation to kings who are "earthly gods" with "anointed bodies" and in the renunciation of his child, who has chosen a "dukeling mushroom" for a husband. Daliell cuts through this mood of the older man, and with a more humble, continuing, and faithful love adds a tincture of consolation to their meeting. When Huntley asks for pardon for slighting Daliell's suit, the younger man offers him "a love, a service,/ A friendship to posterity," and Huntley expresses his gratitude for "some ease,/ A partner in affliction," after which the two men together endure the remainder of the wedding feast. They next appear after Warbeck has been rejected by King James, and although they enter together, they leave separately. Huntley, after a moving farewell to his daughter, returns to Scotland, but Daliell, in an act of faithfulness resembling that of Lear's Kent, asks permission to join Katherine and her husband in their sojourn to Cornwall. When Huntley appears for a brief moment at the end of the play, he does not converse with Daliell, but the two men are obviously united in their attitudes toward Katherine.

The major examination of love in the play involves Katherine. Although when Daliell begins to address her, Huntley suspects that an arrangement has already been made between them, the passion which he supposed to exist is the one thing lacking. Instead of responding to his suit, Katherine pleads duty to her father as an excuse to say no. Highly appreciative of his virtues, she gently and coolly suggests a Platonic courtly-love relationship. In sharp contrast to this is Katherine's first response to Warbeck. She merely watches his arrival in court from the sidelines, when the Countess of Crawford, observing her, remarks, "Madam, y'are passionate." To this passion is added the press of duty to accept Warbeck for a husband, but it is not duty to her father. In spite of Huntley's vociferous objections to the match, King James himself has insisted upon it, claiming an "Instinct of Sovereignty" to authenticate his choice. Katherine is nothing loath to accept this higher authority. She must be hurt deeply, however, when her father refuses his blessing upon the match and goes off to commiserate with Daliell.

From this point on, Katherine's love is a blend of commitment, duty, and faithfulness marked by a desire to share every life experience with her husband. She begs to go off to war with him, and when she is denied this, she extracts from him a promise that he will never again leave without her. Later, when Warbeck is dismissed by King James, his first reaction is not concern for his kingdom but a fear that James will find a way to retract the marriage and separate him from his new wife. Kate affirms her faithfulness to her husband. With bravery and courage, she is ready for what amounts to exile, exhibiting no bitterness toward the king, who commanded her into the marriage. She evinces a majestic sense of pride, vowing that she will not return as long as Warbeck is banished from the king's presence.

At the end of the play, Katherine is not allowed to share Warbeck's death, but she does share the humiliation which he has already turned into triumph by royally refusing to capitulate either to the king's taunts or to Lambert Simnel's demeaning compromise. In a magnificent bit of stagecraft, characteristic of Ford, Katherine climbs up onto the stocks in which he has been fixed. Though the Earl of Oxford is shocked and angered by the indignity, Katherine answers him with an affirmation of her marriage vows and her intention to live or die with her husband. Fate, however, which plays an important part in this play, as it does in Ford's others, decrees otherwise, and Perkin is taken off to his death, while Katherine is escorted to her apartment, her true love thwarted by a tragic misconception of birth and role.

The question of love is again examined in *The Lady's Trial* and this time it is social: Is it possible for love and marriage to succeed across socioeconomic lines? The well-born Auria has married Spinella with no dowry except her youth and beauty. His bosom friend, Aurelio, had warned him against this move, and indeed, shortly after the marriage, Auria is forced to leave Genoa to seek his fortune in the desperate arena of fighting Turkish pirates—not without an "I told you so" from Aurelio. Spinella's real dowry is faithfulness, honor, and an inner nobility. With humility and scorn, she spurns the suit of the ranking lord, Adurni, who, in her husband's absence, has trapped her into a bedroom replete with seductive music and a full banquet spread for the two of them. Aurelio, who discovers them together, threatens to expose her infamy. Although by hiding at Auria's return, she evinces some doubt of his willingness to believe her innocence, a mutual, perfect trust is reestablished at the close of the play, and all is well.

The theme is perhaps even more expressly considered in the subplots of the play. Levidolche has married beneath her station one Benatzi, whom her uncle, Martino, has designated a mere "trencher-waiter." The upper ranks of society beckon, however, and after becoming the mistress of Adurni, she divorces her husband, whose fortunes then degenerate until he becomes a galleyslave to the Turks. When Adurni's affections begin to cool (as he plans his seduction of Spinella), Levidolche writes a passionate letter seeking to enter into a relationship with Malfato, a lowly gentleman of the court, Spinella's uncle and ward. She confides her thoughts on rank to Futelli, whom she has hired to deliver the letter (and who betrays her by bringing it to Adurni first). "The properest men," she states, "should be preferr'd to fortune." Futelli leads her to admit that Adurni is not a man she admires by suggesting that "The title of a lord was not enough/ For absolute perfection," which she answers by describing the real perfections of Malfato. He, however, scorns her letter completely and publicly, mistakenly believing that Adurni was behind the solicitation, seeking to dupe Malfato into a marriage that would serve as both a cover-up for and pregnancy insurance against his own illicit relationship with the woman he would marry off. Infuriated at her betrayal by the two men, Levidolche seeks an avenger and hires Benatzi, who has been freed from the Turks by Auria and is now in disguise as a returned soldier and outlaw. His fee, however, is not money but marriage, and he insists on a wedding before the commission is fulfilled. She confesses her adultery and looseness, but he affirms his faith in her ability to reform. As he leaves, Levidolche smiles, confiding to the audience that "Love is sharp-sighted,/ And can pierce through the cunning of disguises./ False pleasures, I cashier ye; fair truth, welcome!"

This change of heart and life, induced by trust, is evidently genuine and lasting. When Levidolche's uncle, Martino, first sees her with this disheveled, disreputable piece of man-flesh, he accuses her of going public in her whoredom, setting up shop and crying "A market open; to't and welcome," but when he is informed of the marriage and let in on her secret that this creature is in reality her former husband, to whom she now intends absolute fidelity, her uncle is won over and convinced of her ability to achieve faithfulness. In the final scene of the play, Levidolche proclaims her new life-style to the entire court, and they, too, believe, accepting her fully into their society. She blushes to face Malfato but is forgiven by him, and she is supported financially in her new start by Adurni, Spinella, and her sister Castanna. This is indeed what Robert Grams Hunter would call "comedy of forgiveness."

The theme is reiterated on still another level of society, in which it approaches farce. Amoretta has a fixation: Although lacking social status herself, she refuses to marry anyone less than a count and believes that she is really fit for a duke. Futelli and his friend Piero plot to cure her of this disease by having her courted by one Guzman, in the disguise of a Spanish grandee, and by Fulgoso, one of the newly rich who has devised for himself a long and honorable family tree. In four long and delightful pages, Futelli coaches Guzman on the proper method to approach Amoretta, describing correct courtship in terms of military strategy. When Piero enters, counseling Fulgoso, the two would-be lovers challenge each other to a bloody resolution of their rivalry, but when they discover their mutual gluttony, they decide to have a sumptuous dinner together instead. In the wooing scene, in which Amoretta's heavy lisp adds to the foolishness, both Guzman and Fulgoso plead their cases by giving long and hilarious recitations of their family ancestries, and eventually they become so ridiculous that they are literally kicked off the stage with a cruelty reminiscent of Ben Jonson. Amoretta is cured and readily agrees to accept the mate of her father's choice, who later turns out to be Futelli.

Although there may be no such genre, this play can surely be best classified as a revenge comedy. It is almost as if Ford looked at his earlier tragedies and asked what psychological factors might have kept the blood from the stage. Many elements of revenge tragedy are present. There is an age-discrepancy between Auria and Spinella, and when Auria leaves court, he warns his young wife not to give even the slightest appearance of infidelity, charging her to remember "whose wife thou art." Against this charge, Aurelio, who has the innate potential to become an Iago figure, is commissioned to watch her. His love for Auria, which is twice mentioned in the play, is enough to create jealousy. He has warned Auria that his wife's youth and beauty are "baits for dishonour," and would naturally like to prove his forebodings justified. Further motivation is provided in that Auria has made Aurelio his heir, to inherit all of his assets except "Some fit deduction for a worthy widow/ Allow'd, with caution she be like to prove so." In addition to this, Aurelio is provided with "occular proof" which seems totally convincing to him when he finds Spinella locked in the bedroom with Adurni. His threat to inform his newly returned friend of this infidelity is ominous, and it is little wonder, remembering Auria's departing charge, that Spinella chooses to hide rather than to face her husband after he has heard Aurelio's accusations. Hiding, however, could well be interpreted as an admission of guilt, adding one more bit of evidence to the already convincing testimony.

What is the psychological ambience that resolves all of these elements into comedy rather than tragedy? The answer is in the quality of love in the play. Auria answers Aurelio's accusations with common sense and a luminous sense of trust in his wife, a quality that is completely absent in revenge tragedy. The evidence against her is circumstantial, he explains to Aurelio, and other interpretations are equally satisfactory. It is Auria's relationship with his friend that is threatened, not that with his wife. What a refreshing current this is in the murky waters of Renaissance drama: One can trust the person he loves; accusations dissolve into nothing in the clear, binding matrix of love. The one thing that hurts Auria is that Spinella's absence seems to say she did not trust him to have faith in her. His dealing with this seems a bit cruel, for upon their meeting, he pretends not to recognize her. Spinella retains her dignity and is eloquent against both liars and those who believe them. To this, Aurelio confesses that his accusations were engendered more by his suspicions than knowledge, but Auria then suggests the disparity in their ages as a possible cause of her dissatisfaction, to which she answers that there was none. Adurni, who had previously confessed to Auria that his confrontation with Spinella had changed his entire attitude toward women, convincing him that good women exist, enters to ask pardon of Spinella. When Auria seems not to accept even this as evidence of her innocence, Spinella strikes at the heart of their relationship: "You can suspect?/ So reconciliation, then, is needless." To allay Auria's suspicions would be irrelevant; if he has suspicions, the relationship is already beyond salvation. The reader, however, knows that he has none, but is worried about *her* suspicions of him. This worry removed, their relationship of mutual trust is reaffirmed. The real "lady's trial," then, appears not to be the obvious external assault on her virtue, portrayed in the first half of the drama, but the inward trial of the mutual trust, the real basis of love and marriage—the kind that makes tragedy impossible.

The other strain in which the play skirts on tragedy is in Levidolche's cry for revenge, which seems genuine and threatening. Her method of hiring a revenger is also typical of revenge tragedy, as she drops a purse with a note in it from a second-story window in the dark of night, so that it appears mysterious to all those on the lower stage. Benatzi, disguised as Parado, is certainly a fit instrument for revenge. Like Bosola, he has been both a soldier and a galley slave, and he makes a ragged appearance on the stage— an outsider to society. It is only when her renewed love for him proves to be genuine and permanent that the audience knows the revenge will not take place, though some suspense is maintained right up to the moment that he is disarmed in court. The play ends in merriment as Futelli is to wed Amoretta, Adurni is betrothed to Spinella's sister Castanna, and Fulgoso and Guzman enter to make their final foolish speeches before Auria dismisses all to attend the revels celebrating both marriages and his own promotions.

Love is not the only theme of Ford's drama, but it does, perhaps, best illustrate the deep and pervasive interest in psychological motivation which is evident in all of his extant works.

Other major works

POETRY: *Fame's Memorial: Or, The Earl of Devonshire Deceased*, 1606; *Christ's Bloody Sweat: Or, The Son of God in His Agony*, 1613.

NONFICTION: *Honor Triumphant: Or, The Peer's Challenge*, 1606; *The Golden Mean*, 1613; *A Line of Life*, 1620.

MISCELLANEOUS: *The Works of John Ford*, 1869 (Alexander Dyce, editor; includes previously uncollected poetry).

Bibliography

Anderson, Donald K., Jr. *John Ford*, 1972.

Ewing, S. Blain, Jr. *Burtonian Melancholy in the Plays of John Ford*, 1940.

Farr, Dorothy M. *John Ford and the Caroline Theatre*, 1979.

Leech, Clifford. *John Ford and the Drama of His Time*, 1957.

Oliver, Harold J. *The Problem of John Ford*, 1955.

Sargeant, M. Joan. *John Ford*, 1935.

Sensabaugh, George F. *The Tragic Muse of John Ford*, 1944.

Stavid, Mark. *John Ford and the Traditional Moral Order*, 1968.

Howard C. Adams

BRIAN FRIEL

Born: Omagh, Northern Ireland; January 9, 1929

Principal drama

A Doubtful Paradise (The Francophile), pr. 1959; *The Enemy Within*, pr. 1962, pb. 1979; *The Blind Mice*, pr. 1963; *Philadelphia, Here I Come!*, pr. 1964, pb. 1965; *The Loves of Cass Maguire*, pr. 1966, pb. 1967; *Lovers*, pr. 1967, pb. 1968; *Crystal and Fox*, pr. 1968, pb. 1970; *The Mundy Scheme*, pr. 1969, pb. 1970; *The Gentle Island*, pr. 1971, pb. 1973; *The Freedom of the City*, pr. 1973, pb. 1974; *Volunteers*, pr. 1975, pb. 1979; *Living Quarters*, pr. 1977, pb. 1978; *Faith Healer*, pr. 1979, pb. 1980; *Aristocrats*, pr. 1979, pb. 1980; *Translations*, pr. 1980, pb. 1981; *Three Sisters*, pr. 1981 (adaptation of Anton Chekhov's play); *The Communication Cord*, pr., pb. 1983.

Other literary forms

Brian Friel has published two collections of short stories, *The Saucer of Larks* (1962) and *The Gold in the Sea* (1966). A selection from these works has appeared as *Selected Stories* (1979), reprinted as *The Diviner* (1982).

The short stories in these collections are gentle, well-turned tales of ordinary people caught, largely, in the toils of personal circumstances. They belong firmly in the tradition of pastoral frustration, to which the majority of modern Irish short stories belong. The narrative tone of Friel's stories is genial, quizzical, and often humorous, and while their subject matter is not carried over into the author's drama, their tone anticipates the affection and dignity which Friel's plays typically accord the common man.

Achievements

After a modest but assured beginning as short-story writer, Friel has grown, thanks to his plays, into one of the most important figures in the cultural phenomenon which will surely come to be known as the Ulster Renaissance. Like many other artists from the North of Ireland, Friel has had his work deepened and darkened by the recent history of his native province, yet it is also true that his willingness to face that history and its web of cultural subtexts has thrown into bolder relief the innate humanity of all of his work, rendering it all the more estimable.

Throughout his plays, Friel has persistently exposed stereotype, cliché, and narrowness of various kinds. In their place, he has substituted joy, openness, and individuality, qualities which enhance the human lot and for which his birthplace has not been noted. A deep sense of division informs both his characters and his dramatic practice, yet acknowledgment of division is an avenue to sympathy, not a recipe for impairment. Emphasizing with increasing vigor, range, and sophistication the value of spontaneity and the necessity of love, Friel's work is a moving—and stirring—statement of human solidarity in a dark time.

This statement is constantly renewed by the author's formal innovations. Friel's technical brilliance, however, does not permit him to break faith with the heritage of twentieth century Irish drama, its attachment to a sense of locale, its concern for the common lot, its resistance to institutionalized modes of thought. In fact, Friel makes these elements interrelate fruitfully and unexpectedly by subjecting them to the clear, unblinking light of his moral intelligence.

Historically and artistically, Friel's place as Ulster's most important dramatist ever, and as one of Ireland's most significant dramatists in the twentieth century, is secure. Friel's achievements have been acknowledged with numerous drama awards on both sides of the Atlantic, and in 1981, *Translations* received the Ewart Biggs Memorial Prize, instituted to recognize outstanding contributions to Anglo-Irish understanding.

Biography

Order, industry, fixity, and quiet are the hallmarks of Brian Friel's life. He was born in Omagh, County Tyrone, Northern Ireland, on January 9, 1929, the son of a teacher. The family lived in Omagh for ten more years before moving to Derry, the second city of Ulster and the place which, along with its County Donegal hinterland, may be properly considered to be Friel's homeland.

Friel was educated at St. Columb's College, Derry, and at Maynooth, the Irish national seminary, where he was graduated in 1948, though it was not his intention to study for the priesthood. He attended St. Joseph's Teacher Training College, Belfast, from 1949 to 1950, and for the next ten years taught in various schools in Derry.

During this period, Friel began to write in his spare time, and from the mid-1950's, he was a regular contributor of short stories to *The New Yorker.* During this period also he turned to drama as a form, beginning with two radio plays, which were broadcast in 1958, and at the end of the 1950's, he branched out into staged drama.

In 1960, Friel resigned from teaching to devote himself to writing. The wisdom of that decision has been confirmed by the continuing string of international successes which has ensued. English and, particularly, American audiences have greeted his plays at least as enthusiastically as have Irish ones. Friel's rapid development as a playwright was decisively influenced by the celebrated director Tyrone Guthrie, at whose theater in Minneapolis Friel spent some months in 1968, in his words, "hanging around." Since 1980, a more public Friel has been in evidence as the moving spirit behind Field Day Productions, a theater company formed in collaboration, chiefly, with the actor Stephen Rea. Based in Derry, the company's objective is to renew the theatrical life of provincial Ireland by means of touring productions. Friel has also been instrumental in establishing Field Day Publications. This imprint has issued, most notably, an important series of pamphlets on Irish cultural matters by leading contemporary Irish poets and critics.

Analysis

Brian Friel's dramatic output, wide-ranging in subject matter though it is, possesses a notable consistency of theme, tone, and attitude to the stage. Whether a Friel play's pretext is the mission of St. Columbia, Derry's patron saint, to the island of Iona in the sixth century *(The Enemy Within)*, or the living room of decaying gentlefolk *(Aristocrats)*, a hedge school in nineteenth century rural Ireland *(Translations)*, or the encampment of a traveling show *(Crystal and Fox* or rather differently, *Faith Healer)*, familiar themes recur. Their recurrence, however, is invariably fresh, given new life by the author's unfailing sympathy and the suppleness with which he shapes unexpected cultural nuances. Such flexibility and control may be seen as an expression of the author's essential good nature. In his plays, one can also see, however, one of his oeuvre's most consistent traits, his daring use of theater itself. Friel's work shows a marked flair for dramaturgical experimentation, but the experiments themselves are exclusively in the service of broader human concerns, revealing how hollow yet how inevitable ritualized behavior can be, for example, or economically contrasting characters' public and private spaces. A consummate orchestrator of theatrical space and (as is increasingly evident from his recent work) the possessor of a light, though commanding, touch with ensemble work, Friel's is preeminently a writer's theater rather than a director's or a star's.

Foremost among Friel's broad human preoccupations is love—its persistence, its betrayal, its challenge. Few of Friel's characters manage to rise fully to the challenge of loving adequately. Their inadequacy is transmitted from one play to another, like a cynosure of frailty. What is significant, however, is not success but the apparent inevitability of exposure to a sense of human limitation and imperfection. Love generates many other important Friel themes. The affection for common people—uneducated, shrewd street-folk—which is unsentimentally present in all of his plays has a sympathetic loving-kindness in it which his characters themselves generally decline to embody. The destructiveness of family life, particularly the unhappy effects that parents may have on children—in Friel's world an unredeemable original sin—is also a feature of the author's preoccupation with love. Love likewise informs such concerns as fidelity to place and to cultural inheritance. A marked sharpness in attitude toward behavior which is determined by cultural institutions rather than by the vigor of the individual psyche is, again, motivated by Friel's concern with love. In fact, love has developed in Friel's work from being, in early plays, a matter of impossible romance, family bitterness, or sexual buoyancy to being the finely calibrated optic of a worldview. Friel's manipulation of the optic in recent plays reveals love as a saving grace, not only personally but also culturally—and usually both, interdependently—offering at once the tolerance of charity and the zest of passion, a healing ethic and a moral force.

Yet division, symptomatic of love's failure, is very much in evidence in Friel's work. In *Philadelphia, Here I Come!* — his first and major international success—the dichotomy between self and world is given novel dramaturgical embodiment through the device of having two actors play different aspects of the protagonist, Gar O'Donnell: Public Gar and his alter ego, Private Gar. The world sees only the former, while the audience readily perceives that it is the latter who has the greater authenticity, by virtue of his ability to satirize Public's gaucherie and emotional timidity. (Gar O'Donnell is the most winning representative of the naïve, ardent youth, a type beloved of Friel, first seen as the novice in *The Enemy Within*.)

The action takes place on the night before, and early morning of, Gar's emigration to the United States, and consists less of a plot than of a tissue of what Friel in later plays calls "episodes." In effect, Gar's past life passes before him. The passage takes place in two dimensions—the public, by means of farewells, and the private, by means of Private's somewhat manic and mordantly witty analysis of that life's nugatory achievements. The only thing which will relieve life at home in Ballybeg of his abiding sense of depletion, as far as Gar is concerned, is an expression of affection by his father. It is never made; Gar is obliged to carry his incompleteness with him. In that case, staying or going becomes moot.

As in *The Enemy Within*, the conclusion is inconclusive. The difference is that in the earlier play, inconclusiveness was enacted in a condition; here, rather more satisfyingly, it is embodied in a character. *Philadelphia, Here I Come!* also benefits from having its cultural resonances localized, as well as having its treatment of division given clever dramatic form. This play launched Friel's mature playwriting career. It contains an affectionately critical characterization of restlessness and brio, as well as failed love and a lament for it, and longings for a fuller life and a fear of it.

Friel's preoccupation with love, familial relations, and romance is offered in a delicate, bittersweet blend in *Crystal and Fox*, one of his most effective works. Crystal and Fox, a man-and-wife team, own a traveling show of no particular distinction. When we first encounter it, audience response is poor and Fox, in a typical fit of recklessness, fires some of the players. The company is now reduced to four, one of whom is Crystal's ailing and incompetent father who is soon hospitalized. The traveling show, for so long an expression of Fox's restlessness, now attains a stasis, a condition which makes Fox mean and destructive. All that can save the situation is the unwavering romantic attachment, tantamount to worship, that Crystal and Fox have for each other. Into their impoverished encampment comes Gabriel, their son. Gabriel has spent years in England, like Cass in *The Loves of Cass Maguire,* the victim of a family row. Now, however, all is forgiven, and Gabriel is seen as an embodiment of renewal. He soon tells Fox that he is on the run from the English police, having, in desperation, committed robbery with violence. This information is kept from Crystal until Gabriel is arrested before her eyes. As a result, Crystal and Fox sell the show's remaining properties in order to help Gabriel, but en route to Gabriel's trial, Fox lies, telling Crystal that he informed on his son for the sake of the police reward. A demented Crystal leaves her husband, allowing the play to conclude with a statement from Fox about the motivation for his destructiveness. He wanted the whole of life to be reduced to one ardent form—namely, his romantic love of Crystal. Such a love, he believes, expresses the best in him. Everything else is tainted with contingency, incompleteness, mortality. Yet the finality and totality of his love for Crystal is what prompts treachery and ruin.

The play is satisfying on a number of levels. Its spare language complements its essentially violent action. Friel's metaphoric use of playing and roles is deeply ingrained in the piece's fundamental texture. Bleakness and joy are communicated with great clarity and economy. The need for romance—the desire that there be something more to life than the mere role one plays in it—is boldly established and subjected to an impressively unsentimental critique. In all, *Crystal and Fox* is a fitting culmination of Friel's early phase. From this point onward, his work, while not forsaking love as a theme or the family setting as its representative focus, has engaged more public issues and has placed less emphasis on individual destiny than on collective experience, a departure which has meant the virtual elimination of the often stereotyped minor characters present in his early work.

With *The Freedom of the City,* Friel began his major phase. Innovative dramaturgy, a marriage of private and public themes, a major renovation of the part played by love in human affairs, all make this play a work of notable theatrical events.

The city in question is Derry, and the play is inspired by, though it does not mimic, the events of Bloody Sunday, January 30, 1972, when British forces killed thirteen civil rights demonstrators. Friel opens the play's action by having his three protagonists flee from the violent disruption by army and police of a banned civil rights demonstration. They seek refuge successfully in the Mayor's parlor of the Guildhall (the ease with which they do so being one of the play's many ironies about "security"), and, with nothing better to do, they have a party. They drink the Mayor's liquor, smoke his cigars, dress up in ceremonial robes, and parody official ceremonies, including the conferring of the freedom of the city. Skinner, the most restless, deprived, and anarchistically inclined of the threesome, does a minimal amount of damage to property, stabbing a city father's portrait with a ceremonial sword. His opposite is Michael, a clean-cut embodiment of civil rights aspirations, who, without skepticism, wants nothing more than a fair chance to better himself. Between them stands Lilly, a blowsy mother of eleven, who approves of Michael's respectability yet is stimulated by Skinner's vitality. Eventually, summoned by military bullhorn to emerge, the three (now thought of, thanks to rumor, as forty) emerge from the circumscribed freedom of their refuge, to be shot in cold blood on the Guildhall steps.

The play's action, however, is only one of its levels. It is surrounded by frameworks of judicial and intellectual evaluation. Thus, from the outset, we are privy to the findings of the court of inquiry, which examines and distorts the protagonists' actions and characters. We are also periodically subjected to an analysis of the culture of poverty voiced by an American sociologist. These two framing devices—sophisticated revisions of an ironic use of omniscience, introduced in *Lovers* and used most tellingly in *Living Quarters*—help us appreciate the informal, living texture of the trio's activities, as it is that very quality which the processes of evaluation and formal discourse are unable to admit.

Perhaps the play is overloaded with framing devices. In addition to the two central ones mentioned, there are also two which derive from the trio's own cultural constituency, represented by the Church and by a ballad-singer. These two also distort what the characters embody. The aim to be comprehensive is no doubt laudable, and the resultant verbal range is an impressive feature of the play, but the ensuing emphasis on the distorting effects of objectification is overdone. At the same time, however, such an emphasis also draws attention to *The Freedom of the City* as a hymn to the theater, both in the value it implicitly locates in the spontaneous antics of the three victims and in the sense that the stage is large enough for spontaneity and formality to play opposite each other.

In *Volunteers*, Friel also uses an event and a set of issues from contemporary Irish history. The matter in question is the Wood Quay, Dublin, excavation, where, during groundbreaking for a new office block, invaluable remains of Viking Dublin were unearthed. Efforts to preserve the site on the part of local *bien-pensants* led to ugly clashes with the developers, the law, and Dublin's city fathers, and also, ultimately, to frustrated defeat for the preservationists.

Out of this volatile material, Friel fashioned a marvelous play. His volunteers are jailed social activists of a not very well-defined variety; inasmuch as they have a social philosophy, it generally seems to speak in favor of a more abundant life. (The play's one ideologue, a student radical who is one of the supervisors, in the end lets down the volunteers rather seriously.) The play is set in a hole in the ground, and the action takes place on the last day of the dig, a closing date which has been peremptorily hurried forward and which will leave the work unfinished. When this state of affairs is brought to the attention of Keeney and his fellow volunteers, it increases the audience's appreciation of the magnitude of their contribution as well as exposing the sterility of orthodox socially instituted planning. Indeed, the spontaneous gesture of volunteering has placed Keeney and his mates in danger of their narrow-minded fellow prisoners. Those who give freely, it seems, will be regarded with the most suspicion.

This conclusion is reinforced by the attitude of George the foreman. Superior to the volunteers in social status alone, his inability to have anything other than a master-servant relationship with them expresses insufferable moral smugness on the part of one who watches but does not dirty his hands. The only figure with whom the volunteers can feel kinship is the skeleton they have disinterred and named "Lief," and who seems to have been the victim of a ritual execution. Lief is the authentic representative of a past common to all in the play, a past which is only properly visible to the volunteers. Thus, Lief is to be cherished much more than the vase which George has assembled out of fragments rescued by the volunteers, and when one of them deliberately breaks the vase, the symbolic resonance is as great as that provided by their ceremonial reburial of Lief.

The volunteers, then, are those who come in closest contact with the texture of the past, its earthbound treasures and human blemishes—and this contact is all the more estimable for being freely given. Prisoners of the state, menaced by their own kind and by their masters, the volunteers give unlikely expression to *pietas,* which is in cultural terms what love is in personal affairs. Yet all this is communicated in anything but solemn terms; the breezy satire of *The Mundy Scheme* is here deepened and tightened almost beyond recognition. Finally, in Keeney, Friel has created a character who is in total command of himself and prepared to face whatever comes, a character whose abundant energies, verbal pyrotechnics, and keen mind equip him superbly to be the onstage director of what Seamus Heaney has memorably called "a masque of anarchy."

To end a discussion of Brian Friel's drama with *Translations* is entirely fitting, as this is his finest achievement, as well as being, both intellectually and culturally speaking, his most ambitious. Set in the 1830's among the Irish peasantry, it discourses wittily, economically, and profoundly on the clash between the English and the Irish cultures, on language and its imprecision, on violence and its distortions.

The play opens with young adult peasants entering the hedge school of

Hugh O'Donnell for their evening class in Latin, Greek, and arithmetic. In itself, such a scene is replete with noteworthy cultural resonances, being both a far cry from the stage Irishman and a vivid introduction to contemporary peasant life, down to the aging "infant prodigy" in the background who relishes Homer in the original. Hugh's son, Manus, takes the class this particular evening, because of his father's inebriation. One of the students is Manus' sweetheart, ambitious Maire, who is anxious for a fuller life for both of them. She plans to emigrate to America, while Manus, to some extent his father's prisoner, possesses a fierce loyalty to the local native life he loves so well.

In a sense, Maire resembles Manus' brother, Owen. He, too, desires a wider arena for himself, as is clear from his entry into the schoolroom with two well-disposed British soldiers, Captain Lancey and Lieutenant Yolland. These two are members of a detachment of troops engaged on an ordinance survey of Ireland, an enterprise which has as one of its features the translation of Irish place-names into English. Owen is employed in this work, under Yolland's supervision, and he is painfully aware of the offense against *pietas* constituted by the effective divorce of native tongue from native place which will inevitably result. His awareness is ironically contrasted with Yolland's onset of a vague, fashionable, romantic attachment to the locals, and Owen's situation is further underlined by the deft trick of showing that when the native characters speak among themselves, the soldiers do not understand them. In other words, at certain points, the audience must accept English to be Irish.

In the hope that the cultural conflict will not come to a head, Owen arranges for Yolland to attend a local dance. There, Yolland meets Maire, and despite linguistic barriers, hilarious at the time (Friel's flair for representing gaucherie is brilliantly displayed here), she seduces him. Having seen Maire home, however, Yolland is never seen again, and the play ends with peasant hegemony broken beyond repair by the threat of dire reprisal by Lancy, and by Manus' flight from the place whose main hope he was. The situation is left in the hands of Hugh, who is impotently eloquent about its linguistic implications, and Jimmy, the "infant prodigy," whom language has deluded to the extent of his announcing his impending marriage to Homer's *glaukopis Athene*.

The play's effectiveness is not solely derived from the novelty and richness of its cultural scenario: In addition, this scenario enabled Friel to marshal areas of interest which had hitherto existed separately in his works. Here one finds the intersection of public and personal history, the suffocation of love by unpromising family circumstances, the destructiveness and inevitability of passion, the author's devotion to the common people and to that sense of Ireland which Ballybeg connotes. The coalescence of these themes certainly makes *Translations*, in the words of the review in

The Times of London, "a national classic." The play also sets the seal on Brian Friel's reputation as the most resourceful, most engaging, and most serious voice in postwar Irish drama.

Other major works

SHORT FICTION: *The Saucer of Larks*, 1962; *The Gold in the Sea*, 1966; *Selected Stories*, 1979 (reprinted as *The Diviner*, 1982).

RADIO PLAYS: *A Sort of Freedom*, 1958; *To This Hard House*, 1958.

Bibliography

Deane, Seamus. "Brian Friel," in *Ireland Today.* CMLXXVIII (July/ August, 1981), pp. 7-10.
Hogan, Robert. *After the Irish Renaissance: A Critical History of the Irish Drama Since "The Plough and the Stars,"* 1967.
Maxwell, D. E. S. *Brian Friel*, 1973.
Schlueter, June. "Brian Friel," in *Dictionary of Literary Biography, Volume XIII: British Dramatists Since World War II, Part I,* 1982.

George O'Brien

CHRISTOPHER FRY

Born: Bristol, England; December 18, 1907

Principal drama

The Boy with a Cart, pb. 1939, pr. 1950; *Thursday's Child*, pr. 1939; *The Firstborn*, pb. 1946 (revised 1962), pr. 1948; *A Phoenix Too Frequent*, pr., pb. 1946; *The Lady's Not for Burning*, pr. 1948, pb. 1949; *Thor, with Angels*, pr., pb. 1948; *A Sleep of Prisoners*, pr. 1950, pb. 1951; *Venus Observed*, pr., pb. 1950; *The Dark Is Light Enough*, pr. 1954, pb. 1955; *Three Plays*, 1960; *Curtmantle*, pr., pb. 1961; *Plays*, 1963-1971; *A Yard of Sun*, pr., pb. 1970; *Paradise Lost*, pr., pb. 1978 (adaptation of John Milton's poem).

Other literary forms

Christopher Fry is well-known for his many translations of plays into English verse, which have had successful productions both for the stage and, in some cases, for the cinema. His first published translation was of Jean Anouilh's *L'Invitation au Château* as *Ring Round the Moon* (pr., pb. 1950), Fry's only effort in prose, followed by several translations, including *The Lark* (pr., pb. 1955; of Anouilh's *L'Alouette*), *Tiger at the Gates* (pr., pb. 1955; of Jean Giraudoux's *La Guerre de Troie n'aura pas lieu*), *Duel of Angels* (pr., pb. 1958; of Giraudoux's *Pour Lucrèce*), *Judith* (pr., pb. 1962; of Giraudoux's *Judith*), and *Cyrano de Bergerac* (pr., pb. 1975; of Edmond Rostand's *Cyrano de Bergerac*). Fry has also published critical prose, including *An Experience of Critics* (1952) and several important essays on the use of verse in drama. He has worked on television productions and screenplays in recent years, and his work for the British Broadcasting Corporation, *The Brontës of Haworth*, was published in 1975. His screenplay credits include *Ben Hur* (1959) and *The Bible* (1966).

Achievements

Fry is one of the most popular and prolific of twentieth century English verse playwrights; only T. S. Eliot and William Butler Yeats exercised a greater influence on the development of twentieth century verse drama. Fry differs from Eliot and Yeats, however, in that he did not establish a reputation as a poet before turning to the stage: Fry began with an early and practical interest in the theater as an actor and director.

It is a fact worth noting that, with the exception of his translation of Jean Anouilh's *L'Invitation au Château*, all of Fry's plays are in verse in a century which has provided primarily a theater of realistic prose—a prose which Fry claims has lost all contact with anything other than surface reality. Fry insists that his use of verse is in the service of reality, that verse provides a medium for his attempt to shake the world alert again to the deeper reality of every human being's ability to experience afresh the eternal miracle of life—a reality at present obscured and staled by custom. In Fry's view, mankind has domesticated the enormous miracle of life and become deadened to the wonder which is everywhere available. Fry attempts to give voice to his sense of the miracle of life with the language of poetry; he derisively identifies prose on the stage with the tinkle of breakfast cups. In a 1951 article in *Saturday Review*, Fry makes it clear that "poetry is the language in which man explores his own amazement."

This worldview probably accounts for much of the adverse criticism Fry's plays have received, for his work sometimes rings false or hollow, irresponsibly separated from the world the theatergoer accepts as real. Sometimes the reader or viewer senses that Fry protests too much for a man firmly grounded in the "enormous miracle" of the world, and the atmosphere of his plays often has the unfortunate effect of sheer fantasy. The use of distant times and scenes adds to a sense of unreality, and it would seem particularly unfortunate that, if Fry's aim is to reestablish wonder in modern man, he should feel the necessity for setting his dramas in a world removed from the present by time and distance. *A Sleep of Prisoners* and *A Yard of Sun* are exceptions, and *Venus Observed* and even *The Dark Is Light Enough* can be viewed as fairly direct comments on the contemporary dilemma, but Fry's plays are never "modern" in the same sense that Eliot's, W. H. Auden's and Christopher Isherwood's, or Stephen Spender's are.

Fry seldom seeks to come to grips with the modern world by taking it as the arena of his explorations; rather, he works by indirection, indicating in the world of his plays the importance of the individual, the meaning of humanity, the futility and needless cruelty of wars, and the possibilities for redeeming life through love. Having demonstrated the vitality latent in the world, Fry feels that he has made sufficient comment on the modern situation. This approach is misleading in view of Fry's claim to be interested in the problems of his own time, for the emphasis in his work appears to be not on modern man, but on mankind, as if Fry thought he could best restore human life to its proper heritage not by showing the paltry thing it has become in the twentieth century, but by showing what it has been and yet may be. Thus, Fry's dramaturgy stems from his romanticism, which expresses itself in an undaunted humanism and draws its vocabulary from natural and biblical sources. In Fry, there is little of the peculiarly modern vocabulary that one finds in other contemporary playwrights; as a general rule, the science Fry draws upon for his images is that of alchemy or astronomy; his psychology is that of the theory of humours; his textbook, Robert Burton's *The Anatomy of Melancholy* (1621). It is not surprising, then, to find the charge of romantic escapism leveled against Fry: The dangers inherent in his approach are obvious.

Given his orientation, the problem Fry faces in terms of language is perhaps clearer when one considers that the mainstream of poetic idiom for
the modern verse play is that established by Eliot and manipulated by Auden and others. This is an idiom, on the whole, expressive of the modern
world as it has appeared to these poets, and such a language can be of little use to Fry. He needs a language not to embody the dreary failure and,
at best, partially reclaimed successes of the modern world, but a language
to carry as much as possible the wonder, the miracle, the exuberance of a
world that, most likely, never was. Against Eliot's habitual understatement,
Fry's project demands a language of overstatement, resulting in excesses:
the riot of images which often impede the dramatic progress of a passage,
the wit or whimsy which sometimes seems to exist for the sake of its own
good nature, and the verbal coinages which can be effective theater for a
time but begin to pall before the end of the third act.

Fry's linguistic debts have been traced to various and varying sources,
and if all of the critics are right in their assumptions about sources, his
verse has an impressive (but impossible) cosmopolitan paternity. Fry's work
has been linked to that of the Georgians, but the Elizabethan playwrights
as well as the Jacobeans, Francis Beaumont and John Fletcher, are most
often named as his literary ancestors. Fry's desire to recapture a sense of
life and wonder does suggest certain early seventeenth century parallels, as
do specific literary borrowings from William Shakespeare's comedies. In
this respect also, Fry's dominant rhythmic pattern is usually blank verse,
although he makes extensive use of variations involving a four-stress line
and the anapestic foot, which give his verse its characteristic speed.

Clearly, Fry's verse drama has taken a direction quite opposite from
Eliot's, and one need only compare Eliot's *The Cocktail Party* and Fry's *Venus Observed*, both published in 1950 and both dealing thematically with
the acceptance of limitations and the discovery of identity, to discern the
differences in verse and treatment. In the Eliot play, the verse is sub-
merged, approximating in general the common speech of modern man, rising to poetry only in moments of emotional intensity. In the Fry play, the
verse is insistent throughout the play. Although both playwrights are concerned with the human being in his social context, the verse of *The Cocktail Party* seems much more solid, genuinely grounded in an action which in
itself has a depth that the action in the Fry play lacks.

Fry, as a dramatist, has not consistently mastered the third voice of poetry identified by Eliot in "The Three Voices of Poetry" as "the voice of
the poet when he attempts to create a dramatic character speaking in
verse: when he is saying, not what he would say in his own person, but
only what he can say within the limits of one imaginary character address-
ing another imaginary character." Fry's characters, no matter how exor-

bitant their humors, generally reveal in their speech the voice of the poet, slightly academic and a little self-conscious, and it is for this reason that so many of Fry's characters sound alike.

Biography

Christopher Fry's work was virtually unknown to playgoers or readers until the success of *The Lady's Not for Burning* in 1949, although he seems to have been on his way to the creation of this play throughout most of his life. Born Christopher Fry Harris, the son of an architect, Charles Harris, Fry was reared in an intensely religious home. His father had been a lay missionary in the Bristol slums and his mother was a devout Quaker. Fry was still young at the time of his father's death, and his mother took in boarders in order to send her only son to the Bedford Modern School. She also did much to encourage his natural musical talents, translated, in his later writing career, into an appreciation for the music of language. His early performances as a solo musician may also have given him a taste for the more multifaceted world of the professional stage toward which he aimed his life. Fry did not pursue a university education but left school at age eighteen to become a teacher, around this time beginning to use his mother's maiden name, Fry—the name by which he has since been known.

Between periods of teaching, Fry joined the Bath Repertory Company. His next experience with the theater was eight difficult years during which he stubbornly tried to make a living with repertory troupes, performing in plays by William Shakespeare, George Bernard Shaw, Oscar Wilde, Sir James Barrie, and Noël Coward. When he moved to London in search of a career at the center of England's dramatic activities, he found that economic necessity once again forced him to try other work—as an editor, cartoonist, secretary, writer of children's plays, and even songwriter. From 1934 until its demise, he was director of the Wells Repertory Players at Tunbridge Wells. According to Fry, through all of this time his desire to write plays in verse never faltered.

Two years after his 1936 marriage, Fry received a small legacy from a cousin which enabled him to begin sustained work on his plays. In the following year, his first published play, *The Boy with a Cart*, was conceived and first performed as a pageant play for the fiftieth anniversary of a village church, and *Thursday's Child* was produced in Albert Hall, London, with the attendance of the queen at one performance. In 1939, Fry became director of the Oxford Playhouse, but, as a conscientious objector, he spent the war years in civilian service, fighting fires and clearing bomb damage in various parts of England.

In 1946, *A Phoenix Too Frequent*, the first of Fry's mature achievements in verse drama, was performed in London's private Arts Theatre Club, followed by sixty-four performances in a West End theater. The play, despite its success, drew critical reviews that saw it as too facile in its verse and too lightweight in its philosophical implications, in spite of the fact that Fry's original source was a tale from Petronius. The play, the first of Fry's to cross the Atlantic for a commercial performance, closed after only five nights in New York in April of 1950. New York critics almost unanimously condemned the play for being overwritten and too slight with regard to dramatic conception.

The Lady's Not for Burning was championed by John Gielgud for London production in 1948, a production in which Gielgud also had a hand in staging and a major character role in performance. This first of Fry's "seasonal comedies" brought him recognition and success on both sides of the Atlantic, and the play won the prestigious Shaw Prize as the best play of the year. *Venus Observed*, the "autumnal" play, followed the "spring" mood of *The Lady's Not for Burning* two years later when Sir Laurence Olivier successfully staged and acted in it. The "seasonal" round of Fry's intentions was interrupted by *A Sleep of Prisoners* published the year following, which was a religious festival play like *The Boy with a Cart* and *The Firstborn*. Published in 1955, *The Dark Is Light Enough* provided the "winter" comedy, and finally, in 1970, after slightly more than twenty years and the publication of *Curtmantle* in 1961, his Beckett play, Fry completed his expressed intention to write a play for each season of the year with *A Yard of Sun*, displacing *A Phoenix Too Frequent*, which some impatient critics had tried to take for the "summer" comedy needed for the cycle of the seasons.

Fry continues to be active as a translator and as a writer for film and television.

Analysis

A Phoenix Too Frequent and *A Sleep of Prisoners* are Christopher Fry's two most successful one-act plays, a length which Fry easily mastered, but of the two, *A Sleep of Prisoners* is the more interesting because it is one of the few plays in which Fry tries to deal with a contemporary setting, and it is, formally, the most experimental of Fry's plays. In many ways his most complex undertaking, *A Sleep of Prisoners* can be described as one of the most immediately modern of Fry's plays, not simply because it has as its characters four prisoners of war, and as its setting an interlude in World War II, but also because in this play, Fry draws on the experimental formal techniques of the modern theater. The scene of the play is a church converted into a temporary prison for four captured soldiers who, under the pressure of their surroundings, reenact biblical scenes in their dreams. Within this framework, Fry describes his intent and his design in the play's prefatory letter to Robert Gittings: "I have tried to make a more simple statement though in a complicated design where each of four men is seen through the sleeping thoughts of the others, and each, in his own dream, speaks as at heart he is, not as he believes himself to be."

This structure achieves a welding together of the spiritual history of mankind and the dreams of the four sleepers in an expressionistic fantasy which expresses the theme of the play. The dreams are made up of significant moments in the growth of vision Fry hopes to express, and the treatment of the material, the weaving of the patterns of the dreams and the final dream shared in common, suggests that the technique of the play owes more than a little to the Jungian idea of a racial memory, or perhaps to the tendency in modern poetry to suggest a composite experience and protagonist, as in Eliot's *The Waste Land* (1922) and in William Carlos Williams' *Paterson* (1946-1958).

The dreams of the four soldiers involve moments of passion, of suffering, of sacrifice, and the dream-lives of the men are determined by their temperaments, which are established in the brief exchange which opens the play. Peter Abel, outwardly easygoing, uncommitted, and even-tempered, is attacked by his friend, David King, whose nerves are frayed by the whole experience and by his concern for Peter's apparent untroubled acceptance of the situation in which they find themselves. In their subsequent dreams, these two reenact the conflict in the roles which their names and natures suggest—Abel and Cain, Absalom and David, Isaac and Abraham—until they finally join Corporal Adams in his dream, and the three of them become Shadrac, Meshac, and Abednego in the fiery furnace, the crucible of man's experience.

The creation of their dreams in terms of army life gives the whole play a sense of immediacy while underwriting the repetitive nature of history and the cumulative meaning of man's experience. The mixing of biblical situations and military terminology provides a very effective vocabulary for the verse of the play, creating the same kind of tensions which the larger design of the play encompasses.

The fourth character, Meadows, a man beyond the maximum age for enlistment, has accepted his involvement with mankind by the symbolic act of voluntary enlistment, and he provides the structural links between the waking and sleeping worlds, For the most part, as the other dreamers act out their passions, Meadows lies awake in his bunk; the others wake fitfully from time to time, and the waking men interact on the edge of their dreams. For example, after Adams, as Joab, has cut down Absalom with his tommygun, David (no longer the king) awakens, and in the anxiety of his guilt, which had been objectified by his dream, he asks Meadows, who has been awake, if he has heard a shout (the cry of the dying Absalom). Meadows' reply, "Nobody shouted," indicates the complexity of the formal convention of the dream, which is to be compared to the interior monologue technique in the sense that the world of the dream creates its own significant content and form although its larger setting is the external world.

There is a progression in the dreams which David and Peter enact, moving from the wrathful killing by Cain when Abel wins at dice to the meaningful but averted sacrifice of Isaac by Abraham. In the final experience of the furnace, when all three join in a single dream, Meadows appears as Man, who undergoes with the others the purgatorial fires in which mankind is tried. The fourth figure, the role which Meadows takes, is present in the biblical story and is traditionally identified with Christ; yet only if Christ is to be seen as a type of Everyman—not God but first of all Man, sharing the experiences of man—does this reading of the figure do no violence to accomplishment of the play.

In *A Sleep of Prisoners*, Fry deals more directly with the state of man in the modern world than in any of his other plays. David, for example, has the obsession Auden expressed in the 1930's, that the world is divided into "we's" and "they's" "ours" and "theirs"; "I've got to know which side I'm on./ I've got to be on a side." The intent of the play is to suggest, however, that sides and the wars and hatreds they represent offer no solutions, for no man is an island: "whatever happens on the farthest pitch,/ To the sandman in the desert or the island-man in the sea,/ Concerns us very soon." The involvement of man in his history is a purifying experience, just as the flames in the biblical furnace suggest the purgatorial nature of the dreams the men have endured. The flames in the furnace become human figures, the unquenchable fire of breath and blood, which "can only transform."

Fry comes closer in *A Sleep of Prisoners* to achieving a totally realized verse drama than in any of his other attempts. Fry's problem in moving toward longer plays was to find a form in which to put his particular kind of language into a sustainable relationship to the whole. The most critical problem encountered in the longer play, the three-act or the five-act, appears to be that of a structure in which verse can play an integral part and which will, in turn, justify the use of verse, for the problems of verse drama appear to be intensified and complicated by the necessities of the longer play. In the "seasonal comedies" and in *Curtmantle*, Fry stubbornly attacks the problem of the longer play in verse, only partially succeeding.

Fry's idea of a comedy for each season of the year is not a gimmick, but rather it belongs to the aesthetic notion that the "comedy of mood" or "comedy of seasons" can provide a unity of setting, time, and mood which will create the wholeness symbolized by the year itself.

Mood is everything in *The Lady's Not for Burning*. Two charming, young eccentrics—the rationalistic accused witch and the disenchanted soldier who wants to die—are pitted against two antagonists, one of which represents spring and all the forces of life, and the other the petty world of a society which claims that "The standard soul/ Must mercilessly be main-

tained. No/ Two ways of life. One God, one point of view./ A general ac-
quiescence to the mean."

All in all, this spring comedy is determined to prove that April is *not* the
cruelest month, that human beings can survive the birth pangs of self-
knowledge, accepting finally even the burden of an unreasonable future
and an imperfect world. Typically, love reclaims the characters for life and
an intuitive recognition of the wonder of the universe. In the course of
their reclamation, however, there is a good deal of sheer "talk" for its own
sake of the kind that weakens rather than strengthens Fry's comedies. Even
the eccentricity of the characters cannot excuse a language often so circu-
itously poetic that the most notable thing about it is its derivative quality.
The verbal high jinks, the excesses of language and imagery are as obvious
as the literary derivations, and although Fry intentionally does this sort of
thing at times in a scheme of romantic mockery, the device does not always
work, since he is quite capable of creating a passage bearing the same verbal characteristics when his intention is entirely otherwise.

Venus Observed, the autumnal comedy, is set in the declining season of
the year, and its hero, the Duke of Altair, is well past the green age of
youth; he has a grown son who becomes his rival in love and teaches him
that he must accept the encroachments of age. At the beginning of the
play, the Duke thinks that he has accepted the limitations imposed by his
age, and he has gathered three of his former mistresses in his bedroom
observatory to watch an eclipse of the sun through his beloved telescope.
The Duke's son, Edgar, is to perform the Judgment of Paris for his father
and present one of the three women with the symbolic apple, also appropriate to the day of the year, All Hallow's Eve, and to the autumn harvest.
The apple is further to be identified with the legendary apple of the Fall of
Man, so that through symbol and image, the scene of the play is extended
to include the whole ruined Eden of the contemporary world, although
there is no emphasis in the play on the modern situation.

The memory of Eden, of his first, unspoiled love, remains in the Duke,
in spite of his autumnal resolves. When the eclipse has passed and the first
renewed light of the sun reveals Perpetua Reedbeck standing in its rays,
the Duke forgets that " 'mellow'/ Is the keynote of the hour," and takes the
apple to offer it to her youth and beauty. It is not until one of the Duke's
aging mistresses destroys his observatory, which she sees as symbolic of the
Duke's isolation and his invulnerability, that the Duke is brought to realize
that so much he had "delighted in is all of ash." Out of the ash finally
arises the Duke's acceptance of a love befitting his declining years. The
action of the play brings the Duke into harmony with its autumnal mood—
a mood which, like that of *The Cocktail Party*, leads all the characters to
an examination of their limitations and to the adjustments necessary to
make the best of the fading world in which they find themselves. In this

respect, the play is close to the traditional function of comedy as a revelation of the follies and foibles of mankind, which brings human beings into an acceptable balance with society. As a part of this function, the speeches of certain characters (particularly of the Duke as Age pursuing lost Youth) are self-mocking, like those in *A Phoenix Too Frequent*, although Fry has achieved on the whole a quieter and less highly pitched verse.

The verse in this play shows, in general, a certain flexibility not achieved in the earlier comedies, and it is a verse that wears for three acts with much less friction than the verse of *The Lady's Not for Burning*. The language itself is closer to the contemporary idiom, and it is "poetic" in unobtrusive ways which involve concealed end-rhymes, internal rhymes, and alliteration. This is, on the whole, a more mature play than the earlier three-act comedy, and the language reflects this maturity. The verse almost entirely avoids the nondramatic philosophizing one ordinarily expects in a Fry play, and when such general comments do occur, they are part and parcel of the action or mood of the play.

The Dark Is Light Enough is a "winter comedy" presumable because it involves the physical decline and death (but spiritual victory) of its heroine, who triumphs in death as in life, not so much through her own action as through her influence on those about her. This is a comedy, not of manners, but of the spiritual fiber which informs the world of manners, even in a no-man's-land between two warring forces. As in *The Firstborn*, the play is held together by a single, commanding character, that of the Countess, and her sphere of influence is the area of the play, even in the final moments after she has suffered death and yet controls the action about to be performed. The language, as befits a winter comedy, is sober in comparison to that of the other comedies, but on the whole, it is undistinguished either by Fry's excesses or by his achievements. At its worst, the language of the play suffers from the same sentimentality that mars the whole work. At its best, it is a language which rises out of the situation to catch and hold the mood of the play, as when the dying Countess descends the stairs for a final Thursday evening with her devoted group of admirers and tells them, "We must value this evening as the one/ Thursday in the universe, for the rest/ Have gone, and no more may come,/ And we should be on our most immortal behaviour."

A Yard of Sun is set in an Italian summer during the first Palio to be celebrated following the conclusion of World War II. This ancient contest, with its religious and civic affirmations, becomes the fitting occasion for the trial of individual identity, which is a central action of all of Fry's plays. It is also the occasion to bring the characters into an acceptance of the flawed universe, the world that will not bend itself to their own conceptions and desires, but which is, in spite of this fact (or, more likely, because of it), worthy of acceptance and affirmation. In fact, Ernst Cassirer's definition of comedy in "An Essay on Man" seems to have been made for Fry. Cassirer sees comic art as possessing "in the highest degree that faculty shared by all art, sympathetic vision. By virtue of this faculty it can accept human life with all its defects and foibles, its follies and vices. . . . We live in this restricted world, but we are no longer imprisoned by it."

A Yard of Sun is set in the courtyard of an ancient Siena palazzo, and the scene is never varied, for in a technique reminiscent of John Millington Synge's *The Playboy of the Western World* (pr., pb. 1907), the news of the various stages of the running of the traditional horse race comes to the audience only by report. The contest, an occasion for family reunions, provides the heightened moment which unlocks the potentiality for the real challenges of the play.

The sun in this summer comedy seems to suggest to Fry the light before which the inner shadows of the characters must yield and modify themselves. The "heat of the day" (the original title of the play) is a time for clarity, and into the yard of the palazzo come nine characters, representing a variety of modern views and problems, each related to the others in ways which must be clarified before they can accept the ambiguities of their own experiences. Winning turns out, in the end, not at all to mean what the characters had thought it would.

The verse of *A Yard of Sun* is much more controlled and unobtrusive than in any of Fry's other plays. The people are more nearly people talking to one another than they are characters making poems on the stage, and the action of this play seems to fit its meaning with an ease never before achieved. There is nothing very original in the play itself, but it is original within the Fry canon in the sense that it does not strain toward either the condition of verse or the condition of drama.

The "seasonal" comedies, like all of Fry's plays, reflect his serious commitment to humanist and pacifist values and express the determined democracy of the individual spirit that is a legacy of Fry's Quaker heritage. Fry's insistence on the wonder of human life and the capacities of human beings, individually and collectively, for the growth of soul and conscience, has led him to some of the excesses of language and plotting for which he has been both accused and celebrated. Fry's career seems, ironically, almost a mirror of the effect of his best plays: a relatively brief and dazzling burst of light on the generally dark horizon of modern drama. He has persisted stubbornly through his original efforts and his translations of French playwrights to bring to what he sees as the contemporary theater's dreary realism a sense of delight and celebration that is nowhere else to be found and to wed this hopefully awakened sense of wonder to verse, a fit medium to oppose the dullness of the prevailing dialogue of contemporary realism. Fry's final reputation in the history of twentieth century drama may be that of one of the stubborn eccentrics he so loves to portray on the stage, but he will be respected for his desire to suggest a healthy—and very serious—alternative for his time.

Other major works

POETRY: *Root and Sky: Verse from the Plays of Christopher Fry*, 1975.

NONFICTION: *An Experience of Critics*, 1952; *Can You Find Me: A Family History*, 1978; *Death Is a Kind of Love*, 1979 (lecture).

SCREENPLAYS: *The Beggar's Opera*, 1953 (with Denis Cannan); *Ben Hur*, 1959; *Barabbas*, 1962; *The Bible: In the Beginning*, 1966.

TELEPLAYS: *The Canary*, 1950; *The Tenant of Wildfell Hall*, 1968; *The Brontës of Haworth*, 1973 (4 teleplays); *The Best of Enemies*, 1976; *Sister Dora*, 1977 (adaptation of Jo Manton's book).

CHILDREN'S LITERATURE: *The Boat that Mooed*, 1966.

TRANSLATIONS: *Ring Round the Moon*, 1950 (of Jean Anouilh's play *L'Invitation au Château*); *The Lark*, 1955 (of Anouilh's play *L'Alouette*); *Tiger at the Gates*, 1955 (of Jean Giraudoux's play *La Guerre de Troie n'aura pas lieu*); *Duel of Angels*, 1958 (of Giraudoux's play *Pour Lucrèce*); *Judith*, 1962 (of Giraudoux's play); *Cyrano de Bergerac*, 1975 (of Edmond Rostand's play).

Bibliography
Roy, Emil. *Christopher Fry*, 1968.
Schnelling, Heier M. *Christopher Fry's "Seasonal Comedies,"* 1981.
Stanford, Derek. *Christopher Fry*, 1951.
Wiersma, Stanley M. *Christopher Fry: A Critical Essay*, 1970.

Donna Gerstenberger

ATHOL FUGARD

Born: Middelburg, South Africa; June 11, 1932

Principal drama

No-Good Friday, pr. 1958, pb. 1977; *Nongogo,* pr. 1959, pb. 1977; *The Blood Knot,* pr. 1961, pb. 1963; *People Are Living There,* wr. 1962, pr. 1968, pb. 1969; *The Occupation,* pb. 1964 (one act); *Hello and Goodbye,* pr. 1965, pb. 1966; *The Coat: An Acting Exercise from Serpent Players of New Brighton,* pr., pb. 1967 (with Serpent Players); *Ten One-Act Plays,* pb. 1968 (Cosmo Pieterse, editor); *Boesman and Lena,* pr., pb. 1969; *Friday's Bread on Monday,* pr. 1970 (with Serpent Players); *Orestes: An Experiment in Theatre as Described in a Letter to an American Friend,* pr. 1971, pb. 1978; *Statements After an Arrest Under the Immorality Act,* pr. 1972, pb. 1974; *Sizwe Bansi Is Dead,* pr. 1972, pb. 1973 (with John Kani and Winston Ntshona); *The Island,* pr. 1973, pb. 1974 (with Kani and Ntshona); *Three Port Elizabeth Plays,* pb. 1974 (includes *The Blood Knot, Hello and Goodbye,* and *Boesman and Lena*); *Dimetos,* pr. 1975, pb. 1977; *A Lesson from Aloes,* pr. 1978, pb. 1981; *The Drummer,* pr. 1980 (improvisation); *"MASTER HAROLD" . . . and the boys,* pr., pb. 1982; *The Road to Mecca,* pr. 1984, pb. 1985.

Other literary forms

Although Athol Fugard has written in a variety of literary forms, he is known primarily for his plays. *Tsotsi,* a long-lost novel written between 1959 and 1960 and abandoned until its publication in 1979, offers insight into Fugard's subsequent dramatic development. The eponymous antihero, known only by the South African generic label for thug or hoodlum, undergoes a week's journey into his past and present—only to have his future cut off through self-sacrifice. The novel is set in Sophiatown, then Johannesburg's black slum (where Fugard's first plays were set), and its characterization, graphic language, and sardonic humor foreshadow much in Fugard's drama.

Of Fugard's screenplays—*The Occupation* (1964), *Boesman and Lena* (1973), *The Guest: An Episode in the Life of Eugène Marais* (1977), and *Marigolds in August* (1982)—only the last three, under the superb direction of Ross Devenish, have been filmed and released. Published twice, once in 1964 as a screenplay and again in 1968 as a one-act play, *The Occupation* is a psychological tour de force in which four derelicts (three English, one Afrikaner) smash their way into an abandoned farmhouse and possess it. Their occupation is haunted, however, by the presence of a "native" outside and by the World War II memories of their leader, Cappie.

The film *Boesman and Lena* is Fugard's adaptation of his stage play. The opening shots of a bulldozer that levels the squatter's community make present what is known only retrospectively in the play. There are several other additions, and though Fugard himself portrayed Boesman, he prefers the play to the film. Nevertheless, it was a highlight of the Edinburgh Film Festival in 1973.

The Guest, an episode from the life of Eugène Marais, an early twentieth century South African naturalist, lawyer, philosopher, and drug addict, gave Fugard an opportunity to explore the life of someone who had long fascinated him and with whose addictive personality Fugard could identify. The film has been commended for Fugard's portrayal of Marais and for its stunning, at times almost surreal, cinematography.

Marigolds in August reunited Fugard with actors John Kani and Winston Ntshona for the first time since the three had collaborated in the plays *Sizwe Bansi Is Dead* and *The Island*. The film won the 1980 Johannesburg Film Festival Awards for Best Film, Best Director (Devenish), and Best Actor (Ntshona), as well as a special Berlin Film Festival Bear Award. In New York, the film received mixed reviews. *The Village Voice* charged Fugard with offering too pat a course in Empathy 101, but Vincent Canby in *The New York Times* argued that the film was "wise, tough, and theatrically effective."

Fugard's 1968 television script for the British Broadcasting Corporation, *Mille Miglia*—not published until 1984—explores in flashback the relationship between race drivers Stirling Moss and Denis Jenkinson, who won the last Italian one-thousand-mile race in 1955, and their preparations for the race. Fugard felt constricted by the factual material, and Moss and Jenkinson were not pleased with the telecast, but several critics and at least one major dramatist, Tom Stoppard, applauded Fugard's concern with the tyranny of time, the threat of death, and the game of life.

Finally, Fugard's *Notebooks 1960-1977* (1984) testify to the breadth of the influences upon him and his influence upon others. The notebook entries reflect his political engagement as well as his practical concerns as a dramatist; in addition, they are fascinating for what they reveal about the genesis of his plays.

Achievements

Fugard is South Africa's gift to world drama. Playwright, director, and actor, he is South Africa's most widely produced dramatist abroad. His plays, though rooted in one nation, have earned international acclaim. Like earlier dramatists whose work is identified with a particular region, Fugard meticulously details life in a remote corner of the globe yet raises compelling issues of general interest. Using what some consider to be the old-fashioned conventions of social realism, linear plot development, and naturalistic language graced by metaphor and symbol, Fugard has forged an impressive body of work for the theater, ranging from full-length plays to improvisational exercises for actors. These works from a self-styled white liberal constitute a crucible for South Africa's racially segregated society and for modern man, an alien in a world from which almost all security has diminished, the world of Jean-Paul Sartre, Albert Camus, and Samuel Beckett—Fugard's mentors. Theatrically sparse, with small casts and little, if any, reliance on elaborate sets, costumes, or props, Fugard's deceptively simple plays offer "infinite riches in a little room." They therefore have been read easily on radio and adapted frequently for television and film. On December 4, 1984, Fugard received the Common Wealth Award for Distinction in Dramatic Arts, an award which he shared with Stephen Sondheim.

Fugard's distinction as a playwright is inseparable from his contributions to and influences upon South African theater, as well as on the Yale Repertory Theatre. He has radically affected both the practice and purpose of serious drama in his native land. His interpretation of his world, his use of "poor theater" for its maximum effect, and his dedication to his actors, both black and white, have earned for him a critical respect accorded few modern playwrights. Early in his career, he chose to be a witness against what he called a "conspiracy of silence" about South Africa's apartheid legislation. That silence has been broken now, but Fugard has no illusions about his part in that. He considers theater to be no more—and no less— than a civilizing influence, one which may sensitize, provoke, or anger. He deplores the label "political playwright." He believes that if a playwright tells a story, a good one, the larger implications will take care of themselves. Since they are set in South Africa, Fugard's plays can no more ignore apartheid than William Faulkner's novels could ignore slavery and its aftermath, but Fugard's plays are not agitprop. Thus, aside from the message of his plays, critics and actors commend Fugard's craft, especially his attention to what he calls "carnal reality" and his ability to develop resonant images that repay repeated readings or performances.

Fugard's plays—and his actors—have been honored often. *The New York Times* voted *The Blood Knot* Best Play of the 1964 season. Fugard was elected Man of the Year in the Arts in South Africa in 1969. *Boesman and Lena* received an Obie Award for Distinguished Foreign Play from the *Village Voice* in 1971. Janet Suzman won the London *Evening Standard* Award for Best Actress in 1973 for her portrayal of Hester Smit in Fugard's *Hello and Goodbye*. *Sizwe Bansi Is Dead*, devised by Fugard with actors John Kani and Winston Ntshona, was chosen Play of the Year in 1974 by the London Theatre Critics. Kani and Ntshona went on to share Tony Awards for Best Acting in the 1974-1975 New York season for *The Island*, another Fugard play devised with their help. In 1975, Fugard was commissioned by the Edinburgh Festival to write a new play, *Dimetos*, and in 1980 the Actors Theatre of Louisville (Kentucky) commissioned an improvisational work, *The Drummer*. (These works, along with *Mille Miglia*, a 1968 BBC television play, are not set in South Africa.) *A Lesson from Aloes* was awarded the New York Drama Critics Circle Award for Best New Play of the 1980-1981 season, while *"MASTER HAROLD"* . . . *and the boys* won both the Drama Desk Award and the Outer Critics Circle Award for Best Play of 1982, as well as a Tony Award for Zakes Mokae as Outstanding Featured Actor and the *Evening Standard* Award for Best Play of 1983. The play also won South Africa's largest cash award for theater: the AA Mutual Life/Vita Award for Best New South African Play, 1983-1984.

Moreover, Fugard has been given honorary doctorates by three South African universities—the University of Natal, Durban, in 1981; Rhodes University, Grahamstown, 1983; and the University of Capetown, in 1984. Two American universities—Yale, in 1983, and Georgetown, in 1984— have also honored Fugard with doctorates. According to the May 28, 1984, *The Washington Post*, the Georgetown degree lauded Fugard "for his compassion and his faith, for the compelling moral vision of his plays, for the quiet beauty of his craft, and for his struggle as an artist in South Africa to 'fly kites on rainy days'"—an allusion to a crucial incident and central metaphor in *"MASTER HAROLD"* . . . *and the boys*.

Fugard's reputation has grown with the world premieres of two plays written at Yale. Fugard finds a "beautiful irony" and "massive affirmation" in the fact that his present artistic leader, Lloyd Richards, is a black man, according to *The New York Times*. Richards considers his friendship with Fugard "fascinating, strange, and subtle," but one that definitely affects "our theater, the theater." Richards is the only person to whom Fugard has ever shown rough drafts of his plays, yet Richards says, "I can't teach Athol anything; I just remind him what he already knows."

Fugard is also a gifted director; the range of his interests may be inferred from the plays he chose to direct at The Rehearsal Room in Johannesburg in the late 1950's and to stage with the Serpent Players in New Brighton from 1963 to 1973: Harold Pinter's *The Dumb Waiter* (pr. 1960), Samuel Beckett's *Waiting for Godot* (pb. 1952), John Steinbeck's *Of Mice and Men* (pb. 1937), and Jean-Paul Sartre's *Men Without Shadows* (pr. 1946) in Johannesburg; Niccolò Machiavelli's *Mandragola* (pr. 1520), Georg Büchner's *Woyzeck* (pb. 1879), Bertolt Brecht's *The Caucasian Chalk-Circle* (pr. 1948), Sophocles' *Antigone* (pr. c. 422 B.C.), August Strindberg's *The Father* (pr. 1887), Wole Soyinka's *The Trials of Brother Jero* (pr. 1960), William Shakespeare's *Coriolanus* (pr. c. 1607-1608), Albert Camus' *The Just Assassins* (pr. 1949), and Jean Genet's *Deathwatch* (pb. 1954) in New Brighton. Fugard's talents as an actor have enabled him to perform in many of his own plays when they were first staged and now have earned for him "mega-extra" status in such films as *Gandhi* (1981, as General J. C. Smuts) and *The Killing Fields* (1984, as a United Nations official).

Fugard, preeminently a thinking playwright, is prolific. Still flexible, but wedded to telling stories with ambiguous outcomes and working from images rooted in his world, he defies categorization. His influence, national and international, is considerable, but it is too early to say what his final contribution to world drama will be. Like Helen, the reclusive seventy-year-old sculptor in and on *The Road to Mecca*, Fugard's works endure to challenge the silence and keep darkness at bay.

Biography

Harold Athol Lannigan Fugard (pronounced *fewgard*) was born June 11, 1932, in Middelburg, a town in the Great Karoo, a semidesert region of Cape Province, South Africa. The son of an Anglo-Irish father and an Afrikaner mother, Fugard is an ethnic hybrid. English is his first language, but, because of his mother's dominant personality, Afrikaner culture profoundly affected him. Fugard simultaneously honors and excoriates his Afrikaner roots. The two major abstractions of Fugard's work—love and truth—he saw fleshed out as he grew up in Port Elizabeth, a multiracial, industrial, windswept town on the eastern Cape to which his family moved when he was three.

Fugard's father lost a leg in a shipboard accident as a child, and in spite of successfully leading a series of jazz bands, he retired early, when Fugard was young, to a life of sloth and alcoholism. Fugard's ambivalent feelings about his father color much of his work, especially *Hello and Goodbye* and *"MASTER HAROLD"... and the boys*. His mother supported the family, first by running a boardinghouse, the Jubilee Hotel, and then by operating the St. George's Park Tea Room, the scene of *"MASTER HAROLD"... and the boys*. Early in life, Fugard thus learned about failed expectations, a major theme in his work, and about hard times.

As a schoolboy, Fugard, then known as Hally, shunned his peers and spent his free time with his mother's waiters, Sam Semela and Willie Malopo. (These men appear in *"MASTER HAROLD" ... and the boys* under their real names.) Sam, in particular, though middle-aged, became Fugard's friend and his most influential adult figure. Fugard looked up to Sam as a man in the fullest sense of that word; while Sam taught Fugard about being a man, Fugard shared his schoolroom experiences and books with him. For some inexplicable reason, one day Fugard insulted Sam; he did not expiate his guilt for this act until he wrote *"MASTER HAROLD"... and the boys*. In real life, Sam Semela forgave Fugard almost immediately, and they remained friends until Sam died in 1983, shortly before the play in his honor opened in Johannesburg.

Fugard studied philosophy at the University of Cape Town from 1950 to

1953, but he quit immediately before his final examinations to hitchhike up Africa with a poet friend, deciding that the academic life was not for him. From 1953 to 1955, he traveled around the world on a merchant ship on which he was the only white crewman. He was married in 1956 to Sheila Meiring, who introduced him to the theater. When they moved to Johannesburg in 1958, Fugard was employed for three months as a clerk in the Fordsburg Native Commissioner's Court; then he began working with amateur black actors in Sophiatown, Johannesburg's black ghetto at that time. He also worked as a stage manager for the National Theatre Organization before he and his wife went to England and Europe in 1959.

The Fugards returned to South Africa in 1960, and the initial production of *The Blood Knot* in 1961 and its six-month tour around South Africa were crucial to Fugard's development as a playwright. In 1962, Fugard instigated a boycott of South Africa's segregated theaters by British playwrights, but by 1967 he had decided that even in such compromising circumstances, voices were preferable to silence. Fugard visited the United States briefly in 1964 and returned to England in 1966; both trips involved productions of *The Blood Knot*. His government withdrew his passport from 1967 to 1971. From 1963 to 1974, he directed and produced European plays as well as collaborating on indigenous South African material with the New Brighton actors known as the Serpent Players; many of these actors were arrested between 1965 and 1967. The Sharpeville Massacre of 1960, the Rivonia Treason Trial of 1964, the crackdown on all supporters of the banned African National Congress from 1963 to 1966, and the 1976 Soweto riots were major political upheavals which occurred while Fugard was writing. Since 1977, Fugard's reputation has been such that he divides his time between South Africa and the rest of the globe: America, Europe, Asia, and India. America, however, is the only place he could live, he claims, if he could not live in South Africa.

The early highlights of Fugard's life are many, but he has singled out some as of particular importance. For example, he says that his experience as a sailor cured him of any racial prejudice he might have had. His wife's prodding him into helping her establish a theater workshop in Cape Town, the Circle Players, in 1956 and 1957 led to the evolution of his lean, one-room dramaturgy. The move to Johannesburg and his work in the Commissioner's Court caused him to see the worst of apartheid legislation; there, an African was sent to jail every two minutes. Fugard turned this ugly nightmare to dramatic use when he devised *Sizwe Bansi Is Dead* with actors John Kani and Winston Ntshona in 1972; the play is an exposé of the passbook law, which requires every African over sixteen to carry an identity book that restricts his employment opportunities and his movements inside South Africa.

The rejection of Fugard's scripts by the Royal Court Theatre in London in 1960, the hand-to-mouth existence the Fugards shared there, and Fugard's sense of isolation from his roots convinced him that he was a regional writer. Prior to the Fugards' return to South Africa in 1960, in response to the Sharpeville Massacre, they helped form—with Tone Brulin, David Herbert, and Clive Farrell—the short-lived New Africa Group, dedicated to the staging of original South African plays in Europe. Fugard played Okkie, the Greek who tries to pass for white, in Herbert's *A Kakamas Greek* (pr. 1960), which was set in the Karoo, Fugard's birthplace. This production won the Best Entry Award at the Festival of Avantgarde Theatre in Brussels in 1960 and toured thereafter in the Flemish part of Belgium, Holland, and Germany—performed in English. The question of racial identify in *A Kakamas Greek* also haunts Fugard's first critical success, *The Blood Knot.*

While he was writing, in solitude, *The Blood Knot, People Are Living There, Hello and Goodbye,* and *Boesman and Lena,* which detail claustrophobic relationships, Fugard was also experimenting with adapting European plays to South African life and with improvising from the raw material of his actors' lives. *The Coat* in 1967 and *Orestes* in 1971, which actress Yvonne Bryceland considers "the most important single thing" in Fugard's career, are examples of improvisations from life.

The "Statements" plays (*Statements After an Arrest Under the Immorality Act, Sizwe Bansi Is Dead,* and *The Island*), which secured Fugard's reputation outside South Africa, also evolved from collaborative theater. These plays together constitute Fugard's most outspoken indictment of apartheid. An early version of *Statements After an Arrest Under the Immorality Act* was the inaugural production in 1972 of The Space, an "open" theater in Cape Town that evaded audience segregation rulings. *Sizwe Bansi Is Dead* was next, followed by an early version of *The Island* in 1973. These two plays did not exist in written form until Fugard and actors Kani and Ntshona were safely in London, later in 1973, for the South African Season at the Royal Court Theatre. (A Beckett season ran concurrently, and Fugard finally met the playwright whom he most admires.) Nevertheless, in 1977 and 1978, Kani and Ntshona performed *Sizwe Bansi Is Dead* and *The Island* in Johannesburg at the Market Theatre, an "open" venue.

In 1974, after Fugard's success in London, *Three Port Elizabeth Plays*— including *The Blood Knot, Hello and Goodbye,* and *Boesman and Lena*— was published by Oxford University Press, with a detailed introduction by Fugard of excerpts from his then unpublished notebooks. This introduction, combined with that to *Statements After an Arrest Under the Immorality Act,* constituted the clearest summary of Fugard's aesthetics—as well as a biographical gloss on his plays—before 1984, when *Notebooks 1960-1977* appeared. In 1978, the "Statements" plays were performed and published in German; in 1979, *The Island* was translated and performed in French, while *Boesman and Lena* was translated and presented in Afrikaans in Cape Town.

Fugard returned to solo composition when *Dimetos* was commissioned by the Edinburgh Festival in 1975, but in spite of rewriting and a cast headed by Paul Scofield for the London West End run in 1976, *Dimetos* failed with critics and audiences alike. Its poetic allegory and nonregional setting are atypical of Fugard, yet the play remains one of his favorites. Like *Statements After an Arrest Under the Immorality Act*, another play that Fugard cherishes, *Dimetos* attempts to use prose musically and frequently becomes too elliptical and ambiguous.

Between 1978 and 1984, Fugard produced three major plays: *A Lesson from Aloes*, *"MASTER HAROLD" . . . and the boys*, and *The Road to Mecca*. Fugard's tenure at Yale, with which these plays are associated, began in January, 1980, and he later bought a house in rural New York State so that he could continue his hobby of birdwatching when he was not at the Yale Repertory Theatre.

In 1964, the Fugards moved from his mother's apartment in Port Elizabeth to a seaside cottage seven miles away. In a letter to his friend Mary Benson, Fugard wrote: "The sea is at our doorstep, there is enough land and need for the highly moral activity of tree planting and the beginning of a vegetable patch. . . . I've never realized fully how much of an Afrikaner I really am, until this moment when I kicked off my shoes and stood barefoot on the earth. I keep looking at my toes to see if roots haven't appeared." In *The Road to Mecca*, the pastor, Marius, enters with a basket of vegetables and proceeds sincerely to glorify a homegrown potato: "A pinch of salt and you've got a meal, . . . add a little butter and you have indeed got a feast." Fugard is kin to pastor Marius in his fervent embrace of nature—from snakes and aloes to men. Few playwrights know as much about plants and animals as he; his films *The Guest* and *Marigolds in August* exemplify this knowledge, but his work as a whole is pervaded by a reverence for life in all of its multiplicity. In this, as in other ways, Fugard's life and work are a testament to wholeness in a world of fragmentation.

Analysis

Athol Fugard's plays satisfy a major criterion of good drama: the creation of vivid, lifelike characters. His characterization is immature in his early plays, *No-Good Friday* and *Nongogo*—with their black-ghetto gangsters, hustlers, musicians, whores, pimps, dreamers, and even a white priest—but these stereotypes foreshadow such fully developed characters in the 1960's plays as the half brothers in *The Blood Knot*, the landlady in *People Are Living There*, the siblings in *Hello and Goodbye*, and the destitute couple Boesman and Lena, in the play of that title. In the 1970's, Fugard created such powerful characters as the miscegenational lovers in

Statements After an Arrest Under the Immorality Act, the urban and country blacks in *Sizwe Bansi Is Dead*, the prisoners in *The Island*, and the isolated Anglo-Afrikaner couple and their "colored" friend in *A Lesson from Aloes*. In his later plays, Fugard presents two black waiters and a teenage schoolboy (*"MASTER HAROLD"* . . . *and the boys*), and an elderly, reclusive sculptor, her young friend, and a local pastor (*The Road to Mecca*). Fugard's characters, who seem so specific and concrete as to personify South Africa, are at the same time universal in their humanity.

Most of these characters do little or nothing except validate their existence through words that cry out to be heard. Their language ranges from the harshly naturalistic to the eloquently poetic; their rhythms are acutely South African, yet they cross linguistic barriers just as Hamlet and Lear do. Fugard's *Notebooks 1960-1977* record the South African images from which his plays come: two brothers in a shack; a landlady who stays in her nightclothes for a whole day; a woman arriving with a suitcase and a man on crutches; a couple with their worldly possessions on their backs; six police photographs of two naked lovers; a self-confident black with a cigarette in one hand, a pipe in the other; two prisoners putting sand into wheelbarrows; a lonely man studying an aloe plant. Program notes for *"MASTER HAROLD"* . . . *and the boys* and *The Road to Mecca* provide images of ballroom dancing and a magical room of light and color. From such images, Fugard has crafted works of art as solid as steel, as fragile as china. Sturdy yet delicate, his plays wear well—the ultimate tribute to a master artist.

Fugard has long acknowledged his debt to Albert Camus and Samuel Beckett. In Camus, he found a kindred spirit for his worldview and his role as an artist; in Beckett, he found a dramaturgy of maximum import with minimum theatrical outlay. Confined to one room or space, two or three characters recollect, recriminate, role-play, and resign themselves to their existence in a world without meaning and little hope for change. They delude themselves with false hopes and dreams, amuse themselves with games to pass the time; such nobility as they possess comes in the fleeting, lucid moments when they acknowledge their condition—and their dependence upon each other. As does Camus, Fugard opts for a "courageous pessimism" born of the clear-sighted recognition of modern man's plight— trapped in a world as capricious as Ariadne's web and as mazelike as the Cretan Minotaur's labyrinth.

In his 1957 Nobel address at the University of Uppsala, Camus said, "To create today is to live dangerously"; he continued, "The suffering of mankind is such a vast subject that it seems no one could touch it unless he was like Keats so sensitive . . . that he could have touched pain itself with his hands." In an interview with Barrie Hough in 1977, prompted by *The Guest*, Fugard's film about Eugène Marais, Fugard commented that "one of the major Marais statements was that all living, survival, is grounded on pain. . . . It's really a theme that has gone through all my work; it's the string that holds all the beads together to make a necklace." Fugard has touched pain in his plays, as much as he has touched love and truth. He revels in the palpable, the tangible. In the realities of daily living—sore feet, tired bodies, arthritic hands, mounting stress, and cruel insults— Fugard reminds us that we are the sum of our pain. The whole is greater than the sum of its parts, but their interdependence is undeniable. Fugard forces us to recognize this interdependence preeminently in *The Blood Knot*, *Boesman and Lena*, *The Island*, *A Lesson from Aloes*, and *"MASTER HAROLD" . . . and the boys*, the most representative of his plays, as well as in *The Road to Mecca*.

The two plays that began and ended Fugard's work in the 1960's, *The Blood Knot* and *Boesman and Lena*, illustrate his talent for full-bodied characterization, as well as his progression toward structural sparseness and multileveled, resonant language. The half brothers of *The Blood Knot*, bound inextricably in a union of opposites, reveal themselves completely in a long play of seven scenes that builds to a harrowing climax. The Nomadic outcasts and mixed breeds, or "Coloreds," Boesman and Lena, hover on the edge of life and death in what appears to be a cyclic pattern of eviction, of breaking and making camp, of Boesman's beating Lena, and of Lena's manic search for her identity, in two acts that are half as long as *The Blood Knot*. Unlike Beckett's tramps in *Waiting for Godot* (the closest analogue to *Boesman and Lena*), however, whose essence is not to change, Fugard's characters do change in the course of the play. Superficially, more happens in *The Blood Knot*'s shanty over a much longer period of time than the one cold evening under the stars of *Boesman and Lena*, but the latter's reduction in plot and stage business results in a thematic and symbolic complexity that allows for greater character revelation as well as greater character development.

In both plays, two characters diametrically opposite in temperament and goals explode in words and acts when confined in a small space. Such conflicts are the heart of Fugard's drama, beginning with *The Blood Knot*. Morris, the light-skinned brother, suffers from agoraphobia—fear of open spaces—after wandering ten years trying to pass for white, while Zach, the dark-skinned brother, has suffered from claustrophobia ever since Morris returned to minister to him by ordering his life. In his notebook entry on the brothers, Fugard said, "Morris, if anything, hates himself. Zach hates the world that has decided his blackness must be punished. . . . Morris is the better equipped mentally for this last fight—also, weakened by thought and sympathy. Zach has the physical strength and impetus of hate. Zach wins." The tyrannical alarm clock that regulates the brothers' lives rings just in time to keep Zach's violence at bay. When Zach asks Morris for an explanation of why their game of black-white domination has gone awry, Morris responds, "I'll keep the clock winded, don't worry. One thing I'm certain is sure, it's a good thing we got the game. It will pass the time. Because we got a lot left, you know! Almost a whole life . . . stretching ahead. . . . I'm not too worried at all. . . . I mean, other men get by without a future. In fact, I think there's quite a lot of people getting by without futures these days." Condemned at birth to have no future, the brothers reconstructed a brief childhood reprieve in which they took an imaginary, wild, car ride—stopped only by a flock of butterflies—chased donkeys in the veld, climbed trees, teased girls, stole fruit, and caught birds. In contrast, the humor of their adult games is sardonic and menacing, their laughter double-edged. They are two particular South African brothers, yet avatars of Cain and Abel.

Like Morris and Zach, Boesman and Lena are locked in an intimate love-hate relationship as mates—one they have fallen into years before the play opens, and one which Lena chooses to reassert as the play ends, in spite of her open rebellion throughout. Motifs that recall *The Blood Knot*'s birds, donkeys, and aimless walking recur in the later play, while staccato, contrapuntal speeches are interleaved with poetic monologues in both. Lena's frenzied songs and dances on the mudflats parallel the brothers' childhood games, but the violence talked about in *The Blood Knot* actually happens in *Boesman and Lena*. Lena's bruises are real, and the old African whom she befriends dies before dawn; he literally becomes the white man's refuse that Boesman has said he and Lena are, and since they cannot dispose of him, they must resume walking. Though she threatens to remain behind, Lena prepares to follow Boesman; in response, he tells her the correct sequence of their journeys, which she had so desperately tried to get straight throughout the play—as if that knowledge would explain how she got where she is. "It doesn't explain anything," she says, but her parting shot, "I'm alive, Boesman. There's daylights left in me," is believable because she has demonstrated repeatedly her will to live.

Suicide is out of the question for Boesman and Lena. As absurd as their existence is, they endure it; they even tried to perpetuate it, but only one of Lena's babies was born alive, and it lived only six months. In recounting her past to the old African, who cannot understand her language any more than Boesman and Lena can understand his, Lena defines pain: "Pain? Yes! . . . One night it was longer than a small piece of candle and then as big as darkness. Somewhere else a donkey looked at it. . . . Pain is a candle *entjie* [end] and a donkey's face." Such metaphoric language typifies Fugard, as it does Beckett. Moreover, both have been accused of writing plays of despair or bitter comedy. Fugard defends Beckett against such charges, as many critics defend Fugard. Fugard finds Beckett's humor, combined with his love and compassion for man's "absurd and bruised carnality," positive and life-affirming; describing Beckett's humor to his wife, Fugard once said, "Smile, and then wipe the blood off your mouth." *Boesman and Lena* is Fugard's most pessimistic play, in mood and theme, but it is not morbid or maudlin; it is his most profound response to the world as he sees it, a world in which endurance and survival alone may be the only card man holds in a stacked deck.

In *The Island*, collaborative and improvisational in origin, Fugard experimented with the theories of Polish director Jerzy Grotowski, as he did in the unpublished *Friday's Bread on Monday*, in 1970, and *Orestes*, whose 1971 performance is described only in a letter. *The Island* is a tribute to actors' theater, but once written, it has stood on its own merits as a strong play for actors other than John Kani and Winston Ntshona, Fugard's original performers and collaborators. It reads as well as it plays. Unified structurally and centrally focused, it demonstrates Fugard's mastery of the one-act form. Its companion piece, *Sizwe Bansi Is Dead*, another virtuoso play for actors, comes closer to a stream-of-consciousness novella than to a drama built upon the classical unities of time, space, and action that Fugard observes in *Boesman and Lena* and his three subsequent critical successes. Yet Fugard has always practiced what he calls "actors' theater."

As early as 1962, Fugard defined the pure theater experience: "the actor and the stage, the actor *on* the stage. Around him is space, to be filled and defined by movement and gesture; around him is also a silence to be filled with meaning. . . ." The actor, space, and silence—Fugard continued exploring these dramatic requisites after a reading of Grotowski's *Towards a Poor Theatre* (1969) that validated the use of the actor as a creator, not simply as an interpreter. *The Island* could not have been written without Kani and Ntshona's experiences as South African blacks or without what they and Fugard knew of the Serpent Players, who had been sent to Robben Island, South Africa's hard-labor, maximum security prison primarily for political prisoners; some returned to tell their stories. (Kani and Ntshona have never been imprisoned on Robben Island, though they were arrested in 1976 before a performance of *Sizwe Bansi Is Dead* and imprisoned briefly until an international actors' protest secured their release.) Fugard credits Grotowski with giving him the courage to "write directly into . . . space and silence via the actor," using the basic device of "challenge and response"; he also credits Brian Astbury, the founder of The Space in Cape Town, for his "vision and tenacity of purpose" in providing the venue for the "Statements" plays.

The Island, like *The Blood Knot* and *Boesman and Lena*, features two characters who are polar opposites in every sense. John and Winston (both the actors' actual names and the names of the characters) wrestle with fundamental questions of identity and purpose. The play opens and closes with the two convicts miming the futile labor of putting sand into wheelbarrows, pushing a barrow to where the other has been digging, and emptying the sand into that hole; the piles of sand therefore remain the same. A whistle blows, and the prisoners mime being handcuffed together and shackled at the ankles before the whistle blows again to send them off on a torturous three-legged run. They do not run fast enough to avoid being beaten. Bruised and bleeding, they collapse in their cell before uttering a word. After they nurse their wounds and curse their sadistic warder, John gives a news broadcast and weather report: "Black domination was chased by White domination. . . . Conditions locally remain unchanged—thunderstorms with the possibility of cold showers and rain. Elsewhere, fine and warm!" Soon, John begins to rehearse *Antigone* for a prison show. Winston does not want to play a woman, and his reluctance to appear as such is comic until the very end, when his identification with Antigone becomes complete. Condemned to life in prison, he faces the audience and cries, "Brothers and Sisters of the Land! I go now to my last journey"; he tears off his wig and confronts them with, "I go now to my living death, because I honoured those things to which honour belongs." (John had been sentenced for burning his passbook in front of a police station.)

The Island is more, however, than an anguished cry of defiance. Like all of Fugard's plays, it focuses on close human relationships; John and Winston are linked in a bond almost as indissoluble as that of Morris and Zach or Boesman and Lena—almost, because midway through the play, John discovers that he will be free in three months, while Winston must remain for life. Before receiving that news, they talked on an imaginary telephone to their friends in New Brighton, another funny game of the many that Fugard's characters play; after John's news, Winston re-creates John's release and welcome home. Ultimately, Winston recovers from his agony and, like Antigone, comes to terms with his fate. *The Island* is as compelling as Fugard's earlier plays because, once again, its particulars are transcended in a work of universal significance, a study of man's inhumanity to man and his capacity to endure that entrapment through a joy in embracing ideals—regardless of their consequences.

In *A Lesson from Aloes*, isolation, neurosis, and exile are the cost that Fugard's characters must pay for their fidelity to the ideals of love and friendship; there is little laughter here. The three characters are Fugard's first attempt to portray his own kind: literate, well-meaning South Africans caught in their government's crackdown on dissent in 1963, which led many to flee the country. Every Fugard play can be seen as an exploration of the effects of public policy on individual lives, but *A Lesson from Aloes* is Fugard's most quietly anguished portrait of this phenomenon.

Aloes are thorny, spiky, cactuslike plants which survive without water in very harsh environments. Piet Bezuidenhout, a middle-aged Afrikaner, once an active member of an antiapartheid group that was silenced by the police, grows aloes in his back garden. Identifying them by name is his chief pleasure, other than reciting English poetry. Piet's English-speaking wife, back home after a stay in the Fort English mental home, and his "colored" friend and former comrade, Steve Daniels—preparing to leave South Africa on a one-way exit permit and just out of jail for breaking his banning order—are the other characters in this subtle but searing study of personal desolation. All three characters have internalized the shocks that their world has given them.

The first act opens with Piet trying to identify a rare aloe; this leads to a revelation of the bitterness that mars his relationship with Gladys. For her part, Gladys cannot forget the police seizure of her personal diaries during a raid prompted by Piet's political involvement; Piet broodingly wonders why his old friends suspect him of being an informer. Tension builds as Piet and Gladys await the arrival of the Daniels' family for a farewell celebration. When Steve does arrive, in the second act—without his family and a bit drunk—the party fails miserably. Playing a very nasty game, Gladys tells Steve that Piet had informed on him, but then she withdraws the charge. Piet refuses, however, to say anything: "Hell, Steve, you know why. If you could have believed it, there was no point in denying it." Apparently reconciled with Piet, Steve leaves. Gladys decides to return to the hospital, and Piet is left alone with his unidentified aloe. In spite of its explicit title and insistent metaphor, *A Lesson from Aloes* is not didactic. There are no clear-cut answers and few, if any, happy endings in Fugard's plays. Like Piet, Fugard cultivates a private garden with unidentifiable species.

In *"MASTER HAROLD"... and the boys*, Fugard returned to the humor associated with his earlier plays to underscore the point that personal choice and action define a life worth living. Set still further back in Fugard's past than *A Lesson from Aloes*, and his most autobiographical play, *"MASTER HAROLD"... and the boys* takes place in a Port Elizabeth tearoom one rainy afternoon in 1950. A long one-act play—too long perhaps—it opens with two black waiters, Sam and Willie, joking and practicing ballroom dancing for a contest two weeks away. Both men will compete if Willie can appease the partner whom he has recently beaten for not getting the quickstep right. Sam hits upon an ingenious solution for Willie's future practice sessions: "Give her a handicap. . . . Give her a ten-second start and then let Count Basie go. Then I put my money on her. Hot favorite in the Ballroom Stakes: Hilda Samuels ridden by Willie Malopo." As Sam demonstrates his superior skills, Hally, the teenage son of the tearoom owner, enters and applauds. Hally's long friendship with the waiters—especially with Sam—is soon apparent, but Hally is tense because of his father's imminent release from the hospital. Hally loves but is ashamed of his crippled, bigoted, alcoholic father and looks to Sam as a role model instead. Fugard lovingly re-creates Hally's camaraderie with the waiters; he focuses particularly on a kite that Sam made for Hally from scrap materials—a kite that miraculously flew. Nevertheless, Hally's "second family" cannot stand up against the demons of his first. These malign forces are unleashed in the play's climax, when Hally insists that the "boys" call him "Master Harold," tells them a crude racial joke, and, when Sam responds, spits in his face. Sam almost literally turns the other cheek, but Hally is too wracked with guilt to apologize. He leaves, and the curtain falls on the two waiters dancing once again—after Willie has used what was to be his bus fare home to start up the juke box.

A play about growing up and the real meaning of family as much as it is about racism, *"MASTER HAROLD" . . . and the boys* is at once exhilarating, sobering, exuberant, and wrenching. Like all of Fugard's plays, it relies upon resonant language; here, the governing metaphor is that of life as a ballroom dance, which leads Sam to dream of a world without accidents or collisions if men and nations can only get the steps right. The game that Hally and Sam play to identify "men of magnitude" who have benefited all mankind leads to some provocative choices by Hally—Charles Darwin, Leo Tolstoy, Socrates, Karl Marx, and Friedrich Nietzsche among others; Sam's choices are Abraham Lincoln, William Shakespeare, Jesus Christ, and Sir Alexander Fleming. Sam's poor-looking kite becomes the most splendid thing Hally has ever seen aloft, and the bench to which Sam ties it when he has to return to work becomes the "Whites Only" bench of Sam's final words to Hally: "If you're not careful . . . Master Harold . . . you're going to be sitting up there by yourself for a long time to come, and there won't be a kite up in the sky. . . . I reckon there's one thing you know. You don't have to sit up there by yourself. You know what that bench means now, and you can leave it any time you choose. All you've got to do is stand up and walk away from it." Avoiding sentimentality in a play that revels in sentiment is Fugard's rare achievement here; *"MASTER HAROLD" . . . and the boys* is a masterwork from a master craftsman.

Fugard's experiments as a dramatist have been within the confines of social naturalism or realism. His modes are representational rather than expressionist or surreal; his plots are convincing; his language is often poetic but rarely abstruse, colloquial but rarely vulgar. In short, Fugard is not an innovator but a conservator: He emulates the best of his predecessors, but he translates their voices and techniques into his own uniquely South African vision. Over the years—a quarter of a century—he has become inimitable, and no more so than in *The Road to Mecca*. A three-character play, like *"MASTER HAROLD" . . . and the boys*, *The Road to Mecca* is one of Fugard's most daring experiments.

The play is set in the autumn of 1974, and all three of its characters are white: two proud Afrikaners who live in New Bethesda (a village in the Great Karoo) and an equally proud young English-speaking schoolteacher from Cape Town. The plot is essentially uncomplicated. The young woman, Elsa Barlow, drives eight hundred miles for an overnight visit with her old friend, Miss Helen—a reclusive sculptor whom the local pastor, Marius Byleveld, wants to put in a nursing home for her own security. In the first act, the two women slowly reestablish their long-standing friendship, but Marius arrives at the opening of the second act and begins to undermine Miss Helen's confidence in her ability to cope and to create. Elsa briefly adopts Marius' point of view when he tells her that Miss Helen almost set her house on fire earlier. Finally, in a moving reverie about the purpose of her Mecca, Miss Helen becomes courageous enough to dismiss Marius and assert her right to live with the danger of her creative impulses. Disheartened by his failure to convert Helen—and to make her love him—Marius leaves. The play ends with the women trusting each other once again.

While this plot is fairly conventional, Fugard's choice of characters, the importance of the set, and the focus on the self-realization of the artist mark this play as a genuine advance for Fugard, a widening of his range. While women and their concerns crop up obliquely in other Fugard plays— especially in *People Are Living There* and *Boesman and Lena*—*The Road to Mecca* is Fugard's first attempt to fill space with two women talking, arguing, and nurturing each other. It is also the first time Fugard has dramatized the necessary isolation of the artist. Fugard's epigraph for *The Road to Mecca* is an Emily Dickinson poem: "The soul selects her own society/ Then shuts the door./ On her divine majority/ Obtrude no more." An extended metaphor for the artist's vision—its genesis and its consequences—*The Road to Mecca* may also be read as a parable about pain, the pain of loving and not being loved. Apartheid comprises only the subtext of the play, but Fugard's initial title was "My English Name Is Patience." These are the words of the young, barefoot Afrikaner woman whom Elsa befriends en route to Helen's house. This absent character pervades *The Road to Mecca* from beginning to end—like so many of Fugard's striking offstage presences, whose silences become virtually audible. What all of these silent characters share is a need for love.

Near the end of *The Road to Mecca*, candles flicker in mirrors, and the light on the walls—a stunning witness to Fugard's belief that the "candle burns brighter because the night is dark" and an answer to his question, "Would the making of meaning be so moving without the eternal threat of chaos and nothingness?" Miss Helen's laboriously crafted garden of statues—all manner of animals, camels, wisemen, mermaids, and earth goddesses pointing East—does exist, at the home of the real Helen, Helen Niemand, in New Bethesda, South Africa. Created over a remarkable twenty years of Helen's life, from age fifty to seventy, by a small, slight woman using broken bits of glass and hand-mixed cement, the statues are mute witnesses to her courage, integrity, and imagination. Thought mad by her myopic neighbors, she persevered alone. In her life and work, Fugard found the perfect fusion of symbol and referent, fiction and fact. All artists try to give meaning to matter, form to the formless, but only rarely does an artist give meaning to beauty, truth, love, and trust in so magical a form as *The Road to Mecca*. Significantly, one of Fugard's major concerns in his last three plays is the relationship between teacher and learner and the frequent shifts in their roles. To Miss Helen—his master teacher—Fugard gives the words that sum up his life's work: "Light just one little candle in here, let in the light from just one little star, and the dancing starts." Candles, stars, and dancing, healing images from art for a suffering world: Such is the theater of Athol Fugard.

Other major works

NOVEL: *Tsotsi*, 1979.

NONFICTION: "The Gift of Freedom," in *At the Royal Court: Twenty-five Years of the English Stage Company*, 1981 (Richard Findlater, editor); *Notebooks 1960-1977*, 1984.

SCREENPLAYS: *The Occupation*, 1964; *Boesman and Lena*, 1973; *The Guest: An Episode in the Life of Eugène Marais*, 1977; *Marigolds in August*, 1982.

TELEPLAY: *Mille Miglia*, 1968.

Bibliography

Benson, Mary. "Keeping an Appointment with the Future: The Theatre of Athol Fugard," in *Theatre Quarterly*. VII, no. 28 (1977), pp. 77-87.

Collins, Michael J. "The Sabotage of Love: Athol Fugard's Recent Plays," in *World Literature Today*. Summer, 1983, pp. 368-371.

Gray, Stephen. *Athol Fugard*, 1982.

_____ . *Theatre One: New South African Drama*, 1978.

Green, Robert J. "Politics and Literature in Africa: The Drama of Athol Fugard," in *Aspects of South African Literature*, 1976. Edited by Christopher Heywood.

Gussow, Mel. "Witness," in *The New Yorker*. LVII (December, 1982), pp. 47-94.

Hauptfleisch, Temple, et al. *Athol Fugard: A Source Guide*, 1982.

Kroll, Jack. "Love and Freedom in the Karoo," in *Newsweek*. CIII (May 28, 1984), p. 85.

Rich, Frank. "Stage: 'To Mecca,' by Athol Fugard," in *The New York Times*. III (May 15, 1984), p. 17.

Ross, Laura. "A Question of Certainties," in *American Theatre*. I, no. 5 (September, 1984), pp. 4-9.

Vandenbroucke, Russell. "Athol Fugard: Bibliography, Biography, Playography," in *Theatre Quarterly*, 1977.

_____ . *"Truths the Hand Can Touch": The Theatre of Athol Fugard*, 1985.

Weales, Gerald. "The Embodied Images of Athol Fugard," in *The Hollins Critic*. XV, no. 1 (February, 1978), pp. 1-12.

Nancy Kearns

JOHN GALSWORTHY

Born: Kingston Hill, England; August 14, 1867
Died: London, England; January 31, 1933

Principal drama

The Silver Box, pr. 1906, pb. 1909; *Joy,* pr. 1907, pb. 1909; *Strife,* pr., pb. 1909; *Justice,* pr., pb. 1910; *The Little Dream,* pr., pb. 1911; *The Eldest Son,* pr., pb. 1912; *The Pigeon,* pr., pb. 1912; *The Fugitive,* pr., pb. 1913; *The Mob,* pr., pb. 1915; *A Bit o'Love,* pr., pb. 1915; *The Little Man,* pr. 1915, pb. 1921; *The Foundations,* pr. 1917, pb. 1919; *Defeat,* pr. 1920, pb. 1921; *The Skin Game,* pr., pb. 1920; *A Family Man,* pr. 1921, pb. 1922; *The First and the Last,* pr., pb. 1921; *Hall-marked,* pb. 1921; *Punch and Go,* pb. 1921, pr. 1924; *The Sun,* pb. 1921, pr. 1922; *Loyalties,* pr., pb. 1922; *Windows,* pr., pb. 1922; *The Forest,* pr., pb. 1924; *Old English,* pr., pb. 1924; *The Show,* pr., pb. 1925; *Escape,* pr., pb. 1926; *Exiled,* pr., pb. 1929; *The Roof,* pr., pb. 1929.

Other literary forms

There are six multivolume editions of John Galsworthy's collected works; the most important and comprehensive is the thirty-volume Manaton edition (1922-1936). Galsworthy wrote prolifically, composing many novels, poems, stories, addresses, sketches, and essays.

Achievements

Galsworthy's literary reputation rests soundly upon his fiction, especially the novels and stories collected in *The Forsyte Saga* (1922). Adapted for television by the British Broadcasting Corporation, *The Forsyte Saga* appeared in Great Britain, Canada, the United States, and other countries during the late 1960's and early 1970's, reviving interest in his fiction.

Several of Galsworthy's plays gained critical and popular approval at the time of their first production or early revival in England, Europe, and America; they were translated into many languages, and their popularity in the 1920's contributed to the recognition which culminated with the Nobel Prize in 1932. Galsworthy wrote realistic, often almost documentary "problem plays," which focused on social problems far more impartially than was usual in contemporary social melodrama. Social issues such as labor unrest, prison reform, and anti-Semitism, all of which Galsworthy addressed dramatically, continue to be of great concern, but Galsworthy's plays, however much they spurred reform in attitudes or legislation in their own day, are now out of date. Their topicality and their uneasy tension between didactic moralizing and melodramatic theatricality have ensured that there is little interest in reviving his plays.

Biography

John Galsworthy was born August 14, 1867, at Kingston Hill, Surrey, to John Galsworthy, a kind, charming, and prosperous London lawyer and company director whom his son idolized, and Blanche Bartleet, an unimaginative, fussy, and religious woman to whom Galsworthy was never close. The Galsworthys were a newly rich, upper-middle-class family; their wealth came from house and shop rentals and from speculations and investments in real estate which were begun by Galsworthy's grandfather, a merchant who came from Devon to settle in London.

Because of the family's wealth, Galsworthy enjoyed a childhood of privilege and luxury; his family could afford the kind of education his father had not had, so Galsworthy was privately tutored before being sent at age nine to a preparatory school at Bournemouth. He went on to Harrow, where he distinguished himself as an athlete, and then entered New College, Oxford, where he seemed more interested in behaving like a gentleman of leisure, dressing well, and gambling on the horses than in studying. He was graduated in 1889 with a second-class degree in jurisprudence and continued to study law until 1894 at Lincoln's Inn in London; apparently, he wanted to please his father by following in his footsteps. He found the study and work boring and completed only one law case; he preferred hunting, shooting, and the company of a young singing teacher. His father disapproved of the infatuation and sent Galsworthy on several trips abroad to cure him of it. Sailing home from the South Pacific islands and Australia in 1893, Galsworthy met Joseph Conrad, then second mate on the *Torrens*; Conrad afterward became Galsworthy's lifelong friend. Galsworthy had undertaken the trip partly in the hope of meeting Robert Louis Stevenson, whose fiction he admired, but he showed no serious interest in becoming a writer himself for two more years.

In 1895, Galsworthy's acquaintance with his cousin Arthur's wife, Ada Nemesis Pearson Cooper Galsworthy, turned into an adulterous affair. Ada, the illegitimate daughter of Anna Pearson of Norwich, had been adopted by a Norwich physician, Emanuel Cooper, who provided for her and her brother in his will. Ada married unwisely; her escape from the unhappy marriage to Arthur had a profound emotional effect on her and on John Galsworthy, who transformed the episode into fiction several times, most notably into the marriage of Soames and Irene Forsyte in *The Man of Property* (1906). With Ada's advice and encouragement, and with support from a private income provided by his father, Galsworthy abandoned his abortive career at law and and began writing fiction; his first stories appeared pseudonymously in 1897. Between 1895 and 1905, Galsworthy and Ada continued their affair, living separately in London but traveling together on vacations abroad. Galsworthy published three novels and two books of stories before his marriage to Ada in 1905 and made friends with a group of writers that included Conrad, Ford Madox Ford, Constance Garnett, and Edward Garnett, all of whom provided encouraging criticism of his work.

In 1906, Galsworthy scored a double success, publishing *The Man of Property*, the first and best novel of the Forsyte series, and *The Silver Box*, his first play. Produced at the Royal Court Theatre by the Barker-Vedrenne management, the play attracted favorable attention for its unsparing portrayal of one law for the rich and another for the poor. Its concern for issues of social importance set the tone for Galsworthy's best plays, *Strife*, *Justice*, *Loyalties*, and *Escape*. Galsworthy was soon spoken of, together with George Bernard Shaw, James M. Barrie, and Harley Granville-Barker, as part of a new renaissance in English drama.

Galsworthy's new literary prominence coincided with the social respectability he enjoyed by being married, and he soon felt able to speak out and to write pamphlets, letters, and essays on a number of subjects, such as humane slaughtering of animals, prison reform, and censorship in the theater. He told Ada that after coming down from Oxford to London and being sent to collect rents on some of his family's properties in poor neighborhoods, his social conscience had been awakened, and throughout the remainder of his life, he showed sympathy and concern for those less fortunate than he. He not only wrote on their behalf but also provided charitable assistance in the manner of his character Wellwyn in *The Pigeon*. Not a religious man, Galsworthy was disgusted with people who claimed to be Christians yet would not act charitably toward those in need. His novel *The Island Pharisees* (1904) portrays the rebellion of a young gentleman against upper-class social and religious hypocrisy. Particularly during his ten-year affair with Ada, during which he was ostracized from polite society, he seems to have felt strongly a sense of identity with social outsiders such as prisoners (he visited Dartmoor Prison to study conditions of servitude) and the poor.

After their marriage, the Galsworthys lived comfortably and pleasantly in London and in the countryside. Ada, plagued by illnesses during the English winters, liked to travel to warmer countries, and the Galsworthys made frequent and extensive trips abroad. Galsworthy seemed to be able to write copiously wherever they traveled. Yet success and comfort had their penalties: Though his books usually sold quite well, the quality of Galsworthy's writing did not improve significantly, and the onset of World War I severely shook his optimistic belief in the possibility of humanity's progress toward a better world.

After the war, Galsworthy's reputation grew with the publication of *The Forsyte Saga* and with the popular success of three plays, *The Skin Game*, *Loyalties*, and *Escape*. Galsworthy refused a knighthood but accepted many honorary degrees, the Order of Merit (1929), and the 1932 Nobel

Prize for Literature. He was an active member of PEN, the international writers' association, from 1921 until his death, probably caused by a brain tumor, on January 31, 1933.

Analysis

John Galsworthy's strengths and weaknesses as a dramatist both derive from his commitment to the ideas and methods of realistic drama. He was neither a religious man nor a political activist, and his plays spoke for no specific ideology or orthodoxy, but he believed that "every grouping of life and character has its inherent moral; and the business of the dramatist is so to pose the group as to bring that moral poignantly to the light of day." This meant, as he said in "Some Platitudes Concerning Drama," that "a drama must be shaped so as to have a spire of meaning."

Such a theory of drama attempts two mutually contradictory tasks: first, the objective, balanced, impartial depiction of reality, and second, the embodiment of the playwright's subjective, ethical, emotional response in the posing or shaping of a moral spire of meaning. Galsworthy's plays are secular morality plays; his gentlemanly didacticism issues in dramatic sermons which attempt to evoke sympathy and understanding for the human condition and which teach the humanistic creeds of civility, compromise, and fair play. In Galsworthy's plays, the sentimental or melodramatic pointing of a moral frequently undercuts the attempt to depict faithfully the problems of individual characters or social groups.

The realistic problem play was not a new form when Galsworthy took it up; its development in England can be traced back to the middle of the nineteenth century, when Tom Taylor and Thomas William Robertson attempted to leaven their melodramas with realistic settings and restrained social comment. (Robertson's *Caste*, produced in 1867 and notable for dramatizing a marriage across class lines, was Galsworthy's favorite play when he was at Oxford.) In the late nineteenth century, this English tradition drew strength from the influence of Henrik Ibsen's realistic social dramas, which were championed in England by William Archer and also by Shaw, who published *The Quintessence of Ibsenism* during this period (1891, 1913). Following Ibsen's example but lacking his genius, Henry A. Jones and Arthur Wing Pinero combined upper-middle-class marriage problems with the form of the well-made play; the result was a rejuvenation of English drama. Though he wrote comedy in the paradoxical mode pioneered by W. S. Gilbert and Oscar Wilde, Shaw's challenging and idiosyncratic variety of dramatic realism was also inspired by Ibsen. Shaw's plays and polemics helped to create an atmosphere of critical acceptance in England for the realistic theater of ideas and social problems. Shaw's *Candida* (pr. 1897) appeared in 1904 at the Royal Court Theatre as part of the Barker-Vedrenne management's effort to raise the level of English drama. When Galsworthy sent the manuscript of *The Silver Box* to Harley Granville-Barker, it arrived on a Saturday, was read by Barker and Shaw on Sunday, and was accepted for production at Shaw's urging on Monday.

In a letter, Galsworthy remarked that the "main idea" of *The Silver Box* was "that 'one law for the rich, another for the poor' is true, but not because society wills it so, rather, in spite of society's good intentions, through the mere mechanical wide-branching power of money." Galsworthy's play contrasts the unprincipled, propertied, and pragmatic upper-middle-class characters with their lower-class victims in the manipulation of the judicial system. The audience knows from the beginning who the culprits are in two related cases of petty thievery, but Galsworthy creates suspense through gradual revelation of their guilt to their families. The first thief is young Jack Barthwick, down from Oxford on vacation, who, while out drinking with a female companion, steals her purse containing seven pounds. The play opens as Jack returns to the Barthwick home with Jones, a drunken, unemployed groom. When Jack passes out, Jones steals the purse and a silver cigarette box. Jack's theft is revealed to his family but is concealed in court at Jones's trial until after Jones's sentencing, when he can only cry out in helpless frustration, thus giving the audience the "main idea" of the play: "It's '*is money* got '*im* off—*Justice!*"

The Barthwicks' cowardly hypocrisy is illustrated throughout the play, especially in one scene at the end of act 2. Jack's father, John Barthwick, a Liberal Member of Parliament, is so concerned that the scandal of a trial will damage his political and social reputation that he betrays his "Liberal" sympathy for the poor. One of the Jones children is heard sobbing outside the Barthwicks' window because the child cannot find Mrs. Jones, his mother and the Barthwicks' housekeeper (she has been wrongly accused, arrested, and imprisoned with her husband, even though he has admitted his guilt). The sound of the child's suffering moves Mrs. Barthwick to suggest that the case be dropped, but Mr. Barthwick says the matter is out of their hands and refuses to help; the curtain drops on a melodramatic tableau, as Mrs. Barthwick turns her back on the crying, Mr. Barthwick covers his ears, and a servant closes the window to shut out the noise of suffering.

Galsworthy teaches his dramatic lesson through contrasts and parallels, too. In order to illustrate further the disparity between the lives of rich and poor, he sets one scene in the Joneses' lodgings during their meager meal of potatoes and onions and contrasts it with the following scene of the Barthwicks' elaborate dinner. In act 3, the trial for theft is preceded by a hearing to remand the children of an out-of-work father to court custody. The court-ordered breakup of a family arouses Barthwick's liberal sentiments, but Galsworthy shows that liberal zeal for social reform is quickly sacrificed to self-interest as Barthwick seeks to suppress all evidence of

Jack's involvement in Jones's case.

In *The Silver Box*, Galsworthy attempts to portray realistically a serious issue of injustice without resorting to the heroics of melodrama. He imagines the characters as social types and describes their "keynotes" in a letter to Granville-Barker; the play has no hero, and if there is a villain, it is a social class rather than an individual. The drawback of this method was once its virtue, but the sense of recognition to be gained from its topical documentary realism has been lost, and one is left with a double overdose of obvious didacticism and melodramatic attempts to arouse pathos, as in the crying child scene.

The rise to real power of the English labor movement early in the twentieth century provided a subject suited to Galsworthy's realistic method: *Strife* comes closest, among his plays, to a work of lasting value. Through the careful dramatic opposition of ideas, characters, metaphors, and structural elements, the play presents the tragedy of two fanatically iron-willed leaders who battle against each other at great cost to themselves and their followers. The play takes place during six hours on a February afternoon and evening at the Trenartha Tin Plate Works on the English-Welsh border, where a strike has lasted for five months, crippling the company and bringing suffering, hunger, and a winter without heat to the laborers. The deadlock results from the conflict between the leaders of the opposing sides, David Roberts of the strikers and John Anthony of the company directors.

Galsworthy constructed the play so that its spire of meaning would arise from the dialectic of opposing concepts represented by Anthony and Roberts. In a letter to a director who wanted to revive the play in 1931, Galsworthy insisted that "the play's real theme" was not the battle between capital and labor but rather "*hubris*, or violence; *Strife* is, indeed, a play on extremism or fanaticism." Both Anthony and Roberts refuse to compromise their principles by giving in to the other side; their rigidity of purpose shows a kind of heroic intellectual vainglory, producing bitterness, suffering, waste, and death. Galsworthy once more created "type" characters, but Anthony and Roberts are types as extremists, not as members of any social class—such men may be found in any class.

Galsworthy imposes structural balance on the action to achieve the resonant effect of contrast and parallelism of idea, character, and situation. The confrontations of labor and management in the first and third acts balance each other, as do the separate meetings of directors and strikers in the second and third acts, in which each side rejects its leader's plan for action and decides to accept instead the terms for compromise proposed by the union representative. Galsworthy handles his large cast of characters with an almost schematic balancing of psychological and social types. He also uses settings, properties, and dramatic language appropriate to the theme of *Strife*: In several scenes, he contrasts the excesses of cold and heat, hunger and plenty, luxury and deprivation. Metaphoric language carries the idea that if Anthony and Roberts are like gods in their power over men, they are also like devils in the way they use power to cause suffering for the sake of their principles. The play has its melodramatic moments, such as the fight among the workers at the end of the second act, but overall, it is much less encumbered by the sentimentality and overly theatrical scenes which spoil many of Galsworthy's plays.

Strife, in an understated and bitter conclusion, neither celebrates nor condemns the opposing sides in the struggle of labor versus capital; instead, it portrays the need for civility and compromise in human affairs. The plan proposed by the union representative at the beginning of the play finally is adopted; Anthony and Roberts have a moment of mutual recognition after their followers have rejected the inhumanity of blind, proud adherence to principle. The theme of hubris is, if anything, too carefully and obviously portrayed in Galsworthy's systematic balancing of scenes, characters, and metaphors, and in the working out of a metaphoric dialectic of opposed ideas. *Strife*, nevertheless, remains Galsworthy's best problem play and the best realization of his theory of drama.

Galsworthy wrote in his diary for 1921: "During the summer *Loyalties* was written. . . . This was the only play of mine of which I was able to say when I finished it: 'No manager will refuse this.'" The play's popular success proved Galsworthy to be correct; he had adapted his realistic techniques to his audience's preference for entertainment instead of sermons. As in *The Silver Box*, he used a crime plot but spent far more effort creating a suspenseful modern melodrama which, along with his peek into the lives of the postwar, aristocratic, horse-racing set, includes a critique of upper-class anti-Semitism, hypocrisy, and misplaced loyalty to its own members. For the first time since *The Silver Box*, Galsworthy employed neither a pattern of recurrent imagery nor a central emblematic property or setting to underline his theme. The ideas in the play emerge in short speeches closely related to the action; the closest Galsworthy comes to a debate in *Loyalties* is the exchange between Ferdinand De Levis, a young, rich, Jewish social outsider, and General Canynge, the patrician elder statesman of Establishment values and taste. De Levis has (rightly) accused Captain Ronald Dancy, "a soldier and a gentleman," of stealing one thousand pounds. Canynge regards De Levis as an arrogant, insolent bounder and makes no secret of his distaste for De Levis' disregard of "the *esprit de corps* that exists among gentlemen." Other significant words or phrases, such as "unwritten code," "duty," and "honour," occur infrequently and unobtrusively; in context, they are appropriate to the plot and are not overly obvious guideposts to Galsworthy's moral. Just as Galsworthy does not unduly underline the theme of intolerance, neither does he follow his usual practice of overtly pointing up the merit of charity and unselfishness. Instead, the action embodies his theme of uncharitable Christians versus charitable non-Christians in implicit and understated ways.

The play's three acts emphasize three different kinds of loyalties in three appropriate settings. In the first act, at a country estate near Newmarket, De Levis' accusations against Dancy are attacked by Canynge and Charles Winsor out of personal loyalty, the code of the gentleman. In the second act, at a London club, social loyalty is the subject: Canynge and Winsor fear for the reputation of the club and the army; De Levis' loyalty to his race motivates him to refuse to sign an apology. In act 3, at the law office, loyalty to an institution, the profession of law, is emphasized. Finally, in the last scene, the Inspector embodies loyalty to a similar but more abstract institution, the Law itself.

Galsworthy appropriately structures the plot to carry the dramatic presentation of these types of loyalty and their conflicts. The controlled balancing of plot, character, and language which made *Loyalties* not only a popular success but also Galsworthy's best postwar social drama served him well again in *Escape*, which also places less importance on ideas than on action. In a series of ten episodes organized almost cinematically, an escaped prisoner evades capture, meets a variety of characters from all social classes, and eventually, acting out of conscience, gives himself up, having come to terms with the gentleman's code that Barthwick and Dancy betray in *The Silver Box* and *Loyalties*, respectively.

Throughout Galsworthy's dramatic works, there is a tension between oppressive moralism and melodramatic theatricality. As Allardyce Nicoll has observed, "Galsworthian realism and Socialist Realism tend to suffer from the same pathetic complaint—deplorable and even tawdry sentimentalism." In plays such as *Strife*, *Loyalties*, and *Escape*, however, Galsworthy successfully combined realistic representation with dramatic presentation of theme. His plays remain historically interesting because they embody his perceptions of English social and ethical attitudes in the early twentieth century. As examples of realistic drama, his plays have merit as the works of a sincere and careful craftsman who wrote in a tradition made great by the true artists who made it their own: Henrik Ibsen, August Strindberg, Anton Chekhov, and George Bernard Shaw.

Other major works

NOVELS: *Jocelyn*, 1898 (as John Sinjohn); *Villa Rubein*, 1900 (as John Sinjohn); *The Island Pharisees*, 1904; *The Man of Property*, 1906; *Fraternity*, 1909; *The Patrician*, 1911; *The Dark Flower*, 1913; *The Little Man*, 1915; *The Burning Spear*, 1919, 1923; *In Chancery*, 1920; *To Let*, 1921; *The Forsyte Saga*, 1922 (includes *The Man of Property*, "Indian Summer of a Forsyte," "Awakening," *In Chancery*, *To Let*); *The White Monkey*, 1924; *The Silver Spoon*, 1926; *Swan Song*, 1928; *A Modern Comedy*, 1929 (includes *The White Monkey, The Silver Spoon, Two Forsyte Interludes, Swan Song*).

SHORT FICTION: *From the Four Winds*, 1897 (as John Sinjohn); *A Man of Devon*, 1901 (as John Sinjohn); *Five Tales*, 1918; *Captures*, 1923; *Caravan: The Assembled Tales of John Galsworthy*, 1925; *Two Forsyte Interludes*, 1927; *On Forsyte 'Change*, 1930; *Soames and the Flag*, 1930.

POETRY: *The Collected Poems of John Galsworthy*, 1934 (Ada Galsworthy, editor).

NONFICTION: *A Commentary*, 1908; *A Motley*, 1910; *The Inn of Tranquility*, 1912; *A Sheaf*, 1916; *Another Sheaf*, 1919; *Tatterdemalion*, 1920; *Castles in Spain*, 1927; *Candelabra: Selected Essays and Addresses*, 1932; *Letters from John Galsworthy, 1900-1932*, 1934 (Edward Garnett, editor).

MISCELLANEOUS: *The Works of John Galsworthy*, 1922-1936 (30 volumes).

Bibliography

Barker, Dudley. *The Man of Principle: A View of John Galsworthy*, 1963, 1970.

Dupré, Catherine. *John Galsworthy: A Biography*, 1976.

Marrot, Harold V. *The Life and Letters of John Galsworthy*, 1935, 1970.

Nicoll, Allardyce. *English Drama 1900-1930*, 1973.

Sauter, Rudolf. *Galsworthy the Man: An Intimate Portrait*, 1967.

Stevens, Earl E., and H. Ray Stevens, eds. *John Galsworthy: An Annotated Bibliography of Writings About Him*, 1980.

Philip E. Smith II

GEORGE GASCOIGNE

Born: Cardington, England; c. 1539
Died: Stamford, England; October 7, 1577

Principal drama

Jocasta, pr. 1566, pb. 1573 (with Francis Kinwelmershe; translation of Lodovico Dolce's play *Giocasta*); *Supposes*, pr. 1566, pb. 1573 (translation of Ludovico Ariosto's *I suppositi*); *A Devise of a Maske for the Right Honorable Viscount Mountacute*, pr. 1572, pb. 1573; *The Glasse of Governement*, pb. 1575; *The Princely Pleasures at Kenelworth Castle*, pr. 1575, pb. 1576 (with others).

Other literary forms

In addition to his masques and plays, George Gascoigne wrote in a number of genres in verse and prose; whatever the genre, his style is generally direct, lucid, and idiomatic. Several of his works were the first of their kind in English literature.

Gascoigne's later moralistic writings, however, lack interest for most students of literature. In prose, these works include *The Droomme of Doomes Day* (1576) and *A Delicate Diet, for Daintiemouthde Droonkardes* (1576), and, in rhyme royal, *The Grief of Joye* (1576).

Two expository works in prose have special importance. Gascoigne's eyewitness account *The Spoyle of Antwerpe* (1576), originally written as a government report, is perhaps the best journalistic writing of the Elizabethan period, while his "Certayne Notes of Instruction Concerning the Making of Verse," included in *The Posies of George Gascoigne Esquire* (1575), is the earliest extant treatise on poetry in the English language.

Also included in that collection, and of even greater interest, is the prose narrative *The Discourse of the Adventures Passed by Master F. J.* (1573), revised and reissued as *The Pleasant Fable of Ferdinando Jeronimi and Leonora de Valasco* (1575). With lyric poems spaced throughout the prose, the experimental narrative tells the story of a young man's disillusioning love affair with a more experienced woman who is also having adulterous relations with her male secretary. The narrative, lacking in event, nevertheless deals slyly, often humorously, with courtly love conventions as they might apply in real life.

Gascoigne's best original compositions are his poems, numbering more than one hundred. Among the longer poems, two deserve to be singled out, for they share the skepticism toward life and society that is characteristic of much of his best writing: The part of *The Fruites of Warre* (1575) dealing with his own military experiences is lively reading, while *The Steele Glas, a Satyre* (1576) uses the device of a mirror to expose what the poet saw as the decline of social and moral responsibility in the Elizabethan world.

Gascoigne's finest poems, however, are to be found among the shorter poems in various forms published in *A Hundreth Sundrie Flowres Bounde Up in One Small Poesie* (1573), later revised as *The Posies of George Gascoigne Esquire.* Some of this volume's poems that are preferred by critics are "The Lullabie of a Lover," in which an aging lover sings to sleep his fading powers; "Gascoigne's Woodmanship," in which the poet likens his bad marksmanship to his other failures in life; and "The Praise of Phillip Sparrowe," a light celebration of the poet's pet bird. These and other of the poems may still delight and instruct a reader.

Achievements

George Gascoigne died in 1577, when a new generation of writers such as John Lyly, Sir Philip Sidney, and Edmund Spenser were beginning an outburst of literary creativity that lasted from 1578 to the start of the Commonwealth period in 1642. Comparison of Gascoigne's works to the great literature that followed shortly afterward causes Gascoigne to be considered, and perhaps correctly, a minor writer, but his literary achievements won recognition during his own time and strongly influenced the development of English poetry and drama; at least some of his pieces may still be read with enjoyment.

That Gascoigne achieved stature as a writer during his own time is shown by his dealings between 1572 and 1577 with some of the great nobility. He seems to have enjoyed at least some patronage from Lord Grey of Wilton, later a patron to Spenser. Recognition of his ability is implied by Gascoigne's having been asked by the family of Viscount Montague to provide the masque for the Montague-Dormer wedding, and even more by his being chosen by the Earl of Leicester to provide entertainment for the queen's visit to Kenilworth. The poet's appointment to government service very likely resulted from favorable notice by the queen herself.

Modern scholars continue to be interested in Gascoigne primarily because of his contributions to the development of English poetry and drama. During his lifetime, serious English writers, confronted by native and foreign traditions that differed radically, experimented in order to discover the means by which literature might best be created in the vernacular. "Certayne Notes of Instruction Concerning the Making of Verse," a pioneer work in literary criticism, provides insight both into the state of poetics at the time and into Gascoigne's own aims and methods. Consistent with his literary theory, most of his poetry uses plain English words directly and lucidly, maintaining in poetry a native English tradition bridging the gap between Sir Thomas Wyatt and such later poets as John Donne and Ben Jonson. In addition, *The Steele Glas, a Satyre* has historical interest both because it may be the first satire of the era and because it was the first original poem in English written in blank verse.

Literary historians have long recognized the importance of Gascoigne's contributions to the development of Elizabethan drama. As an example of the prodigal-son play, *The Glasse of Governement* has some historical interest but exercised little influence on later plays. Of greater significance was *Jocasta*, which was produced in 1566 and which Gascoigne, in collaboration with Francis Kinwelmershe, had translated from Lodovico Dolce's *Giocasta* (wr. 1549, an adaptation of a Latin translation of Euripides' *The Phoenician Women*, c. 411 B.C.). *Jocasta* was the first Greek tragedy produced on the English stage, though the text was not translated directly from the Greek. Using blank verse, a five-act structure, and dumb shows before each act, the tragedy reinforced the tendency toward the classical mode in tragedy established in 1561 by the production of Thomas Norton and Thomas Sackville's *Gorboduc*, also at the Inns of Court. *Supposes*, Gascoigne's translation of Ludovico Ariosto's *I suppositi* of 1509, exercised an even greater influence on English drama: It not only provided William Shakespeare with the idea for the Bianca subplot in *The Taming of the Shrew* but also helped to establish prose as the medium for comic drama and introduced Italian comedy to the English stage.

Biography

The life of George Gascoigne, probably the greatest writer of the early years of Queen Elizabeth's reign, illustrates some of the worst and some of the best aspects of the life of the Renaissance gentleman. An elder son of prosperous parents, young Gascoigne first undertook the study of law but then chose to pursue life at court. As presented and popularized by the Italian Count Baldassare Castiglione in *The Courtier* (1528), the ideal courtier was to be gracious, attractive, witty, intelligent, learned, wise, and skilled in warfare and in the arts and sciences; such a servant of the king was worthy of fame and fortune. In reality, few people had the character or ability even to approach such an ideal, and the extravagance and intrigue associated with life at court were not often conducive to strength of character. Gascoigne's adult life was characterized by legal difficulties, many of which were caused by his own financial excesses and strained personal relationships. His literary accomplishments, however, were extraordinary: He did much to prepare the way for the greater writers who followed him, and he earned a solid reputation as a lyric and satiric poet.

Relatively little is known about Gascoigne's early life, the period before his admission to Gray's Inn in 1555. His father, Sir John Gascoigne, had inherited a considerable estate at Cardington and had married Margaret Scargill, coheir to the estate of her father, Sir Robert Scargill of Yorkshire. Although Sir John served as a public official in his shire, legal records indicate that he and his men became violent with a neighbor over hunting rights, that Sir John was taken in adultery with a female servant, and that he could be unscrupulous in financial dealings. None of the father's failings, however, seems to have seriously damaged the family's fortune. The family could well afford the sort of education necessary to a young gentleman of prosperous family. Sometime between 1547 and 1555, George Gascoigne entered Trinity College, Cambridge. In 1555, he was admitted to Gray's Inn, to study and practice law. Probably while still pursuing a legal career, Gascoigne entered Parliament on January 20, 1558, and was probably present to hear announced the death of Queen Mary and the succession of Elizabeth. As a substitute for his father, Gascoigne assisted as almoner in the coronation proceedings. Soon afterward, he gave up the idea of a law career in order to take up life at court.

Apparently sharing some of his father's tendencies, Gascoigne seems to have spent money extravagantly and to have earned a reputation as a ruffian. In any case, he did not soon gain preferment at court, and his financial dealings led to expensive legal actions. His marriage to Elizabeth Bretton Boyes, the widowed mother of later poet Nicholas Bretton, did little to repair Gascoigne's finances, though she had inherited substantial wealth from her first husband. When she married Gascoigne she was still, at least in the eyes of the law, the wife of an Edward Boyes, who had in his possession property and money belonging to Elizabeth and her children by Bretton. Gascoigne became involved in even more conflict, both in and out of court. In 1562, as the legal actions multiplied, Gascoigne and Boyes and their retainers came to blows in Redcross Street in London. Probably needing to live more frugally, George and Elizabeth resided in Willington in 1563 and 1564, after which George returned to Gray's Inn, evidently to resume legal training; during this sojourn at Gray's Inn, however, he seems to have written much. In *A Hundreth Sundrie Flowres Bounde Up in One Small Poesie*, he published five poems written on themes provided by friends from this period. Both *Supposes* and *Jocasta* were staged at Gray's Inn in 1566. Soon, however, Gascoigne abandoned Gray's Inn again, to try his hand at farming at Cardington during 1567-1568, the latter the year of his father's death. Although Sir John seems on his deathbed to have considered disinheriting his elder son, George did receive a legacy, but it was not, evidently, sufficient to meet his obligations, for by April of 1570, he was in Bedford jail for debt.

At this low point in his life, Gascoigne redoubled his efforts and applied them in new ways: to win fame and fortune by volunteering to fight for William of Orange in the Low Countries and to gain patronage by exhibiting his writing in print. His military experience was disillusioning, though it provided material for his poetry, particularly *The Fruites of Warre*. In May, 1572, he departed from Greenwich with the first group of English volunteers but returned to England in the fall, after a disappointing campaign. His poetry at this point seems to have gained favorable notice from Lord Grey of Wilton, and Gascoigne was engaged to provide a masque for the Montague-Dormer wedding in October, 1572. He began preparing for the press *A Hundreth Sundrie Flowres Bounde Up in One Small Poesie*, which may include some lyric poems by other writers. The last material for the book was sent from the Low Countries, since he departed on March 19, 1573, for a second attempt in the wars. Worse than the first campaign, his second venture at war ended with his being imprisoned for four months by the Spaniards and abandoning the soldier's life. Upon his return to England in October, 1574, he discovered that *A Hundreth Sundrie Flowres Bounde Up in One Small Poesie* had created a scandal and had been seized by the authorities.

During the last three years of his life, Gascoigne did much writing, most of it repenting the sins of his earlier life. Almost immediately he began revising *A Hundreth Sundrie Flowres Bounde Up in One Small Poesie*; the revised version was published as *The Posies of George Gascoigne Esquire*, some copies of which were also seized by the authorities. Shortly afterward, he published *The Glasse of Governement*, an original play, and for the entertainment of Queen Elizabeth at Kenilworth in July, 1575, he provided most of the literary tribute later published as *The Princely Pleasures at Kenelworth Castle*. While performing the role of Sylvanus in one of his compositions for this entertainment, Gascoigne seems to have received favorable notice from the queen.

Even as Gascoigne was winning favor, his writing continued at a brisk pace. Shortly after April, 1576, he published in a single volume *The Steele Glas* and *The Complaynt of Phylomene*. In the same year, he published *The Droomme of Doomes Day*, a long repentance tract; *A Delicate Diet, for Daintiemouthde Droonkardes*, a temperance tract very like a sermon; and *The Grief of Joye*, a group of elegies which he presented to the queen as a New Year's gift. Also in 1576, he was appointed to government service by Sir Francis Walsingham and sent to Antwerp, where he witnessed and reported on the sacking of the city by the Spanish. *The Spoyle of Antwerpe* was originally written as a government report addressed to Lord Burleigh.

Ironically, Gascoigne did not live long enough to enjoy the success that his writing had brought him. During 1576, he had referred to his own ill health. On October 7, 1577, he died at Stamford, England.

Analysis

Both the state of development of drama during the 1560's and 1570's and the nature of George Gascoigne's dramatic efforts, including the masques and plays, mitigated against Gascoigne's achieving a level of art in drama equal to that in his better poems. His mastery of style may have been sufficient, if the lively prose dialogue of *Supposes* and the verse of his better poems are accepted as evidence, but the court masque, even at its best in the early 1600's, has generally been considered a minor form of art, existing primarily to grace a particular occasion and to honor powerful people. As for the plays, when *Supposes* and *Jocasta* were first produced in 1566, English playwrights had not yet learned how to combine native and classical traditions in order to create great drama. Indeed, much of the impetus behind the production of plays at the Inns of Court during the 1560's probably came from the desire of men educated in the classical tradition to influence the development of English drama. Translations such as *Jocasta* and *Supposes* seem to have exerted a timely and beneficial influence, but the lesser art of translation, no matter how well done, does not evoke the sort of praise given creators of good original works of art. Gascoigne's one original play, *The Glasse of Governement*, has artful touches but lacks theatricality. An examination of the masques and plays may help to explain how Gascoigne's contributions to drama have earned for him a permanent place in literary history even though he is not regarded as a great playwright.

Performed in October, 1572, Gascoigne's first known attempt at the masque omits many of the conventional elements of the form, which usually included mumming, music, dance, verse spoken by more than one character, spectacular costumes and properties, and mythological characters. Of all of these elements, Gascoigne's *A Devise of a Maske for the Right Honorable Viscount Mountacute* uses only spectacular costumes and verse spoken by a single character.

The writer's preface suggests a cause for the masque's peculiarities. Eight men of the Montague family had decided to provide a masque for the Montague-Dormer wedding and had already purchased Venetian costumes. They asked Gascoigne to write something to be spoken by a professional actor that would give a pretext for the Venetian costumes. From the Montague coat of arms he gained information that served his purpose: There was an Italian branch of the Montague family.

In the masque, a boy actor, an imaginary descendant of the English Montagues, tells of his father's death and his own capture by Turks at the siege of Famagusta and of his rescue by Venetians, who are members of the Italian branch of Montagues. On the way to Venice their ship was driven ashore in England by a storm. After using 348 lines of poulter's measure to explain the presence of the Venetians, the boy presents them to the wedding party in ten lines, praises the newly married couples in eighteen lines, and speaks a two-line farewell that ends the masque.

It is true, as Ronald C. Johnson points out in *George Gascoigne* (1972), that the narrative moves well in *A Devise of a Maske for the Right Honorable Viscount Mountacute*, but except for its flattery of the Montagues, the boy's tale has little connection with the wedding. Further, the poet has relied too much on words, neglecting the dialogue, physical motion, and spectacle innate in drama, even in a form of drama as static as the masque.

By July 9, 1575, Gascoigne had learned more about courtly shows. The entertainment of Elizabeth commissioned by the Earl of Leicester and later published as *The Princely Pleasures at Kenelworth Castle* was a series of presentations written by Gascoigne and five other men, each of whose compositions was identified as such in the published text. At least two of the five, as Charles T. Prouty observes, had some experience with similar entertainments at court and therefore may have given Gascoigne valuable information.

Gascoigne himself spoke the first section he had written. As a savage man draped in ivy, he met the queen in the forest as she returned from hunting and spoke poetry expressing the natural man's admiration of the great people gathered at Kenilworth, especially flattering the queen and, fairly subtly, calling her attention to the Earl of Leicester, her suitor. Although this performance still relied primarily on recitation of poetry, Gascoigne made clever use of the character Echo, presumably hidden in the woods, to produce a special effect by repetition of endings of lines spoken by the savage man.

The second section composed by Gascoigne is a full-scale masque. It employs spectacular costumes, music, song, elaborate stage effects, and mythological characters that express a meaning. Diana, goddess of chastity, and four of her nymphs are passing through the forest when Diana remembers Zabeta, a favorite nymph who has abandoned her. Fearing that Juno has won Zabeta away from chastity, Diana sends her nymphs to find the lost follower. Through the help of Mercury, Diana learns that Zabeta is not yet committed to Juno. After Diana leaves, content to allow Zabeta to use her own judgment, Iris descends to earth and ends the masque by urging Zabeta to wed.

The masque was never performed, perhaps because its meaning was too clear: Zabeta was Queen Elizabeth, and she was being urged to marry the Earl of Leicester.

By order of the earl, Gascoigne also wrote a performance bidding the queen farewell. Again Gascoigne relied primarily upon recitation, this time a prose tale spoken extemporaneously. As Sylvanus, god of the woods, Gascoigne met the queen as she went out to hunt and told her the story as he walked beside her horse. Sylvanus' tale concerns the gods' sorrow at her departure and the good things they will shower on Kenilworth if she remains. An abrupt shift to the subject of a goddess who changes her followers into trees and shrubs leads to a holly bush from which Deep Desire speaks verse entreating the queen to stay, concluding the performance with a song lamenting her determination to leave.

The end of the presentation thus incorporates elements other than recitation, but Gascoigne as Sylvanus has depended on words to the point of excluding other desirable elements of the masque or pageant.

Gascoigne's place in the history of drama, however, was earned roughly nine years before the entertainment of Kenilworth, in 1566, when the translations *Jocasta* and *Supposes* were produced at Gray's Inn. The title pages of the plays, first published in *A Hundreth Sundrie Flowres Bounde Up in One Small Poesie*, provide the year and location of production, but there is no indication of precisely when the translations were done or of the order in which the plays were staged.

The tragedy *Jocasta*—its second, third, and fifth acts translated by Gascoigne, the first and fourth by Kinwelmershe—has much historical importance. Even though the title page states that the play is a tragedy written in Greek by Euripides "translated and digested into Acte," the translators actually worked from Lodovico Dolce's *Giocasta*. Still, *Jocasta* was the first Greek tragedy presented in England. By following the earlier *Gorboduc* in the use of five-act structure, blank verse, dumb shows before each act, and Senecan emphases, the play reinforced modes in tragedy that later served playwrights such as Thomas Kyd and Christopher Marlowe.

The translation of the particular play may have had bad as well as good effects on Gascoigne's development as a dramatist. As Johnson comments, *Jocasta* appealed to Elizabethans for several reasons, some of which are its concern with strife over succession to the throne, its use of dumb shows and long set speeches, and its dwelling upon accounts of violence and horror. There is no shortage of subject matter: The tragedy covers almost all the events in Sophocles' trilogy on the Oedipus myth. Scene by scene, the play shifts the focus from one major character to another, emphasis falling at different times on Jocasta, Servus, Antigone, Polynices, Eteocles, Creon, Tyresias, Meneceus, and Oedipus. The shifting causes a lack of focus; moreover, the play's use of long speeches may have encouraged a similar tendency in Gascoigne, primarily a maker of poems. The play, true to its origins in classical tragedy, persistently narrates action instead of showing it onstage.

Ariosto's *I suppositi* was a much better choice for translation than was Dolce's tragedy, and Gascoigne's treatment of the play reflects much skill with language. Carefully unified, Ariosto's comedy imitates Plautus' *Captivi* (c. 200 B.C.) and Terence's *Eunuchus* (161 B.C.) by having a master and slave exchange identities so that the master can enter the house of an attractive girl as a household servant. The young master (really Erostrato) comes to Ferrara from his home in Sicily in order to study at the university, bringing his servant Dulypo with him. Seeing the beautiful Polynesta, Erostrato exchanges roles with his servant and enters service in the house of Damon, Polynesta's father. Using the nurse Balia as an intermediary, Erostrato secretly becomes intimate with Polynesta and wishes to marry her, but her father is inclined to give her hand to Cleander, a rich but miserly old lawyer who offers a large marriage settlement. In order to delay the marriage, Erostrato has his slave pretend to court Polynesta, outbidding Cleander for her hand, but Damon demands that the younger suitor's father guarantee the arrangements. The crafty slave contrives to have a Sienese traveler pose as Philogano, the father of Erostrato. Just as the real Philogano arrives in Ferrara to pay a surprise visit to his son, the real Erostrato has been caught in intimacy with Polynesta and has been imprisoned. Through Pasiphilo, the parasite, the confusion about the father's and the son's identities is resolved, and Cleander discovers his lost son in Dulypo, the crafty slave. No longer needing a marriage to beget an heir, Cleander is happy at the end of the comedy when Philogano and Damon agree on a marriage between Erostrato and Polynesta. The comic resolution is complete and satisfying.

Unlike the masques and *Jocasta*, *Supposes* has sufficient action to appeal to a large audience, and Gascoigne's translation is in light, idiomatic style. He had access to both prose and verse versions in Italian but had the good judgment to opt for prose in English, influencing large numbers of later comedies. In addition, *Supposes* brought the first Italian adaptation of Roman comedy to the English stage, which would make use of many of Roman comedy's type characters and of such devices as disguise, mistaken identity, and love intrigue. If *Supposes* had been Gascoigne's original creation, the play would have earned for him literary immortality as a playwright.

Unfortunately, Gascoigne's one original play, *The Glasse of Governement*, lacks theatrical appeal even though it has interesting touches in characterization and structure. The first of Gascoigne's moralistic writings, the play is written in the tradition of the prodigal-son plays popularized by Dutch Humanists, a tradition to which Gascoigne was probably exposed during his military service in the Low Countries.

Structured in five acts, the story line is clear. Two rich citizens and neighbors of Antwerp, Phylopaes and Philocalus, have two sons each, paired by age with the sons of the other. Anxious for their sons to go to the university but wanting the boys to be prepared both morally and academically, the fathers entrust their sons to the teacher Gnomaticus, who teaches in accordance with the ideals of Christian Humanists. The two elder sons learn very quickly but are soon bored. They are easily lured to the house of Lamia the harlot by the parasite Echo. The two younger sons are slower to learn but eager to understand their morally based instruction.

Learning that their elder sons have been seen in bad company, the fathers consult Gnomaticus, who agrees that the four sons should be sent to the University of Douai so that the elder boys will be separated from evil company. Accompanied by the evil servant Ambidexter, the boys go to

Douai. Quickly the elder sons neglect their studies and, with Ambidexter, frequent taverns and brothels. The younger sons study. Hearing news of the elder sons' conduct, the fathers send the good servant Fidus to help them, but Fidus arrives too late. He returns with news that one elder son has been executed for robbery at the Palsgrave's court in the presence of his successful younger brother, who is now secretary to the Palsgrave. Another elder son has been publicly whipped and banished from Geneva for fornication, even though his younger brother, now a famous preacher there, tried to intercede on his brother's behalf. Thoroughgoing in its use of poetic justice, the play ends after all the evil characters have been punished by the law and the virtue of the two younger sons has been rewarded by social advancement.

For a play of its time, *The Glasse of Governement* has many good features. It is well organized by five-act structure, and the dialogue is in clear prose. Its greatest strength, however, lies in its characterization, which avoids mere stereotypes. The fathers are concerned and sympathetic; Gnomaticus is a kind and tolerant teacher with little practical knowledge of human nature; Severus is an officer of the law who refuses to punish offenders without firm evidence against them; and Lamia is a girl from a prosperous family who drifted into prostitution because she rejected her society's stifling restrictions on the conduct of proper young ladies.

Despite its virtues, the play seems not be have been produced, perhaps because of its untheatrical qualities. Its use of paired characters—fathers, sons, and servants—offers theatrical possibilities through comparison and contrast, but there is little differentiation between the individuals in the sets of pairs. The play's heavy-handed didacticism poses more serious problems: It creates a mood more appropriate to a pulpit than to the stage; it leads to the oversimplified morality of poetic justice; and it results in static scenes in which Gnomaticus and, less frequently, the good sons recite extremely long and moral speeches. Finally, the focus of the action depicted onstage is misdirected. The elder sons' wild behavior and the younger sons' triumphs are merely narrated, whereas the lectures of Gnomaticus take place onstage. This misdirected focus prevents the conflict between good and evil from coming alive in the play.

Gascoigne's tendency to rely on long recitations in drama may suggest a weakness in his sense of the dramatic, or more likely may reflect the immature state of English drama during his time. In any event, George Gascoigne created no original work of lasting fame, but through his translations, particularly his *Supposes*, he did help to make possible the greatest age of English drama.

Other major works

NOVEL: *The Discourse of the Adventures Passed by Master. F. J.*, 1573 (revised as *The Pleasant Fable of Ferdinando Jeronimi and Leonora de Valasco*, 1575).

POETRY: *The Fruites of Warre*, 1575; *The Complaynt of Phylomene*, 1576; *The Grief of Joye*, 1576; *The Steele Glas, a Satyre*, 1576.

NONFICTION: "Certayne Notes of Instruction Concerning the Making of Verse," 1575; *A Delicate Diet, for Daintiemouthde Droonkardes*, 1576; *The Droomme of Doomes Day*, 1576; *The Spoyle of Antwerpe*, 1576.

MISCELLANEOUS: *A Hundreth Sundrie Flowres Bounde Up in One Small Poesie*, 1573 (poetry and prose; revised as *The Posies of George Gascoigne Esquire*, 1575).

Bibliography

Baskervill, Charles Read, Virgil B. Heltzel, and Arthur H. Nethercot, eds. *Elizabethan and Stuart Plays*, 1934.

Helgerson, Richard. *The Elizabethan Prodigals*, 1977.

Herford, C. H. *Studies in the Literary Relations of England and Germany in the Sixteenth Century*, 1886.

Johnson, Ronald C. *George Gascoigne*, 1972.

Lewis, C. S. *English Literature in the Sixteenth Century Excluding Drama*, 1954.

Mills, Jerry L. "Recent Studies in Gascoigne," in *English Language Review*. III (1973), pp. 322-326.

Prouty, Charles T. *Gascoigne: Elizabethan Courtier, Soldier, and Poet*, 1942.

Schelling, Felix E. *The Life and Writings of George Gascoigne*, 1893.

Wilson, F. P. *The English Drama, 1485-1585*, 1969.

Millard T. Jones

JOHN GAY

Born: Barnstaple, England; June 30, 1685
Died: London, England; December 4, 1732

Principal drama

The Mohocks, pb. 1712; *The Wife of Bath*, pr., pb. 1713, 1730 (revised); *The What D'ye Call It*, pr., pb. 1715; *Three Hours After Morning*, pr., pb. 1717 (with Alexander Pope and John Arbuthnot); *Dione*, pb. 1720 (verse tragedy); *The Captives*, pr., pb. 1724 (verse tragedy); *The Beggar's Opera*, pr., pb. 1728 (ballad opera); *Polly*, pb. 1729, pr. 1777 (ballad opera); *Acis and Galatea*, pr. 1731, pb. 1732 (libretto; music by George Frederick Handel); *Achilles*, pr., pb. 1733 (ballad opera); *The Distress'd Wife*, pr. 1734, pb. 1743; *The Rehearsal at Goatham*, pb. 1754.

Other literary forms

In addition to his plays, John Gay is well-known for his poetry, principally *Trivia: Or, The Art of Walking the Streets of London* (1716), the two series of *Fables* (1727 and 1738), and numerous songs and ballads. All of these writings are available in the 1926 edition of Gay's poetic works, edited by G. C. Faber, which also includes most of the plays, or in the two-volume *John Gay: Poetry and Prose* (1974), edited by Vinton A. Dearing with the assistance of Charles E. Beckwith. The entire canon, including all of Gay's dramatic works, is contained in the six-volume *Poetical, Dramatic, and Miscellaneous Works of John Gay* (1795, reprinted 1970). The poet's correspondence is collected in *The Letters of John Gay*, edited by C. F. Burgess (1966).

Achievements

Gay's abilities and significance as a dramatist have often been underestimated. Overshadowed by his more famous friends and sometime collaborators Alexander Pope and Jonathan Swift, Gay has generally been designated, as he was by Samuel Johnson, a poet of a "lower order." While his dramatic work may be uneven, it is generally well crafted and interesting; at its best, it displays originality, dramatic power, and a serious social concern. Gay's central theme is the corruption of English society, but while his criticism is often severe, his satire is more gentle and good-humored than that of his more famous literary friends. His work is also marked by a willingness to explore and reevaluate traditional forms, a practice which results sometimes in literary satire and burlesque and other times in experimentation and innovation. His experiments with mixed forms led him to the creation of a new dramatic type, the ballad opera, of which his masterpiece, *The Beggar's Opera*, is the first and finest example. While Gay's reputation rests principally on this unique work, his other plays abound with the same originality, good-natured satire, gifted lyric expression, and genuine comic spirit which have made *The Beggar's Opera* one of the few plays outside the Shakespearean canon to find a permanent place in the English theatrical repertory.

Biography

John Gay was born on June 30, 1685, at Barnstaple, in Devonshire. Apprenticed from 1702 to 1706 to a London silk mercer, Gay left the business world to make his living as a writer. For most of his life, he was plagued with financial problems, in part because of poor investments and in part because of difficulties in finding a long-standing patron. In 1712, he became secretary to the Duchess of Monmouth, and in 1714, he joined the household of Lord Clarendon, a position he kept less than a year. During these years, he became an active and well-liked member of the circle surrounding Alexander Pope and Jonathan Swift and remained close friends with both men all of his life.

In 1723, Gay received a government appointment which, along with an offer of lodgings at Whitehall, gave him a measure of financial security. His friendships with the royal circle, however, always made him hope for more substantial support, a hope which was perhaps unrealistic, since most of Gay's friends were Tories, and the Whigs, led by Prime Minister Robert Walpole, were in control of the government. Gay may have become concerned that the acceptance of a government post would mean the loss of his literary freedom, for in 1727, he turned down the offer of the position of Gentleman Usher to the two-year-old Princess Louisa.

Although Gay is consistently described as honest and congenial, and his works reflect his basically good-humored disposition, his struggles to achieve recognition and support left him somewhat disillusioned and disappointed. His dissatisfaction with the ruling party and with Walpole, whom he believed was responsible for blocking his own hopes, resulted in the strong vein of political satire which runs through his works. Walpole's displeasure with the satire in *The Beggar's Opera*, Gay's most financially successful play, led to the Lord Chamberlain's prohibition of its sequel, *Polly*, in 1728. The resulting squabble cost Gay his lodgings at Whitehall, and he spent the last years of his life, increasingly bothered by a chronic ailment, with his patrons, the Duke and Duchess of Queensberry. Gay died suddenly in London on December 4, 1732; he is buried in Westminster Abbey.

Analysis

John Gay's reputation rests primarily on *The Beggar's Opera*, to the extent that the rest of his work has gone largely unappreciated. Although none of his plays is as successful as *The Beggar's Opera*, a number of them show, in experimental form, the same characteristics that give Gay's masterpiece its unique form and spirit. Throughout his work, Gay is concerned with the emptiness and corruption of society, and his plays are distinguished by the innovative strategies he developed to present this theme: the use of pastoral forms to achieve a comparison between high and low classes, the inclusion of songs set to popular tunes, the use of literary satire and burlesque side by side with scenes of sincere feeling, the grafting of heroic qualities onto low characters, the use of carefully observed realistic detail, and the blending of several literary forms into a cohesive work. In those plays, principally the later ones, in which Gay is less innovative and more single-minded in purpose, there is a considerable loss of power. Gay's best plays—*The Beggar's Opera* and some of the earlier works—are characterized by a complex and original use of multiple dramatic forms which gives them a unique power and a surprisingly modern flavor.

Gay's interest in experimentation can be seen in his first two plays, *The Mohocks* and *The Wife of Bath*. Both plays have a clear literary ancestry, the first from Shakespearean comedy and the second from Geoffrey Chaucer's *The Canterbury Tales*. Described as a "tragi-comical farce," *The Mohocks* satirizes a group of bullies who roam London at night terrorizing the citizens. The aristocratic men of the gang are confronted by a group of watchmen strongly reminiscent of Dogberry's crew in William Shakespeare's *Much Ado About Nothing*. *The Wife of Bath* imagines the further adventures of Chaucer and some of the Canterbury pilgrims at a stop along their route. Both plays are essentially comic in form, ending in reconciliation and appropriate marriages. *The Mohocks* contains a great deal of literary burlesque, while *The Wife of Bath* gently mocks both Chaucer and the eighteenth century society from which its characters are drawn by a process of deflation, a technique Gay used in a more serious and sophisticated way in *The Beggar's Opera*. Both plays, with their combination of literary burlesque, topical satire, and farce and with their use of songs set to popular music, show Gay experimenting with techniques he later blended more effectively in *The Beggar's Opera*.

Perhaps the most complex and interesting of Gay's early plays is *The What D'ye Call It*. The play mystified its audience at first but eventually became a success. Its title, which recalls Shakespeare's *As You Like It* or *Twelfth Night*, leads one to expect literary parody, but that is only a part of the play's complex effect. Gay works here with the technique, also reminiscent of Shakespeare, of the play-within-a-play. A group of rustics are performing a tragedy, especially created for the occasion, before a country lord and his friends. The couplet verse and excessive sentiment of the tragedy are deflated by being delivered by the simple rustics. At the same time, the real problems and emotions of the lower-class characters are given a measure of dignity through their expression in poetic form. Gay uses the exaggeration of farce to create a blend of laughter and sympathy, an effect not unlike that of modern tragicomedy or Theater of the Absurd. This complex combination disorients the audience and destroys any idea it may have about the proper hierarchy or use of dramatic forms. At the same time, Gay resolves both inner and outer plays through a marriage that cuts across class lines and fittingly caps the play's social comment. With its combination of social satire and literary burlesque, its use of ballads, and its ability to contain and evoke genuine feelings, *The What D'ye Call It* was a major step on Gay's path toward *The Beggar's Opera*.

In his two verse tragedies *Dione* and *The Captives*, Gay abandoned his experiments with literary form to work in a single literary mode without questioning its conventions. Both plays are concerned with fidelity in love, a theme which also appears in *The Beggar's Opera*; they also examine the social conditions that affect fidelity and independence. In *Dione*, the shallowness and infidelity of Evander and the unhappiness of court life are contrasted to the fidelity of Dione and the simple goodness of the pastoral life. This contrast is developed more fully in *The Captives*, in which the imprisoned prince and princess, who have lost all wealth and power, remain faithful to each other and to those who have befriended them in the midst of a court characterized by lust, bribery, and political intrigue. The scheming queen, who uses the king's devotion and wealth to maintain her power, is not far removed from those characters in *The Beggar's Opera* who thrive on a system of bribes and payoffs.

In *The Beggar's Opera*, Gay brought to fulfillment both his experiments with dramatic form and his increasingly serious criticism of society. While it may be true that the initial idea for *The Beggar's Opera* lay in Swift's often quoted suggestion that Gay write a "Newgate pastoral," the actual work that Gay produced has a much more complex genesis. Certainly his central theme, the sameness of all men whatever their social position, was a logical development from his earlier works, especially *The What D'ye Call It*. The unorthodox form, a combination of pastoral, burlesque, satire, tragedy, and opera, was also a logical extension of his experiments with mixed form. The realistic detail of the criminal world and the inspiration for some of the major characters came from recent publicity surrounding the capture and execution of several notorious London criminals. In addition, *The Beggar's Opera* was designed as a response to the Italian opera, which, with its artificiality, unbelievable plots, and foreign music, was becoming increasingly popular in England. The innovative form of the ballad opera allowed Gay both to satirize the extravagance of the foreign opera and to offer a native entertainment as a replacement.

A final ingredient in Gay's dramatic mixture was political satire. Gay had criticized the corruption of city life previously, but before *The Beggar's Op-*

era, most of his criticism had been general. In *The Beggar's Opera*, he turned his wit directly on English politics through a sustained comparison between the London underworld and the British political system. Gay's turn to more specific and more biting political satire was probably a result of his gradual disillusionment with English society and his immediate disappointment over his own lack of recognition.

The Beggar's Opera, like most of Gay's plays, has its roots in the pastoral tradition. An essential element of pastoral is the comparison of upper and lower classes, a comparison Gay used in his earlier plays primarily to ridicule the upper class. In *The Beggar's Opera*, however, it is the similarities rather than the differences between the two classes that are stressed. The lower class is dignified by being portrayed as just as good as the upper. At the same time, the aristocrats are described as no better than the thieves and prostitutes of Newgate. In *The Beggar's Opera*, Gay pictures a society that is corrupt on all levels.

Gay's thesis is established in the opening scene of the play, a scene that also establishes the central organizing principle of both high and low societies. The inhabitants of this world are motivated solely by self-interest. Peachum protects the thieves as long as it is profitable to do so; when they are no longer useful, he turns them in for the reward money. Lockit similarly turns his charges over to the justices, or, if the criminals can offer a better deal, arranges for their release. When Polly announces that she has married Macheath, her parents' primary concern is for their own safety. Even Polly's attachment to Macheath is motivated in part by self-interest.

The one exception to this dedication to self-interest is Macheath, who displays a greater moral integrity than anyone else in the play. He is open and generous with his comrades, polite and considerate with women, and aloof from the vices of the gentlemen with whom he must associate. He is more than once referred to as a great man and is often given phrases reminiscent of Shakespearean heroes. His struggle for independence from the system controlled by Peachum gives him a kind of tragic stature; his dangerous attraction to women may be seen as his tragic flaw. He is genuinely surprised and disappointed by betrayal, first by Jenny and then by Jemmy Twitcher. The second betrayal is particularly disheartening, for it shows that there is no honor even among his comrades.

As engaging as Macheath's character is, Gay does not allow him to remain unblemished. His lack of courage as he faces death and the improbable appearance of four more wives with a child apiece seriously undermine the character's attractiveness. The deflation of Macheath's character also reduces Polly's stature somewhat, although her loyalty remains admirable. As Macheath approaches death, the author's and the audience's attitude toward him and Polly is ambiguous.

Macheath's execution is interrupted by the Beggar and Player, whose opening conversation introduced the play. The Player, voicing the audience's lingering sympathies for Macheath and Polly, protests Macheath's death. The Beggar, supposedly the author of the opera, points to the perfect poetic justice of his intended ending but agrees to a reprieve, since an opera must end happily, "no matter how absurdly these things are brought about." Thus, the "taste of the town" dictates not only an absurd ending, a thrust at the conventions of Italian opera, but also an immoral one, for none of the characters is punished. The way of the world will not allow Macheath a heroic end, but insists that he be drawn back into society and reduced to its level. The playwright cannot afford to take a moral stand; his integrity, like everything in the play, can be had for a price. Gay's final attack is not only against society but also, in a sense, against himself.

The Beggar's Opera was an instant critical and popular success; it has also had considerable influence on the English theater. Gay's attack on Italian opera is generally considered responsible for the decline in that genre's popularity during the next few years. Gay's innovative form, the ballad opera—a play including ballads sung to the tunes of popular songs—continued to be popular for many years and is one of the ancestors of the modern musical comedy. The success of the political satire in *The Beggar's Opera* encouraged other writers to attack the ruling party from the stage, leading eventually to the closing of the theaters and the Licensing Act of 1737. *The Beggar's Opera* remained popular during the eighteenth and nineteenth centuries and found new life in the twentieth century through Bertolt Brecht's adaptation of it, *The Threepenny Opera* (1928). While the play's initial success was partially the result of its treatment of contemporary art and politics, its lasting popularity attests both Gay's originality and his exploration of permanent and universal problems of human experience.

Perhaps to capitalize on the success of *The Beggar's Opera* and perhaps to answer criticism of the play's moral stance, Gay quickly produced a sequel, *Polly*, also a ballad opera. In it, Macheath, stripped of all heroic qualities, has been transported to the West Indies, where he lives with Jenny Diver as head of a band of pirates. Polly travels there to find him, but her quest is interrupted by a war between the pirates and the European planters and native Indians. Disguised as a boy, Polly captures Macheath, who is disguised as a black, and unknowingly sends him to his death. The play is more melodramatic and sentimental than *The Beggar's Opera*, but it contains some biting satire and clever literary burlesque. The contrast between high and low classes becomes a contrast between civilized and natural man, suggesting that the faults Gay finds in society are cultural, not part of man's nature. Unfortunately, Gay labors his moral point too heavily, and *Polly* never reaches the emotional or satiric heights of *The Beggar's Opera*.

Gay's final ballad opera, *Achilles*, is even more single-minded and less satisfying than *Polly*. To prevent her son from going to the Trojan War, Achilles' mother hides him, dressed as a girl, among the daughters of King Lycomedes. Gay exploits the farcical elements of the situation, but the characters never become fully human, and the play lacks the dramatic tension and ambiguities of Gay's more complex and experimental works. The same can be said of the comedy of manners *The Distress'd Wife*, another variation on the city-country comparison, but with little new to offer.

The short satire *The Rehearsal at Goatham* is more interesting and seems to refer more directly to Gay's own experiences with *The Beggar's Opera* and *Polly*; the Lord Chamberlain had prohibited the production of *Polly* without what Gay and his friends considered to be a fair hearing. Inspired by a scene in Miguel de Cervantes' *Don Quixote de la Mancha*, *The Rehearsal at Goatham* portrays a performance of the puppet show *Melisandra*. The performance is prohibited by the town aldermen because it supposedly contains material offensive to the local citizens. The townsmen agree to watch a rehearsal of the piece to see if it is acceptable and proceed to find scandalous references to themselves in the most innocent phrases of the play, thus exposing their own foolishness and misconduct. *The Rehearsal at Goatham* has some of the complexity of Gay's early works, with literary and social satire developed simultaneously, but it lacks the human characters and ability to evoke a full emotional response which characterizes *The Beggar's Opera*.

While Gay's reputation rests principally on *The Beggar's Opera*, his other plays are not without merit. He produced a number of delightful comedies, and his two verse tragedies are well crafted, if somewhat sentimental. The early plays show a development of theme and technique that leads directly to the powerful thesis and original form of *The Beggar's Opera*. The later plays, although weaker, continue to explore the central thematic concerns of Gay's masterpiece—the corruption of society and the difficulty of the individual, especially the artist, in maintaining his honor and independence. Gay's greatest achievement lies in his experimentation with traditional forms. This formal exploration, which gives even his less successful plays great complexity and vitality, led to the creation of a new dramatic form, the ballad opera, and one brilliant play which has had an important place in the English theatrical repertory for more than two hundred years.

Other major works

POETRY: *Rural Sports*, 1713; *The Fan*, 1714; *The Shepherd's Week*, 1714; *Trivia: Or, The Art of Walking the Streets of London*, 1716; *Fables*, 1727, 1738; *Gay's Chair: Poems Never Before Printed*, 1820; *The Poetical Works of John Gay*, 1926 (G. C. Faber, editor; includes plays).

NONFICTION: *A Letter to a Lady*, 1714; *The Letters of John Gay*, 1966

(C. F. Burgess, editor).

MISCELLANEOUS: *Poetical, Dramatic, and Miscellaneous Works of John Gay*, 1795, 1970 (6 volumes); *John Gay: Poetry and Prose*, 1974 (2 volumes; Vinton A. Dearing with Charles E. Beckwith, editors).

Bibliography

Armens, Sven M. *John Gay: Social Critic*, 1954.

Bateson, F. W. *English Comic Drama, 1700-1750*, 1929.

Burgess, C. F. "The Genesis of *The Beggar's Opera*," in *Cithara*. II (1962), pp. 6-12.

Donaldson, Ian. *The World Upside Down: Comedy from Johnson to Fielding*, 1970.

Empson, William. *Some Versions of Pastoral*, 1935.

Erskine-Hill, Howard. "The Significance of Gay's Drama," in *English Drama: Forms and Development*, 1977. Edited by Marie Axton and Raymond Williams.

Gagey, Edmond McAdoo. *Ballad Opera*, 1937.

Irving, William Henry. *John Gay: Favorite of the Wits*, 1962.

Klein, Julie Thompson. *John Gay: An Annotated Checklist of Criticism*, 1974.

Schultz, William Eben. *Gay's "The Beggar's Opera": Its Content, History and Influence*, 1923.

Spacks, Patricia Ann (Meyer). *John Gay*, 1965.

Kathleen Latimer

JACK GELBER

Born: Chicago, Illinois; April 12, 1932

Principal drama

The Connection, pr. 1959, pb. 1960; *The Apple*, pr., pb. 1961; *Square in the Eye*, pr. 1965, pb. 1966; *The Cuban Thing*, pr. 1968, pb. 1969; *Sleep*, pr., pb. 1972; *Barbary Shore*, pr. 1973 (adaptation of Norman Mailer's novel); *Jack Gelber's New Play: Rehearsal*, pr. 1976.

Other literary forms

Most of Jack Gelber's plays have appeared in print. Gelber has also translated Francis Xavier Kroetz's play *Farmyard*, with Michael Roloff. The work was produced at the Yale Theatre in New Haven, Connecticut, on January 22, 1975, and published by Urizen the following year. In addition, the film version of *The Connection*, released in 1962, was based on Gelber's screenplay adaptation. The movie, directed by Shirley Clarke, was screened at the Cannes Festival (1961) and banned as obscene by New York State, though the New York State Supreme Court later found the language in the movie not to be obscene. Gelber's only nontheatrical literary endeavor has been a novel, *On Ice* (1964); some of the concepts that he deals with in this prose work reappear in *Sleep*.

Achievements

Whether fairly or not, Jack Gelber is primarily known for *The Connection*. The drama was popular enough to be made into a motion picture, and it achieved critical success as well, bringing the playwright the Obie, the Vernon Rice Award, and the New York Drama Critics Poll Award for most promising playwright of the 1959-1960 season. There were three reasons for the startling success of the dramatist's first play. First, and most obvious, are the nontraditional characters, setting, subject matter, and plot line. Gelber did in the American theater what John Osborne had done in the British theater with *Look Back in Anger* three years earlier; he exposed the theatergoing public to a new world, in this case, that of skid-row junkies waiting for their heroin connection to arrive with a fix. Second, the play's thematic content is important; it goes far beyond the dreary, desolate, frustrated life of the characters portrayed, for the addicts are really metaphors for modern mankind, much as Vladimir and Estragon are in Samuel Beckett's *Waiting for Godot*. Finally, Gelber's emphasis on improvisation has had a major impact on contemporary drama. Just as free verse has a special appeal to bad poets and is easily misused by them, this approach to playwriting can lead to horrendous results, but when used by someone with Gelber's ability, the improvisational ingredient reinforces one of the theater's basic strengths, its immediacy, and enhances the participatory nature of drama, involving the audience in a way that recalls, indeed reincarnates, the origins of the genre in public ceremonies.

Much of Gelber's writing since *The Connection* has been intended to broaden the theater's possibilities even further; it should never be forgotten that drama, even when based on a text and literary conventions, is essentially rooted in performance. Some of Gelber's subsequent efforts have extended the innovative strategies of *The Connection*, while others have moved in new directions. The dramatist continues to progress, but he has yet to equal the success, either popularly or critically, of *The Connection*.

Biography

Jack Gelber was born in Chicago, Illinois, on April 12, 1932, the son of Harold and Molly (née Singer) Gelber. The playwright has said that as a high school student, he passed the time playing the tuba and attending movies and burlesque shows, but he never went to the legitimate theater, that he did not even know the theater existed until he went to college. Even today, he mentions with respect the Russian novelists—Ivan Turgenev, Maxim Gorky, and Nikolai Gogol—who originally attracted him as well as Rainer Maria Rilke and the German Expressionists. He has also expressed an interest in Buddhism and in "religious states of being."

During the summers of his undergraduate years at the University of Illinois, Urbana, Gelber followed his father's trade as a sheet-metal worker; he has also been a shipfitter's helper in San Francisco and a mimeograph operator for the United Nations. Gelber was graduated from the university with a B.S. in journalism in 1953, and he wrote poetry before turning to dramaturgy. He became involved in Julian Beck and Judith Malina's Living Theatre, an experimental theater group, which mounted *The Connection* under Molina's direction for a run of 768 performances. *The Apple* was also written to be performed by the Living Theatre (sixty-four performances). These first two plays have been performed in a number of foreign countries, including Brazil, England, France, Germany, and Italy. *Square in the Eye* (thirty-one performances) was intended to be staged by the Living Theatre, too, though by 1965, the group was no longer based in the United States. Meanwhile, Gelber visited Cuba in 1963 and again in 1967, and *The Cuban Thing* (one performance) grew out of his experience in that country under Fidel Castro's rule. *Sleep* (thirty-two performances) followed in 1972, and *Jack Gelber's New Play: Rehearsal* was mounted in 1976. In 1981, Gelber was reportedly writing a new play, tentatively titled "Starters."

In addition to writing for the theater, Gelber also has been active as a director. Besides his own *The Cuban Thing, Jack Gelber's New Play: Rehearsal*, and his adaptation of Norman Mailer's *Barbary Shore*, the dramatist has directed Arnold Wesker's *The Kitchen* (in 1966), Arthur Kopit's *Indians* (for the Royal Shakespeare Company at the Aldwych Theatre, in London, in 1968), Merle Molofsky's *Kool Aid* (in 1971), Frank Chin's *The Chickencoop Chinaman* (in 1972), Robert Coover's *The Kid* (in 1972), Tennessee Williams' *A Streetcar Named Desire* (in 1976), Miguel Rinero's *Eulogy for a Small-Time Thief* (in 1977), and Sam Shepard's *Seduced* (in 1979). In 1973, he received an Obie Award for his direction of *The Kid* the previous year. Gelber's experience as a director establishes him as a man of the theater in the fullest sense. More important, working as a director provides him with a wider perspective on the potentials and limitations of drama that he can apply in his writing.

Since 1963, Gelber has alternated between fellowships and teaching to support his writing. In 1963, he received a Guggenheim Fellowship for creative writing for the theater; he was a writer-in-residence at the City College of New York from 1965 to 1966; he received a second Guggenheim Fellowship in 1966; from 1967 to 1972, he was employed as an adjunct professor of drama at Columbia University; in 1972, he was awarded a Rockefeller grant as playwright-in-residence at the American Place Theatre; and he has been a professor of drama at Brooklyn College of the City University of New York since 1972. In 1974, Gelber was the recipient of a Columbia Broadcasting System-Yale University Fellowship, and the following year he received a National Endowment for the Arts Fellowship.

Analysis

In *The Connection*, his first, most famous, and best play, Jack Gelber established himself as an innovative force in the American theater. His experimental approach to his themes wedded form and content far more successfully than would have been possible in a conventionally constructed drama.

The Connection is an exploration of universal human need, metaphorically expressed as a heroin fix; Gelber's play contains little action in any traditional dramatic sense. There is essentially no movement in the plot of this two-act play, since the characters are so desperate in their need that they remain in Teach's room, the only setting in the play, afraid to leave for fear that Cowboy, their dope supplier, might come while they are gone. This is not to say that nothing happens in the play or that no dramatic tension is created. Tension evolves out of the relationships between the room's inhabitants, the question of whether Cowboy will ever come, and the question of what will happen when he arrives. This atmosphere is reinforced by the emotions and physical discomfort displayed by the characters. More traditional plays have dealt with similar themes—Clifford Odets' *Waiting for Lefty* (pr., pb. 1935), Eugene O'Neill's *The Iceman Cometh* (wr. 1939, pr., pb. 1946), and even O'Neill's *Long Day's Journey into Night* (wr. 1941, pb. 1955, pr. 1956)—and invariably plays of this nature are condemned by imperceptive critics who demand constant action onstage. In this play, Gelber's form and content come together with an unexpected result. Following the approach of the Theater of the Absurd, the plot does not appear to be carefully and logically structured. Events that do not seem related (in an Aristotelian sense) occur one after another. Things simply happen onstage, and the feeling of improvisation that Gelber so carefully cultivates is very frustrating to those members of the audience who expect, or need, to have everything carefully spelled out in a strict format as the play progresses.

For other members of the audience, the mood of improvisation is intellectually stimulating; a sophisticated audience soon realizes that the supposedly random happenings and the tedious waiting reflect the drama's theme. If the audience feels frustrated by Cowboy's not coming, they can better imagine how the characters onstage feel (much as film director Michelangelo Antonioni bored the audience of his 1964 film *The Red Desert* for nearly three hours to demonstrate how boring life is for a certain class of Italians). The way jazz music is used here also serves to emphasize the playwright's theme: The essential character of jazz is improvisational, and the music in the play varies according to the musicians' moods rather than corresponding to events transpiring onstage, as would be expected in a musical. At the same time, the music itself provides some movement and a feeling of transition (though, again, in a nontraditional way, frequently increasing the audience's frustration and anxiety, since the changes that appear to be signaled by the musical breaks often remain unrealized).

In accordance with the stage directions, *The Connection* begins with the players coming onstage and arranging themselves around the set, giving the appearance of fourth-wall realism, which maintains the fiction of characters acting out their lives with no interaction between spectator and actor. As the actors move about, they are unhurried and seem to have no plans; they merely walk onstage and stand or sit randomly. Gelber emphasizes the spontenaity of the situation by indicating in the stage directions that "perhaps" there is a sign on the wall, or "perhaps" a painting or an orange-crate bookcase is in the room.

Two actors stroll down the theater aisle, and act 1 has begun. The first words are spoken by Jim Dunn, who introduces himself and Jaybird to the audience as the producer and author of *The Connection*, respectively. Those who feel that the play is about heroin should be alerted by these statements that Gelber wants the audience to be aware that they are watching a play, and that they should not take what happens onstage to be literally true. Throughout the play, one character or another directs his dialogue at the audience to make sure that they do not exercise a willing suspension of disbelief and accept the action onstage as real, even momentarily. Gelber does not want his audience to become absorbed in what is happening in the play; instead, he wants them to be constantly drawing analogies between what is transpiring in front of them and other areas in their lives. Moreover, to make sure that the audience understands exactly what the author intends, these asides clearly state the point that he wants to make. For example, Dunn announces that most recent studies of drug addiction, an "anti-social habit," have not had much to do with the subject of narcotics, per se.

As soon as the dialogue directed at the audience is completed, the Fourth Musician asks if Cowboy has come back yet, thereby immediately establishing the concept of waiting. Within a few moments, Jaybird interrupts the action to lecture the audience, reminding them that they are watching an art form, improvised theater, and noting that if they perceive a relationship between jazz and narcotics they are making their own "connection," not his.

Suspense is generated when there is a knock at the door of Teach's room, but it is not Cowboy who enters. Soon after this, two more characters enter, the First and Second Photographers. One is a black man dressed in a white suit, who is swift and agile; the other is a white man in a black suit, who moves slowly, "clodlike." During the course of the play, these two exchange their personalities and their clothing, piece by piece, as Gelber underscores the artificiality of his play so that his themes will receive more attention than the context in which they are presented.

The various characters are introduced by Dunn (Ernie is a "dope-addict psychopath," Sam is an "expert in folk lore," and so on), and the question about Cowboy's whereabouts is continually rephrased. Gelber continually reminds his audience that dope is not his subject, as when Sam, in a tirade attacking society, asserts that people who work and worry about money and new clothes are addicts ("chlorophyll . . . aspirin . . . vitamin") who are hooked worse than he is. Solly, the intellectual, agrees, commenting that everybody is looking for a fix, a fix of "hope"—to forget, to remember, to be sad, to be happy, to be. Later, he says that everyone is his own connection. At one point, Solly theorizes about Jaybird's intentions in writing the play. Sam ironically undercuts Solly's pronouncements, noting that Solly may be educated and know a lot, but that he is in the room waiting just as everybody else is. As the play progresses, a bit is revealed about the background and nature of most of the characters, yet when act 1 ends, Cowboy has still not appeared and everyone is still waiting for him.

Act 2 opens with a jazz break, and then Cowboy enters. Ironically, as Cowboy takes each of the characters into the bathroom to give them a fix, Sister Salvation visits with those remaining in the room, preaching religious salvation to them, unaware of what is going on about her. The men, including the Second Photographer and Jaybird, get stoned and begin telling stories, and again they turn to Jaybird intermittently to see if they have discovered the meaning that he is trying to convey. Teach takes an overdose, and this leads the characters to discuss why narcotics, particularly marijuana, are illegal. The play ends with Jaybird distressed that he has failed to get his characters to kick their habit, presumably because the actors have actually taken drugs onstage in their play-within-a-play. He has learned one lesson from this evening's experience: "It all fits together," and it fits together on the stage, he tells Dunn. By way of the final exchange in the play, Gelber has reiterated his two major themes—all people need a connection, and innovative theater is an excellent medium for expressing this message.

Besides these devices, Gelber extends the traditional boundaries of the stage in other ways. For example, during the intermission between the two acts, several of the actors mingle with the audience members in the lobby, panhandling, and later, an actor who is pretending to be a member of the audience engages an actor onstage in conversation. At first glance, the drama is chaotic. Underneath, however, it is a carefully structured work, much in the style of the early plays of Luigi Pirandello.

In Gelber's second play, *The Apple*, several of the devices employed in *The Connection* are extended to further blur the boundary between art and reality, as when the actors use their real names onstage, and when the painting that has been created onstage during the performance is auctioned off at the end of the show. Based on an incident involving cast members that took place in a nearby coffee shop during the time that *The Connection* was in rehearsal, this three-act drama is set in a "restaurant or coffee shop." Like *The Connection*, *The Apple* has no formal beginning; there is no curtain, and the actors and actresses move from the audience to the stage and begin to deliver their lines. Similarly, throughout the performance, the actors remind the audience that they are watching a play: Anna announces that she is in charge of the box office; Jabez comments on "control," stating that "art is precision." Gelber purposely confuses and misleads his audience as to the significance of the play's title; the audience tries to determine how apples operate symbolically in the play, but the numerous clues that the dramatist presents appear to be unrelated. In act 1, Anna enters with a bowl of apples, and Iris starts to eat one (which Ajax takes from her); in act 2, Iris tells Jabez that she is his apple; in act 3, Tom pulls a rotten, half-eaten apple out of Jabez's mouth and throws it at the mannequin that has been onstage for most of the play. The characters talk about acting the Adam and Eve story, and Ace concludes the play with the revelation that the apple "is a golden Chinese apple and stands for knowledge." It is likely that this is, indeed, what Gelber means for the fruit to symbolize, and this makes some sense within the various contexts in which apples are represented, but ultimately, the play is so disjointed that it does not seem to matter whether any meaning can be affixed to or drawn from the apples. The multiple possibilities of interpretation engender confusion, to the point that the audience becomes bored rather than gaining any insight.

The premise for *The Apple* is simple, even though its realization is muddled. In a coffee shop during rehearsals for a play, one of the actors goes mad. In act 1, the audience observes the madman; in act 2, the presentation is from the point of view of the madman; and act 3 again puts the audience in the observing position, with Ace trying to tie everything together. Gelber has said that the title of the play originally referred to New York City, but "now I just say it's a satire on death." Perhaps the death of individuality, art, society, and intellectuality, killed by prejudice and lack of understanding and human sympathy, is implied in the play, but none of this holds together very well.

Gelber is to be admired for trying to extend the limits of theater even further than he did in *The Connection*, through a combination of straight dramatic techniques, Theater of the Absurd devices, mime, blackouts, parody, slapstick, and masks, with frequent outright social commentary and philosophizing about the nature of art and the artist. Unfortunately, *The Apple* has neither the intensity nor the underlying structural stability of *The Connection*, and ultimately it fails, both as an intellectual statement and as a piece of theater.

Gelber's next play, *Square in the Eye* (which originally had the working title "Let's Face It"), is more conventional and more successful, up to a point. The play covers a multitude of subjects: life, death, sex, art, and relationships between husbands and wives, friends, lovers, parents and children, and teachers and students. It begins with traditional dramatic exposition, in which Ed tells the audience about his life, family, and work, but the exposition is delivered in an unconventional manner, because the actor enters from the auditorium and delivers his speech like a stand-up comedian. There are devices throughout the play that are reminiscent of experimental techniques used by Bertolt Brecht, Thornton Wilder, and Tennessee Williams—movies, still photographs, and so on.

Gelber has called *Square in the Eye* "a tale and instant replay, about art and artists, marriage and death." To make his point, the dramatist uses flashbacks, a technique that presents the plot out of chronological order. Scene 1 of act 1 takes place before Sandy's death, scene 2 is in the hospital immediately after her death, and scene 3 records Ed's second marriage, six weeks later. Scene 1 of act 2 flashes back to a time before Sandy's death, and scene 2 occurs on the day before her death. This play contains more humor than does Gelber's earlier work, and despite occasional confusion because of flashbacks, the narrative is basically straightforward. Unlike *The Apple*, *Square in the Eye* is about real people with whom an audience can sympathize, although some of the techniques used in it can be disturbing.

Some critics claim that Gelber's next work, *The Cuban Thing*, is not really a play but a political "happening." The production shows the effects of Castro's revolution on an upper-middle-class Cuban family from 1958 to 1964, as their alliance changes from Fulgencio Batista to Castro. On the night before the actual premiere of the play, the fifth of a series of preview performances was marred by the explosion of five powder bombs. The play was considered pro-Castro by many, and poor reviews, claims that the dramatist had researched his material poorly, threats to the actors, active opposition by Spanish-language television and newspapers, and audience fears about physical violence led to the drama's closing after a run of only one night. An example of the "theater of commitment" or the "theater of revolution," *The Cuban Thing* was presented as a happening, a free-form event popular in the early and mid-1960's. As part of a Cuban Action Night, the play was mounted during an evening of Cuban music, Cuban food, and various other activities centering on all aspects of Cuban culture (including politics). By all accounts, however, *The Cuban Thing* was antitheater at its worst—bad writing that could not be salvaged by Gelber's own directing.

Square in the Eye was written during the playwright's first term as a Guggenheim fellow; *Sleep* was written while the playwright held a Rockefeller Foundation grant as playwright-in-residence at the American Place Theatre. Like *Square in the Eye*, *Sleep* is more conventional in form and content than those works that immediately preceded it. The play revolves around experiments into the nature of sleep conducted by two scientists, and one of the subjects of their experimentation, a young man named Gil. The play features a simple plot line and a good deal of humor as well as commentary on mind control (supposedly induced by means of sleep deprivation) and the role of the scientist in society. There are also dream sequences (the play-within-a-play technique) simulated within the framework of the experiment; several of the sequences bear some resemblance to *Interview* (pr. 1964), a revue sketch by Harold Pinter. For the first time, Gelber focuses on character rather than on events or abstract concepts, an extension of certain lines begun in *Square in the Eye*. In his novel *On Ice*, Gelber's protagonist has dreams that sometimes prove to be realities. In *Sleep*, Gil's dreams may not be identical to reality, but they reflect his reality outside the sleep laboratory more accurately than he perceives the reality that he experiences within the lab. Replacing the blackouts used to separate sketches in *The Apple* (particularly in act 2, the madman's act) are interruptions by the scientists as they check their subject between dream sequences. To some extent, the theme of appearance versus reality runs through all of Gelber's works, but in *Square in the Eye* it is dealt with on a conscious level and in an imaginative though relatively traditional way. The result is one of his most conventional and, ironically, most successful works.

Jack Gelber's New Play: Rehearsal depicts the casting, rehearsal, and, finally, the cancellation of a play about prison life (the stage author and one of the actors are convicts). Whereas *Sleep* was patently not about art and the theater, this play's subject is expressly the theater. The convicts are present merely as theatrical counters, not to provide a means to comment on convicts and prison life.

Like John Osborne, Gelber burst on the theatrical scene with a startling, innovative first play. In the twenty-some years since then, he has not written a great deal, and he has suffered several failures. He has also constantly tried to expand theatrical boundaries, and even his failures in this area have been important. When he has been successful, he has altered the nature of contemporary American drama.

Other major works
NOVEL: *On Ice*, 1964.
SCREENPLAY: *The Connection*, 1962.
TRANSLATION: *Farmyard*, 1976 (with Michael Roloff; of Francis Xavier Kroetz's play *Stallerhof*).

Bibliography
"American Playwrights of the Seventies: Some Problems and Perspectives," in *Theatre Quarterly*. VIII (Spring, 1978), pp. 45-50.
Bermel, Albert. "Jack Gelber Talks About Survival in the Theatre," in *Theatre*. IX (Spring, 1978), pp. 46-58.
Biner, Pierre. *The Living Theatre*, 1972.
Brustein, Robert. *Seasons of Discontent: Dramatic Opinions 1959-1965*, 1964.
_____. *The Theatre of Revolt*, 1964.
Burns, Elizabeth. *Theatricality*, 1972.
Driver, Tom F. *History of the Modern Theatre: Romantic Quest and Modern Query*, 1970.
Esslin, Martin. *The Theatre of the Absurd*, 1961, 1969.
Gilman, Richard. *Common and Uncommon Mask*, 1971.
_____. "Introduction," in Gelber's *The Apple and Square in the Eye*, 1974.
Gussow, Mel. "Talk with the Author," in *Newsweek*. LVIII (December 18, 1961), p. 72.
Kostelanetz, Richard. *The Theatre of Mixed Means*, 1968, 1971.
Little, Stuart. *Off Broadway*, 1972.
Taylor, Karen. *People's Theatre in Amerika*, 1973.
Tynan, Kenneth. *Tynan: Right and Left*, 1968.

Wellworth, George E. *The Theatre of Protest and Paradox: Developments in the Avant-Garde Drama*, 1964, 1971.
Wilcox, Agnes. "Jack Gelber," in *Dictionary of Literary Biography*, 1978.
"Young Playwright," in *The New Yorker*. XXXVI (July 9, 1960), pp. 24-25.

Steven H. Gale

WILLIAM GIBSON

Born: New York, New York; November 13, 1914

Principal drama

I Lay in Zion, pr. 1943, pb. 1947; *A Cry of Players*, pr. 1948, pb. 1969; *Dinny and the Witches: A Frolic on Grave Matters*, pr. 1948, pb. 1960; *The Ruby*, pb. 1955, pr. 1957 (libretto; as William Mass); *The Miracle Worker*, pr. 1957 (televised), pr. 1959 (staged), pb. 1959; *Two for the Seesaw*, pr. 1958, pb. 1959; *Golden Boy*, pr. 1964, pb. 1965 (musical; adaptation of Clifford Odets' play, music by Charles Stronse, lyrics by Lee Adams); *John and Abigail*, pr. 1969; *American Primitive*, pr. 1971, pb. 1972 (revision of *John and Abigail*); *The Body and the Wheel: A Play Made from the Gospels*, pr. 1974, pb. 1975; *The Butterfingers Angel, Mary and Joseph, Herod the Nut, and the Slaughter of Twelve Hit Carols in a Pear Tree*, pr. 1974, pb. 1975; *Golda*, pr. 1977, pb. 1978; *Goodly Creatures*, pr. 1980; *Monday After the Miracle*, pr. 1982, pb. 1984.

Other literary forms

Although William Gibson is primarily a dramatist, his initial successes were as a poet and novelist. His first book, *Winter Crook* (1948), is a collection of his early verse, which is marked by complex use of nature imagery and metaphor to explore highly personal concerns. His only novel, *The Cobweb* (1954), a best-seller, introduced many of the themes important in his drama: the isolation of the individual, the potentially redeeming capacity of love to form bonds, and the power of language to define the self and its world. Set in a mental institution, the novel explores the relationships that develop among the psychiatric staff, members of their families, and the patients. As the image of the cobweb suggests, these relationships, while not always healthy, connect the characters in complex ways.

Gibson has also written several nonfiction "chronicles." The first of these, *The Seesaw Log*, an account of the writing and producing of his first successful play *Two for the Seesaw*, was published in 1959 with the text of the play. By chronicling the complexities of producing a play in mid-century America, Gibson demonstrates that a play, unlike a poem or novel, is a collaborative effort that both tests and invigorates the playwright, who has to work with producer, director, and actors, all of whom can truthfully call the play theirs.

Gibson's second chronicle, *A Mass for the Dead* (1968), is one of his most moving works. A mixture of poetry and prose loosely organized along the lines of the Catholic Mass for the Dead, the book recounts the lives of members of Gibson's family, especially his grandparents and their relatives as well as his mother and father. The book is Gibson's attempt to make sense of his ancestors' lives, tracing their progress from working-class roots to middle-class respectability.

In *Shakespeare's Game* (1978), Gibson turns his attention to practical drama criticism and critical theory. The book grew out of his experience in teaching a university course on playwriting—an experience which forced him to review all the basics of drama. As a result, he developed a terminology with which to discuss the craft and art of playwriting, and in *Shakespeare's Game* Gibson applies this terminology to the work of the greatest English-language dramatist. At the book's end, Gibson reveals the essentially psychological nature of his theory of drama, which has its roots in cognitive psychology. A play's structure, Gibson argues, like the human mind, works to achieve equilibrium; when in the uncomfortable state of disequilibrium, the play moves toward an object that promises relief. This movement dashes against barriers that prevent the easy relief of tension in the play and its characters. Using this theory, Gibson demonstrates how a single structure underlies all of William Shakespeare's best plays.

Achievements

William Gibson will be remembered for his development of the popular biographical play; for his creation of strong women characters, many of whom have been portrayed by actress Anne Bancroft; and for his commentary on mid-century drama.

Gibson's most successful play, *The Miracle Worker*, was originally written for *Playhouse 90* and in 1957 won the Sylvania Award for the year's best television drama. This play pioneered the contemporary biographical drama. In it, Gibson exploited the dramatic qualities in Helen Keller's autobiography, centering on her discovery of the power of language under the tutelage of Annie Sullivan, a master teacher who transformed Keller from a wild animal into a human being. Part of the play's power derives from Gibson's ability to dramatize a historical event. Gibson continued developing this genre in later works, such as *American Primitive*, based on the letters of John and Abigail Adams, and *Golda*, based on the autobiography of Golda Meir, one of Israel's most famous prime ministers. While Gibson's subject matter in these plays is limited by his historical sources— in *American Primitive* the dialogue, except for some verse commentary that Gibson added, comes directly from the Adamses' letters—he uses modern stagecraft to make these lives significant.

Gibson will also be remembered for his creation of strong women characters in a period when such roles were the exception. In *Two for the Seesaw*, one of his most successful Broadway plays, the character of Gittel Mosca, the Jewish girl from the Bronx, overpowers that of Jerry Ryan, the lawyer from Nebraska. As Gibson recounts in *The Seesaw Log*, Henry

Fonda, who originally played Ryan, never felt comfortable in the role, partly because of Ryan's paleness compared to Gittel's fullness. *The Miracle Worker*, as well as its sequel, *Monday After the Miracle*, also developed strong women characters, as did *Golda*.

Finally, one of Gibson's most important contributions to the history of the theater is *The Seesaw Log*. By chronicling the composition and production of his play, he details how the mid-century American theater functioned, from the writing through the selling to the production of a Broadway play. Even though the chronicle is admittedly limited to Gibson's perspective, it re-creates for future audiences the texture and development of a work in progress as the producer, director, and actors, all with their own expertise, transform the playwright's initial creation into their own. Gibson has published other logs ("Preface: A Momento" with *Golden Boy* and "Notes on How to Turn a Phoenix into Ashes" with *Golda*), but none as detailed or as intriguing as *The Seesaw Log*.

Biography

William Gibson was born in New York on November 13, 1914, the son of lower-middle-class parents. The families of both parents were musical. Several of Gibson's maternal uncles belonged to the most famous banjo band of the early 1900's, and his mother's family operated a music school, where Gibson's mother had met his father, who was a talented popular pianist. Gibson himself mastered the piano and, in his late teens and early twenties, he tried to become a professional musician. This background explains his lifelong attraction to music, an interest reflected in his writing of pieces such as the libretto for the operetta *The Ruby* (which he wrote under the name of William Mass) and the text for the 1964 musical *Golden Boy*, a project that he finished for Clifford Odets, who died before it was completed.

Although Gibson was graduated at age sixteen from Townsend Harris Hall, a high school for academically talented boys that was affiliated with the City College of New York, he found college stultifying. He took his most rewarding classes at City College of New York from English professor Theodore Goodman, who encouraged his writing. After attending college sporadically for about two years, Gibson dropped out to educate himself, to become a musician, and to launch his writing career. During his years in college and immediately after, he became a Depression-era Communist and lectured on street corners to support this cause.

In 1940, Gibson married Margaret Brenman, a psychoanalyst, whom he had followed first to her graduate school and then to her psychiatric positions in Topeka, Kansas (where they married), and later in Stockbridge, Massachusetts. His first literary success came as a poet when a group of his poems published in *Poetry* won for him the 1945 Harriet Monroe Memorial

Prize. In 1954, he published a best-selling novel, *The Cobweb*, which he sold to Hollywood. The movie of the same name starred Lauren Bacall, Charles Boyer, and Richard Widmark and appeared in 1955 after Gibson helped rewrite the screenplay.

Gibson became interested in drama early in his career. After dropping out of college, he acted at the Barter Theatre in Abingdon, Virginia, where he wrote several unproduced plays. While in Topeka, Kansas, he acted in the community theater and wrote his first produced play, *I Lay in Zion*, which was staged at the Topeka Civic Theatre in 1943. His next play, *A Cry of Players*, a three-act drama about the young Shakespeare, won the Topeka Civic Theatre Award in 1947 and was staged in 1948. In the fall of 1950, Gibson met Clifford Odets, one of America's most important leftist playwrights, who admitted him to a playwright's seminar organized at the Actors' Studio. During this seminar, Gibson "learned more from him than I believed was possible from any man." After the course, while working at a psychiatric institution, Gibson directed Odets' *Rocket to the Moon* (pr. 1938) with a cast of mental patients. Odets saw this production and became a lifelong family friend.

Gibson's first national successes as a playwright were spectacular. In July of 1958, after an agonizing process (recounted in *The Seesaw Log*), *Two for the Seesaw*, which starred Henry Fonda and Anne Bancroft, opened at Broadway's Booth Theatre to enthusiastic reviews. The play ran for 750 performances and became one of the most successful plays of its era. It was also produced as a movie in 1962 starring Robert Mitchum and Shirley MacLaine. At about the same time, *The Miracle Worker*, which was originally written for television, became a Broadway hit in 1959, starring Anne Bancroft as Annie Sullivan and Patty Duke Astin as Helen Keller. These actresses re-created their roles in the popular 1962 film.

With the money he made selling *The Cobweb* to Hollywood, Gibson bought a house in Stockbridge, Massachusetts. In 1969, he cofounded and became the first executive officer of the Berkshire Theatre Festival in Stockbridge. There, *John and Abigail*, which he later revised as *American Primitive*, was first produced.

In 1971, Gibson almost died of a bleeding ulcer, an ailment from which he had suffered for years. This experience prompted him to reevaluate his life, and, during Christmas of 1972, he went to the Maharishi International University in La Antilla, Spain, to visit his son, who had enrolled in the University. There, Gibson studied under Maharishi Mahesh Yogi and was trained in the theory and practice of transcendental meditation. His interest in religion rekindled, he returned to the Catholic Church, in which he had been reared. He proceeded to write three liturgical dramas: *The Body and the Wheel*, a Passion play; *The Butterfingers Angel*, performed in Lennox, Massachusetts, in 1974; and *Goodly Creatures*, performed in 1980 at the

Roadhouse Theatre in Silver Spring, Maryland.

Two major Broadway plays by Gibson that have been neither as critically nor as financially successful as his earlier works are *Golda* and *Monday After the Miracle*. In 1977, *Golda* was plagued by problems and closed after several months. In 1982, a similar fate befell *Monday After the Miracle*, the sequel to *The Miracle Worker*.

Analysis

William Gibson's plays are marked by impressive literary as well as dramatic qualities. Like much contemporary drama, they deal with existential themes, particularly the social and psychological isolation of the individual. To explore these themes, Gibson uses a variety of approaches, including a mixture of comedic and serious elements and an array of innovative production techniques, most notably the split stage to emphasize the psychological isolation of characters. Despite his emphasis on themes of isolation and loneliness, Gibson is not ultimately pessimistic: He shows that love has the potential to unite lonely individuals and that language sheds light on the human condition. Indeed, the consistent weakness in his plays is his tendency toward the sentimental.

Gibson's first major Broadway play was *Two for the Seesaw*, produced in 1958 and directed by Arthur Penn. Set in New York City, the play explores the relationship between Jerry Ryan, a Nebraska lawyer who is being divorced by his wife, and Gittel Mosca, a Jewish girl from the Bronx. Although much of the play's humor results from the cultural differences between the characters, the true conflict grows from the contrasts in their psychological makeup. Because of this psychological emphasis, *Two for the Seesaw* shares more similarities with Gibson's novel, *The Cobweb*, than with his later biographical drama.

Gibson uses *Two for the Seesaw* to explore one of his most important themes, the isolation of the individual and the need people have for human contact. The stage setting emphasizes this by creating two spaces. One is Jerry's apartment, the other Gittel's. The lighting serves to isolate and emphasize one or the other, and the set registers the passing of time and changes in Jerry and Gittel's relationship. At the play's beginning, for example, Jerry's cheap apartment is bare and impoverished. As their relationship develops, the rooms begin to take on life because of Gittel's womanly touch. When Jerry moves into Gittel's apartment, his clothes and legal papers pile up in corners and on the table. Throughout much of the play, the two characters in their isolated areas are connected only by the telephone, which symbolizes the emotional distance between them.

The central problem of the play grows from the different needs that Gittel and Jerry have for each other, and this makes the play too clichéd to be completely successful. Gittel is a giving woman who allows herself to be used by men; Jerry, on the other hand, is used to taking from the people in his life. His career in Nebraska was successful largely because his father-in-law made him a law partner and bought him a fashionable home. Part of his reason for going to New York was his desire to escape from this kind of support. Because Gittel appears weak and vulnerable, she brings out in him for the first time the need to assist and care for others, and these nurturing feelings are intensified in Jerry when her stomach ulcer hemorrhages and he has to nurse her.

From the start, the play's problem is the unsympathetic nature of Jerry, which is heightened by the basic likability and charm of Gittel. Gibson's dialogue captures her character perfectly and infuses her with humor and spirit. Jerry, on the other hand, is too self-absorbed and self-centered to be likable. Henry Fonda, who originally played Jerry on Broadway, objected to the character's self-centered behavior, arguing that Gittel would have kicked him out rather than put up with his meanness. Although Fonda can be faulted for not understanding Jerry's psychological motivation—his attachment to his Nebraskan wife conflicts with his need for Gittel's support and love—Gibson was guilty of not infusing the male character with the lifelike qualities that Gittel possesses.

The play's ending exposes the imperfections of its characters and structure. Jerry decides to return to his wife, a wiser man because of Gittel's love. Although this desertion is believable, it makes Jerry distasteful, because it is clear that Gittel is left alone and pathetic. Gibson has her claim that she, too, has learned from the experience—she gives up her illusions of being a dancer, for example—but the audience has little hope that she will find a meaningful relationship. This bleak ending suggests that Gibson was uncertain whether *Two for the Seesaw* was to be comic or tragic, and the mixture of Gittel's comic antics and Jerry's morose irony further confuses the audience about the play's intentions.

Gibson's reputation rests on his second major Broadway play, *The Miracle Worker*, originally a television play. It opened on Broadway in 1959 under the direction of Arthur Penn and starring Anne Bancroft and Patty Duke. In 1962, after a long run, it was made into a United Artists motion picture starring Bancroft and Duke. Gibson's first major biographical play, *The Miracle Worker* is based on the lives of Helen Keller and her teacher, Anne Sullivan.

The characters and situation are perfect vehicles for two of Gibson's major themes, the isolation of the individual and the power of love to do good and harm. Because of Helen's afflictions—an early illness has left her blind and deaf—she has been cut off from all meaningful human contact. Because of her family's misguided love, she has been pampered and allowed to run wild like an untrained animal. It is only when Annie (as Sullivan is known in the play), herself partially blind, comes to live with the family and insists on disciplining Helen that progress is made.

Two major conflicts arise in the play. The first is between Helen and Annie. When forced to behave in a civilized manner, Helen rebels by attacking Annie, throwing food, and playing for sympathy from her parents Eradicating this behavior is Annie's first job. The second conflict is between Annie and Helen's parents, Captain and Kate Keller. Captain Keller is an Alabama autocrat who expects Annie, a young Bostonian, to obey without question. His major concern is that she control Helen rather than educate her. Kate Keller feels guilty for Helen's condition and pampers the child. Annie, on the other hand, is a forceful woman who has grown up in terrible circumstances. After her mother's early death and the desertion of her alcoholic father, she was reared in a Massachusetts almshouse and blinded by trachoma. By strength of character and determination, she talked her way into an expensive Boston school for the blind, where she underwent nine eye operations in six years. She consequently has little patience with the Kellers coddling Helen.

One of the central symbols of the play is the water pump that stands outside the Kellers' home. It is there, after months of work, that Annie manages to make Helen recognize the connection between words and things, when she signs the word "water" on the girl's palm as actual water flows across it. It is language that allows Helen to become fully human, and this development is Annie's major triumph in the play. By sticking with her demanding teaching methods, by insisting that Helen learn the importance of language despite her parents' conviction that their daughter could never do so, Annie becomes, in Gibson's eyes, the perfect teacher.

One important theme that the play does not handle well concerns Annie's reactions to Helen's miraculous progress. Because of her horrible childhood, Annie, Gibson implies, has not learned to love, only to fight. At the end of the play, when she clutches Helen to her and proclaims her love for the child, the audience is not prepared for such a transformation in character. The ending does not grow out of the play and seems added to give television viewers the warm glow they have come to expect.

Like many television dramas, *The Miracle Worker*'s answers to complex questions are too pat. At the play's end, all problems are resolved, even though in actuality Captain Keller later tried to charge the public an admission fee to view his "freakish" daughter. Nevertheless, the play remains a profound statement on the importance of faith and hard work and, in part for this reason, has become one of the twentieth century's best-known dramas.

Gibson takes up a darker strain in *Monday After the Miracle*, the sequel to *The Miracle Worker*. Unlike the earlier play, which is comic in structure because of its happy ending, *Monday After the Miracle* explores Annie's and Helen's personal discontentments as Helen becomes internationally famous, first as a writer and then as a lecturer. Gibson continues exploring the nature of love, but in this play he examines the gloomier side of that feeling.

The conflict in the play develops among its three major characters: Annie, Helen, and John Macy. When the play opens, Helen, now in her twenties, and Annie, now in her late thirties, have established a unique bond. As "Teacher," Annie has created Helen much as an artist creates a work of art. This project, her lifework, has both invigorated and limited her: She has functioned as Helen's eyes and ears for almost two decades. The love the two women feel for each other is powerful, but it also has become a burden on Annie, who now longs for freedom. Macy complicates matters when he completes the emotional triangle. He comes to help Helen write, and he edits her first major work, her autobiography (Keller published her autobiography, *The Story of My Life*, in 1902), which includes selections from Annie's letters describing her teaching techniques. Both Helen (who is closer to Macy's age) and Annie fall in love with him, and this competition tests the women's relationship.

When Macy falls in love with and marries Annie, other conflicts develop. First, Helen fears that Annie will desert her. This fear is confused by Helen's certainty that Macy had been falling in love with her, not the older Annie. Annie, on the other hand, must struggle with her feelings of guilt about letting someone other than Helen into her life; at the same time, she yearns for marriage, love, and children. After their marriage, Annie and Macy must resolve the conflicts that arise when he becomes sexually drawn to Helen. This situation develops not only because Macy and Helen live in the same household and work closely together but also because Macy feels neglected by his wife, whose major interest in life remains Helen. By the end of the play, Macy's character has disintegrated because of heavy drinking and his humiliating financial dependence on Helen's income from writing and speaking.

If *The Miracle Worker* glorifies the power of love to connect people, *Monday After the Miracle*, like *Two for the Seesaw*, exposes its power to harm and destroy people, especially those who are weak, such as Macy. The relationship between Annie and Helen survives all the pain and conflict, but that between Macy and Annie does not. Indeed, the failure of the marriage results in part from the intensity of Annie and Helen's love, which began with Annie's need to mold Helen into a full human being and which has become, for better or worse, the central passion of Annie's life.

Gibson is a popular Broadway playwright whose considerable dramatic talent allows him to fuse comic and tragic elements in a satisfying whole. While not always complete artistic and formal successes, his plays explore significant aspects of the human condition, especially the dangers and joys of love and the need humans have to connect with their fellows.

Other major works

NOVEL: *The Cobweb*, 1954.

POETRY: *Winter Crook*, 1948.

NONFICTION: *The Seesaw Log*, 1959; *A Mass for the Dead*, 1968; *A Season in Heaven*, 1974; *Shakespeare's Game*, 1978.

SCREENPLAY: *The Cobweb*, 1954 (based on his novel).

Bibliography

Coy, Stephen C. "William Gibson," in *Dictionary of Literary Biography, Volume VII: Twentieth Century American Dramatists, Part 1*, 1981.

Current Biography Yearbook, 1983.

Moe, Christian H. "William Gibson," in *Contemporary Dramatists*, 1977, 1982. Edited by James Vinson.

"On the Seesaw," in *The New Yorker*. XXXIII (February 15, 1958), pp. 23-24.

Michael G. Moran

W. S. GILBERT

Born: London, England; November 18, 1836
Died: Harrow Weald, England; May 29, 1911

Principal drama

Ruy Blas, pb. 1866 (in *Warne's Christmas Annual*); *Dulcamara: Or, The Little Duck and the Great Quack*, pr., pb. 1866 (based on Gaetano Donizetti's opera *L'elisir d'amore*); *Allow Me to Explain*, pr. 1867; *Highly Improbable*, pr. 1867; *Harlequin Cock Robin and Jenny Wren: Or, Fortunatus and the Water of Life, the Three Bears, the Three Gifts, the Three Wishes, and the Little Man Who Woo'd the Little Maid*, pr., pb. 1867; *The Merry Zingara: Or, The Tipsy Gipsy and the Pipsy Wipsy*, pr., pb. 1868; *Robert the Devil: Or, The Nun, the Dun and the Son of a Gun*, pr., pb. 1868; *No Cards*, pr. 1869, pb. 1901 (libretto; music by Lionel Elliott); *The Pretty Druidess: Or, The Mother, the Maid and the Mistletoe Bough*, pr., pb. 1869; *An Old Score*, pr., pb. 1869; *Ages Ago: A Ghost Story*, pr., pb. 1869 (libretto; music by Frederick Clay); *The Princess*, pr., pb. 1870; *The Gentleman in Black*, pr. 1870 (libretto; music by Frederick Clay); *The Palace of Truth*, pr., pb. 1870; *A Medical Man*, pb. 1870, pr. 1872; *Randall's Thumb*, pr. 1871, pb. 1872; *A Sensation Novel*, pr. 1871, pb. 1912 (libretto; music by Florian Pascal); *Pygmalion and Galatea*, pr. 1871, pb. 1872; *Thespis: Or, The Gods Grown Old*, pr., pb. 1871 (libretto; music by Sir Arthur Sullivan); *The Brigands*, pb. 1871, pr. 1889 (libretto; music by Jacques Offenbach); *On Guard*, pr., pb. 1872; *Happy Arcadia*, pr., pb. 1872 (libretto; music by Frederick Clay); *The Wicked World*, pr., pb. 1873; *The Happy Land*, pr., pb. 1873 (with Gilbert à Beckett); *The Realm of Joy*, pr. 1873; *The Wedding March*, pr. 1873, pb. 1879 (adaptation of Eugène Labiche's *Le Chapeau de paille d'Italie*); *Charity*, pr. 1874; *Ought We to Visit Her?*, pr. 1874 (with Annie Edwards); *Committed for Trial*, pr. 1874, pb. 1930 (adaptation of Henri Meilhac and Ludovic Halévy's *Le Réveillon*, later revised as *On Bail*); *Topsy Turveydom*, pr. 1874, pb. 1931; *Sweethearts*, pr. 1874, pb. 1878; *Trial by Jury*, pr., pb. 1875 (libretto; music by Sullivan); *Tom Cobb: Or, Fortune's Toy*, pr. 1875, pb. 1880; *Eyes and No Eyes: Or, The Art of Seeing*, pr. 1875, pb. 1896 (libretto; music by Pascal); *Broken Hearts*, pr. 1875, pb. 1881; *Princess Toto*, pr., pb. 1876 (libretto; music by Frederick Clay); *Dan'l Bruce, Blacksmith*, pr., pb. 1876; *Original Plays*, 1876-1911 (4 volumes); *On Bail*, pr. 1877, pb. 1881 (revision of *Committed for Trial*); *Engaged*, pr., pb. 1877; *The Sorcerer*, pr., pb. 1877 (libretto; music by Sullivan); *The Ne'er-do-Weel*, pr., pb. 1878; *H.M.S. Pinafore: Or, The Lass That Loved a Sailor*, pr., pb. 1878 (libretto; music by Sullivan); *Gretchen*, pr., pb. 1879; *The Pirates of Penzance: Or, The Slave of Duty*, pr. 1879, pb. 1880 (libretto; music by Sullivan); *Patience: Or,*

Bunthorne's Bride, pr., pb. 1881 (libretto; music by Sullivan); *Foggerty's Fairy*, pr., pb. 1881; *Iolanthe: Or, The Peer and the Peri*, pr., pb. 1882 (libretto; music by Sullivan); *Comedy and Tragedy*, pr. 1884, pb. 1896; *Princess Ida: Or, Castle Adamant*, pr., pb. 1884 (libretto; music by Sullivan); *The Mikado: Or, The Town of Titipu*, pr., pb. 1885 (libretto; music by Sullivan); *Ruddigore: Or, The Witch's Curse*, pr., pb. 1887 (libretto; music by Sullivan); *The Yeomen of the Guard: Or, The Merryman and His Maid*, pr., pb. 1888 (libretto; music by Sullivan); *Brantinghame Hall*, pr., pb. 1888; *The Gondoliers: Or, The King of Barataria*, pr., pb. 1889 (libretto; music by Sullivan); *Rosencrantz and Guildenstern*, pr. 1891, pb. 1893; *The Mountebanks*, pr., pb. 1892 (libretto; music by Alfred Cellier); *Haste to the Wedding*, pr., pb. 1892 (libretto; music by George Grossmith); *Utopia, Limited: Or, The Flowers of Progress*, pr., pb. 1893 (libretto; music by Sullivan); *His Excellency*, pr., pb. 1894 (libretto; music by Osmond Carr); *The Grand Duke: Or, The Statutory Duel*, pr., pb. 1896 (libretto; music by Sullivan); *The Fortune Hunter*, pr., pb. 1897; *Fallen Fairies*, pr., pb. 1909 (with Edward German); *The Hooligan*, pr., pb. 1911; *Gilbert Before Sullivan: Six Comic Plays*, 1967 (Jane Stedman, editor).

Other literary forms

Apart from his writing for the theater, W. S. Gilbert's principal literary accomplishment is *The Bab Ballads* (1869), whimsical verses which he illustrated himself. Originally published in comic journals such as *Fun* and *Punch*, they are generally regarded as the well from which Gilbert drew many of the songs and situations of his comic operas.

Achievements

The comic operas of W. S. Gilbert and Sir Arthur Sullivan are the product of one of the most successful collaborations in theatrical history, for while other teams of librettist and composer have achieved comparable distinction, in no other pair have the talents so complemented each other. Both chafed at the fact that their more serious accomplishments were less well regarded, and both tried, without great success, to work with other collaborators. Gilbert's whimsy and legalistic paradoxes would have been little more than quaint if they had not been humanized by Sullivan's melodies, and Sullivan's choral and orchestral virtuosity and his propensity to parody found their focus in Gilbert's preposterous plots. Their initial collaborations took place over a span of six years, during which they were engaged in other artistic enterprises as well. With the composition of *H.M.S. Pinafore*, however, they began a decade of enormous popularity, with virtually one new opera a year, each with a measure of uniqueness yet all derived from a recognizable formula. Although the later operas are somewhat more musically complex and more extravagantly plotted, these advances are less the consequence of artistic maturity than of technical confidence. Gilbert's not too serious social criticism, his tongue-twisting lyrics, and his gentle spoofs of romantic conventions appealed to a middle-class audience that had only recently been persuaded that the theater might be a respectable institution after all. The two operas Gilbert and Sullivan produced after the great breach that lasted from 1889 to 1893 are not sufficiently inferior to the others as to account for their unpopularity. The vogue of Gilbert and Sullivan had not ended, for the earlier operas continued to be revived. It is more likely that the collaborators had produced enough operas to keep their public happy. For almost a century, these operas have remained favorites on both sides of the Atlantic, kept alive largely by the D'Oyly Carte Opera Company, holders of the copyright, from whose elaborately stylized and insistently Victorian productions other professional and amateur renditions have been derived. Although changes in the company's finances forced its closure in 1982, interest in the operas was not noticeably diminished, with both Joseph Papp's 1980 revival and the 1983 film version of *The Pirates of Penzance* being well received.

Biography

William Schwenck Gilbert was born at 17 Southampton Street, Strand, London, on November 18, 1836, the son of a fairly well-to-do naval surgeon, who turned to a literary career at about the same time as young William did. At the age of two, while on holiday with his parents in Italy, Gilbert was kidnaped from his nurse and ransomed for twenty-five pounds. He later claimed to have a perfect recollection of the incident. At any rate, his plots frequently hinge on the removal of infants from their real parents.

Educated at Boulogne, France, and Great Ealing School, he then attended King's College, London, hoping to obtain a commission in the Royal Artillery. The sudden end of the Crimean War made a military career less appealing, and he obtained, by competitive examination, a clerkship in the Education Department of the Privy Council Office, a post he occupied from 1857 to 1862. Coming into an unexpected sum of money, Gilbert was able to free himself from that "ill-organised and ill-governed office." Having already entered the Inner Temple, Gilbert was called to the Bar in 1863. He did not thrive as a barrister, however, earning no more than seventy-five pounds in his first two years of practice. He never wholly abandoned either his military or his legal aspirations, for he held a commission in the Fifth West Yorkshire Militia, the Royal Aberdeen Highlanders, and, from 1893, was a justice of the peace for the county of Middlesex.

Gilbert's career as a writer had been launched as early as 1857, when he accepted a commission to translate a French song for a theater program. His first play to be produced, *Dulcamara*, a travesty based on Gaetano Donizetti's opera *L'elisir d'amore* (1832), was followed in succeeding years by similar treatments of operas by Donizetti, Vincenzo Bellini, Giacomo Meyerbeer, and others. In 1867, Gilbert was confident enough of his abilities to marry Lucy Blois Turner, a woman fourteen years his junior. Despite the example of the tempestuous marriage of Gilberts' parents, his own irascibility, and his almost total absorption in his work, the union appears to have been a happy one. The 1860's were also the years of the composition of *The Bab Ballads*. In 1869, he became a contributor of short comic plays for the German Reeds' Gallery of Illustration, which provided a kind of family entertainment mixing song with improbable fable, presented without the elaborate trappings of the stage. He also began writing full-length comedies, such as *The Palace of Truth*, *Pygmalion and Galatea*, and *Broken Hearts*, whose plots involve the intervention of fairies or other supernatural agencies in human affairs.

The first meeting of Gilbert and Sullivan took place at the Gallery of Illustration and was brought about through a common friend. Though each knew the work of the other, it was another two years before Gilbert proposed that Sullivan set to music the draft of *Thespis* (the musical score has since been lost). Neither appears to have taken this first collaboration very seriously, and four years were to elapse before they worked together on another opera, a curtain raiser prodded into being by Richard D'Oyly Carte, then the manager of the Royalty Theatre, in the Soho district of London. The extraordinary success of this piece, *Trial by Jury*, prompted D'Oyly Carte to lease the Opéra Comique as the home of the Comedy Opera Company and to commission Gilbert and Sullivan to write a third opera, *The Sorcerer*.

One success followed another. To frustrate theatrical piracy, a continuing problem as the popularity of their work increased, the premiere of *The Pirates of Penzance* took place in New York. By 1881, the trio of Gilbert, Sullivan, and D'Oyly Carte had opened their own theater, the Savoy, the first in the world to be illuminated by electric light. All of their subsequent operas were produced here. That two men so temperamentally different— Gilbert, robust and litigious, and Sullivan, frail and affable—should have collaborated at all is more remarkable than that their association became strained during the decade of their greatest artistic and commercial success. Each considered that he was being asked to yield too much to the other. These differences were precipitated by the famous "carpet breach." Believing that D'Oyly Carte had wrongly charged the theater's new carpeting as a cost of production of *The Gondoliers*, rather than as one of building maintenance, and that Sullivan and he were thereby aggrieved, Gilbert insisted on an immediate renegotiation of the agreement among them. When D'Oyly Carte demurred and Sullivan proved insufficiently vigorous in his support of Gilbert's demands, Gilbert became furious and actually took legal action against both of them. Although a compromise was eventually worked out, and two more operas followed the reconciliation, the heyday of the team of Gilbert and Sullivan was over.

Gilbert continued to be active with other collaborators in the 1890's, and he reverted as well to the fairy comedies of his pre-Sullivan days. Gout and other ailments, however, compelled him to lead a life of greater retirement. In 1907, some twenty-four years after Sullivan had received a similar honor, Gilbert was knighted for services to the theater—as a playwright rather than with the more prestigious designation he had craved, that of dramatist. Though rancor figured significantly in Gilbert's life, his death was gallant. Diving to rescue a young woman swimming in the lake on his estate, Sir William suffered a fatal heart attack on May 29, 1911.

Analysis

W. S. Gilbert has occasionally been called "the English Aristophanes"; however extravagant that designation, it may serve as a useful point of departure. Assuredly Aristophanic is Gilbert's capacity to create in his plays worlds in which recognizable institutions—the legal system, the military, the rigid caste system of Victorian society—are transformed into absurdities. In *Trial by Jury*, the legal wrangling between the counsels of the jilted Angelina and the flirtatious defendant are resolved by the judgment of the judge—to marry Angelina himself. In *The Pirates of Penzance*, a pirate must first serve an apprenticeship, as though he were an artisan or skilled mechanic; furthermore, the pirate gang is pardoned of all of their offenses because "they are all noblemen who have gone wrong." Also Aristophanic, though functioning in a different way, to be sure, are Gilbert's choruses—the sisters, cousins, and aunts of Sir Joseph Porter in *H.M.S. Pinafore*, the giggling schoolgirls of *The Mikado*, or the professional bridesmaids in *Ruddigore*—which serve to accentuate the ludicrousness of the situations.

The essential distinction, however, between the absurdities of Aristophanes and those of Gilbert is that for the Greek dramatist, the source of the comedy lay in some social or political aberration that he meant to expose, if not to correct. For Gilbert, on the other hand, though his plays are not devoid of social or political implications, the source of the comedy lies in the pursuit of some intellectual crotchet or paradox to its ultimate conclusion. The topsy-turviness of Gilbert's plays originates in legalisms and logic-chopping. As a slave of duty, Frederic, the hero of *The Pirates of Penzance*, feels that he cannot betray his pirate comrades, loathsome though their trade is to him, until he is discharged of his indentures on his twenty-first birthday. Having been born on the last day of February in a leap year, however, he discovers that he is, in terms of birthdays celebrated, only a little boy of five. Similarly, through an ancestral curse, each baronet of Ruddigore must commit a crime daily or perish in unutterable agony. Failure to commit a crime is thus tantamount to committing suicide, which is itself a crime. Not only are the dilemmas of the characters resolved by similar sophistry, but also it appears that the complications have been conceived with no other purpose in mind.

One Gilbert and Sullivan work that does not quite fit this description is *Princess Ida*. This opera, however, is essentially a reworking of an earlier Gilbert play, *The Princess*, a "respectful perversion" of Alfred, Lord Tennyson's poem of same name (1847), that odd composition whose central subject is the education of women. Even here, however, Gilbert treats the topic not as a timely social issue but as an occasion to explore the comic implications of the attempted isolation of one sex from the other. To say that Gilbert's plays take place in artificial environments hardly accounts for the intense intellectual pressure that has gone into their formation. The clash between the fairies and noblemen in *Iolanthe*, for example, originates in the play on the words "peri" and "peer." The officers of the dragoon guards in *Patience* readily abandon their military garb and their military bearing to become aesthetic poets, because only in that guise can they successfully woo the chorus of rapturous maidens.

Each opera enunciates a topsy-turvy premise, which is then examined. In *H.M.S. Pinafore*, it is the notion that "love can level ranks"; in *Patience*, it is that true love is disinterested; and in *Iolanthe*, it is that a race of immortal and insubstantial beings can exhibit all the characteristics of human beings. All of these, it should be noted, are romantic notions derived very largely from literature. Gilbert's fancies are drawn as well from some of his own early works, particularly his parodies and *The Bab Ballads*. Very little seems to come from direct observation of life or reflection on personal experience, except for the minutiae, the little personal quirks and foibles that make a caricature. The result is a series of plays often quite rich in references or allusions to contemporary life but as remote from that life as animated cartoons are from the life of animals. The characters and plots have been reduced to formula.

Although some of the variations on them are quite subtle, the character-types encountered in Gilbert's plays are almost as rigid as those in classical New Comedy. In addition to the fresh and innocent heroine and her equally ingenuous hero, there is the fastidious and querulous authoritarian (who usually gets to sing the patter song)—Sir Joseph in *H.M.S. Pinafore*, Major-General Stanley in *The Pirates of Penzance*, the Lord Chancellor in *Iolanthe*, King Gama in *Princess Ida*, Ko-Ko in *The Mikado*, and the Duke of Plaza Toro in *The Gondoliers*—as well as the elderly, decayed contralto, who is physically repulsive yet longing for affection—Buttercup in *H.M.S. Pinafore*, Ruth in *The Pirates of Penzance*, Lady Jane in *Patience*, Katisha in *The Mikado*, Dame Carruthers in *The Yeomen of the Guard*, and the Duchess in *The Gondoliers*. The easy classification of roles in these operas makes them particularly attractive to repertory companies.

For all the variety of locales in Gilbert's works, the most frequent form of action involves what has been called the invasion plot. That is, the territory of a more or less settled group is overrun by another, the situation demanding some kind of compromise, if not retreat. Sir Joseph Porter and his female relations board H.M.S *Pinafore*; Major-General Stanley's daughters innocently decide to picnic in the pirates' lair; the procession of peers invades the Arcadian landscape in act 1 of *Iolanthe*, only to have the fairies troop in force to Westminster in act 2. There is actual combat between military units in *Princess Ida*, and in *The Mikado*, the imperial retinue sweeps into Titipu, demanding of its inhabitants the appearance of conformity to decrees from on high.

This reduction of character and plot to a formula, although it is more commercially palatable (thanks to Sullivan's music) than the insipid paradoxes of Gilbert's earlier straight plays, does not initially seem conducive to the generation of enduring art. Yet in at least two ways, it has secured Gilbert's place in the theater, even if not as a dramaturge. First, it provided a vehicle for some of the most versatile metrical and verbal extravagances in the English language. As a lyricist, Gilbert is unsurpassed in his ability to provide both singable *and* memorable words not only to arias, ballads, duets, and choruses but also to part-songs of considerable complexity and to patter songs for single and multiple voices. (Patter songs, which sound like tongue twisters sung at top speed, include "I am the very model of a modern Major-General," from *The Pirates of Penzance*.) The challenge produced the tuneful and rollicking songs familiar to almost everyone, such as "Faint Heart Never Won Fair Lady," from *Iolanthe*, or "For He Is an Englishman," from *H.M.S. Pinafore*. Yet it also produced tender and haunting songs, such as Ko-Ko's "The Titwillow Song" in *The Mikado* (which must surely have originated as a parody of Desdemona's "Willow Song" in William Shakespeare's *Othello*) and Jack Point's "I Have a Song to Sing, O" in *The Yeomen of the Guard*.

Moreover, it is in these lyrics, rather than in the large themes or preposterous situations of the operas, that Gilbert executes his greatest satiric thrusts. On the whole, like the audience for whom he wrote, Gilbert felt enormously pleased with the general state of things in the world around him and was vexed only by ideas, such as socialism or evolution, that threatened to rend society or by fads, such as aestheticism, that tended to distract it. Yet for all his conservatism, he did not wholly succumb to philistine complacency. In his songs, he frequently targets time-honored objects of satire: the abuse of privilege, the vanity in pride of ancestry, or the posturings of the *nouveau riche*. At the beginning of the second act of *The Mikado*, for example, Yum-Yum is adorning herself in preparation for her wedding day. She sings a song ingenuously identifying her with the world of nature, a song whose operation, like that of Alexander Pope's description of Belinda at the beginning of *The Rape of the Lock*, simultaneously elicits wonder and censure at the fair creature. As in this song, Gilbert's satire is often ironically self-deprecating, requiring a good deal of attention to be understood.

This demand for attentiveness constitutes Gilbert's second significant contribution to the English theater. He educated a generation of middle-class theatergoers to listen carefully to what was being said onstage and to expect paradox at every turn. Though himself unwilling or unable to use the stage for serious mockery of social institutions, he made it possible for others to do so. He prepared audiences to receive the witty comedies of Oscar Wilde and the more intellectually provocative plays of George Bernard Shaw.

Trial by Jury demonstrated that Gilbertian humor could successfully be translated to the operatic stage; *The Sorcerer*, that Sullivan could actually compose for Gilbert. In *H.M.S. Pinafore*, the collaboration attained its full flowering. The first and least complicated of their more popular operas, it is also the most familiar. The plot hinges on two threadbare conventions of comedy, a pair of lovers whose union is thwarted by their being of different social classes and a pair of babies, also of different classes, who have been switched in infancy. The discovery of the second circumstance conveniently resolves the difficulty of the first. Gilbert apparently believed in a fluid class structure: Josephine may marry up (although not too far up) but not down the social ladder, and Sir Joseph Porter, while his rise from office boy to First Lord of the Admiralty is a source of some amusement, is not repudiated, either as a cad or as a snob, for rejecting Josephine when she proves to be the daughter of a common seaman. His behavior is seen as quite understandable and serves to refute the absurd egalitarian sentiments he has uttered earlier, sentiments overwhelmed by the jingoistic sailors' chorus and glee. As is usual in Gilbert, the satire against the ruling class is mild. It manifests itself through the self-revelation of an authority figure who is on the whole rather likable, however pompous. In the final analysis, such satire is seen as secondary to the larger purpose of amusement. Sir Joseph and his retinue of sisters, cousins, and aunts are there to provide a complication and a chorus.

The Pirates of Penzance is, as many have observed, *H.M.S. Pinafore* brought to land. All the color of the nautical talk and the costuming has been preserved in the pirates, the female chorus of Sir Joseph's relations has become that of Major-General Stanley's daughters, and there is even an additional male chorus of policemen. Buttercup, who had been responsible for the mixup of babies in *H.M.S. Pinafore*, has metamorphosed into Ruth, whose blunder is to confuse words, apprenticing the young Frederic to a pirate instead of a pilot. There are distant echoes here of Shakespeare's *The Tempest* as Frederic, who has grown up knowing no women other than his nurse, Ruth, discovers the true nature of female beauty in Mabel. The complication is that, as a pirate, he is a sworn foe of legitimate authority, as represented by Mabel's father. Once again, the comic resolution undercuts any serious social criticism: Because they are really renegade noblemen, who owe fealty to Queen Victoria, the pirates surrender in her name and become suitable mates for the Major-General's daughters. There is far less occasion for criticism of social institutions in this opera, however, than in *H.M.S. Pinafore*. Rather, Gilbert takes delight in puncturing romantic myths. Instead of a band of lawless Byronic outcasts, Gilbert's pirates are a guild of credulous, tenderhearted incompetents, whose evil purposes dissolve at once if their intended victim claims to be an orphan (a weakness that Major-General Stanley is quick to exploit). Their antagonists, the local constabulary, prove to be as unheroic as the pirates are unvillainous. Major-General Stanley, like Sir Joseph Porter, is a mere functionary. In the modern world, Gilbert seems to be saying, romantic idealization is no longer tenable, and the conflict between good and evil dwindles into banality.

Although *Patience* appears to be one of the most topical of Gilbert's works, taking aim at the whole Aesthetic movement, the play's origins belie that contention. The central situation derives from "The Rival Curates," one of *The Bab Ballads*, in which two provincial clergymen compete for a title in abnegation or, in Gilbert's term, "mildness." Unlike the opera, the twenty-three-stanza ballad presents no motive for the eccentricity beyond that of a desire for reputation. The essential topsy-turvy premise of the opera, then, is that an affected mannerism extended to one's whole demeanor will excite admiration. Gilbert confessed that he had difficulty sustaining the conceit through the two acts of the opera without falling into bad taste or blasphemy, and this may account for the transformation of the rival curates into poets. The emergence of the young Oscar Wilde as a flamboyant exponent of Aestheticism made him appear to be a perfect prototype of Bunthorne, the fleshly poet, an association that proved profitable both for Wilde and the three partners of the D'Oyly Carte Opera Company. Love interest in the opera is supplied by Patience, a dairymaid sensible enough not to be attracted by bizarre behavior yet sufficiently innocent of passion to believe that love must be totally disinterested. It is through the characterizations of the fleshly and idyllic poets, however, that *Patience* achieved its popularity and has maintained its interest. Gilbert's attack was timely, to be sure, but somewhat off the mark. The eccentricity and languor of his poets are fair enough targets of satire, but he invests them as well with a kind of puritanism more appropriate to his curates. Elsewhere, Gilbert administers occasional mild jolts to middle-class complacency; in *Patience*, however, by portraying his poets not merely as fools but also as conscious hypocrites, he panders to philistine anti-intellectualism.

Iolanthe brings together the world of Gilbert's earlier fairy plays and the world of reality, particularly legal and political reality. As in *The Pirates of Penzance*, Gilbert insists upon looking at romantic matter in a matter-of-fact way. Like the Greek satirist Lucian, Gilbert endows his supernatural creatures not only with immortality, discretionary corporeality, and magical powers, but also with human emotions. The opening chorus of dancing fairies complains of boredom since the exile of Iolanthe for having married a mortal (Iolanthe is subsequently forgiven). The offspring of that union, the shepherd Strephon (a fairy from the waist up), is in love with Phyllis, the ward of the Lord Chancellor, who intends to marry her himself. Needless to say, both the young and the middle-aged lovers are properly sorted out by the end of the opera, but not before several clashes have taken place between the romantic and pragmatic worlds. Phyllis, seeing Strephon in the company of his very youthful-looking mother, is driven to jealousy; he, backed by the powerful influence of the fairies, takes over Parliament, where he proceeds to confound the whole political system by instituting competitive examinations for admission to the peerage and by eliciting assent to all of his proposals. *Iolanthe* is quite remarkable for the good-naturedness of its critical observations on parliamentary democracy. At the beginning of act 2, Private Willis' song ponders the division of people into parties, by which they relinquish their private intellects and submit to the discipline of a leader upon entering the House of Commons. Two songs later, Lord Mountararat extols the House of Lords for doing precisely nothing and doing it "very well": Britain's glory is contingent upon the assurance that "noble statesmen do not itch/ To interfere with matters which/ They do not understand." Taken together, the two songs seem to express Gilbert's belief that, however riddled with anomalies, the British system of government works very well indeed.

The Mikado signaled a change of direction for Gilbert and Sullivan. With the exception of *Thespis*, whose setting is Olympus, and *Princess Ida*, which, like Tennyson's poem, is laid in a legendary atmosphere, all of their operas up to *The Mikado* had been contemporary. However outlandish the premises or exaggerated the manners, they could be seen as obvious extrapolations of the familiar. Whether Gilbert felt that he had exhausted this vein or whether the possibility for more elaborate productions was the inducement, *The Mikado* initiated a movement away from the familiar. Though topical allusions abound, the last six operas all take place either in a locale definitely not English or at a time decidedly not the present. They are also characterized by more complicated plots. The simple invasion formula gives way to more intricate maneuverings, and the songs are made to carry a greater burden of exposition and development. Though *The Mikado* may be no less popular than *H.M.S. Pinafore* or *The Pirates of Penzance*, it is more difficult to unravel and its satire is more oblique. Most obviously, in its portrayal of excessive ceremony and politeness masking bloodthirstiness and tyranny, *The Mikado* sardonically congratulates Englishmen for choosing not to belong to any other nation and laughs at the Victorian fascination for things Oriental. It is equally obvious, however, that Gilbert's Japanese have no more authenticity than his fairies: The opening choruses of *Iolanthe* and *The Mikado* are strikingly similar. In both, the singers proclaim themselves creatures of artistic convention, doomed to perform antics they know to be meaningless. The world of *The Mikado*, then, is one of stylized behavior, in which the law no longer serves society but enslaves it. The Lord Chancellor in *Iolanthe* had proclaimed, "The Law is the true embodiment/ Of everything that's excellent," but it remains for Ko-Ko, the Lord High Executioner, to have "a little list" of society's offenders who can be dispatched whenever a victim must be found, and for the Mikado himself to invent cruel and unusual punishments to "fit the crime." The plight of the thwarted lovers, Nanki-Poo and Yum-Yum, is central; what is topsy-turvy is their entire milieu, in which forms are preserved at the expense of substance.

The Yeomen of the Guard was Gilbert's response to Sullivan's repeated requests for more human situations, for characters less eccentric, and for songs whose sentiments were not continually undercut by irony. Though rich in comic turns, it aspires to the condition of grand, rather than comic, opera. It is quite likely that the setting—the Tower of London in the sixteenth century—with its potential for costuming and design, may have first suggested itself to Gilbert, and that only then did he begin to work on a plot. Sergeant Meryll, a yeoman of the guard, and his son, Leonard, and daughter, Phoebe, plan to effect the escape of Colonel Fairfax, who is destined to be executed on trumped-up charges of sorcery. Meanwhile, Fairfax, knowing nothing of their scheme, is resigned to dying, but desires to marry first and thus thwart the plan of his kinsman, who concocted the charges in order to inherit Fairfax's estate. A hasty marriage is concluded with Elsie Maynard, a strolling singer. Fairfax, disguised as young Meryll, disappears from his cell, and his jailer, Wilfred Shadbolt, who in his love for Phoebe Meryll has unwittingly assisted the plot, is in danger of suffering the penalty in his stead. Shadbolt allies himself with the jester Jack Point, who, as Elsie's lover, has also been discomfitted by Fairfax's disappearance, and together, they concoct a tale. Like that of Ko-Ko and Pooh-Bah in *The Mikado*, the explanation given for Fairfax's absence is filled with "corroborative detail, intended to give artistic versimilitude to an otherwise bald and unconvincing narrative," maintaining that Shadbolt shot Fairfax dead as he tried to escape. Phoebe, in love with Fairfax and in distress at seeing him woo Elsie in the guise of her brother, reveals his true identity to Shadbolt. As Phoebe and Shadbolt are now in possession of each other's secret, they agree to marry in order to purchase each other's silence. Fairfax, who has actually been reprieved, is genuinely attracted to the wife he has acquired out of convenience, Sergeant Meryll pairs off with Dame Carruthers, the housekeeper to the Tower, and only Jack Point is left pathetically without a mate at the opera's conclusion. The substitution of intrigue for topsy-turviness obviously distances *The Yeomen of the Guard* from *H.M.S. Pinafore*, yet the work is recognizably Gilbertian; for all their melodramatic pretensions, the characters have affinities with those of the other operas. Even Jack Point, who falls insensible as the curtain descends, is cousin to the Lord Chancellor and Ko-Ko. The plight of these characters, however, has been more poignantly imagined.

Composed in the midst of mounting strife between Gilbert and Sullivan, *The Gondoliers* is their last major theatrical success. In many ways it is the most colorful and lyric of the whole series. The richness of its foreign setting may be rivaled by that of *The Mikado*, but musically, it is unequaled; for this opera, Sullivan added to his usual array of arias, duets, part songs, and choruses the rhythms of Spain and Italy. Gilbert worked what must be the ultimate variation on the baby-swapping convention: Throughout the opera, the audience waits to find out which of the two gondoliers is the rightful king of Barataria, only to discover what may have already been guessed—that neither is. During the last few minutes of the opera, an even earlier switch is announced as having taken place, conveniently preventing the marriage of royalty with the lower orders. Indeed, it often appears that Gilbert is engaging in self-parody in *The Gondoliers*, for the situations of the earlier operas are here piled on one another. Topsy-turviness is present not merely in the mixup of the infants but also in the joint rule of the two gondoliers while they await the determination of their status and in their ludicrous attempts to introduce republican monarchy. In the antics of the Duke and Duchess of Plaza Toro, Gilbert is not repudiating the aristocratic ideal—the Grand Inquisitor sings persuasively of the need for degree in a stable society. Rather, Gilbert portrays in them examples of a decayed and venal aristocracy. Like Pooh-Bah in *The Mikado*, they have pride but no honor. For all of its sprightliness, however, *The Gondoliers* lacks the integrity of the earlier operas: Themes and characters are introduced capriciously because they have worked before.

Alone among the comic versifiers of his age—Lewis Carroll, Edward Lear, C. S. Calverley, Richard Barham, and others—Gilbert succeeded in converting comic verse to comic song, thereby transcending whimsy. For this, he certainly owes much to Sullivan. Yet in how many operas, comic or grand, does the work of the lyricist or librettist count for much? Gilbert has earned classic status not because he is timeless and universal, but because even after a century, he can impose a Victorian sensibility upon his audience.

Other major works

POETRY: *The Bab Ballads*, 1869; *More Bab Ballads*, 1873; *Songs of a Savoyard*, 1898.

Bibliography

Baily, Leslie. *Gilbert and Sullivan and Their World*, 1973.
_____. *The Gilbert and Sullivan Book*, 1953.
Goldberg, Isaac. *The Story of Gilbert and Sullivan*, 1929.
Pearson, Hesketh. *Gilbert: His Life and Strife*, 1957.
Searle, Townley. *Sir William Schwenck Gilbert: A Bibliographic Adventure*, 1931.
Sutton, M. K. *W. S. Gilbert*, 1975.

Ira Grushow

FRANK D. GILROY

Born: New York, New York; October 13, 1925

Principal drama

Who'll Save the Plowboy?, wr. 1957, pr., pb. 1962; *The Subject Was Roses*, pb. 1962, pr. 1964; *That Summer—That Fall*, pr., pb. 1967 (includes his teleplay *Far Rockaway*); *The Only Game in Town*, pr., pb. 1968; *Present Tense*, pr. 1972, pb. 1973 (4 one-act plays: *So Please Be Kind*, *'Twas Brillig*, *Come Next Tuesday*, *Present Tense*); *The Next Contestant*, pr. 1978, pb. 1979 (one act); *Dreams of Glory*, pr. 1979, pb. 1980 (one act); *Last Licks*, pr. 1979 (also as *The Housekeeper*, pr. 1982).

Other literary forms

Frank D. Gilroy's career as a writer has been devoted primarily to drama, although he collaborated with his wife, Ruth G. Gilroy, on a children's book, *Little Ego* (1970), and he is also the author of two novels: *Private* (1970), a fictionalized account of his experiences in the Army, and *From Noon till Three* (1973), a comical Western.

In addition, Gilroy has had an active career as a television scriptwriter and as a screenwriter. During the 1950's he was a contributor to many of the television programs that stimulated a new interest in drama in the United States: *Studio One*, *Kraft Theatre*, *U.S. Steel Hour*, *Playhouse 90*, *Omnibus*, *Lux Video Theater*, the *Armstrong Theater*, and *The Dick Powell Show*. Gilroy's screenwriting career developed initially out of his work for television. *The Last Notch* (1954), a Western drama he wrote for television, became the source of his first screenplay, *The Fastest Gun Alive* (1956). In the 1960's, he adapted two of his own plays for the screen, *The Subject Was Roses* (1968) and *The Only Game in Town* (1969). In the 1970's, Gilroy was the director as well as the writer of *Desperate Characters* (1971), *Once in Paris* (1978), and the film version of *From Noon till Three* (1976).

Achievements

Gilroy's most impressive accomplishment has been his ability to master the techniques of three genres of drama, television, film, and the theater, and to gain recognition for his writings in each field. He not only wrote for television during its golden age; he was one of the playwrights who made it golden. As a screenwriter, Gilroy earned a national reputation for his adaptation of *The Subject Was Roses* as well as for his play. Patricia Neal was nominated for an Academy Award for her role as Nettie Cleary, and Jack Albertson won the Academy Award for Best Supporting Actor in the role of John Cleary. In 1971, Gilroy received international attention as writer, director, and producer of *Desperate Characters*, which won a Silver Bear Award at the Berlin Film Festival.

Gilroy's achievements and contributions as a writer for the stage are more substantial. His reputation as a dramatist is assured by the literary and theatrical merits of *Who'll Save the Plowboy?* and *The Subject Was Roses*. Not only have his first two plays been more highly regarded by critics and audiences than his later works, but also they continue to be produced. *Who'll Save the Plowboy?* won the Obie Award for the best American play produced Off-Broadway during the 1961-1962 season. *The Subject Was Roses* was the choice of many as the best play of 1964-1965; it won the Outer Circle Award (1964), the New York Drama Critics Circle Award (1964), the New York Theatre Club Award (1964-1965), the Antoinette Perry (Tony) Award (1965), and the Pulitzer Prize for Drama (1965). Gilroy received an honorary doctor of letters degree from Dartmouth College in 1966.

Gilroy has also been recognized by his fellow dramatists as a spokesman and advocate for the writing profession. His well-publicized campaign to get and keep *The Subject Was Roses* on the stage set an example for other playwrights in challenging the play-financing establishment and in having drama produced on the playwright's own terms. In 1965, he filed suit against two publishers, a television network, and two television production companies for misappropriating his property as a writer. When Gilroy won his case eleven years later (1976), his lawyer, Robert Ehrenbard, was quoted in *Publishers Weekly* as saying, "It is a very important victory for writers and supports their rights in a way that the law hasn't done before." It is evidently for efforts such as these that Gilroy was chosen to be a member of the Council of the Dramatists Guild and then its president (1969-1971).

Biography

Frank Daniel Gilroy was born and grew up in New York City. He was the only child of Bettina and Frank B. Gilroy. His father, like John Cleary in *The Subject Was Roses*, was in the coffee business. The family lived in an apartment in the West Bronx. Memories of his early family life and his relationship with his parents eventually provided material for *Last Licks* as well as for *The Subject Was Roses*. By the time Gilroy was graduated from DeWitt Clinton High School in 1943, he had shown an interest in writing but little promise as a student; his father was evidently willing to send him to college, but his grades were not good enough. Gilroy's autobiographical novel *Private* opens with an account of a visit to New Haven and the humiliating return trip to New York after Yale University had rejected his application.

Gilroy was drafted into the United States Army ten months after his high school graduation. He would say later that during his tour in the army his life underwent "some good and productive changes." In Europe, however, attached to the Eighty-ninth Infantry Division Reconnaissance Troop, he also faced degradation and the threat of death and witnessed the depravity of the final days of the war. *Private* records the indelible impression of his army experiences; war memories both trivial and serious also surface in *Who'll Save the Plowboy?* and *The Subject Was Roses*.

In 1946, Gilroy came out of the army with the determination to go to college and with the desire to write. He applied to forty colleges and was accepted by only two of them—Davis and Elkins, and Dartmouth. He chose Dartmouth and was graduated *magna cum laude* with a bachelor of arts degree in 1950. In college, he wrote stories and was an editor of the paper, but a playwriting course convinced him that drama was the form best suited to his talents. During his junior and senior years, he wrote and was accorded productions of two full-length plays and six one-act plays. In both years, he won the Frost Playwriting Award. Following his graduation, Gilroy attended the Yale School of Drama with the help of a scholarship, but his funds ran out after six months.

The growing popularity of television provided a new market for playwrights, and Gilroy began writing scripts for television in the early 1950's. To support himself during this period, he held a series of jobs—including messenger, trumpet player, and cabana salesman—but by the mid-1950's he was making a good living from television. He wrote regularly for two popular Western series, *The Rifleman* and *Have Gun, Will Travel*, in addition to having plays produced by the leading network drama programs. Only a few of his unpublished scripts can still be identified. He wrote at least three plays for *Studio One*: *A Likely Story* (1955), *Uncle Ed and Circumstances* (adaptation of a story by Jackie Gleason), and *The Last Summer* (1958). Two of his plays appeared on *Kraft Theater*: *Run for the Money* (1954) and *Ten Grapefruit to Lisbon* (1956). *A Matter of Pride* (1957; adaptation of John Langdon's story "The Blue Serge Suit") was shown on the *U.S. Steel Hour*. For *Playhouse 90* he adapted two works by John P. Marquand, *Sincerely, Willis Wayde* (in 1956) and *Point of No Return* (in 1958).

In 1954, Gilroy married Ruth Gaydos, and by the time *The Subject Was Roses* was produced, ten years later, they had three sons and lived in Upstate New York. For several years at the end of the 1950's, however, while Gilroy was employed as a studio screenwriter, California was his home. This experience was evidently the inspiration for *'Twas Brillig*, a one-act comedy about a writer's first day on a studio lot. In 1960, Gilroy collaborated with Beirne Lay, Jr., on *The Gallant Hours*, a biographical film about Admiral William Halsey, starring James Cagney. Gilroy's work for television and films gave him enough time and income to write for the stage and enabled him to complete *Who'll Save the Plowboy?* in 1957.

Gilroy moved his family back to New York in 1961, and in 1962, after searching for five years, he found a producer for *Who'll Save the Plowboy?* Although its reviews were generally favorable and it won an Obie Award, the play did not enjoy a long run—a month at the Phoenix Theatre and another month at the Orpheum Theatre. Its production at the Haymarket Theatre in the spring of 1963 introduced Gilroy's work to London audiences. On May 25, 1964, *The Subject Was Roses* opened at the Royale Theatre on Broadway, then moved to the Winthrop Ames Theatre on September 7, 1964. Although it ended up being Gilroy's longest-running drama and greatest achievement, he worked steadily for two years to get it produced and then faced the threat of an early closing. The play not only survived but also received 832 performances in New York, toured the United States, and was produced in a number of other countries. *The Subject Was Roses* won almost every award given for the best play of 1964-1965. In *About Those Roses: Or, How Not to Do a Play and Succeed* (1965), Gilroy gives a diary account of his struggles for the play from its completion in the spring of 1962 to its opening night in the spring of 1964. In a 1966 interview with Joseph Blank in *Reader's Digest*, Gilroy summed up the meaning of the experience for him: "It's amazing how much *can* be accomplished if you believe in what you want to do. The strength of your belief makes others believe."

In a story in *Life* three months after the opening of *The Subject Was Roses*, Tom Prideaux reported that Gilroy had become a "hot property" and had received offers "to adapt sixteen books into movies, to write four musicals and six TV pilot films." Gilroy may never have committed himself to any of these projects, but the decade between 1965 and 1975 was to become the most active period of Gilroy's writing career. In 1965, *Far Rockaway*, a very brief expressionistic play in thirteen scenes, was presented on National Educational Television. When it was printed with the Random House edition of *That Summer—That Fall*, Gilroy claimed that the little drama demonstrated that he was not exclusively dedicated to the "real." *That Summer—That Fall*, Gilroy's updated dramatization of the Phaedra story, opened on March 16, 1967, at the Helen Hayes Theatre in New York, and closed on March 25. The film of *The Subject Was Roses* was released in 1968, and on May 23, 1968, Gilroy's Las Vegas love comedy, *The Only Game in Town*, opened at New York's Broadhurst Theatre, only to close on June 1. The film of the comedy, for which Gilroy wrote the screenplay, was released a year later with Elizabeth Taylor and Warren Beatty as the lovers. *Little Ego*, the children's book which Gilroy wrote with his wife, Ruth, was published in 1970; the same year saw the publication of *Private*, Gilroy's autobiographical war novel. The novel is written in an impressionistic style, resembling in its form and its evocative power the interchapter vignettes of Ernest Hemingway's *In Our Time* (1924, 1925).

Gilroy produced, directed, and wrote the screenplay for *Desperate Characters* in 1971; the film was adapted from a novel by Paula Fox and starred Shirley MacLaine. A program of four of his one-act plays—*Come Next Tuesday*, *'Twas Brillig*, *So Please Be Kind*, and *Present Tense*, opened at the Sheridan Square Playhouse July 8, 1972, and closed July 23. Gilroy's Western novel, *From Noon Till Three*, was published in 1973. Its comic irony develops from two versions of a frontier romance told first by a lady and then by her outlaw lover. Gilroy adapted the story for the screen and produced and directed the film, which was released in 1976 and featured Charles Bronson and Jill Ireland in the leading roles. In the same year, Gilroy returned briefly to television to adapt stories by John O'Hara for *Gibbsville*, a short-lived series that he directed.

In 1976, Gilroy also realized a great profit, however indirectly, from another television play, *Who Killed Julie Greer?* (1961), which he had written for *The Dick Powell Show* fifteen years earlier. In the play, he created the character of Amos Burke, a wealthy detective, who became the main character in the television series *Burke's Law* two years later (1963). In 1965, Gilroy filed suit against two publishers, a television network, and two television production companies which had misappropriated the Burke character, and after eleven years of litigation a jury awarded Gilroy one million dollars in compensation and interest.

Since then, Gilroy has written the screenplay for *Once in Paris*, which he also produced and directed. His full-length play *Last Licks* focuses on the relationship between father and son and reveals an unhappy marriage and a family triangle in their past. With its autobiographical roots, the comedy is a sequel to *The Subject Was Roses*. *Last Licks* opened at the Longacre Theatre on November 20, 1979, and closed December 1. The plays that Gilroy has written since 1964 have survived for only a short time on stage, yet Gilroy has retained a dramatist's interest in the theater and in theater groups devoted to developing and showcasing new plays. Two of his one-act plays, *The Next Contestant* and *Dreams of Glory*, were produced by the Ensemble Studio Theatre in its annual play festivals.

Analysis

Most of Frank D. Gilroy's plays—both comic and serious, full-length and one-act—may be identified by their development of themes and situations that are related to marriage or family problems and by their ironic style. Unhappy or failed marriages are directly or indirectly responsible for complications in *Who'll Save the Plowboy?*, *The Subject Was Roses*, *That Summer—That Fall*, *The Only Game in Town*, *Last Licks*, *So Please Be Kind*, and *Come Next Tuesday*. Family problems centering on the relationship between father and son or on an Oedipal triangle are sources of conflict in *The Subject Was Roses*, *That Summer—That Fall*, *Last Licks*, and

Present Tense. Gilroy's realistic drama, like Henrik Ibsen's, is distinguished not so much by its verisimilitude in dramatizing these problems as by its mastery of irony. In each of his full-length plays, in the manner of Ibsen's *Hedda Gabler* (pb. 1890), Gilroy creates patterns of irony through triangular character relationships: in *Who'll Save the Plowboy?*, Albert and Helen Cobb and Larry Doyle; in *The Subject Was Roses*, John and Nettie Cleary and their son, Timmy; in *That Summer—That Fall*, Angelina and Victor Capuano and Victor's son, Steve; in *The Only Game in Town*, Fran Walker, Joe Grady, and Thomas Lockwood; and in *Last Licks*, Matt and Dennis Quinlan and Fiona (but also Matt and Dennis Quinlan and Margaret Quinlan, the dead mother). This triangular design allows for developments, in the relationship and dialogue between two characters, that are concealed from the third character but revealed to the audience. The complexities of the pattern may be expanded by shifts in the balance of the triangle that give each character a turn as the victim of irony.

The inciting action in *Who'll Save the Plowboy?* is deceptively simple, because only two of the characters who will form the ironic triangle are onstage when the play opens. An unhappily married couple, Albert and Helen Cobb, argue as they await the visit of Larry Doyle, Albert's buddy during the war. Larry risked his own life and was wounded in carrying out a miraculous battlefield rescue that saved Albert's life. Helen suspects that Larry is coming to ask for something, and, in an ironic way, he is. Albert, who considers Larry to be the best friend he ever had, anticipates an opportunity of some kind, perhaps a job offer. A bitter quarrel erupts when Helen balks at Albert's plan that they act like a loving couple and welcome Larry into a happy home. They exchange insults and threats, and Albert slaps his wife when she makes fun of the "Plowboy" image he is reviving for Larry's sake. Before Larry arrives, Albert warns Helen not to mention the "farm" or the "boy."

Albert and Larry have not seen each other for fifteen years, but the joy of their reunion is quickly dissipated. Each man is surprised and disappointed by the changes in the other. Albert is made increasingly uncomfortable by Larry's questions about the "boy," the son who was named after Larry and is supposedly visiting relatives. Larry is evasive in speaking about his own life and work. Both men are disturbed by Helen's cutting remarks. The first scene ends in a violent argument between the two men after Albert reveals to Larry the sordidness of his life—the failure of the farm he bought after the war, his drinking problem, and his unfaithfulness to his wife. As Albert pleads with him to save the Plowboy again, Larry, disgusted, leaves the apartment but collapses on the stairs.

The first scene provides the exposition necessary to understand the relationships among the three central characters and the basic situation in the play, yet the scene is even more important in setting up the ironies that develop in the second scene of act 1 and in act 2. Before Larry arrives, the dramatic interest is created and sustained not by irony but by the strident verbal exchanges between Albert and Helen and particularly by Helen's sarcasm and ridicule of Albert. In her self-hatred ("Every night before I go to bed I hope I won't wake up in the morning") and in the destructive power of her words, she resembles Martha of *Who's Afraid of Virginia Woolf?*, the Edward Albee play that opened eight months after Gilroy's drama. After Larry enters, the first pattern of irony is introduced in the reversal of the two friends' expectations. Albert remembers Larry as a joking, hell-raising, hard-drinking woman-chaser, and he finds that Larry is serious, single, and no longer drinks. Larry discovers that Albert, who never took a drink, now drinks heavily. He finds it even harder to believe that the young man whom he had nicknamed the "Plowboy" and who had talked constantly about owning a farm is living in a run-down apartment in New York City and reading meters for a living.

In the second scene of act 1, Gilroy introduces the first of a series of discoveries that contribute to the ironic design which gives focus and dramatic force to the play. Mrs. Doyle, Larry's mother, reveals to the Cobbs her son's secret and his purpose in visiting them. Mrs. Doyle tells them that Larry has been in and out of hospitals for years and does not have long to live. He is dying of cancer that developed from the wound he sustained in saving Albert. Shortly after the war, when Larry discovered that his condition was terminal, he dropped out of medical school, where he was the top student, and broke off his engagement to spare the girl he loved. Mrs. Doyle lets Albert know that she blames and hates him for ruining her son's life. She also suggests that Larry has come to the Cobbs in the hope of proving before his death that Albert's life and family were worth the life and happiness he gave up. The scene ends with Albert, tormented by guilt, vowing to convince Larry that he is happy in his life and marriage. Helen agrees to join him in the masquerade and to pretend that Mrs. Doyle never called or told her story.

While the irony at the end of act 1 depends on the Cobbs's discovery of Larry's secret, the irony in act 2 is created by Larry's discovery of the Cobbs's secret, which provides both the climax and the resolution of the play. Larry's first discovery on the morning after his illness, however, merely develops the incidental irony that Helen has been just as unfaithful as Albert. After Albert has left the apartment to meet his boss, Larry tries to get Helen to tell him why she hates him. She breaks down, and when Larry plays the piano to get her to stop crying, she becomes even more upset. The trumpet player who lives upstairs appears at the door, and Larry deduces that Helen uses her piano as a signal for her lover. Promising not to reveal her secret yet unable to learn the reason for her hatred, Larry tells Helen that he intends to stay in New York until he meets the "boy" who bears his name. The "boy" is Larry's last hope of giving meaning to the life he sacrificed by saving Albert. Realizing that Larry will not heed her warning to spare himself by leaving, and "sick of lies," Helen reveals the secret about the "boy" that became a psychological cancer for her and Albert and destroyed their marriage: "I gave birth to a monster. . . . Not boy. Not girl. Not anything. . . . It took something in him and something in me. Something bad in the both of us to produce this thing." Helen's confession and the irony of its grotesque response to Larry's hope form the climax of the play. The monster child and its malignant effects on Helen, Albert, and their marriage are comparable to the imaginary child and its effects on George and Martha in *Who's Afraid of Virginia Woolf?* The monster would never have been born if Larry had not saved Albert, and that is why Helen has hated Larry. She suggests that Albert also regrets that he was not left to die.

In releasing her pent-up feelings, Helen inadvertently reveals that she and Albert know that Larry is dying. What follows this disclosure is one of the two moments of warmth and compassion in the play. After Larry tells Helen that the truth has drained away her hatred of him, she takes his head in her hands and kisses him on both cheeks and the forehead. The secrets that Helen and Larry now share and keep from Albert create the final ironies of the play's resolution. Albert returns with a boy whom he has picked up on the street and passes him off as his son. Although Larry is almost disgusted enough to spoil Albert's plan, he creates the second compassionate moment by accepting the boy as his namesake and, in effect, saving the Plowboy again. It is possible to interpret the close of the play as an act of compassion on Helen's part, as she answers "Yes" when Albert asks her if she thinks Larry believed the boy was their own. What makes the ending ambiguous and contributes the final irony is the sound of the trumpet in the background as Albert says, "Well, it was worth it. . . . He believed me. . . . I owed him that."

The Subject Was Roses is a more appealing play than *Who'll Save the Plowboy?*, and its three characters are more fully realized and more intrinsically interesting than Larry Doyle or the Cobbs. The irony, too, is more subtle and sympathetic and develops more directly from the characterizations of John, Nettie, and Timmy Cleary and from their relationships with one another. Although *The Subject Was Roses* is a "comedy drama," Gilroy's Cleary family may be compared with the Tyrones of Eugene O'Neill's *Long Day's Journey into Night* (pb. 1955). Like Edmund Tyrone, Timmy Cleary overcomes his resentment of his father and his blind loyalty to his mother and achieves a better understanding of both parents. Like Mary Tyrone, Nettie Cleary was devoted to her father as a girl and feels that her marriage was a mistake—a comedown in class and something of a fall from innocence. She will not forgive John his past infidelities. John

Cleary, like James Tyrone, grew up in abject poverty and is tightfisted with his money. Vital and gregarious as a young man, in his middle years he has trouble expressing his emotions and seems to be much more unfeeling than he actually is. Yet the form and substance of Gilroy's play has more to do with character relationships than with individual characterizations. A triangle is formed by the conflict between Nettie and John over Timmy, as each attempts to secure his love and allegiance. The shape of the triangle changes during the play as Timmy feels more strongly the pull of ties first to one parent and then to the other. It is only in the end that, in Timmy's eyes, all sides of the triangle are equal and the family relationships are balanced.

The first act of the play focuses on the realignment of family loyalties that begins when Timmy returns home after three years in the army. It is clear from conversations between Nettie and John and from Timmy's own remarks that in the years before he left home, he was much closer to his mother than to his father. In the exchange between Nettie and John that begins the play, John voices the hope that his relationship with his son will improve now that his son is a man, and everything that happens in the first act seems to support his hope, as Timmy displays not only a new understanding of his father but also similar personality traits. They drink together, take in a ballgame, and team up for an impromptu vaudeville routine after a night on the town. More important, they talk together, and for the first time Timmy is able to form his own impressions of his father. As a boy, he saw his father through his mother's eyes and accepted her judgments of him. Timmy gains a new appreciation of his father's humor, his fighting spirit, and his successful struggle out of poverty.

In the first act, as Timmy draws closer to his father, he pulls back gently but firmly from his mother. It is not that Timmy loves his mother less but that he realizes better his position at the center of his parents' conflict with each other. He is also aware that his identity is no longer defined solely by his role as a son and that he must claim his independence. Timmy's withdrawal from his mother's hold on him is dramatized in an emotionally intense moment in the first scene. When Nettie says she cannot believe he is home again, Timmy extends his hand and tells her to pinch him. His mother takes his hand, holds on, and will not let go until Timmy becomes agitated and "jerks" his hand free. Much of the irony in the first act comes as Timmy pulls away from his mother's grip on his life, and there is a reversal in her expectations of continuing their past relationship. Nettie is surprised and upset not only because Timmy is doing things with John instead of with her, but also because he shows signs of taking after his father—telling jokes, repeating John's favorite expressions, and drinking too much.

Act 1 concludes with a bitter argument between Nettie and John following the family's evening in New York. After Timmy has gone to his room, John grows amorous, and Nettie resists. Their struggle becomes ugly when John resorts to force; it ends with Nettie smashing the vase of roses she has been led to believe were a present from John. She has been moved by the roses, but she will not forgive his unfaithfulness—his "hotel lobby whores"—and refuses to renew their sexual relationship. In his frustration at the end of the scene, John tells her that the roses were Timmy's idea. What has appeared to be friction between them over their son is revealed to be a much more serious marital problem.

Nettie tells John that "what's wrong" between them "has nothing to do" with Timmy, but it does. The second act opens the morning after, and John, still smarting from Nettie's rejection, vents his anger on Timmy as well as Nettie. The scene suggests the tone of John's relationships with his wife and son before Timmy left home. His petulance gives way to outraged disbelief when Timmy declines to attend Mass with him because he no longer considers himself to be a Catholic. When Nettie defends Timmy's right as a man to choose for himself, John speaks bitterly of the "familiar alliance" between mother and son. Ironically, after John leaves the house, Timmy stands up for his father and tries to get his mother to admit that it was "always us against him." It is evidently the first time Timmy has ever argued seriously with his mother or sided with his father: "You, and him, and me, and what's been going on here for twenty years. . . . *We've* got to stop ganging up on him." Timmy also accuses Nettie of bolstering the alliance against John by maintaining close ties and daily contact with her mother and sister. The irony is doubled at the end of the scene when Nettie, angered by Timmy's accusations, thanks him for the roses and stalks out of the apartment with fifty dollars in coins which she has saved.

Irony is created in the second scene of act 2 in its reversal of one of the more melodramatic scenes of the Cleary's prewar family life. It is ten o'clock on a Sunday night, and it is Nettie, not John, who has not returned home. As the father and son wait and seek news of her, it is John who is frantic and Timmy who is drunk—but well aware of the irony of his father's position. He recalls for his father the dreaded ritual that was repeated throughout his childhood of lying awake listening for his father's return from a late-night adventure and for the argument between his parents that inevitably followed. The irony of the scene is complete when Nettie comes home but refuses to respond to John's angry demands for an explanation. Instead, she uses John's favorite alibi of having been to a movie. Finally, as John presses her for an answer, Nettie insinuates that she has been with another man. She never reveals the truth of her absence to husband or son and will say only that her twelve hours away from them gave her the only "real freedom" she has ever known. Regardless of whether Nettie walked out with the intention of teaching her son a lesson, her rebellious act has that effect. Timmy's memories of his father's irresponsible behavior bring a further adjustment in his relationship with both parents.

The proof of a new evenness in Timmy's attachments to his parents is provided in the scene that follows. At two in the morning, Timmy and Nettie, who have been unable to sleep, talk together in the living room. Timmy tells his mother that he must leave home, and she accepts his decision. Nettie then tells Timmy the story of how she met and married John. Like Mary Tyrone, she describes her marriage in a litany of regret as the inevitable tragic turning point of her life. It is at this point that Timmy speaks of the shifts in his loyalties and of his new and more balanced view of his parents: "When I left this house three years ago, I blamed *him* for everything that was wrong here. . . . When I came home, I blamed *you.* . . . Now I suspect that no one's to blame. . . . Not even me."

The play ends as it began, by focusing on John and Timmy and on the final adjustment that ensures Timmy's balanced relationship with his parents and his own independence. Unsuccessful in his appeal to Nettie to persuade Timmy to stay, John himself tries to talk Timmy out of going. He tells him that he is willing to let him do as he pleases in the house, and, confessing that he was wrong in his treatment of Timmy in the past, he promises to change. Timmy insists that he must leave, but he gives his father an assurance of his love that makes his leaving bearable for both. Timmy tells his father of a childhood dream that he had dreamed again the night before—that his father would die without ever saying he loved him. Then, Timmy says, "It's true you've never said you love me. But it's also true I've never said those words to you. . . . I say them now—I love you, Pop." Timmy's declaration and what follows—the father and son in tears and embracing each other—provide the emotional climax of the play and a happy ending for Timmy, but there is no happy resolution of his parents' marital problems. Gilroy spoke openly of the play's roots in his own family life. In his interview for *Reader's Digest*, he explained that the play had been written several years after his parents' deaths as his "way of saying how [he] came to love them." By including unpleasant recollections as well as happy memories and by treating them honestly, Gilroy avoided the sentimentality that would have spoiled the play.

That Summer—That Fall, Gilroy's most ambitious drama, fails because it neglects the proven strengths of his first two plays—psychological realism and irony. Gilroy may also have made a mistake in taking the material for his play from a classical tragedy, turning away from his own experience. In another sense, however, the Phaedra story, with its unhappy marriage and its father-son conflict, was a logical choice for the author of *The Subject Was Roses*.

The play is given a contemporary setting in a run-down Italian neighborhood of New York City; with the exception of the opening and closing scenes in a playground, the action takes place in the apartment of Victor and Angelina Capuano. In his delineation of his characters and their relationships, Gilroy shows the influence of Jean Racine's *Phèdre* (pr. 1677) as well as Euripides' *Hippolytus* (428 B.C.). Victor, whose role is comparable to that of Theseus in the original story, is a successful restaurant owner in his mid-fifties. His wife Angelina, who is thirty-six, is Gilroy's modern Phaedra and, like Racine's heroine, is the dominant character in the play. Angelina falls in love with Steve Flynn before Victor brings him home and identifies him as his illegitimate son. Steve resembles Racine's Hippolytus more closely than he does Euripides' chaste woman-hater. By the end of the play, he is dating Josie, a teenage neighbor girl who has fallen in love with him. Zia Filomena, Angelina's aunt, plays the part of go-between that Euripides assigned to Phaedra's nurse and Racine expanded for Oenone, the nurse and lady-in-waiting of his Phaedra.

The plot of *That Summer—That Fall* follows Euripides' tragedy more closely than Racine's. When the play opens, Angelina is already tormented by her secret passion for Steve. From papers his mother left after her death, Steve has discovered that Victor is his father, and he has hitchhiked from California to meet him. Victor accepts Steve as his son, all the more eagerly because he and Angelina are childless. A close, trusting relationship grows quickly between father and son, and they are soon working together as partners. At the same time, Angelina's desire and frustration are intensified by living with Steve under the same roof.

The turning point of the play comes on a night on which Josie and Steve have gone to a dance. Angelina attempts to dull her pain with wine, and in an inebriated stupor she confesses to Zia her love for Steve. The following morning, after Victor has told her that Steve will be staying, Angelina's thoughts turn to suicide. Zia realizes what Angelina plans to do and promises to help her. With the idea of bringing Angelina and Steve together to save her niece's life, Zia sends the young man to Angelina's bedroom.

The climax and resolution follow very quickly. Mistaking Steve's intentions in visiting her room, Angelina kisses him passionately and confesses her love. Steve is repulsed by her passion and tells her to go back to the playground and find another boy. When Steve returns to the apartment late that night, he finds Victor sitting alone in the dark. Angelina has killed herself, leaving a letter accusing Steve of raping her. Steve tells his father that the letter is a lie, but Victor will not believe him. After Steve runs out of the apartment, Victor confronts Zia with Steve's denial, and she finally confesses the truth—that Angelina loved Steve, "was dying for him," but that nothing happened between them. A hysterical Josie rushes in to tell Victor that Steve has crashed his car and is dying. The play ends with Steve, who lies dying in his father's arms, saying, "Raise me up," and Victor replying, "To heaven if I could."

Gilroy was upset by the hostile reception his play received and by its failure, and he offered his defense in a foreword to the Random House edition: "It was my intention that *That Summer—That Fall* should work both realistically and as ritual. Unfortunately, the latter element has, so far, escaped detection. . . ." The problems with *That Summer—That Fall*, however, have nothing to do with realism or ritual: The play lacks adequate plot development and convincing motivation for Angelina and Steve. At the end of the play, each crucial scene—from the moment that Steve enters Angelina's bedroom to the moment of his death—is unusually brief and is developed in dialogue that is monosyllabic and frequently stichomythic. As a consequence, there is little opportunity for the development of irony. Angelina's attraction to Steve comes across as lust, not love, since she registers her feelings most strongly whenever she sees Steve bare-chested. Unrequited lust is not a believable motive for suicide or revenge, and, since nothing happens, Angelina has no reason to feel guilty or sinful. Steve has even less motive for suicide, if indeed that is the way his automobile wreck is to be taken. He has no reason to blame himself for Angelina's death, and his father's wrongheaded rejection hardly seems motive enough to take his own life. Indeed, the best explanation of the motives of Angelina and Steve would seem to be that they behave as they do because that is the way Phaedra and Hippolytus behave.

The Only Game in Town is worth mentioning because it is Gilroy's only full-length comedy, and Gilroy is a talented comic writer—as is evident in *The Subject Was Roses* and *Last Licks*, as well as in the short comedies *'Twas Brillig, So Please Be Kind*, and *Dreams of Glory*. The plot complications in *The Only Game in Town* may be contrived, but the humor of the dialogue is as sharply honed and as quickly paced as Neil Simon's. The play also makes good use of comic irony to develop an idea that is treated seriously in Gilroy's other full-length plays: that marriage is a gamble at long odds. Appropriately enough, the comedy is set in Las Vegas, the action taking place in Fran Walker's apartment over a period of two years. Fran, one of the players in the love game, is a nightclub dancer who has not yet had the courage to bet on matrimony. It is revealed at the end of the play that she has feared and avoided marriage because her father deserted the family when she was ten years old. The other player is Joe Grady, a piano player who is also a compulsive gambler and a two-time loser at marriage. The first act traces the development of the relationship between Fran and Joe from a casual sexual liaison into a love that each feels but conceals from the other. In the second act, having lived together for almost two years, Fran and Joe remove the obstacles to their marriage and reluctantly agree to wed. Joe licks his gambling problem, and Fran, although she is still "scared," finally takes a chance. The theme of the comedy and its underlying attitude toward marriage are expressed by Joe in proposing to

Fran: "Granted that marriage is a most faulty, pitiful, and wheezing institution, right now it's the only game in town and *we're* going to play it."

As a realistic playwright in the 1960's and 1970's, Gilroy often faced the hostility or indifference of critics who were embracing the Absurdists and who dismissed realistic drama as dull and outmoded. Gilroy also found himself challenging the values of producers who dismissed as a bad investment any play that was serious and had no music or lyrics. He succeeded in overcoming the opposition of both groups by the sheer power of his writing in *Who'll Save the Plowboy?* and *The Subject Was Roses.* In these plays and occasionally in his later works, Gilroy has contributed to an evolving tradition in the best modern American drama, which refines and applies the techniques of psychological realism to a focus on the family and marriage.

Other major works

NOVELS: *Private,* 1970; *From Noon Till Three,* 1973 (also as *For Want of a Horse,* 1975).

NONFICTION: *About Those Roses: Or, How Not to Do a Play and Succeed,* 1965.

SCREENPLAYS: *The Fastest Gun Alive,* 1956; *The Gallant Hours,* 1960 (with Beirne Lay, Jr.); *The Subject Was Roses,* 1968 (adaptation of his play); *The Only Game in Town,* 1969 (adaptation of his play); *Desperate Characters,* 1971 (adaptation of Paula Fox's novel); *From Noon Till Three,* 1976 (adaptation of his novel); *Once in Paris,* 1978.

TELEPLAYS: *The Last Notch,* 1954; *Run for the Money,* 1954; *A Likely Story,* 1955; *Uncle Ed and Circumstances,* 1955; *Sincerely, Willis Wayde,* 1956 (adaptation of John P. Marquand's play); *Ten Grapefruit to Lisbon,* 1956; *A Matter of Pride,* 1957 (adaptation of John Langdon's story "The Blue Serge Suit"); *The Last Summer,* 1958; *Point of No Return,* 1958 (adaptation of Marquand's play); *Who Killed Julie Greer?,* 1961; *Far Rockaway,* 1965.

CHILDREN'S LITERATURE: *Little Ego,* 1970 (with Ruth G. Gilroy).

Bibliography

Bonin, Jane. *Prize-Winning American Drama: A Bibliographical and Descriptive Guide,* 1973.
Frank, Leah D. "Frank D. Gilroy," in *Contemporary Dramatists,* 1982.
Laufe, Abe. *Anatomy of a Hit,* 1966.
Weales, Gerald. *The Jumping-Off Place: American Drama in the 1960's,* 1969.

Ted R. Ellis III

OLIVER GOLDSMITH

Born: Ballymahon, Ireland; November 10, 1730
Died: London, England; April 4, 1774

Principal drama

The Good-Natured Man, pr., pb. 1768; *She Stoops to Conquer: Or, The Mistakes of a Night*, pr., pb. 1773.

Other literary forms

Although best remembered as a dramatist, Oliver Goldsmith is also known for his work in several other genres. His only novel, *The Vicar of Wakefield* (1766), the comic and sentimental tale of a village curate's attempts to guide his children through the tribulations of growing up, remains a minor classic. *The Citizen of the World* (1762), a recasting of Charles de Montesquieu's *Persian Letters* (1721), is a collection of fictitious letters, purportedly written by a Chinese philosopher who is living in London, describing English customs and English society from an outsider's point of view.

Goldsmith's poetry was often comic as well (as in his parodies of "An Elegy on the Death of a Mad Dog," of 1766, and "An Elegy on the Glory of Her Sex: Mrs. Mary Blaize," of 1759), but when his sympathies were touched, he produced some creditable serious poems, the most notable of which is *The Deserted Village* (1770), a protest against the economic and social conditions that were forcing a massive shift of the populace from small villages to cities.

Like other eighteenth century authors, Goldsmith earned his living by writing whatever publishers thought would sell: histories of Rome and England, biographical sketches, epilogues for the plays of others, translations, and introductions to the natural sciences as well as plays, novels, and poems. The best modern edition of Goldsmith's varied canon is *The Collected Works of Oliver Goldsmith* (1966), in five volumes, edited by Arthur Friedman for Oxford University Press.

Achievements

Goldsmith's success rate as a dramatist is virtually unmatched: two plays written, the first very good, the second a masterpiece. Goldsmith was the preeminent English comic dramatist in the period of almost two centuries between William Congreve and Oscar Wilde. Only his contemporary Richard Brinsley Sheridan—who wrote more plays and had better theatrical connections—came close to matching Goldsmith's talent.

The qualities which make *The Good Natured Man* and *She Stoops to Conquer* wonderful theater are the qualities that mark all Goldsmith's writings: an eye for human foibles, a knack for creating the scene or situation in which such foibles can best display themselves, and a willingness to laugh at folly rather than to be irked by it. Goldsmith expresses his comic vision of human experience in language that induces the reader's continuing attention and seduces the reader's affection.

Goldsmith was a writer who believed that it was his duty to entertain his audience. Like a stage performer, he used every device, trick, and resource which gives pleasure. No reader finds Goldsmith's prose a chore to read; no theatergoer finds his plays too long.

Biography

Tony Lumpkin in *She Stoops to Conquer* is one of those classic ne'er-do-wells in English literature who would rather eat, drink, and play a merry prank than work for a living. Tony may have been Oliver Goldsmith's favorite male character in the play; at the very least, he was a kindred spirit, because the playwright himself had lived a ne'er-do-well's existence before successful authorship brought him some stability and an income, however irregular it may have been.

Goldsmith began life as the second son in the large family of an Anglo-Irish clergyman. What limited wealth the family had was destined to become part of his older brother's inheritance or of the dowry for an older sister who "married above herself"; nothing much was left for Oliver. Goldsmith seems to have been equally slighted by Nature: He was a sickly child, badly disfigured by smallpox contracted at age seven, and he was considered dull by his first teachers. From this inauspicious background, it took a number of years for Goldsmith to discover his niche in the world as a writer.

Goldsmith was graduated from Trinity College, Dublin, in 1749, after fitful periods of study that were punctuated by riotous parties and pranks, clashes with administrators, and attempts to run away. Two years later, he applied for ordination in the Church of England, but the red trousers he wore to the interview seem not to have made a favorable impression on the local bishop. Goldsmith's uncle, the Reverend Thomas Contarine, gave him the money to study medicine, first at the University of Edinburgh and then at the University of Leyden, but the fledgling physician preferred to spend the time and money otherwise, wandering the Continent as a tourist. In 1756, when Goldsmith returned to London, he found it hard to support himself. His casual medical knowledge was no help in obtaining a doctor's commission in the Royal Navy (which at the time appointed as "surgeon" almost anyone who could wield a scalpel without self-mutilation). Goldsmith tried teaching, but he proved less disciplined than the young boys he was supposed to instruct.

Not until he began work as a proofreader for novelist-printer Samuel

Richardson did Goldsmith find a task that focused his energies. Drawing upon his Continental wanderings, the proofreader turned author in 1759 when his *An Enquiry into the Present State of Polite Learning in Europe* was published with some success. His achievement brought Goldsmith freelance assignments from other publishers, and he contributed essays, reviews, and poems to several periodicals. From these, Goldsmith gained popular applause, the recognition of fellow writers, and a modest though unsteady income. The most notable sign of his success was his admission to the Literary Club in the early 1760's. There, Goldsmith dined and conversed with the most prominent London intellectuals, among them the painter Sir Joshua Reynolds, the politician Edmund Burke, the actor David Garrick, and the writer-critic Samuel Johnson. In the Literary Club, Goldsmith found and immersed himself in a sophisticated version of the lively fellowship Tony Lumpkin enjoys at the Three Pigeons Tavern.

Club members helped channel Goldsmith's efforts in new literary directions. When Goldsmith was threatened with arrest for nonpayment of rent, Samuel Johnson sent the unfinished manuscript of *The Vicar of Wakefield* (on which Goldsmith had been working intermittently for several years) to a publisher, who bought it for sixty pounds. Because Goldsmith did not get along with David Garrick, who was manager of the Drury Lane Theatre, Reynolds wrote a letter of recommendation to Garrick on behalf of Goldsmith's recently finished first foray into drama, *The Good-Natured Man*. Though Goldsmith was no doubt anxious to become a playwright, with a chance of making hundreds of pounds if his play ran until the third night (which was the performance known as the "author's benefit"), *The Good-Natured Man* was not produced until two years later. Garrick and Goldsmith had argued over revisions and payments; eventually, Goldsmith had to take the play to another theater.

The profits from his first play were enough to provide Goldsmith with new quarters, new furnishings, and several new coats; they also whetted his desire to repeat his success. By 1771, he had finished a second comedy, *She Stoops to Conquer*, which was produced by a recalcitrant theater manager who procrastinated over the production for more than a year until Johnson again intervened. Through his reasoned arguments and bearlike presence, Johnson convinced the manager to put the play into production, and from the moment it opened on March 15, 1773, it was a huge success. Goldsmith, however, would have only thirteen months left in which to enjoy these financial rewards.

Even after he turned novelist and dramatist, Goldsmith never stopped racing from literary project to literary project. He continued to write essays, biographies, and general histories as well as to compile translations and anthologies. Despite his remarkable output in the last decade of his life, he was never far out of debt. Fortunately, publishers were always eager for his services, because they knew that Goldsmith's name on the title page increased their chances of a brisk sale.

Goldsmith wrote almost until the hour of his death. His last effort was the poem "Retaliation," a verse response to Garrick's epigrammatic remark (that Goldsmith "wrote like an angel, but talk'd like poor Poll"). Goldsmith died on April 4, 1774, the victim of both a fever and the remedy prescribed to cure it.

Analysis

The Good-Natured Man and *She Stoops to Conquer* were written to spite the prevailing taste in comedy. In an essay written just after he completed the second play, Oliver Goldsmith explained that the comedy of his time, which he called sentimental comedy, was a degeneration of a genre that had been clearly defined since the days of Aristotle. Comedy, Goldsmith lamented, had become a kind of tragedy that sought to influence the audience by appealing to its sympathy.

Sentimental comedy was a dramatic subgenre that developed at the beginning of the eighteenth century. The Restoration comedy of manners, which had delighted audiences with contrasting manners, sharp wordplay, and sexual innuendo, had been attacked by Jeremy Collier and others as immoral. To save drama, some writers began to make sure that every rake reformed by the fifth act and that sober, sensible lovers got as much attention as witty, scandalous ones. Sir Richard Steele, in the influential *The Conscious Lovers* (pr. 1722), had shown that lovers could be entangled in plots of parental opposition and mistaken identities so complicated that only the playwright could untie the fifth-act knots. Audiences, it seemed, would watch good people suffer through complex but manageable difficulties and would cheer when the protagonists swept all before them. Sentimental comedy was a part of Sensibility, a movement which characterized much literature after 1740. Sensibility invited readers and audiences to prove their humanity by sympathizing with the plight of fictional or dramatic heroes and heroines; it promised that their sympathy would be rewarded because all would work out in the end, leaving viewers with emotions stirred, teased, and satisfied.

In his essay on "laughing comedy," Goldsmith described the typical sentimental play

> in which the virtues of private life are exhibited . . . and the distresses rather than the faults of mankind made our interest. . . . In these plays almost all the characters are good, and exceedingly generous; they are lavish enough of their *tin* money on the stage; and though they want humor, have abundance of sentiment and feeling.

Whatever claim to merit such plays have is reduced by the fact that they— like modern television situation comedies—are too easily written. Goldsmith scoffed that in sentimental comedies, it was enough

> to deck out the hero with a riband, or give the heroine a title; then to put an insipid dialogue, without character or humor into their mouths, give them mighty good hearts, very fine clothes, furnish a new set of scenes, make a pathetic scene or two, with a sprinkling of tender melancholy conversation through the whole. . . .

The essay concludes with a lament on the art of making audiences laugh, an art that Goldsmith thought had disappeared with plays of Sir John Vanbrugh and Colley Cibber at the start of the eighteenth century. Determined to show that whatever delight sentimental comedies gave, laughing comedies gave better, Goldsmith submitted his own two plays as evidence.

The Good-Natured Man, which debuted while Hugh Kelly's latest sentimental play, *False Delicacy* (pr. 1768), was dominating theatrical London, teased contemporary taste in two ways. First, Goldsmith created scenes which are ironic, farcical, or witty enough to generate laughter. Second, he delineated—that is, in traditional terms, offered up to ridicule—the folly of a culture hero of the age, the "good-natured man." The good-natured man is the sentimental hero, the one who thinks with his heart rather than his head and who leaps to help solve life's smallest distresses. This generous instinct, Goldsmith's good-natured man discovers, has its limitations: One so inclined to sympathize with others may be in danger of losing himself. The twin purposes of the play—literary and moral—actually work together because the laughter which the play generates makes the lesson easier for the audience to accept.

The Good-Natured Man traces Sir William Honeywood's attempt to test and reform his nephew and heir, whose easy generosity (that is, good nature) has led him into extravagance and foolishness. Sir William's plan is to involve young Honeywood in enough fictitious distresses that he will be jailed for debt. Young Honeywood, then, the uncle reasons, would learn a valuable lesson by seeing which of his friends come to his assistance and which of them have only been taking advantage of his generosity. Sir William willingly admits that his nephew's universal benevolence is "a fault near allied to excellency," but as far as Sir William is concerned, it is still a fault to be corrected.

Sir William's plot is intended to demonstrate the need for the sentimental, good-natured man to be shown his follies, and most of the play's other characters reinforce the same idea. Sir William himself is a not very subtle mouthpiece for the dramatist, expostulating precisely and exactly upon the hero's mistakes. Honeywood's friend Croaker is the exact opposite of Honeywood; as a man who sees everything gloomily and selfishly, he lets the audience see the defects of the other extreme. Another friend, Lofty, is a character who counterfeits benevolence (pretending to use influence at court on his friends' behalf) in order to puff himself up in the eyes of the world. Lofty is a conscious pretender, while Honeywood is sincere, but the latter comes to see that "in attempting to please all," he "fed his vanity" as much as Lofty did.

Once Honeywood has been arrested for debt, Sir William is pleased to learn, Miss Richland, a woman of independent fortune and a close friend, has secured his release. Honeywood, however, does not need his uncle's conniving to find himself in difficulties. His benevolence, good nature, and sensibility generate other problems, one of the most knotty being his relationship with Miss Richland. Honeywood loves her deeply, but he is content to be only a friend. "Never let me harbour," he proclaims sentimentally, "a thought of making her unhappy by a connection with one so unworthy her merits as I am." In addition to being modest about his worth to her, Honeywood fears that he could never please her guardians, Mr. and Mrs. Croaker. Rather than tackle such obstacles directly, as would the witty hero of a Restoration comedy, Honeywood is content to sigh and wring his hands in distress.

Circumstances, however, refuse to let Honeywood remain uninvolved. Honeywood must watch while Croaker tries to marry his son, Leontine, to Miss Richland, despite the fact that Leontine is really in love with Olivia, an orphan whom he has brought to England from France in place of the long-absent sister he was sent to fetch. Honeywood must not only watch Croaker's matchmaking, but he must also intercede for Lofty's wooing of Miss Richland. Lofty, pretending to sentimental friendship, calls upon Honeywood to court the young heiress for him. Honeywood is on an emotional rack, stretched between the desire to please a friend and the agony of speaking love in another person's name: "What shall I do! Love, friendship, a hopeless passion, a deserving friend! . . . to see her in the possession of another! . . . Insupportable! But then to betray a generous, trusting friend!—Worse, worse."

Honeywood's dilemmas are solved in the last two acts by accident and by Sir William's intercession. He lends money to Leontine and Olivia that they may elope, but when Croaker intercepts what he thinks is a blackmail letter, Honeywood accidentally sends him after the "blackmailer" to the very inn where the lovers are hiding. Catching his son and "daughter," Croaker praises Honeywood for his help and Leontine damns him for his apparent betrayal. Meanwhile, in speaking to Miss Richland on Lofty's behalf, Honeywood coaxes an admission of love from her. Not realizing that the one she confesses to loving is himself, Honeywood decides that "nothing remains henceforward for me but solitude and repentance."

As the characters gather at the inn for the last act, Sir William sets all to rights on his nephew's behalf. First, he persuades Croaker to accept Olivia as Leontine's bride: She is, Sir William testifies, the daughter of an old acquaintance, of good family, and an orphan with a fortune. Next, Sir William exposes the pretentions of Lofty so that Honeywood sees he is no friend. Now that his sentimental dilemma between love and friendship is understood to be no dilemma after all, a pleased but surprised Honeywood receives Miss Richland's hand in marriage. The events have been a lesson for the good-natured man, who closes the play with the promise that "it shall be my study to reserve pity for real distress, my friendship for true merit, and my love for her, who first taught me what it is to be happy."

Goldsmith generates "laughing comedy" in the play by several devices: a farcical scene in which a bailiff and his deputy dress as gentlemen, humorous characters such as Croaker and Lofty whose foibles are played upon repeatedly, and dialogue at cross-purposes. Dialogue at cross-purposes is one of Goldsmith's favorite comedic devices, one of several dialogue strategies that had made the Restoration comedy of manners so rich in wit. When characters speak at cross-purposes, they manage to hold what appears to be a logical conversation although each is talking about a different subject. The result is confusion among the characters onstage and delight for the audience, which appreciates the ironic interplay of one attitude with another.

The best of these scenes in *The Good-Natured Man* are Leontine's marriage proposal to Miss Richland in act 1, Honeywood's plea on Lofty's behalf in act 4, and Honeywood's interview with the Croakers in act 4. In the first instance, Leontine twists himself into verbal knots as he tries simultaneously to convince his father that he is making an ardent proposal and to make it lukewarm enough to ensure that Miss Richland will reject it. In the second, Honeywood pleads so eloquently for another that Miss Richland is convinced he speaks for himself. In the third, Honeywood counsels Croaker on how to forgive the eloping lovers—counsel which the old man mistakes for advice on how to treat a blackmailer.

What Goldsmith does well in *The Good-Natured Man*, he does brilliantly in *She Stoops to Conquer*. The second play dispenses with the mouthpiece figure of Sir William, offers more entanglements more dextrously resolved, and satirizes sentimental comedy more subtly. *She Stoops to Conquer* has no thesis at all in the usual sense. It is a play that is not *about* something; instead, it is a play that *is* something: a recipe for laughing comedy.

Talking about *She Stoops to Conquer* is somewhat like trying to explain a joke. *She Stoops to Conquer* is an inventory of dramatic tricks for making comedy: juxtaposing high-class and low-class characters, creating farcical situations, putting witty dialogue in the mouths of several characters and having them converse at cross-purposes, establishing several good intriguers to initiate the action, and adding a generous helping of mistaken identities. *She Stoops to Conquer* is one of the purest pieces of entertainment ever written; it stands above its time and historical circumstances to such a degree that it has been a theatrical staple since its first production. To enjoy Goldsmith's comedy, an audience needs no special knowledge or moral perspective; it needs only a willingness to react instinctively to high spirits, confusion, and surprise. The play is a delight for actors as well as audience because all the principal characters are good roles; it is a play for an acting company rather than a vehicle for one or two stars. Although there are two plots, they are so nicely balanced that no audience wishes to see one enhanced at the expense of the other.

Goldsmith manages throughout the play to keep the audience informed of all that occurs while the characters onstage usually act under some mistaken impression. By constantly shifting who-knows-what-about-whom, Goldsmith keeps the plot throttle on "full ahead," the characters in unexpected predicaments, and the audience wide awake. Casting the whole in clever dialogue adds to the delight. In the hands of actors capable of playing the physical comedy broadly, *She Stoops to Conquer* becomes three hours of fast-paced merriment.

So much seems to be occuring simultaneously that *She Stoops to Conquer* is a difficult play to summarize. Perhaps reviewing the *dramatis personae* and sketching the action of the two plots best reveals Goldsmith's dexterity at introducing contrasting parts while keeping the whole moving forward. This dramatist is a theatrical juggler of rare skill; once set into motion, no character, action, or situation falls from his hand.

"The mistakes of a night" occur at the country residence of Mr. and Mrs. Hardcastle, a mismatched couple, each of whom is married for a second time. Mr. Hardcastle loves the country and its old-fashioned ways; Mrs. Hardcastle yearns for the city and the latest styles. Like another literary couple grown accustomed to each other's hobbyhorses, Mr. and Mrs. Bennet in Jane Austen's *Pride and Prejudice* (1813), each Hardcastle takes an independent path while poking fun at the spouse's preference.

Living at the Hardcastle residence are three young persons on the verge of independence and love. First, there is Tony Lumpkin, Mrs. Hardcastle's son by her first marriage. He is about to turn twenty-one and come into his own estate. Mr. Hardcastle regards him as a lazy and useless child, while Mrs. Hardcastle dotes on him, one minute sure he has the makings of a scholar and the next worried that he is consumptive. Tony prefers to ignore both parents and to concentrate on drinking and singing at his favorite tavern, the Three Pigeons. Here he entertains his fellows with practical jokes and lyrics that make clear his values:

> Let schoolmasters puzzle their brain
> With grammar, and nonsense, and learning;
> Good liquor, I stoutly maintain,
> Gives genius a better discerning.

Tony, the alehouse hero, is rather a bold protagonist for Goldsmith to portray to audiences accustomed to central male characters dressed in fine linen and attentive to providing themselves with life's essentials: a pretty wife and a sufficient income.

The second resident is Constance Neville, Mrs. Hardcastle's orphaned niece. Constance is treated with as much restraint as Tony is indulged. She is anxious to marry George Hastings but cannot, because her dowry, a substantial sum in jewels, is closely kept by her aunt. Mrs. Hardcastle is reluctant to give the jewels into Constance's care because she hopes to force her niece to marry Tony. Mrs. Hardcastle's matchmaking is having no luck: The sober Constance and the lighthearted Tony thoroughly dislike each other. Constance is a typical dramatic heroine of the time: pleasant but not especially bright, rich but without control of her fortune, and restless but not very disobedient.

The third person is Kate, Hardcastle's daughter by his first marriage. She and her father get along much better than do mother and son or aunt and niece. They are honestly affectionate with each other and speak frankly to each other; they care enough for each other to indulge each other's preferences. Kate, for example, who shares her stepmother's interest in fashion, moderates her indulgence by dressing for one half of the day in current styles and the other half in a plain country style that pleases her father. Mr. Hardcastle, in turn, has allowed Charles Marlow, the son of an old friend, to become Kate's suitor only after knowing that he is financially sound, handsome, and modestly spirited. As the play begins, Kate anxiously awaits her first look at this prospecting and prospective husband.

When young Marlow and Hastings (the man Constance loves), arrive at the Hardcastle house, they mistakenly believe that they are at a public inn. This false impression is entirely Tony's fault. Tony recognizes the two London beaux when they stop to ask for directions at the Three Pigeons. Irritated by their affected manners, desirous of playing a trick on his stepfather, and anticipating no consequences but a solid embarrassment, Tony directs them to his stepfather's house, telling them that he is sending them to the best inn of the neighborhood. This first mistake of the night begins a series of events that will turn the household topsy-turvy.

Expecting the modest young men described by his old friend Sir Charles Marlow, Hardcastle greets the two weary travelers generously and familiarly. Surprised at the supposed innkeeper's behavior, Marlow and Hastings react with hauteur and sarcasm. To Hardcastle's every offer of hospitality, they respond with increased demands. This scene (act 2, scene 1) is a classic instance of Goldsmith's spectacular handling of dialogue at cross-purposes.

Soon afterward, Hastings encounters Constance and learns how Tony has deceived him and Marlow. The reunited lovers plan to elope as soon as Constance can gain possession of her jewels; to protect their plot, they decide to keep Marlow in the dark about where he is. They introduce him to Miss Hardcastle as if she had just alighted at the inn. Throughout the play these two couples will maintain distinct characteristics. Constance and Hastings, whose mutual affection is a given, will struggle against external obstacles; Marlow and Kate, having just met, will try to discover what mutual affection, if any, exists between them.

Kate is anxious to meet the man who has come to court her. In a complete reversal of the bold, brash character that he showed to Mr. Hardcastle, Marlow becomes shy and stuttering in Miss Hardcastle's presence. It seems that proper young ladies of rank intimidate Marlow with their genteel and sentimental conversation. He bumbles his way through a conversation saved only by Kate's promptings:

> MISS HARDCASTLE: You were going to observe, Sir—
> MARLOW: I was observing, Madam—I protest, madam, I forget what I was going to observe.
> MISS HARDCASTLE: . . . You were observing, sir, that in this age of hypocrisy—something about hypocrisy, sir.
> MARLOW: Yes, madam. In this age of hypocrisy, there are few who upon strict inquiry do not a-a-a-
> MISS HARDCASTLE: I understand you perfectly, sir.
> MARLOW: (*aside*) Egad! and that's more than I do myself.
> MISS HARDCASTLE: You mean that in this hypocritical age there are few that do not condemn in public what they practise in private, and think they pay every debt to virtue when they praise it.

While Constance enlists Tony's help to get the jewels from his mother and thus free both of them from her matchmaking, Kate and Mr. Hardcastle try to decide who is the real Marlow: the overbearing puppy who insulted his host or the tongue-tied dandy who courted the daughter? The mystery begins to clear a little when Kate, now wearing her plain country dress, meets Marlow a second time. The young man makes his second mistake of the night. Not recognizing Miss Hardcastle in what appears to be a barmaid's outfit, Marlow is immediately and frankly attracted to the pretty servant. He proves not shy at all in the presence of lower-class women. With them he can wittily compliment, flirt, and steal a kiss. When Mr. Hardcastle sees Kate receiving this impudent attention, he is ready to order Marlow from his house. Kate, however, having seen what a charming wooer the young man can be, protests that this is the same modest man she interviewed earlier. She asks her father for the chance to show Marlow's real character; he begins to wonder if the usually sensible Kate is not now afflicted by that same malady that makes all young people undecipherable by their elders. At a second interview, Marlow begins to fall in love with the girl he assumes to be a household servant.

For one frantic moment the two plots intertwine before going separate ways. Tony filches Constance's jewels from his mother's bureau and gives them to Hastings. To get them out of sight, Hastings hands the jewels to Marlow. Thinking that such valuable gems must not lie around unguarded, Marlow gives them to Mrs. Hardcastle for safekeeping. Mrs. Hardcastle, alerted by the odyssey of the jewels that something is afoot, is quickly suspicious when her illiterate Tony receives a letter. Neither Constance's extemporaneous excuses nor Tony's obstinacy can prevent Mrs. Hardcastle from snatching the letter and discovering instructions from Hastings about the elopement. Determined to frustrate her niece and Hastings, Mrs. Hardcastle orders her carriage made ready for a trip to London: Constance is going to be taken where she can be better watched.

Thus, by the end of act 4, Goldsmith has every character's fate up in the air. The dramatist who knotted things into such a delightful tangle, however, has enough legerdemain to unravel the confusion. Goldsmith will not have to step in to rescue the characters: Kate by her stooping and Tony by his prankstering will set all to rights.

Kate has quite a tangle to undo: first, her father's impression that Marlow is a rude guest and an inconsiderate lover; second, Sir Charles' fear that the son he thought to be honest and modest is really the lout that Hardcastle has described and an indifferent lover to his friend's daughter; third, Marlow's belief that he can be gallant in the pantry but *must act* stand-offish in the parlor. She accomplishes all three ends by having the fathers witness the third interview of Kate the maid and Marlow. He professes his love for her—and learns to his shock that he has wooed the redoubtable Miss Hardcastle as well as the pliant Kate.

Meanwhile Tony has been frustrating his mother's flight to London. In the darkness, he has led her carriage on repeated rounds of the estate before driving it into a pond; Mrs. Hardcastle is convinced that she is stranded "forty miles from home." Determined to torment her further, Tony leads his mother into a gloomy thicket where even Mr. Hardcastle, out for a walk in his yard, may look like something more sinister. Although Tony's prank is soon exposed, he at least has had the pleasure of exhausting his mother.

Tony has exhausted the eloping lovers as well. Constance and Hastings decide it will be easier to talk Mrs. Hardcastle into compliance than to escape her this evening. All the cold and sore wanderers in the night return to the house and find Kate and Marlow engaged while the fathers stand beaming. When Mrs. Hardcastle threatens revenge on Tony and Constance, Mr. Hardcastle breaks another surprising bit of news: Tony has already reached the age of majority. The Hardcastles had kept this fact secret to keep the irresponsible Tony from squandering his inheritance, but Mr. Hardcastle now resents his wife's misuse of her authority. Tony's first act as an independent gentleman is to renounce any claim to Constance.

George Hastings quickly grabs the marriageable hand that Tony surrenders. Everyone except Mrs. Hardcastle now sees that the mistakes of a night have turned out happily indeed.

Even this account of the play omits some of its brighter moments: Hardcastle's amusingly futile efforts to turn rough farm laborers into stylish drawing-room valets; the rousing but innocent debauchery of Tony's friends at Three Pigeons; and Kate's dumb-show wooing that quickly heals Marlow's embarrassment after his mistakes were revealed. Actually nothing but reading or viewing can give a complete idea of the brilliance of *She Stoops to Conquer*. It is a rare play, in which no situation is unexploited, no detail wrong, and no word wasted.

Even without the historical interest, many readers still find Goldsmith enjoyable for his prose style and his sense of humor. He is one of the masters of the middle style; his informal, almost conversational prose and his humane and humorous observations of individuals make his work accessible and pleasurable even to those who have never met a lord or made the Grand Tour. Goldsmith's characters and comments are rooted in universal experience.

Other major works

NOVEL: *The Vicar of Wakefield*, 1766.

SHORT FICTION: *The Citizen of the World*, 1762 (collection of essays first published in *The Public Ledger*, 1760-1761).

POETRY: "An Elegy on the Glory of Her Sex: Mrs. Mary Blaize," 1759; *The Traveller: Or, A Prospect of Society*, 1764; "Edwin and Angelina," 1765; "An Elegy on the Death of a Mad Dog," 1766; *The Deserted Village*, 1770; "Threnodia Augustalis," 1772; "Retaliation," 1774.

NONFICTION: *An Enquiry into the Present State of Polite Learning in Europe*, 1759; *The Bee*, 1759 (essays); *A History of England in a Series of Letters from a Nobleman to His Son*, 1764 (2 volumes); *An History of the Earth, and Animated Nature*, 1774 (8 volumes; unfinished).

MISCELLANEOUS: *The Collected Works of Oliver Goldsmith*, 1966 (5 volumes; Arthur Friedman, editor).

Bibliography

Kirk, Clara. *Oliver Goldsmith*, 1967.
Scott, Temple. *Oliver Goldsmith, Bibliographically and Biographically Considered*, 1928.
Sells, A. Lytton. *Oliver Goldsmith: His Life and Works*, 1974.
Sherwin, Oscar. *Goldy: The Life and Times of Oliver Goldsmith*, 1961.

Robert M. Otten

HARLEY GRANVILLE-BARKER

Born: London, England; November 25, 1877
Died: Paris, France; August 31, 1946

Principal drama

The Weather Hen: Or, Invertebrata, pr. 1899 (with Berte Thomas); *The Marrying of Ann Leete*, pr. 1902, pb. 1909; *Prunella: Or, Love in a Dutch Garden*, pr. 1904, pb. 1906 (with Laurence Housman, music by Joseph Moorat); *The Voysey Inheritance*, pr. 1905, pb. 1909; *A Miracle*, pr. 1907; *Waste*, pr. 1907, pb. 1909; *The Madras House*, pr. 1910, pb. 1911; *Rococo*, pr. 1911 (one act); *The Morris Dance*, pr. 1913 (adaptation of Robert Louis Stevenson and Lloyd Osborne's play *The Wrong Box*); *The Harlequinade*, pr. 1913, pb. 1918 (with Dion Calthrop); *The Dynasts*, pr. 1914 (adaptation of Thomas Hardy's verse drama); *Vote by Ballot*, pr. 1917 (one act); *Three Plays*, pb. 1917 (3 one-acts: *Rococo, Vote by Ballot,* and *Farewell to the Theatre*); *Deburau*, pr. 1920, pb. 1921 (adaptation of Sacha Guitry's play); *The Secret Life*, pb. 1923; *His Majesty*, pb. 1928.

Other literary forms

Harley Granville-Barker's concern for a serious drama, and for a serious theater to interpret that drama, informs much, if not all, of his prose writings. With William Archer, Granville-Barker compiled *A National Theatre: Scheme and Estimates* (1907, revised by Granville-Barker in 1930), a working blueprint for a national repertory theater. *The Exemplary Theatre* (1922) presents Granville-Barker's conception of the theater from the perspective of a director-actor-playwright. His other writings on the theater, *On Dramatic Method* (1931), *The Study of Drama* (1934), *On Poetry in Drama* (1937), and *The Use of Drama* (1945), focus primarily upon his conception of a theatrically viable drama. This particular concern is evident as well in his famous series, *Prefaces to Shakespeare* (1927-1947) and in its predecessor, the various prefaces and introductions Granville-Barker wrote for the volumes of *The Player's Shakespeare* (1923-1927). The remainder of Granville-Barker's literary works comprises a handful of articles on drama and on the theater; six short stories, of which only three have been published; and numerous translations.

Achievements

In addition to his full-length plays, Granville-Barker wrote three one-act plays, *Rococo, Vote by Ballot,* and *Farewell to the Theatre*. "Agnes Colander" (wr. 1901) and the unfinished "The Wicked Man" (wr. 1910-1914), were never published or produced. Also never published were the four plays Granville-Barker wrote in collaboration with Berte Thomas between

1895 and 1899. Two of his other collaborations, however, *Prunella: Or, Love in a Dutch Garden*, with Laurence Housman, and *The Harlequinade*, with Dion Calthrop, were published. The remainder of Granville-Barker's dramatic writing consists of translations or adaptations, most notably a translation of Arthur Schnitzler's *Anatol* (pr. 1911) and an adaptation of Sacha Guitry's *Deburau*. He also translated plays by Jules Romains and, with his wife, Helen Huntington Barker-Granville, by Gregorio Martínez Sierra, and by Serafín and Joaquín Álvarez Quintero.

Granville-Barker's reputation as an *homme de théâtre* began to suffer a decline after he left active theater work and became a "mere professor." His plays, already looked upon with suspicion by his contemporaries, suffered an even greater decline. Although Granville-Barker's plays were lauded by such fellow dramatists as George Bernard Shaw, John Masefield, and Gilbert Murray, external factors, such as the growing dominance of Shaw and changes in dramatic and theatrical styles, hastened the decline of his plays into obscurity. Recent years, however, have seen a revival of interest in the plays of Granville-Barker (*The Madras House*, for example, was produced for television by the British Broadcasting Corporation). This revival of interest in Harley Granville-Barker betokens his significance as a dramatist.

The Granville-Barker play is singular among plays of the Edwardian period in its use of heterosexual relationships to define the worth of human actions and to signify the larger moral concerns that are the prime concern of his plays: the necessity of what he termed "the secret life," the inner reality that puts into perspective the trivialities of everyday life. Granville-Barker was lauded by his fellow dramatists not only for the superb "actability" and polish of his plays but also for his dramatic portrayal of the real, vital dilemmas of human sensibility and of absolute morality beneath the superficialities of daily existence. Granville-Barker's greatest achievement as a dramatist, and his significance as a dramatist to our age, lies in his successful deployment of heterosexual relationships as signs of our fragile hold on our essential selves and our humanity.

Biography

Harley Granville-Barker was, in a manner of speaking, born into the theater in 1877. Granville-Barker's mother, Mary Elizabeth Barker, formerly Bozzi-Granville, was a professional entertainer. The family traveled around together to her engagements, and young Harley was brought up to appear and to recite poetry with her professionally. Little is known of the extent and the nature of his formal education, but, at the age of fourteen, he was enrolled in Sarah Thorne's theatrical school at the Margate Theatre. During his six-month sojourn at the school, Granville-Barker met Berte Thomas, with whom he collaborated in the writing of his first four plays.

Granville-Barker's first major acting job was touring with Ben Greet's Shakespeare Company, which included Lillah McCarthy, whom he was later to marry. In 1899, at the age of twenty-two, Granville-Barker took the main role in William Poel's Elizabethan Stage Society production of William Shakespeare's *Richard II*. Poel's production led Granville-Barker to become involved in the newly founded Stage Society, for which he functioned as both an actor and a director. One of the results of his involvement with the Stage Society was his long and close friendship with George Bernard Shaw and, through his involvement with Shaw, his membership in the Fabian Society.

Another, more significant result of Granville-Barker's work with the Stage Society was the revolutionary Vedrenne-Barker management at the Court Theatre from 1904 to 1907; J. E. Vedrenne acted as business manager, and Granville-Barker directed all the plays and acted in many. The Vedrenne-Barker seasons at the Court Theatre were revolutionary not only in the plays they presented (by John Galsworthy, Henrik Ibsen, Maurice Maeterlinck, Gerhart Hauptmann, and Shaw, to name a few), but also in their format of repertory. In 1906, Granville-Barker married Lillah McCarthy, who also had been involved in the Vedrenne-Barker productions. Following the Vedrenne-Barker management, Granville-Barker's involvement with the theater took the form of efforts to establish a repertory theater in London. Such efforts defined the nature of his management of the Duke of York Theatre in 1910 (a venture backed by the American impresario Charles Frohman), the McCarthy-Granville-Barker management of the Little Theatre in 1911, and the Granville-Barker management of the St. James Theatre in 1913. In 1912, Granville-Barker gave his last performance as an actor, preferring to devote his time and his energy to directing, to the establishment of a repertory theater, and to the writing of plays.

On a trip to America in 1914, Granville-Barker met Helen Huntington, his future second wife. Upon his return to England, Granville-Barker became involved in World War I, serving with the Red Cross. He later enlisted in the Royal Horse Artillery and was soon transferred to Army Intelligence. Lillah McCarthy and Harley Granville-Barker were divorced in 1917, and the following year he married Helen Huntington; it was also at this time that he hyphenated his name. Granville-Barker's second marriage marked the beginning of the end of his friendship with George Bernard Shaw. Moreover, the new Mrs. Granville-Barker's dislike of Shaw in particular and theater people in general, coupled with Granville-Barker's own disillusionment with the theater, led to his retirement from active theater work in 1921.

Beginning in 1922, Granville-Barker devoted himself entirely to the program of writing that he began with his first attempts at playwriting. In 1930, the Granville-Barkers moved to Paris, where they lived until the German invasion of France. They spent the remainder of the war years in New York, where Granville-Barker worked for the British Information Services until 1942. After the war, the Granville-Barkers returned to England and then to Paris, where Granville-Barker died in 1946, a few months before his seventieth birthday, of arteriosclerosis.

Analysis

Harley Granville-Barker's early dramatic efforts—his apprentice plays— reveal that from the beginning, his plays were preoccupied with, if not generated by, the question of how a heterosexual relationship delineates and nurtures that moral strength or secret life essential to confront absolute moral dilemmas. The protagonist of a Granville-Barker play (Shaw preferred "worm" to "protagonist" in his letters to Barker) is thrust into a moral dilemma through a conflict between his outer, public life and his inner, secret life. The dramatic action of the play, then, is ordered by this conflict between the inner and the outer life of the protagonist. Granville-Barker heightens this basic conflict by means of his deft interweaving of theatrical symbol, dialogue, and theme. The dialogue itself, condensed, close-textured, and elliptical to the point of appearing disjointed, further underscores the central conflict of the play. In addition, much of the power of a Granville-Barker play is generated by what is implied through theatrical symbol rather than what is verbally stated. Granville-Barker's stage directions are decidedly Shavian in their wealth, precision, and breadth of detail and description. In *The Madras House*, for example, much of Jessica Madras is revealed through the description of her as "the result—not of thirty-three years—but of three or four generations of cumulative refinement. She might be a race horse!"

The basic conflict inherent in all the plays naturally imposes a similar structural pattern upon them. The protagonist is faced with a moral dilemma in which he is opposed by a figure of authority, refuses the negative examples of his close associates, and ends by accepting a mate under his own difficult conditions. The crucial point in this pattern is the protagonist's great refusal to accept the prevailing conditions and the prevailing wisdom in favor of his own conditions and his own wisdom. This great refusal invariably involves a sexual conclusion—that is, a consideration by the protagonist and his mate of how to continue in a world made difficult by the action of the inner life upon the outer. The element of sex in Granville-Barker's plays is not the "farmyard world of sex" denounced by Philip Madras but the relationship that prevails between the sexes, as in the case of Ann Leete and Abud, in the new world that the protagonist strives to create.

In *The Marrying of Ann Leete*, the conflict of the inner and the outer life takes the form of marriage. Carnaby Leete, a parliamentarian out of favor with his party, attempts to revive his career through the marriage of his daughter Ann to Lord John Carp, as he had once before salvaged his career by marrying his daughter Sarah to a member of the opposite party. Sarah's marriage, now falling apart in acrimonious mutual contempt, is a negative example for Ann. Her brother George provides another negative example of marriage; in defiance of his father, he has married a woman beneath his station who reveals herself to be little more than a vulgar social climber. Although Ann presumes that she will be married, she refuses to permit her father to sell her into marriage.

When Carp tells Ann he loves her, she responds: "It suddenly occurs to me that sounds unpleasant." For Ann, marriage is the union of male and female in the service of life; it requires no metaphysical justification. Her decision to marry John Abud, the gardener, is a manifestation of her inner life, of her need to forge a sexual relationship that is true to the fundamental moral purpose of men and women. The reference to Ann as a "new woman" and as the "new generation" underscore not only her determination not to repeat the marital mistakes of her brother and her sister, but also the role she forges for herself: the new Eve who will bring the future into the world. Ann's marrying, however, is left at the play's close as a frail gesture against the unlivable present. The class suspicions that emerge in the wedding scene, along with Ann's recognition of the experimental nature of her marriage, suggest that whatever the private significance of Ann's marrying, its public significance is minimal. Ann's marital experiment must bear fruit in the private life before it can be recognized by the public life.

Although *The Voysey Inheritance* also ends with a marriage, the focus of the play is not upon marriage per se. The central conflict of the play is structured in terms of capitalism and creativity. The elder Voysey, like his father before him, has placed the family's small solicitor's firm on the brink of ruin by systematically defrauding clients' accounts for personal profit through financial speculation. Moreover, the elder Voysey has managed this fraud with an artistic flair and a brilliance that ensures not only the prolongation of the game but also the temporary well-being of his clients. The elder Voysey's death pitches his son and heir, Edward Voysey, into the moral dilemma of continuing the family "practice" or turning himself in to the authorities, thereby atoning for the family's financial sins.

Edward is persuaded into accepting his inheritance by his potential wife, Alice Maitland. She encourages Edward to persist in his father's game of fraud to rectify the past and to ensure the economic future of his clients and of his firm. Although he never approaches the elder Voysey's talent for creative fiscal management, Edward's inheritance does save him from the morally flaccid existence of the "well-principled prig" and from the morally compromising positions of his brothers: the cold legality of Trenchard, the moral conventionality of Booth, and the uncontrolled creativity of Hugh.

In the final scene, a new Edward, with his new fiancée, Alice, charts the implications of their new life of benevolent fraud and of mutual help. Moreover, the final scene strongly suggests that Edward Voysey's inheritance is not the moral dilemma of financial corruption but the moral resolution of an admixed creativity and capitalism, the merging of the inner life with the outer.

Of all Granville-Barker's dramas, *Waste* is the most concerned, outwardly, with politics; its inner subject, however, is again the sexual relationship that unlocks the secret life. In fact, *Waste*'s open reference to sex—an abortion—prompted its censorship until 1936. Henry Trebell's suicide superficially results from his disappointment in the loss of a cabinet seat and in the rejection of his life's work by his party. In reality, his suicide is the direct result of his lack of a secret life. A meaningless sexual encounter with a married woman that culminates in her death in a back-alley abortion forces Trebell to a recognition of his own back-alley act of spiritual abortion: His angry hatred of women, and his powerful reason (he is described at various times as a machine) have killed his human sensibility, his secret life, before it was born.

Trebell's lack of a secret life, his incapability of loving another human being, is matched by that of his mate of the moment, Amy O'Connell, who is incapable of accepting the fact of life and of her womanhood without the placebo of love. Without a secret life and without a sexual means of engendering a secret life, Trebell is destroyed by the assumption of the void within him by his outer, political life. The motif of waste in the play achieves its final, most powerful resonance in the waste of Trebell. Without the supportive strength of the secret life, Trebell becomes the plaything of the Edwardian political oligarchy that controls government policy by Machiavellian infighting and that deliberately uses the bogey of public morality to destroy the threat posed to it by the able man with the good cause.

Implicit in all of Granville-Barker's plays is the question of the social and moral position of women. This question is made explicit in *The Madras House*, becoming, in fact, the dominant theme of the play. The play's action proceeds in a documentary fashion that suggests the simultaneous existence of contrasting groups of women within the great Edwardian middle class. Each act shows a different kind of woman and a different perspective—familial, marital, and professional—upon women's economic dependence upon men. Act 1 counterpoints Mrs. Huxtable, the paragon of that respectability that inhibits all spontaneous impulses and reduces life to domestic conventions, to her six, no longer young, daughters. This particular gaggle of spinsters is indistinguishable. The Huxtable daughters have no expressive language of their own, only a code of verbal behavior imposed upon them that governs them and threatens all who approach them. Act 2 presents the economic slavery of the independent woman. Most of the employees of Huxtable and Roberts and of the Madras House live on the premises under the morally vigilant eye of Miss Chancellor. When it is discovered that Miss Yates, one of Miss Chancellor's charges, is pregnant, an inquisition into her morals is held. Miss Yates's secret life, which has its source in her pregnancy, permits her to scoff at the world's equation of virtue with gainful employment. Her ability to rise above her moral dilemma throws into relief the pathos of Miss Chancellor, whose life has been stunted by the conventional morality imposed upon her spirit by thirty years of economic slavery to the drapery firm of Huxtable and Roberts.

Act 3 is the antithesis of act 1, as it presents a male banquet of articulateness in a fantastic seraglio setting. The masters of the drapery trade, enthroned in the "Moorish" rotunda of the Madras House, are shown engaged in the business of reducing women to sexual automata for economic exploitation in haute couture. Mr. State, an American millinery magnate, idolator of the "woman-spirit" and admirer of the women's movement as womanly sartorial self-expression, defines the middle-class woman as "one of the greatest Money Spending Machines the world has ever seen." The only women to appear in the act are barely women at all. The grotesquely dehumanized fashion mannequins, members of the industrial seraglio, are present only because actual automata are inefficient and uneconomical in comparison to flesh-and-blood automata.

The fourth and final act of the play attempts to bring to a resolution the question of womanhood delineated in the preceding acts. Philip Madras, the play's connecting character, by rejecting a position in the Madras House, rejects the prevailing conceptions of womanhood. Rather than exploit women, and through them, men, Philip chooses to change prevailing conditions by joining the County Council. Jessica Madras, the epitome of the Edwardian middle-class lady, supports her husband provided that he, in his new world, creates a meaningful place for her by his side. More disgusted than her husband by the farmyard world of sexual games symbolized by the Madras House, Jessica yearns for a world in which men and women can be friends. The play closes with the unresolved, because it is unresolvable, discussion between Philip and Jessica as to the place of woman in this new life. Like Ann Leete and John Abud, Philip and Jessica Madras must make their marriage the testing ground for the moral dilemma represented by their redefinition of the sexual relationship and their need to realize the secret life of both man and woman.

The Secret Life, written after Granville-Barker left the theater, is his finest, fullest dramatic exploration of sexual relationships and the secret life. *The Secret Life* is an exploration of the potential hazards of middle age, with its loss of purpose and of conviction, its desires that fail to come to fruition, and the extreme difficulty of bringing the inner life to bear upon the outer. As in *Waste*, to which it is the natural pendant, the outer life of the play unfolds in the political arena. Evan Strowde, who left politics years ago to write a multivolume industrial history, is being wooed back into politics at the start of the play by his parliamentarian friends. Strowde himself is attempting to renew his courtship of his old love, Joan Westbury. Evan and Joan are presented throughout the play as antithetical yet complementary. Strowde, like Trebell, has a full outer life but no inner life, whereas Joan, stripped of her outer life by the deaths of her husband and her sons and by the destruction of her home, has a rich inner life. Although Strowde needs Joan to kindle his inner life and she needs him to structure her outer life, Joan refuses to commit herself to him. Such a commitment would destroy her inner life and, by extension, herself: "I couldn't have lived my love for you, Evan . . . it would have killed me." Joan's secret life is based upon her love for the unattainable in Evan, and its existence depends upon the sanctity of that unattainability. Union with Strowde would make external her secret life, would reduce her secret life to an everyday triviality, and would leave her an empty shell.

Because Joan, like Amy O'Connell and Trebell, refuses to risk her happiness in what is, essentially, a commitment to the absolute morality of life, she condemns herself and Strowde to death. Strowde loses himself in his renewed political career and Joan loses herself in death. Although Joan's great refusal of life destroys both herself and Strowde, it does provide the play's youth, Oliver and Susan, with a negative example of the power of the secret life. In the play's final scene, Oliver, Strowde's illegitimate son, and Susan, Joan's alter ego, reveal the potential to make the great commitment demanded by the conflict of the inner life with the outer life.

Other major works

NONFICTION: *A National Theatre: Scheme and Estimates*, 1907 (with William Archer), 1930 (revised by Granville-Barker); *The Exemplary Theatre*, 1922; *The Player's Shakespeare*, 1923-1927 (prefaces and introductions); *Prefaces to Shakespeare*, 1927-1947; *On Dramatic Method*, 1931; *The Study of Drama*, 1934; *On Poetry in Drama*, 1937; *The Use of Drama*, 1945.

TRANSLATIONS: *Anatol*, pr., pb. 1911 (of Arthur Schnitzler's six playlets); *The Romantic Young Lady*, pr. 1920, pb. 1923 (with Helen Granville-Barker, of Gregorio Martínez Sierra's *Sueño de una noche de agosto*); *The Two Shepherds*, pr. 1921, pb. 1923 (with Helen Granville-Barker, of Martínez Sierra's *Los pastores*); *The Kingdom of God*, pr., pb. 1923 (with Helen Granville-Barker, of Martínez Sierra's *El reino de Dios*); *Wife to a Famous Man*, pb. 1923, pr. 1924 (with Helen Granville-Barker, of Martínez Sierra's *La mujer del héroe*); *Six Gentlemen in a Row*, pr., pb. 1927 (one act, of Jules Romains' *Amédée et les messieurs en rang*); *The Women Have*

Their Way, pb. 1927, pr. 1928 (with Helen Granville-Barker, of Serafín and Joaquín Álvarez Quintero's *Pueblo de las mujeres*); *A Hundred Years Old*, pb. 1927, pr. 1928 (with Helen Granville-Barker, of the Álvarez Quintero Brothers' *Papa Juan: Centenario*); *Fortunato*, pb. 1927, pr. 1928 (with Helen Granville-Barker, of the Álvarez Quintero Brothers' play); *The Lady from Alfaqueque*, pb. 1927, pr. 1928 (with Helen Granville-Barker, of the Álvarez Quintero Brothers' *La consulesa*); *Take Two from One*, pb. 1931 (with Helen Granville-Barker, of Martínez Sierra's play); *Love Passes By*, pb. 1932 (with Helen Granville-Barker, of the Álvarez Quintero Brothers' *El amor que pasa*); *Peace and Quiet*, pb. 1932 (with Helen Granville-Barker, of the Álvarez Quintero Brothers' *La escondida senda*); *Doña Clariñes*, pb. 1932, pr. 1934 (with Helen Granville-Barker, of the Álvarez Quintero Brothers' play).

Bibliography
Morgan, M. M. *A Drama of Political Man: A Study in the Plays of Barker*, 1961.
Purdom, Charles B. *Harley Granville-Barker*, 1955.
Salenius, Elmer W. *Harley Granville-Barker*, 1982.
Shaw, George Bernard. *Barker: Some Particulars*, 1946.

Stella Maloney

SIMON GRAY

Born: Hayling Island, England; October 21, 1936

Principal drama

Wise Child, pr. 1967, pb. 1968; *Dutch Uncle*, pr., pb. 1969; *Spoiled*, pr. 1970 (staged), pb. 1971 (televised 1968); *The Idiot*, pr. 1970, pb. 1971 (adaptation of Fyodor Dostoevski's novel); *Butley*, pr., pb. 1971; *Dog Days*, pr. 1975, pb. 1976; *Otherwise Engaged*, pr., pb. 1975; *Molly*, pr. 1977, pb. 1978 (revision of Gray's television play *Death of a Teddy Bear*); *The Rear Column*, pr., pb. 1978; *Close of Play*, pr., pb. 1979; *Stage Struck*, pr., pb. 1979; *Quartermaine's Terms*, pr., pb. 1981.

Other literary forms

Simon Gray is primarily known as a stage dramatist, but he began his playwriting career as an author of television scripts: *The Caramel Crisis* (1966), *Death of a Teddy Bear* (1967), *A Way with the Ladies* (1967), *Sleeping Dog* (1967), *Pig in a Poke* (1969), *The Dirt on Lucy Lane* (1969), *Style of the Countess* (1970), *The Princess* (1970), *The Man in the Sidecar* (1971), *Plaintiffs and Defendants* (1975), and *Two Sundays* (1975).

Besides being a successful dramatist, Gray has also published novels: *Colmain* (1963), *Simple People* (1965), *Little Portia* (1967), and *A Comeback for Stark* (1968). This last novel was published under the pseudonym Hamish Reade; Gray has also used the pen name James Holliday.

In 1975, the playwright wrote the screenplay version of his play for the film *Butley*, directed by Harold Pinter and starring Alan Bates, re-creating his stage role as the title character. The movie was made as part of the American Film Theatre series.

Finally, Gray coedited with Keith Walker an anthology entitled *Selected English Prose* that was published by Faber in 1967, and he has been editor of *Delta* magazine since 1964.

Achievements

Gray has received many of the highest awards for dramatists. *Death of a Teddy Bear* won a Writers Guild Award, *Butley* received the *Evening Standard* (London) Award for Best Play of the Year in 1972, and *Otherwise Engaged* was voted Best Play by the New York Drama Critics Circle. Moreover, the filming of *Butley* and the option taken to film *Death of a Teddy Bear* are indicators of the dramatist's popularity.

Biography

Simon Gray was born on Hayling Island, Hampshire, England, on October 21, 1936, the son of James Davidson and Barbara Celia Mary (née Holliday) Gray. The elder Gray was a pathologist and first-generation Canadian of Scottish ancestry, and when World War II began, Simon Gray was sent from Great Britain to his grandparents' home in Montreal. He returned to the United Kingdom for a while after the war and then moved back and forth between England, Canada, France, and Spain. He married Beryl Mary Kevern, a picture researcher, on August 20, 1964, and they have one son, Benjamin.

Gray, a lecturer in English, taught at Trinity College, Cambridge, from 1965 through 1966 and has been on the faculty at Queen Mary College of the University of London since 1965. This experience, together with his educational background, serves as the source of many of the dramatist's subjects (and characters) and his literate style alike. He attended the Westminster School in London, and he received a B.A. (honors in English) from Dalhousie University in Canada in 1958, and another B.A. (again with honors in English) from Cambridge University in England in 1962. Between the awarding of his two bachelor's degrees, Gray served as a lecturer at the University in Clermont-Ferrand, France. He resided in France from 1960 to 1961 and in Spain from 1962 to 1963. Subsequently, he returned to live and teach in London.

Analysis

Two important elements in Simon Gray's playwriting career evolved directly from his educational background. The Cambridge experience was clearly an important one. In a sense, when Gray reports, "I went to university when I was seventeen and I never left," he is speaking metaphorically as well as literally. His postgraduate life has been spent in academia, but it is obvious that there are symbolic connections with his everyday life that reappear in his plays. During Gray's tenure at Cambridge, there was an extraordinarily gifted group of other students also in attendance. The intellectual atmosphere was stimulating; a number of undergraduates wrote and acted in satiric revues on campus and then moved on to the London stage immediately afterward (and sometimes even while still pursuing their studies). Peter Cook, a contributor to the immensely successful *Beyond the Fringe* (1959), was one such. Novelist Margaret Drabble, television personality David Frost, actor Derek Jacobi, and Christopher Booker, a cofounder of *Private Eye* magazine, were among Gray's contemporaries. Furthermore, director John Barton was a don at King's College and poet Sylvia Plath lived in the town of Cambridge.

Besides the literary climate of the present and the long line of literati connected with the university in the past, Gray was also exposed to literary and dramatic traditions in his course work. Many of his characters, settings, and plot situations derive from this aspect of his life. The numer-

ous literary allusions that are characteristic of his style are direct out-
growths of Gray's Cambridge experience. Finally, the many references to
Cambridge, typically related to the concept of class distinctions, are similarly attributable to this period in his life.

The second element is Gray's experience as a teacher. A number of the
aspects of his writing that can be traced to his university days extend to his
professional career as well; the origins of several of Gray's dramatic works
reflect the attitude of an academic mind.

Unlike many contemporary playwrights who began writing dramas while
in college, Gray actually became a dramatist as a young man after he was
graduated and while he was trying to write short stories and novels. He
had already published two prose volumes, *Colmain* in 1963 and *Simple People* in 1965, when he adapted a short story that was primarily dialogue and
sold it as a television script. The piece, entitled *The Caramel Crisis*, was
televised in 1966, and within a year *Death of a Teddy Bear*, *A Way with the
Ladies*, and *Sleeping Dog* were also televised. *Death of a Teddy Bear* was
an award-winning script, and *Sleeping Dog* was well received for its examination of the elements of domination and submission in the British national
character (represented by Sir Herbert, a retired colonial administrator, who
imprisons Claud, a black homosexual, in the basement of his manor
house—the theme of ambiguous sexuality is also introduced).

Wise Child was written for television, too, but it was reportedly considered "too bizarre for home viewing," and it became Gray's first play to be
staged in the theater (at the Wyndham on October 10, 1967). The play is
usually considered Gray's best early effort, and it has been favorably compared with the work of Joe Orton. The plot revolves around a criminal who
is wanted for a brutal mail robbery and is hiding from the police by
disguising himself as a woman (creating a sort of black comedy version of
Brandon Thomas' 1896 farce *Charley's Aunt*) while his accomplice poses as
his son. After the pair murder their homosexual landlord, the older man
reverts to wearing men's clothing, and the younger man dons the maid's
clothes. Gray was fortunate that one of the finest actors of all time, Sir
Alec Guinness, took the lead role. The "son's" part was played by Simon
Ward, who would appear in later plays by Gray. Harold Hobson, drama
critic for the London *Sunday Times*, was impressed by the piece.

Dutch Uncle followed *Wise Child* and was considerably less successful.
Mounted by the Royal Shakespeare Company at the Old Vic in London,
the drama shows the academic turn of mind characteristic of Gray's later
works. The play was inspired by the case of police constable Reginald
Christie, a mass murderer who did away with his wife, the wife of his upstairs lodger, and several other women. (Christie walled up the corpses in
his kitchen. Gray's play *Death of a Teddy Bear*, written a few years earlier,
was similarly based on an actual murder case.) In *Dutch Uncle*, the main

character, Mr. Godboy, tries to murder his wife to attract the attention of Inspector "Manly" Hawkins. His motivation is a homosexual obsession for the policeman. Unfortunately for Godboy, he proves ineffectual as a murderer—his wife blissfully and unknowingly avoids his trap—and when the inspector finally becomes interested in the household, it is because the upstairs tenant is the Merritt Street rapist. The play was not well received, and Gray himself described it as a failure "as witless as it was macabre. . . . [It] would goad an audience into an irritated restlessness." He goes on to claim that the London opening was "the worst night in the British theatre." Nevertheless, the husband's distaste for his role as a husband and the dramatist's exploration of the themes of domination and submission (also dealt with in *Wise Child*) mark the play as a contemporary work. It was probably these elements that attracted Harold Pinter to Gray's work.

Next came *Spoiled*, a realistic domestic drama that was televised in 1968 and then adapted for the stage in 1970. The play, which premiered at the Close Theatre Club in Glasgow, Scotland, on February 4, moved to London's Haymarket Theatre on October 31 of the following year. It is about the relationships among a high school French instructor, his pregnant wife, and a young male student. During the course of tutoring the teenager, the teacher seduces him, and the play evolves into a straightforward study of the "unthinking abuse of trust and power." *Spoiled* also serves as a companion piece to *Butley*; both plays involve student-teacher relationships in an academic setting, as well as failed marriages and homosexual activities. There are also some parallels with *Otherwise Engaged*. In contrast with the latter play, however, in which Simon Hench is too detached to be able to maintain a human relationship, Howarth, the teacher in *Spoiled*, falls tragically because he is too emotionally involved.

Butley, one of Gray's most successful dramas, premiered at the Oxford Playhouse on July 7, 1971, and then moved to the Criterion Theatre in London exactly one week later. The first of Gray's works to be directed by Pinter, it starred Alan Bates in the title role. Subsequently the play moved to the Morosco Theatre in New York City, on October 31, 1972.

All the action in the two-act play takes place in Ben Butley's office in a college of London University. Act 1 opens at ten o'clock in the morning on the first day after the midterm break, and the second act begins about two hours later, "shortly after lunch."

Butley is an English teacher at the University. He shares an office with Joseph Keyston, whom he calls Joey. Joey is also an English instructor, a former student of Butley and his current lover.

From the play's beginning, it is clear what kind of person Butley is—even the office set reflects the nature of his mind. His desk, for example, "is a chaos of papers, books, detritus" in contrast to Joey's neat, almost bare desk. Similarly, Butley's bookcase is "chaotic with old essays and mimeographed sheets scattered among the books." Butley's attitude toward his profession is certainly evident, as is the unsettled state of his mind. The photograph of T. S. Eliot indicates the kind of literature that interests Butley and is a visual reference to the source of some of the literary allusions that embellish Butley's conversations. The smeared and curled corner shows that what was once important enough to Butley that he put it on his wall no longer has his attention and has become damaged (and not repaired) as a result. The lamp that will not work for Butley is further evidence of the lack of connections in his life, the way that things no longer work for him.

Butley's egocentrism and the tactics that he uses to isolate himself from others and from his responsibilities are evident in his very first speech. He tells the head of his department, who has called him on the telephone, that he cannot talk at the moment because he is "right in the middle of a tutorial"—and all the while the audience can plainly see that Butley is sitting alone in his office. In a sense, there is dramatic irony involved here, too, and not only because the audience is aware of something that one of the characters (the caller, in this case) is not. Throughout the play people try to get in touch with Butley, and he rejects their attempts; he constantly uses the false tutorial excuse to avoid contact. The comic touch of Butley taking a squashed banana from his pocket and throwing the peel on Joey's desk seems to lighten the effect of Butley's lie, but it soon becomes evident that this is merely another indication of Butley's sloppy habits, his lack of consideration for others, and his conscious attempts to belittle everyone. The piece of toilet paper stuck to his chin to stop the blood from a cut sustained while he was shaving is a parallel to the banana. Obviously Butley does not demonstrate much respect for himself, and he shows even less for those with whom he comes in contact.

In the first act, Gray introduces most of the rest of the characters who play major parts in the protagonist's life. In essence, there is no action and no traditional plot. Joey appears first, and through his conversation with Butley, the various levels of their relationship are exposed, as is Butley's estrangement from his wife and the possibility that Butley is about to be replaced in Joey's life by Reg Nuttall.

The word games, wit, literary allusions (often in the form of direct quotations), and cruelty that characterize Butley are also revealed. Butley emerges as a sad, lonely man who wants some sort of relationship with someone, preferably Joey, but who is unable to give enough of himself or accept enough from anyone else to allow them to penetrate his sarcasm to create a truly emotional relationship. Instead, Butley retreats behind a wall of sterile intellectualism.

Miss Heasman, a minor character, makes an appearance, serving as a bit of comic relief (and creating dramatic irony) when Butley purposely misunderstands her request and then lies about her duties (the audience already knows about his treatment of a student with a similar request previously). There is also a confrontation between Butley and his wife, who informs him that she has decided to take up with an acquaintance of theirs.

In his dealings with all of these people, Butley is consistently sarcastic and offensive, he knows where his victims are most vulnerable, and he sticks the knife in with sadistic pleasure and precision. He jokes about homosexuality, frequently by using double entendres or literary allusions. Other literary allusions (to Eliot, William Blake, Gerard Manley Hopkins, and others) provide further insight into Butley's character (unwittingly on his part), as he uses them as weapons. Butley's use of literary allusions is effective because the other characters in the play recognize their sources; this is an essential part of his game-playing. Also indicated is the probability that patterns are being repeated, implying that they have all engaged in the activity before—and this is reinforced by Butley's expressed appreciation for good comebacks by his targets. One of the games that he plays revolves around Joey's constant use of the tag "in point of fact." When Joey says that Reg's family lives "in a place just outside Leeds, in point of fact," Butley pretends that he thinks that "point of fact" is the name of a suburb. This becomes a running joke in the play and serves a dual purpose by simultaneously drawing attention to Reg's lower-middle-class background. The situation concerning Gardner is prepared for, too.

In act 2, the only major character not met in act 1 appears when Reg comes to collect Joey (and, incidentally, to make sure that Butley does not adversely influence the younger man's decision to leave). Beyond this, about all that happens is a continuation of the lines self-destructively developed by Butley, leaving him as he was when he first came onstage—alone and ineffectually trying to turn on the lamp. Butley's nonstop allusions (to Eliot, nursery rhymes, John Donne, D. H. Lawrence, John Milton, Sir John Suckling, Richard Lovelace, and Beatrix Potter, among others), his use of a Northern dialect to denigrate Reg's social background—all of this epitomizes his hollowness.

In her essay entitled "Literary Allusion as Satire in Simon Gray's *Butley*," Sophia B. Blaydes discusses this important aspect of the writer's technique and demonstrates how the allusions may provide insight into Butley's self-image as an individual "beset by betrayal and mediocrity," a tragic figure rather than the pitiable, "irresponsible, wasted man" that the characters in the play perceive him to be. The truth probably lies somewhere between: Butley is, indeed, surrounded by foolish people, but he cannot see beyond their flaws to their common humanity.

Otherwise Engaged, also directed by Pinter and featuring Bates in the part of Simon Hench, was first presented at London's Queen's Theatre on July 30, 1975. In February, 1977, the production was transferred to the

Plymouth Theatre in New York City, with Tom Courtenay making his long-awaited Broadway debut in the lead role.

The setting for *Otherwise Engaged* is more elegant than that of *Butley*. As in the earlier play, the action is limited to the events that transpire in one room, in this instance over a period of time equivalent to the running time of the drama. That room is Hench's living room in London. The plot has been described as the depiction of a series of events that occur during an afternoon that Hench wishes to spend listening to a newly acquired phonograph recording of Richard Wagner's opera *Parsifal* and which prevent him from accomplishing his goal; that is a bit like saying that *Butley* is about a teacher who is not interested in teaching.

In act 1, Hench, a book publisher, is discovered preparing to listen to his new purchase. He is interrupted by Dave, a dull polytechnic student who is renting a flat from him. This is only the first of a series of interruptions. Hench no sooner gets rid of the young man, who is seeking advice on his love life and money, than Hench's brother, Stephen, enters to expose fears and self-doubts about his professional status. Hench is witty, sociable, and somewhat supportive, but his rather obvious wish is to return to his recording. This pattern is repeated throughout the play.

The next interruption comes in the form of Jeff Golding, a dilettantish literary critic who seems not to be particularly attractive either as a critic or as a person. He confesses, for example, that he does not like literature, and his own description of how he mistreats women is damning. Next, Jeff's current mistress, Davina, appears, searching for her lover, whom she immediately dismisses. After Jeff leaves, Davina tries to seduce Hench. She is unsuccessful, but he does agree to consider for publication a book that she has written.

Hench then records a message on his telephone answering machine to inform anyone who might call that he is "otherwise engaged" for the rest of the day. Bernard Wood enters. Hench and Wood attended Wundale School at the same time, a place where both men engaged in homosexual activities. Wood accuses Hench of seducing his fiancée, Joanna, and Hench admits to the transgression as the curtain falls.

Act 2 opens where act 1 left off; in the continuation it becomes clear that Hench does not consider the seduction as a serious transgression. Wood wants to know if Hench's wife is aware of his activities; the audience soon learns that Mrs. Hench is involved in an affair and that she is considering leaving her husband. Hench finds her choice of partners tasteless, but sees the affair, like his, as posing no threat to their marriage. Wood, on the other hand, has a history of being unstable, and he calls to leave a message on the telephone recorder: He is going to shoot himself in the head because he is despondent about the Hench-Joanna affair, and he wants the act recorded so that Hench can hear it. Hench switches the machine off the instant before Wood squeezes the trigger. The play ends with Jeff returning to sit with Hench, listening to *Parsifal*.

The theme of *Otherwise Engaged* is again that of a man incapable of sustaining human relationships. Unlike Butley, however, Hench does not even seem to desire a meaningful relationship. He is comfortable in his marriage—whether he or his wife, Beth, actually have engaged in affairs is less important to him than his desire that they remain together, mainly because breaking up is a tiresome process, and staying together makes life easier, especially since he does not wish to become emotionally involved with anyone, including his wife, anyway.

There are some contradictory pieces of information provided by the dramatist. In act 1, Hench refuses to be seduced by the attractive Davina, even though she is aggressively willing and he admits that "I fancy you because of your breasts" (which she has exposed by removing her shirt). This scene is in direct contrast with Wood's claim that Hench seduced his fiancée. It may be that Hench does not reject Davina because of feelings of fidelity for his wife, but simply because her personality does not appeal to him. Additionally, in spite of Stephen's protests to the contrary, Hench does seem to have an interest in his brother's well-being. Finally, there is the ironic counterpointing between Hench's apparent attempts to remain emotionally disengaged from those intruders who surround him and his pleasure (and possibly his retreat) into Wagner's *Parsifal*. Wagner's music is lush and romantic in nature, full-bodied and emotional. If Hench enjoys this kind of music, it would indicate that he, too, has a romantic, emotional nature. His seeming lack of concern for Wood or Beth may stem either from his sense of hurt and betrayal, or from his realization that there may be little that he can do to alter the circumstances, or both. On the other hand, it may well be that he has no feelings for people and that he seeks emotional release in the safety of music—which can make no demands upon him, and which does not interrupt his privacy. Somewhat like the characters in *Close of Play* four years later, those in *Otherwise Engaged* are so wrapped up in their own problems that they think that all action focuses on them, and they are insensitive to and inconsiderate of others.

Stylistically, the play is entertaining. Gray is at his witty, literate best, and he handles the language masterfully. There are some echoes from Pinter's plays, particularly *The Caretaker* (pr. 1960), *The Collection* (pr. 1961), and *The Homecoming* (pr. 1965), and there are some amusing plot twists. The repetition of certain tags ("Not as stupid as he seems," for example) and other stylistic devices used in *Butley* reappear in *Otherwise Engaged*. Structurally, the interweaving of reappearing characters, motifs (egotism, fidelity, dominance, sexuality, and so forth), and images (drinks thrown in people's faces) all combine to give the play an operatic texture.

Gray's most recent plays have not significantly developed his earlier themes and style. In *Close of Play* (presented at the National Theatre's Lyttleton Theatre in London on May 24, 1979), Gray returned to an intellectual setting, of sorts. Jasper, a retired academic, sits silently while his wife, children, grandchildren, and assorted in-laws reveal the desperate nature of their lives. *Close of Play* is a dark, mature drama, yet it breaks no new ground for the playwright. With *Stage Struck* (Vaudeville Theatre, London, November 21, 1979), the dramatist tried his hand at a stage thriller in the vein of Ira Levin's *Deathtrap* (pr. 1978) and Anthony Shaffer's *Sleuth* (pr. 1970). In 1981, his play about an ineffectual upper-class Englishman, *Quartermaine's Terms*, opened at Queen's Theatre, London, on July 28. In New York, the Long Wharf Theatre presented the drama at Playhouse 91 in February, 1982.

Gray has shown the potential to become a major playwright, but so far he has not achieved that status. His plays are interesting, witty, and well structured, and his characters are believably drawn. Furthermore, he uses language well, and it is clear that the use of language in his later works has been influenced by Pinter's dramaturgy, improving an already good product.

The major weakness in Gray's dramas is in their subject matter. While he deals with problems of interpersonal communication and the difficulties involved in establishing or maintaining meaningful relationships, his plays are primarily character sketches. They are superficial portrayals of self-destructive people, and they lack the depth of Pinter's plays or the dramas of other contemporary British dramatists.

If Gray's plays lack profound thematic significance, they nevertheless excel in stagecraft and technique, and his works have entertained audiences at home in England and abroad. He does not contend that his plays are meant to convey a message, but he does work at his writing rigorously; *Otherwise Engaged*, for example, required thirty-five drafts. Combining this attention to craftsmanship with a flair for witty dialogue, Gary has achieved both critical acclaim and popular acceptance.

Other major works

NOVELS: *Colmain*, 1963; *Simple People*, 1965; *Little Portia*, 1967; *A Comeback for Stark*, 1968 (as Hamish Reade).

SCREENPLAY: *Butley*, 1975.

TELEPLAYS: *The Caramel Crisis*, 1966; *Death of a Teddy Bear*, 1967; *Sleeping Dog*, 1967; *A Way with the Ladies*, 1967; *Pig in a Poke*, 1969; *The Dirt on Lucy Lane*, 1969; *The Princess*, 1970; *Style of the Countess*, 1970; *The Man in the Sidecar*, 1971; *Plaintiffs and Defendants*, 1975; *Two Sundays*, 1975.

ANTHOLOGY: *Selected English Prose*, 1967 (editor with Keith Walker).

Bibliography

Blaydes, Sophia B. "Literary Allusion as Satire in Simon Gray's *Butley*," in *Midwest Quarterly*. XVIII (July , 1977), pp. 374-391.

Fox, Terry Curtis. "Heart of Grayness," in *The Village Voice*. XXIII, no. 49 (December 4, 1978), pp. 121-122.

Hamilton, Ian. "Simon Gray," in *The New Review*. III (January/February, 1977), pp. 39-46.

Hayman, Ronald. *British Theatre Since 1955: A Reassessment*, 1979.

Hobson, Harold. "Hobson's Choice: 'Close of Play,'" in *Drama*. No. 133 (Summer, 1979), pp. 41-42.

Imhof, Rüdiger. "Simon Gray," in *Essays on Contemporary British Drama*, 1981. Edited by Hedwig Bock and Albert Wertheim.

Kerensky, Oleg. *The New British Drama: Fourteen Playwrights Since Osborne*, 1977.

New, William H. *Dramatists in Canada: Selected Essays*, 1972.

Taylor, John Russell. *The Second Wave*, 1971.

Steven H. Gale

PAUL GREEN

Born: Lillington, North Carolina; March 17, 1894
Died: Chapel Hill, North Carolina; May 4, 1981

Principal drama

Surrender to the Enemy, pr. 1917; *The Last of the Lowries*, pr. 1920, pb. 1922; *The Long Night*, pb. 1920; *Granny Boling*, pb. 1921 (revised as *The Prayer Meeting*, pb. 1924); *The Old Man of Edenton*, pr. 1921, pb. 1925; *Old Wash Lucas (The Miser)*, pr. 1921, pb. 1924; *The Lord's Will*, pr., pb. 1922; *Blackbeard*, pr. 1922, pb. 1925 (with Elizabeth Lay Green); *White Dresses*, pb. 1922, pr. 1923 (one act); *Sam Tucker*, pb. 1923 (revised as *Your Fiery Furnace*, pb. 1926); *Wrack P'int*, pr. 1923; *Fixin's*, pr. 1924, pb. 1934 (with Erma Green); *The Hot Iron*, pb. 1924 (revised as *Lay This Body Down*, pb. 1959, pr. 1972); *In Aunt Mahaly's Cabin: A Negro Melodrama*, pb. 1924, pr. 1925; *The No 'Count Boy*, pr., pb. 1924; *The Lord's Will and Other Carolina Plays*, pb. 1925; *The Man Who Died at Twelve O'Clock*, pr. 1925, pb. 1927; *Quare Medicine*, pr. 1925, pb. 1928; *The End of the Row*, pb. 1926; *In Abraham's Bosom*, pr., pb. 1926 (one-act version); pr. 1926, pb. 1927 (full-length version); *Lonesome Road: Six Plays for the Negro Theatre*, pb. 1926; *The Man on the House*, pb. 1926; *Supper for the Dead*, pb. 1926, pr. 1954; *The Field God*, pr., pb. 1927; *Unto Such Glory*, pb. 1927, pr. 1936; *Blue Thunder: Or, The Man Who Married a Snake*, pb. 1928; *Bread and Butter Come to Supper*, pb. 1928, pr. 1954 (as *Chair Endowed*); *The Goodbye*, pb. 1928; *In the Valley and Other Carolina Plays*, pb. 1928; *Old Christmas*, pb. 1928; *The Picnic*, pb. 1928; *Saturday Night*, pb. 1928; *Tread the Green Grass*, pb. 1929, pr. 1932 (music by Lamar Stringfield); *The House of Connelly*, pr., pb. 1931; *Potter's Field*, pb. 1931, pr. 1934 (revised as *Roll Sweet Chariot*, pr. 1934, pb. 1935; symphonic drama; music by Dolphe Martin); *Shroud My Body Down*, pr. 1934, pb. 1935 (revised as *The Honeycomb*, pb. 1972); *The Enchanted Maze*, pr. 1935, pb. 1939; *Hymn to the Rising Sun*, pr., pb. 1936 (one act); *Johnny Johnson: The Biography of a Common Man*, pr. 1936, pb. 1937 (music by Kurt Weill); *The Southern Cross*, pr. 1936, pb. 1938; *The Lost Colony*, pr., pb. 1937 (symphonic drama); *Alma Mater*, pb. 1938; *The Critical Year*, pb. 1939; *Franklin and the King*, pb. 1939; *The Highland Call*, pr. 1939, pb. 1941 (symphonic drama); *Out of the South: The Life of a People in Dramatic Form*, pb. 1939; *Native Son*, pr., pb. 1941 (with Richard Wright; adaptation of Wright's novel); *The Common Glory*, pr. 1947, pb. 1948 (symphonic drama); *Faith of Our Fathers*, pr. 1950; *Peer Gynt*, pr., pb. 1951 (adaptation of Henrik Ibsen's play); *Serenata*, pr. 1953 (with Josefina Niggli); *The Seventeenth Star*, pr. 1953 (symphonic drama); *Carmen*, pr. 1954 (adaptation of the libretto of Georges Bizet's opera); *Wilderness*

Road, pr. 1955, pb. 1956 (symphonic drama); *The Founders*, pr., pb. 1957 (symphonic drama); *The Confederacy*, pr., pb. 1958 (symphonic drama); *The Stephen Foster Story*, pr. 1959, pb. 1960 (symphonic drama); *The Thirsting Heart*, pb. 1959, pr. 1971; *Five Plays of the South*, pb. 1963; *Cross and Sword*, pr. 1965, pb. 1966 (symphonic drama); *The Sheltering Plaid*, pb. 1965; *Texas*, pr. 1966, pb. 1967; *Sing All a Green Willow*, pr. 1969; *Trumpet in the Land*, pr. 1970, pb. 1972; *Drumbeats in Georgia*, pr. 1973; *Louisiana Cavalier*, pr. 1976; *We the People*, pr. 1976; *The Lone Star*, pr. 1977.

Other literary forms

An extremely prolific writer, Paul Green produced work in all the main literary genres. Related to his numerous stage plays is his work in other dramatic forms. Some of the screenplays he wrote for Hollywood include *Cabin in the Cotton* (1932; adaptation of Harry Harrison Kroll's novel of the same title), *State Fair* (1933, with Sonya Levien; adaptation of Phil Stong's novel of the same title), *Dr. Bull* (1933; adaptation of James Gould Cozzens' novel *The Last Adam*), *David Harum* (1934; adaptation of Edward Noyes Westcott's novel of the same title), *Time Out of Mind* (1947; adaptation of Rachel Field's novel of the same title), and *Black Like Me* (1963; adaptation of John Howard Griffin's novel of the same title).

Green's fiction includes two novels, *The Laughing Pioneer* (1932) and *This Body the Earth* (1935), and several collections of short stories: *Wide Fields* (1928), *Salvation on a String and Other Tales of the South* (1946), *Dog on the Sun* (1949), *Words and Ways* (1968), *Home to My Valley* (1970), and *Land of Nod and Other Stories* (1976). Green's verse appeared in *The Lost Colony Song-Book* (1938), *The Highland Call Song-Book* (1941), *Song in the Wilderness* (1947), *The Common Glory Song-Book* (1951), *Texas Song-Book* (1967), and *Texas Forever* (1967).

Nonfiction by Green includes a critical work, *Contemporary American Literature: A Study of Fourteen Outstanding American Writers* (1925, with Elizabeth Lay Green); a book about teaching, *Forever Growing: Some Notes on a Credo for Teachers* (1945); and four collections of writings on the theater, *The Hawthorn Tree* (1943), *Dramatic Heritage* (1953), *Drama and the Weather* (1958), and *Plough and Furrow* (1963).

Achievements

Early in his long career as a playwright, Green was hailed as the promising young Eugene O'Neill of the South. The New York drama critics were encouraging and so was a Pulitzer Prize for *In Abraham's Bosom* in 1927. Green's promise, however, was never quite fulfilled, although he continued to write for the New York stage up until World War II. Both Green's initial success and his ultimate failure in New York can be attributed to his folksy images of the South—images which, upon examination, and with repetition and age, proved stereotypical, especially in comparison with the work of more substantial Southern writers, such as Thomas Wolfe and William Faulkner. Green wrote too prolifically for his work to attain consistent quality: In particular, his characters, usually meant to be realistic, tend to be one-dimensional (or, when he tried to make them complex, merely inconsistent), and, for a student and teacher of philosophy, Green's lack of philosophical depth is disappointing.

When the romance with New York waned, Green, who had a down-home lover in the Carolina Playmakers and who had flirted with German experimental drama and with Hollywood, went in other directions. These other directions constitute his main achievement. Along with such groups as the Carolina Playmakers, Green helped to expand the material, techniques, and audiences of legitimate drama in the United States. He brought in more folk and historical material, music, and stylized techniques, and his "symphonic" plays (historical plays usually with patriotic themes), performed in outdoor theaters recalling the original Greek drama, brought drama to the people, particularly in the South. Immensely popular, great tourist attractions, some of the symphonic dramas are still running each summer, including the first one, *The Lost Colony*. Unfortunately, the setting, ritual, and spectacle of the symphonic dramas do not cover up Green's tendency toward stereotypes, which became even more pronounced with the historical material.

Of Green's prodigious output, his best work includes *White Dresses* and *Hymn to the Rising Sun* among the one-act plays, *In Abraham's Bosom* and *Johnny Johnson* among the full-length plays, and *Wilderness Road* among the symphonic dramas.

Biography

Paul Eliot Green was a product of the Cape Fear River farming region of eastern North Carolina. His paternal grandfather, John Green, had owned a plantation and slaves before the Civil War, and his maternal grandfather, William Byrd, was a preacher, singing teacher, and composer of hymns. Green's parents were William Archibald and Betty Byrd Green (William's second wife). His father owned and operated a large farm, where, with the other Green children, Paul played, worked, and got to know the sharecroppers, black and white. This rural background provided a rich source of material for Green's future plays.

After attending public elementary school, Green entered Buie's Creek Academy (now Campbell College) and benefited from the teaching of the academy's dedicated founder, James Archibald Campbell. Upon graduation, Green earned money to attend college by working for two years as the principal of tiny Olive Branch School and as a professional baseball player for the Lillington Cats. (He was an ambidextrous pitcher—a fact in which some critics of his plays might see a symbolic fitness.) He entered the University of North Carolina, Chapel Hill, in 1916, the same year as Thomas Wolfe, but his university studies were interrupted by volunteer service (1917-1919) in the United States Army Engineers. After serving at the front during World War I and in Paris afterward, attaining the rank of second lieutenant, Green left the engineers to resume his university studies. During Green's absence, Frederick Koch had come to the University of North Carolina and established the Carolina Playmakers. Koch and the Playmakers, with their emphasis on folk drama, exercised a profound influence on Green and his subsequent career, although at the university Green majored in philosophy.

Through Green's involvement with the Carolina Playmakers, he met his future wife, Elizabeth Lay, who had written the first play produced by the Playmakers and continued to work for them after her graduation in 1919. She helped produce some of Green's early one-act plays and collaborated with him in writing *Blackbeard*. They were married in 1922, between two years of graduate study in philosophy for Green, first at North Carolina, then at Cornell. In 1923, they returned to Chapel Hill, where they made their home and reared four children and where Green taught at the university, as lecturer and then associate professor of philosophy (1923-1939), as professor of dramatic arts (1939-1944), and as professor of radio, television, and motion pictures (1962-1963).

Green's 1927 Pulitzer Prize for *In Abraham's Bosom* was followed in 1928 by a Guggenheim Fellowship allowing him to study theater for two years in Germany and England. In Berlin, Green was particularly impressed by Alexis Granowsky's stylized productions in the Yiddish Theater (including the actors' imitation of puppets) and by the "epic theater" (deliberately theatrical, didactic drama) of Bertolt Brecht. Also influential was Green's intermittent screenwriting work in Hollywood (1932-1936, 1942, 1964). Finally, in the last part of his life, Green's successful production of patriotic outdoor dramas received further stimulus when he was frequently called upon to represent the United States officially and unofficially: Among other such activities, he was a United States delegate to UNESCO (1950-1952), lectured for UNESCO in Asia (1951), and attended the International Conference on the Performing Arts (Athens, 1962). He received the Freedoms Foundation George Washington Medal three times (1951, 1956, 1966).

Analysis

Paul Green's playwriting career is usually divided into three phases: an early phase when he wrote one-act plays about the South; a middle phase when he advanced to full-length plays, at first traditional but then experimental in form, mostly set in the South but including other settings; and a final phase when he concentrated on historical outdoor plays, the so-called symphonic dramas, still mostly set in the South. Another division scheme is suggested by a surprising break in his career around World War II, when for five years (1942-1946) this prolific playwright produced no work for the stage (though he was writing for Hollywood). The five-year break effectively divides Green's period of concentration on indoor drama from his period of concentration on outdoor drama.

During the five-year period, Green apparently reassessed his dramatic career and emerged not only with a new form but also with new material and new attitudes. Before the break, Green relentlessly criticized social injustice in these United States, particularly the Southern parts, but the born-again Green celebrated the patriotic *Faith of Our Fathers* and became a member of the United States Executive Committee and member of the National Commission, UNESCO (1950-1952). The onetime antiwar playwright filled the stage with battles. Green can be accused of inconsistency here—or at least of going for the popularity by merely reflecting changes in social climate from the 1930's to the 1950's. In his defense, however, it should be noted that his development was dictated, in part, by the opportunities available to him (which perhaps, in turn, were influenced by the prevailing social climate).

More important, the gulf between *Native Son* and *The Common Glory* is not as great as it first appears. The uniting strand is Green's democratic belief in human rights, expressed in a negative, critical form before World War II and in a positive, celebratory form after the war. Green's emphasis changed, but his beliefs remained the same, as can be seen most clearly in his consistently sympathetic portrayal of black Americans. His consistent development is demonstrated by the following analysis of his best work during the various phases.

The one-act plays *White Dresses* and *Hymn to the Rising Sun* both depict brutal social conditions in the South early in the twentieth century. *White Dresses* focuses on the relationship of a white landowner and his black female tenants, while *Hymn to the Rising Sun* shows guards and convicts on a chain gang. Both plays are expository in nature, with little plot, the action serving to demonstrate a sordid condition—the cruel dominance of one party and subjection of another, as though the South knows no other pattern.

In *White Dresses*, the mulatto girl Mary McLean has likings for young Hugh Morgan, the white landlord's son (with whom she has apparently had sexual relations), and talks of going to New York and passing for white. Her aspirations in both directions are crushed by the landlord, Henry Morgan, who forces her to marry another black tenant, Jim Matthews; otherwise, he will evict her sickly old grandmother. Henry Morgan comes across as a Simon Legree, but, as the eye-popping conclusion reveals, he has at least one good reason for preventing a liaison between Hugh and Mary— Mary is Hugh's half sister. Also, because it is Christmas Eve, Henry delivers Mary a present, apparently from Hugh: a white dress matching the one Henry gave Mary's mother to bribe her. The dress is a powerful symbol of Mary's crushed hopes and the cycle of degradation from which she had hoped to escape.

Hymn to the Rising Sun, the chain-gang drama, is also set on an ironic date, the Fourth of July. All the action takes place between dawn's first light and sunrise of another hot Southern day, the nearest thing to Hell in the life of the chain-gang members (black and white here are treated equally). The state legislature and judges have decreed "hard labor" for the convicts, and Captain, the head guard, is there to see that the decree is carried out. A stereotype of the Southern sheriff or "boss" (fat, sombrero-crowned, wearing a whip curled up in one boot), Captain obviously takes pleasure in his work, although he denies it. His easygoing humor loaded with sinister threats, Captain rules by intimidation and sadism. To celebrate the holiday, Captain has the guards blast off their shotguns, makes a speech to the convicts on his concept of democracy (law is of, by, and for the Establishment), and forces the convicts to sing a verse of "America." He then proceeds to routine matters: whipping Bright Boy for talking too much and releasing Runt from eleven days in the sweatbox (unfortunately, the man is dead).

Both *White Dresses* and *Hymn to the Rising Sun* have social implications beyond their immediate themes of race and penal servitude, although Green does not push these wider implications to the fore. *White Dresses* shows the paternalistic economic system by which the few control the many, and *Hymn to the Rising Sun* shows what happens to those who step out of line: They are given a few basic civics "lessons." The chain gang, hired out by the governor to build the railroad, is a microcosm of the whole system, and Captain, with his Mussolini-style harangue on "democracy," in particular suggests the system's totalitarian nature.

Like Mary McLean in *White Dresses*, Abraham McCranie of *In Abraham's Bosom* is a mulatto who hopes to break out of the cycle of Southern degradation. Unlike Mary, Abe aspires to lift his whole race with him. He is, therefore, a much more dangerous character than Mary; Mary only wanted to go to New York, but Abe wants to teach blacks to read and write. A heroic figure who first struggles to teach himself, Abe is feared by both blacks and whites, with the exception of Goldie, a mulatto who becomes his devoted wife, and Colonel McCranie, a white landowner and Abe's father. Although the stereotypical old Colonel whips Abe onstage (because Abe throws the Colonel's mean white son, Lonnie, into a briarpatch), he genuinely likes Abe, encourages him, and eventually helps him to open a school for black children. Unfortunately, when the Colonel dies, the children stop coming, and Abe is run out of town. Eighteen years later, Abe returns and tries to open his school again, but he is beaten by a white mob and, after he kills the abusive Lonnie, he is gunned down in the doorway of his home.

One of the many depressing aspects of *In Abraham's Bosom* is the way other blacks oppose Abe's aspirations. His sarcastic old aunt, Muh Mack, constantly derides him, and his fellow turpentine workers consider him uppity; they are convinced that blacks are hewers of pine trees and pickers of cotton, and they resent any effort to prove otherwise. Such is the heavy weight of oppression upon the blacks that they have internalized white attitudes toward them. Another psychological inversion is represented by Douglass, Abe and Goldie's son, who, though named after a great black leader, turns out no-good and stirs up the white mob against his father. He embodies Abe's self-defeating anger and frustration, which boil forth occasionally (although too abruptly and awkwardly) and lead to Abe's killing of Lonnie, his white half-brother. To complete the Cain-Abel parallel, Abe sometimes thinks, in this cycle of waste and defeat, that even God is against him. In the sense that God has abandoned Abe, the play's multifaceted title seems sardonic, a theological mockery.

Although some of Green's plays might be considered dated, such is not the case with *Johnny Johnson*, an outstanding antiwar satiric comedy. The play is as timely now as when it was written, and audiences have grown more receptive to antiwar themes. In addition, Green's technique in *Johnny Johnson* caught American audiences and critics by surprise in the 1930's; now they should be more prepared. The early critics thought they should pan *Johnny Johnson* for its rambling plot and mix of harsher material with comedy; nevertheless, they felt a strange affinity for the play. The play is in the "epic theater" style of Bertolt Brecht (whose work Green had admired on his German theatrical tour, 1928-1929), complete with music by Brecht's partner, Kurt Weill, who had fled Adolf Hitler's Germany. Besides songs, other Brechtian features include emblematic settings and scenes, folk sayings, signs, vaudeville tricks, and stereotypical characters (here Green's penchant for stereotypes served him well).

Although Johnny Johnson is a Southern bumpkin, he has enough sense to know that peace is better than war. He would rather stay home and marry his girl than fight in the war. His girl, Minny Belle, has other ideas: Swept up by patriotic fervor, she demands his complete sacrifice. Persuaded by President Woodrow Wilson's words that this is the war to end all wars, Johnny finally enlists. Wounded on the Western Front (actually, shot in the behind), he steals a cylinder of laughing gas from the hospital and reduces the Allied High Command to silly ninnies. Having elicited from them orders to stop the fighting, he dons the American commander's cap and coat and, with the spontaneous assistance of like-minded German soldiers, halts World War I. Soon, however, the ruse is discovered, Johnny is arrested, and the war resumes. Johnny is confined in an insane asylum for ten years, during which time Minny Belle marries his rival, the prospering owner of Crystal Mineral Springs, Anguish Howington, whom the army rejected on medical grounds.

An early example of black humor, *Johnny Johnson* mixes farce and horror, but its main components are irony and satire. War is announced at a small-town ceremony to unveil a peace monument, and the populace instantly switches gears. Recruits are enticed by a phonograph blaring "Democracy March," and they are immediately introduced to military dehumanization by a brutal physical examination. The insane asylum's debating society, solving problems and prescribing world order, sounds like Congress or the United Nations. The overriding irony is that the common man, Johnny Johnson, has better sense than his leaders but is declared insane.

As Howington's prosperity shows, war is good for some people's business. As the war hysteria shows, war also encompasses the nature of bloody ritual. War's cyclic nature is suggested by the play's ending, set in the 1930's, that shows the pacified Johnny Johnson selling homemade toys in front of a crowded stadium from which martial noises (music and shouted slogans) are issuing. Along comes Minny Belle, fat and fur-swathed, accompanied by her son, Anguish Jr., who wants to buy a toy soldier. Johnny, however, whom Minny Belle fails to recognize, does not make toy soldiers.

The theme of war as insane ritual and the Cain-Abel theme of brother against brother continue in *Wilderness Road*, Green's symphonic outdoor drama of the Civil War. Named after the road carved into Kentucky by struggling early settlers, *Wilderness Road* was commissioned by Berea College, a distinguished Kentucky college established in 1855 for poor people, black and white. The founding of Berea College (by abolitionists) is closely linked to the action of the play, set in the Kentucky hills nearby. Influenced by Berea's founders, John Freeman struggles to establish a school for mountain children. At first the community supports him, but some of his slave-owning neighbors do not like his radical notion that "God hath made of one blood all nations of men" (Berea's motto). To these fearful neighbors, led by the politician Jed Willis, education itself is a subversive idea. Against such forces, in the midst of brewing civil war, Berea's founders and John Freeman have to travel a "wilderness road," like Abraham McCranie of *In Abraham's Bosom* or like Jesus walking "that lonesome valley" (in the Appalachian hymn so prominent in the play). Eventually, the school board withdraws its support from John; he is beaten and the school vandalized by the hooded Knights of the White Star, also led by Jed Willis.

When civil war comes, the divided community, like neutral Kentucky as a whole, sends men off to both sides. Both sides whoop it up, but, as the dead and wounded come home, the whoops change to lamentations. Performed on three adjacent stages and summarized by the play's narrator, the Civil War panorama unfolds in swift, emblematic scenes like movie montages, but the audience gets a taste of stunning realism from the fireworks going off all around and the sound effects of shells whizzing overhead. Altogether, Green leaves little doubt that war is hell.

A pacifist, John Freeman stays out of the action until the community is overrun by Southern forces, again led by Jed Willis, who gloats that the new social order will reflect his ideas. Willis' temporary triumph provides a shocking glimpse of the totalitarian society which might have emerged if the South had won the Civil War. Faced with this possibility, John Freeman joins the Union forces, leads a raid to destroy a key railroad bridge near his home, and is killed in action. On the railroad bridge, which supplies Southern forces, hangs the fate of Kentucky and, to some extent, the Union; thus, by his death John Freeman strikes a decisive blow for freedom. He leaves behind Elsie Sims, a girlfriend who will now marry his brother and rival, Davie (on the vast outdoor stage, the initial love interest in the play can hardly compete with the cannon fire). Also surviving, minus a leg, is Neill Sims, Elsie's brother and John's best student, who will carry on the school.

To a great extent, *Wilderness Road*, the best example of Green's work in his most successful form, represents the culmination of his development as a playwright. Here his interests in the folk, in music, and in history are integrated; so also are the influences of Brecht and the movies. *Wilderness Road*, in addition, shows the coming together of Green's various themes. Through his portrayal of civil war, of brother against brother, Green comments on the nature of all war: If God has made of one blood all nations of men, then all war is civil war. For purposes of persuasion, Green much preferred education to warfare, yet, as John Freeman illustrates, there are some things worth fighting for: One such thing was whether, as Lincoln said, the United States would be defined as free or slave—a very close call in American history. Green, in his life and work, was still struggling to establish the definition of freedom in the United States. A man of the South and of the folk, Green contributed more than his share to the cause.

Other major works

NOVELS: *The Laughing Pioneer*, 1932; *This Body the Earth*, 1935.

SHORT FICTION: *Wide Fields*, 1928; *Salvation on a String and Other Tales of the South*, 1946; *Dog on the Sun*, 1949; *Words and Ways*, 1968; *Home to My Valley*, 1970; *Land of Nod and Other Stories*, 1976.

POETRY: *The Lost Colony Song-Book*, 1938; *The Highland Call Song-Book*, 1941; *Song in the Wilderness*, 1947; *The Common Glory Song-Book*,

1951; *Texas Forever*, 1967; *Texas Song-Book*, 1967.

NONFICTION: *Contemporary American Literature: A Study of Fourteen Outstanding American Writers*, 1925 (with Elizabeth Lay Green); *The Hawthorn Tree*, 1943; *Forever Growing: Some Notes on a Credo for Teachers*, 1945; *Dramatic Heritage*, 1953; *Drama and the Weather*, 1958; *Plough and Furrow*, 1963.

SCREENPLAYS: *Cabin in the Cotton*, 1932 (adaptation of Harry Harrison Kroll's novel); *Dr. Bull*, 1933 (adaptation of James Gould Cozzens' novel *The Last Adam*); *The Rosary*, 1933; *State Fair*, 1933 (with Sonya Levien; adaptation of Phil Stong's novel); *Voltaire*, 1933 (with Maude T. Howell); *Carolina*, 1934 (adaptation of his play *The House of Connelly*); *David Harum*, 1934 (adaptation of Edward Noyes Westcott's novel); *Time Out of Mind*, 1947 (adaptation of Rachel Field's novel); *Broken Soil*, 1949; *Red Shoes Run Faster*, 1949; *Roseanna McCoy*, 1949 (adaptation of Albert Hannum's novel); *Black Like Me*, 1963 (adaptation of John Howard Griffin's novel).

RADIO PLAY: *A Start in Life*, pr., pb. 1941 (also as *Fine Wagon*).

Bibliography
Adams, Agatha Boyd. *Paul Green of Chapel Hill*, 1951.
Clark, Barrett H. *Paul Green*, 1928.
Dusenberry, Winifred. *Loneliness in American Drama*, 1960.
Kenny, Vincent S. *Paul Green*, 1971.
Lazenby, Walter S. *Paul Green*, 1970.

Harold Branam

GRAHAM GREENE

Born: Berkhamsted, England; October 2, 1904

Principal drama

The Heart of the Matter, pr. 1950 (adaptation of his novel, with Basil Dean); *The Living Room*, pr., pb. 1953; *The Potting Shed*, pr., pb. 1957; *The Complaisant Lover*, pr., pb. 1959; *Carving a Statue*, pr., pb. 1964; *The Return of A. J. Raffles: An Edwardian Comedy in Three Acts Based Somewhat Loosely on E. W. Hornung's Characters in "The Amateur Cracksman,"* pr., pb. 1975; *For Whom the Bell Chimes*, pr. 1980; *Yes and No*, pr. 1980.

Other literary forms

Graham Greene has tried his hand at every literary genre. He has been poet, reporter, critic, essayist, pamphleteer, dramatist, screenwriter, short-story writer, biographer, and autobiographer. His near compulsion to travel has led to published accounts of his numerous journeys. His established place in literature, however, is the result of the worldwide acclaim that has greeted most of his twenty-odd novels. Critics have noted a strong autobiographical element in his fiction and have charted the development of his philosophical, religious, and political thought through his career. Certain themes recur in a recognizable pattern: man as alien at home and abroad, oppressed by evil in a violent world, flirting with suicide as an answer to his despair, seeking salvation, perhaps finding it at last, through the grace of God. Since *Brighton Rock*, published in 1938, most of the novels are decidedly the work of a confirmed Roman Catholic, but Greene himself rejects the label "Catholic writer." Acknowledging his Catholicism as a point of reference, Greene, borrowing the title of one of his novels, prefers to think of himself as a writer exploring the human factor.

From 1929 to the early 1960's, Greene's works, with few exceptions, were published in Great Britain by William Heinemann. From the mid-1960's, his British publisher has been the Bodley Head, a firm in which he served as a director from 1958 to 1968. In 1970, the two British publishing houses became jointly involved in issuing a uniform edition of his collected works, for which Greene has written new introductions. In the United States, his works have been published by the Viking Press and Simon and Schuster.

Achievements

Greene, most highly regarded for his work as a novelist, is not a distinguished dramatist, nor has he been an innovator in dramatic form. His first dramatic work was not even meant for the stage; *The Great Jowett*, a character study of Benjamin Jowett, the late nineteenth century educator and head of Balliol College, Oxford, was written as a radio play for the British Broadcasting Corporation and broadcast in 1939. One of Greene's early plays, for which no manuscript survives, was accepted by a theatrical firm but never reached production. Only five of his plays—*The Living Room*, *The Potting Shed*, *The Complaisant Lover*, *Carving a Statue*, and *The Return of A. J. Raffles*—have been produced in London. Two later plays, *Yes and No*, a curtain raiser consisting of a comic dialogue between a director and an actor, and *For Whom the Bell Chimes*, a black farce in the manner of Joe Orton, have been produced in the provinces.

Greene's major plays—*The Living Room*, *The Potting Shed*, and *The Complaisant Lover*—suggest the influence of the well-made play as they recall the work of Henrik Ibsen in his realist phase. As in Ibsen's work, the present dilemma in which the characters find themselves has been dictated by the irrevocable events of the past. Tradition, superstition, and religion all take their toll on characters torn between a sense of duty and the urgings of love. Despite their serviceable structure and moving content, Greene's plays generally echo his superior fiction without deepening its themes.

Biography

Graham Greene was born on October 2, 1904, in Berkhamsted, a small town twenty-eight miles northwest of London, and was the fourth of six children. His father, Charles Henry Greene, was a teacher, and later headmaster, at the Berkhamsted School. Being the son of the headmaster created difficulties for the sensitive youngster. He was victimized, or so he believed, by his schoolmates and made the butt of their jokes. His bouts of depression led him, at an early age, to several attempts at suicide, which, in later years, he understood to be merely disguised pleas for attention and understanding rather than serious efforts to end his own life. In his teens, he was determined to be a writer, to demonstrate to his schoolmates and to the world that there was something at which he could excel, and several of his stories were printed in the school paper, some even finding their way into the local newspaper.

When Greene was sixteen, his older brother, then studying medicine, suggested to his father that Graham needed psychiatric help. Agreeing, his father sent him to live in London for six months with an analyst, Kenneth Richmond, who helped the boy make some necessary social adjustments. During this period, Greene developed an interest in dreams and the subconscious. He also read widely and later claimed that the works that most influenced him were the melodramatic adventure stories of Anthony Hope, John Buchan, and H. Rider Haggard. Marjorie Bowen's *The Viper of Milan* (1917) enabled him to recognize evil as a force to be dealt with in his everyday life.

From 1922 to 1925, at Balliol College, Oxford, Greene involved himself in the literary life of a great university. He edited the *Oxford Outlook* and published a book of verse, *Babbling April: Poems* (1925). The depression of his early youth was replaced by a boredom which plagued him for much of his life and was the impetus for his frequent travels. His means of relieving boredom during his Oxford days were to engage in excessive drinking, even some Russian roulette, this time the result of an urge to gamble rather than a desire to kill himself. At Oxford, he met Vivien Dayrell-Browning, who wrote to him objecting to his reference in a film review to Catholics "worshiping" the Virgin Mary.

Unsure of his next move, but determined not to be a teacher, Greene applied for work with *The Times* of London but could find employment only with the Nottingham *Journal*. Interested in Vivien, whom he was still seeing, he sought out a Father Trollope in Nottingham to give him Catholic instruction in order to understand her better. As a result, in February, 1926, he converted to Catholicism, a decision which influenced all of his subsequent writing but which first appeared as a thematic concern in the novel *Brighton Rock* in 1938. In 1926, he also became subeditor for *The Times*. Greene and Vivien married the next year and had two children, a son and a daughter. A few years later, the couple separated. Thereafter, Greene protected his family's privacy by maintaining silence in regard to their relationships.

After the publication of *The Man Within* in 1929, Greene expected to support himself as a novelist; the failure of his next works, *The Name of Action* (1930) and *Rumour at Nightfall* (1931), which he later suppressed, proved a setback. In 1932, however, *Stamboul Train: An Entertainment* began a string of successes for Greene. For a time in the 1930's, he supplemented his royalties by serving as film critic for the *Spectator* and *Night and Day*. During the 1930's, he also began a series of extended journeys, such as a walking trip across Liberia which led to *Journey Without Maps: A Travel Book* (1936) and a trip to Mexico which led to both a travel book, *The Lawless Roads: A Mexican Journal* (1939), and a work of fiction, *The Power and the Glory* (1940).

In 1940, Greene became literary editor for the *Spectator* and two years later worked in Sierra Leone, Africa, for British Intelligence under the authority of Kim Philby, who later defected to the Soviet Union. In 1948 and 1949, Greene worked with director Sir Carol Reed on the films *The Fallen Idol* and *The Third Man*, gaining a sound preparation for his coming theatrical endeavors. Before seriously undertaking his own plays for the theater, in 1950 he adapted his novel *The Heart of the Matter* (1948) for the stage with director Basil Dean. Another of his novels, *The Power and the Glory*, was made into a play, but Greene had no hand in its adaptation. His three most significant plays—*The Living Room*, *The Potting Shed*, and *The*

Complaisant Lover—were all produced in the 1950's.

A trip to Indochina in 1954 and 1955 bore fruit in the publication of *The Quiet American* (1955); likewise, a trip to the Belgian Congo led to the publication of *A Burnt-out Case* (1961). *The Comedians* was published in 1966 following a trip to Haiti, and later trips to Paraguay and Chile laid the foundation for *The Honorary Consul* (1973). A strain of anti-Americanism is apparent in some of these works, perhaps traceable in part to a libel suit involving Greene's references to the nine-year-old Shirley Temple as a sexual tease, a contretemps that developed while he was writing film criticism for the short-lived comic weekly *Night and Day*. He also felt harassed by the State Department when, on more than one occasion, his visas for travel to the United States were delayed. He was vociferous in his condemnation of the United States' actions in Vietnam as well.

Greene was awarded an honorary doctorate from Cambridge University in 1962, was made a fellow of Balliol College, Oxford, in 1963, and was named Companion of Honour by Queen Elizabeth in 1966. He is also one of the most widely read, highly regarded, and influential writers of the twentieth century.

Analysis

In the introduction to the 1974 edition of his first thriller-novel, *Stamboul Train*, Graham Greene confesses to an early passion for playwriting. While his earliest attempts at that genre have never come to light, the idea of shaping scenes dramatically has informed much of his work as a novelist. Greene admits that he has sometimes found it essential to escape the liquidity of the novel to play out a situation, a confrontation between two characters perhaps, within the narrow confines of a space approximating the dimensions of a stage. This dramatic method within the form of the novel reached its climax in *The Honorary Consul*, in which most of the story takes place in a hut where the kidnaped victims are held hostage.

Whereas dramatic form has influenced Greene's novels, the theme of what may be his most popular novel, *The End of the Affair* (1951), pervades his most ambitious plays: *The Living Room, The Potting Shed,* and *The Complaisant Lover*. Frequently thought of as a Catholic novelist, Greene, who may have converted to Catholicism out of an intellectual need to find answers to questions ignored by the Anglican Church, makes his most explicit statements about the relationship of God and man in *The End of the Affair*, a first-person narrative in which a novelist, Bendrix, searches through his memories of Sarah Miles, the woman he loved and lost, to attempt some understanding of the role that God has played in his own life. Sarah, who did not remember that she had been secretly baptised a Catholic by her mother against her father's wishes, had undergone a crisis during a London bombing. Finding her lover supposedly dead amid the debris, she had prayed to God to restore him to life. In exchange, she would believe in Him. With Bendrix alive, Sarah broke off the affair and remained with her loving but dull and passionless husband Henry, a civil servant. Unable to cope with the pain of a life without passion at its center, Sarah seems to have willed her own death after a cold is aggravated by her being caught in the rain. Bendrix, who contemplates but rejects suicide, comes to understand Sarah's dilemma, her growing need for God, when he reads her diary and enters his own dilemma as he attempts, but fails, to shut God out of his life. The novel's real miracle is not Bendrix's seeming resurrection after the bombing but his finding and offering of comfort and love in a nonphysical relationship with Henry Miles, whose need for Sarah is as great as his own. God's love offers them all eventual peace.

In *The Living Room*, twenty-year-old Rose Pemberton, the child of a Catholic mother and a non-Catholic father, both deceased, goes to live with her two spinster great-aunts and her great-uncle, a priest who for many years has been confined to a wheelchair as the result of a car crash. Just before coming to her new home, Rose has entered into a physical relationship on the night of her mother's funeral with a man twice her age, Michael Dennis, the executor of her mother's will and a lecturer in psychology at the University of London. Dennis still cares deeply for his neurotic wife, who has a desperate need for him, and he makes clear to Rose that he cannot marry her. When Rose sees Dennis attempting to comfort his wife, she realizes for the first time that there are different kinds of love. Rose tries to overcome her despair by submitting to God's love and mercy as she takes a fatal dose of the pills with which Dennis' wife had threatened to commit her own suicide. Rose's great-uncle, the crippled priest, must explain to Dennis, who understands the mind of man but not the ways of God, that God's realm is eternal. As a woman loves her child after the pain and suffering of bearing it, mankind finds eternal comfort in God's love. Death is the child of mankind. For that death, which leads to God's mercy, to be borne, man must first suffer the pain of life.

The most intriguing aspect of *The Living Room*, a play marred by its too-frequent emotionally charged confrontations, bordering on the melodramatic, is its unusual setting. Rose's elderly great-aunts, Teresa and Helen, practicing Catholics, fear death even more than they love God. Like Luigi Pirandello's character Henry IV (in his 1922 play), in an attempt to freeze time, to keep death at bay, they have made the third-floor nursery of their home its only living room. Every room in the house in which someone has died has been closed off. The dead have been forgotten; their pictures have been removed. The only room still available in the house, the living room, becomes Rose's bedroom, and it is in the living room that Rose makes her choice, reverts to childhood as she seeks God in prayer, and dies.

The sisters Helen and Teresa, the characters in *The Living Room* who undergo a believable change as a result of the play's action, force the theological issues of the play without being at its center. Helen, younger than Teresa but the stronger of the two, prevents Rose from committing the mortal sin of going off with a married man by convincing her nearly senile sister that she is ill and that Rose must stay to help nurse Teresa back to health. Helen has her daily woman, Mary, spy on Rose just as Bendrix, in *The End of the Affair*, hired Parkis, a private detective, to follow Sarah. Like Parkis, Mary comes to sympathize with her prey and regrets her involvement. After Rose's death, Teresa asserts herself by choosing to move into the living room, which Helen wants to abandon. By embracing the memory of her dead grandniece, by choosing to meet her own eventual death in the room in which Rose died, Teresa forces her sister to an acknowledgment that God's mercy could not be served by Helen's unmerciful acts toward Rose, another of God's creatures, for whom, hypocritically, Helen had only professed love. Helen's role as villain, however, is a relative matter. A Catholic audience would understand that her actions have in fact kept Rose within the Church and leave Helen's judgment to God. That same audience would further recognize the ambiguity of the play's ending. Is Rose finally damned because of her suicide or does she achieve salvation? Greene leaves the question—which echoes that posed by Scobie's suicide in the novel *The Heart of the Matter*—unanswered.

Greene's next work for the theater, *The Potting Shed*, adheres to the conventional structure of the well-made play. A secret withheld from the protagonist is eventually revealed to him and to the audience as well. Benefiting from his experience as a writer of some well-plotted novels which he termed entertainments, Greene builds the suspense in what might be considered his religious thriller for the stage with a sure hand for most of the play. What makes *The Potting Shed* a sounder work than *The Living Room* is the author's ability to relax the dramatic tension with humorous dialogue and some nuances of characterization absent from the one-dimensional earlier play. Adding an extra dimension to *The Potting Shed* and contributing greatly to its success was the memorable performance by John Gielgud in its central role. First produced in New York in 1957, *The Potting Shed* was presented in London the following year with some minor changes which reflected Greene's original intentions. The most significant change was in the season of the third act—during the Christmas season in the American version, closer to Easter in the British version.

Like *The Living Room*, *The Potting Shed* is centered on death. The play's premise is the imminent death of one H. C. Callifer, author of *The Cosmic Fallacy* and founder of a rationalist movement to disprove the existence of God (a belief that aligns him with Smythe, to whom Sarah Miles turned for comfort in *The End of the Affair*). Callifer's works, which enjoyed a great vogue during the period in which twentieth century man moved from doubt to disbelief in the existence of a deity guiding his destiny, have in recent years fallen out of fashion. Faith is respectable once again, and Callifer, on his deathbed, has generally been forgotten. Indeed, in the last year, his soon-to-be-widowed wife reports, his masterwork has sold only three copies for export. Mrs. Callifer had instructed her precocious thirteen-year-old granddaughter Anne to send telegrams to absent family members informing them that Callifer is near death. With a mind of her own, Anne has taken it upon herself to add the name of her uncle, James Callifer, the younger of H. C.'s two sons, to those summoned to Wild Grove, the family home, despite her grandmother's deliberate omission of his name.

James Callifer, a newspaperman in his mid-forties who lives and works in Nottingham, has not seen his father in fifteen years and has spent little time at home in the last thirty years after having been sent away to school when he was fourteen. The estrangement from his parents seems to have been their doing. In fact, as his father's death becomes imminent, his mother forbids him to enter Callifer's sickroom.

Curiously, James has no memory of anything in his life before he was fourteen, and his life from that time on has been an empty one. His marriage to Sara, who has also joined the family in the Callifer household, failed when both husband and wife became aware that he had lost interest in the relationship, or perhaps had never had any. James has no close relationship, not even with his dog Spot, who is being housed in the potting shed, where seedlings are prepared for planting and the garden tools are stored. Overcome by an unaccountable fear on the dark path to the shed, James would let his dog spend the night without water rather than go to him.

After the memorial ceremony, marred by Spot's spilling the ashes as they are about to be consigned to the river, James learns that another family member was not notified of Callifer's impending death. His Uncle William's absence, however, is understandable, for William is the family pariah. H. C.'s younger brother did not merely convert to Catholicism; he committed what was for his rationalist brother the ultimate sin: He became a priest.

On the eve of his return to Nottingham, James is informed by his niece Anne that she has heard that something shocking involving him occurred many years ago in the potting shed. In trying to learn something of his past, James has been seeing a psychiatrist in Nottingham. Despairing of a cure, however, he has hinted at suicide, even stolen some pills from his doctor. Prodded by Anne, he eventually learns the family's dark secret when he hunts down his drunken uncle, Father William, in a run-down presbytery in an East Anglian town.

Long ago, James and his uncle were close, and William attempted to teach James basic Christian precepts, which H. C. violently opposed. The confused fourteen-year-old James hanged himself in the potting shed. Finding him dead, William prayed to God for a miracle—a miracle the reverse of that in *The End of the Affair*. In the novel, on finding Bendrix dead, Sarah offered God her belief in Him in exchange for her lover's life. In the play, on the other hand, William, a believer, offered God, in exchange for the boy's life, what he loved most in the world: his faith. Having forgotten the terms of the bargain, Father William has spent the intervening years in despair, with whiskey his only means of getting through an existence without meaning, without hope.

James's journey toward the light is a moving one, and the confrontation between nephew and uncle is as highly charged a scene as any that Greene has written in novel or play. That the mystery is solved at the end of the second act, however, makes an anticlimax of the third act, in which Mrs. Callifer admits to spending her life protecting her husband from an acceptance of the truth of the events in the potting shed. Having accepted God's love, loving Him in return, her son James is at last enabled to love another human being and offers that love to his ex-wife, Sara. Despite the weakness of its final act, *The Potting Shed*, more than *The Living Room*, can, on the strength of its intriguing mystery, engage an audience uncommitted to the author's own religious beliefs.

In *The Complaisant Lover*, Greene returned to that staple of so much of his fiction, the tragic triangle. The relationships of Sarah Miles and the two men in her life, her civil servant husband and her novelist lover, in *The End of the Affair* were obviously still on his mind when he wrote this play about Mary Rhodes, her dull dentist-husband Victor, and her worldly-wise lover, Clive Root, an antiquarian bookseller. In the play, however, in contrast to the novel, Greene chose to rely upon the sense of humor so evident in *The Potting Shed* but absent from *The Living Room*, a humor which should come as no surprise to readers of his fiction. Long an admirer of the comic actors J. Robertson Hare and Alfred Drayton and their Aldwych farces so beloved by London audiences of the 1920's and 1930's, in both *The Complaisant Lover* and his following play, *Carving a Statue*, Greene extended himself by exploring the relationship between farce and tragedy. In *The Complaisant Lover*, he was successful; in *Carving a Statue* he was not. Perhaps the single feature contributing to the success of the former is, surprisingly in a work by Greene, the total absence of any allusion to God. Mary loves both of her men, and both return that love without any of them having to come to terms first with a love for or a hatred of God.

Evident from the start of *The Complaisant Lover*, an obvious advance over his earlier work for the stage, is Greene's ability to sustain a scene in which characters reveal themselves in extended small talk rather than dramatic confrontations. In the after-dinner conversation at the Rhodeses', Victor engages in some mildly boorish behavior as he relates unamusing anecdotes and plays practical jokes on his guests. One of them, Clive Root, who is paying his first visit to the Rhodes household, is obviously unamused. He has recently entered into an affair with Victor's wife, Mary, and he is unable to surrender himself to Victor's jolly mood. Clive is also irritated by the unwelcome advances of yet another guest, a determined but inexperienced nineteen-year-old. Alone with Mary, Clive pleads with her to leave her husband and family, but Mary already understands what Rose had to learn in *The Living Room*: There are different kinds of love. The best Mary can offer Clive is a brief holiday abroad. Telling Victor that she is going to Amsterdam with an imaginary friend whom she spontaneously christens Jane Crane (the rhyming jokes about Mary's friend become the play's running gag), Mary makes plans for a trip with Clive. Her plans further call for Victor to join her after "Jane's" departure.

The comedy of manners of the opening scene becomes the pure farce of the play's second scene, set in a hotel room in Amsterdam. As Clive is about to leave, Victor appears a day earlier than planned, accompanied by a Dutch manufacturer of dental equipment who speaks no English. Entirely without guile, Victor is pleased to see Clive and has no suspicions concerning his wife. When Mary asks Clive, who still wants to marry her, to let matters stand until Victor learns the truth, Clive attempts to force the issue. He dictates to a bewildered hotel valet a letter to be posted to Victor, supposedly from the valet, informing the dentist of his wife's infidelity.

The mood changes again in the second act after Victor reads the letter, part of which the valet has got right, part of which has gone hilariously wrong. The revelation, however, plunges Victor into despair, not at the abandonment of his God but at the possibility of his abandonment by the wife without whom he cannot live. Contemplating suicide but rejecting it as a silly solution for which he is not properly dressed—tragedy requires togas, not the dinner jackets of domestic comedy—the sometime boorish dentist takes on near tragic proportions. In a moving scene with his wife, he pleads with her to stay, making clear Greene's belief that marriage has little to do with sexual satisfaction and more to do with living in a house with someone one loves. Victor had stopped making love to her only when he had become aware that he was no longer giving her physical pleasure. Mary, desirous of a future involving a physical relationship with Clive, cannot turn her back on her past sixteen years with a man who needs her, a man who has been a good husband to her and a good father to her children. With a variation on the ending of *The End of the Affair*, the establishing of a solid relationship between husband and lover after Sarah's death, Victor, eager to be a complaisant husband, suggests that his very-much-alive wife keep both of her men. Reluctantly, Clive enters into the newly formed relationship.

The accommodation at the end of *The Complaisant Lover* is by no means a conventional happy ending. Bendrix and Miles at the conclusion of *The End of the Affair* may in fact be happier in their loss than are the three characters in *The Complaisant Lover* in their resignation. None has exactly what he wants, and Clive is realistic enough to understand that the day will eventually come when he will tire of the arrangement, when Mary, recognizing Clive's pain, will end it. Greene seems unable to refrain from bringing to bear his own religious scruples, here unstated, on his characters' moral dilemma. At any rate, in *The Complaisant Lover* he has fashioned his most successful play and expertly handled its varying moods.

As Ibsen moved toward mysticism in his exploration of artistic creation in *The Master Builder* (pb. 1892) and *When We Dead Awaken* (pb. 1899), Greene, too, turned mystical in *Carving a Statue*, a play about a failed artist and his indifference toward his unhappy child, which Greene may intend as an echo of God's creation and the sacrifice of his Son to redeem it. In the delightful *The Return of A. J. Raffles*, by contrast, Greene for once gave himself over wholeheartedly to the pursuit of fun. The author's subtitle tells all: *An Edwardian Comedy in Three Acts Based Somewhat Loosely on E. W. Hornung's Characters in "The Amateur Cracksman."* As Raffles helps Lord Alfred Douglas get even with his father, the Marquess of Queensberry, in a plot involving the Prince of Wales, Greene sends his characters scampering in and out of an established social order, the conventions of which parallel the bewildering manners and mores of the contemporary world. The play's inability to find an audience despite an elegant and accomplished production by the prestigious Royal Shakespeare Company may well have dampened Greene's enthusiasm for the theater.

Other major works

NOVELS: *The Man Within*, 1929; *The Name of Action*, 1930; *Rumour at Nightfall*, 1931; *Stamboul Train: An Entertainment*, 1932 (also as *Orient Express: An Entertainment*); *It's A Battlefield*, 1934; *England Made Me*, 1935; *A Gun for Sale: An Entertainment*, 1936 (also as *This Gun for Hire: An Entertainment*); *Brighton Rock*, 1938; *The Confidential Agent*, 1939; *The Power and the Glory*, 1940 (reissued as *The Labyrinthine Ways*); *The Ministry of Fear: An Entertainment*, 1943; *The Heart of the Matter*, 1948; *The Third Man: An Entertainment*, 1950; *The Third Man and The Fallen Idol*, 1950; *The End of the Affair*, 1951; *Loser Takes All: An Entertainment*, 1955; *The Quiet American*, 1955; *Our Man in Havana: An Entertainment*, 1958; *A Burnt-out Case*, 1961; *The Comedians*, 1966; *Travels with My Aunt*, 1969; *The Honorary Consul*, 1973; *The Human Factor*, 1978; *Dr.*

Fischer of Geneva: Or, The Bomb Party, 1980; *Monsignor Quixote*, 1982; *The Tenth Man*, 1985.

SHORT FICTION: *The Basement Room and Other Stories*, 1935; *The Bear Fell Free*, 1935; *Twenty-four Stories*, 1939 (with James Laver and Sylvia Townsend Warner); *Nineteen Stories*, 1947; *Twenty-one Stories*, 1954; *A Visit to Morin*, 1959; *A Sense of Reality*, 1963; *May We Borrow Your Husband and Other Comedies of the Sexual Life*, 1967; *Collected Stories*, 1972.

POETRY: *Babbling April: Poems*, 1925; *After Two Years*, 1949; *For Christmas*, 1950.

NONFICTION: *Journey Without Maps: A Travel Book*, 1936; *The Lawless Roads: A Mexican Journal*, 1939 (reissued as *Another Mexico*); *British Dramatists*, 1942; *Why Do I Write: An Exchange of Views Between Elizabeth Bowen, Graham Greene and V. S. Pritchett*, 1948; *The Lost Childhood and Other Essays*, 1951; *Essais Catholiques*, 1953 (Marcelle Sibon, translator); *In Search of a Character: Two African Journals*, 1961; *The Revenge: An Autobiographical Fragment*, 1963; *Victorian Detective Fiction*, 1966; *Collected Essays*, 1969; *A Sort of Life*, 1971; *The Pleasure Dome: The Collected Film Criticism, 1935-40, of Graham Greene*, 1972 (John Russell-Taylor, editor); *Lord Rochester's Monkey: Being the Life of John Wilmot, Second Earl of Rochester*, 1974; *An Impossible Woman: The Memories of Dottoressa Moor of Capri*, 1975 (editor); *Ways of Escape*, 1980; *Getting to Know the General*, 1984.

SCREENPLAYS: *Twenty-one Days*, 1937; *The New Britain*, 1940; *Brighton Rock*, 1947 (adaptation of his novel, with Terence Rattigan); *The Fallen Idol*, 1948 (adaptation of his novel, with Lesley Storm and William Templeton); *The Third Man*, 1949 (adaptation of his novel, with Carol Reed); *The Stranger's Hand*, 1954 (with Guy Elmes and Giorgino Bassani); *Loser Takes All*, 1956 (adaptation of his novel); *Saint Joan*, 1957 (adaptation of George Bernard Shaw's play); *Our Man in Havana*, 1959 (adaptation of his novel); *The Comedians*, 1967 (adaptation of his novel).

TELEPLAY: *Alas, Poor Maling*, 1975.

RADIO PLAY: *The Great Jowett*, 1939.

CHILDREN'S LITERATURE: *The Little Train*, 1946; *The Little Fire Engine*, 1950 (also as *The Little Red Fire Engine*); *The Little Horse Bus*, 1952; *The Little Steam Roller: A Story of Mystery and Detection*, 1953.

ANTHOLOGY: *The Spy's Bedside Book: An Anthology*, 1957 (with Hugh Greene).

MISCELLANEOUS: *The Old School: Essays by Divers Hand*, 1934 (editor); *The Best of Saki*, 1950 (editor); *The Bodley Head Ford Madox Ford*, 1962, 1963 (4 volumes, editor); *The Portable Graham Greene*, 1973 (Philip Stout Ford, editor).

Bibliography

Adler, Jacob H. "Graham Greene's Plays: Technique Versus Value," in *Graham Greene: Some Critical Considerations*, 1963. Edited by Robert O. Evans.
Allain, Marie-Françoise. *The Other Man: Conversations with Graham Greene*, 1983.
Allott, Kenneth, and Miriam Farris. *The Art of Graham Greene*, 1951.
Boardman, Gwenn R. *Graham Greene: The Aesthetics of Exploration*, 1971.
De Vitis, A. A. *Graham Greene*, 1964.
Donaghy, Henry J. *Graham Greene: An Introduction to His Writings*, 1983.
Stratford, Philip. *Faith and Fiction: Creative Process in Greene and Mauriac*, 1964.
Wolfe, Peter. *Graham Greene the Entertainer*, 1972.
Wyndham, Francis. *Graham Greene*, 1955.

Albert E. Kalson

ROBERT GREENE

Born: Norwich, England; July, 1558(?)
Died: London, England; September 3, 1592

Principal drama

Orlando Furioso, pr. c. 1588, pb. 1594; *Friar Bacon and Friar Bungay*, pr. 1589, pb. 1594; *A Looking Glass for London and England*, pr. c. 1588–1589, pb. 1594 (with Thomas Lodge); *John of Bordeaux*, pr. c. 1590–1591 (fragment); *James IV*, pr. c. 1591, pb. 1598; *Complete Plays*, pb. 1909.

Other literary forms

Although Robert Greene is perhaps most respected today for his contribution to English drama, it was as a writer of prose fiction that he was best known to his contemporaries. His novellas made him England's most popular writer of fiction in the 1580's. Among his early works, showing the influence of Italian writers, are *Mamillia: A Mirror or Looking Glass for the Ladies of England* (part 1, 1583; part 2, 1593), *Morando: The Tritameron of Love* (part 1, 1584; part 2, 1587), *Arbasto: The Anatomy of Fortune* (1584), and *Planetomachia* (1585). Turning to the pastoral romance in 1588, Greene published such novellas as *Alcida: Greene's Metamorphosis* (1588), *Pandosto: The Triumph of Time* (1588), *Ciceronis Amor* (1589; also known as *Tullies Love*), and *Menaphon* (1589). Pastorals featuring repentance as a major theme include *Greene's Never Too Late* (1590), *Francesco's Fortunes* (1590), *Greene's Mourning Garment* (1590), and *Greene's Farewell to Folly* (1591).

Greene created still another literary fashion in the last two years of his brief life, as he cultivated another form, the rogue, or "connycatching," pamphlet. His *A Notable Discovery of Cozenage* (1591), *A Disputation Between a Hee Conny-catcher and a Shee Conny-Catcher* (1592), and *The Black Book's Messenger* (1592), as well as other small books in the series, combined London street argot with satire of middle-class greed to produce a form that appealed to all levels of society.

Greene's untimely death in 1592 sparked the publication of two alleged "deathbed" pamphlets, *Greene's Groatsworth of Wit Bought with a Million of Repentance* (1592) and *The Repentance of Robert Greene* (1592), both usually attributed to him but neither closely resembling his style and thus probably spurious. The one surely authentic posthumous work, *Greene's Vision* (1592), follows the pastoral penitent style of 1590 and was probably written during that most fruitful year of his career.

Achievements

Greene's accomplishments as a playwright have always been greatly overshadowed by those of his younger contemporary, William Shakespeare. Still, it is accurate to say that Greene created in comedy the form on which Shakespeare worked his greater miracles, just as Thomas Kyd and Christopher Marlowe led the way for Shakespeare in tragedy. The form Greene developed, the English romantic comedy, as demonstrated most clearly in *Friar Bacon and Friar Bungay*, *James IV*, and the fragmentary *John of Bordeaux*, is strikingly different from its predecessors. Departing from the morality tradition still current on the London stage, Greene chose as his principal theme romantic love between princely men and beautiful women. The popularity of this approach was greatly enhanced by Greene's ability to weave the love plot into a tapestry of affairs of state—usually events from English history—and to convey in dialogue the varied atmospheres of court, city, and countryside.

Greene's most immediate influences were his own prose romances, in which his heroes and heroines become embroiled in the wars of love through their pride, only to be chastened by the disasters they occasion and thus eventually brought to repentance and reconciliation. These romances, in their lengthy, intense monologues and conversations between lovers, created in the 1580's a drama of character, as it were, well before Marlowe's *Tamburlaine the Great* lit up the stage in 1587. The vision of Greene's romances and plays differed from, even opposed, Marlowe's vision of the individual will able to dominate society and bend morality to its own consciousness. Through his thoroughly comic perspective, Greene saw individual attempts to conquer or dominate as ineluctably limited by an inherent human need to form communities and by the ideals of peace and the orderly succession of generations.

The few contemporary assessments of his work that have survived praise Greene as a "plotter of plays." Certainly, his ability to move characters across a stage and from scene to scene is unmatched before Shakespeare, who no doubt profited from Greene's example. Indeed, Shakespeare learned more from Greene than plotting: Greene was also the first English playwright to vary verse and prose significantly in order to imply differences in rank or tone; he also varied rhyme and blank verse for tonal effects. Moreover, Greene was the first to create memorable female characters in English drama (the women in his romances are usually more interesting and important characters than his men). Greene's Margaret, Dorothea, and Ida worthily precede Shakespeare's Rosalind and Viola. Perhaps Greene best prepared the way for Shakespeare by peopling his plays with individuals who could also represent the various levels within a society. In this way, Greene could create for the spectators the illusion that they were witnessing the reactions of an entire nation to critical events.

Though not a satiric dramatist, Greene also influenced the comedy of Ben Jonson and Thomas Middleton through his connycatching pamphlets of London life. These works created a tremendous vogue for tales of the exploits of thieves and confidence men. In these dramatic narratives, Greene brought such figures to life through dialogue rich with the patois of the city. Shakespeare's Falstaff and Autolycus, as well as the rogues of London comedy after 1600, take much of their inspiration from Greene's connycatchers.

Biography

According to the best, albeit sketchy, evidence, Robert Greene was born in Norwich, Norfolk, in 1558, of a saddler and his wife. It is certain that this ambitious son of bourgeois parents went on to St. John's College, Cambridge, in 1576 on a sizar's appointment (a sort of work-study position by which scholars earned their keep, usually as valets for sons of aristocrats). Though Greene's record at St. John's appears to have been undistinguished, he did take his baccalaureate in 1580. Greene continued his studies at Cambridge and received his master of arts degree from there in 1583, the same year in which his first prose romance, *Mamillia: A Mirror or Looking Glass for the Ladies of England*, was published. A second master's, from Oxford, came in 1588; this degree was more a formality than the result of further study. There is no evidence that after 1583 Greene intensely pursued any course other than the winning of a large, eager audience in London for his romances, plays, and pamphlets.

Concerning Greene's no doubt adventurous life as a writer in London from 1583 until his death in 1592, there is much rumor and rancor but little solid fact. His publication record indicates that he was immensely popular; his title pages from 1588 onward include his name within the titles themselves, as in *Greene's Mourning Garment* and *Greene's Never Too Late*. His friend Thomas Nashe declared that printers felt "blest to pay him dear for the very dregs of his wit." Nevertheless, since the London publishing industry, still in its infancy, provided large returns for printers but no royalties for authors, even great popularity guaranteed no security. Thus, Greene survived on the speed of his pen. Curiously, there is no indication that he seriously vied for the relative stability of noble patronage, nor does he seem to have written for the pay of either the Anglican Establishment or their Puritan opponents, as did many, including Nashe and Marlowe.

Perhaps more because of the persistent theme of repentance in his writings than because of his actual life, Greene at his death left a considerable reputation as a rakehell, albeit a penitent one. His vitriolic companion Nashe wrote that he cared only "to have a spell in his purse to conjure up a good cup of wine with the poet Gabriel"; Harvey, whom Greene had insulted in a pamphlet, called him "A rakehell, a makeshift, a scribbling fool/ a famous Bayard in city and school." Gentler wits, such as the critic Francis Meres, ignored the gossip and merely noted Greene's achievement as one of the "best for comedy" among the playwrights.

Of Greene's allegedly bitter feelings toward the acting companies which bought his plays, much has been echoed through four centuries. In the posthumous tract *Greene's Groatsworth of Wit Bought with a Million of Repentance*, there is a thinly veiled attack on the players, one "Shake-scene"—no doubt Shakespeare—in particular. Careful studies, however, have concluded that another, most likely Henry Chettle, the author and printer, wrote these words and passed them off as Greene's. That the playwright's dealings with the actors were not always cordial is certain; Greene himself admits, for example, that he sold the same play, *Orlando Furioso*, to rival companies. Nevertheless, that at least five of his plays were produced in London between 1588 and 1591 attests largely amicable relations between the author and his clients.

Analysis

The most obvious common feature of Robert Greene's two best-known plays, *Friar Bacon and Friar Bungay* and *James IV,* is the love plot, the romantic battle of strong male and female personalities. The women in both plays are particularly striking; it is no wonder that critics have focused much attention on them and that they see Greene's principal dramatic impulse as romantic. Nevertheless, what joins all five of Greene's known plays is not the love interest but rather the playwright's exploration of the individual's role within society; in those plays in which it is central, the love plot is merely one overt vehicle by which Greene asks his characters to choose between the desire to dominate others and the desire to live in harmony.

Greene found a locus for his first known dramatic handling of this theme within Ariosto's long narrative epic, *Orlando Furioso* (1516, 1521, 1532). Greene's play of the same title centers on the affection of the epic hero for Angelica, daughter of the King of Africa. In the play, Orlando, a warrior but not a king, contends with monarchs for the heroine. When he wins her, it is the victory that means everything to him; Angelica herself means nearly nothing to him. So little does he know or trust her that he eagerly believes the lies of Sacrapant, here a minor court attendant, that she has betrayed him with one Medoro. Orlando goes mad with jealousy; he runs wild through a stage forest, killing and dismembering. Symbolic of his ignorance of Angelica is his failure to recognize her when they meet in the forest; rather, he speaks his rage to a dummy (or a clown) made up to look somewhat like his beloved. Only after a woodland priestess, Melissa, is brought in to heal his madness can Orlando understand his fault and beg Angelica's forgiveness.

In *Orlando Furioso*, Greene paints with bold and none too careful strokes his typical portrait of the proud hero who slights his lover, suffers disasters, and comes to repentance. The audience cannot take the ranting Orlando seriously, though he might be more likable than the unbearably pompous kings who are his rivals; before the final scene, Orlando does virtually nothing to win the audience's hearts, nor does the audience sympathize with the slighted Angelica, who (albeit in the fragmentary version of the play that has survived) shows none of the depth of Greene's later heroines. Greene's heavy hand is deliberate here, however, for *Orlando Furioso* is an out-and-out parody of Marlowe's hero, Tamburlaine, the second part of whose history had appeared a few months earlier than Greene's play. Greene had attacked Marlowe's thumping verse and arrogant hero in the preface to his romance *Perimedes the Blacksmith* (1588), and here he burlesques Tamburlaine's megalomania as mere insanity. Critics have misjudged the play as Greene's failed attempt to match Marlowe as a bombastic tragedian; since Greene throughout his prose and verse shows consistent antipathy to the conqueror type, there is no reason to see *Orlando Furioso* as anything other than satire.

If *Orlando Furioso* is misjudged as a serious but inept attempt at what might be called tragicomedy, then it is difficult indeed to account for the skill and sensitivity apparent in Greene's next play, *Friar Bacon and Friar Bungay*, produced most likely in 1589. This play is still only beginning to be appreciated for its plotting, its use of verse and prose structures, and its study of ideas, though scholars have long recognized it as the prototype of English romantic comedy.

As in *Orlando Furioso*, the love story is the primary vehicle for Greene's exploration of the individual's relationship to society. Here, the love intrigue has social consequences that every member of Greene's audience could easily appreciate, particularly in the year following the invasion of the Spanish Armada. Greene sets his play within the reign of Henry III (1216-1272) and focuses his plot on the Prince of Wales, Edward, who must choose between honoring an arranged marriage with Eleanor, Princess of Castile, and pursuing the affections of the beautiful Margaret, an English country maid. The first third of the play is devoted to Edward's stratagems for securing the maid as a mistress, including his hiring the great English scientist (popularly considered a magician) Roger Bacon to use the "art" to win Margaret. When Edward fails to appear at court, his father and the royal Habsburg visitors grow nervous and set out to find him. When the prince is stymied in his illicit suit by Margaret's falling in love with Edward's best friend, Lacy, Earl of Lincoln, the tension almost provokes bloodshed. Finally, however, the deep, honest love of Margaret and Lacy cures Edward's fury. He heads back to court, once again knowing his duty to king, nation, and conscience.

Nevertheless, the play is only half over. The second half beautifully juxtaposes two stories. One is Bacon's attempt to rise at court, at first by overmatching the Habsburg magician in a test of powers, then by conjuring a wall of brass to surround England and thus ward off potential invaders (the audience would have immediately thought of Spain). The other story is Lacy's attempt to assure himself of Margaret's constancy to him despite her being ceaselessly flattered and bribed by rich suitors. Both Bacon's and Lacy's attempts are proved shameful. Not only would Bacon's wall destroy the harmony of nations promised in the marriage of Edward and Eleanor, but also, as Bacon comes to see, the conjuring requires the aid of evil powers. On Lacy's part, his test of Margaret gravely insults her; moreover, his hesitancy to ask her hand leaves her at the mercy of two boorish suitors, Lambert and Serlsby, who grow so incensed at her refusal to choose between them that they fall to swords; both are killed. The tragedy is compounded—and the two plots brought strategically together—when the sons of the combatants, both scholars at Bacon's college in Oxford, witness their fathers' duel through one of Bacon's conjurations, a "perspective glass." The sons turn enemies, and they, too, wound each other mortally. By juxtaposing these plots, Greene allows his audience to see that both Bacon and Lacy have been blinded by their desire for control, Bacon's over the power of magic, Lacy's over the power of Margaret's beauty.

When Lacy eventually gives up the stupid test and comes to claim her, Margaret forgives him heartily, even though he fails to see how much he has hurt her. Then, in the final scene, which celebrates the double wedding of Edward and Eleanor, Lacy and Margaret, this country lass, now Eleanor's attendant, offers to all the royalty present an example of humility and thanksgiving. By stating her thanks to "Jove" rather than to the favor of the court, she implicitly reawakens the awareness of all, especially Edward and Lacy, to the dangers which have providentially been averted. She places the emphasis of the closing scene where it belongs, on the sanctity of marriage rather than on the euphoria occasioned by a successful political match. Friar Bacon, now penitent, is also on hand to lend further solemnity to the celebration.

The final impact of the play is intensified by what might be called the delicate power of Greene's verse. His ability to evoke in diction and line the flavor of the English countryside has been amply noted by critics, but the varying of this accent with the equally accurate rendering of the courtly and academic atmospheres is perhaps just as remarkable. The play affirms the power of language to embody the spirit of place and person. That Greene's style shifts easily from blank verse to Skeltonics to prose, and from images of "butter and cheese, cream and fat venison" to those of "cates, rich Alexandria drugs" helps to create an environment as magical as Bacon's spells or Margaret's beauty. In such an atmosphere, rich with promise, one easily believes in the magic of love to soften hearts and heal wounds of the spirit.

Written in collaboration with the playwright and romance writer Thomas Lodge, *A Looking Glass for London and England* explores England's relations with other countries in a form quite different from the romantic comedy. Neither tragedy nor comedy, *A Looking Glass for London and England* is a dramatic sermon, Greene and Lodge's quite faithful retelling of the biblical story of Jonah and the Ninevites. An enduringly popular play in printed form and on the stage, it was one of the last and best of the religious dramas of the 1570's and 1580's that had developed out of the morality and mystery play traditions. Like *Friar Bacon and Friar Bungay*, *A Looking Glass for London and England* urges the audience to consider ethically its attitudes and actions toward foreign neighbors. The particular focus of the play is on the moral state of nations basking in victory over foreign foes. Though the censure is only implied in the parable of Nineveh, Greene and Lodge judged England to be on the verge of losing its ethical perspective in the wake of its defeat of the "invincible" Armada. Reminiscent of *Orlando Furioso*, the play's opening scenes ring with pompous speeches by vainglorious nobility; these court scenes are juxtaposed to scenes of the merchant and laboring classes lost in greed, drunkenness, and adultery.

One of Greene's presumed contributions to the play (it is impossible to determine each author's influence exactly) is the light touch with which much of the dissipation among the commons is handled. Greene's romances of these years show his increasing skill in creating clowns and cityfolk with whom his audience could identify, and this talent is used here to draw characters who can lull an audience into feeling that all of these dangerous excesses are mere jests and good fun. Having trapped the audience, however, Greene suddenly turns the plot so that dire consequences result; the most dramatic incident of this kind is the jovial drinking bout that leads to a brawl—which in turn leads to murder. Greene uses these scenes not only to prove the prophet Jonas' point about the perils into which the society can fall, but also to compare the typical evils of the populace with the even more dangerous behavior of the nobles, who are expected to lead society.

James IV, probably written shortly after *A Looking Glass for London and England*, retains some of the former play's sermonizing tone while replacing the parabolic structure with that of a masquelike fairy tale. One of Elizabethan drama's most imaginative spectacles, *James IV* combines authentic British history with materials adapted from Italian romance and then invests the story with sweetness and light by means of fairies, clowns, and balladlike verse. As in *Friar Bacon and Friar Bungay*, Greene here uses the pleasing form to move his audience gently toward accepting a controversial political stance, in this case the rightful succession of the Scots king, James VI, to the English throne.

Greene sets his play a century back in history, to the reign of James IV, another Scots monarch who had roused English ire. With the aid of a romance on the same theme by Cinthio (1504-1573), he twists the chronicle to create another love story in which the hero's injury to his beloved leads his nation to the brink of disaster. James, married to Dorothea, daughter of the English king, falls in love with a young gentlewoman, Ida, a peerless beauty. Urged on in his adultery by Ateukin, a Machiavellian adviser who secretly desires the King's overthrow, James banishes Dorothea, whom Ateukin accused of plotting against her husband. When news of the banishment reaches England, King Henry leads an army against James, whose demoralized forces wither before the English. Thousands of soldiers die and many towns fall; then, just as the climactic battle is about to commence, Dorothea, who has lived like a hunted animal, appears on the battleground. She begs her husband and father to throw down their arms. James, at last overcome by his injustice, implores her forgiveness. She replies with renewed vows of obedience to him. Again, the Greene heroine sets the example of humble love.

As in *Friar Bacon and Friar Bungay*, the fairy tale works because several poetic and structural devices conspire to create a magical atmosphere. One key element is the subplot involving Ida and an English officer, Eustace, whose courtship occasions the tenderest wooing scene in Greene's dramatic canon. Their love makes all the more painful the estrangement of James and Dorothea; it also sustains the audience's faith in the potential of romantic relationships to engender love and fidelity. Also vitally important to the fairy-tale magic is Greene's poetry, particularly the frequent alternation between blank verse and ballad stanzas. The rhyme provides minstrel-like distance between the harsh events being portrayed and their poetic evocation by Greene. Particularly in the dialogue between the banished Dorothea and her trusty servant, Nano, the rhyme enhances the poignancy of the situation. Greene's technique is put to a purpose far different from that in *Friar Bacon and Friar Bungay*, in which rhyme forms had been used satirically by Miles, the clown.

In *A Looking Glass for London and England*, Greene and Lodge had used another plotting device, the frame, as a means of relating the Ninevite parable to contemporary England. In the frame plot, a second prophet, Oseas, comments on the action. In *James IV*, Greene again turns to the frame plot to focus the audience's attention on a key issue in the play. Here, two antithetical types, a dour Scots cynic, Bohan, and an immortal optimist, Oberon, King of the fairies, observe the historical pageant as a test of their opposing views of human nature. Though for them the play will merely confirm or deny a point of view, these objective onlookers become more and more emotionally involved as the action proceeds. The intent is obvious: Greene again wants to move the audience to understand how the power of compassion can affect even the most resistant spirits. If even the cynic and the fairy king can feel for these characters, the audience is supposed to ask, how can love not prevail?

Though Greene provides many devices to heighten the artifice of this pseudohistory, the patriotic appeal in *James IV* is even more obvious than that of *Friar Bacon and Friar Bungay*, with its direct references to England's defenses. The marriage of James and Dorothea would have immediately reminded the spectators of the recent marriage of James IV to Anne of Denmark, while the English-Scottish alliance in the play directly foreshadows the likely advance of James VI to the English throne upon the death of Elizabeth. Greene's presentation of James's character indicates the author's sympathy for the fears of the English public toward the current king's suspected reliance on untrustworthy ministers. The romantic ambience of the play, however, and the happy resolution of the plot are meant to ease the fears of the audience. Moreover, the horrors of war depicted in the play are intended to keep spectators aware of the inevitable outcome of opposition to the succession. Thus, the political presentation is balanced, not partisan. Greene's interest, as in his earlier plays, is to encourage in the theatergoing public the same faith in the power of love that his romances tried to evoke in his readers.

Scholars have attributed to Greene various plays otherwise anonymous, since these plays bear some distinguishing marks of Greene's style. Long thought a Greene play is *Alphonsus, King of Arragon* (pr. c. 1587, pb. 1599), which bears the name "R. Green" on its 1599 edition, the only extant; the play itself, however, is little like anything Greene is known to have written, so the attribution is doubtful. A more plausible case can be made for the bitterly satiric *A Knack to Know a Knave* (pr. 1592, pb. 1594), which emphasizes a Greene-like concern for the moral health of the different levels of society and which vividly portrays some of the tricks of characters doubtless drawn from Greene's connycatching pamphlets. *A Knack to Know a Knave* gradually degenerates, however, into a brutally vengeful depiction of the punishments of wrongdoers. Certainly antithetical to Greene's philosophy of forgiveness, this play, as it exists, may be a revision by another writer, perhaps the violent-tempered Nashe, of a work left unfinished by Greene at his death.

The only anonymously produced play definitely of Greene's authorship is *John of Bordeaux*, a sure sequel to *Friar Bacon and Friar Bungay*. Loosely based on the chivalric romance *Duke Huon of Bordeaux*, this play features Roger Bacon, who had renounced his magic in the earlier play, here using his powers to free beggars from prison, relieve their suffering, and confound their enemies. The play seems a perfect vehicle to rehabilitate this popular character from his relative ignomiry at the close of *Friar Bacon and Friar Bungay*. As one might expect, the friar shares center stage with a chaste and loyal woman, Rossalin, the wife of Bordeaux. Her warrior husband gone and feared dead, the constant Rossalin is wooed by a tyrant, then banished, penniless, when she rejects him. Eventually, her endurance, Bacon's magic, and Bordeaux's return win a happy ending.

The appeal of this play is more social than political. Rather than supporting a particular view of a specific national situation, it attempts to move the audience to identify with the poor folk portrayed onstage. In the most affecting scene of the play, Rossalin and her children beg from passersby, who probably resemble members of the audience; they scorn her pleas as the ruses of a begging thief or give her the cold comfort of pious warnings about the wages of sin. That chance can reverse the places of rich and poor is one message of the play, a message which Greene hoped to insinuate through his characteristic appeal to the finer emotions of his audience. *John of Bordeaux* illustrates once again that Greene's way in drama, as in prose, is not to threaten or lecture his audience on their duties to one another, but to create characters of sympathy and courage, humility and humor, who might win their hearts and set examples to follow.

Other major works

FICTION: *Mamillia: A Mirror or Looking Glass for the Ladies of England*, 1583, 1593 (2 parts); *Arbasto: The Anatomy of Fortune*, 1584; *The Mirror of Modesty*, 1584; *Morando: The Tritameron of Love*, 1584, 1587 (2 parts); *Planetomachia*, 1585; *Euphues His Censure to Philautus*, 1587; *Penelope's Web*, 1587; *Alcida: Greene's Metamorphosis*, 1588; *Pandosto: The Triumph of Time*, 1588; *Perimedes the Blacksmith*, 1588; *Ciceronis Amor*, 1589 (also known as *Tullies Love*); *Menaphon*, 1589; *Francesco's Fortunes*, 1590; *Greene's Mourning Garment*, 1590; *Greene's Never Too Late*, 1590; *Greene's Farewell to Folly*, 1591; *Greene's Vision*, 1592; *Philomela: The Lady Fitzwater's Nightingale*, 1592.

POETRY: *A Maiden's Dream*, 1591.

NONFICTION: *The Spanish Masquerado*, 1589; *The Royal Exchange*, 1590; *A Notable Discovery of Cozenage*, 1591; *The Second Part of Conny-catching*, 1591; *The Third and Last Part of Conney-Catching*, 1592; *The Defense of Conny-catching*, 1592; *A Disputation Between a Hee Conny-catcher and a Shee Conny-catcher*, 1592; *The Black Book's Messenger*, 1592; *A Quip for an Upstart Courtier*, 1592; *Greene's Groatsworth of Wit Bought with a Million of Repentance*, 1592; *The Repentance of Robert Greene*, 1592.

MISCELLANEOUS: *Life and Complete Works in Prose and Verse*, 1881-1886.

Bibliography

Bevington, David. *Tudor Drama and Politics*, 1968.
Ellis-Fermor, Una. "Marlowe and Greene: A Note on Their Relations as Dramatic Artists," in *Studies in Honor of T. W. Baldwin*, 1958. Edited

by Don Cameron Allen.
Gurr, Andrew. *The Shakespearean Stage, 1576-1642,* 1970.
Jordan, John Clarke. *Robert Greene*, 1915.
Pruvost, René. *Robert Greene et ses romans*, 1938.
Sanders, Norman. "The Comedy of Greene, and Shakespeare," in *Early Shakespeare,* 1961. Edited by John Russell Brown and Bernard Harris.
Senn, Werner. *Studies in the Dramatic Construction of Robert Greene and George Peele*, 1973.

Christopher J. Thaiss

LADY AUGUSTA GREGORY

Born: Roxborough, Ireland; March 15, 1852
Died: Coole Park, Ireland; May 22, 1932

Principal drama

Spreading the News, pr. 1904, pb. 1905; *The Rising of the Moon*, pb. 1904, pr. 1907; *Kincora*, pr., pb. 1905, pr. 1909 (revised); *The White Cockade*, pr. 1905, pb. 1906; *Hyacinth Halvey*, pr., pb. 1906; *The Canavans*, pr. 1906, pr. 1907, pb. 1912 (revised); *The Gaol Gate*, pr. 1906, pb. 1909; *Dervorgilla*, pr. 1907, pb. 1908; *The Jackdaw*, pr. 1907, pb. 1909; *The Workhouse Ward*, pr. 1908, pb. 1909 (with Douglas Hyde; revision of *The Poorhouse*, pb. 1903, pr. 1907); *The Travelling Man*, pb. 1909, pr. 1910; *The Image*, pr. 1909, pb. 1910; *The Full Moon*, pr. 1910, pb. 1911; *Coats*, pr. 1910, pb. 1913; *The Deliverer*, pr. 1911, pb. 1912; *Grania*, pb. 1912; *Damer's Gold*, pr. 1912, pb. 1913; *The Bogie Men*, pr. 1912, pb. 1913; *The Wrens*, pr. 1914, pb. 1922; *Shanwalla*, pr. 1915, pb. 1922; *The Golden Apple*, pb. 1916, pr. 1920; *Hanrahan's Oath*, pr. 1918, pb. 1922; *The Jester*, wr. 1918, pb. 1923; *The Dragon*, pr. 1919, pb. 1920; *Aristotle's Bellows*, pr. 1921, pb. 1923; *The Story Brought by Brigit*, pr., pb. 1924; *Sancho's Master*, pr. 1927, pb. 1928; *Dave*, pr. 1927, pb. 1928; *Lady Gregory: Selected Plays*, pb. 1962, pb. 1970 (Elizabeth Coxhead, editor); *The Collected Plays of Lady Gregory*, pb. 1970 (8 volumes: Ann Saddlemyer, editor).

Other literary forms

Lady Augusta Gregory would have been a significant figure in Irish literature even if she had never written any plays. Her earliest writing centered largely on the life and correspondence of her deceased husband, Sir William Gregory. In 1894, two years after his death, she completed the editing of *An Autobiography of Sir William Gregory*, and in 1898 she published *Mr. Gregory's Letter Box*.

Lady Gregory also did a number of translations, most notably of Molière's plays. Her plays were published in various collections throughout her lifetime. They now have been collected in *The Collected Plays of Lady Gregory*. A selection of nine plays can be found in Elizabeth Coxhead, *Lady Gregory: Selected Plays*.

Lady Gregory's most valuable work for literature and Irish culture, however, was the gathering and publishing of the myths and legends of Ireland, a love for which began early in her life and lasted until the end. Traveling from village to village and cottage to cottage (including trips to the Aran Islands at the same time as John Millington Synge), she devoted herself to the recording of an oral tradition that she felt was central to the future as well as the past of Ireland. The first of these numerous collections appeared as *Cuchulain of Muirthemne* in 1902, and the last, as *Visions and Beliefs in the West of Ireland* in 1920.

Lady Gregory also wrote for and about the Irish Renaissance itself, particularly about the dramatic revival. In 1901, she edited a book of essays, *Ideals in Ireland*, that called for a renewal of Irish culture and criticized English domination. Her account of the rise of Irish drama and the struggles at the Abbey Theatre are given in *Our Irish Theatre* (1913).

Lady Gregory's other nondramatic writings grow largely out of her personal life. In 1921, she published *Hugh Lane's Life and Achievement*, a memorial to her beloved nephew who died with the sinking of the *Lusitania*, and in 1926 *A Case for the Return of Hugh Lane's Pictures to Dublin*, part of a futile battle to get his French Impressionist collection returned from England. Others oversaw the publication of some of her private thoughts and reminiscences in *Coole* (1931) and *Lady Gregory's Journals 1916-1930* (1946).

Achievements

The achievement of Lady Gregory is not to be found in awards and prizes given to her, but in the gift of her life, possessions, and talents to the literary and cultural awakening of modern Ireland. She would be a significant figure for any one of her contributions, but the sum of them makes her central to one of the most important movements in modern literature.

Lady Gregory's initial contribution to what has been called the Irish Renaissance (or Irish Literary Revival) was the early collecting of the myths and folktales of the Irish people. In so doing, she was participating in the discovery of the richness of so-called primitive cultures that was only beginning at the end of the nineteenth century to engage the interest of the earliest anthropologists and ethnologists. These efforts not only served an important historical function but also became a part of both her own plays and the poetry and plays of William Butler Yeats, and contributed significantly to the Irish people's rediscovery of and pride in their own past.

Lady Gregory's plays, while not greatly influential on other playwrights, were important in their contribution to what has come to be called the Irish dramatic movement (especially in its primary expression, the Abbey Theatre) and as works of art in their own right. They broke new ground for example, in the mixing of the fabulous with the realistic and in the transformation of peasant speech into successful dramatic dialect. Lady Gregory perfected the one-act play; she also led the way in demonstrating that the lives and speech of peasants could be the stuff of dramatic art— and, in fact, the popular success of her plays helped sustain the Abbey Theatre during years of great struggle.

Perhaps her most important and most widely acknowledged achievement was as a motivating and sustaining force behind the Irish dramatic movement. As cofounder, with Yeats and Edward Martyn, of the Irish Literary Theatre at the turn of the century, later to become the Abbey Theatre, she worked tirelessly as director, fund-raiser, playwright, and defender in what seemed times of endless trouble.

Lady Gregory's contribution, however, extended beyond the dramatic movement itself. She also played the important role of encourager, comforter, guide, provider, and friend to fellow writers and laborers in the cultural renewal of Ireland. The symbol for this was her country estate, Coole Park, near Galway in the west of Ireland, where she graciously provided spiritual and material sustenance to many, most famously to Yeats.

Biography

Lady Augusta Gregory was born Isabella Augusta Persse on March 15, 1852, at Roxborough in County Galway, the twelfth of sixteen children. Her staunchly Protestant family was thought to have come to Ireland in the seventeenth century at the time of Oliver Cromwell's suppression of Ireland. The intellectual and aesthetic sterility of her childhood was relieved by the storytelling and quiet nationalism of her Catholic nurse, Mary Sheridan.

An avenue out to the larger world of which she longed to be a part was provided by her marriage in 1880 to Sir William Gregory, a man of sixty-three who had recently resigned as governor of Ceylon and returned to his country estate at Coole Park, not far from Roxborough. As the new Lady Gregory, she found a large library, a kind and intelligent husband, and the beginning of an outlet for her incipient talents.

It was to be many years before Lady Gregory would think of herself as a writer. Her first efforts consisted largely of editing the autobiography and letters of her husband, who died in 1892. Of more importance to her career, however, was the publication in 1893 of Douglas Hyde's *Love Songs of Connacht* and Yeats's *The Celtic Twilight* (both 1893). These two books sparked her own latent interest in the tales and speech of the Irish peasant. She was drawn to their lyric beauty, imaginativeness, and rich spirituality, and she made it her task for much of the rest of her life to record this rich oral tradition.

Lady Gregory first discussed with Yeats in 1894 the possibility of launching a theater devoted to the writers and plays of Ireland. Their dream became a reality in January, 1899, with the founding of the Irish Literary Theatre. This movement was to be the central concern and accomplishment of her life.

Initially, Lady Gregory's contribution was largely practical. She was an organizer, fund-raiser, encourager, and occasional collaborating playwright; it was she who first argued that the theater should be in Dublin, not London, as Yeats proposed. Within a few years, however, she was writing plays of her own, initially, she said, to provide some brief comic relief from Yeats's more esoteric works. These one-act plays proved to be more popular with the Dublin audiences than were Yeats's, and her career as a playwright was well, if late, begun.

The early years of the literary movement also saw the publication of a series of her collections of Irish myth and folklore, beginning with *Cuchulain of Muirthemne* and followed in rapid succession by *Poets and Dreamers* (1903), *Gods and Fighting Men* (1904), *A Book of Saints and Wonders* (1907), and *The Kiltartan Wonder Book* (1910). These were important books because they offered a single coherent telling of previously scattered tales (especially of the mythic hero Cuchulain) and, in so doing, made this heritage more widely known not only in Ireland but also abroad.

The single phrase which sums up all that Lady Gregory aimed for and achieved was her own oft-repeated observation to her fellow laborers that "we work to add dignity to Ireland," and work she did. As one of the directors of the Abbey Theatre (initially with Yeats and Synge), she was involved in constant battles—artistic, political, financial, and personal—to preserve the dramatic movement. As an Anglo-Irish Protestant with strong nationalistic convictions, she was suspected and attacked by both sides in the increasingly politicized and polarized Ireland.

The symbol of all this was the famous riots early in 1907 over Synge's *The Playboy of the Western World*. Considered a slur against Ireland by the ardent nationalists, and immoral by some quarters of the Catholic Church, the play evoked a series of riotous confrontations within the theater and an ongoing controversy without. Lady Gregory defended the play with all of her energies at the time, and during a subsequent tour in America in the winter of 1911 to 1912, even though she personally disliked it.

Lady Gregory's skill as a dramatist grew rapidly and her works were increasingly important to the financial solvency of the Abbey Theatre (especially since she collected no royalties for her plays). The first of a number of collections of her dramas, *Seven Short Plays*, came out in 1909, followed later by *Irish Folk-History Plays* (1912) and *New Comedies* (1913).

The beginning of World War I marks a tragic turn in the life of a remarkable woman who became a central figure in the literary life of a nation, a woman who did not write her first imaginative work until she was fifty. Lady Gregory's beloved nephew, Hugh Lane, died in the sinking of the *Lusitania*. His death left her with the task of trying to get his important collection of French Impressionist art returned from England to its rightful place in Ireland, a battle into which she futilely poured her declining energy until her death. In January, 1918, her only child, Robert Gregory, was killed while flying for the Royal Flying Corps. These personal tragedies, combined with her grief for the suffering of Ireland during the prolonged bloodshed of this nation's struggle for liberation, cast a darkness over Lady Gregory's declining years.

The 1920's were still years of effort on behalf of the Abbey Theatre, however, and were brightened for a time by Lady Gregory's special role in the discovery and encouragement of Sean O'Casey. That too took a sad turn, as he broke relations with her and the Abbey Theatre over their rejection in 1928 of *The Silver Tassie*.

Lady Gregory's last years were spent in poor health and growing loneliness, but she maintained her aristocratic dignity up until her death at Coole Park in 1932.

Analysis

Lady Augusta Gregory's beginnings as a dramatist were modest. Her first efforts involved contributions of pieces of realistic dialogue and plot to Yeats's early poetic drama. Even when she began to write her own plays, she claimed that they were only to serve as brief comic relief from the more serious work of the poet. This situation, however, did not last long. Lady Gregory's plays soon became important in their own right to the Abbey Theatre and to the Irish dramatic movement, and they remain a significant part of one of the most seminal periods in modern literature.

The central motivation behind all that Lady Gregory did is found in her statement that she and others worked "to add dignity to Ireland." Some of the ways in which her plays contributed to this lofty goal are suggested in her remarks on the desired impact of her historical plays, comments which at the same time give telling clues to the nature of her own work:

> I had had from the beginning a vision of historical plays being sent by us through all the counties of Ireland. For to have a real success and to come into the life of the country, one must touch a real and eternal emotion, and history comes only next to religion in our country. And although the realism of our young writers is taking the place of fantasy and romance in the cities, I still hope to see a little season given up every year to plays on history and in sequence at the Abbey, and I think schools and colleges may ask to have them sent and played in their halls, as a part of the day's lesson.

One sees here much that finds dramatic expression in Lady Gregory's plays: the desire to have her work both spring from and appeal to the common people of Ireland; the intention to recover and respect Irish history, particularly as it is found in the stories and songs of the people rather than in the books of academics; the unapologetic combination of didacticism and entertainment; the wish to preserve romance, myth, and imagination in an increasingly skeptical, political, and materialistic age; the hope that Irish drama could be a natural part of the education and life of the Irish people.

These desires find expression in each of the three categories into which

Lady Gregory's plays are usually divided: comedy; tragedy and tragi-comedy (including the historical plays); and plays of wonder and the supernatural. Lady Gregory's first plays were comedies. Like most of her drama, they were largely one-act works which combine a skillful command of structure, plot, and dialogue with genuine insight into human nature.

The recurring locale for Lady Gregory's comedies is the rural community of Cloon, a fictional version of the real town of Gort, near which Lady Gregory lived on her estate, Coole Park. The poor peasants and only slightly less impoverished townspeople with whom she mingled from her earliest childhood became her characters. She tried to capture not only their speech and mannerisms but also the quality of their lives that transcended their poverty and sometime clownishness. That quality had to do with their closeness to the spiritual heart of life, to myth and legend, to a sense of the past and of community, and to other dimensions of reality which Lady Gregory feared were disappearing from Ireland and from the world.

These characters are not idealized. They are often fools, simpletons, and ne'er-do-wells. Hers are not the heroic poor of some literature, yet beneath their gullibility, love of gossip, and simplemindedness is a closeness to the core of life which Lady Gregory admired and tried to capture. This accounts for the consistent sympathy for her comic creations. Lady Gregory laughed with, not at, her characters, and she did not set herself apart from the human foibles that they portray.

One of those foibles, both a weakness and a strength, is the Irish love of talk. This very human desire to share lives manifests itself comically (and sometimes tragically) in Lady Gregory's plays in an unquenchable thirst for gossip, a penchant for exaggeration and misrepresentation, a disposition to argument for its own sake, and an irrepressible urge to know their neighbor's business. This foible is at the heart of two of her most successful works, *Spreading the News* and *The Workhouse Ward*.

The skillfully structured *Spreading the News* turns on the eagerness of a man's neighbors to hear and believe the worst about him. Poor Bartley Fallon, a man convinced that if something bad is to happen it will happen to him, finds that his innocent attempt to do a good deed becomes the basis, through a series of outrageous misunderstandings of everyday speech, of the universally believed story that he has murdered his neighbor and plans to run off with the neighbor's wife. The humor of the situation grows exponentially as each new person who happens on the expanding story embraces it eagerly and adds to its enormity in passing it on. The comic tension builds even beyond where it seems it must be released as the appearance in good health of the supposedly murdered man only prompts the police to arrest him along with Bartley as they set off to find the body of the "real" victim, whom he is assumed to be impersonating.

The Workhouse Ward also turns on the Irish love of talk. Two old men in a poorhouse argue viciously with each other until the sister of one, whom he has not seen for five years, arrives to offer to take him into her home (for largely selfish reasons). He is eager to leave his pitiful surroundings until he learns that his roommate cannot come with him. After the sister leaves, the two old men resume their fighting, hurling objects as well as words at each other.

Both comedies illustrate Lady Gregory's ability to capture the rich dialect of the Irish peasant in all its color, cadence, and natural metaphor. One of the old men in *The Workhouse Ward* responds to the charge of the other in typical fashion: "To steal your eggs is it? Is that what you are saying now? . . . Isn't it a bad story for me to be wearing out my days beside you the same as a spancelled goat. Chained I am and tethered I am to a man that is ramsacking his mind for lies!"

As with most of Lady Gregory's comedies, these two reveal her interest in something more than laughter. The condescending and uncomprehending attitude of the English magistrate in *Spreading the News* is a clear if commonplace indictment of Ireland's oppressor, and his repeated references to his earlier duties in the Andaman Islands indicates that Ireland too is simply another of England's exploited colonies. Both plays also reveal Lady Gregory's fondness for symbolism and near allegory. She later said she wanted the two old men in *The Workhouse Ward* to be seen as symbols of Ireland itself, suggesting that the Irish, as with any family, feel free to fight among themselves but do not desire the interference of outsiders, especially hypocritical ones whose apparent benevolence is only thinly disguised exploitation.

Although it was her comedies that were most popular and are most likely to last, Lady Gregory herself preferred to write tragedy. Her work in this form ranges from the highly condensed power of *The Gaol Gate* to one of her most ambitious works, the three-act *Grania*. One finds in the tragedies the clearest expression of the idealism, patriotism, and respect for the noble lost cause that are so much a part of Lady Gregory's own character. The tragedies generally center on people who have refused to be the passive pawns of circumstance, and who, in insisting on acting independently, come to grief against the harsh realities of life.

In *The Gaol Gate*, the man who has acted thus is dead before the play begins. Refusing to inform on his friends, he is hanged for a political murder he did not commit. The action of the play centers on the discovery of his fate by his wife and mother. As they approach the prison, unaware that he has been executed, they agonize over the rumors that he has in fact informed against his friends. His wife makes excuses for him in preparation for the possibility that it may be true, but his mother, with a longer memory of the suffering of the people, will not tolerate the idea of a son who is not faithful to his neighbors. On learning that her son has died for his loyalty, the mother breaks into a shocking celebration that reveals simultaneously the strength of the code of honor of the nationalist, the woman's own selfish desire to triumph over her son's false accusers, and the mental strain of a grief too great to bear; the latter is reminiscent of Maurya's break with reality at the end of Synge's *Riders to the Sea*.

Given the nature of Irish history, it is fitting that Lady Gregory's historical plays are found among the tragedies and tragicomedies. This is true both of plays based on Ireland's mythological history, such as *Grania*, and of those based on more verifiable history, such as *The White Cockade*, an idiosyncratic account of James II and that infamous turning point for Ireland, the Battle of the Boyne. In *Grania*, a play which Lady Gregory never allowed to be produced during her lifetime, one finds in the treatment of the legendary love triangle between Grania, Diarmuid, and Finn perhaps her most sophisticated exploration of psychological motivation. As a strong woman whose determination to live intensely rather than conventionally leads her into a lifetime of turmoil to which she never succumbs, Grania perhaps contains more elements of Lady Gregory than she herself was ready to make public on the stage.

The third major category comprises the plays of wonder and the supernatural. Here Lady Gregory explored most directly that realm of folk spirituality she loved and valued so much. It was this sense of the spiritual (in both a figurative and literal sense), underlying and giving meaning to the physical, that Lady Gregory feared was disappearing from the modern world. Her plays of wonder and the supernatural, many of them written for children, portray that world where reality is multilayered and the physical world is suffused with beings of another dimension.

The Travelling Man is a case in point. Giving the Christian tradition of entertaining angels, or Christ, an Irish setting, Lady Gregory adapted a story told her by an old peasant woman about a destitute girl who had been directed by Christ to the house of her future husband, but who herself failed years later to show charity to Christ in the guise of a traveling beggar. In the play, the woman readies the house, as she does each year on the anniversary of her rescue, for the possibility that her Saviour from long ago, the King of the World, will return as He had promised. She is so absorbed in preparing only the finest for what she assumes will be His dignified and impressive return, that she turns furiously against the poor beggar who interrupts her preparations, and who, of course, is Christ Himself. In this play, as in many others, Lady Gregory demonstrated her interest in the deeper reality that infused the life of the Irish peasant with a significance that transcended physical deprivation.

This need for a spiritual sustenance to redeem the tragic physical and political burden that had long been Ireland's is the overarching theme of

Lady Gregory's plays. She valued, above all, the mythmakers of Ireland, whether the anonymous poets of ancient legend, or Raftery, the blind wandering poet of the early nineteenth century, or a political mythmaker such as Charles Parnell. She wanted the Irish Renaissance to be a revival of mythmakers, herself among them. The potential for all this rested, she believed, in the Irish people themselves, particularly the peasants, with their natural mythmaking reflected in their common stories, their conception of the world about them, and their very speech.

In their formal character, Lady Gregory's plays can most readily be understood, following critic Ann Saddlemyer, as classical treatments of largely Romantic subject matter. The plays demonstrate economy and balance, are very linear and simple in construction, and generally observe the classical unities of time, place, and action. The tendency to sameness and predictability in structure is relieved by her storyteller's gift for local color and suspense, and by her effective adaption to the stage of the Irish-English dialect that she called Kiltartan (after the district in which she and her peasant models lived).

Lady Gregory was not a great playwright. She was not considered so at the time, by herself or by others, and is only in recent years being rescued from the oblivion into which her reputation fell following her death. She deserves great respect, however, as one of a lesser rank who made a significant contribution at a crucial time and in so doing served both her art form and her country well.

Other major works

NONFICTION: *An Autobiography of Sir William Gregory*, 1894 (editor); *Mr. Gregory's Letter Box*, 1898 (editor); *Ideals in Ireland*, 1901 (editor); *Our Irish Theatre*, 1913; *Hugh Lane's Life and Achievement*, 1921; *A Case for the Return of Hugh Lane's Pictures to Dublin*, 1926; *Coole*, 1931; *Lady Gregory's Journals 1916-1930*, 1946 (Lennox Robinson, editor).

FOLKLORE EDITIONS: *Cuchulain of Muirthemne*, 1902; *Poets and Dreamers*, 1903; *Gods and Fighting Men*, 1904; *A Book of Saints and Wonders*, 1907; *The Kiltartan History Book*, 1909; *The Kiltartan Wonder Book*, 1910; *The Kiltartan Poetry Book*, 1919; *Visions and Beliefs in the West of Ireland*, 1920 (2 volumes).

Bibliography

Adams, Hazard. *Lady Gregory*, 1973.
Coxhead, Elizabeth. *Lady Gregory: A Literary Portrait*, 1961, 1966.
Ellis-Fermor, Una. *The Irish Dramatic Movement*, 1954.
Fay, Gerard. *The Abbey Theatre: Cradle of Genius*, 1958.
Hogan, Robert, and Michael J. O'Neill, eds. *Joseph Holloway's Abbey Theatre: A Selection from His Unpublished Journal, Impressions of a*

  Dublin Playgoer, 1967.
Kopper, Edward A. *Lady Isabella Persse Gregory*, 1976.
Malone, Andrew E. *The Irish Drama*, 1965.
Mikhail, E. H. *Lady Gregory: Interviews and Recollections*, 1977.
Robinson, Lennox. *Ireland's Abbey Theatre: A History, 1899-1951*, 1951.
Saddlemyer, Ann. *In Defence of Lady Gregory, Playwright*, 1966.

Daniel Taylor

JOHN GUARE

Born: New York, New York; February 5, 1938

Principal drama

Did You Write My Name in the Snow?, pr. 1962; *To Wally Pantoni, We Leave a Credenza*, pr. 1964; *The Loveliest Afternoon of the Year*, pr. 1966, pb. 1968; *Something I'll Tell You Tuesday*, pr. 1966, pb. 1968; *Muzeeka*, pr. 1967, pb. 1969 (one act); *Cop-Out*, pr. 1968, pb. 1969; *Home Fires*, pr. 1968, pb. 1969; *A Day for Surprises*, pb. 1970, pr. 1971; *The House of Blue Leaves*, pr. 1971, pb. 1972; *Two Gentlemen of Verona*, pr. 1971, pb. 1973 (with Mel Shapiro, music by Galt MacDermot; adaptation of William Shakespeare's play); *Marco Polo Sings a Solo*, pr. 1973, pb. 1977; *Rich and Famous*, pr. 1974, pb. 1977; *Landscape of the Body*, pr. 1977, pb. 1978; *Bosoms and Neglect*, pr. 1979, pb. 1980; *In Fireworks Lie Secret Codes*, pr. 1979, pb. 1981; *A New Me*, pr. 1981; *Gardenia*, pr., pb. 1982; *Lydie Breeze*, pr., pb. 1982.

Other literary forms

All of John Guare's work to date has been in dramatic form, though not always for the theater. *Kissing Sweet* was one of ten short plays about pollution by Off-Broadway playwrights produced on a New York public television program on November 25, 1969. A satiric, revuelike piece about Americans' obsession with various bodily odors, it is probably more suited to the stage than to television. Guare has been represented on-screen by two films, *Taking Off* (1971) and *Atlantic City* (1981). For the former, he merely helped director Miloš Forman revise a script which Forman and two other writers had already created. The screenplay for the latter film, however, was entirely his own work, inspired by a short trip to Atlantic City with director Louis Malle, who was contracted for a movie production but had no property to film. Guare's screenplay won an Oscar nomination, as well as Best Screenplay awards from the New York Film Critics, the Los Angeles Film Critics, and the National Board of Film Critics, and helped to make *Atlantic City* one of the most acclaimed movies of the year. It demonstrated the same sensitivity to eccentric characters, their distinctive speech and high-flying dreams, the same freshness of imagery, the same sense of comic incongruity and surprise that makes his plays so original and appealing.

Achievements

Guare's work is a combination of horror and hilarity, conveying a vision of the world characteristic of the second half of the twentieth century. The

violence most prevalent in his plays is not emotional violence, as in Edward
Albee or Eugene O'Neill, or cathartic violence, as in William Shakespeare
or the Greek tragedians, but senseless, unexpected violence, quite unprepared for and inadequately motivated—the violence of newspaper head-
lines, often so bizarre as to make one laugh. This violent vision is matched,
however, by a compassion which extends to a wide range of humanity, from
the lost, lower-class, and low-life types of *Landscape of the Body* or *The
House of Blue Leaves* to the rich and powerful in *Marco Polo Sings a Solo*
and *Lydie Breeze*. Guare's plays have roots in the Absurdist tradition, yet
his characters are often realized with great depth and poignance; his work
transcends classification into any movement or school of contemporary
drama.

Biography

John Guare grew up in Queens, in New York City, the son of bright but
unhappy loners; his father was a clerk in the stock exchange. Guare was
reared as a Catholic and attended Catholic schools through Georgetown
University, where he received his A.B. in 1960. He attended the Yale
School of Drama, where he received his M.F.A. in 1963 and had one of his
plays produced in 1962. He had begun writing much earlier; in 1949, when
he was eleven, he appeared in *Newsday* for writing a play performed at
Atlantic Beach, Long Island. After Yale, he spent time in New York, California, and the Air Force Reserve. In Hollywood, the wife of his uncle, a
casting director, gave him money to embark on experiences to further his
writing career, and he proceeded to tour Europe. Guare's 1965 European
trip provided the inspiration for *The House of Blue Leaves* and gave him
the impetus to carry on his writing in New York, helped by several summers at the Eugene O'Neill Foundation Theater in Connecticut, where he
tried out several plays before attempting New York productions for them.

In 1981, Guare married Adele Chatfield-Taylor, director of the New
York Landmarks Foundation. Among his numerous awards are the Obie,
the New York Drama Critics Circle Award, and Outer Critics Circle Award
for *The House of Blue Leaves*, the Tony for *Two Gentlemen of Verona*, and
the *Variety* award for most promising playwright in 1969.

Analysis

The world of John Guare is not that of Eugene O'Neill, hopeless and
humorless, of unrelieved darkness. It is not that of Arthur Miller, with
ordinary people confronted with emotions too big for them but psychologically quite comprehensible. It is not the world of Tennessee Williams, with
characters whose frustrations are evident and clearly derived from incidents
in their pasts. It is not that of Edward Albee, with characters playing subtle games with one another's psyches, intentionally but surreptitiously

wounding one another. It is not that of Sam Shepard, with characters living out mysterious, age-old rituals of the family and the race to learn who they are. It is certainly not the world of Neil Simon, full of neurotic but humorous rationalization, always contained in a socially acceptable framework.

Guare's world is not easily rationalized, not understandable by means of reductive Freudianism, Jungian myth, Bernean game theory, transactional analysis, or gag humor. His world is not so easily explained by particular theories, for it is a world gone awry. Guare is too much a product of the turbulent 1960's—rather than of the 1940's, with its concern with fitting into the social fabric, or the 1950's, with its anguished rebellion against conformity—to find an easy way out of the dilemmas facing the human family. The 1960's showed that reason neither can nor should rule the world, and Guare's plays embody that thesis.

A decade of assassination, revolution, and war plunged the nation into hopelessness, into despair that anything could be done to improve the world. The pervasive violence of the decade was senseless and desensitizing and the increasing explicitness allowed by film and television in the depiction of violence made acts of brutality and meanness somehow palatable. How could an audience be resensitized to the horrors of violent acts? Perhaps by hitting them with such acts when they were quite unprepared. How to "unprepare" them? Through laughter.

The outrageous comedy of *The House of Blue Leaves*, *Muzeeka*, *Cop-Out*, and other Guare plays leaves an audience unprepared for the devastating conclusions of murder and suicide. Julius Novick could not accept this mingling of modes in *The House of Blue Leaves*: "The farce and the agony seem to violate instead of reinforcing each other." Yet this, indeed, seems to have been Guare's purpose, as he suggests in his foreword to the published script: He describes seeing Sir Laurence Olivier perform in August Strindberg's *The Dance of Death* and Georges Feydeau's *A Flea in Her Ear* on consecutive nights, and then feeling "the savage intensity of the first blended into the maniacal intensity of the second. . . . Why shouldn't Strindberg and Feydeau get married, at least live together, and *The House of Blue Leaves* be their child?" It is this marriage of soul-searing drama and madcap farce that Guare effects—not only in *The House of Blue Leaves* but also throughout most of his work—and through this "marriage," he achieves his striking dramatic impact.

Viewing the violence, the frenzy, the madness of contemporary American life, Guare finds the dark seriousness of an O'Neill, a Miller, or a Strindberg play inadequate to his purposes. He finds it much more fitting to place his anguished characters on the running treadmill of farce, with its multiple surprises (for the characters as well as for the audience) and its sense of figures trapped with no escape in mazes of their own designing. The friction between the characters and their treadmill gives rise to plentiful comedy, albeit sometimes drawn from pain.

Guare's characters are usually "little people," society's lost ones (the frustrated songwriting zookeeper Artie and his crazy wife in *The House of Blue Leaves*; the lonely young mother who becomes a porno actress in *Landscape of the Body*; the blind old woman dying of cancer in *Bosoms and Neglect*; the dreaming employee of a piped-in music company in *Muzeeka*), yet even famous people, the movers and shakers of the world, are caught up in this treadmill and cannot escape. Such characters form the entire cast of *Marco Polo Sings a Solo*, "people living without traditional limits," as the author's note to the published text calls them. Yet even without limits, such characters are caught up in their own isolation, their own obsessions, and the overwhelming power of technological marvels that can go amiss: Misdirected bolts from outer space destroy a paper inscribed with the newly discovered cure for cancer, a diplomat ends up half-eaten by tropical piranhas who have been redirected with the Gulf Stream to Norway, a planet that could feed the world with its incredibly abundant fertility is destroyed. The power and control of logic and rationality are thrown to the four winds.

Traditionally, no dramatic genre demands a more careful and consistent use of logic than farce, with its meticulously prepared setups for future comic payoffs and its minute manipulation of resolutions for all the discordances laid out earlier in the play. Guare—who, as a student at Yale Drama School, rejected the emphasis there on logic and careful construction—has chosen instead to emphasize the madness at the heart of farce, deliberately abandoning the climactic imposition of order intended to put the audience at its ease. Guare argues, in the words of a blithe transsexual in *Marco Polo Sings a Solo*, that "We were born for chaos. That's our natural state. Chaos comes natural. Give in to it." Give in to it Guare certainly does, through outrageous plots, incidents, characters, behavior, and theatrical devices.

Marco Polo Sings a Solo, set in 1999, probably has Guare's most outrageous plot. It centers on an astronaut named Frank Schaeffer who is exploring distant planets but who is simultaneously supposed to impregnate his earthbound wife, kidnaped in the White House, by means of an interplanetary bolt of Frank's sperm transferred electronically to a metal disc implanted in his wife. Another character, a transsexual, has a son by becoming impregnated by the sperm her former male self had offered to be saved for such an occasion. The mishaps, technological and human, deriving from such "unnatural" plans are hilarious.

Such bizarre comedy abounds in Guare's work: One of the stone lions in front of the New York Public Library walks into the library and eats a librarian in *A Day for Surprises*; the protagonist of *Rich and Famous* shoots his parents, but they do not die; Jack Argue in *Muzeeka* visits a prostitute for the "Chinese basket job" and while having sex hears from the hospital that his wife has just had a child; the crazy Bananas in *The House of Blue Leaves* swallows a movie star's hearing-aid transistors, and the movie star can only guess what kind of response she should make when people address her; in that same play, three nuns invade Artie's apartment to watch the Pope on television. The comedy comes from incongruity, surprise, and richly fulfilled expectations; comedy is drawn even from acts of violence (those, that is, that do not involve one major character's intentional assault upon another character—many of the acts of violence in Guare's work derive from nonhuman causes).

Guare's originality may be most evident in his creation of characters. Even when he uses familiar character-types (policeman, mistress, nun, cuckolded husband, Latin lover), he twists the stereotype by giving his characters cartoonish eccentricities. Such highly individualizing traits may seem to be merely tacked on for the surprise factor—as with the macho Cuban Raulito in *Landscape of the Body*, who wears a gold lamé dress over his business suit because it represents the wealth that he dreamed of when watching American films as a boy. Yet these traits are usually intricately woven into the fabric of the play. The comic avarice of the nuns in *The House of Blue Leaves* lays the groundwork for their greedy rush to destruction. The broadly drawn caricatures of *Rich and Famous* all contribute to Guare's mockery of the American quest for fame. Moreover, such individual quirks enable Guare's characters to become real by violating dramatic stereotypes.

Beyond the level of plot and character, where Guare breaks down standard expectations for his chosen genre, he challenges more fundamental dramatic conventions. In *The House of Blue Leaves*, as in many of his other plays, characters speak directly to the audience, breaking the notion in realistic theater of the sanctity of the fourth wall. Moreover, the play opens and closes outside the very realistic apartment setting; in a prologue, Artie is seen trying out his songs at amateur night at the El Dorado Bar and Grill, sitting at a piano and talking to the theater audience as if they were the patrons of the El Dorado. After the devastating strangling of Bananas, Artie again appears at the piano, singing one of his awful songs and thanking the management for the blue spotlight he has at last been granted for his performance of a ballad. Meanwhile, the stage becomes filled with blue leaves—associated with the insane asylum where he threatened to put Bananas. The utter inappropriateness of Artie's song ("I'm Here with Bells On") provides a suitably shocking conclusion to a play that relies on the foregrounding of its theatricality.

Others of Guare's plays are even more radical in their refusal to give the audience a comfortable basis for approaching or dealing with the play. *Landscape of the Body*, for example, frames a long sequence of flashbacks—mostly chronological—with a scene of a woman and a man on a boat: The man is a detective; the woman, Betty, a suspect for the murder and decapitation of her son. The flashbacks occur under the aegis of Rosalie, the dead sister of Betty, the suspect, to reveal the true murderer of Betty's son. Along with spoken comments, Rosalie provides occasional cabaret-style songs such as "Hey, Stay a While" and "It's Amazing How a Little Tomorrow (Can Make Up for a Whole Lot of Yesterday)." These songs, with music and lyrics by Guare, as in several of his other plays, give a pseudo-Broadway or nightclub excitement to what are otherwise rather sordid stories of insignificant lives and suggest the triviality that commercial entertainment makes of such lives. Such songs act as a rather unusual, vaguely Brechtian means of commenting on the story—not always as successfully as in *The House of Blue Leaves*, however, in which the songs themselves are part of the plot, Artie's feeble attempts at making an award-winning career as a songwriter.

However complex its structure, *Landscape of the Body* has at least a single narrative thrust that involves the audience immediately: Who killed Betty's son? *Muzeeka*, on the other hand, a long one-act, Guare's first play to receive significant attention, lacks such narrative direction. Rather, it matches the madness of its content with a free-form style, moving from one isolated incident to another in a method reflective of contemporary fragmentation. The scenes are generally expressionistic rather than realistic. The play's only really naturalistic scenes, those at the end between Argue and a fellow soldier in Vietnam, turn out to be the most bizarre in content: Their battalions are under contract to specific networks or magazines for exclusive coverage of their battles, and they must go into combat wearing appropriate makeup for the cameras. Through such devices, Guare comments on the dehumanization, commercialization, and deadening demands for conformity in contemporary American life; such a play has a visceral as well as an intellectual impact.

Despite his preoccupation with the nightmarish reality of the modern world, Guare's outlook is not invariably defeatist. "Only connect" is the E. M. Forster motto that Deirdre quotes to fellow bibliophile Scooper in *Bosoms and Neglect*, and it seems a pervasive motto for Guare's own work: One thinks of the move that Betty makes toward Holahan, the detective, in the final moment of *Landscape of the Body*, or the connection—this time with humanity's primal feelings—that Argue seeks to bring about in *Muzeeka* by eventually piping into elevators, supermarkets, and dentists' offices a music that will make people want to dance wildly, uninhibitedly, like the ancient Etruscans. One can even connect through fighting, as the old couple in the short play *Something I'll Tell You Tuesday* realize, as Deirdre and Scooper discover in their comic but literally wounding attacks on each other in *Bosoms and Neglect*. Such connection is hardly easy:

Scooper's mother, Henny, tries to reach him at the end of that play by telling him about a long past experience that, unknown to her, has haunted him all of his life; her blind eyes do not tell her that he has just left to be with Deirdre—perhaps the knowledge this story could give him is not needed, now that he is embarking on a successful love relationship—and yet Henny's final gesture, a hand outstretched to her absent son, is painful and poignant, a fitting gesture for all humanity's constant and not always answered need.

Although such a theme is certainly universal, Guare's work is distinctly American in its focus on the American dream—the belief in success and the chance to make something of oneself. His characters may fail to recognize their limitations, like Artie, or may become defeated by too lofty a dream, like Jack Argue, but others may reject unrealistic expectations and live in the beauties of the here and now, like Stony McBride in *Marco Polo Sings a Solo*. Guare refuses to accept the deterioration of contemporary American life; his projected tetralogy, of which two parts have appeared on Broadway, *Lydie Breeze* and *Gardenia*, explores the roots of late-twentieth century America in nineteenth century America. The scope of these works is ambitious, encompassing both large social movements—Utopian communities, rising industry—and individual dramas of adultery and murder. On both levels, Guare deplores corruption and mourns abandoned dreams.

At the end of *Landscape of the Body*, a flashback shows Betty and her sister Rosalie talking as adolescent girls. Betty asks, "How am I going to get through my life?" Rosalie explains that spirits float like fish through space until they are caught by fishhooks on earth; thus, "we spend the rest of our stay on this planet trying to free our mouths of that hook, fighting, fighting." In the meantime, says Rosalie, "You travel alone because other people are only there to remind you how much that hook hurts that we all bit down on. Wait for that one day we can bite free. . . . We're gone. We're dead. We're safe." Betty rebels against this vision; the play's final moment presents her move—as an adult woman—toward Holahan, rejecting loneliness, embracing life here on earth. Guare's entire work is a move beyond isolation, embracing human life, however chaotic, however mad it may be.

Other major works

SCREENPLAY: *Atlantic City*, 1981.
TELEPLAY: *Kissing Sweet*, 1969.

Bibliography

Berkvist, Robert. "John Guare Stirs up a 'Breeze," in *The New York Times*. LXXXIV (February 21, 1982), sec. 2, p. 4.

Bernstein, Samuel J. *The Strands Entwined: A New Direction in American Drama*, 1980.

Bosworth, Patricia. "Yes for a Young Man's Fantasies," in *The New York Times*. LXIV (March 7, 1971), sec. 2, p. 1.

Chase, Christopher. "At the Movies: Good Days in the Life of a Screenwriter," in *The New York Times*. LXXXIV (May 29, 1981), sec. 3, p. 8.

Clurman, Harold. Review of *Landscape of the Body*, in *The Nation*. CCXXV (November 12, 1977), pp. 505-506.

_____. Review of *Rich and Famous*, in *The Nation*. CCXXII (March 13, 1976), p. 318.

Eder, Richard. "Guare Play Misses Its Mark," in *The New York Times*. LXXVII (October 13, 1977), sec. 3, p. 17.

Kael, Pauline. Review of *Atlantic City*, in *The New Yorker*. LVII (April 6, 1981), pp. 154-160.

Kauffmann, Stanley. Review of *Rich and Famous*, in *The New Republic*. CLXXIV (March 13, 1976), pp. 28-29.

Kerr, Walter. "John Guare: A Distant Way of Doing Things," in *The New York Times*. LXX (May 2, 1982), sec. 2, p. 5.

_____. "Language Alone Isn't Drama," in *The New York Times*. LXXVI (March 6, 1977), sec. 2, p. 3.

Kroll, Jack. "Laugh When It Hurts," in *Newsweek*. XCIII (May 14, 1979), pp. 85-86.

_____. "Yankee Doodle Deadly," in *Newsweek*. XCIX (March 8, 1982), p. 94.

Lyons, Warren. "No More Crying the 'Blue Leaves' Blues," in *The New York Times*. LXV (July 25, 1971), sec. 2, p. 1.

Marranca, Bonnie, and Gautam Dasgupta. *American Playwrights: A Critical Survey*, 1981.

Wetzsteon, Ross. "The Coming of Age of John Guare," in *New York*. XV (February 22, 1982), pp. 35-39.

Scott Giantvalley